WHEN DO FISH SLEEP?

Other Books by David Feldman

Imponderables™

How to Win at Just About Everything

Why Do Clocks Run Clockwise? and
Other Imponderables™

Who Put the Butter in Butterfly? and
Other Fearless Investigations into
Our Illogical Language

WHEN DO FISH SLEEP?
and Other Imponderables™ of Everyday Life

David Feldman

Illustrated by Kassie Schwan

HARPER & ROW, PUBLISHERS, New York
Grand Rapids, Philadelphia, St. Louis, San Francisco
1817 *London, Singapore, Sydney, Tokyo, Toronto*

Library of Congress Cataloging-in-Publication Data

Feldman, David, 1950–
   When do fish sleep? and other imponderables of everyday life/by David
Feldman.
      p. cm.
   Includes index.

   1. Questions and answers.   2. Questions and answers—Humor.   I. Title.
AG195.F458   1989
031.02—dc20   89-45038

Preface

Imponderables are mysteries that can't be answered by numbers, measurements, or a trip to the reference section of your library. If you worry about why the carbons on airplane tickets are red, or why tennis balls are fuzzy, or why yawning is contagious, you have been struck by the dread malady of Imponderability.

When we wrote the first volume of *Imponderables,* we weren't sure that there were others like us, who were committed to cogitating about the everyday mysteries of life. We needn't have worried. Most of the Imponderables in this book were submitted by readers of the first two volumes of Imponderables.

In *Why Do Clocks Run Clockwise?,* we introduced a new section, Frustables (short for "frustrating Imponderables") and asked for your help in solving them. Your response was terrific, but we don't want you to get complacent. We've got ten new Imponderables that we haven't been able to solve.

And because so many readers offered corrections and caustically constructive comments, we've added a letter section—we couldn't shut you up anymore even if we wanted to.

Would you like to win a free copy of the next volume of *Imponderables?* If you are the first to submit an Imponderable that we use in the next book, you will not only have the relief of finally having the answer to your mystery, but also a free, autographed copy of the book (along with, of course, an acknowledgment).

The last page of the book tells you how to get in touch with us. But for now, sit back and enjoy. You are about to enter the wonderful world of Imponderability.

Imponderables

Why Do Roosters Crow in the Morning?

Because there are humans around to be awakened, of course. Does anyone really believe that roosters crow when they are by themselves? Nah! Actually, they speak perfectly good English.

Ornithologists don't buy our common-sense answer. They insist that crowing "maps territory" (a euphemism for "Get the hell out of my way and don't mess with my women—this is my coop"). In the spirit of fair play, we'll give the last word to one of those nasty ornithologist types (but don't believe a word she says), Janet Hinshaw, of the Wilson Ornithological Society:

> Most of the crowing takes place in the morning, as does most singing, because that is when the birds are most active, and most of the territorial advertising takes place then. Many of the other vocalizations heard throughout the day are for other types of communication, including flocking calls, which serve to keep members of a flock together and in touch if they are out of sight from one another.

Submitted by Rowena Nocom of North Hollywood, California.

Why Do Many Hotels and Motels Fold Over the Last Piece of Toilet Paper in the Bathroom?

This Imponderable was sent in by reader Jane W. Brown in a letter dated May 12, 1986. Jane was clearly a discerning seer of emergent popular culture trends:

> Staying in less than deluxe lodgings has led me to wonder why, and how, the custom of folding under the two outside corners on a roll of bathroom paper was begun. This operation creates a V on the last exposed edge of the tissue. I first noticed this bizarre sight in a LaQuinta Motor Inn. Then I stayed in some Holiday Inns while on a business trip. There, too, the bathroom paper had been tediously tucked in on the outside edges, the large V standing out, begging for attention. Recently, I upgraded my accommodations and spent several nights in a Marriott and an Intercontinental. Right: the bathroom paper was also arranged in this contorted fashion. Why?

Jane, enterprisingly, included an audiovisual aid along with her letter, as if to prove she wasn't crazy: a specimen of the mysterious V toilet paper. Since Jane wrote her letter, the folded toilet paper trick has run rampant in the lodging industry.

We contacted most of the largest chains of innkeepers in the country and received the same answer from all. Perhaps James P. McCauley, executive director of the International Association of Holiday Inns, stated it best:

> Hotels want to give their guests the confidence that the bathroom has been cleaned since the last guest has used the room. To accomplish this, the maid will fold over the last piece of toilet paper to assure that no one has used the toilet paper since the room was cleaned. It is subtle but effective.

Maybe too subtle for us. Call us sentimental old fools, but we still like the old "Sanitized for Your Protection" strips across the toilet seat.

Submitted by Jane W. Brown of Giddings, Texas.

DAVID FELDMAN

Why Do Gas Gauges in Automobiles Take an Eternity to Go from Registering Full to Half-full, and Then Drop to Empty in the Speed of Light?

On a long trek down our illustrious interstate highway system, we will do anything to alleviate boredom. The roadway equivalent of reading cereal boxes at breakfast is obsessing about odometers and fuel gauges.

Nothing is more dispiriting after a fill-up at the service station than traveling sixty miles and watching the gas gauge stand still. Although part of us longs to believe that our car is registering phenomenal mileage records, the other part of us wants the gauge to move to prove to ourselves that we are actually making decent time and have not, through some kind of *Twilight Zone* alternate reality, actually been riding on a treadmill for the last hour. Our gas gauge becomes the arbiter of our progress. Even when the needle starts to move, and the gauge registers three-quarters' full, we sometimes feel as if we have been traveling for days.

How nice it would be to have a gauge move steadily down toward empty. Just as we are about to give in to despair, though, after the gauge hits half-full, the needle starts darting toward empty as if it had just discovered the principle of gravity. Whereas it seemed that we had to pass time zones before the needle would move to the left at all, suddenly we are afraid that we are going to run out of gas. Where is that next rest station?

There must be a better way. Why don't fuel gauges actually register what proportion of the tank is filled with gasoline? The automakers and gauge manufacturers are well aware that a "half-full" reading on a gas gauge is really closer to "one-third" full, and they have reasons for preserving this inaccuracy.

The gauge relies upon a sensor in the tank to relay the fuel level. The sensor consists of a float and linkage connected to a variable resistor. The resistance value fluctuates as the float moves up and down.

If a gas tank is filled to capacity, *the liquid is filled higher than the float has the physical ability to rise.* When the float is at the top of its stroke, the gauge will always register as full, *even though the tank can hold more gasoline.* The gauge will register full until this "extra" gasoline is consumed and the float starts its descent in the tank. At the other end of the float's stroke, *the gauge will register as empty when the float can no longer move further downward, even though liquid is present below the float.*

We asked Anthony H. Siegel, of Ametek's U.S. Gauge Division, why sensors aren't developed that can measure the actual status of gasoline more accurately. We learned, much as we expected, that more precise measurements easily could be produced, but the automakers are using the current technology *for our own good:*

> Vehicle makers are very concerned that their customers do not run out of fuel before the gauge reads empty. That could lead to stranded, unhappy motorists, so they compensate in the design of the float/gauge system. Their choice of tolerances and calibration procedures guarantees that slight variations during the manufacturing of these components will always produce a combination of parts which falls on the safe side. The gauge is thus designed to read empty when there is still fuel left.

Tens of millions of motorists have suspected there is fuel left even when the gauge says empty, but few have been brave enough to test the hypothesis. Perhaps there are gallons and gallons of fuel left when the gauge registers empty, and this is all a plot by Stuckey's and Howard Johnson's to make us take unnecessary pit stops on interstates.

Submitted by Jack Belck of Lansing, Michigan.

DAVID FELDMAN

HOW Is the Caloric Value of Food Measured?

Imponderables is on record as doubting the validity of caloric measurements. It defies belief that the caloric value of vegetables such as potato chips and onion rings, full of nutrients, could possibly be higher than greasy tuna fish or eggplant. Still, with an open mind, we sought to track down the answer to this Imponderable.

Calories are measured by an apparatus called a *calorimeter*. The piece of food to be measured is placed inside a chamber, sealed, and then ignited and burned. The energy released from the food heats water surrounding the chamber. By weighing the amount of water heated, noting the increase in the water's temperature and multiplying the two, the energy capacity of the food can be measured. For example, if ten liters of water surrounding the chamber is 20 degrees Centigrade before combustion and then is measured at 25 degrees after combustion, the difference in temperature (five degrees) is multiplied by the volume of water (ten liters) to arrive at the caloric value (fifty calories of energy).

A calorie is nothing more than the measurement of the ability of a particular nutrient to raise the temperature of one gram of water one degree Centigrade. The calorimeter is a crude but reasonable model for how our body stores and burns energy sources. The calorimeter slightly overstates the number of calories our body can use from each foodstuff. In the calorimeter, foods burn completely, with only some ashes (containing minerals) left in the chamber. In our body, small portions of food are indigestible, and are excreted before they break down to provide energy. The rules of thumb are that two percent of fat, five percent of carbohydrates, and eight percent of proteins will not be converted to energy by the body.

Food scientists have long known the caloric count for each food group. One gram of carbohydrates or proteins equals four calories. One gram of fat contains more than twice the number of calories (nine).

Scientists can easily ascertain the proportion of fat to carbohydrates or proteins, so it might seem that calories could be measured simply by weighing the food. When a food consists exclusively of proteins and carbohydrates, for example, one could simply multiply the weight of the food by four to discover the calorie count.

But complications arise. Certain ingredients in natural or processed foods contain no caloric value whatsoever, such as water, fiber, and minerals. Foods that contain a mixture, say, of water (zero calories), fiber (zero calories), proteins (four calories per gram), fats (nine calories per gram), and carbohydrates (four calories per gram), along with some trace minerals (zero calories), are simply harder to calculate with a scale than a calorimeter.

Submitted by Jill Palmer of Leverett, Massachusetts.

DAVID FELDMAN

The chart reads:

E
VN F U CN
RD THS CHRT
U STL MHT ND
SPCTCLS!

Who Put E on Top of the Eye Chart? And Why?

Professor Hermann Snellen, a Dutch professor of ophthalmology, put the E on top of the eye chart in 1862. Although his very first chart was headed by an A, Snellen quickly composed another chart with E on top.

Snellen succeeded Dr. Frans Cornelis Donders as the director of the Netherlands Hospital for Eye Patients. Donders was then the world's foremost authority on geometric optics. Snellen was trying to standardize a test to diagnose visual acuity, to measure how small an image an eye can accept while still detecting the detail of that image. Dr. Donders' complicated formulas were based on three parallel lines; of all the letters of the alphabet, the capital E most closely resembled the lines that Dr. Donders had studied so intensively. Because Donders had earlier determined how the eye perceives the E, Snellen based much of his mathematical work on the fifth letter.

The three horizontal limbs of the E are separated by an

equal amount of white space. In Snellen's original chart, there was a one-to-one ratio between the height and width of the letters, and the gaps and bars were all the same length (in some modern eye charts, the middle bar is shorter).

Louanne Gould, of Cambridge Instruments, says that the E, unlike more open letters like L or U, forces the observer to distinguish between white and black, an important consitituent of good vision. Without this ability, E's begin to look like B's, F's, P's or many other letters.

Of course, Snellen couldn't make an eye chart full of only E's, or else all his patients would have 20-10 vision. But Snellen realized that it was important to use the same letters many times on the eye charts, to insure that the failure of an observer to identify a letter was based on a visual problem rather than the relative difficulty of a set of letters. Ian Bailey, professor of optometry and director of the Low Vision Clinic at the University of California at Berkeley, says that it isn't so important whether an eye chart uses the easiest or most difficult letters. Most eye charts incorporate only ten different letters, ones that have the smallest range of difficulty.

Today, many eye charts do not start with an E—and there is no technical reason why they have to—but most still do. Dr. Stephen C. Miller, of the American Optometric Association, suggests that the desire of optical companies to have a standardized approach to the production of eye charts probably accounts for the preponderance of E charts. And we're happy about it. It's a nice feeling to know that even if our vision is failing us miserably, we'll always get the top row right.

Submitted by Merry Phillips of Menlo Park, California.

DAVID FELDMAN

Do the Police Really Make Chalk Outlines of Murder Victims at the Scene of the Crime? Why Do They Use Chalk?

As soon as law enforcement officials descend upon a murder scene, a police photographer takes pictures of the corpse, making certain that the deceased's position is established by the photographs. The medical examiner usually wants the body as soon as possible after the murder; the sooner an autopsy is conducted, the more valuable the information the police are likely to obtain.

Right before the body is removed, the police do indeed make an outline of the position of the victim. More often than not the body is outlined in chalk, including a notation of whether the body was found in a prone or supine posture.

A police investigation of a murder can take a long time, too long to maintain the murder site as it appeared after the murder. Forensic specialists cannot rely on photographs alone. Often, the exact position of the victim can be of vital importance in an investigation. By making an outline, the police can return to the murder scene and take measurements which might quash or corroborate a new theory on the case. Outline drawings may also be used in the courtroom to explain wound locations, bullet trajectories, and blood trails.

Herbert H. Buzbee, of the International Association of Coroners and Medical Examiners, told *Imponderables* that chalk is not always used to make outlines. Stick-em paper or string are often used on carpets, for example, where chalk might be obscured by the fabric. Carl Harbaugh, of the International Chiefs of Police, says that many departments once experimented with spray paint to make outlines, but found that paint traces were occasionally found on the victim, confusing the forensic analysis.

The ideal outline ingredient would be one that would show up, stay put, and do no permanent damage to any surface. Unfortunately, no such ingredient exists. Chalk gets high marks for leaving no permanent markings, but is not easily visible on many surfaces. Tape and string (which has to be fastened with tape) have a tendency to mysteriously twist out of shape, especially if they get wet.

None of these flaws in the markers would matter if murder victims were considerate enough to die in sites convenient to the police. Harbaugh says that on a street or highway any kind of outline will do. But what good is a chalk outline on a bed covered with linens and blankets?

Submitted by Pat O'Conner of Forest Hills, New York.

What Do Restaurants that Specialize in Potato Skins Do with the Rest of the Potato? What Do Restaurants that Specialize in Frogs' Legs Do with the Rest of the Frog?

In most restaurants, potato skins are a waste product, served as the casing of a baked potato or not at all. So we assumed that restaurants that specialized in potato skins used the rest of the potato to make mashed potatoes, boiled potatoes, or soups.

Our assumption was correct, but our correspondent mentions that potato skins are often served in bars that do not serve potatoes in any other form. Is it cost-effective for these establishments to serve the skins and dump the potato filling?

Most restaurants that serve potato skins buy the skins *only*, usually in frozen form. Linda Smith, of the National Restaurant Association, sent us a list of the biggest suppliers of potato skins. Most of these companies, not at all coincidentally, also supply restaurants with pre-cut cottage fries, hash browns, and O'Brien potatoes, among others. Ore-Ida isn't about to sell the skin and throw away the potato.

Anyone who has ever dissected a frog in biology class does not want to contemplate the idea of chefs picking apart an entire frog to get at its legs. Suffice it to say that restaurants buy only

DAVID FELDMAN

the legs of frogs. What suppliers of frogs' legs do with the rest of the frog is too gruesome for even us to contemplate.

Submitted by Myrna S. Gordon of Scotch Plains, New Jersey.
Thanks also to Sharon Michele Burke of Menlo Park, California.

If Water Is Heavier than Air, Why Do Clouds Stay Up in the Sky?

What makes you think that clouds aren't dropping? They are. Constantly.

Luckily, cloud drops do not fall at the same velocity as a water balloon. In fact, cloud drops are downright sluggards: They drop at a measly 0.3 centimeters per second. And cloud drops are so tiny, about 0.01 centimeters in diameter, that their descent is not even noticeable to the human eye.

Submitted by Ronald C. Semone of Washington, D.C.

Why Are There More Holes in the Mouthpiece of a Telephone than in the Earpiece?

We just checked the telephone closest to us and were shocked. There are thirty-six holes on our mouthpiece, and a measly seven on the earpiece. What gives?

Tucked underneath the mouthpiece is a tiny transmitter that duplicates our voices, and underneath the earpiece is a receiver. Those old enough to remember telephones that constantly howled will appreciate the problems inherent in having a receiver and transmitter close together enough to produce audible transmission without creating feedback.

Before the handset, deskstand telephones were not portable, and the speaker had to talk into a stationary transmitter. Handsets added convenience to the user but potential pitfalls in transmission. While developing the telephone handset, engineers were aware that it was imperative for the lips of a speaker to be as close as possible to the transmitter. If a caller increases

14   DAVID FELDMAN

the distance between his lips and the transmitter from half an inch to one inch, the output volume will be reduced by three decibels. According to AT&T, in 1919 more than four thousand measurements of head dimensions were made to determine the proper dimensions of the handset. The goal, of course, was to design a headset that would best cup the ear and bring the transmitter close to the lips.

One of the realities that the Bell engineers faced was that there was no way to force customers to talk directly into the mouthpiece. Watch most people talking on the phone and you will see their ears virtually covered by the receiver. But most people do not hold their mouths as close to the transmitter. This is the real reason why there are usually more holes in the mouthpiece than in the earpiece. The more holes there are, the more sensitive to sound the transmitter is, and the more likely that a mumbled aside will be heard three thousand miles away.

Submitted by Tammy Madill of Millington, Tennessee

How Do Fish Return to a Lake or Pond that Has Dried Up?

Our correspondent, Michael J. Catalana, rightfully wonders how even a small pond replenishes itself with fish after it has totally dried up. Is there a Johnny Fishseed who roams around the world restocking ponds and lakes with fish?

We contacted several experts on fish to solve this mystery, and they wouldn't answer until we cross-examined you a little bit, Michael. "How carefully did you look at that supposedly dried-up pond?" they wanted to know. Many species, such as the appropriately named mudminnows, can survive in mud. R. Bruce Gebhardt, of the North American Native Fishes Association, suggested that perhaps your eyesight was misdirected: "If there are small pools, fish may be able to hide in mud or weeds while you're standing there looking into the pool." When you leave, they re-emerge. Some tropical fish lay eggs that develop while the pond is dry; when rain comes and the pond is refilled with water, the eggs hatch quickly.

For the sake of argument, Michael, we'll assume that you communed with nature, getting down on your hands and knees to squeeze the mud searching for fish or eggs. You found no evidence of marine life. How can fish appear from out of thin air? We return to R. Bruce Gebhardt for the explanation:

> There are ways in which fish can return to a pond after total elimination. The most common is that most ponds or lakes have outlets and inlets; fish just swim back into the formerly hostile area. They are able to traverse and circumvent small rivulets, waterfalls, and pollution sources with surprising efficiency. If they find a pond with no fish in it, they may stay just because there's a lot of food with no competition for it.

Submitted by Michael J. Catalana of Ben Lomond, California.

Why Do We Call Our Numbering System "Arabic" When Arabs Don't Use Arabic Numbers Themselves?

The first numbering system was probably developed by the Egyptians, but ancient Sumeria, Babylonia, and India used numerals in business transactions. All of the earliest number systems used some variation of 1 to denote one, probably because the numeral resembled a single finger. Historians suggest that our Arabic 2 and 3 are corruptions of two and three slash marks written hurriedly.

Most students in Europe, Australia, and the Americas learn to calculate with Arabic numbers, even though *these numerals were never used by Arabs*. Arabic numbers were actually developed in India, long before the invention of the printing press (probably in the tenth century), but were subsequently translated into Arabic. European merchants who brought back trea-

DAVID FELDMAN

tises to their continent mistakenly assumed that Arabs had invented the system, and proceeded to translate the texts from Arabic.

True Arabic numerals look little like ours. From one to ten, this is how they look:

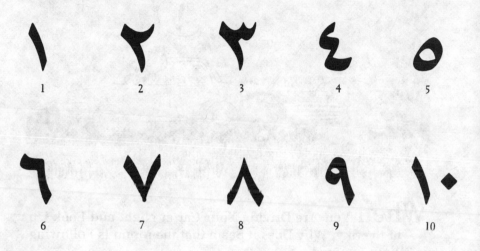

Submitted by Dr. Bruce Carter of Fort Ord, California.

When You Are Driving Your Car at Night and Look Up at the Sky, Why Does It Seem that the Moon Is Following You Around?

If you, like every other literate human being, have read *Why Do Clocks Run Clockwise? and Other Imponderables*, then you know why the moon looks larger on the horizon than up in the sky, even though the moon remains the same size. Clearly, our eyes can play tricks on us.

Without reference points to guide us, the moon doesn't seem to be far away. When you are driving on a highway, the objects closest to your car go whirring by. Barriers dividing the lanes become a blur. You can discern individual houses or trees by the side of the road, but, depending upon your speed, it might be painful to watch them go by. Distant trees and houses move by much more slowly, even though you are driving at the same speed. And distant mountains seem mammoth and motionless.

DAVID FELDMAN

Eventually, as you travel far enough down the highway, you will pass the mountains, and they will appear smaller.

If you think the mountain range off the highway is large or far away, consider the moon, which is 240,000 miles away and bigger than any mountain range (more than 2,100 miles in diameter). We already know that our eyes are playing tricks with our perception of how big and far away the moon is. You would have to be traveling awfully far to make the moon appear to move at all. *Astronomy* editor Jeff Kanipe concludes that without a highway or expanse of landscape to give us reference points "this illusion of nearness coupled with its actual size and distance makes the moon appear to follow us wherever we go."

This phenomenon, much discussed in physics and astronomy textbooks, is called the parallax and is used to determine how the apparent change in the position of an object or heavenly body may be influenced by the changing position of the observer. Astronomers can determine the distance between a body in space and the observer by measuring the magnitude of the parallax effect.

And then again, Elizabeth, maybe the moon really is following you.

Submitted by Elizabeth Bogart of Glenview, Illinois.

When Does a Calf Become a Cow?

The calf's equivalent of a bar mitzvah occurs after it stops nursing, usually at about seven to eight months of age. After they are weaned and/or when they reach twelve months, they are referred to as yearling bulls or yearling calves.

According to Richard L. Spader, executive vice president of the American Angus Association, "calves don't achieve full-fledged bullhood or cowhood until they're in production. We normally refer to a first calf heifer at, say, twenty-four months of age or older, as just that, and after her second calf as a three-year-old, she becomes a cow."

Bulls don't usually reach maturity until they are three. After they wean from their mothers, they are referred to as "yearling bulls," or "two-year-old bulls." Are we now all totally confused?

Submitted by Herbert Kraut of Forest Hills, New York.

When One Has a Cold, Why Does Only One Nostril at a Time Tend to Get Clogged (Even Though Which Nostril Gets Clogged Can Change at Any Time)? Come to Think of It, Why Do We Need Two Nostrils in the First Place?

The shifting of clogged nostrils is a protective effort of your nasal reflex system. Although the nose was probably most important to prehistoric man as a smelling organ, modern humans' sense of smell has steadily decreased over time. The nose is now much more important in respiration, breathing in O_2 to the nose, trachea, bronchi, lungs, heart, and blood, and ultimately the exchange of oxygen and carbon dioxide. As rhinologist Dr. Pat Barelli explains:

> A fantastic system of reflexes which originate in the inner nose sends impulses to the heart and indirectly to every cell in the body. These reflexes, coupled with the resistance of the nose, increase the efficiency of the lungs and improve the effectiveness of the heart action.

We tend to think of the nose as one organ, but we smell or breathe through the nose in stereo, just as we hear through two ears or see with two eyes. Each lung is controlled by one of our "two noses." Without a flow of oxygen from a nostril for a prolonged period, the well-being of the corresponding lung is threatened.

DAVID FELDMAN

The most common reason for congested nostril switching is the sleep process. When we sleep, our body functions at a greatly reduced rate. The heart beats slower and the lungs require less air. Rhinologist Dr. Zanzibar notes that patients

> commonly complain that at night when they lie on one side, the dependent side of the nose becomes obstructed and they find it necessary to roll over in bed to make that side open. Then the other side becomes obstructed, and they roll over again.

When the head is turned to one side during sleep, the "upper nose" has the entire load of breathing and can become fatigued. According to Dr. Pat Barelli,

> one nostril doing solo duty can fatigue in as little as one to three hours, and internal pressures cause the sleeper to change his head position to the opposite side. The body naturally follows this movement. In this way, the whole body, nose, chest, abdomen, neck, and extremities rest one side at a time.

Bet you didn't know your schnozz was so smart. Our motto is "One nostril stuffed is better than two."

Submitted by Richard Aaron of Toronto, Ontario.

Why Do New Fathers Pass Out Cigars?

"What this country needs is a good five-cent cigar" might have been first uttered in the early twentieth century, but in the late seventeenth and early eighteenth centuries, cigars cost much more than five cents. According to Norman Sharp, of the Cigar Association of America, "cigars were so rare and treasured that they were sometimes used as currency."

Two hundred years ago, a baby boy was considered a valuable commodity. He would work the fields all day and produce money for the father, whereas a baby girl was perceived as a financial drain. At first, precious cigars were handed out as a symbol of celebration only when a boy was born.

By the twentieth century, some feminist dads found it in their hearts to pass the stogies around even when, drat, a girl was born. Now the ritual remains a primitive but relatively less costly act of male bonding—a tribute to male fertility while the poor mother recovers alone in her hospital room.

Submitted by Scott P. Frederick of Wilmington, North Carolina. Thanks also to Mike Bartnik of Omaha, Nebraska; and Dan and Patty Poser of San Luis Obispo, California.

What Are Dimples? And Why Do Only Some People Have Them?

Dimples are a generic name for indentations of the skin. Dimples are produced when muscle fibers are attached to the deep surface of the skin, such as in the cheek or chin, or where the skin is attached to bones by fibrous bands, such as the elbow, shoulder, and back.

Dimples are most likely to appear where the skin is most tightly attached to the underlying bone. Anatomist Dr. William Jollie, of the Medical College of Virginia, indicates that "dimples probably are due to some developmental fault in the connective tissue that binds skin to bone."

So all this time we've envied those with dimples but didn't realize that they were exhibiting an anatomical flaw! And the tendency toward dimples seems to be hereditary. You have your father to blame, Michael Douglas.

Submitted by Donna Lamb of Stafford, Texas.

WHEN DO FISH SLEEP?

Why Do Bath Towels Smell Bad After a Few Days When They Are Presumably Touching Only Clean Skin?

Most towels are made of 100% cotton. While it's true that after a shower you have eliminated most of the germs and dirt from your skin, the process of rubbing a towel against the body rubs off dead skin that sticks to the moist towel. Towels become an ideal nesting place for the mildew endemic to humid bathrooms.

Most people flip a fan on or open the windows when showering but then turn off the fan or close the windows when they dry themselves. Jean Lang, director of Marketing at Fieldcrest, says it is much more important to promote circulation *after* the shower. Without dispersing the moisture, the bathroom becomes like a terrarium. The same type of mildew that afflicts plastic shower curtains attacks towels, especially if the towels have never dried completely from their last use.

We remember our windowless high school locker room with little nostalgia. The lack of ventilation and circulation led to mildew and smelly towels. We would have gladly endured the smell of garbage for the odious aroma of schoolmates' moist towels.

Submitted by Merry Phillips of Menlo Park, California. Thanks also to Paul Funn Dunn of Decatur, Illinois.

How Do Stamp Pads Keep Moist When They Are Constantly Exposed to the Drying Influence of Air?

The ink used in stamp pads has a glycol and water base, which forms a mixture that actually absorbs moisture from the air. On a humid day, this hygroscopic effect allows the stamp or stamp pad to replenish any moisture lost on dry days.

Submitted by Russ Tremayne of Auburn, Washington.

DAVID FELDMAN

Why Are Tupperware® Brand Products Sold Only at Parties? Couldn't They Make More Money by Selling the Stuff in Stores Too?

Until Earl Tupper came along, most housewares were made of glass, ceramics, wood, or metal—traditional, dependable materials. In 1945, Tupper established Tupper Plastics and tried to market his containers in retail stores.

Tupper's products bombed. Consumers feared that plastic material would prove flimsy, and they didn't understand or believe that Tupper's innovative airtight seal would keep foods fresh. Two salespeople with experience demonstrating Stanley Home Products on the party plan saw Tupper's products and convinced him that sales would mushroom if his plasticware were demonstrated. Early tests were highly successful. In 1951, Tupperware Home Parties was incorporated, and all Tupper products were removed from store shelves.

Now that the public has learned that Tupperware plastic is durable and effective, why doesn't Tupperware compete with less established brand names in K-Mart's and Macy's? Tupperware is convinced that the party approach has unique advantages. Lawrie Pitcher Platt, Tupperware's director of Public Relations and Community Affairs, explains:

> Tupperware brand products continue to be sold on the party plan because each dealer is like a teacher. He or she demonstrates the many subtle features designed into the pieces shown and discusses product care and the full lifetime warranty. Tupperware brand products are a lifetime purchase, unlike many products manufactured today, and it is management's belief that learning about use and care enhances the value to the customer.

Translation: The Tupperware dealer justifies the higher cost of its product.

As of 1989, Tupperware has 89,000 independent dealers in the United States alone and 325,000 in forty-two countries worldwide. With such a solid sales force base, Tupperware would jeopardize the revenue of its dealers by selling Tupperware brand products on a retail basis again. Why risk a retail rollout when Tupperware already has a dedicated sales force devoted solely to its product? Avon and Fuller Brush have experienced problems with direct sales of late, but Tupperware's success may be partly attributable to its party concept, in which the "sponsor" gets rewarded with free merchandise for throwing the party. And unlike many direct sellers, Tupperware doesn't necessarily invade customers' homes. About 25% of all Tupperware parties in the United States are now held outside the home.

Submitted by Charles Kluepfel of Bloomfield, New Jersey.

Why Do Monkeys in the Zoo Pick Through Their Hair All the Time? Why Do They Pick Through One Another's Hair?

In the wild, primates pick at their own hair frequently but for short periods of time. Usually, they are trying to rid themselves of parasitic insects, insect webs, or remnants of food.

DAVID FELDMAN

Monkeys in captivity are much less likely to be riddled with parasites, but may be afflicted with another skin problem. Monkeys exude salt from the pores of their skin. The salt lands on loose bits of skin, and monkeys will often pick through their hair trying to shed the salty flakes.

A monkey, unlike a human, has no difficulty in scratching its back (or any other part of its body, for that matter). Most animal behaviorists assume that apes—be they gibbons or chimpanzees—search through one another's hair for purely social reasons. One psychologist, H. H. Reynolds, noted that chimpanzees are not altruistic or naturally cooperative: "Grooming behavior appears to be one of the most cooperative ventures in which chimpanzees engage."

Perhaps mutual grooming in monkeys is akin to the human handshake, whose original purpose was to signal that a potential weapon, the outstretched hand, would not turn into a clenched fist.

Why Is Cheddar Cheese Orange?

Unless they've been breeding some pretty strange cows in Wisconsin, we would expect cows to produce white milk. All the folks in the dairy industry assured us that they haven't bred a mutant race of cows just to produce orangeish cheddar cheese.

Cheddar cheese is artificially colored with natural ingredients, most commonly annatto, a seed obtained from the tropical annatto tree, found in Central America. Kraft, the largest seller of cheese in the United States, uses a combination of annatto and oleoresin paprika, an oil extraction of the spice paprika, to color its cheddar cheese. Depending upon the natural color of the milk and the amount of annatto added, cheese can be turned into a bright orange color or a more natural-looking yellow shade.

The only reason why cheesemakers color their product is because consumers seem to prefer it. Regional tastes differ, though. Some areas of the eastern United States prefer white cheese, while most of the rest of the country favors yellow. Kraft even makes white "American Singles," although the artificially colored yellow slices far outsell them.

Submitted by Christoper S. von Guggenberg of Alexandria, Virginia.

What Is the Circle Adjacent to the Batter's Box on Baseball Fields?

This area is known as the fungo circle. Coaches stand in the fungo circle during pregame practice and hit balls to infielders and, more frequently, outfielders.

Why confine the coach to stand in one small area? So he won't wear out the grass on the field!

Submitted by Terrell K. Holmes of New York, New York. Thanks also to Ronald C. Semone of Washington, D.C.

What Exactly Is One Hour Martinizing?

Countless millions have passed dry-cleaning stores with the words ONE HOUR MARTINIZING emblazoned on the sign and wondered: What the heck is "Martinizing"? Can it really be done in one hour? Is it painful, and if so, can an anesthetic be administered?

Don't worry. Be happy. Martinizing is a service mark of Martin Franchises, Inc., the largest chain of franchised dry-cleaning establishments in the United States. Martinizing was first registered with the U.S. Patent Trademark Office in 1950 by the Martin Equipment Corporation, a manufacturer of dry-cleaning machines.

The equipment business and trademarks were later sold to the American Laundry Machinery Company of Cincinnati, Ohio, also a manufacturer of cleaning equipment. Although Martinizing was once part of the sales division of the American Laundry Machinery Company, it has spun off into a separate entity, still located in Cincinnati.

Today if an aspiring dry cleaner wants the know-how and name recognition that a franchise can provide, he or she will likely choose Martin, since it is the best-known name in the dry-cleaning field, and start-up costs are relatively low.

What's special about One Hour Martinizing? As far as we can tell, nothing. They use the same chemicals, solvents, and cleaning methods as other dry cleaners, and can "Martinize" in one hour, just as most dry cleaners can handle a job in one hour.

The folks are relying on the notion that if you patronize another establishment, you can say your clothes have been dry cleaned but you can't brag that they've been Martinized.

Submitted by Dominic Orlando of Arlington, Texas. Thanks also to Peter B. Child of Seattle, Washington.

What Flavor Is Bubble Gum Supposed to Be? Why Is Bubble Gum Usually Pink?

Although in *Imponderables* we managed to ascertain the main flavors in Juicy Fruit gum, we have failed miserably at obtaining the constituents in bubble gum. Perhaps we are losing our powers of persuasion. The best we have been able to wangle from our sources is that "regular" pink bubble gum is a mixture of several natural and artificial fruit flavors.

We thought that the pink color of bubble gum would provide clues to the identity of the flavors, but we were disappointed again. Bubble gum was invented in 1928 by a lone entrepreneur, Walter Diemer, who was an accountant from Philadelphia. From the very beginning, Diemer artificially colored his gum pink. Why? "Because it was the only coloring I had handy at the time!" So much for the sanctity of pink bubble gum.

Now, of course, with Bubble Yum coming in flavors like Bananaberry Split and Checkermint, pink bubble gum looks old

DAVID FELDMAN

hat. But not quite yet. Good old pink bubble gum is still the best seller by far.

Submitted by John Geesy of Phoenix, Arizona.

Why Don't Traffic Signal Light Bulbs Ever Seem to Burn Out? Can We Buy Them?

To answer the second part of the Imponderable first: sure, you can buy the same bulbs that light our traffic signals. But you probably wouldn't want to buy them.

Yes, the bulbs found in traffic lights do last much longer than standard household bulbs. The traffic light bulbs are rated at eight thousand hours, compared to the standard one thousand hours. Incandescent lights can be manufactured to last any length of time. However, the longer life a bulb has, the less efficiently it burns. According to General Electric's J. Robert Moody:

> The incandescent light is like a candle. If you burn it dimly, the candle will last a long time. If you burn the candle on both ends, you get a lot of light but short life. The traffic signal light must use 100 watts to get 1,000 lumens [units of light]. To obtain the same 1,000 lumens a household lamp needs only 60 watts. At an electric rate of $0.10/Kwh, the electric cost for 100 watts is $10.00 per 1,000 hours. For the 60 watts the electric cost is $6.00 per 1,000 hours. Thus, the consumer saves $4.00 per 1,000 burning hours [or 40%] by using a household light bulb rather than a traffic signal light bulb.

Traffic signal bulbs are also specially constructed and are filled with krypton gas rather than the less expensive argon gas used in standard bulbs. Municipalities obviously feel the added expense of the special bulbs is more than offset by the cost of labor for replacing burned-out bulbs and the fewer dangerous situations created by malfunctioning traffic signals.

We're as lazy as the next guys, but even we figure it is worth changing bulbs to save nearly 50% on our lighting needs. Now if we could get a flashing red light, that might be worth it . . .

Submitted by Michael B. Labdon of Paramount, California.

Why Does Mickey Mouse Have Four Fingers?

Or more properly, why does Mickey Mouse have three fingers and one thumb on each hand? In fact, why is virtually every cartoon animal beset with two missing digits?

Conversations with many cartoonists, animators, and Disney employees confirm what we were at first skeptical about. Mickey Mouse has four fingers because it is convenient for the artists and animators who have drawn him. In the early cartoons, each frame was hand-drawn by an animator—painstaking and tedious work. No part of the human anatomy is harder to draw than a hand, and it is particularly difficult to draw distinct fingers without making the whole hand look disproportionately large.

The artists who drew Mickey were more than happy to go along with any conceit that saved them some work. So in Disney and most other cartoons, the animals sport a thumb and three fingers, while humans, such as Snow White and Cinderella, are spared the amputation.

And before anyone asks—no, we don't know for sure *which* of Mickey's fingers got lopped off for the sake of convenience. Since the three nonthumbs on each hand are symmetrical, we'd like to think it was the pinkie that was sacrificed.

Submitted by Elizabeth Frenchman of Brooklyn, New York.
Thanks also to R. Gonzales of Whittier, California.

DAVID FELDMAN

Why Don't Migrating Birds Get Jet Lag? Or Do They?

No, birds don't seem to suffer from jet lag. But then again they don't suffer from airport delays, crowded seating, inedible airline food, or lost luggage either.

Human jet lag seems to be bound inextricably to passing rapidly through time zones. Birds usually migrate from north to south, often not encountering any time change. Veterinarian Robert B. Altman speculates that if you put a bird on an airplane going east to west, it might feel jet lag.

But birds, unlike humans, don't try to fly from New York to Australia in one day. Some migrations can take weeks. Birds don't stretch their physical limits unless they have to (such as when flying over a large body of water). If they are tired, birds stop flying and go to sleep, while their human counterparts on the airplane choose between being kept awake by a screaming baby or the one movie they have assiduously avoided seeing in its theater or cable presentations.

Humans are particularly susceptible to jet lag when they travel at night. As a rule, migration doesn't upset birds' natural sleeping patterns. They sleep when it is dark and awaken when it is light. On airplanes, humans fall asleep only immediately preceding the meal service or the captain's latest announcement of the natural wonders on the ground.

Of course, migration isn't without some perils of its own. The National Audubon Society sent *Imponderables* an article detailing the migration habits of shore birds along the Delaware Bay. Many of these shore birds travel from their breeding ground in the Arctic to the southern tip of South America. The round trip can be in excess of fifteen thousand miles.

When the birds land in warmer climes, they engage in a feeding frenzy not unlike a season-long Thanksgiving dinner. The birds found in the Delaware Bay, who had often flown more than five thousand miles with little rest, often doubled their body weight in two weeks. An official of the New Jersey Division of Fish, Game and Wildlife is quoted as saying that the birds

"get so fat they can hardly even fly." *New York Times* reporter
Erik Eckholm describes these fatted birds as bouncing along
"like an overloaded airplane when trying to take off."

Submitted by Chris Whelan of Lisle, Illinois.

Why Do Some Hard-Boiled Egg Yolks Turn Gray or Green When Soft-Boiled Eggs Don't Discolor?

The discoloring is caused by iron and sulphur compounds that
accumulate when eggs are overcooked. Although gray egg yolks
lack eye appeal, the iron and sulfur don't affect the taste or nutritional value of the eggs.

Probably the most common way of overcooking eggs is to
leave the eggs in hot water after cooking. The American Egg
Board recommends that after eggs are cooked either cold water
should be run over them or they should be put in ice water until
completely cooled. Cooling eggs in this manner will not only
avoid overcooking but will also make the shells much easier to
peel.

DAVID FELDMAN

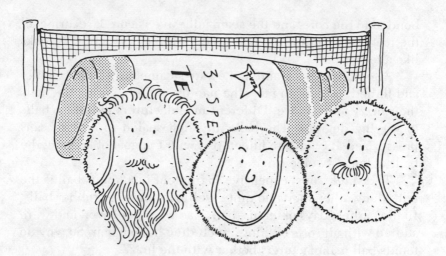

Why Are Tennis Balls Fuzzy?

The core of a tennis ball is made out of a compound consisting of rubber, synthetic materials, and about ten chemicals. The compound is extruded into a barrel-shaped pellet that is then formed into two half shells.

The edges of the two half shells are coated with a latex adhesive and then put together and cured in a double-chambered press under strictly controlled temperature and air-pressure conditions. The inner chamber is pressurized to thirteen psi (pounds per square inch), so that the air is trapped inside and the two halves are fused together at the same pressure.

Once the two halves have been pressed together to form one sphere, the surface of the core is roughened so that the fuzz will stick better. The core is then dipped into a cement compound and oven-dried to prepare for the cover application.

The fuzzy material is felt, a combination of wool, nylon, and Dacron woven together into rolls. The felt is cut into a figure-eight shape (one circular piece of felt wouldn't fit as snugly on a ball), and the edges of the felt are coated with a seam adhesive. The cores and edges of the two felt strips are mated, the felt is

WHEN DO FISH SLEEP?

bonded to the core, and the seam adhesive is cured, securing all the materials and for the first time yielding a sphere that looks like a tennis ball.

After the balls are cured, they are steamed in a large tumbler and fluffed in order to raise the nap on the felt, giving the balls their fuzzy appearance. Different manufacturers fluff their balls to varying degrees. The balls are then sealed in airtight cans pressurized at twelve to fifteen psi, with the goal of keeping the balls at ten to twelve psi.

The single most expensive ingredient in a tennis ball is the felt. Many other sports do quite well with unfuzzy rubber balls. In the earliest days of tennis, balls had a leather cover, and were stuffed with all sorts of things, including human hair. So why do tennis ball manufacturers bother with the fuzz?

Before the felt is added, a tennis ball has a hard, sleek surface, not unlike a baseball's. One of the main purposes of the fuzz is to slow the ball down. The United States Tennis Association maintains strict rules concerning the bound of tennis balls. One regulation stipulates, "The ball shall have a bound of more than 53 inches and less than 58 inches when dropped 100 inches upon a concrete base." The fluffier the felt, the more wind resistance it offers, decreasing not only the bound but the speed of the ball. If the felt were too tightly compacted, the ball would have a tendency to skip on the court.

A second important reason for fuzzy tennis balls is that the fluffy nap contributes to increased racket control. Every time a tennis ball hits a racket the strings momentarily grip the ball, and the ball compresses. With a harder, sleeker surface, the ball would have a tendency to skip off the racket and minimize the skill of the player.

A third contribution of fuzz is the least important to a good player but important to us refugees from hardball sports like racquetball and squash. When you get hit hard by a fuzzy tennis ball, you may want to cry, but you don't feel like you're going to die.

Submitted by Dorio Barbieri of Mountain View, California.

DAVID FELDMAN

What Causes Floaters, or Spots, in the Eyes?

The innermost part of the eye is a large cavity filled with a jelly-like fluid known as vitreous humor. Floaters are small flecks of protein, pigment, or embryonic remnants (trapped in the cavity during the formation of the eye) that suspend in the vitreous humor.

The small specks appear to be in front of the eye because the semitransparent floaters are visible only when they fall within the line of sight. Most people might have specks trapped in the vitreous humor from time to time but not notice them. Eyes have a way of adjusting to imperfections, as any eyeglass wearer with dirty lenses could tell you. Floaters are most likely to be noticed when one is looking at a plain background, such as a blackboard, a bare wall, or the sky.

What should one do about floaters? An occasional spot is usually harmless, although sometimes floaters can be precursors of retinal damage. Most often, a home remedy will keep floaters from bothering you. The American Academy of Ophthalmology suggests:

> if a floater appears directly in your line of vision, the best thing to do is to move your eye around, which will cause the inside fluid to swirl and allow the floater to move out of the way. We are most accustomed to moving our eyes back and forth, but looking up and down will cause different currents within the eye and may be more effective in getting the floaters out of the way.

Although you may be aware of their presence, it is often surprisingly difficult to isolate floaters in your line of vision. Because the floaters are actually within the eye, they move as your eyes move and seem to dart away whenever you try to focus on looking at them directly.

Submitted by Gail Lee of Los Angeles, California.

Does It Ever Really Get Too Cold to Snow?

Having withstood a few snowy midwestern winters in our time, we're not sure we would want to test this hypothesis personally. Luckily, meteorologists have.

No, it never gets too cold to snow, but at extremely low temperatures the amount of snow accumulation on the ground is likely to be much lower than at 25 degrees Fahrenheit. According to Raymond E. Falconer, of the Atmospheric Sciences Research Center, SUNY at Albany, there is so little water vapor available at subzero temperatures that snow takes the shape of tiny ice crystals, which have little volume and do not form deep piles. But at warmer temperatures more water vapor is available, "so the crystals grow larger and form snowflakes, which are an agglomerate of ice crystals." The warmer the temperature is, the larger the snowflakes become.

What determines the size of the initial snow crystals? It depends upon the distribution of temperature and moisture from the ground up to the cloud base. If snow forming at a high level drops into much drier air below, the result may be no accumulation whatsoever. In the condition known as "virga," streaks of ice particles fall from the base of a cloud but evaporate completely before hitting the ground.

Submitted by Ronald C. Semone of Washington, D.C.

Why Do Dogs Have Black Lips?

You would prefer mauve, perhaps? Obviously dogs' lips have to be some color, and black makes more sense than most.

According to veterinarian Dr. Peter Ihrke, pigmentation helps protect animals against solar radiation damage. Because

DAVID FELDMAN

Why Don't Crickets Get Chapped Legs from Rubbing Their Legs Together? If Crickets' Legs Are Naturally Lubricated, How Do They Make that Sound?

If we rubbed our legs together for five minutes as vigorously as crickets do all the time, our legs would turn beet red and we would hobble into the bathroom searching for the talcum powder. How do crickets survive?

Quite well, it turns out. No, crickets don't possess a lubrication system, their legs are made of a tough horny substance not unlike our fingernails, durable enough to withstand this punishment. Like nails, the surface gets worn down with excessive friction, but can grow back.

W. Darryl Hansen, of the Entomological Society of America, explains how the hard, cutaneous surface actually enhances the crickets' chirping:

The hard surface aids in causing the 'scrubbing' board that makes their chirps sound louder. I seriously doubt that there are a sufficient number of nerve endings in the leg that would cause discomfort even if they did get chapped legs from the rubbing.

Submitted by Sandra Baxter of Ada, Oklahoma.

Why Is a Navy Captain a Much Higher Rank than an Army Captain? Has This Always Been So?

When one looks at the ranks of the officers of the four branches of the American military, one is struck by how the Army, Air Force, and Marine Corps use the identical ranks, while the Navy uses different names for the equivalents. But there is one striking disparity: the Navy elevates the rank of captain.

Army, Air Force, Marine Corps	*Navy*
Warrant Officer	Warrant Officer
Chief Warrant Officer	Chief Warrant Officer
Second Lieutenant	Ensign
First Lieutenant	Lieutenant Junior Grade
CAPTAIN	Lieutenant
Major	Lieutenant Commander
Lieutenant Colonel	Commander
Colonel	CAPTAIN
Brigadier General	Commodore
Major General	Rear Admiral
Lieutenant General	Vice Admiral
General	Admiral
General of the Army or General of the Air Force	Fleet Admiral

The word "captain" comes from the Latin word *caput*, meaning "head." In the tenth century, captains led groups of Italian foot soldiers. By the eleventh century, British captains commanded

DAVID FELDMAN

warships. So the European tradition has been to name the head of a military unit of any size, on land or sea, a captain.

Our elevation of the English captain stems from English naval practice. In the eleventh century, British captains were not the heads of ships *per se*. Although captains were in charge of leading soldiers in combat aboard ship, the actual responsibility for the navigation and maintenance of ships fell upon the ranks of master. By the fifteenth century, captains bristled at deferring to the masters they outranked, and captains began to assume the responsibility for the ships heretofore claimed by masters. By 1747 any commander of a ship was officially given the rank of captain.

Meanwhile, on land most European countries named the commander of a company—of any size—captain. By the sixteenth century, military strategists felt that one hundred to two hundred men were the maximum size for a land unit in battle to be effectively led by one person. That leader was known as a captain.

From the inception of the United States military we borrowed from the European tradition. A captain was a company commander and indeed is so today. In the Air Force, a captain commands a squadron, the airborne equivalent of a company. But the Navy captain, because he has domain over such a big and complicated piece of equipment, has a legitimate claim to a higher rank than his compatriots in the other branches. As Dr. Regis A. Courtemanche, of the Scipio Society of Naval and Military History, put it,

> Navy captain isn't only a rank. The senior officer of a ship is always called "Captain" even though his rank may only be lieutenant. So a naval captain may have more responsibility than a military captain who usually commands only a small detachment in battle.

In 1862, the Navy realized that it was no longer practical to make captain its highest rank. They needed a way not only to differentiate among commanders of variously sized and equipped vessels but to reward those who were supervising the captains of warships. For this reason, the Navy split the rank of captain into three different categories. The commodore (and later, the rear admiral) became the highest grade, the commander the lowest, and the captain, once ruler of the seas, stuck in the middle of the ranks.

Submitted by Barrie Creedon of Philadelphia, Pennsylvania.

Why Do Astronomers Look at the Sky Upside Down and Reversed? Wouldn't It Be Possible to Rearrange the Mirrors on Telescopes?

Merry Wooten, of the Astronomical League, informs us that most early telescopes didn't yield upside-down images. Galileo's original spyglass used a negative lens as an eyepiece, just as cheap field glasses made with plastic lenses do now. So why do unsophisticated binoculars yield the "proper" image and expensive astronomical telescopes render an "incorrect" one?

Astronomy editor Jeff Kanipe explains:

> The curved light-gathering lens of a telescope bends, or refracts, the light to focus so that light rays that pass through the top of the lens are bent toward the bottom and rays that pass through the bottom of the lens are bent toward the top. The image thus forms upside down and reversed at the focal point, where an eyepiece enlarges the inverted and reversed image.

Alan MacRobert, of *Sky & Telescope* magazine, adds that some telescopes turn the image upside down, and others also mirror-reverse it: "An upside-down 'correct' image can be viewed correctly just by inverting your head. But a mirror image does not become correct no matter how you may twist and turn to look at it."

O.K. Fine. We could understand why astronomers live with inverted and upside-down images if they had to, but they don't.

DAVID FELDMAN

Terrestrial telescopes do rearrange their image. Merry Wooten says that terrestrial telescopes can correct their image by using porro prisms, roof prisms, or most frequently, an erector lens assembly, which is placed in front of the eyepiece to create an erect image.

Why don't astronomical telescopes use erector lenses? For the answer, we return to Jeff Kanipe:

> Most astronomical objects are very faint, which is why telescopes with larger apertures are constantly being proposed: Large lenses and mirrors gather more light than small ones. Astronomers need every scrap of light they can get, and it is for this reason that the image orientation of astronomical telescopes are not corrected. Each glass surface the light ray encounters reflects or absorbs about four percent of the total incoming light. Thus if the light ray encounters four glass components, about sixteen percent of the light is lost. This is a significant amount when you're talking about gathering the precious photons of objects that are thousands of times fainter than the human eye can detect. Introducing an erector into the optical system, though it would terrestrially orient the image, would waste light. We can afford to be wasteful when looking at bright objects on the earth but not at distant, faint galaxies in the universe.

And even if the lost light and added expense of erector prisms weren't a factor, every astronomer we contacted was quick to mention an important point: There IS no up or down in outer space.

Submitted by William Debuvitz of Bernardsville, New Jersey.

Why Are the Rolls or Bread Served on Airlines Almost Always Cold While Everything Else on the Tray Is Served at the Appropriate Temperature?

We won't even comment on the *taste* of airline food (this is a family book). But if McDonald's can separate the cold from the hot on a McDLT sandwich, why can't the airlines get their rolls within about 50 degrees of the right temperature?

The answer lies in how airline meals are prepared aloft. The salad, bread, and dessert are placed on trays that are usually refrigerated or packed in ice. Entrees are loaded onto separate baking sheets. When it is time to start the meal service, the flight attendant who prepares the meals simply sticks the trays of entrees into ovens (not, by the way, microwaves).

The rolls are cold because they have been sitting all along with the salad and cake. Most airlines offer customers a choice of entrees. The flight attendant who is serving the meal simply

DAVID FELDMAN

selects the entree from the sheets they were cooked in and places it alongside the rest of the meal. Except for the entree choice, every flier's tray will look identical. Note that although most airlines vary the vegetable according to the entree, the vegetable is always cooked on the same plate as the main course because the entree plate will be the only heated element on the tray.

If the bread and salad taste cold, why doesn't the dessert? Airlines, almost without exception, serve cake for dessert. Michael Marchant, vice president of Ogden Allied Aviation Services and the president of the Inflight Food Service Association, told *Imponderables* that the softness of cake fools us into thinking it is being served at room temperature. The gustatory illusion is maintained because in contrast to the roll's hard crust, which locks in the coldness, the soft frosting of a cake dissipates the cold.

The folks in first class, meanwhile, are munching warm rolls, which have been heated. Certainly it is worth an extra five hundred dollars or so to get heated rolls, isn't it?

Why Do Chickens and Turkeys, Unlike Other Fowl, Have White Meat and Dark Meat?

Other birds that we eat, such as quail, duck, or pigeon, have all dark meat. Chickens and turkeys are among a small group of birds with white flesh on the breasts and wings.

Birds have two types of muscle fibers: red and white. Red muscle fibers contain more myoglobin, a muscle protein with a red pigment. Muscles with a high amount of myoglobin are capable of much longer periods of work and stress than white fibers. Thus, you can guess which birds are likely to have light fibers by studying their feeding and migration patterns.

Most birds have to fly long distances to migrate or to find food, and they need the endurance that myoglobin provides. All birds that appear to have all white flesh actually have some red fibers, and with one exception, all birds that appear to be all dark have white fibers. But the hummingbird, which never stops flying, has pectoral muscles consisting entirely of red fibers because the pectoral muscles enable the wings to flap continuously.

The domestic chicken or turkey, on the other hand, lives the life of Riley. Even in their native habitat, according to Dr. Phil Hudspeth, vice president of Quality and Research at Holly Farms, chickens are ground feeders and fly only when nesting. Ordinarily, chickens move around by walking or running, which is why only their legs and thighs are dark. They fly so little that their wings and breasts don't need myoglobin. In fact, the lack of myoglobin in the wing and breast are an anatomical advantage. Janet Hinshaw, of the Wilson Ornithological Society, explains why chicken and turkey musculature is perfectly appropriate:

> They spend most of their time walking. When danger threatens they fly in a burst of speed for a short distance and then land. Thus they need flight muscles which deliver a lot of power quickly but for a short time.

Next time you fork up an extra fifty cents for that order of all-white meat chicken, remember that you are likely paying to eat a bird that racked up fewer trips in the air than you have in an airplane.

Submitted by Margaret Sloane of Chapel Hill, North Carolina. Thanks also to Sara Sickle of Perryopolis, Pennsylvania; and Annalisa Weaver of Davis, California.

Why Haven't Vending Machines Ever Accepted Pennies?

In the second half of the twentieth century, when a child is more likely to think that penny candy is the name of a cartoon charac-

DAVID FELDMAN

ter rather than the actual price of a confection, it is hard to believe that in the early days of vending machines the industry would have loved to be able to accept pennies. When a candy bar cost five cents, vendors undoubtedly lost many sales when frustrated kids could produce five pennies but not one nickel. Now, when a candy bar might cost half a dollar, payment in fifty pennies might clog a receptacle. But why didn't vending machines *ever* accept pennies? We spoke to Walter Reed, of the National Automatic Merchandising Association, who told us about the fascinating history of this Imponderable.

The vending machine industry has always been plagued by enterprising criminals who inserted slugs or relatively worthless foreign coins into machines in the time-honored tradition of trying to get something for nothing. In the 1930s, a slug rejector was invented that could differentiate U.S. coinage from Mexican centavos of the same size. The slug rejector worked by determining the metallic content of the coin. Although the slug rejector could easily differentiate between silver or nickel and a slug, it couldn't tell the difference between a worthless token and the copper in a penny. For this reason, vendors hesitated to accept pennies in the machines.

The slug rejectors of today are much more sophisticated, measuring the serration of the coin, its circumference, its thickness, and the presence of any holes. Whereas the 1930s slug rejector was electromagnetic, current rejectors perform tests electronically.

The vending machine industry was instrumental in pushing for the clad-metal coins that were introduced in 1965. Since that year our quarter, for example, which used to be made of silver, now has a center layer of copper surrounded by an outer layer of copper and nickel. The copper-nickel combination reacts to the electronic sensors in vending machine rejectors much like silver. The government also loves the clad coins because the constituent metals are so much cheaper to buy.

Except in gumball machines, the vending machine industry has never accepted pennies, although they once gave pennies away to consumers. In the late 1950s, a cigarette tax was imposed that drove the retail price of cigarettes a few cents above its long-held thirty-five-cent price. Stores simply charged thirty-seven cents, but vending machines couldn't, for they were not equipped to return pennies.

Vendors had to decide whether to keep charging thirty-five cents and absorb the loss of the two cents on every pack, or charge forty cents and risk loss of sales when grocery stores could undercut them by 10%. So they compromised. Vending machines charged forty cents a pack, but pennies were placed in the pack to restore equity to the consumer.

Submitted by Fred T. Beeman of Wailuku, Hawaii.

NOW that Most Products Sold in Vending Machines Sell for Fifty Cents or More, Why Don't Most Vending Machines Accept Half Dollars or Dollar Bills?

The problem with the half dollar is that the public does not carry it in its pocket. Half dollars are too bulky and heavy. Allowing half dollars would necessitate increasing the size of coin slots in the machines.

The American public loves quarters. Unfortunately, studies have shown that people resist putting in more than two coins in vending machines. And two quarters aren't enough to buy even a soft drink anymore.

So isn't the dollar bill acceptor the panacea? The technology exists to accept dollar bills in vending machines, but the same hassles that plague the consumer using dollar-bill changers are also a nightmare for the vendor. Bills must be placed in the proper position to be accepted. Worn or slightly torn bills are rejected routinely even though they are perfectly legal tender. And worst of all, dollar bills can't be counted by machine. The labor involved in counting paper money is not insignificant.

The vending machine industry lusts after the resuscitation of the silver dollar. Frustrated by the unpopularity of the Susan

DAVID FELDMAN

B. Anthony dollar, trade groups are now pushing for a new gold-colored dollar with a portrait of Christopher Columbus on the obverse. The Treasury supports the proposal, for although coins are more expensive to manufacture than bills, they last much longer in circulation. Walter Reed points out that no other industrialized nation has an equivalent of a one dollar bill in paper currency anymore. The Canadians were the last to fall, with the Looney dollar, the same size as the ill-fated Susan B. Anthony, replacing their dollar bill.

Why Is a Blue Ribbon Used to Designate First Prize?

Most sources we contacted give credit to the English for introducing the blue ribbon. In 1348, King Edward III of England established the Order of the Garter, now considered one of the highest orders in the world. Ribbons had traditionally been used as a badge of knighthood. Members of the Order of the Garter were distinguished by wearing their dark blue ribbon on their hip.

A second theory presented by S. G. Yasinitsky, of the Orders and Medals Society of America, was new to us:

> Another version of the blue ribbon as meaning the highest achievement may have originated among British soldiers who practiced abstinence by belonging to the various army abstinence groups, especially in India, in the latter part of the nineteenth century. Their basic badge for the first six years' total abstinence was a medal worn on a blue ribbon. Hence a 'blue ribbon unit' was one which was comprised of all men who were sporting a blue ribbon in their buttonhole to denote their sobriety. 'Blue ribbon panel' and 'blue ribbon selection' followed this, I'm sure.

Yasinitsky and others have speculated that our ribbon color schemes might have had an astronomical basis. Blue, the highest award, represented the sky and the heavens, the highest point possible. Red (second prize) represented the sun, which was high up in the sky. Yellow (third prize) represented the stars, once thought to be lower than the sun. Yasinitsky mentions that runners-up in fairs and festivals are often given green ribbons as consolation prizes. The green color probably represents the lowly grass on the ground.

What Is the "Cottage" in Cottage Cheese?

Food historians speculate that cottage cheese was probably the first cheese. And it was undoubtedly made by accident. Some anonymous nomad was probably carrying milk on a camel in the desert and at the end of the day found lumps rather than liquid. And much to the nomad's surprise, the lumps tasted pretty good.

According to the United Dairy Industry Association, cottage cheese was made in the home all over Europe as far back as the Middle Ages. "It was called 'cottage' because farmers made the cheese in their own cottages to utilize the milk remaining after the cream had been skimmed from it for buttermaking."

Submitted by Mrs. K. E. Kirtley of Eureka, California.

Why Are There So Many Ads *for* the Yellow Pages *in* the Yellow Pages?

Yellow Pages publishers are smart enough to realize that if you've got a copy of their directory in your grubby hands, you already are convinced of the efficacy of their medium. So why must they pummel us with promotional ads? Phone companies make profits from their directories by selling advertising space —you would think they'd rather have a local plumber buy a small display ad than toot their own horns.

The simple purpose of the promotional ads is to fill space between paid ads. Kenneth Hudnall, executive director of the National Yellow Pages Agency Association, explains why there is a need for filler:

> Mechanically, the composition of the Yellow Pages is quite involved. For a variety of reasons there will be small bits of space left at the bottom of a column of listings or between display ad-

DAVID FELDMAN

vertisements. Rather than leave this space blank, the publishers will throw in "justifiers" to fill up the space. And what is more natural than to put promotional copy for Yellow Pages in this space?

If all advertisements in the Yellow Pages were the same size, it would be easy for designers to lay out the directory without need for filler. But the ads, whether listings or display, come in all different sizes. A catering company won't want its advertisement stranded alone when all the other caterers in town are listed on the two pages before. Justifiers, then, have been a way to make the life of the designer easier and soothe the complaints of advertisers about the placement of their display ads.

One man, Arnie Nelson, had the kind of brilliant idea that can make fortunes: Why should Yellow Pages publishers "waste" the filler space when they could sell advertising in it? Nelson founded a company called Yellow Spots, Inc., whose purpose is to sell small-space display advertising to companies who traditionally do not advertise at all in the Yellow Pages.

According to Nelson and Yellow Spots executive Gabe Samuels, initially there was some resistance from the regional phone companies to giving Yellow Spots an exclusive right to sell display ads. But Yellow Spots mustered some strong arguments to convince them, the most compelling one economic: it would provide a windfall. According to Yellow Spots, anywhere from 6 to 20% of the Yellow Pages consist of filler. Adding 5 or 10% more to gross revenues through new display ads would be most profitable.

Some of the publishers were also reluctant to introduce a new type of advertising into a medium that had thrived without it for more than a hundred years. Nelson and Samuels argued that the Yellow Pages were actually used more by consumers as an information source, a magazine, rather than as an advertising medium. The editorial matter of the *Yellow Pages Magazine* are the directory listings. Yellow Spots would deliver the advertising, billboard ads without addresses or phone numbers. The ads that Yellow Spots would solicit were designed to promote a product rather than tell consumers where to buy it, thus not alienating Yellow Pages' traditional retail clients.

Yellow Spots' second obstacle was to convince corporations, mostly big, national advertisers, to promote their companies in a medium that had heretofore not been considered. There had never been a category in the Yellow Pages that would allow Coca-Cola to promote the image of its beverage, although local bottlers or distributors might have had their addresses and phone numbers printed.

So how did Yellow Spots attract national advertisers and have the temerity to ask up to $8 million from one potential client? They touted the unique advertising climate that the Yellow Pages presents:

- The circulation of all the Yellow Pages directories in the United States is about 100 million, 10 million more than there are homes in America. The Yellow Pages, of course, is usually used by more than one person.
- 50% of all customer references to the Yellow Pages result in a sale.
- 18% of all adults use the Yellow Pages at least once on any given day (and they average one and one-half uses per day). This is the equivalent of a rating of 18 on TV, emblematic of a successful show.
- Advertisers operate in a nonhostile environment in the Yellow Pages. Whereas the clutter of TV commercials is a bone of contention among viewers, users of the Yellow Pages do not feel oppressed by the number of ads. In a recent survey, 65% of Americans surveyed felt the number of ads in the Yellow Pages were "just about right"; 18% said they wished there were *more* ads; and only 8% complained there were too many ads.
- Yellow Pages are kept in the home all year long and, in many cases, much longer. Magazines—even those passed around within a family—tend to be thrown out within weeks.

Yellow Spots has already signed up Budget car and truck rentals and Sears Discovery card as major accounts, with others soon to follow. Although we admire the ingenuity of Yellow Spots, we're glad that the homely graphics of the promotional

DAVID FELDMAN

fillers won't totally disappear. Even Nelson and Samuels concede that they'll never take over all of the possible remnant space. They will be quite content with about 50 to 60% of it, thank you.

Submitted by Calvin Wong of Chapel Hill, North Carolina.

Why Is Flour Bleached?

Wheat isn't white. Flour is made out of wheat. So why is flour white?

First of all, all of the major flour producers, such as Pillsbury and General Mills, do make unbleached flour, which many breadmakers prefer. But the vast majority of flour sold to consumers is in the form of all-purpose bleached white flour, which is a combination of hard wheat flour (high in protein and best for making breads) and soft wheat flour (lower in protein and the best consistency for cakes and pastries).

Freshly milled white flour has a yellowish tinge, much like unbleached pasta, which consumers reject in favor of a pristine white. Flour processors have two ways to eradicate the yellow from wheat flour. If flour is stored and allowed to age naturally for several months, the yellow disappears as it is exposed to oxygen. But the cost of storing the bulky flour is prohibitive, so commercial flour is bleached artificially with bleaches such as benzoyl peroxide. Artificial bleaching works better than natural aging, which doesn't yield uniformity of color or maturation.

Mature flour produces better baking results and has a longer shelf life. So along with being bleached, all-purpose flour is artificially aged. While benzoyl peroxide merely bleaches flour, other agents such as azodicarbonamide and potassium bromide artificially age the flour as they bleach. The whole process is performed in twenty-four hours, and the bleach eventually decomposes into a harmless residue called benzoic acid when the flour is used.

Is there a down side to the bleaching process? Certain nutrients are lost, which is why all-purpose flour by law is enriched with nutrients. Some nutritionists are not sanguine about the results. The late Adele Davis was particularly rabid about the subject. She felt the machinery that grinds flour overheats it and gives it a precooked taste "comparable to last night's chops reheated." But she was particularly skeptical about the value of enriched flour:

> So-called "enriched" flour is my idea of outright dishonesty; at least 25 nutrients are largely removed during refining, and one-third of the original amount of iron, vitamin B and niacin may be replaced. Such flour is "enriched" just as you would be enriched by someone stealing 25 dollars from you and returning 99 cents.

Flour enrichment was mandated by the federal government in the early 1940s to compensate for the loss of nutrients that are eliminated from white flour. The flour industry contends that Adele Davis and other critics' objections to enrichment overstate the case. Although they concede that the bran and germ of wheat kernels in whole-wheat flour contain more nutrients than white flour, those nutrients lost (e.g., calcium, phosphorus, and potassium) tend to be found in other foods, and few consumers look toward baked goods as a source for these nutrients.

Although health-food advocates tend to belittle the nutritional value of white flour, the flour companies stress that bleaching in itself has never been a health hazard. The alternative to bleached flour, they say, is vastly more expensive flour.

What Is Goofy?

Goofy can't be a dog, claims our correspondent, or else he would look like Pluto, wouldn't he? Goofy is indeed a dog. Chihuahuas don't look like Doberman pinschers, so why should Goofy look like Pluto? Although we must admit that we don't know too

DAVID FELDMAN

many dogs who speak English and walk on two feet.

Pluto appeared several years before Goofy, in a tiny role in a Mickey Mouse short called "Chain Gang." Pluto's original name was Rover, and he was Minnie's dog, not Mickey's. But Mickey soon gained ownership, and Rover was renamed Pluto the Pup. Animator John Canemaker observes that Pluto's lack of speech and doglike walk were used to emphasize that Pluto was Mickey's pet and not his equal.

Goofy, on the other hand, was nobody's pet. His dogginess is indisputable, since his original name was Dippy Dawg. But Dippy had to pay his dues before he reached the summit of Goofyness. Dippy first played small roles in Mickey Mouse shorts in the early 1930s, and it wasn't until he was featured in the syndicated Mickey Mouse newspaper cartoons that he gained prominence in animated shorts.

Although Goofy was as loyal and loving as Pluto, he was not subservient. As his popularity grew, Goofy became a part of "The Gang," with costars Mickey Mouse and Donald Duck in a series of twelve cartoons in the late 1930s and early 1940s. Few remember that Goofy was married (to Mrs. Goofy) and that he was a proud parent (of Goofy, Jr.).

This Imponderable has been thrust at us many times since the release of the movie *Stand By Me*, in which a character muses about this question. How people can accept that a duck can survive being squashed by a refrigerator and then not believe that Goofy can be a dog, we'll never understand.

Submitted by Ashley Hoffar of Cincinnati, Ohio.

How Did the Toque Become the Traditional Chef's Hat? Does It Serve Any Functional Purpose?

Most men, in their daily lives, wear neither rags nor haute couture. We don a pair of pants and a shirt—maybe a sports coat or suit and tie if the occasion warrants it. But in the kitchen headware has always been schizophrenic. Cooks wear either ugly but functional hair nets or *toques blanches* ("white caps"), smart-looking caps with tops long enough to camouflage the heads of the entire Conehead family. Isn't there a middle ground? Why can't a chef wear a baseball cap or a derby? Can there possibly be a logical function for the shape of toques?

As early as the Roman and Greek Empires, master chefs were rewarded for their achievements by receiving special headware. For the ancients, laurel-studded caps were the honor.

In France up until the seventeenth century, chefs were awarded different colored caps depending upon their rank. Apprentices wore ordinary skull caps. During the early eighteenth century, Talleyrand's chef required his entire staff to don the toque blanche for sanitary reasons. The toque blanche was designed not only to keep the chef's hair from entering food but to register any stains upon the white background.

But this original cap was flat. The high hat gradually gained popularity not as a fashion statement, not to hide Mohawk hairdos, but to provide some ventilation for the head, as chefs frequently work under extremely hot conditions.

Viennese chef Antonin Careme, not willing to leave well enough alone, decided that the toque blanche needed still more oomph. He put a piece of round cardboard inside his toque to give the cap a stiffer, more dashing appearance. The cardboard has been replaced today by starch.

The toque blanche is no more functional than a hair net, and almost as silly looking. But as Shriners or Mouseketeers can testify, any hat bestowed upon someone as an honor is likely to be worn proudly by the recipient, regardless of how funny it looks.

Submitted by William Lickfield of Hamburg, New York.

When and Where Do Police Dogs Urinate and Defecate?

Our fearless correspondent, Eric Berg, notes that he trains his eyes for police dogs whenever he is in a big city and has yet to see nature call one of our canine protectors. "Have the police bred some sort of Bionic Dog?" Eric wonders.

Natural urges dog police dogs just as often as any Fido or Rover, but the difference is in the training; police dogs are much more disciplined than other dogs, or for that matter, most dog owners. Before the animals go on duty, trainers allow police dogs to run and go to the bathroom (well, not *literally* a bathroom) in the area where they are kept.

Part of the training of police dogs involves teaching the dog to control itself while on patrol and when in front of the public.

The dog is taught to signal when it has to "go," but is trained to keep itself under control in all circumstances.

Gerald S. Arenberg, editor of the official journal of the National Association of Chiefs of Police, alludes to the fact that "the dogs are given walks and care that is generally not seen by the public," the only hint we received that occasionally a dog might relieve itself while on duty.

Let's end this discussion here, before we run out of euphemisms.

Submitted by Eric Berg of Chicago, Illinois.

How Can Hurricanes Destroy Big Buildings But Leave Trees Unscathed?

Think of a hurricane as heavyweight boxer Sonny Liston, a powerful force of nature. A building in the face of Liston's onslaught is like George Foreman, strong but anchored to the ground. Without any means of flexibility or escape, the building is a sitting target. A building's massive size offers a greater surface area to the wind, allowing greater total force for the same wind pressure than a tree could offer.

But a tree in a hurricane is like Muhammad Ali doing the rope-a-dope. The tree is going to be hit by the hurricane, but it yields and turns and shuffles its way until the force of the hurricane no longer threatens it. In this case, the metaphor is literal: by bending with the wind, the tree and its leaves can sometimes escape totally unscathed.

Richard A. Anthes, director of the National Center for Atmospheric Research, offers another reason why we see so many buildings, and especially so many roofs, blown away during a hurricane. "Buildings offer a surface which provides a large aerodynamic lift, much as an airplane wing. This lift is often what causes the roof to literally be lifted off the building."

DAVID FELDMAN

We don't want to leave the impression that trees can laugh off a hurricane. Many get uprooted and are stripped of their leaves. Often we get the wrong impression because photojournalists love to capture ironic shots of buildings torn asunder while Mother Nature, in the form of a solitary, untouched, majestic tree, stands triumphant alongside the carnage.

Submitted by Daniel Marcus of Watertown, Massachusetts.

Why Are Downhill Ski Poles Bent?

Unlike the slalom skier's poles, which must make cuts in the snow to negotiate the gates, the main purpose' of the downhill ski poles is to got the skier moving, into a tuck position . . . and then not get in the way.

According to Tim Ross, director of Coaches' Education for the United States Ski Coaches Association, the bends allow the racer "to get in the most aerodynamic position possible. This is extremely important at the higher speeds of downhill." Savings of hundredths of a second are serious business for competitive downhill skiers, even when they are attaining speeds of 60–75 miles per hour.

If the bends in the pole are not symmetrical, they are designed with careful consideration. Dave Hamilton, of the Professional Ski Instructors of America, reports that top-level ski racers have poles individually designed to fit their dimensions. Recreational skiers are now starting to bend their poles out of shape. According to Ross, the custom-made downhill ski poles may have as many as three to four different bend angles.

Funny. We haven't seen downhill skiers with three to four different bend angles in their bodies.

Submitted by Roy Welland of New York, New York.

Why Do So Many Mail-Order Ads Say to "Allow Six to Eight Weeks for Delivery"? Does It Really Take that Long for Companies to Process Orders?

This is a mystery we have pondered over ourselves, especially since these same companies that warn us of six-to-eight-week delivery schedules usually send us our goods within a few weeks. We talked to several experts in the mail-order field who assured us that any reasonably efficient operation should be able to ship items to customers within two to three weeks.

Many manufacturers farm out much or all of the processing of mail orders to specialized companies, called fulfillment houses. Some fulfillment houses do everything from receiving the initial letters from customers and obtaining the proper goods from their own warehouses to producing address labels, maintaining inventory control, and shipping out the package back to the customer.

DAVID FELDMAN

Dick Levinson, of the fulfillment company H.Y. Aids Group, told *Imponderables* that a fulfillment house should be able to gurarantee a client a turnaround of no more than five days from when a check is received until the package is shipped to the customer. A two- or three-day turnaround is the norm.

Do the mail order companies blame the post office? Why not? Everybody else does. But despite a few carpings, all agreed that even third-class packages tend to get delivered anywhere in the continental United States within a week.

Being paranoid types, we thought about a few nefarious reasons why mail-order companies might want to delay orders. Perhaps they want to create a little extra cash flow by holding on to checks for an extra month or so? No, insisted all of our sources.

How about advertising goods they don't have in stock? As checks clear, companies could pay for their inventory out of customer money rather than their own. It's possible but unlikely, said our panel. Stanley J. Fenvessey, founder of Fenvessey Consulting and perhaps the foremost expert on fulfillment, said that only a fly-by-night operation would try to get away with such shenanigans. He offered a few more benign explanations.

Sometimes a mail-order company, particularly one that specializes in imports or seasonal items, might run out of stock temporarily. By listing a delayed delivery date, the company forestalls complaints, even though it expects to deliver merchandise in half the stated time.

And in the magazine field, fledgling efforts sometimes try a "dry test," in which prospective subscribers are solicited by mail even though no magazine yet exists. Only if there is a high enough response rate will the magazine ever be produced.

The most compelling reason is the Federal Trade Commission's Mail Order Rule. The rule was established in 1974 after consumers complained in droves about late or nonexistent shipments of merchandise by mail-order operations. The President's Office of Consumer Affairs reported that the number of complaints registered against mail-order firms was second only to complaints about automobiles and auto services.

The Mail Order Rule states that a buyer has the right to

assume that goods will be shipped within the time specified in a solicitation and, "if no time period is clearly and conspicuously stated, within thirty days after receipt of a properly completed order from the buyer." Furthermore, when a seller is unable to ship merchandise within the time provisions of the rule, the seller must not only notify the buyer of the delay but also offer the option to the buyer to cancel the order.

Refunding money is not exactly any company's favorite thing to do, but the provisions about sending the notice of delay and option to cancel is perhaps more onerous to mail-order firms. Not only must the seller spend money on mailing these notices, but must somehow track the progress of each order to make sure it hasn't exceeded the 30-day limit. The bookkeeping burden is enormous.

Finally, we have arrived at the answer: By putting a shipping deadline of much longer than they think they will ever need, mail-order firms avoid having to comply with the provisions of the thirty-day rule whenever they run out of stock temporarily.

But don't these disclaimers discourage sales? After all, most items ordered by mail are available in retail stores as well. Dick Levinson suggests that most items ordered from magazines and newspapers are impulse items rather than necessities, and that most buyers are flexible about delivery schedules. Lynn Hamlin, book buyer for New York's NSI Syndications Inc., commented that space customers (those who order from newspapers and magazines) are less demanding than those who order from catalogs with toll-free phone numbers and who have the ability to ask a company operator how long the delivery will take. NSI advertisements guarantee shipment within 60 days, but usually are filled in two or three weeks. Ms. Hamlin notes that she has not seen any detrimental effect of the sixty-day guarantee on her company's sales, although she admits that around December 1, some potential customers might fear whether merchandise would arrive by Christmas.

Stanley Fenvessey informs us that about 75 to 90% of all catalog merchandise is delivered within two weeks, and insists

DAVID FELDMAN

that no large catalog house would ever print "six to eight weeks for delivery." One of Fenvessey's smaller clients, who owned a catalog company, printed "please allow four to five weeks for delivery" on his catalog. Fenvessey asked his client whether it really took this long to fulfill orders. The client replied that most orders were delivered in two weeks.

"So why put four to five weeks in the catalog?" asked Fenvessey.

"Because this way we avoid hassles when we are a few days late."

Fenvessey was convinced that the client couldn't see the forest for the trees. Fenvessey conducted a test in which two sets of catalogs were printed and shipped; the only difference between the two was that one announced that delivery would be between two to three weeks; the other, four to five weeks. The two to three week catalog drew 25% more orders, a huge difference.

Maybe many space advertisers are losing sales by scaring potential customers into thinking they're going to have to wait longer than they really will to get merchandise.

Submitted by Susie T. Kowalski of Middlefield, Ohio.

Why Are Silos Round?

The poser of this Imponderable, Susan Diffenderffer, insisted she had the correct answer in hand: "In a square silo, grain could form an air pocket and cause spontaneous combustion. There are no corners in a round silo."

Well, we think the spontaneous combustion theory is a tad apocalyptical, but you have the rest of the story right. Actually, at one time silos were square or rectangular. Fred Hatch, a farmer from Illinois, built a square wooden silo in 1873. But the square corners didn't allow Hatch to pack the silo tightly enough. As a result, air got in the silo and spoiled much of the feed. To the rescue came Wisconsin agricultural scientist, Franklin H. King, who built a round silo ten years later. The rest is silage history.

Why is it so important to shut air out of a silo? The mold that spoils grain cannot survive without air. Without air, the grass and corn actually ferment while in the silo, inducing a chemical change in the silage that makes it palatable all through the winter season.

Before silos were invented, cows gave less milk during winter because they had no green grass to eat. Silos gave the cows the lavish opportunity to eat sorghums all year long.

Submitted by Susan C. Diffenderffer of Cockeysville, Maryland.

DAVID FELDMAN

DIAL '9'
for
"outside"

Why Does Dialing 9 Usually Get You an Outside Line in a Hotel? And Why Does 8 Open a Long-Distance Line?

For many years we've been looking at want ads in the newspaper and seeing positions open for PBX operators. We've always wondered what the heck they did. "PBX" sure sounds threateningly high-tech. Little did we know that we were already experts in the field.

PBX systems are simply telephone lines designed for communication within one building or business that are also capable of interfacing with the outside world. Most large hotels have a PBX system. When you lift your phone up in your room, you become a PBX station user whether you like it or not.

Most PBX systems reserve numbers one through seven for dial access to other internal PBX stations. In a hotel, this allows a guest in one room to call another room directly. Decades ago, one might have dialed for the operator to perform this function, but hotels found that patrons preferred the greater speed of direct access; and of course, direct dialing saved hotels the labor costs of operators.

There is no inherent reason why 4 or 2 *couldn't* be the access code for an outside line or long-distance access, but Victor J. Toth, representing the Multi-Tenant Telecommunications Association, explains how the current practice began:

> The level "9" code is usually used by convention in all commercial PBX and Centrex as the dialing code for reaching an outside line. This number was chosen because it was usually high enough in the number sequence so as not to interfere with a set of assigned station numbers (or, in the case of a hotel, a room number).

Likewise, the 8 is sufficiently high in the number sequence to not interfere with other station numbers and has become the conventional way to gain access to long-distance services.

Toth adds that it is easy to deny level 9 class of service to a particular phone or set of phones if desired. Most hotels, for example, make it impossible for someone using a lobby phone to dial outside the hotel, let alone long distance.

Why Can't (Or Won't) Western Union Transmit an Exclamation Mark in a Telegram?

Many of the origins of the customs we now take for granted are lost in obscurity. We are thankful to Paul N. Dane, executive director of the Society of Wireless Pioneers, who led us to two gentlemen, W.K. "Bill" Dunbar, and Colonel Ronald G. Martin, who could answer these two Imponderables authoritatively.

Mr. Dunbar informs us that the original Morse code alphabet (but not the international code used for cablegrams and radiograms) did indeed provide for the exclamation mark: - - - · expressed it. "The early teletype machines with a three-row keyboard may not have provided for the exclamation mark, and although later equipment did, it might not have been capable of conveying the exclamation point into a Telex circuit."

DAVID FELDMAN

According to Colonel Martin:

> It is very easy to cause an error during the transmission of a message with a lot of punctuation therein. Therefore, Western Union, in order to prevent lawsuits, abolished it.

Even if there were technological problems in printing an exclamation mark, a more compelling reason existed to shun it and other punctuation: Punctuation marks were charged as if they were words.

Submitted by Fred T. Beeman of Wailuku, Hawaii.

Why Do Telegrams End Sentences with STOP Rather than with a Period?

Western Union, throughout most of its history, has charged extra for periods as well as exclamation marks. But the reasons for the exclusion of periods and the inclusion of STOP are fascinating and highly technical. Bill Dunbar, president of the Morse Telegraph Club, explains:

> In certain instances the word STOP, when used as a period, was free. I believe this was the case with transoceanic cablegrams. Hollywood sometimes showed STOP in domestic telegrams, which may have given the impression it was common usage. At one time when competition between Western Union and Postal Telegraph was keen, STOP was free, but this did not last long and usually it was a chargeable word, so naturally it wasn't used much.
>
> The main reason for periods not appearing was a procedural one—the period was used to indicate the beginning and end of the body of a message. The preamble (i.e., call letters of sending office, the number of words in a message, type of service, and type of payment), origin city, the time and date were sent first. This was followed by the word TO, after which the receiving operator would drop down a line or two and move to the left of the page to write the address.

At the end of the address, a period was sent, signifying that the next characters would begin the text of the message. At the end of the message, the sender would send another period and say SIG (signature), and the copying operator would drop down two lines to write the signature; he would also add the time the message was copied. If there *was* a period in the message, it was converted to STOP for transmission.

The words TO, SIG and the periods were not written on the telegram, since they were procedural signals. Decimals were transmitted by sending the word DOT as 18 DOT 5. This might seem clumsy, but it eliminated any ambiguity as to whether a decimal point or the end of a message was indicated.

PERIOD must have been considered instead of STOP to signify the period, but probably was rejected for one simple reason: STOP is two letters shorter. Colonel Martin adds that the word PERIOD is more likely to cause confusion when a telegram concerns time.

Both Martin and Dunbar emphasize how important brevity of language and speed of transmission has always been to Western Union. But customers have proven to be just as frugal in their own way. Traditionally, Western Union charged a basic rate that allowed for ten free words. Any extra words or punctuation marks cost extra. Sometimes the need to squeeze a lot of information into ten words tested the ingenuity of the sender, as Mr. Dunbar's story illustrates:

> The story is told of a man who sent the following message: BRUISES HURT ERASED AFFORD ERECTED ANALYSIS HURT TOO INFECTIONS DEAD
> Translated it reads: "Bruce is hurt he raced a Ford he wrecked it Aunt Alice is hurt too in fact she's dead"

Writers who are paid by the word try to be as verbose as possible. But a writer who has to *pay* by the word will try to squeeze nineteen words into ten.

Submitted by Eileen LaForce of Weedsport, New York.

DAVID FELDMAN

Why Are Most Snack-Food Items, Such as Chips, Cakes, and Popcorn, Prepriced (on the Package) by the Manufacturers?

How often have you scoured the aisles of your local supermarket looking for the elusive item on your grocery list? You despair of ever finding what you need when you encounter a young man arduously arranging packages on the shelf. "Where can I find the artificial coloring?" you inquire.

"I don't know. I don't work here," replies the man.

Why can't you ever find the people who supposedly *do* work at the damn store? This poignant episode, repeated in grocery stores throughout the land, explains—believe it or not—why most snack items are prepriced by the manufacturers.

Most items in a supermarket, such as canned goods, are sent to the store by a warehouse distributor who handles many different brands. Snack-food manufacturers work on "store-door distribution," providing full service to retailers. Potato chips or popcorn are brought to the stores in trucks displaying the logo of one company. The agent for the manufacturer rids the shelves of any unsold packages with elapsed expiration dates, restocks, and straightens up the shelves to make the company's selling environment look attractive.

Retailers have come to expect this kind of full-service treatment from the snack-food industry. Next to the expense of cashiers, pricing items is one of the costliest labor costs of grocery retailers: Stores welcome prepricing by the industry.

Why do snack-food manufacturers go along with providing extra service to stores? Although manufacturers like retaining the control of pricing, according to Chris Abernathy, of the Borden Snack Group, fear of retail overcharging is not the main purpose for the practice. By stamping the price themselves, Borden and other snack-food companies can run citywide or regional promotions by cutting the price on the package itself.

Al Rickard, of the Snack Food Association, stresses that by stamping prices on packages themselves, manufacturers can guarantee *equality* of prices to outlets that sell their products. Snack foods are sold not only in grocery stores but in convenience stores, bowling centers, service stations, and other venues that are not used to putting price stickers on food items. Those establishments are more likely to sell snacks when they don't feel they will be undercut in price by supermarkets.

Most important, with store-door distribution manufacturers can assure themselves that their products are not languishing on the shelves because retailers are refusing to pull old goods. What all of the food items with prepricing have in common is their perishability. Most salted snack foods have shelf lives of approximately two weeks. Other prepriced items, such as doughnuts and bread, may have even shorter expiration dates. If they have to preprice snack items to guarantee the proper rotation of their goods, it is a small price to pay.

Submitted by Herbert Kraut of Forest Hills, New York.

DAVID FELDMAN

Why Are the Commercials Louder than the Programming on Television?

Having lived in apartments most of our adult lives, we developed a theory about this Imponderable. Let us use a hypothetical example to explain our argument.

Let's say a sensitive, considerate yet charismatic young man —we'll call him "Dave"—is taking a brief break from his tireless work to watch TV late at night. As an utterly sympathetic and empathic individual, "Dave" puts the volume at a low level so as not to wake the neighbors who are divided from him by tissue-thin walls. Disappointed that "Masterpiece Theatre" is not run at 2:00 A.M., "Dave" settles for a rerun of "Hogan's Heroes." While he is studying the content of the show to determine what the character of Colonel Klink says about our contemporary society, a used-car commercial featuring a screaming huckster comes on at a much louder volume.

What does "Dave" do? He goes up to the television and

WHEN DO FISH SLEEP?   81

lowers the volume. But then the show comes back on, and "Dave" can't hear it. Ordinarily, "Dave" would love to forgo watching such drivel, so that he could go back to his work as, say, a writer. But he is now determined to ascertain the sociological significance of "Hogan's Heroes." So for the sake of sociology, "Dave" gets back up and turns the volume back on loud enough so that he can hear but softly enough not to rouse the neighbors. When the next set of commercials comes on, the process is repeated.

Isn't it clear? Commercials are louder to force couch potatoes (or sociological researchers) to get some exercise! When one is slouched on the couch, the walk to and from the television set constitutes aerobic exercise.

Of course, not everyone subscribes to our theory.

Advertising research reveals, unfortunately, that while commercials with quick cuts and frolicking couples win Clio awards, irritating commercials sell merchandise. And it is far more important for a commercial to be noticed than to be liked or admired. Advertisers would like their commercials to be as loud as possible.

The Federal Communications Commission has tried to solve the problem of blaring commercials by setting maximum volume levels called "peak audio voltage." But the advertising community is way ahead of the FCC. Through a technique called "volume compression," the audio transmission is modified *so that all sounds, spoken or musical, are at or near the maximum allowable volume.* Even loud rock music has peaks and valleys of loudness, but with volume compression, the average volume of the commercial will register as loudly as the peaks of regular programming, without violating FCC regulations.

The networks are not the villain in this story. In fact, CBS developed a device to measure and counterattack volume compression, so the game among the advertisers, networks, and the FCC continues. Not every commercial uses volume compression, but enough do to foil local stations everywhere.

Of course, it could be argued that advertisers have only the best interests of the public at heart. After all, they are offering free aerobic exercise to folks like "Dave." And for confirmed couch potatoes, they are pointing out the advantages of remote-control televisions.

Submitted by Tammy Madill of Millington, Tennessee.
Thanks also to Joanne Walker of Ashland, Massachusetts.

Why Is U.S. Paper Money Green When Most Countries Color-Code Their Currency?

Until well into the nineteenth century, paper money was relatively rare in the United States. But banknotes became popular in the mid-1800s. These bills were printed in black but included colored tints to help foil counterfeiters.

However, cameras then in existence saw everything in black, rendering color variations in bills meaningless when reproduced photographically. According to the U.S. Treasury, the counterfeiters took advantage:

> the counterfeiter soon discovered that the colored inks then in use could easily be removed from a note without disturbing the black ink. He could eradicate the colored portion, photograph the remainder, and then make a desired number of copies to be overprinted with an imitation of the colored parts.

Tracy R. Edson, one of the founders of the American Bank Note Company, developed the solution. He developed an ink that could not be erased without hurting the black coloring. Edson was rewarded for his discovery by receiving a contract from the U.S. government to produce notes for them. Edson's counterfeit-proof ink had a green tint.

In the nineteenth century, notes were produced by private firms as well as the treasury. But all notes, regardless of where they were printed, were issued in green, presumably to provide uniformity.

Could Edson have chosen blue or red instead of a green tint? Certainly. Although our sources couldn't tell us why green was the original choice, the treasury does have information about why the green tint was retained in 1929, when small-sized notes were introduced:

> the use of green was continued because pigment of that color was readily available in large quantity, the color was relatively high in its resistance to chemical and physical changes, and green was psychologically identified with the strong and stable credit of the Government.

And besides, "redbacks" or "bluebacks" just don't have a ring to them.

Other countries vary the coloring of their bills as well as their size. And why not? Different sizes would enable the sighted but especially the legally blind to sort the denominations of bills easily. But despite occasional rumblings from legislators, the Treasury Department stands by its greenbacks.

Submitted by Paul Stossel of New York, New York. Thanks also to Charles Devine of Plum, Pennsylvania; and Kent Hall of Louisville, Kentucky.

Why Do We Have to Close Our Eyes When We Sneeze?

We thought we'd get off easy with this mystery. Sure, a true Imponderable can't be answered by a standard reference work, but would a poke in a few medical texts do our readers any harm?

We shouldn't have bothered. We understand now that a sneeze is usually a physiological response to an irritant of some sort. We learned that there is a $10 word for sneezing (the "sternutatory reflex") and that almost all animals sneeze. But what exactly happens when we sneeze? Here's a short excerpt from one textbook's explanation of a sneeze:

DAVID FELDMAN

When an irritant contacts the nasal mucosa, the trigeminal nerve provides the affect limb for impulses to the pons, and medullai Preganglionic efferent fibers leave these latter two structures via the intermediate nerve, through geniculate ganglion to the greater petrosal nerve, through the vividian nerve and then synapse at the sphenopalatine ganglion . . .

Get this outta here! Until Cliff Notes comes out with a companion to rhinology textbooks, we'll go to humans for the answers.

Our rhinologist friend, Dr. Pat Barelli, managed to read those textbooks and still writes like a human being. He explains that the sneeze reflex is a protective phenomenon:

The sneeze clears the nose and head and injects O_2 into the cells of the body, provoking much the same physiological effect as sniffing snuff or cocaine. When a person sneezes, all body functions cease. Tremendous stress is put on the body by the sneeze, especially the eyes.

As Dr. G. H. Drumheller, of the International Rhinological Society, put it, "we close our eyes when sneezing to keep the eyes from extruding." While nobody is willing to test the hypothesis, there is more than a grain of truth to the folk wisdom that closing your eyes when you sneeze keeps them from popping out, but probably not more than three or four grains.

Submitted by Linda Rudd of Houston, Texas. Thanks also to Michelle Zielinski of Arnold, Missouri; Helen Moore of New York, New York; Jose Elizondo of Pontiac, Michigan; Amy Harding of Dixon, Kentucky; and Gail Lee of Los Angeles, California

Why Don't Grazing Animals that Roll in or Eat Poison Ivy Ever Seem to Get Blisters or Itching in Their Mouths?

A few of the many veterinarians we spoke to had seen allergic reactions to poison ivy among animals but all agreed it was exceedingly rare. Poison ivy is not really poison. Humans develop an allergic reaction because of a local hypersensitivity to the oil in the plant. Veterinarian Anthony L. Kiorpes, a professor at the University of Wisconsin-Madison School of Veterinary Medicine, informed us that the same plant that may cause a severe reaction in one human may not affect another person at all.

Elizabeth Williams, of the University of Wyoming College of Agriculture, notes that she has never seen an allergic reaction in deer, but allows:

> It's possible some deer might be allergic to it but we just don't see the reaction because they are covered with hair. Or it may be that only a very few deer are allergic, and they learn to stay away from poison ivy.

DAVID FELDMAN

Veterinarian Ben Klein feels that most domestic animals have a built-in immunity to contact allergy dermatitis, such as poison ivy. Furthermore, that same hair Dr. Williams mentioned hiding an allergic reaction also shields the skin against potential reactions, according to veterinary dermatologist Peter Ihrke.

Why don't ruminants break out when they eat poison ivy or poison oak? Dr. Don E. Bailey, secretary-treasurer of the American Association of Sheep and Goat Practitioners, explains that even if these animals had a tendency toward allergic reactions, which they don't, the mucus membrane in their mouths is very thick and heavy.

The one animal that most often seems to contract allergic reactions to poison ivy is the dog. Dogs love to roll around in the worst imaginable things. Dr. Ihrke notes that most dogs can withstand the exposure to poison ivy but many of their owners cannot. The owners pet the dogs and come down with severe reactions. Similarly, an innocent vet will examine a dog and break out in a rash, the victim of a communicable disease that doesn't afflict the carrier.

Submitted by Karole Rathouz of Mehlville, Missouri.

Why Don't Queen-Sized Sheets Fit My Queen-Sized Bed?

Queen-sized beds expanded from 60" x 75" to 60" x 80" in the early 1960s. You would think that more than twenty-five years would be a sufficient amount of time to manufacture sheets large enough to cover the expanded surface area. And it was.

The problem is that sheets are designed to cover mattresses, and the linen industry has no control over what the mattress manufacturers are doing. And what the bed companies are doing lately is driving sheetmakers nuts. As Richard Welsh, senior vice president of Cannon Mills Company, succinctly summarizes:

The sheet industry has experienced problems with fitted sheets for all sizes, not only queen size. The problem is primarily due to the fact that mattress manufacturers have been increasing the depth of their mattresses. As one tries to get an edge on the other, they outsize them by half an inch. There are no standard mattress depths.

When Mr. Welsh first wrote to *Imponderables*, in December 1986, he complained about how the sheet industry, accustomed to fitting six-and-one-half- to seven-inch-deep mattresses, watched in horror as depth inflation hit. In the early 1980s, Cannon increased the length of their sheets to accommodate mattresses from eight to eight-and-one-half inches deep. But soon, the nine-inch barrier was broken. Cannon responded to this problem in 1987 by manufacturing sheets "guaranteed to fit." These sheets could cover a mattress nine-and-one-half inches thick.

But the mattressmakers never stopped. They invented a whole new genre of bed, the "pillow top" mattress, with pockets of polyester fill on top. Pillow tops have increased the crown space (the highest point of padding) on some mattresses to as high as one foot to twelve-and-one-half inches.

The standard queen-size flat sheet is now 90" x 102", which is more than sufficient to cover the 60" x 80" queen-size beds if they don't continue the creep upward. But creep they probably will. On the low end of the market, six-inch-thick mattresses still are available. If you have sheets that are longer than you need, have compassion for the sucker with the pillow top. The same sheet that is too long for you probably isn't long enough to tuck under his mattress.

P.S. It was inevitable. Fieldcrest and Wamsutta, among others, are now manufacturing sheets specifically for pillow top mattresses.

DAVID FELDMAN

Why Is There Cotton Stuffed in Prescription and Over-the-Counter Medicine Bottles? What Happens If I Take Out the Cotton? Why Aren't Alka-Seltzer Containers Stuffed with Cotton?

The main purpose of the cotton stuffed in medicine vials is to prevent rattling and subsequent breakage of pills during shipment. But why cotton? Because of its absorbency, cotton helps keep medications dry. David G. Miller, associate director of the National Association of Retail Druggists, points out that moisture will destroy most drugs.

Still, all the druggists we spoke to recommended taking out the cotton once the container is opened for use. Melvin T. Wilczynski, of the Lane Drug Company, explains that the absorptive characteristics of cotton, which help keep pills dry during shipment, also are capable of absorbing moisture from the environment. If the cotton gets wet and re-enters the bottle, the effectiveness of the medication is jeopardized.

Excess heat and light are also capable of breaking down medications. For this reason, it makes no sense to keep pills in the kitchen, where they are exposed to the heat of ovens, or outside the medicine cabinet in the bathroom, where they could be exposed to harsh light or space heaters.

At one time, Miles Laboratories did put cotton into Alka-Seltzer containers, but found that consumers couldn't be trusted. If you accidentally get an Alka-Seltzer tablet wet, you get premature fizz—a temporary thrill perhaps, but one that will do you no good when a bout of indigestion sets in.

Miles provides a styrofoam cushion to protect tablets during shipping, but they recommend throwing away the cushion once the bottle is opened. Although styrofoam is not as absorbent as cotton, it is perfectly capable of generating bubbles when wet.

Submitted by Andrew Neiman of Dallas, Texas.

Why Do Bagels Have Holes?

In *Why Do Clocks Run Clockwise? and Other Imponderables*, we explained why doughnuts have holes. We were pretty smug about our accomplishment too. Then a letter arrives from Jay Howard Horne asking us why bagels have holes. Will there ever be a stop to this mania for knowledge about hole origins?

Nobody knows for sure who created the first bagel. Chances are, it was an accident precipitated by a piece of yeast-laden dough falling into hot water. But we do know who first called a bagel a "bagel." In 1683, the first Viennese coffeehouse was opened by a Polish adventurer, who introduced a new bread called the *beugel*. When Austrians emigrated to the United States in the next two centuries, the beugel was re-christened the bagel.

So what was a Polish man doing opening a coffeehouse in Vienna and creating a hole-y bread?

The king of Poland, Jan Sobiesky, had become a hero in Austria in the late seventeenth century by driving off armed invaders from Turkey. In their escape, the Turks left behind sacks of enough coffee to keep every citizen of Vienna up nights for a month, inspiring the opening of many a coffeehouse in Vienna.

The coffeehouse owner took a popular yeast bread called kipfel and reshaped it into the bagel shape we know and love today. The bread was meant to resemble the stirrups of brave King Sobiesky, who fought on horseback to save Vienna from the Turks. "Bagel" is derived from the German word for stirrup, "bugel."

Submitted by Jay Howard Horne of Pittsburgh, Pennsylvania.

Do the Digits in a Social Security Number Have Any Particular Meaning?

Now that the Social Security number has become a virtual citizenship identification number, paranoid types have become convinced that each digit is another way for Uncle Sam to poke into our private lives. No, the government can't tell by looking at our Social Security number whether we are registered Democrats or Republicans, whether we are in the highest income-tax bracket or are on welfare, or even whether we have committed a crime.

Under the current system, the first three digits of a Social Security number indicate the state of residence of the holder at the time the number was issued. The remaining digits have no special meaning.

Before 1973, Social Security numbers were assigned by local Social Security offices. The first three digits were assigned based on the location of the Social Security office rather than the residence of the issuee. Opportunists used to scoop up several different Social Security numbers by applying for cards at several different offices, which led to the current practice of issuing all numbers from the central Social Security office in Baltimore. According to Dorcas R. Hardy, commissioner of Social Security, the first three digits of a person's Social Security number are now determined by the ZIP code of the mailing address shown on the application for a Social Security number.

Although the first three digits of the Social Security number do not correspond exactly to the first three digits of that state's zip codes, the lowest Social Security numbers, like their ZIP code counterparts, start in New England and then get progressively larger as they spread westward. Numbers 001–003 are assigned to New Hampshire, and the highest numbers assigned to the 50 states are Hawaii's 575–576. The Virgin Islands (580), Puerto Rico (580–584, 596–599), Guam (586), American Samoa (586), and the Philippine Islands (586) are also assigned specific three-digit codes.

Until 1963, railroad employees were issued a special series of numbers starting with the digits 700–728. Although this practice is now discontinued, these numbers remain the highest ever issued. No one has ever cracked the 729 plus barrier.

Submitted by Douglas Watkins, Jr. of Hayward, California. Thanks also to Jose Elizondo of Pontiac, Michigan; Kenneth Shaw of San Francisco, California; and Rebecca Lash of Ithaca, New York.

DAVID FELDMAN

Why Do the Light Bulbs in My Lamps Loosen After I've Put Them in Place?

An unscientific poll conducted by the Imponderables Research Board indicates that creeping bulb loosening is a problem for many, although a majority of respondents never faced the problem. Is some sadist running around loosening the bulbs of selected victims?

Perhaps, but a natural explanation is more likely. The greatest culprit in loosening light bulbs is vibration. Friction keeps the socket threads of a light bulb tightly fitted into the base threads of a fixture. J. Robert Moody, of General Electric, informed Imponderables that "vibration weakens the friction force, allowing the light bulb to back out of the socket on its own. If the vibration is intense, like on an automobile or an airplane, then a bayonet base must be used in place of the screw-threaded base."

Perhaps that incessant bass drone emanating from the

heavy-metal freak upstairs caused your problem. The only solution might be the purchase of a bayonet base for your lamp or a bayonet to use on your neighbor.

Submitted by Darryl Williams of New York, New York.

How Are Olives Pitted? How Do They Stuff Olives?

Until recently, the vast majority of olives were stuffed by hand. Olives were held in cups, and a crude machine operated with a foot treadle would punch out the pit while another element cut a hole on top of the olive simultaneously. A worker would then inspect the olive. If it was acceptable, she would take a pimento, onion, anchovy or other filling and manually stick it in the hole.

Obviously, olive companies were desperately in need of a high-tech solution to the slowness of their production line. Not only was the pitting and stuffing operation labor-intensive, but the machines would rip olives to shreds and leave pit fragments as a "bonus" for unsuspecting consumers. Even more damaging, the U.S. Food and Drug Administration would routinely refuse to allow importation of mangled olives (almost all green olives are imported from Spain).

Automation revolutionized the olive industry in the early 1970s. Modern machines, typically containing twenty-four separate stations, are capable of stuffing twelve hundred to fifteen hundred olives a minute. The olives are pitted in one movement, and the pimento is inserted with ease.

The down side to this otherwise lovely story is that automation has encouraged olive distributors to dump natural pimentos in favor of pimentos "enhanced" with paste and binders. These additives enable the pimento to be fashioned into an endless ribbon of red stuff. The machine then cuts the ribbon to exact specifications prior to stuffing the cavity, so that larger olives receive wider strips of pimento–red stuff. Of course, the pimento–red stuff tastes more like red stuff than pimento, but this is the price we pay for progress.

Machines now exist to sort olives by size, to inject brine into a jar, to pack olives in jars, to stuff olives with pimentos, to slice olives, and to seal olive jars. Until the 1980s almost all olives were packed into jars by hand. Fancy Spanish olives are often placed in geometric patterns to induce impulse purchases by consumers. According to Edward Culleton, of the Green Olive Trade Association, American consumers have never developed brand loyalty, so shoppers have traditionally been receptive to eye-catching arrangements of olives. About 90% of green olives are now packed by machine rather than by hand, so "place packs" (hand-packed jars) are likely to be a specialty item in the future. In fact, Spain now exports hand-pitted stuffed olives in beautiful crystal jars as a luxury gift item—and the olives are stuffed with real pimentos.

Submitted by Helen Tvorik of Mayfield Heights, Ohio.

Why Is One Side of a Halibut Dark and the Other Side Light?

With the price of halibut these days, we might assume that we are paying extra for the two-tone job. But nature supplies halibut with two colors for a less mercenary reason.

The eyeless side of the halibut is light, requiring no camouflage. But the side with eyes is dark. Like other flat fish that swim on one side, the halibut is dark on the side exposed to the light. Robert L. Collette, associate director of the National Fisheries Institute, describes the coloring as "a natural defense system." The dark side is at top "so that predators looking down upon halibut are less likely to detect their presence."

This camouflage system is adapted for fish and mammals that swim upright. They have dark backs and white undersides to elude their predators.

DAVID FELDMAN

What Is the Difference Between a "Mountain" and a "Hill"?

Although we think you are making a mountain out of a molehill, we'll answer this Imponderable anyway. Most American geographers refer to a hill as a natural elevation that is smaller than 1,000 feet. Anything above 1,000 feet is usually called a mountain. In Great Britain, the traditional boundary line between hill and mountain is 2,000 feet.

Still, some geographers are not satisfied with this definition. "Hill" conjures up rolling terrain; "mountains" connote abrupt, peaked structures. A mound that rises two feet above the surrounding earth may attain an elevation of 8,000 feet, if it happens to be located in the middle of the Rockies, whereas a 999-foot elevation, starting from a sea-level base, will appear massive. For this reason, most geographers feel that "mountain" may be used for elevations under 1,000 feet if they rise abruptly from the surrounding terrain.

WHEN DO FISH SLEEP?   97

The *Oxford English Dictionary* states that "hill" may also refer to non-natural formations, such as sand heaps, mounds, or, indeed, molehills.

Submitted by Thomas J. Schoeck of Slingerlands, New York.
Thanks also to F. S. Sewell of San Jose, California.

Why Aren't There License Plates on the Back of Many Big Trucks on the Highway?

Fewer than two-thirds of the fifty states require license plates on both the front and back of a commercial truck. Why do truckers, unlike automobile owners, only have to display one plate in many states?

Presumably, tractors will be pulling trailers most of the time, so the only time we are likely to see a tractor with two plates is when it is "deadheading" (not towing a trailer). Then, the back license plate is likely to be obscured by the trailer anyway, and be of little use to police.

Because many tractors are crossing borders constantly, the licensing of commercial tractors and trailers can be complicated. According to Jan Balkin, of the American Trucking Associations,

> All trailers must have license plates from the state in which it is licensed. That state may not necessarily be the same as the state in which the tractor is licensed; carriers may license the tractor and trailer in different states, depending upon certain financial decisions as to which state(s) the carrier chooses.

DAVID FELDMAN

Why Do Mayors Hand Out Keys to Their City?

We've all seen those silly ceremonies on TV where a grinning mayor hands a three-foot-long key to a minor celebrity as flashbulbs pop. But we have always wondered: Why does the recipient need a key to the city? He's already *in* the city.

Actually, this ceremony has legitimate historical antecedents. In the Middle Ages, most large cities were walled. Visitors could enter and exit only through gates that were locked at sundown and reopened at dawn.

Mike Brown, of the United States Conference of Mayors, told *Imponderables* that gatekeepers used keys to open and close the gates. These keys were closely guarded, for they were crucial in preventing military attacks. If a key was passed to an honored visitor, it indicated total trust in him.

Today, a mayor no longer threatens the security of her domain by handing out the key to the city, and the honor is more likely a public relations stunt than in gratitude for service or accomplishment. But the meaning is the same. By handing out the key to the city, the mayor says, "Come back any time and you don't even have to knock. We trust you."

What Is the Purpose of the Beard on a Turkey?

All of our poultry experts felt that the beard has no specific anatomical function, but this doesn't mean the beard has no purpose. The beard is a secondary sex characteristic of the male, a visual differentiation between the sexes. How could a hen possibly resist the sexual allure of the beard of a strutting Tom?

Submitted by Mrs. Anabell Cregger of Wytheville, Virginia.

WHY Are Banking Hours So Short?

Nine to three, five days a week. Not a bad job if you can get it, eh? Short banking hours have always fit the needs of bankers and industry, but have not been convenient for retail customers. The banks are open only when the average person is working or going to school.

Mind you, workers in the bank industry don't get to leave the door at the stroke of three. Tellers, for example, must count cash and report their balances to a central processing center. Before automation, reconciling their books might have taken a little longer, but not significantly so.

Executives in the banking industry, who do not have to mind the day-to-day transactions of retail customers, have plenty of phone and social contacts to make after banking hours. When we posed this Imponderable to Joan Silverman, of Citibank, she was incredulous that we had not heard of the rule of 3/6/3.

"What is the rule of 3/6/3?" we asked.

"It's simple," she replied. "If you want to be a successful

DAVID FELDMAN

banker, you pay 3% to depositors; you charge 6% on loans to customers; and you hit the golf course by 3 P.M." Based on the interest rates mentioned, this obviously is a very old rule.

Government regulations once restricted the hours during which banks could be open for business. Gentleman bankers conducted most of their business on the golf course while tellers were back at the ranch settling their ledgers.

With computerization, there is no reason why banks couldn't have much longer hours. The tradition of the 9 A.M. to 3 P.M. Monday through Friday bank is preserved because of the bottom line: The banks figure that if they stay open later or open on weekends, they will increase retail customers' simple—and to the bank, often unprofitable—transactions, such as depositing or withdrawing money from checking and savings accounts. Most other businesses are closed on weekends and evenings— *they* don't have demanding, long hours.

Bank hours generally are extended only when there is a competitive marketing reason to do so, usually when a new bank or new branch needs to build new accounts and can advertise extended hours. Ohio's Banc One, Dayton, for example, opens many branches on Saturdays and even Sundays. Many of their branches are located in malls; before Banc One opened on weekends, it was often the only business closed in the whole shopping center. Much to Banc One's surprise, according to *American Banker:*

> the volume of teller activity during Sunday's four-hour shift has been greater than the amount of teller activity during a normal seven-hour weekday.

Obviously, if it were cost-effective for most banks to be open longer, they would do it. Automated teller machines have effectively opened the doors of many banks twenty-four hours a day anyway. Unlike bank employees, ATMs don't complain when they aren't excused to leave for the golf course at 3 P.M.

Submitted by Dorio Barbieri of Mountain View, California. Thanks also to Herbert Kraut of Forest Hills, New York.

Speaking of ATMs . . . When They Were Introduced, ATMs Were Supposed to Save Labor Costs for the Banks and Ultimately Save Money for the Customers. Now My Bank Is Charging Money for Each ATM Transaction. What Gives?

The banking industry is being squeezed from two sides. On the one hand, customers now demand interest on checking accounts and money-market rates on savings accounts. Yet they also want services provided for free.

While it is true that an ATM transaction generally is cheaper for the banks than the same transaction conducted by a teller, banks have spent a fortune buying and installing these machines. As David Taylor, of the Bank Administration Institute put it, "As the customer gets more and more convenience and control of his banking options, he will have to pay for each option one at a time." The alternative would be a return to having no service fees but also to customers getting lower interest rates

102   DAVID FELDMAN

on CDs and checking and savings accounts, which banks know would be suicidal for them. As bank deregulation accelerates and banks are allowed to compete with brokerages and other financial institutions, expect to see increasing service charges.

Most banks do not charge for ATM transactions. If there are two big banks in a town, each knows that if it charges for ATM transactions, the other bank will advertise that its machines are free. So the choice between free and pay ATMs is left to what the banking business calls "competitive reasons," which is fiduciary lingo for "if we think we can get away with charging for it, we will."

Why Does Granulated Sugar Tend to Clump Together?

It ain't the heat, it's the humidity. Sugar is hygroscopic, meaning that it is capable of absorbing moisture from the air and changing its form as a result of the absorption. When sugar is subjected to 80% or higher relative humidity, the moisture dissolves a thin film of sugar on the surface of the sugar crystal. Each of these crystals turns into a sugar solution, linked to one another by a "liquid bridge."

According to Jerry Hageney, of the Amstar Corporation, when the relative humidity decreases, "the sugar solution gives up its moisture, causing the sugar to become a crystal again. The crystals joined by the liquid bridge become as one crystal. Thus, hundreds of thousands of crystals become linked together to form a rather solid lump."

Although we can't see the moist film on sugar exposed to high humidity, it won't pour quite as smoothly as sugar that has never been exposed to moisture. But when it dries up again, the liquid bridge is a strong one. Bruce Foster, of Sugar Industry Technologists, told us that the technology used to make sugar cubes utilizes this natural phenomenon.

To make sugar cubes, water is added to sugar in a cube-shaped mold. After the sugar forms into cubes, it is dried out, and voilà! you have a chemical-free way to keep sugar stuck together.

Submitted by Patty Payne of Seattle, Washington.

Why Do Two Horses in an Open Field Always Seem to Stand Head to Tail?

Horses, unlike people, don't bother to make the pretense of listening to what companions have to say. And also, unlike humans, horses have tails. Rather than stand around face-to-face boring each other, figures the horse, wouldn't it be more practical to stand head to tail? This way, with one swish of the tail, a horse can rid its body of flies and other insects while knocking the bugs off of the head of the other horse.

In cold weather, horses are more likely to stand head-to-head, so they can help keep each other warm with their breaths. In this one respect, horses are like people—they are full of an inexhaustible supply of hot air.

Submitted by Mrs. Phyllis A. Diamond of Cherry Valley, California.

Why Does Your Whole Body Ache When You Get a Cold or Flu?

When a virus enters your bloodstream, it releases several compounds that mount your body's defense against infection. Interferon, interleukin, and prostaglandins are among the body's most

DAVID FELDMAN

valuable compounds. They raise a fever, shift the metabolism, and increase blood flow to areas of the body that need it.

Frank Davidoff, of the American College of Physicians, suggests that although science hasn't yet precisely defined their function, there is much evidence to suggest that these compounds are responsible for the aching feeling that accompanies colds and flus. More of the compounds are usually found in the bloodstream during the aching phase than before any symptoms start. And when doctors inject a purified form of each compound into a patient, many of the symptoms of a virus, including fever, sweating, and aching, occur without actually causing the entire illness.

These compounds are effective without anyone knowing precisely *how* they work, but there are logical explanations for *why* they work. Davidoff sums it up well:

> the aching and other symptoms seem to be the "price" that's paid for mounting a defense against the infection. Whether the price is inseparable from the defense isn't clear. Thus, on the one hand, the symptoms might actually be a holdover from some mechanism that was important earlier in evolution but that is unnecessary now in more complex creatures. On the other hand, symptoms like aching may be part and parcel of the defense; I don't believe anyone knows for sure.

Submitted by James Wheaton of Plattsburgh Air Force Base, New York.

How Did Romans Do the Calculations Necessary for Construction and Other Purposes Using Roman Numerals?

Our idea of a good time does not include trying to do long division with Roman numerals. Can you imagine dividing CXVII by IX and carrying down numbers that look more like a cryptogram than an arithmetic problem?

The Romans were saved that torture. The Romans relied on the Chinese abacus, with pebbles as counters, to perform their calculations. In fact, Barry Fells, of the Epigraphic Society, informs us that these mathematical operations were performed in Roman times by persons called "calculatores." They were so named because they used *calcule* (Latin for pebbles) to add, subtract, multiply, and divide.

Submitted by Greg Cox of San Rafael, California.

Why Do Some Ice Cubes Come Out Cloudy and Others Come Out Clear?

A caller on the Merle Pollis radio show, in Cleveland, Ohio, first confronted us with this problem. We admitted we weren't sure about the answer, but subsequent callers all had strong convictions about the matter. The only problem was that they all had *different* convictions.

One caller insisted that the mineral content of the water determined the opacity of the cube, but this theory doesn't explain why all the cubes from the same water source don't come out either cloudy or clear.

Two callers insisted that the temperature of the water when put into the freezer was the critical factor. Unfortunately, they couldn't agree about whether it was the hot water or the cold water that yielded clear ice.

We finally decided to go to an expert who confirmed what we expected—all the callers were wrong. Dr. John Hallet, of the Atmospheric Ice Laboratory of the Desert Research Institute in Reno, Nevada, informed us that the key factor in cloud formation is the temperature of the *freezer*.

When ice forms slowly, it tends to freeze first at one edge. Air bubbles found in a solution in the water have time to rise and escape. The result is clear ice cubes.

DAVID FELDMAN

The clouds in ice cubes are the result of air bubbles formed as ice is freezing. When water freezes rapidly, freezing starts at more than one end, and water residuals are trapped in the middle of the cube, preventing bubble loss. The trapped bubbles make the cube appear cloudy.

Why Are Most Pencils Painted Yellow?

Pencils came in various colors before 1890, but it was in that year the Austrian L & C Hardtmuth Company developed a drawing pencil that was painted yellow. Available in a range of degrees of hardness, the company dubbed their product Koh-I-Noor.

In 1893, L & C Hardtmuth introduced their Koh-I-Noor at the Chicago World's Colombian Exposition, and Americans responded favorably. Ever since, yellow has been synonymous with quality pencils.

Monika Reed, product manager at Berol USA, told *Imponderables* that although Berol and other manufacturers make pencils painted in a wide range of colors, yellow retains its great appeal. According to Bill MacMillan, executive vice president of the Pencil Makers Association, sales of yellow-painted pencils represent 75% of total sales in the United States.

Submitted by Robert M. Helfrich of Pittsburgh, Pennsylvania.
Thanks also to Beth Newman of Walnut Creek, California.

DAVID FELDMAN

Why Do You Have to Use #2 Pencils on Standardized Tests? What Happens If You Use a #1 Pencil? What *Is* a #2 Pencil?

If only we could blame our SAT scores on using #1 or #3 pencils! But it's hard to find any other besides #2s anyway.

All-purpose pencils are manufactured in numbers one through four (with half sizes in between). The higher the number, the harder the pencil is. Although the numbers of pencils are not completely standardized, there is only slight variation among competitors.

The #2 pencil, by far the most popular all-purpose pencil, is considered medium soft (compared to the #1, which is soft; to #2.5, medium; to #3, medium hard; and to #4, hard). Pencils are made harder by increasing the graphite content and made softer by increasing the clay content of the lead.

Why do some administrators of standardized tests insist on #2 pencils? Because the degree of hardness is a happy compromise between more extreme alternatives. A hard pencil leaves marks that are often too light or too thin to register easily on mark-sensing machines. Too soft pencils, while leaving a dark mark, have a tendency to smudge and thus run into the spaces left for other answers.

Even some #2 pencils might not register easily on mark-sensing machines. For this reason, Berol has developed the Electronic® Scorer. According to Product Manager Monika Reed, "This pencil contains a special soft lead of high electric conductivity," which eases the burden of today's high-speed marking machines.

Unfortunately, even the Electronic Scorer doesn't come with a guarantee of high marks, only accurately scored answers.

Submitted by Liz Stone of Mamaroneck, New York. Thanks also to John J. Clark of Pittsburgh, Pennsylvania; Gail Lee of Los Angeles, California; William Lush of Stamford, Connecticut; and Jenny Bixler of Hanover, Pennsylvania.

WHEN DO FISH SLEEP?

Why Do Fish Eat Earthworms? Do They Crave Worms or Will Fish Eat Anything that Is Thrust upon Them?

We have to admit, earthworms wouldn't be our first dining choice. What do fish see in worms that we don't see (or taste)?

R. Bruce Gebhardt, of the North American Native Fishes Association, emphasizes that just about any bait can entice a fish if the presentation is proper. Human gourmets may prefer a colorful still life on white china, but fish prefer a moving target. And they are a little less finicky than humans:

> A pickerel, for example, will attack a lure before it's hit the water. It must instantly assess the size of the bait; if it's a pine cone, it will worry about spitting it out after it is caught.

Most fish are attracted to food by sight, and prefer live bait. Fish are often attacking and testing as much as dining:

> It is unnecessary to *completely* convince the fish that the bait is alive. Most fish encountering anything strange will mouth it or closely examine it as potential food; the less opportunity it's liable to have, the more vigorously it will attack.

While the fisherman might think that every pull on his line means the fish finds his worm irresistible, the fish may well be

DAVID FELDMAN

nibbling the worm to determine the identity of the bait—by the time it finds out it has caught a worm, it's too late: It is hooked.

Our Imponderable also assumes that fish may go out of their way to eat earthworms, but Gerry Carr, director of Species Research at the International Game Fish Association, assures us that given a choice, most fish will go after food native to their environment:

> Nature is constituted in a way that everything has its place and is in ecological balance. Fish eat the foods that nature provides for them. The fly fisherman is acutely aware of this. He or she knows that trout, for example, at a certain time of year, seem to crave and feast on the type of nymphs that are hatching and falling into the water at that moment. Any other kind of artificial fly will not work, only the one that best imitates the hatch.
>
> Of course, not all fish are that finicky. Catfish eat anything that stinks. Logical! Their purpose in nature is to clean up the bottom, eliminating dead, rotting carcasses that rob water of oxygen and might cause all the fish to die. Nature's vacuum cleaner! And they survive because they have carved out or been given an ecological niche in the system that is not overly in competition with other species.

But why will worms attract even finicky fish? Carr continues:

> Worms, actually, are probably more of a side-dish in the diets of some fishes, a sort of aperitif. Worms look tasty, so the fish eats them. I do not think fish go looking for worms, specifically, unless they have got their appetite whet up for them by an angler conveniently drowning them.

Even if worms aren't native to a fish's environment, they fulfill most of the prerequisites for a favorite fish fast food. The size and shape are good for eating, and the fact that worms are wiggling when alive or look like they are moving even when dead adds to their allure. Carr mentions that barracudas cannot resist any appropriately sized bait or lure that is long and slender or cigar-shaped and moving at the right speed. "But offering them a worm that just sits there would be tantamount to a human asking for jelly instead of 'All-Fruit.' "

WHEN DO FISH SLEEP?   111

One other point needs to be stated. The popularity of earthworms as bait is undoubtedly enhanced by the cheapness, easy availability, and convenience of them. As Gebhardt put it, "It's probably anglers' convenience that has given earthworms their reputation for delectability rather than petitions signed by fish."

Submitted by Roy Tucker of Budd Lake, New Jersey.

Why Are Stock Prices Generally Quoted in Eighths?

In *Why Do Clocks Run Clockwise? and Other Imponderables* we discussed the derivation of our expression "two bits." In Spain, a *bit* was one of the "pieces of eight," an actual pie-shaped slice of a peso. Two bits were one-quarter of a peso.

Spanish coins circulated freely in the New World before and during colonial times for at least two reasons. There weren't enough native coins to go around, and Spanish gold and silver specie were negotiable just about anywhere in the world (like in the good old days when foreign nations sought American dollars) because they were backed by gold.

Was it a coincidence that two bits of a peso happened to equal two bits of a dollar? Not at all. Peter Eisenstadt, research associate at the New York Stock Exchange archives, told *Imponderables* that when U.S. currency was decimalized in 1785,

> the U.S. silver dollar was established with a value equivalent to the Spanish silver peso. Though the official divisions of the dollar were in decimals, many continued to divide the new U.S. dollar into eighths and this practice was followed in securities trading.

Stocks were usually traded in eighths from the inception of securities trading in the United States in the 1790s. Eisenstadt believes that Americans simply borrowed the practice of quoting in eighths from the Europeans. As he notes, most early stockbrokers were part-timers, devoting most of their attention to the merchant trade, which had long quoted prices in eighths.

By the 1820s, stocks traded on the NYSE were universally quoted in eighths, but this was an informal arrangement; it became a requirement in 1885. The American and Pacific Stock Exchanges followed suit.

Although the history of our quoting stock prices in eighths makes historical sense, we don't understand why the exchanges still maintain the practice. When a stock dips to near zero, prices now are quoted in sixteenths and even thirty-seconds of a dollar, forcing financial tycoons to rely on their memory of grade-school fractional tables when doing calculations. And what happens when someone wants to sell his one share of stock quoted at 48⅜? Who gets the extra half-cent?

Wouldn't it make more sense to quote all stocks in hundredths of a dollar? Why should two-dollar stocks have to rise or fall more than ten percent at a time when a 2% change in most stocks is considered significant? Roy Berces, of the Pacific Stock Exchange, acknowledges that our system is probably archaic, but sees no groundswell for changing tradition.

Submitted by E. B. Peschke of St. Charles, Missouri. Thanks also to John A. Bush of St. Louis, Missouri; Christopher Dondlinger of Longmont, Colorado; and Dave Klingensmith of Fulton Canal, Ohio.

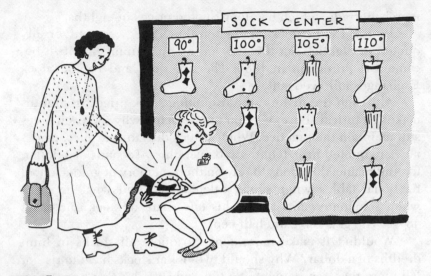

Why Are Socks Angled at Approximately 115 to 125 Degrees When the Human Foot Is Angled at About 90 Degrees?

Not all socks are angled, of course. Tube socks are "angled" at 180 degrees. Tube socks are so named because they are a straight tube of fabric closed on one end by sewing. The tube sock is constructed by "full circular knitting" (i.e., the knitting head on the machine knits in a full circle).

A tube sock doesn't contain a designated position for the heel, but more conventional socks do. Most socks are knitted with a feature called the "reciprocated heel." Sid Smith, president and chief executive officer of the National Association of Hosiery Manufacturers, told *Imponderables* how the reciprocated heel is made:

> Imagine a full circular knitting machine starting at the top of the sock and knitting in a complete circle all the way down the top of the sock, until it hits the point where the heel is to be knitted in. At this point, the machine automatically enters what is called the "reciprocated function." Instead of knitting in a complete circle,

DAVID FELDMAN

it knits halfway to each side and then back again, until the heel portion is knitted in.

After this is completed, the machine automatically reverts to full circular knitting to finish the sock. This reciprocation is what causes the finished sock to be angled.

The 115- to 125-degree angle of the sock, then, is the result of, rather than the purpose of, the knitting process. The fabrics used for socks will give or stretch to conform to the contours of the foot. Since a 180-degree tube sock can fit comfortably on the human foot, there is no reason why a conventional sock won't.

Submitted by Vernon K. Hurd of Colorado Springs, Colorado.

Why Do Cattle Guards Work?

No, there aren't demons underground shooting BB pellets between the bars of the cattle guards. Cows are afraid to walk where their feet can't get solid footing.

Our correspondent mentions that he has seen painted white strips used as cattle guards, presumably tricking cows into thinking that the unpainted area is a black hole. Cows are evidently as subject to phobias as cowboys and cowgirls.

Submitted by A. M. Rizzi of Torrey, Vermont.

Why Are There No A- or B-Sized Batteries?

Because they are obsolete. A- and B-sized batteries once existed as component cells within much larger zinc carbon battery packs. The A cell contained a low-voltage filament, while the B cell was high-voltage. These batteries were used in early radios and crank telephones.

Of course, the descendants of the old A- and B-sized batteries are still with us. As electronic devices have gotten smaller, so have the batteries that power them. As might be expected, the A cell came first, then B, C, and D cells. The batteries were lettered in ascending order of size. James Donahue, Jr., of Duracell, Inc., says that as cells smaller than the original A cells were developed, they were designated as AA and then AAA cells. Donahue reports that there is even a new AAAA battery.

So the old A- and B-sized batteries are no longer in production. It's no use having a battery larger than the device it powers.

Submitted by Larry Prussin of Yosemite, California. And thanks also to Herman E. London of Poughkeepsie, New York; Nancy Ondris of Kings Park, New York; and Ronald Herman of Montreal, Quebec.

What Are Those Little Plastic Circles (that Sometimes Have Rubber in the Middle) Found on the Walls of Hotels?

If you've noticed, those circles are located about three feet off the ground and usually near the entrance. They are called wall protectors, and their sole function in life is to keep doorknobs from slamming against the walls. And with some of the paper-thin walls we've encountered in motels, wall protectors may be responsible for keeping the structural integrity of the building intact.

Submitted by Carol Rostad of New York, New York.

WHEN DO FISH SLEEP? 117

Why Does Starch Make Our Shirts Stiff?

Starch is a type of "sizing," a filler used to add body, sheen, and luster to limp clothing. All shirts come off the rack with sizing, but cotton is water-soluble; every time the shirt is washed, sizing comes out of the shirt. The main purpose of adding starch, then, is to restore the original body of a garment.

The main ingredient in starch is wheat or, less frequently, corn. The grain is mixed with water, resins, and chemicals. As Bill Seitz, of the Neighborhood Cleaners Association, describes it, the starch is literally absorbed by the fabric. Cotton plus wheat is stiffer than cotton alone.

Norman Oehlke, of International Fabricare Institute, adds that starch also enhances soil resistance, facilitates soil removal for the next wash, and makes ironing easier.

Synthetic fabrics aren't as receptive to starch as all-cotton garments, so extra chemicals are added to the starch, such as polyvinyl acetate, sulfated fatty alcohols, silicones, and our personal favorite, carboxymethylcellulose.

Submitted by Kris Heim of De Pere, Wisconsin.

How Does the Campbell Soup Company Determine Which Letters to Put in Their Alphabet Soup? Are There an Equal Number of Each Letter? Or Are the Letters Randomly Inserted in the Can?

We spoke to a delightful young woman at Campbell's named Ginny Marcin, who, astonishingly, did not have the answers to these questions at her fingertips. But she spoke to the vice president of Letter Distribution and obtained the following information.

DAVID FELDMAN

Campbell's makes two sizes of letters for their soups. Small letters go into some of the prepared soups (such as the Chunky line). Slightly larger letters bejewel their vegetable and vegetarian vegetable soups.

It is the stated intention of the Campbell Soup Company not to discriminate against any letter. All are equally represented. However, Campbell's cannot control the distribution of letters while inserting the letters and soup into the can, so irregularities can result. You might find a can with eight q's and only three u's, screwing up your plans to use the letters as Scrabble tiles.

Come to think of it, if the letters really are distributed randomly, why does Campbell's need a vice president of Letter Distribution?

Submitted by Tom Carroll of Binghamton, New York.

What Is the Purpose of Corn Silk?

These strands, which bedevil shuckers and flossless eaters alike, actually do have an important purpose. The longer threads of corn silk stand outside of the husk in tufts to collect pollen. The pollen then travels the silk to the ear of corn and fertilizes it.

Edith M. Munro, director of Information of the Corn Refiners Association, told *Imponderables* one of the critical factors exacerbating the loss in the corn harvest during the 1988 drought was that the "lack of moisture delayed the development of silks or dried the silks up, so that no silks were present when pollen was released." Without sufficient pollination, the growth of the corn is stunted, resulting in ears of corn with only a few kernels.

Submitted by Denise Dennis of Shippensburg, Pennsylvania.

DAVID FELDMAN

Why Are U.S. Government Department Heads Called "Secretaries" Instead of "Ministers," as in Most Other Countries?

The word "secretary" comes from the same Latin root as the word "secret." In medieval days, a secretary was a notary or a scribe, someone privy to secret and often important information. Over time, secretaries became not only men and women in charge of correspondence for an employer but trusted advisors to heads of state and royalty. So although today's office secretaries may now be a neglected and abused lot, Europeans have long called important officeholders "secretaries."

We wrote to several historians who were kind enough to unravel this Imponderable. They concurred that although Americans appropriated their governmental vocabulary from the English, no single term was used to describe cabinet-level officials in England at the time the United States Constitution was drafted.

The parliamentary-cabinet style government of England was not established until the early 1700s, and many of the titles from feudal governments still existed. Thomas L. Purvis, of the Institute of Early American History and Culture, elaborates on the mishmash of English titles:

> members of the cabinet carried titles both feudal and modern, such as Chancellor of the Exchequer and Prime Minister. Intermediate in age were the secretaries of various departments, such as the former Secretary of State for the Southern Department (whose purview extended over the American Colonies) and the ad hoc Secretary *at* War.

Americans, in their revolutionary ethos, were not about to give a nod to the hated English king and his ministers. The terms "president" and "vice president" were chosen to distinguish elected leaders from the dreaded monarchy.

None of the framers of the Articles of Confederation wrote why "secretary" was designated as the term for America's executive officers. The Department of the Treasury conducted an investigation into this Imponderable and found that the Library of Congress, the National Archives, and the Office of Protocol at the Department of State could provide no documentary evidence for the choice.

But all of our sources indicated that the attempt to distance the United States from any trappings of a monarchy contributed to the selection of "secretary." Samuel R. Gammon, executive director of the American Historical Association, told *Imponderables* that "the older English tradition of terming the monarch's chief executive assistants 'Principal Secretary of State' may also have been in their [the framers of the Constitution] minds."

"Secretary" was a solid, middle-of-the-road choice. As Purvis points out, the title seems honorific yet confers no indication of aristocracy and could be applied to any department in the government.

Submitted by Daniel Marcus of Watertown, Massachusetts.

Why Is Prepackaged Chocolate Milk Thicker in Consistency than the Chocolate Milk You Make at Home?

Gravity.

If you make a batch of chocolate milk at home and put it in the refrigerator to cool, you will notice something when you fetch it ten hours later. The chocolate sinks to the bottom.

All is not lost. Simply shaking up the container will redistribute the chocolate throughout the milk.

But this kind of separation is unacceptable in a commercial product, especially one that is sold in a transparent container. So commercial dairies use stabilizers and emulsifiers to assure that the chocolate and milk remain mixed. Although the job of the (usually natural) stabilizers and emulsifiers is to keep the choc-

DAVID FELDMAN

olate from falling to the bottom of the carton, the by-product is a thicker consistency than home-style chocolate milk.

Submitted by Herbert Kraut of Forest Hills, New York.

Why Do Fingernails Grow Faster than Toenails?

This is not the kind of question whose solution wins Nobel Prizes for scientists or garners prestigious grants for research hospitals, yet the answer is not obvious. The average severed fingernail takes four to six months to grow back to its normal length. The average toenail takes nine to twelve months.

Dermatologist Dr. Fred Feldman says that although nobody knows for sure why toenails lag behind fingernails in growth, there are many possible explanations:

1. Trauma makes nails grow faster. Dermatologists have found that if a patient bites a nail down or loses it altogether, the traumatized nail will grow faster than on one left alone. Fingernails, in constant contact with many hard or sharp objects, are much more likely to be traumatized in everyday life than toenails. Even nonpainful contact can cause some trauma to nails. Because we use our fingers much more often than our toes, toenails do not tend to get the stimulation that fingernails do.
2. All nails grow faster in the summer than the winter, which suggests that the sun promotes nail growth. Even during the summer, most people cover their toenails with socks and shoes.
3. Circulation is much more sluggish in the feet than in the hands.

Our medical consultants did not suggest the obvious: The faster growth of fingernails is nature's way of providing us with a constant tool with which to open pistachio nuts.

Submitted by Dave Bohnhoff of Madison, Wisconsin.

Why Do We Dream More Profusely When We Nap than We Do Overnight?

According to the experts we consulted, we dream just as much at night as we do when we take a nap. However, we *recall* our afternoon-nap dreams much more easily than our dreams at night.

While we are dreaming, our long-term memory faculties are suppressed. During the night, our sleep is likely to go undisturbed. We tend to forget dreams we experience in the early stages of sleep. The sooner that we wake up after having our dreams, the more likely we are to remember them.

Any situation that wakes us up just after or during the course of a dream will make the sleeper perceive that he or she has been dreaming profusely. Dr. Robert W. McCarley, the executive secretary of the Sleep Research Society, told *Imponderables* that women in advanced stages of pregnancy often report that they are dreaming more frequently. Dr. McCarley believes that the perceived increase in dreaming activity of pregnant women is prompted not by psychological factors but because their sleep is constantly interrupted by physical discomforts.

Why Do Place Kickers and Field-Goal Kickers Get Yardage Credit from Where the Ball Is Kicked and Yet Punters Only Get Credit from the Line of Scrimmage?

Well, who said life was fair? It turns out that this blatant discrimination occurs not because anyone wants to persecute punters particularly but for the convenience and accuracy of the scorekeepers. Jim Heffernan, director of Public Relations for the National Football League, explains:

DAVID FELDMAN

Punts are measured from the line of scrimmage, which is a defined point, and it sometimes is difficult to determine exactly where the punter contacts the ball. Field goals are measured from the point of the kick because that is the defined spot of contact.

Submitted by Dale A. Dimas of Cupertino, California.

How Does a Gas Pump "Know" When to Shut Off When the Fuel Tank Is Full?

A sensing device, located about one inch from the end of the nozzle, does nothing while fuel is flowing into the gas tank, but is tripped as soon as fuel backs up into the nozzle. The sensing device tells the nozzle to shut off.

Because of the location of the sensing device and the relatively deep position of the nozzle, a gas tank is never totally filled unless the customer or attendant "tops off" the tank. Topping off tanks is now illegal in most states and is a dangerous practice anywhere.

Submitted by Stephen O. Addison, Jr. of Charlotte, North Carolina.

Inside the illustration:
ASSESSOR
of
Old,
Oily and Gross
Paper
Currency

U. S.
Bureau
of
Engraving

How Does the Treasury Know When to Print New Bills or Mint New Coins? How Does it Calculate How Much Money Is Lost or Destroyed by the Public?

There are more than two hundred billion dollars in coins and currency in circulation today in the United States. Determining the necessary timing for the minting and printing of new monies is therefore far from a simple task.

Most of the demand for new money comes from banks. When a bank receives more checks to cash than it can comfortably accommodate with its cash on hand, the bank orders new money from one of the twelve Federal Reserve Banks. Of course, the bank doesn't get the new money for free; it uses a special checkbook to order new cash. When a bank has excess cash, it can deposit money into an account at the Federal Reserve Bank to offset its withdrawals.

What happens when the Federal Reserve Bank itself runs out of coins or notes? It places an order with the U.S. Mint for new coins or the Bureau of Engraving and Printing for the new

DAVID FELDMAN

currency. So demand from individual banks, funneled through a larger "distributor"—a Federal Reserve Bank—is responsible for the decision to issue new currency.

The average life-span of a dollar bill is fifteen to eighteen months. Larger denominations tend to have a longer life because they are circulated less frequently. The perishability of paper notes is the second major factor in calculating the requirements for new currency. In 1983 alone, the twelve Federal Reserve Banks destroyed more than 4.4 billion notes, worth more than $36 billion. The constant retirement of defective bills explains why almost one out of every four notes the Federal Reserve Bank sends to local banks is a newly printed one.

Every time a Federal Reserve Bank receives currency from a local bank, it runs the notes through high-speed machines designed to detect unfit currency. The newest machines can inspect up to sixty thousand notes per hour, checking each bill for dirt by testing light reflectivity (the dirtier the note, the less light is reflected) and authenticity (each note is tested for magnetic qualities that are difficult for counterfeiters to duplicate).

Notes valued at $100 or less are destroyed by the local Federal Reserve Bank. Unfit bills used to be burned and processed into mulch (we kid you not), but they are now shredded and compressed into four-hundred-pound bales. Most of these bundles of booty are discarded at landfills. Federal Reserve notes in denominations of $500 or more are canceled with distinctive perforations and cut in half lengthwise. The local Federal Reserve Bank keeps the upper half of each note and sends the other half to the Department of Treasury in Washington, D.C. When the Treasury Department verifies the legitimacy of the notes, it destroys its halves and informs the district bank that it may destroy the upper halves.

Coins have a much longer life in circulation, but the Mint still produces more than 50 million coins a day (compared to "only" twenty million notes printed per day). A U.S. Mint official told us that shipping coins across country is not a trivial task logistically—five-hundred-thousand pennies, for example, are a tad bulky. Huge tractor-trailer trucks, up to 55 feet in length and

13½ feet high, are used to transport coins from the Mint to Federal Reserve Banks. Dimes, quarters, and half dollars are transported by armored carriers.

The demand process for coins works the same way as for paper notes. Although the Mint has learned that seasonal peaks run true from year to year (the demand for coins goes up during prime shopping seasons, such as Christmas), the Mint yields to the demands of its constituent Federal Reserve Banks.

Submitted by Hugo Kahn of New York, New York.

DAVID FELDMAN

What Is the Purpose of that Piece of Skin Hanging from the Back of Our Throat?

No, Kassie Schwan's illustration to the contrary, the purpose of that "hanging piece of skin" is not to present targets for cartoon characters caught inside other characters' throats. Actually, that isn't skin hanging down, it's mucus membrane and muscle. And it has a name: the uvula.

The uvula is a sort of anatomical tollgate between the throat and the pharynx, the first part of the digestive tract. The uvula has a small but important role in controlling the inflow and outflow of food through the digestive system. Dr. William P. Jollie, chairman, Department of Anatomy, the Medical College of Virginia, explains: "The muscle of both the soft palate and the uvula elevates the roof of the mouth during swallowing so that food and liquid can pass from the mouth cavity into the pharynx."

Dr. L.J.A. DiDio, of the Medical College of Ohio, adds that the uvula also helps prevent us from regurgitating our food during swallowing. Without the uvula, some of our food might enter the nasal cavity, with unpleasant consequences.

Submitted by Andy Garruto of Kinnelon, New Jersey.

Why Don't Birds Tip Over When They Sleep on a Telephone Wire?

A telephone wire, of course, is only a high-tech substitute for a tree branch. Most birds perch in trees and sleep without fear of falling even during extremely windy conditions.

The secret to birds' built-in security system is their specialized tendons that control their toes. The tendons are located in front of the knee joint and behind the ankle joint. As it sits on its perch, the bird's weight stretches the tendons so that the toes flex, move forward, and lock around the perch.

Other tendons, located under the toe bones, guarantee that a sleeping bird doesn't accidentally tip over. On the bottom of each tendon are hundreds of little projections. These fit perfectly into other ratchetlike sheaths. The body weight of the bird pressing against the telephone wire (or tree branch) guarantees that the projections will stay tightly locked within the sheaths.

Barbara Linton, of the National Audubon Society, adds that while this mechanism is most highly developed in perching birds and songbirds, many other birds do not perch to sleep. They snooze on the ground or while floating on water.

Submitted by Dr. Lou Hardy of Salem, Oregon. Thanks also to Jann Mitchell of Portland, Oregon.

Why Is It Sometimes Necessary to Stroke a Fluorescent Lamp to Get It to Light?

All fluorescent bulbs require a ground plane to start. If the fluorescent lamp is inside a metal fixture, any piece of metal, such as the reflector, can serve as a ground plane. Richard H. Dowhan, manager of Public Affairs for GTE Products Corporation, told *Imponderables* that the closer the ground plane is to the tube, the easier it is to start the fluorescent. "Placing your hand on the tube or stroking it creates a very effective ground plane." Magicians have been lighting "naked" fluorescent bulbs for quite a long time by serving as the ground plane.

But most of us aren't magicians, and most of us use fluorescent lamps inside of metal fixtures. Why do the lamps usually light with a flick of the switch at some times and then other times require a little massage? J. Robert Moody, of General Electric's Lighting Information Center, was kind enough to supply an answer that doesn't require a physics degree to understand.

Under normal conditions, fluorescent lamps should light without difficulty, with the electric current flowing inside the fluorescent tube. But if the lamp has a combination of a light coating of dust and a small amount of moisture from the air, the coating will allow "some of the electric current to flow on the outside of the tube, and the current on the outside of the bulb will prevent the lamp from lighting. Under this condition, stroking the tube will interrupt the flow of current on the outside of the tube and cause the light to come on."

Submitted by Harold J. Ballatin of Palos Verdes, California.

Why Is There an Expiration Date on Sour Cream? What's the Matter, Is It Going to Get More Sour?

We've gotten this Imponderable quite often on radio interviews, usually from smug callers sure that expiration dates are a capitalist plot to force us to throw away barely used sour cream. But mark our words: if you think sour cream is tart when you open it, just leave it in the refrigerator too long and taste the difference. As the expiration date on sour cream becomes a dim memory, bacteria acts upon the sour cream, making it unbearably tart. Given enough time, mold will form on the sour cream, even if it is properly refrigerated.

Sour cream has about a month-long life in the refrigerator. Wait much longer and we'll bet that you won't want to test just how sour cream can get. If you think we're wrong, there's one way to find out for sure.

Go ahead and taste it. Make our day.

DAVID FELDMAN

Who Translates the Mail When a Letter Is Sent to the United States from a Foreign Country that Uses a Different Alphabet?

If the United States Postal Service has problems sending a letter across town in a few days, we wondered how they contended with a letter sent to Nebraska from a remote village in Egypt. Does every post office hire a staff of linguists to pore over mail and route it in the right direction?

No, not every post office. But the USPS does employ linguists at their International Exchange Offices, located at the major ports (New York, San Francisco, Miami, and Boston) where foreign mail is received. All mail is separated and sorted at these border points and sent on its merry way.

We contacted some foreign consulates to find out how they solved the problem of indecipherable mail. A representative of the Greek consulate told *Imponderables* that if foreign mail is written in one of the international languages, multilingual personnel have no problem sorting it. If no postal worker can translate an address, the postal service will likely do what we did— call the embassy or consulate of the country of the sender and hope for the best.

Submitted by Charles F. Myers of Los Altos, California.

Why Do Roaches Always Die on Their Backs?

We couldn't believe that three readers actually had experienced the good fortune to see a dead roach and had torn themselves away from the subsequent celebration long enough to note the posture of the deceased insect. But we trudged on nevertheless, contacting entomologists who actually get paid to study stuff like this.

WHEN DO FISH SLEEP?   133

Professor Mary H. Ross, affiliated with Virginia Polytechnic Institute and State University, told *Imponderables* that when a roach dies, its legs stiffen and the cockroach falls on its side. Because most roaches have a flattened body form with narrow sides, the momentum of the fall rolls them onto their backs.

John J. Suarez, technical manager of the National Pest Control Association, adds that small cockroaches, such as the German and the brown-banded, are more likely to die on their backs. Larger cockroaches with lower centers of gravity, such as the American and the Oriental, occasionally die face down.

Needless to say, we can't guarantee the position of dead roaches contained in traps. Maybe the lifeless occupants of Roach Motels lie perfectly prone. Unfortunately, there is only one way to find out and only entomologists have the stomach for it. Please don't try to verify this at home!

Submitted by Gloria Stiefel of Orange Park, Florida. Thanks also to Irma Keat of Somers, New York; and Gregg Hoover of Morgan Hill, California.

Why Does Warmth Alleviate Pain?

A caller on Tom Snyder's radio show posed this Imponderable. We had no idea of the answer, but it was surprising that so many physicians we spoke to didn't know the answer either.

We finally got the solution from Daniel N. Hooker, Ph.D., coordinator of Physical Therapy/Athletic Training at the University of North Carolina at Chapel Hill. His answer included plenty of expressions like "receptors," "external stimuli," and "pain sensors." So let's use an analogy to simplify Hooker's explanation.

If a pneumatic drill is making a ruckus outside your window, you have a few choices. One is to do nothing, which won't accomplish much until the drill stops. But another option is to go

DAVID FELDMAN

to your stereo and put on a Led Zeppelin record at full blast. The pneumatic drill is still just as loud—you may still even be able to hear it. But the music will certainly distract you (and for that matter, your next-door neighbors as well), so the drilling doesn't seem as loud.

Hooker emphasizes that most of us associate warmth with pleasant experiences from our youth. By placing heat on the part of our body that hurts we stimulate the sensory receptors, which tell our brain that there has been a temperature change. This doesn't eliminate the pain, but the distraction makes us less aware of the pain. As our body accommodates to the high temperature, we need fresh doses of warmth to dampen the pain. When we receive the renewed heat treatment, we *expect* to feel better, so we do.

Why Can't We Use Both Sides of a Videotape like We Do with an Audio Tape?

Don French, chief engineer of Radio Shack, is getting a little testy with us: "If you keep using me as a consultant on your books, we are going to have to start charging for my service!"

We have read all of the bestselling business management books. They all reiterate that most people aren't motivated by higher pay but by recognition of their effort and accomplishments. So to you, Don French, we want to acknowledge our heartfelt appreciation for the efforts you have expended in educating the American public on the wonders and intricacies of modern technology in our contemporary culture of today. Through your efforts, our citizens will be better equipped to handle the challenges and complexities of the future.

But not one penny, bub.

Luckily, Mr. French couldn't resist answering this Imponderable anyway.

DAVID FELDMAN

It turns out that even though some audio cassette recorders require the tape to be flipped before recording on the other side, the recorder doesn't actually copy on both sides of the tape. It copies on both edges into the middle of it.

Because videotape requires an audio and a video track, recorders use both sides of the tape each time.

Submitted by Jae Hoon Chung of Demarest, New Jersey.

Why Are the Toilet Seats in Public Restrooms Usually Split Open in the Front?

This has become one of our most frequently asked Imponderables on radio shows. So for the sake of science and to allay the anxiety of unspoken millions, here's the, pardon the expression, poop on a mystery whose answer we thought was obvious.

Try as they might, even the most conscientious janitors and bathroom attendants know it is impossible to keep a multiuser public toilet stall in topnotch sanitary condition. Let's face it. Pigs could probably win a slander suit from humans for our comparing our bathroom manners to theirs. Too many people leave traces of urine on top of toilet seats. Men, because of a rather important physiological distinction from women, particularly tend not to be ideally hygienic urinators, but most sanitary codes make it mandatory that both male and female toilets contain "open-front" toilet seats in public restrooms. In fact, at one time, "open back" seats were mandated as well, but the public wouldn't stand (or sit) for them.

If they are more hygienic, why not use open-front toilet seats at home? The answer is psychological rather than practical. An open-front seat would imply to the world that one's bathroom habits were as crass as those employed by the riffraff who use public restrooms. Still, we would think that open-front toilet seats in home bathrooms might lessen the number of divorce-causing arguments about men keeping the toilet seats up.

Submitted by Janet and James Bennett of Golden, Colorado. Thanks also to Tom Emig of St. Charles, Missouri; Kate McNeive of Scottsdale, Arizona; and Tina Litsey of Kansas City, Missouri.

DAVID FELDMAN

How Are the First Days of Winter and Summer Chosen?

This Imponderable was posed by a caller on John Dayle's radio show in Cleveland, Ohio. John and the supposed Master of Imponderability looked at each other with blank expressions. Neither one of us had the slightest idea what the answer was; the first day of summer certainly didn't mark the longest day of the year. What did it signify?

We received a wonderful answer from Jeff Kanipe, an associate editor at *Astronomy*. His answer is complicated but clear, clearer than we could rephrase. So Jeff generously has consented to let us quote him in full:

> The first day of winter and summer depend on when the sun reaches its greatest angular distance north and south of the celestial equator.

Imagine for a moment that the Earth is reduced to a tiny ball floating in the middle of a transparent sphere and that we're on the "outside" looking in. This sphere, upon which the stars seem fixed and around which the moon, planets, and sun seem to move, is called the celestial sphere. If we simply extend the earth's equator to the celestial sphere it forms a great circle in the sky: the celestial equator.

Now imagine that you're back on the Earth looking out toward the celestial sphere. You can almost visualize the celestial equator against the sky. It forms a great arc that rises above the eastern horizon, extends above the southern horizon, and bends back down to the western horizon.

But the sun doesn't move along the celestial equator. If it did, we'd have one eternal season. Rather, the seasons are caused because the Earth's pole is tilted slightly over 23 degrees from the "straight up" position in the plane of the solar system. Thus, for several months, *one hemisphere tilts toward the sun while the other tilts away*. The sun's apparent annual path in the sky forms yet another great circle in the sky called the ecliptic, which, not surprisingly, is inclined a little over 23 degrees to the celestial equator.

Motions in the solar system run like clockwork. Astronomers can easily predict (to the minute and second!) when the sun will reach its greatest angular distance north of the celestial equator. This day usually occurs about June 21. If you live in the Northern Hemisphere and note the sun's position at noon on this day, you'll see that it's very high in the sky because it's as far north as it will go. The days are longer and the nights are shorter in the Northern Hemisphere. The sun is thus higher in the sky with respect to our horizon, and remains above the horizon for a longer period than it does during the winter months. Conditions are reversed in the Southern Hemisphere: short days, long nights. It's winter there.

Just reverse the conditions on December 22. In the Northern Hemisphere, the sun has moved as far south as it will go. The days are short, while the lucky folks in the Southern Hemisphere are basking in the long, hot, sunny days.

The first days of spring and fall mark the vernal and autumnal equinox, when the sun crosses the equator traveling north and south. As astronomer Alan M. MacRobert points out, the seasonal divisions are rather arbitrary:

> Because climate conditions change continuously, there is no real reason to have four seasons instead of some other number. Some cultures recognize three: winter, growing, and harvest. When I lived in northern Vermont, people spoke of six: winter, mud, spring, summer, fall, and freezeup.

Why Do Most Cars Have Separate Keys for the Ignition and Doors? Doesn't This Policy Increase the Chances of Locking Yourself Out of the Car?

The automakers aren't so concerned about *you* getting into your car. They are worried about thieves getting into your car.

Ford Motor Company, for example, now uses one key for the ignition and doors and a separate key for the glove compartment and trunk. Ford once used the same key for the door and the trunk, but changed. A Ford representative, Paul Preuss, explains:

> At one time, it was a relatively easy matter for a car thief to work open a car door and make an imprint so that it was possible to produce a key that also worked the ignition. Hence, a separate ignition key. Changing from a five-cut key to the present ten-cut key accomplishes the same thing. Five of the cuts activate the door lock and a different five operate the ignition. Taking an imprint of the door lock does not provide the proper cuts for the ignition lock.

General Motors also provides a separate key for doors and ignition and explains its decision as an attempt to foil aspiring thieves.

A two-key approach also allows the car owner to stash valuables in the trunk or glove compartment while leaving only the ignition key with a parking lot attendant or valet. And if you misplace the door key? Well, there's always the coat hanger.

Submitted by Doris Hosack of Garfield Heights, Ohio. Thanks also to Charles F. Myers of Los Altos, California; and Loretta McDonough of Frontenac, Missouri.

P.S. News Flash. Just as this book was going to press, we received a note from the Ford Parts and Service Division. Although the company felt that separate door and ignition keys made sense for security reasons, Ford is returning to its roots: "The consumer prefers one key for both door and ignition; therefore, we will phase in one key for both in the near future."

What's the Difference Between Popcorn and Other Corn? Can Regular Corn Be Popped?

There are five different types of corn: dent, flint, pod, sweet, and popcorn. Popcorn is the only variety that will pop consistently. Gregg Hoffman, of American Popcorn, told *Imponderables* that other corn might pop on occasion but with little regularity.

The key to popcorn's popping ability is, amazingly, water. Each popcorn kernel contains water, which most popcorn processors try to maintain at about a 13.5% level. The water is stored in a small circle of soft starch in each kernel. Surrounding the soft starch is a hard enamel-like starch. When the kernel is heated for popping, the water inside heats and begins to expand. The function of the hard starch is to resist the water as long as possible.

When the water expands with such pressure that the hard starch gives way, the water bursts out, causing the popcorn kernel to explode. The soft starch pops out, and the kernel turns inside out. The water, converted into steam, is released (fogging the eyeglasses of four-eyed popcorn makers), and the corn pops.

DAVID FELDMAN

The other four varieties of corn are able to store water effectively. But their outer starch isn't hard enough to withstand the water pressure of the expanding kernel, and so nothing pops.

Submitted by David Andrews of Dallas, Texas.

What Does It Mean When We Have 20–20 or 20–40 Vision?

The first number in your visual acuity grade is always twenty. That's because the 20 is a reference to the distance you are standing or sitting from the eye chart. The distance is not a coincidence. Rays of light are just about parallel twenty feet from the eye chart, so that the muscle controlling the shape of the lens in a normal eye is in a state of relative rest when viewing the chart. Ideally, your eyes should be operating under optimal conditions during the eye test.

The second number represents the distance at which a normal eye should be able to see the letters on that line. The third from the bottom line on most eye charts is the 20–20 line. If you can see the letters on that line, you have 20–20 ("normal") vision. A higher second number indicates your vision is subnormal. If you have 20–50 vision, you can discern letters that "normal" observers could see from more than twice as far away, fifty feet. If you achieve the highest score on the acuity test, a 20–10, you can spot letters that a normal person could detect only if he were 50% closer.

We also got the answer to another Imponderable we've always had about the vision test: Are you allowed to miss one letter on a line and still get "credit" for it? Yes, all you need to do is identify a majority of the letters on a line to get full credit for reading it. If only our schoolteachers were such easy graders.

HOW Does Yeast Make Bread Rise? Why Do We Need to Knead Most Breads?

Yeast is a small plant in the fungus family (that's ascomycetous fungi of the genus *Saccharomyces*, to you botanical nuts), and as inert as baker's yeast might seem to you in that little packet, it is a living organism. In fact, it works a little like the Blob, feeding and expanding at will.

Yeast manufacturers isolate one healthy, tiny cell, feed it nutrients, and watch it multiply into tons of yeast. One gram of fresh yeast contains about ten billion living yeast cells, thus giving yeast the reputation as the rabbit of the plant world.

To serve the needs of bakers, manufacturers ferment the yeast to produce a more concentrated product. But the yeast isn't satisfied to idly sit by in the fermentation containers—it wants to eat. So yeast is fed its favorite food, molasses, and continues to grow. A representative of Fleischmann's Yeast told *Imponderables* that under ideal conditions, one culture bottle of yeast holding about two hundred grams will grow to about one hundred fifty tons in five days, enough yeast to make about ten million loaves of bread.

After it has grown to bulbous size, the yeast is separated from the molasses and water and centrifuged, washed, and either formed into cakes or dried into the granulated yeast that most consumers buy. When the baker dissolves the yeast in water, it reactivates the fungus and reawakens the yeast's appetite as well.

Yeast loves to eat the sugar and flour in bread dough. As it combines with the sugar, fermentation takes place, converting the sugar into a combination of alcohol and carbon dioxide. The alcohol burns off in the oven, but small bubbles of carbon dioxide form in the bread and are trapped inside the dough. The carbon dioxide gas causes gluten, a natural protein fiber found in flour, to stretch and provide a structure for the rising dough without releasing the gas. When the dough doubles in size, the

DAVID FELDMAN

recommended amount, it is full of gas bubbles and therefore has a lighter consistency than breads baked without yeast.

By kneading the bread, the baker toughens the gluten protein structure in the dough, stretching the gluten sufficiently to withstand the pressure of the expanding carbon dioxide bubbles. You don't need to knead all dough, however; for instance, batter breads, which are made with less flour and have a more open, coarse grain, don't need it.

Submitted by Jim Albert of Cary, North Carolina.

Why Do Doctors Tap on Our Backs During Physical Exams?

We've always been suspicious about this tapping. From a patient's point of view, it has two strong attributes: It doesn't hurt and it doesn't cost anything extra. But nothing ever seems to happen as a result of the tapping. No doctor has ever congratulated us on how great our back sounded or for that matter looked worried after giving us a few whacks on the back. At our most cynical, we've even wondered whether this is a physical examination equivalent of a placebo: The doctor gets a break from the anxious gaze of the patient, and the patient is reassured that at least the back part of his body is O.K.

Doctors insist that there is a sound reason to tap our backs. Short of an X ray, the tap is one of the best ways to collect information about the lungs. The space occupied by the lungs is filled with air. The two lungs are contained in the two pleural spaces, full of air, and lung tissue itself contains air.

Dr. Frank Davidoff, associate executive vice president, Education, for the American College of Physicians, told *Imponderables* about the fascinating history of the practice of tapping:

> In 1754, a Viennese physician named Leopold Auenbrugger discovered that if you thumped the patient's chest, it would give off

a more hollow sound when you tapped over the air-filled lung space, and a more "flat" or "dull" sound if you tapped over a part of the chest that was filled with something more solid, like muscle, bone, etc. Auenbrugger's father was a tavern keeper in Graz, Austria, who used to judge the amount of wine left in the casks by tapping on them—the hollow note indicating air, the flat note indicating wine.

Auenbrugger found that by thumping a patient's chest—somewhat as his father rapped on a cask—abnormal lesions in the chest cavity, such as fluid or a solid tumor in the cavity where air-filled lung ought to be, produced a sound different from that given off in a healthy air-filled chest. Auenbrugger tested out his new method of physical diagnosis over a period of seven years of drumming on his patient's chests, and in 1761, he put before the medical profession the result of his experiments, in a book called *New Invention to Detect by Percussion Hidden Diseases in the Chest.*

Dr. Davidoff adds that the technique used today is virtually the same as the one Auenbrugger invented more than two hundred years ago.

Dr. William Berman, of the Society for Pediatric Research, says that the technique is a good, obviously cheap alternative to an X ray and has even other attributes. Tapping on the front of the chest can determine the size of a patient's heart, because the heart is much more solid than the lungs as it is muscular and full of blood.

Submitted by Richard Aaron of Toronto, Ontario.

Why Do Military Personnel Salute One Another?

Every Western military organization we know of has some form of hand salute. In every culture, it seems the inferior initiates the salute and is obligated to look directly into the face of the superior.

The origins of the hand salute are murky. In ancient Europe, where not only military officers but freemen were allowed to carry arms, the custom for men about to encounter one another was to lift their right hand to indicate they had no intention of using their sword. Many of our friendly gestures, such as tipping hats, waving, and handshaking, probably originated as ways of proving that one's hand was not reaching for a sword or a convenient rock.

By the time of the Roman Empire, salutes were a part of formal procedure among the military. Soldiers saluted by placing their right hands up to about shoulder height with the palm out. The hand never touched the head or headgear during the salute.

In medieval times, when knights wore steel armor that covered their bodies from head to toe, two men often encountered each other on horseback. To display friendship, two knights supposedly would raise their visors, exposing their faces and identities to view. Because they held their reins in the left hand, they saluted with their right (sword) hand, an upward motion not unlike the salute of today.

Whether or not our modern salute stems from the rituals of chivalry, we know for a fact that we Americans borrowed our salute from modern British military practices. In 1796, British Admiral Earl of St. Vincent commanded that all British officers must henceforth take off their hats when receiving an order from a superior "and not to touch them with an air of negligence." Although the British Navy made salutes compulsory, it didn't codify the precise nature of the salute. In many cases, inferiors simply "uncovered" (doffed their caps).

The American military salute has also undergone many changes over the years. At one time, Marines didn't necessarily salute with their right hand, but the hand farthest from the officer being saluted. Even today, there are differences among the branches. Although the Army and Air Force always salute with their right hand, Navy personnel are allowed to salute with the left hand if the right is encumbered. And while Air Force and Army men and women may salute while sitting down, Naval officers are forbidden to do so.

Even if the motivations of ancient saluters were to signal friendly intentions, the gesture over the years has been transformed into a ritual signifying respect, even demanding subjection, and a tool to enforce discipline. The United States Marine Corps, though, has maintained a long tradition of shunning any symbols of servility. In 1804, Marine Commandant William Ward Burrows knowingly discarded the European tradition of inferiors uncovering before superiors and issued this order:

DAVID FELDMAN

> No Marine in the future is to take his hat off to any person. When the officer to be saluted approaches, he will halt, face the officer and bring his right hand with a quick motion as high as the hat, the palm in front.

As a Marine publication notes, Burrows' order did much for the esprit de corps:

> We can be certain of one fact—the newly initiated salute was popular with enlisted personnel, for an English traveler of that period (Beachey) reported that "the Marines, although civil and well disciplined, boast that they take their hats off to no one."

Submitted by Wally DeVasier of Fairfield, Iowa. Thanks also to George Flower of Alexandria, Virginia.

Why Do Recipes Warn Us Not to Use Fresh Pineapple or Kiwifruit in Gelatin? Why Can We Use Canned Pineapple in Gelatin?

Both pineapple and kiwifruit contain enzymes that literally break down gelatin into a pool of glop. The enzyme in pineapple, papain, is also found in papaya and many other tropical fruits. According to the president of the California Kiwifruit Commission, Mark Houston, kiwifruit contains a related enzyme, actinidin, that similarly breaks down gelatin, preventing jelling.

Papain is a particularly important enzyme that has more functions than turning your Jell-O mold into a Jell-O pool. Papain is the active ingredient in meat tenderizers. Just as papain splits the protein in gelatin, it also attacks proteins in meat. Ever experience a stinging sensation in your mouth while eating a fresh pineapple? Papain is attacking your throat.

How can we contain this rapacious enzyme? Just as Kryptonite incapacitates Superman or garlic renders Dracula useless, so heat is the enemy of protein-splitting enzymes such as papain or actinidin. Canned pineapple can be used effectively in gelatin because the heat necessary to the process of canning fruit inactivates the enzymes. Canned pineapple might not taste as good as fresh, but it is much easier on the throat.

Submitted by Marsha Beilsmith of St. Charles, Missouri. Thanks also to David Freling of Hayward, California; and Susan Stock of Marlboro, Massachusetts.

Where Is Donald Duck's Brother?

"We see Donald Duck's nephews, Huey, Dewey, and Louie, but we never see their Dad, Donald's brother. Why not?" wails our concerned correspondent.

The main reason we never see Donald's brother is that he doesn't have one. He does have a sister with the infelicitous name of Dumbella. In a 1938 animated short, *Donald's Nephews*, Donald receives a postcard from his sister informing him that she is sending her "three angel children" for a visit.

Poor Donald, excitedly anticipating the arrival of Masters Huey, Dewey, and Louie, had no idea either that the little visit would turn into a permanent arrangement or, since his sister really thought they were little angels, that she had really earned her name. The three ducklings, indistinguishable in their personalities and equally adept in their propensity for mischief, continued to torture Donald and Scrooge McDuck in many cartoon shorts.

In a 1942 short, *The New Spirit*, Donald lists the three dependents in a tax form as adopted, indicating that Donald was a most generous brother, a certified masochist, and just as dumb as Dumbella.

Submitted by Karen S. Harris of Seattle, Washington.

What Causes Bags Under the Eyes?

Let us count the ways, in descending order of frequency:

1. Heredity. That's right. It wasn't that night on the town that makes you look like a raccoon in the morning. It's all your parents and grandparents' fault. Some people are born with excess fatty tissue and liquid around the eyes.
2. Fluid retention. The eyelids are the thinnest and softest skin in the entire body, four times as thin as "average" skin. Fluid tends to pool in thin portions of the skin.

    What causes the fluid retention? Among the culprits are drugs, kidney or liver problems, salt intake, and very commonly, allergies. Cosmetics drum up more business for dermatologists and allergists than just about anything else. Allergic reactions to mascara and eyeliner are the usual culprits.
3. Aging. The skin of the face, particularly around the eyes, loosens with age. Age is more likely to cause bags than mere sleepiness or fatigue.
4. Too many smiles and frowns. These expressions not only can build crow's feet but bags. We can safely disregard this answer to explain Bob Newhart's bags, however.

Another less fascinating explanation for many sightings of bags under the eyes was noted by Dr. Tom Meek, of the American Academy of Dermatology, in the *New York Times:* "The circles are probably caused by shadows cast from overhead lighting. . . ."

Submitted by Stephen T. Kelly of New York, New York.

How Do Blind People Discriminate Between Different Denominations of Paper Money?

Sandra Abrams, supervisor of Independent Living Services for Associated Services of the Blind, points out that the government defines "legally blind" as possessing 10% or less of normal vision. Legally blind people with partial vision usually have few problems handling paper money:

> Individuals who are partially sighted may be able to see the numbers on bills, especially in certain lighting conditions. Some people with low vision must hold the money up to their noses in order to see the numbers; some people have been asked by members of the public if they are smelling their money. Other persons with low vision might use different types of magnification. Some people with partial sight have pointed out that the numbers on the top corners of bills are larger than those on the bottoms.

The U.S. government certainly doesn't make it easy for blind people to identify currency. Virtually every other nation varies the size and color of denominations. One reader asked

DAVID FELDMAN

whether a five-dollar bill *feels* different from a twenty-dollar bill. Although suggestions have been made to introduce slight differences in texture, a blind person can't now discriminate between bills by touching them.

Initially blind people must rely on bank tellers or friends to identify the denomination of each bill, and then they develop a system to keep track of which bill is which. Gwynn Luxton, of the American Foundation for the Blind, uses a popular system with her clients:

- One-dollar bills are kept flat in the wallet.
- Five-dollar bills are folded in half crosswise, so that they are appproximately three inches long.
- Ten-dollar bills are folded in thirds crosswise, so that they are approximately two inches long.
- Twenty-dollar bills are folded in half lengthwise, so that they are half the height of the other bills and sit down much farther in the wallet or purse than the other bills.

Machines have been created to solve this problem as well. The relatively inexpensive Talking Wallet reads out the denomination of bills it receives. The more expensive Talking Money Identifier can be hooked up to cash registers and be used for commercial use. Many newspaper vendors are blind, and the Money Identifier can save them from being shortchanged.

Blind people have so many pressing problems imposed on them by a seeing culture that identifying paper money is a minor irritant. As Sandra Abrams puts it, "Frankly, of all the things I do daily, identifying money is one of the easiest."

Submitted by Jon Gregerson of Marshall, Michigan.

When Not Flying, Why Do Some Birds Walk and Others Hop?

Birds are one of the few vertebrates that are built for both walking and flying. Physiologically, flying is much more taxing on the body than walking. Usually a bird without fear of attack by predators in its native habitat will eventually become flightless. New Zealand, an oceanic island with few predators, has flightless cormorants, grebes, wrens, and even a flightless owl parrot. As Joel Carl Welty states in *The Life of Birds:*

> Why maintain splendid wings if the legs can do an adequate job? This principle may well explain why birds who are good runners fly poorly or not at all. And some of the best fliers, such as hummingbirds, swifts, and swallows, are all but helpless on their feet.
>
> More birds are hoppers than walkers. Birds that walk or run characteristically possess long legs and live in wide open spaces. While the typical tree dweller has four toes on each foot, many walkers have only two or three. Most tree-dwelling birds are hoppers, because it is easier to navigate from branch to branch by hopping than by walking. Most birds that hop in trees will hop on the ground. Although each hop covers more ground than a step would, the hop is more physically taxing.

Dr. Robert Altman, of the A & A Veterinary Hospital, points out that some birds will hop or walk depending on the amount of ground they plan to cover. "For a few steps, it might be easier for a bird to hop from place to place as he would from perch to perch in trees. To cover longer distances, the bird would walk or run."

Submitted by Jill Clark of West Lafayette, Indiana.

DAVID FELDMAN

Why Does String Cheese "String" When Torn Apart?

If you read *Why Do Clocks Run Clockwise? and Other Imponderables,* and shame on you if you haven't, you know that news papers tear easily in a vertical position because all the fibers are lined up in the same direction when pulp is put into the paper-making machine. String cheese works on exactly the same principle.

When producing string cheese, the cheese curd is formed into a large mass and then stretched mechanically. The stretching causes the protein fibers to line up in a parallel fashion. According to Tamara J. Hartweg, of Kraft, "This physical modification of the protein structure is what causes the stringing quality of the cheese. When peeled, the protein fibers, which are aligned in one direction, come off in strings."

Submitted by Lee Hand of Newbury Park, California.

Who Got the Idea of Making Horseshoes? Why are Horseshoes Necessary? What Would Happen If Horses Weren't Shod?

If horses weren't shod, they would probably have trouble getting served at fast-food establishments. Maybe they can get away with no shirts. But no shoes?

But seriously, folks, horses have the Romans to blame for the end of their barefoot existence. Horses were perfectly happy galloping around without shoes until the leaders of the Roman Empire decided that it would be a good idea to build paved roads. Without support, horses' hooves would split and crack on the hard pavement.

The paving of roadways hastened the time when horses, used to riding the range in the wild, were domesticated and forced to carry loads and pull heavy carts. These added burdens put strain on horses' feet, so the Romans used straw pads as the first horseshoes.

Karen L. Glaske, executive secretary of the United Professional Horsemen's Association, says that although evolution has bred out some of the toughness of horses' feet, many can still live a barefoot life:

> Shoes are not essential to a horse that is left to pasture or used only as an occasional trail mount. However, the stresses which horses' feet endure when jumping, racing, showing, or driving make it necessary for the conscientious owner to shoe the animal. It is a protective measure.

DAVID FELDMAN

Why Are Tattoos Usually Blue (With an Occasional Touch of Red)?

Most tattoos are not blue. The pigment, made from carbon, is actually jet black. Since the pigment is lodged *underneath* the skin, tattoos appear blue because of the juxtaposition of black against the yellowish to brown skin of most Caucasians. Although red is the second most popular color, many other shades are readily available; in fact, most tattoo artists buy many different colorings, premade, from Du Pont.

We spoke to Spider Webb, perhaps the most famous tattooist in the United States and leader of the Tattoo Club of America, about the prevalence of black pigment in tattoos. Webb felt that most clients, once they decide to take the plunge, want to show off their tattoos: Black is by far the strongest and most visible color. Webb added that in the case of one client, albino guitarist Johnny Winter, a black tattoo does appear to be black and not blue.

Submitted by Venia Stanley of Albuquerque, New Mexico

Why Is the Width of Standard Gauge Railroads Four Feet Eight-and-One-Half Inches?

When tramways were built in England to carry coal by cart or coach, the vehicles were built with wheels four feet eight-and-one-half inches apart. Legend has it that this was the same distance apart as Roman chariot wheels, but we doubt it for one important reason: There is a more logical explanation. Track gauges are determined by measuring from the *inside* of one rail to the *inside* of the other. However, the rails themselves occupied three-and-one-half inches of space. In other words, fifty-six-

and-one-half inches was almost certainly derived by starting with a measurement of five feet and deducting the width of the rails themselves.

When steam railroads were later constructed in England, the tramway gauge was retained for the most part, and in 1840 Parliament made it official, decreeing four feet eight-and-one-half inches as the standard gauge in Great Britain.

If only the United States were as logical. The first railroad in America, in Massachusetts, featured locomotives from England, built for standard gauge tracks, so the U.S. started with the same track dimensions. But no one in the fledgling American rail industry seemed to consider that it might be nice to have an interlocking system of compatible railways.

As companies from different states started their own lines, anarchy ruled. The Mohawk & Hudson stretched the standard gauge only one half inch, but the Delaware & Hudson featured a six-foot behemoth. In the early and mid-nineteenth century, gauges ranged between a little more than three feet to more than six feet.

Faced with incompatible rolling stock, long delays were common, yet to be preferred to the numerous accidents that ensued when engineers tried to roll locomotives on gauges a few inches too wide at the usual breakneck speeds.

When Union Pacific was about to be built, Abraham Lincoln tried to fix five feet—then the most popular width in the South and California—as the standard gauge for the whole country. But the established railroads in the North and the East objected on financial grounds and managed to lobby to retain fifty-six-and-one-half inches as the standard.

According to railroad expert Alvin Harlow in "The Tangle of Gauges,"

> In 1871 there were no fewer than twenty-three gages, ranging from 3 feet up to 6 feet on the railroads of the United States. Less than fifteen years later there were twenty-five; a considerable group of roads in Maine had been born only two feet wide, whilst

DAVID FELDMAN

a logging company in Oregon had built one that sprawled over 8 feet of ground.

The proliferation of gauges was caused not only by regional stubbornness but because no railroad company seemed willing to spring for the cost of converting its tracks. Finally, Illinois Central broke the logjam. In one wild, torchlit night, Illinois Central workers narrowed six hundred miles of track. Southern railroad companies, reluctant to adopt the Yankee standard, followed suit years later.

Even more difficult than relaying track was the task of refitting the rolling stock. Locomotives and cars were dragged into shops all along their routes. Harlow mentions that although the companies tried to return cars to their home lines for conversion, the logistics were a nightmare. Usually cars were converted wherever they were when the tracks were remodeled. Sufficient numbers of new workers had to be hired temporarily to have crews working twenty-four hours a day resetting locomotive truck wheels, removing the tires from truck wheels, and resetting them for the standard gauge.

A few gauges with oddball widths survived into the twentieth century, mostly in New England and the Pacific Northwest, but they were anomalies. The United States eventually rejected the "new and improved" and returned to the standard gauge of the English.

Why Is the Bathtub Drain Right Below the Faucet? Why Isn't the Bathtub Drain on the Opposite Side of the Bathtub from the Faucet?

"Wouldn't this configuration be easier for rinsing purposes?" asks our correspondent Pam Lebo. No doubt it would, but there are plenty of reasons why the plumbing industry is going to continue to make you and the makers of Woolite unhappy.

Now hard as it may be to believe, some people actually use the bathtub for bathing. These heathens would not appreciate having to sit on the drain (or for that matter, having the spigot clawing at their backs). John Laughton, of American Standard, raises another legitimate objection: A dripping faucet in Pam's configuration would cause a stain on the whole length of the bathtub.

Your dream configuration would have other practical drawbacks. Peter J. Fetterer, of Kohler Company, explains why:

> The bathtub drain is generally at the same location as the water supply because of the piping required for both. Drains and supplies run through buildings in plumbing chases, vertical spaces for pipes that move water from floor to floor. Drains are attached to vent pipes that run through the chases and vent to the outside of a structure. These chases use up living space and are kept to a minimum for economic reasons.

So must we resign ourselves to a lifetime of boring bathtubs? Not necessarily. Pam's configuration might attract some who take only showers, but it will probably never be popular. However, American Standard has created a bathtub that presents interesting possibilities for extracurricular activities besides rinsing. Their avant garde bathtub places both the faucet and the drain halfway along the bath with, offers John Laughton, "a back slope at both ends so that two could bathe together in comfort and save water." Save water. Sure, Mr. Laughton.

Submitted by Pam Lebo of Glen Burnie, Maryland.

Do Fish Sleep? If So, When Do Fish Sleep?

Our trusty *Webster's New World Dictionary* defines sleep as "a natural, regularly recurring condition of rest for the body and mind, during which the *eyes are usually closed* and there is *little or no conscious thought or voluntary movement.*" Those strategically placed little weasel words we have italicized make it hard for us to give you a yes or no answer to this mystery. So as much as we want to present you with a tidy solution to our title Imponderable, we feel you deserve the hard truth.

Webster probably didn't have fish in mind when he wrote this definition of "sleep." First of all, except for elasmobranchs (fish with cartilaginous skeletons, such as sharks and rays), fish don't have eyelids. So they can't very well close them to sleep. No fish has opaque eyelids that block out vision, but some have a transparent membrane that protects their eyes from irritants.

Pelagic fish (who live in the open sea, as opposed to coasts), such as tuna, bluefish, and marlins, *never* stop swimming. Jane Fonda would be proud. Even coastal fish, who catch a wink or two, do not fall asleep in the same way humans do. Gerry Carr, director of Species Research for the International Game Fish Association, wrote us about some of the ingenious ways that fish try to catch a few winks, even if forty winks are an elusive dream:

Some reef fishes simply become inactive and hover around like they're sleeping, but they are still acutely aware of danger approaching. Others, like some parrot fishes and wrasses, exude a mucus membrane at night that completely covers their body as though they've been placed in baggies. They wedge themselves into a crevice in the reef, bag themselves, and remain there, semicomatose, through the night. Their eyes remain open, but a scuba diver can approach them and, if careful, even pick them up at night, as I have done. A sudden flurry of movement, though, will send them scurrying. They are not totally unaware of danger.

In many ways, fish sleep the same way we plod through our everyday lives when we are awake. Our eyes are open but we choose, unconsciously, not to register in our brains most of the sensory data we see. A fish sleeping is in a state similar to the poor fish depicted watching the slide show in Kassie Schwan's illustration. We stare at the screen with our eyes open, but our minds turn to mush. If a crazed assassin burst into the room, we could rouse ourselves to attention, but if someone asked us to describe what fabulous tourist attraction we were watching, we couldn't say whether it was Stonehenge or the Blarney Stone.

If you accept that a fish's blanking out is sleeping, then the answer to the second part of the mystery is that fish sleep at night, presumably because of the darkness. Anyone with an aquarium can see that fish can float effortlessly while sleeping. They exude grace—which is more than we can say for how most humans look when they are sleeping.

Submitted by Karole Rathouz of Mehlville, Missouri. Thanks also to Cindy and Sandor Keri of Woodstock, Georgia; and Heather Bowser of Tulsa, Oklahoma.

DAVID FELDMAN

Why Do We Seem to Feel Worse at Night When We Have a Cold?

For the same reason that your feet swell up and hurt after a long day standing up. To quote Dr. Ernst Zander, of Winthrop Consumer Products:

> Nasal obstruction, produced by a great variety of conditions, usually seems worse to a patient when he is lying down. This is because tissue fluids and blood tend to pool in the head more when he is recumbent than when he is standing.

Of course, one is generally more likely to feel tired and worn out at night. But the doctors who *Imponderables* consulted indicated that reclining for long periods of time will worsen symptoms—one reason why often we feel lousy despite the "luxury" of being able to lie in bed all day long when we are sick.

Why Do Many Dry Cleaning Stores Advertise Themselves as "French" Dry Cleaners? Is There Any Difference Between a French Dry Cleaner and a Regular Dry Cleaner?

To answer the last part of this Imponderable first, there is a BIG difference between a French dry cleaner and a regular dry cleaner: about one dollar per garment.

Sure, some justification exists for calling any dry cleaning establishment "French." Dry cleaning was supposedly discovered in the 1830s by one Jolie Belin, a Frenchman who reputedly tipped over a kerosene lamp on a soiled tablecloth and found that the oil eliminated the stains. The story of Jolie Belin might be apocryphal, but dry cleaning definitely started in France.

Most Yankees are so cowed by the image of anyone who can speak French and order fancy wines in restaurants that we not only entrust our best clothing to them but are willing to pay extra for the artistry of the French dry cleaner.

DAVID FELDMAN

We conveniently forget, though, that the owner of the French dry cleaning store is as likely to be Japanese as French. And the French dry cleaner is unlikely to tell you that there is absolutely no difference between the way he and the One Hour Martinizing store down the block cleans your clothes.

Submitted by Mrs. Shirley Keller of Great Neck, New York.

Why Do Kellogg's Rice Krispies "Snap! Crackle! and Pop!"?

Kellogg's Rice Krispies have snapped, crackled, and popped since 1928. Kellogg's production and cooking process explains the unique sound effects.

Milled rice, from which the bran and germ have been removed, is combined with malt flavoring, salt, sugar, vitamins, and minerals and then steamed in a rotating cooker. The rice, now cooked, is left to dry and temper (i.e., sit while the moisture equalizes). The rice is then flattened and flaked as it passes through two cylindrical steel rollers. The Krispies are left to dry and temper for several more hours.

The cereal then moves to a toasting oven. The flattened rice is now exposed to hot air that puffs each kernel to several times its original size and toasts it to a crisp consistency. This hot air produces tiny air bubbles in each puff, crucial in creating the texture of Rice Krispies and their unique sound in the bowl.

When milk is added to the prepared cereal, the liquid is unevenly absorbed by the puffs, causing a swelling of the starch structure. According to Kellogg's, "This swelling places a strain on the remaining crisp portion, breaking down some of the starch structure and producing the famous 'Snap! Crackle! and Pop!' "

Submitted by Kevin Madden of Annandale, New Jersey.

Why Do So Many Cough Medicines Contain Alcohol?

No, the alcohol isn't there to make you forget the taste of the cough medicine. *Nothing* could do that.

Some drugs don't mix well with water. Alcohol is the best substitute. Although the alcohol may help some people sleep, the alcohol in the recommended doses of most cough medicines isn't high enough to affect the average person (one teaspoon has less than 10% the alcohol of a shot of whiskey).

Why Do Letters Sent First Class Usually Arrive at Their Destination Sooner than Packages Sent by Priority Mail?

When we send a package through the United States Postal System, we have alternatives. We can send them third class (and for certain goods, fourth class) for considerably less than Priority Mail, the package equivalent of first-class mail. But our experience is that packages invariably take longer to arrive. So we asked the USPS why. Their answers:

1. Packages are canceled and processed by hand. Almost all letters are canceled and processed by machines. Letters are sorted by OCR (Optical Character Reader) machines capable of processing up to thirty thousand letters in one hour. These machines "read" the last line of the address and sort the envelopes by zip code. Even if the OCRs can't read a letter, another machine helps humans to do so. The letter is transferred to an LSM (Letter Sorting Machine), which pops up a letter one second at a time before a postal worker who routes the letter to the proper zip code.
2. Samuel Klein, public affairs officer of the United States Postal Service, says that if a package is larger than a shoe box or weighs more than two pounds, it must be delivered by a parcel-post truck, which also carries nonpriority packages.

DAVID FELDMAN

3. Postal workers inadvertently treat Priority Mail as fourth-class mail. Dianne V. Patterson, of the Office of Consumer Affairs of the USPS, warns that "If the Priority Mail or First-Class stamps or stickers are not prominently placed on the parcel, it stands a good chance of being treated as fourth-class mail."

It isn't hard to understand the tremendous logistical difficulties in delivering mail across a large country, or even why mail might be delivered more slowly than we would like. But it is hard to understand exactly how the post office discriminates between processing a first-class and a fourth-class delivery. In the days when airmail was a premium service and fourth-class mail was transported by rail, we understood the distinction. But are postal workers now encouraged to malinger when processing fourth-class mail? Are they taught to let it sit around delivery stations for a few days so as not to encourage customers to use the slower service?

Despite our grumbling, we've found the USPS to be dependable in delivering all the free books we sent out to Imponderables posers. But we'll share a nasty secret. The books we send out at Special Fourth Class (book rate) seem to arrive no later than the books we send by the costlier Priority Mail.

Why Isn't There a Holiday to Commemorate the End of the Civil War?

Reader Daniel Marcus, who sent in this Imponderable, stated the mystery well:

> We observe a national holiday to commemorate the end of World War I on November 11 [Veteran's Day], and newspapers always note the anniversaries of V-E and V-J Days regarding the end of World War II. The Revolutionary War is honored, of course, on July 4. Why isn't there a national holiday to celebrate the end of the Civil War, the second most important and only all-American war in our history?

Good question, Daniel, but one that assumes a false premise. Memorial Day (also known as Decoration Day), celebrated on the last Monday of May, now honors the dead servicemen and servicewomen of all wars. But originally it honored the Civil War dead.

In his book *Celebrations*, historian Robert J. Myers credits Henry C. Welles, a druggist in Waterloo, New York, for originating the idea of decorating the graves of dead Civil War veterans in 1866. Originally the holiday was celebrated on May 5, when townspeople would lay flowers on the servicemen's graves.

John A. Logan, commander in chief of the Grand Army of the Republic (a veterans' support group), declared in 1868 that Decoration Day should be observed throughout the country. New York State was the first to make the day a legal holiday in 1873. Although Memorial Day never officially became a national holiday, it is celebrated in almost every state on the last Monday in May.

As with most holidays, the average person does not necessarily celebrate the occasion with the solemnity the founders of the holiday envisioned. In his study of the Civil War era, *The Expansion of Everyday Life, 1860–1878*, historian Daniel E. Sutherland notes that the new Memorial Day conveniently filled the void left by the declining popularity of George Washington's birthday: "Brass bands, picnic lunches, baseball games, and general merrymaking soon attached themselves to the new holiday, as it became as much a celebration of spring as a commemoration of the nation's honored dead." Today, the holiday is more often viewed as a kickoff to summertime than a serious tribute to the war dead.

Southerners, as might be expected, didn't particularly cotton to the concept of the northerner's Memorial Day. They countered with Confederate memorial days to honor their casualties, and many southern states still observe these holidays today. Florida and Georgia's Confederate Memorial Day is April 26; and Alabama and Mississippi celebrate on the last Monday of April. Not coincidentally, the president of the Confederacy, Jefferson Davis, was born on June 3. Kentucky and Louisiana celebrate the day as a state holiday.

Submitted by Daniel Marcus of Watertown, Massachusetts.

WHEN DO FISH SLEEP? 169

Is It True that Permanents Don't Work Effectively on Pregnant Women?

No, it isn't true, despite the fact that our correspondent has been told that it *is* true by her hairdressers. And you are not alone; we have been asked this Imponderable many times.

Everett G. McDonough, Ph.D., senior vice president of Zotos International, Inc., is one of the pioneers of permanent waving (he has worked at Zotos since 1927), and he is emphatic. He has seen or read the results of fifty thousand to one-hundred thousand perms given in the Zotos laboratory over the past sixty years. He has never seen the slightest evidence that pregnancy has any effect on permanent waving. And for good reason:

> a hair fibre after it emerges from the skin has no biological activity. Whether it remains attached to the scalp or is cut off, its chemical composition will remain the same. In either case the chemical composition can be altered only by some external means.

Louise Cotter, consultant to the National Cosmetology Association, reiterated McDonough's position and explained how a permanent wave actually works.

> A hair is held together by a protein helix consisting of salt, hydrogen, and disulphide bonds. The words "permanent wave" refer to the chemical change that takes place when those bonds are broken by a reducing agent having a pH of 9.2 (thioglycolate acid). The hair, when sufficiently softened, is re-bonded (neutralized) with a solution having a pH of 7.0–7.9. This causes the hair to take the shape of the circular rod on which it is wound, creating full circle curls or a wave pattern, depending upon the size and shape of the rod.

Although Cotter says that poor blood circulation, emotional disturbances, malfunctioning endocrine glands, and certain drugs may adversely affect the health of hair, none of these factors should alter the effectiveness of a perm on a pregnant woman. Pregnancy isn't an illness, and none of these four factors is more likely in pregnant women. Even if a pregnant woman takes hor-

DAVID FELDMAN

mones that could conceivably affect the results of a perm, a cosmetologist can easily compensate for the problem.

John Jay, president of Intercoiffure, answers this Imponderable simply:

> I have never had a permanent-wave failure due to pregnancy. Should failure occur for whatever reason, pregnancy may be the most convenient excuse available to some hairdressers.

Submitted by Jeri Bitney of Shell Lake, Wisconsin.

Why Do Some Escalator Rails Run at a Different Speed from the Steps Alongside Them?

The drive wheel that powers the steps in an escalator is attached to a wheel that runs the handrails. Because the steps and the rails run in a continuous loop, the descending halves of the stairs and handrails act as a counterweight to their respective ascending halves. The handrails, then, are totally friction-driven rather than motor-driven.

If the escalator is properly maintained, the handrail should move at the same speed as the steps. The handrails are meant to provide a stabilizing force for the passenger and are thus designed to move synchronously for safety reasons. Handrails that move slower than the accompanying steps are actually dangerous, for they give a passenger the impression that his feet are being swept in front of him. Richard Heistchel, of Schinder Elevator Company, informed *Imponderables* that handrails were once set to move slightly faster than the steps, because it was believed that passengers forced to lean forward were less likely to fall down.

Submitted by John Garry, KTAE Radio, Pittsburgh, Pennsylvania. Thanks also to Jon Blees of Sacramento, California; Robert A. Ciero, Sr. of Bloomsburg, Pennsylvania; and David Fuller of East Hartford, Connecticut.

Why Are There Lights Underneath the Bottom Steps of Escalators and Why Are They Green?

Those emerald lights are there to outline the periphery of the step on which you are about to hop or hop off. The majority of accidents on escalators occur when a passenger missteps upon entering or exiting the escalator. The lights, which are located just below the first step of ascending stairs (and the last step of descending stairs), are there to show the way for the unproficient escalator passenger.

Escalator lights are green for the same reason that traffic lights use green: Green is among the most visually arresting colors.

Submitted by John T. Hunt of Pittsburgh, Pennsylvania.

Why Are Rented Bowling Shoes So Ugly?

We know that taste in art is a subjective matter. We are aware that whole books have been written about what colors best reflect our personalities and which colors go best with particular skin tones.

But on some things a civilized society must agree. And rented bowling shoes *are* ugly. Does anybody actually believe that maroon-blue-and-tan shoes best complement the light wood grain of bowling lanes or the black rubber of bowling balls?

Bruce Pluckhahn, curator of the National Bowling Hall of Fame and Museum, told us that at one time "the black shoe—like the black ball—was all that any self-respecting bowler would be caught dead using." Now, most rented bowling shoes are tricolored. The poor kegler is more likely to be dressed like Cindy Lauper (on a bad day) than Don Carter.

We spoke to several shoe manufacturers who all agreed that their three-tone shoes were not meant to be aesthetic delights. The weird color combinations are designed to discourage theft. First, the colors are so garish, so ugly, that nobody *wants* to steal them. And second, if the rare pervert does try to abscond with the shoes, the colors are so blaring and recognizable that there is a good chance to foil the thief.

Of course, rented bowling shoes get abused daily. A bowling proprietor is lucky if a pair lasts a year. Gordon W. Murrey, president of bowling supply company Murrey International, told *Imponderables* that the average rental shoe costs a bowling center proprietor about $10 to $25 a pair. The best shoes may get rented five hundred times before falling apart, at a very profitable $1 per rental.

Even if rentals were a dignified shade of brown, instead of black, tan, and red, they would get scuffed and bruised just the same. Bowlers don't expect fine Corinthian leather. But can't the rented bowling shoes look a littler classier, guys? Isn't a huge 9 on the back of the heel enough to discourage most folks from stealing a shoe?

Submitted by Shane Coswith of Reno, Nevada.

What's the Difference Between Virgin Olive Oil and *Extra* Virgin Olive Oil?

We promised ourselves that we wouldn't make any jokes about virgins being hard to find and extra-virgins being impossible to find, so we won't. We will keep a totally straight face while answering this important culinary Imponderable.

We may have trouble negotiating arms reductions, but on one issue the nations of the world agree; thus, the International Olive and Olive Oil Agreement of 1986. This agreement defines the terms "virgin olive oil" and "extra virgin olive oil."

Any olive oil that wants to call itself virgin must be obtained from the fruit of the olive tree solely by mechanical or other physical means rather than by a heating process. The oil cannot be refined or diluted, but may be washed, decanted, and filtered.

DAVID FELDMAN

The lowest grade of virgin olive oil is semi-fine virgin olive oil, which is sold in stores as "virgin." This oil must be judged to have a good flavor and no more than three grams of free oleic acid per hundred grams of oil.

The next highest grade, fine virgin olive oil, cannot exceed one and a half grams of oleic acid per hundred grams and must have excellent taste.

Extra virgin olive oil must have "absolutely perfect flavour" and maximum acidity of one gram per hundred grams. According to José Luis Perez Sanchez, commercial counselor of the Embassy of Spain, extra virgin olives are often used with different kinds of natural flavors and are quite expensive, which any trip to the local gourmet emporium will affirm.

As with many other food items, the prize commodity (extra virgin olive oil) is the one that achieves quality by omission. By being free of extraneous flavors or high acidity, the "special" olive oil is the one that manages what wouldn't seem like too difficult a task: to taste like olives.

Submitted by Phyllis M. Dunlap of St. George, Utah.

Why Are There Cracks on Sidewalks at Regular Intervals? What Causes the Irregular Cracking on Sidewalks?

Believe it or not, those regularly spaced cracks are there to prevent the formation of irregular cracks.

We tend to see concrete as lifeless and inert, but it is not. Concrete is highly sensitive to changes in temperature. When a sidewalk is exposed to a cool temperature, it wants to contract.

Gerald F. Voigt, director of Engineering–Education and Research at the American Concrete Pavement Association, explains that concrete is very strong in compression but only one tenth as strong in tension.

> It would be much easier to break a piece of concrete by pulling on two opposite ends, rather than push it together. Cracking in concrete is almost always caused by some form of tensile development.
>
> In many cases the concrete slabs are restricted by the friction of the base on which they were constructed. This frictional resis-

DAVID FELDMAN

tance will put the slabs in tension as they contract; if the resistance is greater than the tensile strength of the concrete, a crack will form. Something has to give.

Without any form of restraint, the concrete will not crack.

Concrete tends to shrink as it dries, and tends to gain strength over time. Thus, sidewalks are most vulnerable to cracking the first night after the concrete is placed. Two strategies are employed to combat cracking.

Arthur J. Mullkoff, staff engineer at the American Concrete Institute, told *Imponderables* that properly positioned reinforcing steel is often used to reduce cracks. But the most effective method of minimizing cracks is to predetermine where the cracks will be located by installing joints in between segments of concrete.

Those spaces that threaten the well-being of your mother's back are a form of "tooled joints," strategically positioned cracks. These joints are placed in all types of concrete slabs. Gerald Voigt elaborates:

> The concrete is sawed or tooled to approximately one-quarter of the thickness of the slab, which creates a "weakened plane." The concrete will crack through the "weakened plane" joint, because that joint is not as strong. As you can see on almost any sidewalk, tooled joints are placed about every four to eight feet. These joints are placed to control where cracks develop and avoid random cracking which is usually considered unattractive. . . . Typically sidewalks are four inches thick; joint depth must be at least one-quarter of the sidewalk thickness.

Perhaps the most surprising element in the story of concrete cracks is that although so much effort is put into preventing them, cracks are not particularly troublesome. The National Ready-Mixed Concrete Association says that cracks rarely affect the structural integrity of concrete. Even when the cracks are wide enough to allow water to seep in, "they do not lead to progressive deterioration. They are simply unsightly."

Incidentally, our correspondent asked how the superstition "Step on a crack, break your mother's back" originated. We've never found a convincing answer to this Imponderable, but Gerald Voigt offered a fascinating theory:

> Since a concrete sidewalk consists of many short segments (slabs) of white concrete, it can be imagined that it is like a human spine. The spine also consists of many short segments (vertebrae) of white bones. The weak links in each system are the joints. Stepping on a sidewalk crack, or joint, is analogous to stepping on the weakest area of the spine. I imagine if I were walking down a spine, I would avoid stepping on a vertebrae link, wouldn't you?

Submitted by Mrs. Harold Feinstein of Skokie, Illinois.
Thanks also to Henry J. Stark of Montgomery, New York.

Why Do We Have to Shake Deodorant and Other Aerosol Cans Before Using?

If you could see inside a can of deodorant, you would see that the ingredients are not arranged uniformly in the can. The propellant is not soluble and so won't mix with the active ingredients in the deodorant.

In many cases, you would see three or four levels of ingredients in a can. The top layer would contain the hydrocarbon gas used as a propellant. Other active ingredients, such as aluminum salt, emollient, and fragrance, also might seek their own level. By shaking up the can, you would guarantee spraying the proper proportion of ingredients.

Any effort expended in shaking the can is well worth the appreciation from friends and loved ones. But a stiff spray of hydrocarbon gas simply isn't sufficient to take care of a nasty body odor problem.

Submitted by Mark Fusco of Northford, Connecticut.

DAVID FELDMAN

Why Do Airlines Use Red Carbons on Their Tickets?

The dominant manufacturer of airline tickets is Rand McNally, the same company that makes maps and atlases. We spoke to Chris George, of Rand McNally's Ticket Division, who told us that there are two explanations for the tradition of red carbons.

In the early years of commercial aviation, black carbons were used. This we know for a fact. But Mr. George says the problem with black carbons was that in high humidity specks of black would fall off the ticket. Women, in particular, were upset that their hands or gloves were befouled with black crud. So the airlines did market research that revealed women did not object as much to traces of red on their hands because they were used to rouge and lipstick stains. This, Mr. George adds wryly, is the romantic explanation.

The unromantic explanation (a.k.a. the truth) is as follows: Once your ticket form is torn by the ticket agent, it is sent to the accounting department of the airline. The major carriers have long used optical scanners to read the serial numbers found on each ticket. An OCR (Optical Character Recognition) scanner can't read the ticket when black flecks of carbon land on the serial number because it can only register information printed in black ink. Much as a photocopier will not read blue ink, an OCR scanner won't read red ink. Who would have thought that accountants would be responsible for the daring flash of red on airline tickets?

In a time of high-tech stationery, why don't the airlines use carbonless paper? Part of the answer again relates to the OCR equipment. Carbonless paper contains blue specks that OCRs won't read. Furthermore, with chemically sensitized noncarbon paper, legibility is good for only about five copies. Old-fashioned carbon paper can render nine legible copies, sometimes necessary for the daunting itineraries of business travelers.

Now that most airlines are issuing automated ticket boarding passes—the ones that look like computer cards—the decline of the carbonized form is inevitable. Because not all ticket counters possess the equipment to issue these boarding passes, Mr. George predicts that the beloved red carbonized forms will continue to play a part in aviation for the foreseeable future.

Submitted by Niel Lynch of Escondido, California.

I Have a Dollar Bill with an Asterisk After the Serial Number: Is It Counterfeit?

The *Imponderables* staff will gladly accept your dollar bill if you don't want it. No, it's not counterfeit. You are holding a "star note," a replacement for a defective bill that has been destroyed.

In 1910, the Bureau of Engraving and Printing started printing ★ B and later ★ D as prefixes before the serial numbers of replacement notes. No star notes were issued for national bank notes, which were replaced by new notes that matched the missing serial numbers.

Now that notes are issued in series of one hundred million at a time, it is obvious why the Bureau would rather not have to renumber replacement notes, especially since, as Bob Cochran,

DAVID FELDMAN

secretary of the Society of Paper Money Collectors, told us, errors are quite common in the printing process:

> The most common errors are in inking, cutting, and in the overprinting operation. With inking there can be too much, not enough, or unacceptable smears. Notes are printed in sheets of 32; the back is printed in all green ink and then the face is printed in all black ink. If one side or the other is not registered properly, the designs will not match up on both sides after the sheets are cut up; if the registration is very poor, the notes will be replaced. A third separate printing operation adds the serial number and Treasury Seal; the major error possibilities are in inking and placement, since the basic note design already exists at this point.

You have probably noticed that serial numbers on U.S. currency are preceded by a letter. That letter designates which of the twelve Federal Reserve districts issued the note (this is why the letters span A through L). For example, all serial numbers preceded by D (the fourth letter of the alphabet) are issued by the Fourth District of the Federal Reserve (Cleveland). Here is a list of the twelve Federal Reserve Bank districts and the letter designations for each:

District	Letter	City
1	A	Boston
2	B	New York
3	C	Philadelphia
4	D	Cleveland
5	E	Richmond
6	F	Atlanta
7	G	Chicago
8	H	St Louis
9	I	Minneapolis
10	J	Kansas City
11	K	Dallas
12	L	San Francisco

The star note enables the treasury to issue a new set of serial numbers rather than attempting to reassign all the missing serial numbers of defective notes. On U.S. notes, a star substitutes for the prefix letter. A replacement U.S. note might look like this: ★ 00000007 B. On Federal Reserve notes, a star substitutes for the letter at the end of the serial number, so that the location of the Federal Reserve district is kept intact: D 00000007 ★.

William Bischoff, associate curator of the American Numismatic Society, adds that there is one other use for the star note. The Bureau of Printing and Engraving uses printers with eight-digit numbering cylinders to produce one hundred million notes at a time. But for the one-hundred-millionth note, a ninth digit is needed. Rather than bothering to add another digit on the cylinder that would literally be used on one out of a hundred million notes, the one-hundred-millionth note is a hand-inserted star note.

To What Do the Numbers Assigned to Automotive Oil Refer?

Thirty years ago, 10–30 was considered a premium automotive oil. Today, one can buy 10–50 or even 10–60 oil, but few people know what these numbers mean.

The numbers measure the viscosity of the oil. The higher the number, the higher the viscosity (meaning the oil is less likely to flow). Although the viscosity of a liquid is not always directly correlated to thickness, high-viscosity oils are thicker than their low-viscosity counterparts.

The numbers on engine and transmission oils are assigned by the Society of Automotive Engineers. Their numbers range from 5W to 60. The W stands for winter. When a W follows a number, it indicates the viscosity of the oil at a low temperature. When there is no W following a number, the viscosity is measured at a high temperature.

All oil companies promote multigrade oils, which are designed to perform well in hot or cold temperatures. Thus 10W–40 doesn't indicate a range of viscosity, but rather the low

DAVID FELDMAN

viscosity of oil during winter (when one desires greater flow capabilities) and high viscosity in the summer.

Submitted by Tom and Marcia Bova of Rochester, New York.

When I Put One Slice of Bread in My Toaster, the Heating Element in the Adjacent Slot Heats Up as Well. So Why Does My Toaster Specify Which Slot to Place the Bread in If I Am Toasting Only One Slice?

Considering that the pop-up toaster has proven to be perhaps the most durable and dependable kitchen appliance, we were surprised to learn that toasting technology varies considerably from model to model. The earliest toasters browned one side of bread at a time; one had to decide when to flip the bread over by hand, a problem not unlike the momentous decision of when to flip over a frying pancake or hamburger.

Now that even the simplest pop-up toaster has a toast selector dial to allow the user to choose the preferred degree of doneness, most of the guesswork in toasting has been eliminated. We are not even allowed to select which of two or four slots to put in our one meager slice of bread. Why not?

Actually, nothing dire will result if you don't use the slot marked ONE SLICE. The worst that will happen is that the toaster will pop up an underdone or overdone piece. But why is the same well that manages to produce wonderful toast when it has company next door suddenly rendered incompetent when forced to work alone?

The answer depends upon the type of technology the toaster uses to determine doneness. The simplest toasters, now passé, worked from a simple time principle. The darker the brownness dial was set for, the longer the timer set for the toaster to heat the bread. Toasters that worked on a timer alone did not need a ONE SLICE notation because they always cooked the bread for the same amount of time, as long as the brownness dial wasn't changed. Using a timer alone guaranteed that a second set of toast would come out overdone, because the toaster was already warmed up yet toasted the second set for the same period of time as the first batch that was heated from a "cold start."

To solve the problem, appliancemakers inserted a thermostatic switch in toasters, which measured the heat of the toaster rather than the time elapsed in cooking. The thermostat alone caused a reverse problem. A second batch of bread would come out underdone because the first cycle had already caused the heating element to charge. The toaster didn't "know" that the second batch of bread hadn't been exposed to the toaster long enough; it knew only that the toaster had achieved the desired temperature.

The solution to the problem was to use a combination timer-thermostat. Today, the timer is not set off until the thermostat tells the timer that the toaster has reached the preset temperature (determined by the setting of the brownness dial). With this technology, it might take a minute for the thermostat to tell the timer to start ticking with the first set of toast but only a few seconds for the second or third.

We spoke to an engineer at Proctor-Silex who told us that most of their toasters have the thermostat close to—or in some cases, inside—the well that is marked ONE SLICE so the thermostat can do a more accurate job of "reading" the correct temperature for that slice. Some toasters that have ONE SLICE markings are "energy saver" toasters, specifically designed so that the heating element in the second slot will not be charged if it does not contain bread.

Sunbeam has long produced the 20030 toaster, an elegant two-slicer that selects the proper brownness of the bread by a radiant control that "reads" the surface of the bread to determine the degree of doneness. As far as we know, the Sunbeam 20030 is the only toaster that doesn't work on a time principle. The 20030 actually measures the surface temperature of the bread by determining its moisture level and can accurately measure the time needed to toast any type of bread. Wayne R. Smith, of

DAVID FELDMAN

Sunbeam Public Relations, told *Imponderables,* "There's no point in having radiant controls in both slots when having a control in one slot works just as well."

Submitted by Lisa M. Giordano of Tenafly, New Jersey. Thanks also to Muriel S. Marschke of Katonah, New York; and Jim Francis of Seattle, Washington.

Why Are Almost All Cameras Black?

Black isn't the most obvious color we would pick for cameras. Not only is black an austere and a threateningly high-tech color to amateurs, it would seem to have a practical disadvantage. As Jim Zuckerman, of Associated Photographers International, explained, black tends to absorb heat more than lighter colors, and heat is the enemy of film.

Of course, there was and is no reason why the exteriors of cameras need to be black. For a while, chromium finishes were popular on 35 millimeter cameras, but professional photographers put black tape over the finish to kill any possible reflections. Sure, some companies now market inexpensive cameras with decorator colors on the exterior. Truth be told, the persistence of black exteriors on cameras has more to do with marketing than anything else. As Tom Dufficy, of the National Association of Photographic Manufacturers, told us: "To the public, black equals professional."

Submitted by Herbert Kraut of Forest Hills, New York.

WELL, THEY SAID MY NEW SHIRT WOULD IRON ITSELF!!

SHIRT PERMA PRESS #39⁹⁵

Why Is There a Permanent Press Setting on Irons?

We buy a permanent press shirt so that we won't have to iron it. Then after we wash the shirt for the first time, it comes out of the dryer with wrinkles. Disgusted, we pull out our iron only to find that it has a permanent-press setting. Are iron manufacturers bribing clothiers to renege on their promises? Is this a Communist plot?

The appliance industry is evidently willing to acknowledge what the clothing industry is reluctant to admit: A garment is usually permanently pressed only until you've worn it—once. Wayne R. Smith, consultant in Public Relations to the Sunbeam Appliance Company, suggested that "permanent press" was chosen to describe the benefits of some synthetic materials be-

DAVID FELDMAN

cause "it has a far more attractive sound to consumers than 'wrinkle-resistant.' "

We know what Mr. Smith means. We've always felt that the difference between a water-resistant watch and a waterproof watch was that the waterproof one would die the moment *after* it hit H_2O.

What Causes Double-Yolk Eggs? Why Do Egg Yolks Sometimes Have Red Spots on Them?

Female chicks are born with a fully formed ovary containing several thousand tiny ova, which form in a cluster like grapes. A follicle-stimulating hormone in the bloodstream develops these ova, which will eventually become egg yolks. When the ova are ripe, the follicle ruptures and an ovum is released. Usually when a chicken ovulates, one yolk at a time is released and travels down the oviduct, where it will acquire a surrounding white membrane and shell.

But occasionally two yolks are released at the same time. Double-yolk eggs are no more planned than human twins. But some chickens are more likely to lay double-yolk eggs. Very young and very old chickens are most likely to lay double yolks; young ones because they don't have their laying cycles synchronized, and old ones because, generally speaking, the older the chicken, the larger the egg she will lay. And for some reason, extra-large and jumbo eggs are most subject to double yolks.

If a chicken is startled during egg formation, small blood vessels in the wall may rupture, producing in the yolk blood spots—tiny flecks of blood. Most eggs with blood spots are removed when eggs are graded, although they are perfectly safe to eat.

DAVID FELDMAN

Submitted by Lewis Conn of San Jose, California. Thanks also to Melody L. Love of Denver, North Carolina.

Why Are Barns Red?

We first encountered this Imponderable when a listener of Jim Eason's marvelous KGO-San Francisco radio show posed it. "Ummmmm," we stuttered.

Soon we were bombarded with theories. One caller insisted that red absorbed heat well, certainly an advantage when barns had no heating system. Talk-show host and guest agreed it made some sense, but didn't quite buy it. Wouldn't other colors absorb more heat? Why didn't they paint barns black instead?

Then letters from the Bay area started coming in. Donna Nadimi theorized that cows had trouble discriminating between different colors and just as a bull notices the matador's cape, so a red barn attracts the notice of cows. She added: "I come from West Virginia and once asked a farmer this question. He told me that cows aren't very smart, and because the color red stands out to them, it helps them find their way home." The problem with this theory is that bulls are color-blind. It is the movement of the cape, not the color, that provokes them.

Another writer suggested that red would be more visible to owners, as well as animals, in a snowstorm. Plausible, but a stretch.

Another Jim Eason fan, Kemper "K.C." Stone, had some "suspicions" about an answer. Actually, he was right on the mark:

> The fact is that red pigment is cheap and readily available from natural sources. Iron oxide—rust—is what makes brick clay the color that it is. That's the shade of red that we westerners are accustomed to—the rusty red we use to stain our redwood decks. It's obviously fairly stable too, since rust can't rust and ain't likely to fade.

WHEN DO FISH SLEEP? 189

The combination of cheapness and easy availability made red an almost inevitable choice. Shari Hiller, a color specialist at the Sherwin-Williams Company, says that many modern barns are painted a brighter red than in earlier times for aesthetic reasons. But aesthetics was not the first thing on the mind of farmers painting barns, as Ms. Hiller explains:

> You may have noticed that older barns are the true "barn red." It is a very earthy brownish-red color. Unlike some of the more vibrant reds of today that are chosen for their decorative value, true barn red was selected for cost and protection. When a barn was built, it was built to last. The time and expense of it was monumental to a farmer. This huge wooden structure needed to be protected as economically as possible. The least expensive paint pigments were those that came from the earth.

Farmers mixed their own paint from ingredients that were readily available, combining iron oxide with skim milk—did they call the shade "2% red"?—linseed oil and lime. Jerry Rafats, reference librarian at the National Agricultural Library, adds that white and colored hiding pigments are usually the most costly ingredients in paints.

K.C. speculated that white, the most popular color for buildings in the eighteenth and nineteenth centuries (see *Why Do Clocks Run Clockwise? and Other Imponderables* for more than you want to know about why most homes are and always have been painted white), was unacceptable to farmers because it required constant cleaning and touching up to retain its charm. And we'd like to think that just maybe the farmers got a kick out of having a red barn. As K.C. said, "Red is eye-catching and looks good, whether it's on a barn, a fire truck, or a Corvette."

Submitted by Kemper "K.C." Stone of Sacramento, California. Thanks also to Donna Nadimi of El Sobrante, California; Jim Eason of San Francisco, California; Raymond Gohring of Pepper Pike, Ohio; Stephanie Snow of Webster, New York; and Bettina Nyman of Winnipeg, Manitoba.

DAVID FELDMAN

Why Are Manhole Covers Round?

On one momentous day we were sitting at home, pondering the imponderable, when the phone rang.

"Hello," we said wittily.

"Hi. Are you the guy who answers stupid questions for a living?" asked the penetrating voice of a woman who later introduced herself as Helen Schwager, a friend of a friend.

"That's our business, all right."

"Then I have a stupid question for you. Why are manhole covers round?"

Much to Helen's surprise, the issue of spherical manhole covers had never been important to us.

"Dunno."

"Guess!" she challenged.

So we guessed. Our first theory was that a round shape roughly approximated the human form. And a circle big enough to allow a worker would take up less space than a rectangle.

"Nope," said Helen, friend of our soon-to-be ex-friend. "Try again."

Brainstorming, a second brilliant speculation passed our lips. "It's round so they can roll the manhole cover. Try rolling a heavy rectangular or trapezoidal manhole cover on the street."

"Be serious," Helen insisted.

"O.K., we give up. Tell us, O brilliant Helen. *Why are manhole covers round?*"

"It's obvious, isn't it?" gloated Helen, virtually flooding with condescension. "If a manhole were a square or a rectangle, the cover could fall into the hole when turned diagonally on its edge."

Helen, who was starting to get on our nerves just a tad, went on to regale us with the story of how she was presented with this Imponderable at a business meeting and came up with the answer on the spot. With tail between our legs, we got off the phone, mumbling something about maybe this Imponderable getting in the next book. First we get humiliated by this woman; then we have to give her a free book. Isn't there any justice?

Of course, after disconnecting with Helen we did what any self-respecting American would do: We tortured our friends with this Imponderable, making them feel like pieces of dogmeat if they didn't get the correct answer. And very few did.

Of course, we can't rely on an answer provided by the supplier of an Imponderable, even one so intelligent as Helen, so we contacted many manufacturers of manhole covers, as well as city sewer departments.

Guess what? The manufacturers of manhole covers can't agree on why manhole covers are round. Some, such as the Vulcan Foundry of Denham Springs, Louisiana, immediately confirmed Helen's answer but couldn't resist throwing a plug in as well ("Then, again, maybe manhole covers are round to facilitate the use of the Vulcan Classic Cover Collection").

But the majority of the companies we spoke to said not only do manhole covers not have to be round but many aren't. Manhole covers sit inside a frame or a ring that is laid into the concrete. Many of these frames cover the hole completely and are not hollow, so there is no way that a cover any shape could fall into the hole.

Most important, as Eric Butterfield, of Emhart Corporation, told *Imponderables*, manhole covers have a lip. As long as the lip of the cover extends long enough, any shape will do. Usually the manhole cover is at least one inch longer in diameter for each foot of the diameter of the hole.

Round manholes are more convenient in other ways. Lathe workers find spherical products easier to manufacture. Seals tend to be tighter on round covers. And Lois Hertzman, of OPW, a division of Dover Corporation, adds that round manholes are easier to install because there are no edges to square off.

Everyone we spoke to mentioned that many manholes are not round. Many older manhole covers are rectangular. The American Petroleum Institute wants oil covers to be the shape of equilateral triangles (impractical on roadways, where this shape could lead to covers flipping over like tiddlywinks).

Engineers at the New York City Sewer Design Department could find no technical reason for round manhole covers. They assumed, like most of the fall-through theory dissenters, that the round shape is the result of custom and standardization rather than necessity.

So, Helen, we have wreaked our revenge. Perhaps your answer is correct. But then, maybe it is wrong. Maybe the real reason manholes are round is so that they can facilitate the use of the Vulcan Classic Cover Collection.

Submitted by Helen Schwager of New York, New York.
Thanks also to Tracie Ramsey of Portsmouth, Virginia.

Frustables

OR

The 10 Most Wanted   Imponderables

In *Why Do Clocks Run Clockwise?*, we broke down and admitted we were haunted and rendered sleepless by our inability to answer some Imponderables that were sent to us. Often we found fascinating explanations, tantalizing theories, or partial proof. But burdened by the strict ethical codes that the custody of the body Imponderability places upon us, we can't rest until we positively nail the answers to these suckers.

So we asked our readers for help with the ten most Frustrating Imponderables (or Frustables, for short). The fruits of your labors are contained in the following pages. But before you get totally smug about your accomplishments, may we lay ten more on you?

These are ten Imponderables for which we don't yet have a conclusive answer. Can you help? A reward of a free, autographed copy of the next volume of *Imponderables,* as well as an acknowledgment in the book, will be given to the first reader who can lead to the proof that solves any of these Frustables.

FRUSTABLE 1: *Why is Legal Paper 8½" × 14"?*

We have located the first company to manufacture a legal-sized pad. We've also contacted the largest manufacturers of paper and stationery and many legal sources. But no one seems to know the reasons for lengthening regular paper and dubbing it "legal size." And yes, we know that many courts have abandoned legal-sized paper and now use 8½" × 11".

FRUSTABLE 2: *Why Do Americans, Unlike Europeans, Switch Forks to the Right Hand After Cutting Meat?*

Did someone give the Pilgrims radical etiquette lessons on the *Mayflower?* Is there any sense to the American method?

FRUSTABLE 3: *How, When, and Why Did the Banana Peel Become the Universal Slipping Agent in Vaudeville and Movies?*

Vegetable oil would work better, no?

FRUSTABLE 4: *Why did the Grade E Disappear from Grading Scales in Most Schools?*

An F makes sense as the lowest mark (F = failure); but why did the E get lost?

FRUSTABLE 5: *How Did They Lock Saloon Doors in the Old West?*

Were saloons in the old West open 24 hours? If they weren't, a couple of swinging doors three feet off the ground wouldn't provide a heckuva lot of security. Were there barriers that covered the entrance, or are swinging saloon doors a figment of movemakers' imaginations?

DAVID FELDMAN

FRUSTABLE 6: *Why Do So Many People Save* National Geographics *and Then Never Look at Them Again?*

A visit to just about any garage sale will confirm that most people save *National Geographics.* An unscientific poll confirms that nobody ever looks at the issues they've saved. What gives?

FRUSTABLE 7: *Why Do People, Especially Kids, Tend to Stick Their Tongues Out When Concentrating?*

Theories abound, but no one we contacted had any confidence about their conjectures.

FRUSTABLE 8: *Why Do Kids Tend to Like Meat Well Done (and Then Prefer It Rarer and Rarer as They Get Older)?*

Are kids repelled by the sight of blood in rare meat? Do they dislike the texture? The purer taste of meat? What accounts for the change as they get older?

FRUSTABLE 9: *Why Does Whistling at an American Sporting Event Mean "Yay!" When Whistling Means "Boo!" in Most Other Countries?*

FRUSTABLE 10: *Why Are So Many Restaurants, Especially Diners and Coffee Shops, Obsessed with Mating Ketchup Bottles at the End of the Day?*

We have been in sleazy diners where we couldn't hail a waitress if our lives depended on it and were lucky if our table was cleaned off. Where was the waitress? She was grabbing all the ketchup bottles and stacking them so that the remains of one bottle flowed into a second bottle.

Who cares whether the ketchup bottle on the table is one third filled or completely full? Doesn't the ketchup flow more easily out of a less than full bottle? Do restaurateurs mate ketchup bottles to please patrons, or do they have other, perhaps nefarious, reasons?

Frustables Update

Captured!!! The Ten Frustables from Why Do Clocks Run Clockwise?

FRUSTABLE 1: *Why Do You So Often See One Shoe Lying on the Side of the Road?*

They say that every parent has a favorite. In this case, we'll admit it. This isn't only our favorite Frustable, it's probably our favorite Imponderable ever, partly because it has been a difficult "child." We spoke to endless officials at the Department of Transportation and the Federal Highway Safety Traffic Administration. All of them were aware of the phenomenon; none had a compelling explanation.

In *Why Do Clocks Run Clockwise?* we talked about some of

the theories proffered by readers of Elaine Viets, columnist for the *St. Louis Post-Dispatch:*

- They are tossed out of cars during fights among kids.
- They fall out of garbage trucks.
- Both shoes are abandoned at the same time, but one rolls away.
- They are disentangled, discarded newlywed shoes.
- They are thrown out of school buses and cars as practical jokes.

We asked if our readers could come up with anything better.

We needn't have worried. You guys came through in spades. Your answers fell into three general categories: theoretical, empirical, and confessional. So profound were your insights into this important subject that we have given thirteen of them official *Imponderables* Awards of Merit.

Award-Winning Theoretical Explanations

Best Supply-Side Argument by a Noneconomist. Provided by Stefan Habsburg of Farmington Hills, Michigan: "Because if there were a pair, someone would pick them up!"

Best Conspiracy Theory. Provided by Morry Markovitz of Croton Falls, New York:

If a lost pair of shoes were found intact, the shoe industry might lose a sale as these old shoes were pressed into service by a new owner. Has the shoe industry secretly hired "road agents" to scour the country-side, picking up one of each pair they find?

Best Explanation Involving Eastern European Influence Upon the One-Shoe Problem. Provided by Rick La Komp of Livermore, California: "Barefoot field-goal kickers decided they didn't need more than one shoe and threw the other away."

Best Explanation by an Obnoxious Anthropomorphic Cartoon Animal. Provided by David Selzler of Loveland, Colorado. David sent us a "Garfield" cartoon in which the cat muses, "Why do you find only one shoe in the trash? One shoe on a sidewalk? One shoe in the street?" He wonders about why people don't throw things away in pairs. So Garfield sees one shoe in a trash can and knocks on the door of the adjacent house. Guess who answers? A pirate with a peg leg.

Most Logical Theory. Provided by Russ Tremayne of Auburn, Washington, and Maria N. Benninghoven of Kensington, Maryland. Both of these readers assume that most shoes found on the side of the road are thrown out of moving cars. They also assume that most people toss both shoes out one at a time. Russ assumes it would be most natural to throw out the shoes with one dominant hand:

> Most people's hands aren't large enough to comfortably grasp a pair of shoes, even if the laces are tied. Therefore, one shoe gets thrown at a time as the vehicle continues to travel. Perhaps one shoe, thrown weakly, lands on the edge of the highway, while the other, thrown with more force, lands off the road to lie invisibly among tall grass or brush.

Empirical Theories

Best Exploitation for Personal Profit of the One-Shoe Phenomenon. Provided by R.E. Holtslander of Lake Wales, Florida.

> About 20 years ago when I lived in Missouri and was coming home from California on a windy day, I noticed a large cardboard box on the highway in New Mexico. Papers were flying from it. Shortly after that, I saw an almost new broom, so I pulled off the road and picked it up.
>
> Soon other things appeared by the road. I saw a shoe for the right foot. As I had a sore toe at the time and thought the shoe was big enough to give my foot comfort, I picked it up, too.
>
> I saw a man in a pickup truck at the side of the road. He too had stopped to retrieve something. From then on it was like a treasure hunt I picked up several things and then he would pass us and then we would pass him. Soon we passed into Texas, and there I found the mate to the shoe I had picked up in New Mexico!
>
> I kept the shoes for several years and showed my guests a pair of shoes, one of which I got in New Mexico and the other in Texas . . .

WHEN DO FISH SLEEP?

Best Explanation for the Unsalutary Effect of Poor Nutrition and Sleeping Habits Upon the Retention of Shoes. Provided by Dave Sodovy of Hamilton, New York: Dave recounts the story that a few summers ago he had a job with two other kids who were the sons of the boss. Father and sons lived an hour's drive away from work, necessitating leaving their house at 7:15 because the boss wanted to get coffee and doughnuts to fortify him for the road. The sons retaliated for having to get up at this barbaric hour by sleeping through the trip.

From this evolved a routine in which the time between waking up and later falling asleep in the car was spent in "semi-sleep."

One morning, the two boys and their dad arrived as usual, but the younger son was wearing only one shoe! A few questions revealed the reason. In his state of semi-sleep, with one shoe on, one shoe in one hand, and a bag lunch in the other hand, he set the shoe on the roof of the car to open the car door.

Since his main concern was to go to sleep in dad's car, he didn't retrieve his shoe—he just closed the door and got comfortable. Dad and his other son had been in the car waiting; the three took off as soon as my one-shoed friend closed the door. The shoe was still on the roof of the car, and apparently survived the 25- and 35-mph speed limits of the neighborhood in which they lived. Once on the highway, the shoe was doomed. Indeed, once the three arrived at work, they called Mom, who sought out the missing shoe, locating it on the side of the highway.

I doubt that this is the definitive answer that you're looking for, but it does explain how at least one shoe got on the road by itself.

The Margaret Mead Field Research Award. Goes to Laurie McDonald of Houston, Texas. Laurie once lived in Providence, Rhode Island, and found scores of single shoes alongside the highway between Warwick and Pawtucket while driving to and from work. Laurie collected seventy shoes in a period of six months.

Among her discoveries were mostly tennis shoes, most left-footed; "very early on Sunday mornings, I would inevitably find a few brand-new patent leather platform shoes sitting upright on the side of the road, waiting to be plucked."

DAVID FELDMAN

In 1979, Laurie was inspired to write a series of short stories, consisting of hypothetical explanations of how single shoes landed off the highway. In one, the protagonist was a hippie, sticking out his hand to hail a car. Instead, the outstretched hand became a shooting target for unneeded boots of army servicemen.

Although Laurie offers no theoretical breakthroughs, we nevertheless owe her a great deal for proving conclusively that single shoes are deposited on the highway at an alarming rate, at least in Rhode Island.

Confessions

The "10–4, Good Buddy" Award. Goes to Robin Barlett of Erie, Pennsylvania. Robin writes:

> My husband is a truck driver and I went with him on a run. He got tired and pulled off to the side of the road to sleep, and I went back into the bunk and took my shoes off.
>
> We got up late at night and my husband had to go to the bathroom. Nobody was on the highway so he just hopped out to go and he must have kicked my shoe out, for it was not there when I tried to find it.

The Foot Out the Window Routine Award. Goes to Brian Razen Cain of Chipley, Florida, the last honest man in the world. Many readers theorized that single shoes are remnants of passengers who nap with one (or both) shoes dangling out car windows. But Brian was the only one to admit it. Brian fell asleep on the Florida Turnpike and woke up to find himself semishoeless. His response? The normal one: "I simply threw the other one out the window too."

The Dog Ate My Homework Award. Goes to Jay Lewis of Montgomery, Alabama.

> The shoes were dropped there by animals. Various beasties are attracted by the taste and smell of salt-impregnated leather. Since animals have trouble getting more than one shoe in their mouths,

they only carry one of the pair away. Where they finally discard it is where you see it—invariably without its mate.

C. Lynn Graham of Pelham, Alabama, adds that dogs tend to think that they will carry a shoe in their mouths forever. But as soon as they are distracted by a car coming down the road, the shoe pales compared to the chance to chase a passing car.

Surprisingly only one soul, Jennifer Ballmann of Jemez Springs, New Mexico, was willing to admit that she was the personal victim of doggy single-shoe syndrome. Two questions arise: Can a Saint Bernard carry two shoes at a time? Can a Pekingese carry one shoe at a time?

I Did it for the Sake of Science Award. Goes to an anonymous caller on a Detroit, Michigan, radio show hosted by David Newman. This caller, a paramedic, confessed that he was personally responsible for dropping several single shoes in the past week.

When administering CPR paramedics are trained to take off the victim's shoes, in order to promote better circulation. Many times in transporting a heart attack victim from a residence the shoes are taken off hastily and get lost before the patient enters the ambulance.

Will insurance companies pay for the missing shoes of patients not responsible for their loss?

The Motorcycles are Dangerous Even WITH a Helmet Award. Goes to Tom Vencuss of Newburgh, New York. Several readers speculated that single shoes were discarded wedding shoes. "Well," claims Tom, "not quite . . . "

> I was scheduled to be the best man at my cousin's wedding in Schenectady, New York, a two-hour ride from my home in Poughkeepsie. Prior to the wedding, I needed to make a quick run up to get fitted for my tuxedo. It was a beautiful afternoon so I decided to ride my motorcycle. I dressed in my normal riding gear but took a pair of dress shoes to wear at the fitting. I decided not to take a bag along since I would not be spending the night. So I strapped the shoes to the back of the bike.

DAVID FELDMAN

Several hours later, as I pulled into the parking lot for the tuxedo rental, I reached back to find only one shoe. The other, no doubt, was sitting lonely on a stretch of the New York State Thruway. Though it was an expensive afternoon, it did solve one of life's little mysteries.

Do we have the definitive, smoking-gun solution to this Frustable? We're afraid not. But after all, philosophers have been arguing over less important topics for thousands of years. Together we have raised the level of discourse on this topic to stratospheric heights. Maybe our grandchildren will find the ultimate answer.

Submitted by Julie Mercer of Baltimore, Maryland. Thanks also to Bess M. Bloom of Issaquah, Washington; and Sue S. Child of Red Bluff, Louisiana.

A free book goes to Laurie McDonald of Houston, Texas, to inspire her to conduct further hard research on this important topic. Thanks also to Elaine Viets of the St. Louis Post-Dispatch, *for her generosity.*

FRUSTABLE 2: Why Are Buttons on Men's Shirts and Jackets Arranged Differently From Those on Women's Shirts?

Of all the Frustables, none yielded less new ground than this one. Although more readers tried to answer this Frustable than any other but number three, few added much beyond the speculations we offered in *Why Do Clocks Run Clockwise?*

This much we know for sure: Buttons were popularized in the thirteenth century, probably in France. Before that, robes tended to be loose and unfitted and were fastened by strings, hooks, or pins.

Many readers said that men in the thirteenth century wore swords on the left hip under their coats. When they cross-drew their sword, they risked catching their sword if their garments were arranged right over left. By changing the configuration so that left closed over right, they could unfasten jacket buttons with their left hand and draw their sword with their right hand more quickly and safely.

An equal number of readers insisted that the different button configurations come from the custom of rich women having handmaidens who dressed them. Because clothes, as everything else, were designed for right-handers, the women's arrangement made it easier for maids to button their mistresses' blouses and dresses. Male aristocrats presumably dressed themselves.

The third popular answer is that women's button arrangement is most convenient for breast-feeding, so that the mother can unbutton her blouse with her right hand and rest the baby on her left arm.

None of the three popular explanations is convincing to us. All of the clothing historians we spoke to did not accept these pat answers either. Only the second theory explains why men's and women's buttons need to be different, and there is one inherent problem with this theory—many rich men were indeed dressed by servants. We don't put much stock in the breast-feeding theory either. One book we found mentioned that the women's arrangement made it easier for women who were breast-feeding while holding their babies in their right arms.

Much of the written material we have read on this subject mentions all three of these nonrelated theories, an indication to us that these explanations are based more on supposition after the fact than solid evidence. Robert Kaufman, reference librarian in the Costume Division at the Metropolitan Museum of Art in New York, told *Imponderables* that this Frustable has been among his most often asked questions. He and others have done considerable research on the subject and found no credible evidence to sustain any particular argument.

DAVID FELDMAN

A few readers offered some imaginative answers to this Frustable. A surprising number mentioned an intriguing variation of the handmaiden theory: By switching the button arrangement for the two sexes, it's easier for the two sexes to unbutton each other's clothing during a sexual encounter. Hmmmmmm.

Along the same garden path comes our favorite contribution to this discussion, from Erik Johnson of Houston, Texas: "The button arrangement is so that when a couple is driving in a car, with the man driving, they can peek inside each other's shirts."

Submitted by Julia Zumba, of Ocala, Florida. Thanks also to Kathi Sawyer-Young of Encino, California; Mathew Gradet of Ocean City, Maryland; Jodi Harrison of Helena, Montana; Sheryl K. Prien of Sacramento, California; Harry Geller of Rockaway Beach, New York; Terry L. Stibal of Belleville, Illinois; Mary Jo Hildyard of West Bend, Wisconsin; Tom and Marcia Bova of Rochester, New York; Robert Hittel of Fort Lauderdale, Florida; and many others.

FRUSTABLE 3: Why Do the English Drive on the Left and Just About Everybody Else on the Right?

Quite a few readers, justifiably, took us to task for the phrasing of this Frustable. By saying "just about everybody else" drives on the right, we didn't mean to slight the rest of the United Kingdom, Ireland, India, Indonesia, Australia, South Africa, Kenya, Thailand, Japan, and many other nations, all of which still drive on the left side of the road. But because most of these other countries adopted their traditions while a part of the British Empire, we wanted to give the "credit" where it was due.

WHEN DO FISH SLEEP?   209

So how did this left-right division start? All historical evidence indicates that in ancient times, when roads were usually narrow and unpaved, a traveler would move to the left when encountering another person on foot or horse coming toward them. This allowed both parties to draw their sword with their right hand, if necessary. If the approaching person were friendly, one could give the other a high five instead. Military policy, as far back as the ancient Greeks, dictated staying to the left if traveling without a shield, so that a combatant could use his left hand to hold the reins and need not brandish the sword or lance crosswise, risking the neck of the horse.

Richard H. Hopper, a retired geologist for Caltex, has written a wonderful article, "Why Driving Rules Differ," the contents of which he was kind enough to share with *Imponderables* readers. Hopper believes that the custom of mounting horses on the left-hand side also contributed to traffic bearing left. In many countries, pedestals were placed alongside the curbs of the road to help riders mount and dismount from their horses. These approximately three-feet-high pedestals were found only on the left side of the road. Long before the pedestals were erected, horsemen mounted and dismounted on the left, probably because their scabbards, slung on the left, interfered with mounting the horse; the unencumbered right leg could be more easily lifted over the horse.

Until 1300 A.D., no nation had mandated traffic flow. But Pope Boniface VIII, who declared "all roads lead to Rome," insisted that all pilgrims to Rome must stick on the left side of the road. According to Hopper, "This edict had something of the force of law in much of western Europe for over 500 years."

The movers and shakers of the French Revolution weren't excited about having a pope dictate their traffic regulations. Robespierre and other Jacobins encouraged France to switch to right-hand driving. Napoleon institutionalized the switch, not only in France but in all countries conquered by France.

Why did the United States, with an English heritage, adopt the French style? The answer, according to Hopper and many others, is that the design of late-eighteenth-century freight wag-

DAVID FELDMAN

ons encouraged right-hand driving. Most American freight wagons were drawn by six or eight horses hitched in pairs; the most famous of these were the Conestoga wagons that hauled wheat from the Conestoga Valley of Pennsylvania to nearby cities. These wagons had no driver's seat. The driver sat on the left-rear horse, holding a whip in his right hand. When passing another vehicle on a narrow ride, the driver naturally went to the right, to make sure that he could see that the left axle hub and wheel of his wagon were not going to touch those of the approaching vehicle.

In 1792, Pennsylvania passed the first law in the United States requiring driving on the right-hand side, although this ordinance referred only to the turnpike between Lancaster and Philadelphia. Within twenty years, many more states passed similar measures. Logically, early American carmakers put steering wheels on the left, so that drivers on two-lane roads could evade wavering oncoming traffic. Although Canada originally began driving on the left-hand side, the manufacture of automobiles by their neighbors to the south inevitably led to their switch to the right. Although Ontario adopted right-hand driving in 1812, many other provinces didn't relent until the 1920s.

Great Britain, of course, stayed with the ancient tradition of left-side driving and not just out of spite. Their freight wagons were smaller than Conestoga wagons and contained a driver's seat. Hopper explains why the driver sat on the right-hand side of the wagon:

> The driver sat on the right side of the seat so that he could wield his long whip in his right hand without interference from the load behind him. In passing oncoming wagons, the drivers tended to keep to the left of the road, again to be able to pass approaching vehicles as closely as necessary without hitting.
>
> In passenger carriages, the driver also sat on the right, and the footman, if there was one, sat to the driver's left so that he could quickly jump down and help the passengers disembark at the curb.

Needless to say, a coachman wouldn't have felt quite as secure sitting to the right of the driver. Every time a right-handed driver

WHEN DO FISH SLEEP?

got ready to crack the whip, the coachman would have had to duck and cover.

The British built their cars with the steering wheel on the right because their wagons and carriages at the time still stuck to the left side of the road. Their foot controls, however, have always been the same as American cars.

Well more than a hundred readers sent responses to this Frustable, most of them containing fragments of this explanation. Hopper's article is the best summary of the conventional wisdom on this subject that we have encountered. But there are dissenters. Patricia A. Guy, a reference librarian at the Bay Area Library and Information System in Oakland, California, was kind enough to send us several articles on this subject, including a fascinating one called "The Rule of the Road" from a 1908 periodical called *Popular Science Monthly*. Its author, George M. Gould, M.D., argues that Americans had adopted right-hand side travel before the development of Conestoga wagons, as had the French, whose wagons were driven by postilion riders (mounted on the left-rear horse). Dr. Gould couldn't come up with a convincing theory for the switch and argued that this Imponderable was likely to be a Frustable for all time.

We include this dissent to indicate that we tend to lunge at any answer that neatly solves a difficult question. We can give you a logical reason why Americans and the French switched the traditional custom of driving on the left; but we wouldn't risk our already precarious reputations on it.

Submitted by Claudia Wiehl of North Charleroi, Pennsylvania. Thanks also to John Haynes of Independence, Kentucky; Kathi Sawyer-Young of Encino, California; Larry S. Londre of Studio City, California; David Andrews of Dallas, Texas; Hugo Kahn of New York, New York; Barbara Dilworth of Bloomsburg, Pennsylvania; Pat Mooney of Inglewood, California; Stephen Murphy of Smithfield, North Carolina; Frederick A. Fink of Coronado, California; and many others.

A free book goes to Richard H. Hopper of Fairfield, Connecticut.

DAVID FELDMAN

Speech bubble text (part of illustration): YAWN, WARNING, YAWNING EPIDEMIC, HELP! HELP! THAT MAN IS CONTAGIOUS!, War and PEACE

FRUSTABLE 4: *Why Is Yawning Contagious?*

After the publication of *Imponderables,* this question quickly became our most frequently asked Imponderable. And after years of research, it became one of our most nagging Frustables. We couldn't find anyone who studied yawning, so we asked our readers for help.

As usual, our readers were bursting with answers, unfortunately, conflicting answers. They fell into three classes.

The Physiological Theory. Proponents of this theory stated that science has proven that we yawn to get more oxygen into our system or to rid ourselves of excess carbon dioxide. Yawning is contagious because everybody in any given room is likely to be short of fresh air at the same time.

The Boredom Theory. If everyone hears a boring speech, why shouldn't everyone yawn at approximately the same time, wonders this group.

The Evolutionary Theory. Many readers analogized contagious yawning in humans to animals displaying their teeth as a
sign of intimidation and territoriality. Larry Rose of Kalamazoo,
Michigan, argued that yawning might have originally been a
challenge to others, but has lost its fangs as an aggressive maneu-
ver as we have gotten more "civilized."

Several readers pointed us in the direction of Dr. Robert
Provine, of the University of Maryland at Baltimore County, who
somehow had eluded us. You can imagine our excitement when
we learned that Dr. Provine, a psychologist specializing in psy-
chobiology, is not only the world's foremost authority on yawning, but has a special interest in why yawning is contagious! In
one fell swoop, we had found someone who not only might be
able to answer a Frustable but a fellow researcher whose work
was almost as weird as ours.

Dr. Provine turned out to be an exceedingly interesting and
generous source, and all the material below is a distillation of
his work. As usual, experts are much less likely to profess cer-
tainty about answers to Imponderables than are laymen. In fact,
Provine confesses that we still don't know much about yawning;
what we do know is in large part due to his research.

Provine defines yawning as the gaping of the mouth accom-
panied by a long inspiration followed by a shorter expiration.
This definition seems to support the thinking of some who believe the purpose of a yawn is to draw more oxygen into the
system, but Provine disagrees. He conducted an experiment in
which he taped the mouths of his subjects shut. Although they
could yawn without opening their mouths, they felt unsatisfied,
as if they weren't really yawning, even though their noses were
clear and were capable of drawing in as much oxygen as if their
mouths were open. From this experiment, Provine concludes
that the function of yawning is not related to respiration.

In other experiments, Provine has proven that yawning has
nothing to do with oxygen or carbon dioxide intake. When he
pumped pure oxygen into subjects, for example, their frequency
of yawning did not change.

DAVID FELDMAN

Provine's research also supports the relationship between boredom and yawning. Considerably more subjects yawned while watching a thirty-minute test pattern than while watching thirty minutes of rock videos (although he didn't poll the subjects to find out which viewing experience was more bearable— we wouldn't yawn while watching and listening to thirty minutes of fingernails dragged across a blackboard, either). Did the subjects yawn for psychological reasons (they were bored) or for physiological reasons (boredom made them sleepy)?

When Provine asked his students to fill out diaries recording their every yawn, certain patterns were clear. Yawning was most frequent the hour before sleep and especially the hour after waking. And there was an unmistakable link between yawning and stretching. People usually yawn when stretching, although most people don't stretch every time they yawn.

Yawning is found throughout the animal kingdom. Birds yawn. Primates yawn. And, when they're not sleeping, fish yawn. Even human fetuses have been observed yawning as early as eleven weeks after conception. The child psychologist Piaget noted that children seemed susceptible to yawning contagion by the age of two. It was clear to Provine that yawning was an example of "stereotyped action pattern," in which an activity once started runs out in a predictable pattern. But what's the purpose of this activity?

Although Provine is far from committing himself to an answer of why we yawn, he speculates that yawning and stretching may have been part of the same reflex at one point (one could think of yawning as a stretch of the face). Bolstering this theory is the fact that the same drugs that induce yawning also induce stretching.

The ubiquity of yawning epidemics was obvious to all the people who sent in this Imponderable. Provine told *Imponderables*, "Virtually anything having to do with a yawn can trigger a yawn," and he has compiled data to back up the contention:

- 55% of subjects viewing a five-minute series of thirty yawns yawned within five minutes of the first videotaped yawn, com-

pared to the 21% yawn rate of those who watched a five-minute tape of a man smiling thirty times.
- Blind people yawn more frequently when listening to an audiotape of yawns.
- People who read about yawning start yawning. People who even think about yawning start yawning. Heck, the writer of this sentence is yawning as this sentence is being written.

If we are so sensitive to these cues, Provine concludes that there must be some reason for our built-in neurological yawn detectors. He concludes that yawning is not only a stereotyped action pattern in itself, but also a "releasing stimulus" that triggers *another* consistently patterned activity (i.e., another yawn) in other individuals. Yawns have the power to synchronize some of the physiological functions of a group, to alter the blood pressure and heart rate (which can rise 30% during a yawn).

Earlier in our evolution, the yawn might have been the paralinguistic signal for members of a clan to prepare for sleep. Provine cites a passage in I. Eibl-Eibesfeldt's *Ethology*, in which a European visitor to the Bakairi of Central Brazil quickly noted how yawns were accepted behavior:

> If they seemed to have had enough of all the talk, they began to yawn unabashedly and without placing their hands before their mouths. That the pleasant reflex was contagious could not be denied. One after the other got up and left until I remained . . .

Yet, Provine is not willing to rule out our evolutionary theory either. Perhaps at one time, the baring of teeth sometimes apparent in yawning could have been an aggressive act. Or more likely, combined with stretching, it could have prepared a group for the rigors of work or battle. When bored or sleepy, a good yawn might have revivified ancient cavemen or warriors.

So even if Dr. Provine can't yet give us a definitive answer to why yawning is contagious, it's nice to know that someone out there is in the trenches working full-time to stamp out Frustability. If Dr. Provine finds out any more about why yawning is contagious, we promise to let you know in the next volume of Imponderables.

DAVID FELDMAN

Submitted by Mrs. Elaine Murray of Los Gatos, California. Thanks also to Esther Perry of Clarks Summit, Pennsylvania; Julie Zumba of Ocala, Florida; Jo Ellen Flynn of Canyon Country, California; Hugo Kahn of New York, New York; Steve Fjeldsted of Huntington Beach, California; Frank B. De Sande of Anaheim, California; Mark Hallen of Irvington, New York; Raymond and Patricia Gardner of Morton Grove, Illinois; Jim White of Cincinnati, Ohio; Renee Nank of Beachwood, Ohio; and many others.

A free book goes to Christine Dukes of Scottsdale, Arizona, for being the first to direct us to Dr. Provine.

FRUSTABLE 5: *Why Do We Give Apples to Teachers?*

This Frustable has remained remarkably resistant to reasoned replies. Although few readers could supply hard evidence to back their claims, a lot of people sure seemed to think they knew the answer to this one.

Two theories predominated. The most popular answer was the Biblical explanation. In Genesis, the forbidden fruit comes from the tree of knowledge. Although the forbidden fruit is never specified, the apple has over time been given that distinction. As Lou Ann M. Gotch of Canton, Ohio, puts it:

> the apple has come to signify knowledge. Perhaps by giving an apple to the teacher our children are admitting that they're little devils. Or perhaps they are intimating that the teachers could use a little more knowledge.

The second camp traces the custom to early rural America, when teachers were given free room and board but little pay. Students and their families traditionally brought something to

DAVID FELDMAN

contribute to the school and/or the teacher, be it wood for a fire or fruit for consumption.

But why an apple? As Georgette Mattel of Lindenhurst, New York, points out, apples were cheap and plentiful. Donald E. Saewert adds that the apple is the only fruit that can be stored for long periods of time without canning. In the winter, it might have been the only fresh fruit that was available in many areas. And Ann Calhoun of Los Osos, California, closes this argument with an impressive volley: "Sure would beat dragging a twelve-foot stalk of corn to school."

Both of these arguments are plausible but certainly not proven. Two readers sent us evidence of other possible solutions to this Frustable.

Ann Calhoun mentions that perhaps the apple-teacher connection was made up by an illustrator in one of the nineteenth-century illustrated magazines ("Every illustration I've seen . . . includes a very pretty young teacher, a blushing hayseed boy of nine, and a classroom of giggling sniggerers.")

Calhoun speculates that the boy gives the teacher an apple not as a symbol of knowledge but as a symbol of beauty. For according to ancient Greek legend, the highly prized golden apples that grew in the Garden of the Hesperus were awarded for beauty at the Judgment of Paris. Calhoun continues:

> In every Rockwellian illustration of this theme . . . the teacher is young and beautiful. Since older generations were heavily schooled in the classics (as ours is not) the teacher and kids would get the reference immediately. And yes, there are satiric variations with the teacher depicted as old, fat, gray, ugly, and scowling. The reason for her sour expression is that *she* also knows the original reference, knows the satiric content of the gesture and is about to send that little hypocritical, mendacious, miscreant presenter out behind the barn for a thrashing he so richly deserves. . . . I truly can't imagine a spindly young cleric presenting his medieval monkish tutor with an apple for beauty. Such impertinence would only earn him a thrashing outside the castle walls. So when and where did all this apple presenting and polishing start?

WHEN DO FISH SLEEP?   219

Good question. We've heard from only one person who dares to speculate on this. We received a fascinating letter from Henry C. Hafliger, member of the Board of Trustees of the San Jacinto Unified School District. He traces the custom back to Switzerland and cites the book *Bauerspiegel*, written by Jeremiah Gotthelf in the early nineteenth century. Gotthelf was a disciple of Johann Pestalozzi, the Swiss educator and reformer who had a tremendous influence on American education in the nineteenth century.

In effect, *Bauerspiegel* chronicles a Swiss equivalent to our rural explanation for the custom. Hafliger summarizes:

> when education was first offered to all classes of children in Switzerland, salaries of teachers were subsistence at best. Parents would supplement teachers' salaries with food, and one of the easiest foods to bring to school was the apple. Farmers would keep apples in their cellars all year long because in those days apples were not considered a dessert but a staple. Gotthelf writes that children soon learned that the child who brought the apple received the least amount of swats with the pointer or switch that the teacher always carried. The children from the poor families, some of whom did not have enough food themselves, were at a distinct disadvantage.

Hafliger's theory, then, was that the fruit was originally given on the premise that "an apple a day keeps the switch away."

Submitted by Malinda Fillingion of Savannah, Georgia. Free books go to Ann Calhoun of Los Osos, California; and Henry C. Hafliger of San Jacinto, California.

DAVID FELDMAN

FRUSTABLE 6: *Why Does Looking up at the Sun Cause Many People to Sneeze?*

Of all the Frustables, we came closest to getting a definitive solution to number six. Most of the people who responded were sun-sneezers themselves, and some said that just looking up at a bright light or even at the reflection from a car bumper was enough to set off the achoo mechanism.

The more than one hundred letters we received on this topic almost all carried some variation of the same theme. After a little digging, we found out that the most popular explanation was far from the only possible one.

We do know this much: Somewhere between 25 to 33% of the population is afflicted with "photic sneeze reflex." It is almost certainly a hereditary condition. Reader Margy D. Miller of DeKalb, Illinois, reports that she and all four of her children all sneeze when they first step out of doors into the bright sun.

The most accepted explanation for the photic sneeze reflex is that light signals that should irritate the optic nerves somehow trigger receptors that play a part in the sneezing process. The neural tracts for the olfactory and optic sensory organs lie adjacent to each other and have close (but not identical) insertion points in the brain.

When some people with this particular genetic predisposition encounter a bright light for the first time, the pupils do not contract as rapidly as they should, and the eyes are irritated. Somehow—neurologists we spoke to could not specify *how*—the olfactory and neural tracts cross-circuit.

The result: The nerves fool the brain into thinking that there is a foreign irritant in the nasal mucosa. The brain does what comes naturally, it tries to rid the sinuses of the phantom dust or pollen. The brain sends out a sneeze reflex.

Case closed?

Not quite. Reader John W. Lawrence, M.D., who specializes in internal medicine and rheumatology, gave us a variation of the above. He concurs that the original cause of the sneeze is eye irritation, but believes that the tears caused by the irritation actually trigger the sneeze:

> Many people develop eye sensitivity to light. This sensitivity results in a lacrimal outburst (making of excess tears) in response to the irritation. The excess tears then run off down the lacrimal duct, which is present for this purpose. The lacrimal duct empties into the back of the nasopharynx. A drippage of liquid into the back of the nose triggers the sneeze.
>
> Only when tearing exceeds the lacrimal duct's capacity to carry runoff do tears overflow and "run down the cheeks."

William J. Dromgoole, a reader from Somerdale, New Jersey, sent us a newspaper clip indicating that scientists at Scripps Clinic and Research Foundation in La Jolla, California, have found evidence that certain allergy treatments for runny noses can cause photic sneeze reflex. Simply switching medications has rid some people of this mildly vexing problem.

Several readers have written to ask why they always seem to sneeze a particular number of times (sometimes twice, but usually three times). ENT specialists we talked to pooh-poohed it. Anyone have a theory to explain this phenomenon?

Submitted by Rick Stamm of Redmond, Washington. Thanks also to William Debuvitz of Bernardsville, New Jersey; and Lisa Madsden of Minneapolis, Minnesota.

A free book goes to James Miron, R.N., of Republic, Michigan.

DAVID FELDMAN

FRUSTABLE 7: *Why Does the First Puff of a Cigarette Smell Better than Subsequent Ones?*

As we indicated in *Why Do Clocks Run Clockwise?*, the research departments of the major cigarette companies couldn't (or wouldn't) answer this Imponderable. Similarly, the Tobacco Institute and the Council For Tobacco Research—U.S.A., Inc., claimed that although much research has been conducted on the sensory awareness of cigarette smoke, this phenomenon was neither universal nor verifiable.

Luckily, *Imponderables* readers aren't as reticent as the professionals in the field. We don't have a definitive answer to this Frustable, but readers supplied us with three plausible explanations.

The Physiological Theory. Richard H. Hawkins, D.D.S., president of Medical Innovators of North America, argues that the first puff of a cigarette smells best because the olfactory nerve endings within the nasal cavity are able to interpret the smell sensation only after a rest period. "With repeated puffs, the olfaction perception goes to zero." This argument might explain why a smoker derives increasingly less satisfaction from subsequent puffs, but doesn't explain why nonsmokers, who might find cigarette smoke irritating and obnoxious, find the aroma of the first puff pleasant.

Reader Albert Wellman of Santa Rosa, California, speculates that the difference between first puffs and subsequent ones is the physical process of burning the tobacco leaves. "I suspect that once the major portion of the chemical responsible for the 'good smell' of cigarette smoke has been vaporized by the first puff of smoke, there is not enough left in the tobacco to provide a comparable olfactory experience from the remainder of the cigarette."

Wellman also hypothesizes that perhaps the olfactory nerves are temporarily blocked by some other active biochemical agent in the smoke. This theory is bolstered somewhat by research that indicates that although olfactory organs are easily fatigued, the fatigue is limited to one particular flavor. Usually, the nose will respond to a new or different smell, and there are 685 different chemical compounds found in leaf tobacco smoke.

Most of the (little) hard research we have been able to find on the sensory response to cigarette smoke doesn't corroborate these physiological explanations. Dr. William S. Cain, of the departments of Epidemiology and Public Health and Psychology at Yale University, argues that smokers don't really "taste" cigarettes in the conventional sense. The four tastes—sweet, sour, salty, and bitter—don't play much of a role in cigarette enjoyment; of the four, only the bitter is perceived by the smoker.

But Cain argues that the sense of smell is not very important either, and in the last words of the following, hints at the problem posed in this Frustable:

> it matters little for smoking enjoyment whether the smoke is exhaled through the nose or through the mouth. Smell may play a role at the moment the smoker lights up, but adaptation rapidly blunts olfactory impact.

DAVID FELDMAN

The Tobacco as Filter Theory. Reader Jack Perkins of San Francisco, California, writes:

> As a long-time heavy smoker, I can tell you that the first puff not only smells better, it's milder. The reason for this is that the tobacco acts as a filter catching tars, nicotine, and chemicals. The further down you smoke, the greater the build-up of these substances, resulting in harsher smoke.

Rev. David C. Scott, of Bethany Presbyterian Church in Rochester, New York, agrees, adding, "The first puff has the advantage of being filtered both by the longest filter and cleanest filter. . . . Each subsequent puff both shortens the filter and dirties even more what remains. Andrew F. Garruto of Kinnelon, New Jersey, compares smoking the stub of a cigarette to making a pot of coffee through used grains.

All of these arguments explain why the purity of taste and smell deteriorate as a cigarette has been smoked. But none explains to the nonsmoker why the first puff smells fine but then deteriorates immediately.

The Burning Wood, Sulfur, and Butane Theory. Even if we can't confirm any of these theories for sure, we like this modest explanation the best. Perhaps the reason why the first puff smells better is that the aroma of the lighting agent, not the tobacco, is what we are responding to. We received this letter from Allison Rosenthal, of Rancho Palos Verdes, California:

> People have always loved the smell of burning wood. By burning tree branches, pine needles, and pine cones, many not only warm their houses but improve the smell therein. If you have ever gone for a walk in Mammoth [California] in the winter, you would surely be familiar with this wonderful scent. A burning match smells much the same, maybe even a little better. Not only do you have a form of wood on a match but also sulfur, which is very pleasing when mixed with wood smoke. If you use a large 'Diamond' wood match and pull on the cigarette hard enough when lighting it, you can actually taste the sulfur and wood mixture. Even though it doesn't taste so good, it *does* smell nice.

WHEN DO FISH SLEEP?

Although Allison Rosenthal hasn't noticed that the first puff of a lighter-lit cigarette smells better, several other readers, including Judith R. Brannon of Santa Clara, California, feel that the smell of butane is the hero. As connoisseurs of gas station fumes, we would agree.

The match/lighter argument is the only theory that explains how an odor perceived as pleasant by smoker and nonsmoker alike can suddenly turn unpleasant, at least for the nonsmoker. If the hard research in sensory reactions to cigarette smoke can be believed, what a smoker perceives as a response to the taste of the flavor of a cigarette is actually a camouflage, masking a chemical response to the relief from nicotine deprivation.

A free book goes to Allison Rosenthal of Rancho Palos Verdes, California.

FRUSTABLE 8: *Why Do Women in the United States Shave Their Armpits?*

The recorded history of armpit shaving is a spotty one indeed. The earliest reference we have found was that the ancient Babylonians, more than one thousand years before the birth of Christ, developed depilatories to remove unwanted body hair.

Julius Caesar reported that the early Britons "had long flowing hair and shaved every part of their bodies except the head and upper lip," but this quotation may refer only to men. We do know that barbers removed superfluous hair from the eyebrows, nostrils, arms, and legs from male customers around this time.

The first direct reference to the specific topic at hand is contained in Ovid's *Art of Love*, written just before the birth of

DAVID FELDMAN

Christ: "Should I warn you to keep the rank goat out of your armpits? Warn you to keep your legs free of coarse bristling hair?"

In Chaucer's day (the fourteenth century), the mere sight of any hair was considered erotic. Women were required to wear head coverings; caps were worn indoors and out by women of all ages.

These ancient antecedents predict our current duality about body hair on women. On the one hand, underarm hair is considered unsightly and unhygienic, and yet on the other, sexy and natural.

None of the many razor companies or cosmetic historians we contacted could pinpoint when women first started shaving their armpits. The earliest reports concerned prostitutes during the gold rush days in California. Terri Tongco, among other readers, posited the theory that prostitutes shaved their underarms to prove they had no body lice, which were rampant in the old West.

Many older readers were able to pinpoint when their mothers and grandmothers started shaving their armpits. Not-so-old historian C.F. "Charley" Eckhardt of Seguin, Texas, is the only person we have found who has actually studied this Frustable:

> My paternal grandmother, born in 1873, and my maternal grandmother, born in 1882, did not shave their armpits. My wife's maternal grandmother (1898), my mother (1914), and my mother-in-law (1921) all did or do.
>
> Eadweard Muybridge's photographic studies of the nude human figure in motion and Hillaire Belloc's photographs of New Orleans prostitutes, all taken before or immediately after the turn of the century, show hairy armpits, as do nude photos of prostitutes known to have been taken in El Paso, Texas, prior to 1915. In addition, still photographs taken from pornographic motion pictures known to have been made prior to 1915 show the women with unshaven armpits, as do surviving pornographic photographs of the "French postcard" variety which are documented as having been made in the United States prior to 1915.
>
> Theatrical motion pictures released about and after 1915, including *Cleopatra* (starring Theda Bara), the biblical sequences

from D.W. Griffith's *Intolerance*, and several others, show shaven armpits. Something, then, happened about 1915 that would cause not merely stars but impressionable teenagers (as my wife's grandmother was) but not necessarily older family women (like my grandmothers) to start shaving their armpits.

So what caused these women to start shaving their armpits around 1915? Many readers, including Charley Eckhardt, give the "credit" to Mack Sennett:

> The first moviemaker to show the feminine armpit extensively in non-pornographic films was Mack Sennett, in his Bathing Beauty shorts . . . Sennett's Bathing Beauties had shaven armpits, and they are the first direct evidence we have of the armpit-shaving phenomenon. Whether or not Mack actually said 'That looks like hell—have 'em shave' is a moot point, though the statement is completely in character with what we know about Sennett.

We do know that flappers of the Roaring Twenties adopted the sleeveless clothing that seemed so daring in the Sennett shorts.

We heard from several women who were more concerned about why the custom persists rather than how and when it started. Typical was this letter from Kathy Johnson of Madison, Wisconsin:

> I am one of the apparently few U.S. women who has never shaved her armpits or legs. It never made logical sense to me, so why do it? I've heard the argument that shaving those regions is more sanitary. Then why, I volley back, don't men shave their armpits? Why, in fact, doesn't everyone shave their heads if lack of hair is so sanitary? Stunned silence . . .

Several psychologists and feminists have speculated that men like the shaven look because it makes women look prepubescent —young, innocent, and unthreatening. Diana Grunig Catalan of Rangely, Colorado, who subscribes to the prepubescent theory, speculates that "American women, unlike their European counterparts, were not supposed to do anything with all those men they attracted with their revealing clothing. A childlike, helpless look can be a protection as well as an attractant."

DAVID FELDMAN

In defense of men, it has been our experience that many women have visceral reactions to the presence or lack of body hair in men. Why does the same woman who likes hair on the front of the torso (the chest) not like it on the back? Why is hair on the arms compulsory but excess hair on the hands considered repugnant? Are women, as well as men, afraid to face the animal part of our nature? Hairy questions, indeed.

Submitted by Venia Stanley of Albuquerque, New Mexico.

A free book goes to C.F. "Charley" Eckhardt of Seguin, Texas.

FRUSTABLE 9: *Why Don't You Ever See Really Tall Old People?*

This Imponderable-turned-Frustable was submitted by Tom Rugg, who stands six foot six inches and understandably has a vested interest in the answer.

Many readers sent us lists of reasons why people get shorter as they get older. Some of the reasons include gravity; the degeneration, rigidification, and compression of the vertebral column as we get older; osteoporosis; curvature of the spine. All of these phenomena explain why we might lose two or three inches over a lifespan, but don't explain why we haven't seen the six-foot-nine person who has "shrunk" to six foot six.

Several people wrote to say that improved nutrition has made our population taller than it used to be. Presumably, our generation will grow old and "really tall" with a lifetime of Twinkies and Diet Coke in our systems. Yes, we have grown taller but on average little more than a half inch in the last twenty-five years and fewer than two inches since the beginning of the century.

Dr. Alice M. Mascette of Tacoma, Washington, and Cindy West of Towson, Maryland, mentioned that a portion of our really tall population is afflicted with Marfan's syndrome, a genetic affliction of the connective tissue of the body. Sufferers of Marfan's syndrome have abnormally large hands and feet and a subpar heart. Many die of a ruptured aorta after an aneurism.

So far, these Marfan's syndrome sufferers—only a small fraction of all very tall people—are the only identifiable group of tall people who have been proven to have a short lifespan. But it is not at all clear that the tallness per se is what causes their deaths.

The way to unlock this Frustable is by asking: Do very tall people have shorter lifespans than other people? Surprisingly, there is no scientific data to support the proposition. We heard from more than fifteen doctors, health agencies, and insurance companies, and none of them study mortality based on height alone. Metropolitan Life conducts countless studies on the relationship between height-weight ratios and longevity, but doesn't feel that there is any reason to believe that tall people have a higher morbidity rate than the population as a whole.

In fact, the only quasi-scientific study we've seen (sent to us by reader David Jordan) that claims that very tall people live shorter lives was conducted by an aerospace engineer, Thomas T. Samaras. He tracked the lifespans of three thousand professional baseball players and found that the tallest players (six foot six or taller) lived, on average, to only the age of fifty-two. On the other hand, the shortest group (under five foot four) lived more than sixty-six years on average.

All of the medical and insurance experts we spoke to doubted the validity of Samaras' results, as well as his reasoning. Samaras speculated that the heart of a tall person must work overtime to pump blood a longer distance than a short person. Johns Hopkins University heart specialist Dr. Solbert Perlmutt disagreed with this argument and added, "Besides, you don't see mice living long. But you see elephants doing quite well."

DAVID FELDMAN

And evidently some old people only slightly shorter than elephants are doing pretty well, too, though the scarcity of the really tall old person is evidenced by the fact that of the hundreds of thousands of people who read *Why Do Clocks Run Clockwise?* only one person stepped up to the plate and offered himself as a specimen. Robert Purdin of Tinton Falls, New Jersey, is sixty-five (is that old?) and six foot five (is that really tall these days?).

Dr. Emil S. Dickstein of Youngstown, Ohio, says that he sees many tall old people, as does Gwen Sells, a member of Tall Clubs International. Reader George Flower, who once encountered a six foot seven man in his seventies, reminds us that Jimmy Stewart, if not "really" tall, is pretty tall.

But our favorite sighting was sent in by Andy Stone of Denver, Colorado, who told us about Randy "Sully" Sullivan, who weighs trucks at the Port of Entry in Cortez, Colorado:

> Sully is six foot ten inches. I've never asked his age but his hair is white, his posture stooped (that's right, stooped), and I estimate he's about seventy.

So, Tom Rugg, there's hope for you yet.

Submitted by Tom Rugg of Sherman Oaks, California.
Thanks also to Joanna Parker of Miami, Florida.

A free book goes to David Jordan of Greenville, Mississippi.

FRUSTABLE 10: *Why Do Only Older Men Seem to Have Hairy Ears?*

How appropriate that we saved the most frustrating Frustable for last. In *Why Do Clocks Run Clockwise?*, we mentioned that we consulted endocrinologists who professed ignorance on the subject. "If this condition is only found in males, why don't you speak to geneticists," they chimed in unison.

So we talked to geneticists. Guess what they said.

"Why don't you talk to endocrinologists? They'd know about this stuff."

So we put this in as our last Frustable and waited for the mail to roll in. It did.

Most of the mail had much the same answer as this one, from Bryan, Texas:

> I am Stacey Lero, a seventh grader at Anson Jones School. . . . We are studying genetics in science. On the Y chromosome there is a gene for hairy ears. It matures throughout your lifetime and as men reach the late forties or early fifties (sometimes earlier or later), it has matured enough to be expressed and the hair begins to grow. I hope I've answered your question.

What??? Heads of genetic departments at prestigious universities can't answer this Imponderable and Stacey Lero is studying it in a seventh grade science class? What's going on here?

Then several other readers, including Richard Landesman, associate professor of zoology at the University of Vermont, and R. Alan Mounier of Vineland, New Jersey, sent me clips from genetics textbooks that confirmed Stacey Lero's letter. One text said that hypertrichosis (excessive hair) of the ear is passed directly from father to son. Reader Derek E. King of Los Angeles, California, adds that color blindness and pattern baldness are also traits residing on the small Y chromosome.

Feeling humbled by the knowledge of our readers, we consulted some more geneticists. They replied that the Y-chromosome theory had been largely discounted—no hard research supports this belief. "Why don't you talk to an endocrinologist," said one soothingly.

Are we the only ones who feel a little queasy about medical textbooks printing untrue facts? Or are scientists and doctors not believing what is in medical textbooks?

Peter H. Lewis, a reporter at the *New York Times*—the

DAVID FELDMAN

paper of record, for darn's sake—called us excitedly to say that they had run an article in 1985 about hairy ears being signs of susceptibility to heart attacks. In 1984, two doctors in Mineola, Long Island, reported to the *New England Journal of Medicine* that there was a "significant statistical link" between men (but not women) who had hair in their ear canal and people they had treated for coronary artery disease. The doctors did not overplay the significance of this finding. In fact, the hubbub their findings released prompted Dr. Richard F. Wagner and Dr. Karen Dineen to issue a poetic disclaimer:

> If on the ear there is a crease
> Do not assume that life will cease.
> If hair is noted in the ear,
> Do not assume that death is near.
> So, if when walking down the street
> An ear with hair and crease you meet,
> Don't give the gent a dreadful fright—
> Don't hint infarction is in sight.

Needless to say, the medical authorities we consulted would neither affirm nor deny the viability of the androgen theory.

We give up. Some Frustables are too frustrating even for us, and we're masochists.

We figure that Stacey Lero will be going to high school soon. She's obviously very bright and will probably become a science major in high school. She will then enter college, where she will become a double endocrinology/genetics major. She'll choose between MIT and Cal Tech for her graduate work. In the year 2011, Stacey will win the Nobel Prize for answering this Frustable. The world will be a better place. And it will all be due to that seventh-grade science teacher in Bryan, Texas. Well, and maybe a little to the inspiration provided by that free copy of *When Do Fish Sleep?*

A free book goes to Stacey Lero of Bryan, Texas.

LETTERS

We have received more than two thousand letters since the publication of *Why Do Clocks Run Clockwise?*. Most of them posed Imponderables or tried to answer Frustables. But some corrected or added information to our answers or contained priceless comments about the topics in our first two volumes of *Imponderables*. Here are some of our favorites.

On the Relative Merits of Round vs. Flat Toothpicks

We commented that even the manufacturers of flat toothpicks couldn't provide any reason why they were superior to round toothpicks, except for their lower price. Who would have thought that this topic could rouse emotions? Some letters were thoughtful, others passionate.

Flat toothpicks have uses round ones don't have, such as smearing small amounts of various kinds of goo onto surfaces (epoxy cement is one) and in being able to enter crevices closed to round toothpicks. Flat picks, with their greater surface, are in my experience superior to round ones for testing doneness of cakes, custards and so on. . . .

MAX HERZOG
Augusta, Georgia

When I read your slam at flat toothpicks in *Imponderables*, I thought, "Gee, I hope I can find this guy's address so I can straighten him out." And lo and behold, there it was. You even invited comment. You must be a brave man. If you can't stand the thought of reading a defense of flat toothpicks, skip this part.

I *hate* round toothpicks, The damn things are too fat and too close to their little pointy ends, which means that they won't go between my teeth at the gum line far enough to push out the bits of whatever gets stuck in there. Flat toothpicks will. So what if I have to throw a few away when they break before I can accomplish much; they're cheap, as you pointed out.

Furthermore, being pointed on both ends, round toothpicks are worthless for polishing the front surfaces of my teeth, unless I chew them down a bit first. I think the makers of flat toothpicks should square off those big ends, but at least those ends aren't pointy as on those round jobbers, and I can do some good with them.

Whenever a restaurant has only round toothpicks, I take out my pocket knife and whittle 'em down so they'll go through the gaps. I haven't worked up the nerve yet to do this in front of the maître d', but one of these days I will, scattering toothpick slivers on the carpet, to make sure the message is absorbed.

ALAN M. COURTRIGHT
Seattle, Washington

On Why Countdown Leaders on Films Don't Count Down to One

Your information is correct until you reported that the number one is the start of the picture. Although there isn't a one on Academy Leader, the picture actually starts on what would be zero. The forty-seven frames of black film that follow the single frame bearing a "2" are for the projectionist to open the dowser and allow light through the projector. A quick "beep" is usually heard along with the number two, indicating that the sound is in sync with the picture.

In theaters that alternate between two projectors, there is a mark that appears in the upper right-hand corner of the picture, which tells the projectionist to start the other projector up to speed, and then a second mark, which is when the projectionist actually should change over to the new reel. This countdown leader allows a precise amount of time for the projector to get up to speed, so that when the changeover occurs the viewer will not have missed any of the movie.

BRIAN M. DEMKOWICZ
Chief Projectionist, IMAX Theater
Baltimore, Maryland

DAVID FELDMAN

On Why American Elections Are Held on Tuesday

Election day is not the second Tuesday in November but is the first Tuesday after the first Monday in November.

STEVEN J. RIZZO
Islip, New York

On Why Balls Are on Top of Flagpoles

I was always taught that the answer was longevity of the pole. In the days when flagpoles were wooden, the end grain of the wood was exposed if not capped by a ball or other type of finial. End grain absorbs dampness more readily than any other part of the wood. . . .

GAVIN DUNCAN
Tabb, Virginia

Several veterans, including retired Army Sergeant Robert E. Krotzer of Hephzibah, Georgia, wrote to say that they were taught that the purpose of the ball was to keep the flag from being caught on the pole when the wind blew the flag upward. The flag experts we spoke to admit that this is the reasoning the Army provides, but insist that even a sphere doesn't stop a flag from getting stuck on top of a pole.

On Why the Sound of Running Water Changes When Hot Water Is Turned On

I do not deny the validity of the causes you discussed, however the *pitch* of that sound at a given rate of flow depends on the density of the water. Hot water is substantially less dense than cold water. . . . The fundamental fact of physics is that different density fluids have different natural frequencies of vibration while flowing through a given orifice.

Just turn on any hot-water faucet that has been off long enough for the water content to get cold some distance down the pipe. Then stand back and listen. You will clearly hear a change in pitch as the hot water arrives. The change is sudden and cannot be explained by any adaptive change of the pipes. It is the direct result of the change in the natural frequency of the water itself. The noisier the flow the more noticeable the change.

STEFAN HABSBURG
Farmington Hills, Michigan

On Why We Aren't Most Comfortable in 98.6° F Temperature

In *Why Do Clocks Run Clockwise?*, you wrote we would feel most comfortable when it is 98.6° F in the ambient air—if we were nudists.

Not *exactly* so. Human beings use up caloric energy, derived from food, to make motions with our muscular bodies. This process yields a certain amount of excess energy in the form of heat. Our bodies radiate this excess heat into the ambient air. When severely overheated, our bodies hasten the action by evaporating sweat. But we must have a means to *keep* our body temperature at 98.6° F or we die of heat prostration.

If we were all nudists and the ambient air *everywhere* was 98.6° F, we'd feel discomfort the moment we began to move. Lacking a temperature differential in the ambient air, our bodies could no longer radiate heat easily. First we'd sweat, and then we'd all die.

The only hope to remain alive would be to remain as motionless as possible for as long as possible, but sooner or later the excess heat from involuntary motions (like the heart and lung muscles) would build up.

So a 98.6° F temperature wouldn't be "comfortable" very long. . . . We need a slightly lower temperature in the air sooner or later.

DON SAYENGA
Bethlehem, Pennsylvania

DAVID FELDMAN

On Bird Droppings

You can't get away with anything with Imponderables readers. We simplified a little by calling the white stuff surrounding the black dot in bird droppings "urine." One reader noticed.

Mammals and amphibians get rid of nitrogenous waste in the form of urea dissolved in water. This is the material we commonly call urine. Birds and reptiles cannot accomplish this. They get rid of their nitrogenous wastes in a white semisolid form called uric acid. This is the white material in the birds' droppings.

There are two reasons why birds and reptiles use uric acid for waste disposal. One is because it is a water conservation technique. The other reason is perhaps more important. Bird and reptile embryos develop inside a hard shell. If they were to produce water-soluble urea while developing, it would end up poisoning the embryo before it could fully develop and hatch.

This leads us to the answer of another interesting question, "What is that 'gooky' stuff inside the shell after a baby bird hatches?" It is the remains of what is called the "allantois," the garbage can where nonsoluble uric acid is deposited while the embryo is developing.

SANDY JONES
Manassas, Virginia

On the Purpose of the Half Moons on Fingernails

Although our explanation—lunula are trapped air and serve no biological purpose—was correct, one reader did find a way to use them:

When preparing a patient prior to surgery requiring a full anesthetic, I was told to remove all nail polish prior to admission. When I asked why, I was told that recovery room personnel can monitor blood pressure by observing changes in the color of half moons.

MICHEALE WILLIAMS
Portland, Oregon

WHEN DO FISH SLEEP?   241

On the Mysterious Fruit Flavors Contained in Juicy Fruit Gum

When I was in college, I made the synthetic flavors of oil of pineapple (ethyl butyrate) and oil of banana (amyl acetate). I found when mixed in precisely a certain ratio, I got the distinct aroma of Juicy Fruit. . . .

Incidentally, if one wishes to synthesize ethyl butyrate, be prepared. Butyric acid is one stinking, sickening smelling acid. But once mixed with ethyl alcohol and concentrated sulfuric acid, the ethyl butyrate emerges with a sweet pineapple aroma.

HAROLD E. BLAKE
Tampa, Florida

On the Purpose of Pubic and Underarm Hair

Most of the experts we contacted speculated that this body hair served as a sexual attractant. But in a letter to Human Evolution, *one reader dissented. We reprint part of the letter with his permission:*

Pubic and axillary hair have been assumed to be biologically non-functional and therefore relegated to a role of mere sex attractants or to signal sexual maturity. Yet if one examines the action of axillary and pubic hair it can be seen that these patches serve as a kind of lubricant for arm and leg movements repectively and must have been retained in that capacity or evolved separately when other body hair was lost. One can easily observe the friction-reducing function of axillary hair by shaving under one arm and noting the added friction of the shaved arm. The fact that pubic hair extends up the abdomen beyond the point where it facilitates leg movement may mean that body hair was lost while our fore-bears were still walking in a crouch or on knuckles; for it comes into function, particularly the lateral portions, in that position. It would serve well for a semicrouched or sometimes-crouched proto-hominid that had lost most of its body hair. As our ancestral mothers began losing their body hair, fatty breasts and pubic and axillary hair could have all evolved simultaneously. The hair patches were selected for the purely biological function of reducing friction whereas general loss of body hair gave rise to the

DAVID FELDMAN

necessity of fatty breasts for providing the crucial psychological role of softness, comfort, and security for the infant.

NOEL W. SMITH
State University of New York
Plattsburgh, New York

On Why Ranchers Hang Old Boots Upside-down on Fence Posts

The longest chapter in Why Do Clocks Run Clockwise? *was a futile attempt to answer this Imponderable. We confirmed that Nebraska was the epicenter of boot-hanging activity. We even found the son of the man reputed to have started the practice. But even he didn't know why his father hung the boots. Some readers had their own ideas.*

Marla Bouton, of Kearney, Nebraska, sent us an article by Roger L. Welsch, professor of English and anthropology at the University of Nebraska–Lincoln, published in the October 30, 1983, Sunday World-Herald Magazine *of the Midlands. Along with repeating all of the theories we advanced, Welsch recounted many other stories he was told by boot-hangers, including the number of boots indicated the number of sons in the family; the toes point toward the nearest graveyard; the toes point toward the main house in case someone was lost in a snowstorm; and the boots are a token of good luck.*

Welsch concludes that although there may not be one single answer, hanging boots is probably some form of territorial marker. He notes that boot hanging is most prevalent in arid flatlands.

In a geography like this, long arrays of boots are striking, even stunning, and that is precisely their purpose. They are markers. They announce that someone lives here in this moonscape, that there are inhabitants, no matter how "deserted"—a perfect word, "deserted!"—things appear to be. . . .

WHEN DO FISH SLEEP? 243

Several readers insisted there was a more practical explanation for the custom.

The ranchers may be trying to stop the absorption of water. . . . In Alabama, a lot of farmers turn empty cans onto the tops of fence posts for this reason, or they will nail the tops that were taken from cans, onto the tops of the posts. This keeps the posts from absorbing large amounts of water when it rains. Wooden posts absorb quite a bit of water through the tops. Putting boots on the posts might prevent the wood from rotting prematurely.

C.A. "JUNIOR" WEAVER
Millbrook, Alabama

In West Virginia, some of the older farmers, including my grandparents, used to put on tin cans, old pieces of tires, roof shingles, or something else that would cover the top and hang down the sides of the fence posts.

This practice was done mostly to fence posts that still had bark on them. The farmers felt there was no reason to put objects on posts that had the bark stripped off.

Still asking why? Believe it or not, the reason was to keep the fence posts from rotting.

The idea was to keep the rain and snow from laying on the top of the post and soaking or running behind the bark. They believed the rain or snow would run down behind the bark, become trapped and rot the wood faster than if there was no bark at all on the posts. . . .

My husband and I have fence posts in our backyard (they are over 10 years old) and the bark has been stripped off. They show no signs of rot so far. They are so hard you can't hardly drive a nail into them.

Every once in awhile when I am traveling on some of the older, less busier country roads in the state, I see a fence with something on the top of the fence posts, and I remember asking my grandfather why he was doing it. I am glad that I was curious enough to ask because I may have helped you solve an Imponderable that seemed to be driving you nuts.

ELAINE K. SOUTHERN
Clarksburg, West Virginia

DAVID FELDMAN

If most of our letters on this subject came from the South and the Midwest, we received at least one sighting considerably farther to the north.

I was very surprised to see this in your book as I thought this practice was only done in my old territory.

I was a district rep for a car manufacturer and my territory included the central east of Alberta, Canada. This included Drumheller and Trochu, two small towns on either side of the Deer River.

Drumheller is famous for being the site of one of the first large dinosaur finds in North America. It now has a large scientific museum that attracts thousands of visitors every year. Trochu is not famous for anything, although it does have a very good ice-cream stand open during the summer.

Anyway, the back road from Drumheller to Trochu is one of the most pleasant drives you can find on the prairie. . . .

After crossing the river and driving toward Trochu and the ice-cream stand, there is a rancher who has put hundreds of boots on his fencing along the road. I asked about them and was told that they were to stop the aging of the fence posts. If the tops of the posts are covered and not left exposed, they will last that much longer. And since I once had a job replacing an old fence, I can assure you that anything that can be done to make them last longer would be tried.

KEVAN TAYLOR
Niagara Falls, Ontario, Canada

Acknowledgments

The single most gratifying part of my job is receiving the thousands of letters that readers of *Imponderables* have sent me. Your ideas have supplied most of the mysteries answered in this book. Your support and encouragement have supplied the inspiration.

I have kept my promise to answer all letters that have included self-addressed stamped envelopes. I'll continue the practice, but please be patient. When deadline pressure mounts, so does my response time. I cherish your letters and pounce on each one like a child encountering a wrapped birthday present.

In Harper & Row, I have a found a publishing house that provides me with all the benefits of a family—without the in-laws. Excepting that he is taller and wears clothes better than me, Rick Kot is all I could ask for in a person or an editor. His assistant Scott Terranella is exhibiting annoying tendencies toward becoming as perfect as Rick, but Scott has been so kind to me it's hard to get mad at him.

From the top down the folks at Harper & Row have been gratuitously nice to me. The publisher, Bill Shinker, has been constantly supportive and enthusiastic. The beloved Brenda Marsh and the sales reps (sounds like a Motown act!) have, wonder of wonders, gotten my books into the stores. Roz Barrow, with skill and graciousness, made sure there were enough books to ship to the stores. Steve Magnuson has been full of great marketing ideas. Debra Elfenbein, with a sharp mind and several sharp red pencils, helped tighten and focus this manuscript. The publicity department, headed by Karen Mender, helped thrust me upon an innocent North America. Special thanks to my publicist and rock 'n' roll heartthrob, Craig Herman, and to Allison Koop, Susie Epstein, and Anne Berman. And to the trinity in Special Markets, Connie Levinson, Barbara Rittenhouse, and Mark Landau: You have a friend for life, whether you like it or not.

In *Why Do Clocks Run Clockwise?*, I complained that my agent, Jim Trupin, didn't laugh enough at my jokes. I'm happy and proud to announce that he has corrected this egregious flaw and can now lay claim to be the last Renaissance man. Jim and his wife, Elizabeth, are two of my favorite people. Speaking of favorite people, Kassie Schwan, illustrator and semiprofessional gardener, continues to produce terrific illustrations. And the late (not dead, just late) Mark Kohut has taught me more than anyone about how the book business works. Lovely Joann Carney is the only person who has ever gotten me to sit in front of a camera for more than five minutes without wiggling uncontrollably, let alone to enjoy the process of being photographed.

Over the last few years, I've had a chance to meet an underpaid, unsung but fabulous group of people—booksellers. From the president and CEO of Waldenbooks, Harry Hoffman, to the managers of mall stores, Julie Lasher and Brian Scott Rossman; from B. Dalton's manager of Merchandise Planning and Communication, Mattie Goldberg, to all the folks at the Benjamins Bookstore in the Pittsburgh Airport, the booksellers I've met have been intelligent, committed, and inordinately good company. Thanks for providing me with an on-the-job education.

My friends and family have helped me survive a difficult year. Thanks to all who have lent support: Tony Alessandrini; Michael Barson; Rajat Basu; Ruth Basu; Jeff Bayone; Jean Behrend; Brenda Berkman; Cathy Berkman; Sharon Bishop; Carri Blees; Christopher Blees; Jon Blees; Bowling Green State University's Popular Culture Department; Jerry Braithwaite; Annette Brown; Arvin Brown; Herman Brown; Joann Carney; Janice Carr; Alvin Cooperman; Marilyn Cooperman; Judith Dahlman; Paul Dahlman; Shelly de Satnick; Linda Diamond; Joyce Ebert; Steve Feinberg; Fred Feldman; Gilda Feldman; Michael Feldman; Phil Feldman; Phyllis Fineman; Kris Fister; Linda Frank; Seth Freeman; Elizabeth Frenchman; Michele Gallery; Chris Geist; Jean Geist; Bonnie Gellas; Bea Gordon; Dan Gordon; Ken Gordon; Judy Goulding; Chris Graves; Christal Henner; Marilu Henner; Melodie Henner; David Hennes; Paula Hennes; Sheila Hennes; Sophie Hennes; Steve Hofman; Uday Ivatury; Terry Johnson; Sarah Jones; Mitch Kahn; Dimi Karras; Mary Katinos; Robin Kay; Stewart Kellerman; Harvey Kleinman; Mark Kohut; Claire Labine; Randy Ladenheim-Gil; Debbie Leitner; Jared Lilienstein; David Lynch; all my friends at the Manhattan Bridge Club; Phil Martin; Jeff McQuain; Julie Mears; Phil Mears; Carol Miller; Barbara Morrow; Phil Neel; Steve Nellisen; Millie North; Milt North; Charlie Nurse; Debbie Nye; Tom O'Brien; Pat O'Conner; Joanna Parker; Jeannie Perkins; Merrill Perlman; Joan Pirkle; Larry Prussin; Joe Rawley; Rose Reiter; Brian Rose; Paul Rosenbaum; Carol Rostad; Tim Rostad; Susie Russenberger; Leslie Rugg; Tom Rugg; Gary Sanders;

Joan Sanders; Mike Sanders; Norm Sanders; Cindy Shaha; Patricia Sheinwold; Kurtwood Smith; Susan Sherman Smith; Chris Soule; Karen Stoddard; Kat Stranger; Anne Swanson; Ed Swanson; Mike Szala; Josephine Teuscher; Carol Vellucci; Dan Vellucci; Hattie Washington; Julie Waxman; Roy Welland; Dennis Whelan; Devin Whelan; Heide Whelan; Lara Whelan; Jon White; Ann Whitney; Carol Williams; Maggie Wittenburg; Karen Wooldridge; Maureen Wylie; Charlotte Zdrok; Vladimir Zdrok; and Debbie Zuckerberg.

Well more than one thousand educators, institutions, experts, foundations, corporations, and trade associations were contacted for this book. Because we can't go to reference books to get our answers to Imponderables, we are dependent upon the generosity of the folks listed below. Although many other people supplied help, those listed below gave us information that led directly to the solution of Imponderables in this book: Sandra Abrams, Associated Services for the Blind; Richard B. Allen, Atlantic Offshore Fishermen's Association; Dr. Robert D. Altman, A & A Veterinary Hospital; American Academy of Dermatology; American Hotel and Motel Association; Carl Andrews, Hershey Foods; Richard A. Anthes, National Center for Atmospheric Research; Gerald S. Arenberg, National Association of Chiefs of Police; Dr. Edward C. Atwater, American Association for the History of Medicine.

Dr. Don E. Bailey, American Association of Sheep and Goat Practitioners; Dr. Ian Bailey, School of Optometry, University of California, Berkeley; Jan Balkin, American Trucking Associations; Dr. Pat A. Barelli, American Rhinologic Society; Nancy Beiman, National Cartoonists Society; Roy Berces, Pacific Stock Exchange; Dr. William Berman, Society for Pediatric Research; Dr. William Bischoff, American Numismatic Society; Ed J. Blasko, Eastman Kodak Company; Dr. Peter Boyce, American Astronomical Society; Richard Brooks, Stouffer Hotels; Edwin L. Brown, American Culinary Federation; Bureau of the Mint, Department of the Treasury; Dr. Walter F. Burghardt, American Veterinary Society of Animal Behavior; Herbert H. Buzbee, International Association of Coroners and Medical Examiners.

John Canemaker; Gerry Carr, International Game Fish Association; Carel Carr, Yellow Pages Publishers Association; Helen Castle, Kellogg's; Louis Chang; Bob Cochran, Society of Paper Money Collectors; Lyndon Cole, Society of Actuaries; Linda W. Coleman, Department of the Treasury, Bureau of Engraving and Printing; Robert

L. Collette, National Fisheries Institute; Dr. James D. Conroy, College of Veterinary Medicine; Charles T. Conway, Gillette Company; Philip S. Cooke, Inflight Food Service Association; Captain K.L. Coskey, Navy Historical Foundation; Louise Cotter, National Cosmetology Association; Danny J. Crawford, Marine Corps Historical Foundation; Edward Culleton, Green Olive Trade Association.

Hubert R. Dagley II, American College of Sports Medicine; Paul N. Dane, Society of Wireless Pioneers; Neill Darmstadter, American Trucking Association; Dr. Frank Davidoff, American College of Physicians; Professor Michael De L. Landon, American Society for Legal History; Brian M. Demkowicz, Maryland Academy of Sciences; Dr. Liberato John A. DiDio, International Federation of Associations of Anatomists; James J. Donahue, Duracell Inc.; Richard H. Dowhan, GTE Products; Don R. Duer, Still Bank Collectors Club of America; Thomas Dufficy, National Association of Photographic Manufacturers; W.K. Bill Dunbar, Morse Telegraph Club.

Susan Ebaugh, Serta Inc.; Dr. William G. Eckert, INFORM; Carole L. Edwards, Mobil Oil Corporation; Peter Eisenstadt, New York Stock Exchange Archives; Kay Engelhardt, American Egg Board.

Raymond E. Falconer, Atmospheric Sciences Research Center, SUNY at Albany; Dr. Fred Feldman; Dr. Barry Fells, Epigraphic Society; Stanley Fenvessey, Fenvessey Consulting; Peter C. Fetterer, Kohler Company; Deidre Flynn, Popcorn Institute; Bruce A. Foster, Sugar Industry Technologists; Don French, Radio Shack; Lester Frey, Villamarin Guillen.

Samuel R. Gammon, American Historical Association; Dr. James Q. Gant, International Lunar Society; Bruce R. Gebhardt, North American Native Fishes Association; Chris George, Rand McNally; Gerontology Research Center, National Institute of Aging; Karen L. Glaske, United Professional Horsemen's Association; Jacqueline Greenwood, Black & Decker; Patricia A. Guy, Bay Area Information System Reference Center.

Susan Hahn, United States Tennis Association; Dr. John Hallett, Desert Research Institute; Korynne Halverson, Evans Food Group; David A. Hamilton, Professional Ski Instructors of America; Lynn Hamlin, National Syndications Inc.; Darryl Hansen, Entomological Society of America; Carl Harbaugh, International Association of Chiefs of Police; Dorcas R. Hardy, Commissioner of Social Security; John Harrington, Council for Periodical Distributors; Tamara J. Hartweg, Kraft; Connie Heatley, Direct Marketing Association; Jim Heffernan,

National Football League; Richard Heistchel, Schinder Elevator Company; Jacque Hetrick, Spalding Sports Worldwide; Shari Hiller, Sherwin-Williams Company; Janet Hinshaw, Wilson Ornithological Society; Robert C. Hockett, Council for Tobacco Research; Dick Hofacker, AT&T Bell Laboratories; Greg Hoffman, Jolly Time; Beverly Holmes, Frito-Lay Inc.; Dr. Daniel Hooker, University of North Carolina at Chapel Hill, Student Health Service; Richard H. Hopper; Donald Hoscheit, Osco Drug; Mark R. Houston, California Kiwifruit Commission; Professor Barbara J. Howe, National Council on Public History; Kenneth Hudnall, National Yellow Pages Agency Association; Hyde Athletic Industries, Inc.

Dr. Peter Ihrke, American Academy of Veterinary Dermatology; International Bank Note Society; Helen Irwin, National Tennis Hall of Fame.

John Jay, Intercoiffure America; Dr. William P. Jollie, American Association of Anatomists; Larry Josefowicz, Wilson Sporting Goods Company.

Jeff Kanipe, *Astronomy*; Robert Kaufman, Metropolitan Museum of Art; Edward E. Kavanaugh; Dr. Thomas P. Kearns, American Ophthalmological Society; Michele Kelley, American Hotel and Motel Association; Dr. Anthony L. Kiorpes, University of Wisconsin, Madison, School of Veterinary Medicine; Dan Kistler, Christian Research Institute; Dr. Ben Klein; Samuel Klein, United States Postal System; Ken Klippen, United Egg Producers; Dr. Kathleen Kovacs, American Veterinary Medicine Association; Stanley Kranzer, Metropolitan Life.

Jean Lang, Fieldcrest, Keith Lattislaw, National Center for Health Statistics; John Laughton, American Standard; Mary Jane Laws, American Dairy Association; Cathy Lawton, Shulton Inc.; Dr. Beverly Leffers, Milton Helpern Institute of Forensic Medicine; Professor Alfonz Lengyel, Eastern College; Dick Levinson, H.Y. Aids Group; Peter H. Lewis, *New York Times*; Pierre Lilavois, New York City Sewer Department; Barbara Linton, National Audubon Society; Kenneth M. Liss, Liss Public Relations; John Loftus, Society of Collision Repair Specialists; Joan G. Lufrano, Foote, Cone & Belding; Lynne Luxton, American Foundation for the Blind.

William L. MacMillan III, Pencil Makers Association; Alan MacRobert, *Sky & Telescope*; Dr. M. Mackauer, Center for Pest Management; Joseph D. Madden, Drug, Chemical and Allied Trades Association; Reverend Robert L. Maddox, Americans United for

Separation of Church and State; Mail Order Association of America; William C. Mailhot, Gold Medal Flour; Michael Marchant, Ogden Allied Aviation Services; Ginny Marcin, Campbell Soup Company; Colonel Ronald G. Martin; Howard W. Mattson, Institute of Food Technologists; Dr. Robert McCarley, Sleep Research Society; James P. McCauley, International Association of Holiday Inns; Dr. Everett G. McDonough, Zotos International; William F. "Crow Chief" Meyer, Blackfeet Indian Writing Company; Mary D. Midkiff, American Horse Council; Jerry Miles, American Baseball Coaches Association; David G. Miller, National Association of Retail Druggists; Dr. Stephen Miller, American Optometric Association; Robert J. Moody, General Electric; Rita Moroney, Office of the Postmaster General; Pete Morris, C.H. Morse Stamp Company; Bill Mortimer, Life Insurance Marketing and Research Association; George Motture, Wise Foods; Meg Wehby Muething; Arthur J. Mullkoff, American Concrete Institute; Edith Munro, Corn Refiners Association; Gordon W. Murrey, Murrey International; D.C. Myntti, American Bankers Association.

Dr. David Nash, American College of Physicians; National Institute on Aging, National Institute of Health; Arnie Nelson, Yellow Spots; David Nystrom, U.S. Geological Survey.

Norman Oehlke, International Fabricare Institute; Carl Oppedahl.

Dr. Lawrence Charles Parish, History of Dermatology Society; Dianne V. Patterson, United States Postal System; William R. Paxton, Federal Railroad Administration; Peggy Pegram, Bubble Yum; Joy Perillo, AT&T Archives; Pillsbury Company; Leslye Piqueris, American Foundation for the Blind; Lawrie Pitcher Platt, Tupperware Home Parties; Bruce Pluckhahn, National Bowling Hall of Fame and Museum; Proctor-Silex; Dr. Robert Provine, University of Maryland; Roy S. Pung, Photo Marketing Association, International; Thomas L. Purvis, Institute of Early American History and Culture.

Jerry Rafats, National Agriculture Library; Dr. Salvatore Raiti, National Hormone and Pituitary Program; Monika Reed, Berol USA; Walter Reed, National Automatic Merchandising Association; Al Rickard, Snack Food Association; Bob Riemer, Gasoline and Automotive Service Dealers; R.J. Reynolds; Robert S. Robe, Scipio Society of Naval and Military History; Dr. Robert R. Rofen, Aquatic Research Institute; Tim Ross, U.S. Ski Coaches Association; Professor Mary H. Ross, Virginia Polytechnic Institute; Rosemary Rushka, American Academy of Ophthalmology.

Micael Saba, Attiyeh Foundation; Gabe Samuels, Yellow Spots;

ACKNOWLEDGMENTS

José Luis Perez Sanchez, Commercial Office of the Embassy of Spain; Ronald A. Schachar, Association for the Advancement of Ophthalmology; Schick Division, Warner-Lambert; Janet Seagle, U.S. Golf Association; William Seitz, Neighborhood Cleaners Association; Gwen Sells, Tall Clubs International; Dale Servetnick, Department of the Treasury; Norman F. Sharp, Cigar Association of America; Anthony H. Siegel, Ametek; Dr. M.S. Silberman; Joan Silverman, Citicorp; Dave Smith, Disney Company; Linda Smith, National Restaurant Association; Sid Smith, National Association of Hosiery Manufacturers; Wayne Smith, Sunbeam Appliance Company; Bruce V. Snow, Dairylea Cooperative; Dona Sorensen, Fleischmann's Yeast; Marshall Sorkin, Carter-Wallace; Richard Spader, American Angus Association; Dr. Bob Spanyer, American College of Physicians; John J. Suarez, National Pest Control Association; Amy Sudol, Chase Manhattan; Richard J. Sullivan, Olive Oil Group.

David Taylor, Bank Administration Institute; Thomas A. Tervo, Stearns and Foster Bedding; William D. Toohey, Tobacco Institute; Victor Toth, Multi-Tenant Telecommunications Association; Bob Toy, Telephone Pioneers of America; Jim Trdinich, National League.

Ralph E. Venk, Photographic Society of America; Dennis Vetock, U.S. Army Military History Institute; Elaine Viets, St. Louis *Post-Dispatch*; Gerald F. Voigt, American Concrete Pavement Association; Vulcan Foundry.

Al Wagner, AFC Computer Services; Debbie Walsh, American Federation of Teachers; Belinda Baxter Walsh, Procter & Gamble; Spider Webb, Tattoo Club of America; Monique Wegener, Lenders Bagel Baker; Richard H. Welsh, Jr., Cannon Mills; S.S. White Industrial Products, Pennwalt Corporation; Melvin T. Wilczynski, Lane Drug Company; Dr. Elizabeth Williams, Wyoming State Veterinary Laboratory; Dr. Jack Wilmore, University of Texas; Frank C. Wilson, American Orthopedic Association; Donald W. Wilson, U.S. Ski Educational Foundation; Jerry Wiseman, Atlantic Gelatin; Dr. Robert M. Wold, College of Optometrists in Vision Development; Merry Wooten, Astronomical League; World Impex Bowling.

S.G. Yasinitsky, Orders and Medals Society of America.

Dr. E. Zander, Winthrop Consumer Products; Linda Zirbes, Hyatt Hotels Corporation; Jim Zuckerman, Associated Photographers International.

And to my sources who, for whatever reason, preferred to remain anonymous, thanks for your contribution.

ACKNOWLEDGMENTS

Help!

After finishing this book, we are an empty shell. We are physically and spiritually depleted.

    Only one thing can help us: new Imponderables.

    We need letters. Lots and lots of letters.

    Stacks of letters full of witty Imponderables.

    Gobs of letters answering Frustables.

    Piles of letters patting us on the back or letting us have it.

    Join the slightly deranged community of folks plagued by Imponderability. If you are the first to submit an Imponderable we use in the next volume, we'll send you a free copy, along with a sycophantic acknowledgment in the book.

    If you send a self-addressed stamped envelope, we promise to reply (although it may take us awhile). Even without the SASE, we cherish every letter we receive.

    So send those Imponderables, Frustables answers, and comments, along with your name, address, and phone number to:

IMPONDERABLES

BOX 24815

LOS ANGELES, CALIFORNIA 90024

Index

INDEX

INDEX

El fiscal

Augusto Roa Bastos

El fiscal

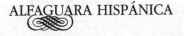

EL FISCAL,
© 1993, Augusto Roa Bastos

De esta edición:
© 1993, Aguilar, Altea, Taurus,
Alfaguara, S.A. de C.V.
Av. Universidad 767, Col. del Valle
México, 03100, D.F.
Teléfono 604 9209

- Ediciones Santillana S.A.
  Carrera 13 N° 63-39, Piso 12. Bogotá
- Santillana S.A., Avda San Felipe 731. Lima
- Editorial Santillana S.A.
  4ª, entre 5ª y 6ª, transversal. Caracas 106. Caracas
- Editorial Santillana Inc.
  P.O. Box 5462 Hato Rey, Puerto Rico, 00919
- Santillana Publishing Company Inc.
  901 W. Walnut St., Compton, Ca. 90220-5109. USA

Primera edición en México: septiembre de 1993

ISBN: 968-19-0177-0

Diseño:
Proyecto de Enric Satué
© Cubierta: Carlos Aguirre

Impreso en México

A Morena Tarsis,

*Tú me animaste a reescribir esta
historia, la viviste tú misma y eres
escrita por ella.*
A. R. B.

Con Hijo de hombre y Yo el Supremo, El Fiscal
compone la trilogía sobre el "monoteísmo" del poder, uno
de los ejes temáticos de mi obra narrativa. Después de casi
veinte años de silencio, la primera versión de esta obra fue
escrita en los últimos años de una de las tiranías más largas y
feroces de América Latina. En 1989 una insurrección abatió
al tirano. La novela quedó fuera de lugar y tuvo que ser
destruida. El fruto estaba inmaduro. Un silencio de lápida
resulta siempre ensordecedor. El mundo había cambiado no
menos que la visión del mundo del autor. Esas cenizas resul
taron fértiles. En cuatro meses, de abril a julio, una versión
totalmente diferente surgió de esos cambios. Era el acto de fe
de un escritor no profesional en la utopía de la escritura
novelesca. Sólo el espacio imaginario del no-lugar y del no-
tiempo permite bucear en los enigmas del universo humano
de todo tiempo y lugar. Sin esta tentativa de busca de lo real
desconocido, el trabajo de un autor de ficciones tendría apenas sentido.

A. R. B.

Toulouse, 1993

Primera parte

Anoche llamó Clovis de Larzac desde París.

—Tengo algo urgente que comunicarte. Ven lo más pronto que puedas —me ha dicho con su voz inconfundible y un cierto tonillo zumbón como si hablara silbando a través de la comisura de los labios.

—Mañana estaré ahí.

Me sorprendió esta repentina invitación. Hacía rato que no lo veíamos. Decidí ir. Después de lo que me había pasado en París era casi natural que me castigara visitando de nuevo la "carroña dorada". Por asociación inconsciente tal vez, cuando me habló Clovis, volví a ver incrustada en el cielo la lápida de mármol negro del general La Fayette, situada en los fondos del jardín del hospital Rothschild, 33 Boulevard de Picpus.

Suelo acudir raramente a París y esto sólo cuando no puedo evitarlo. A fuerza de perderlo se vuelve uno mezquino de su tiempo. Para mí París, que me perdonen los mitólogos metropolitanos, continúa siendo, de otro modo, la antigua y pantanosa Lutecia donde galos y romanos batallaban con el barro hasta el pecho. Ahora pululan allí emigrados de todo el mundo. Una verdadera infección. Hay atracadores de alto y bajo copete, asaltantes de bancos, ardorosos y feroces secuestradores de mujeres, de niños. Hay políticos lo suficientemente mediocres como para aspirar a los más altos cargos. Y casi todos arriban a ellos sin mucho esfuerzo. Hay, en fin... ¿Pero no lo dijo ya Balzac hace más de un siglo? No hago más que repetir sus injustas y excesivas palabras. "Uno de los espectáculos del mundo que más horrores contiene es, sin duda, el aspecto general de la población parisiense, horrenda visión de un pueblo macilento, de color amarillo." Perdón, don Honorato, pero ¿no cree usted que hoy en la población parisiense apenas hay franceses?

La Ciudad Luz está ahí con su aureola de belleza eterna. La aborrezco porque me fascina. Es una cuestión personal; nada tiene que ver con la gratitud y simpatía que siento hacia el país. En Francia, el extranjero, el apátrida que fui —como otros millones de advenedizos— volvió a nacer ciudadano de una república, orgullo del mundo occidental. Aquí se me restituyó la dignidad del ser humano, sin exigírseme nada a cambio.

Sólo he tenido que tomar un nombre falso, despojar al yo de su imposible sinceridad, mudar de aspecto, inventarme nuevas señas particulares: espesa barba tornasolada por canas rubiáceas, una honda hendidura en el arco cigomático, y sobre todo, dominar perfectamente la lengua con el acento y la entonación de provincias. Aprendí a simular a la perfección la renguera del inválido y la parquedad silenciosa del que no quiere papar ni tragarse moscas, habida cuenta de que más pronto cae el hablador que el cojo, y de que la renguera siempre inspira compasión y antipatía, dos elementos siempre útiles en la relación con el prójimo prepotente.

La obsesión de todo exiliado es volver. No puedo regresar con la cara del proscrito. He tenido pues que adoptar un nombre seudónimo y un cuerpo seudónimo que tornara irreconocible el propio, no digo el verdadero porque ése ya tampoco existe. Puede uno inventarse otra forma de vida, pero no disfrazarse de otro para seguir siendo el mismo. Ahora me llamo Félix Moral, profesor asociado a la Universidad de X.

Trato de hacer de la opacidad virtud, de pasar inadvertido, de ser apenas nadie y sin pena nada. Un rechazo instintivo me opone visceralmente a todo lo que huela a manada, a sectas de cualquier índole, a honores togados, a gloriolas académicas, a coloquios seudoliterarios o científicos. Actividades en las que hispanistas y americanistas resplandecemos como templarios barbudos con la luz propia de las sectas ilustradas. Enciclopedistas de lo exótico. Para mí el más genuino de los americanistas es Mr. Antoine Augustin Parmentier que dio carta de nobleza a la patata e instituyó a perpetuidad y con carácter universal el culto de la *frite*, que es en realidad la mejor del mundo y no la "papa frita" que comemos en América como importada de Francia.

El exilio es el mayor destructor de almas —me escribió en los primeros tiempos, para confortarme, mi abuelo Ezequiel Gaspar. Cualquier clase de exilio, aun el de quien se va a la esquina a comprar cigarrillos y no vuelve nunca más, como si él mismo se hubiera desvanecido en humo. Y el exilio político, aun el de los que no hacen política, como usted, es el peor de todos, garrapateaba en su carta el viejo soldado-niño que guerreó en la Guerra Grande cuando apenas tenía 13 años. Sólo salía de tanto en tanto de su amada Asunción para viajar en una destartalada diligencia de fines del siglo a su estancia de las Misiones, en los campos que fueron legados a los oficiales ex-combatientes, cuando se vendieron en subasta las tierras públicas. "Vivo —solía ironizar el viejo— en una pequeña fracción de las tierras que el Mariscal regaló a la Lynch, un poco antes de Cerro-Corá."

Las malas lenguas murmuraban que el garrido anciano tenía allí un pequeño harén de muchachas jóvenes. De mañana las mandaba a caballo a la escuela del pueblo de San Ignacio, a cinco leguas de la estancia. Por las noches, de a una o dos por vez, como el rey David, las llevaba a su inmenso lecho de trama de cuero para estudiar con ellas el libro eterno al calor de la inocencia primitiva. Si esas murmuraciones no eran mentirosas, el viejo Ezequiel Gaspar había encontrado su fuente de juvencia en ese gineceo de sílfides pastoriles, puesto que vivió hasta los 108 años y dejó, naturalmente, un montón de hijos naturales.

"Sobreviví a tres guerras internacionales —me decía en su carta con la confusa voracidad que los viejos tienen del tiempo—, a media docena de revoluciones intestinas, a dieciocho golpes de Estado y a catorce dictaduras militares. No sé si el país resistirá esta última del alemán, el caníbal más salvaje de los que se han ensañado con este país. En tiempos de López, éste lo hubiera puesto a Tembelo a lustrarle las botas y a rasquetearle su caballo *Manduví*... ¡Y ahora este gringo miserable de la colonia Hoeneau se ha declarado su heredero y sucesor!"

El viejo Ezequiel Gaspar formulaba un vaticinio escalofriante: "Los militares y los malos políticos, que son casi todos, vienen empeñándose desde hace más de un siglo en destruir nuestro hermoso país, ponerlo en liquidación y entregar sus chatarras a una potencia extranjera... Menos mal que yo ya no estaré aquí para ver esta última infamia. Acuérdese usted de lo que le digo, mi querido nieto. Ojalá venga un terremoto que acabe con esta plaga que dejó sembrada el López carapé desde su muerte en Cerro-Corá..." Agregaba una letanía de insultos, anatemas y maldiciones contra "la vil raza de los milicos y los politicastros", y concluía su carta con un típico arranque de su genio cerril: "Aunque los viera arder en montón ni siquiera les mearía encima. Tan codiciosos y avaros son que negarían su mierda a los cuervos y preferirían convertirse en cenizas... El único grande fue mi jefe, el general don Bernardino Caballero. ¡Ése sí que fue un paraguayo de ley! Pero lo metieron en política y lo jodieron..."

Para entonces, el viejo veterano de la guerra muy suelto de lengua y chismoso ya no andaba muy bien de la cabeza, y había que tolerarle sus desvaríos. Un año antes de su muerte, en un juicio sumarísimo, el tribunal militar le confiscó sus campos y su casa en Asunción "por traición a la patria". No se dieron a conocer los detalles. Creo que ni siquiera le incoaron una causa. Todo fue decidido por la inapelable "Orden superior" que pone y quita ley, y manda "empaquetar" a millares de opositores que son enterrados vivos, luego de salvajes sesiones de torturas, o arrojados desde los helicópteros del ejército sobre lo más espeso de las selvas vírgenes.

Lo cierto es que el viejo más que centenario se quedó, como se suele decir, sin un lugar donde caerse muerto. Murió —de un síncope, según algunos, y según otros, de un tiro en la nunca— cuando venía en su desvencijada diligencia a presentarse al Estado Mayor para reclamar sus derechos de veterano de la Guerra Grande. Lo enterraron entre gallos y medianoche, sin mayores requilorios, en el Panteón Militar de la Recoleta. Ezequiel Gaspar, considerado uno de los mejores granaderos del Ejército Grande, fue oficial de Bernardino Caballero y acompañó a Solano López hasta su muerte en Cerro-Corá. El Gran Tembleo no podía "empaquetarlo" tan fácilmente como a otros infelices. Ezequiel Gaspar llevó una vida cumplida y murió como un patriarca en exilio, cuya memoria a toda honra se arroja al basural del olvido.

Todos los recursos del disimulo son necesarios para ocultar las taras del exilio. Pero la clave de eficacia en esta existencia seudónima es no mantener ningún contacto con los exiliados del mismo origen. He logrado evitar por completo las relaciones con mis connacionales, cortar todo vínculo con el país que tuvo la desdicha de ser el lugar de mi nacimiento. Pero el exilio dejó de ser hace tiempo el mal de un país. Es una plaga universal. La humanidad entera vive en exilio. Desde que ya no existen territorios patrios —y, menos aún, esa patria utópica que es el lugar donde uno se encuentra bien—, todos somos beduinos nómadas de una cabila extinta. Objetos transnacionales, como el dinero, las guerras o la peste.

El exilio, efectivamente, es la peor de las enfermedades que pueden atacar a un ser humano. El contacto con otros apestados no hace más que agravarla. No es sólo la consunción del cuerpo y del espíritu; es la degradación moral que un individuo puede sufrir a límites extremos y que lo lleva a la locura, al crimen, a los delirios místicos o políticos y finalmente al suicidio físico o moral. Llega un momento en que el enfermo deja de sufrir. Queda reducido a una sombra saciada y tranquila, lamentable y satisfecha en su rozagante ruina, como la de los débiles mentales en los que ha desaparecido por completo la fuente de toda emoción.

Mi gratitud hacia Francia comienza en Jimena. En París conocí a esta mujer que iba a llenar por entero mi vida después de habérmela salvado por dos veces. Jimena es mi mejor juez y crítico, no sólo con respecto a mi trabajo intelectual; también con respecto a mi renovada apariencia física. Me conoció antes de que la cirugía plástica me dibujara esta nariz judía y la cicatriz de un hachazo en el pómulo izquierdo sin olvidar la remodelación de mis rejillas dactilares y algunos otros detalles que sólo ella conoce. Me suele decir con sorna que la reparación me ha mejorado.

A Jimena le debo también la radical transformación de mi carácter. Reconozco que, antes de encontrarla, yo no era más que un nómada del neolítico. Antes de conocerla, todos estos años de exilio valían para mí menos que nada. No me habrían permitido comprar una hora de vida. Vivía en medio de lo incomprensible, de lo que no tiene ningún sentido. Jimena me ayudó a recuperar el sentido de mi vida y del mundo. Ella acarrea consigo una asistencia múltiple e inesperada; ofrece a cada momento compañías distintas: es ella misma siempre, pero proteica de maneras y de tonos. Basta una sonrisa que ilumina su rostro y la unidad queda restablecida, su presencia recupera toda su plenitud. Está *siempre* allí. A su lado, el reposo no es sosiego solamente sino la plenitud activa del ser. Todo en ella me inspira una confianza absoluta. Entre nosotros hay respeto y aceptación total del otro. Admiro y amo en ella el secreto de su personalidad. Sólo un gran secreto define y precisa la expresión de un rostro y lo hace a la vez infinitamente cambiante y misterioso.

Lo que la hacía sufrir, al comienzo, era ignorar los detalles de una vida, la mía, de la que no había formado parte. La dio vuelta del revés y se apegó a ella como la uña a la carne. Ahora ella *sabe* todo lo que yo ignoro de mí. Lo bueno y lo malo de mi vida, lo conocido y lo desconocido, incluso tal vez lo que va a ser de mí. Mi destino humano ha penetrado profundamente bajo la piel del suyo. Ignora mis recuerdos pero adivina mis presentimientos. Yo no puedo darle más que mi adhesión sin límites, necesaria al par de la pareja sola. Vivimos bajo un mismo techo, bajo el mismo signo de una vida compartida como en una fiebre intensa y poderosa, que encuentra en su ardor su propia calma.

A Jimena, en la intimidad, la llamo Morena, con lo que el nombre de la esposa del Cid Campeador pierde en magia heroica lo que gana en aureola de afecto y de hogareña intimidad. Jimena Tarsis, de los Tarsis de Castilla la Vieja. Realmente su madera humana tiene la calidez, la nobleza, la salud de la caoba o del ébano. Su cabellera, sus ojos, su carácter reflejan ese obstinado color del resplandor oscuro sobre la tez mate y aterciopelada, levemente dorada: ese color que parece teñir la piel de la mujer hispana, heredada por las mujeres de mi tierra.

Jimena no podía reconstruir mi pasado. Pero entonces restauró para ambos en su casa-museo la Ventana del Poniente, esta especie de gran nicho abovedado que da hacia el ocaso. En ella vivimos gran parte de tiempo. Al caer la noche, por un curioso fenómeno de refracción, el gran ventanal se convierte en una especie de puente de un navío navegando en la oscuridad. Entonces Jimena corre el cortinado y el mundo a oscuras queda del otro lado; la luz y el sosiego se quedan adentro. Pero esa quietud de la vida no se parece en absoluto a la paz de un sosegado retiro. Es la quietud de algo implacable que acecha y que parece meditar una amenaza inescrutable.

Antes de pasar a manos de Jimena, la propiedad había sido posesión durante dos siglos de una misma familia. Tenía una capilla ruinosa donde se amontonaban libros de himnos religiosos, cuadros y tallas de santos, colgaduras de iglesia, carcomidos por insectos con ojos y patas de moho. No sé si esto correspondía a la realidad de esa casa; si me lo imagino ahora, confundido por mis recuerdos de antes de la internación, o por haberlo leído en la novela de *La princesse de Clèves*, una de las obras preferidas de Jimena quien siente a la vez gran admiración por su autora. Considera a Madame de Laffayette una de las precursoras del feminismo ilustrado ya en tiempos de la vida cortesana de Luis XIV.

La princesa era una de nuestras lecturas en la Ventana del Poniente. La leíamos como una crónica viva de Nevers. El palacio ducal y la mansión de la familia de Clèves formaban parte del decorado de la ciudad que el tiempo había vuelto menos vivo y real que en las páginas de su novela. Es imposible comunicar la sensación de una época determinada de nuestra propia existencia; eso que constituye la esencia sutil y penetrante de una experiencia humana. Vivimos solos, igual que en los sueños. De pronto aparece alguien que es capaz de leer esos sueños, de entrar en ellos transformándolos en una fantástica realidad. Eso logró Jimena con mi vida. Se entrega por entero a la causa de los demás, sin dejar nada para sí. Su destino es el de las personas que han nacido desprovistas de todo, salvo de generosidad. La ha concentrado en mí por creer tal vez que yo era alguien a quien todavía se podía salvar. A veces, sin embargo, se queja de haber tenido que lidiar siempre con exiliados: su padre, su madre, Jimena incluida y, como remate, yo mismo. Pero estos reproches no son sino efusiones de un alma satisfecha de dar más que de recibir, de haber sostenido almas en pena, en el verdadero sentido de la palabra.

Jimena mandó desmontar toda la faramalla gelatinosa, casi fósil, que abarrotaba la casa. Obsequió al doctor Maurel un curioso tintero gótico. El doctor dijo que no era un tintero sino una bacía para sangrar apopléticos en la Edad Media. Jimena quemó y donó todo lo que había que donar y quemar, e instaló su propio museo de muebles, objetos y *souvenirs* de España, de México y otros países. Había hasta reliquias de las Misiones jesuíticas: un altar, un reclinatorio, tallas de santos y angelotes en el más puro estilo del barroco hispano-guaraní, comprados a unos embajadores del Paraguay, duchos en todo género de contrabando y extraperlo, actividad que justamente forma parte de su misión diplomática, además de ser inversores y agentes de bolsa del tiranosaurio.

Jimena amuebla un incierto porvenir con esos restos de otras épocas, acaso por aquello de que el recuerdo del pasado es todo el futuro que nos queda. Ella permanece fuera del ordenado hacinamiento como si el tiempo no la tocara y sólo ella pudiese manipularlo en esos objetos con sus manos largas y flexibles sin que su aire distante y concentrado se altere. Con rápidos toques de plumero desviste de polvo todas esas cosas que están destinadas a ser polvo. Jimena *vive* en la casa; yo la ocupo, sólo a medias, con el obsesivo pensamiento del retorno que me carcome sordamente como una gran caries; una cavidad en el hueso del alma donde resuena con eco fuerte y permanente, sólo audible para mí, el llamado de la tierra natal.

La actividad cotidiana de Jimena es rápida y variada, pero todo lo hace en un susurro sin que apenas se noten sus movimientos: preparar sus clases, algún frugal refrigerio, amasar y hornear el pan hacia el atardecer y el chipá o pan paraguayo para los mates de sábados y domingos. El cuidado del jardín quedaba a mi cargo; a veces también la limpieza de la vajilla. Pronto volveré a reanudar estas tareas auxiliares en las que pongo más gusto y empeño que en enseñar literatura y civilización hispanoamericana.

Una señora portuguesa la ayuda por la mañana en los quehaceres menores. Mme. Alves viene muy temprano, antes de la salida del sol. Entra por la puerta del fondo que se la dejamos abierta porque no quiere llevarse la llave. Es mucha responsabilidad, dice. Se queda hasta media mañana, antes de que nos levantemos nosotros. Nos despierta el olor de sus apetitosos guisos. Deja preparada la mesa, con una rosa tierna de rocío en el fino florero de cristal de Bohemia, obsequio de Clovis, y se va a hacer su trabajo en otras casas de las inmediaciones.

Silenciosa, lenta, siempre vestida de luto, Mme. Alves ama a Jimena, como a la hija que se le murió cuando tenía la edad de Jimena. Según Mme. Alves, su hija era muy parecida en carácter y presencia física a Jimena. Se comunican en el lacónico pero elocuente lenguaje de los gestos y de los monosílabos. Mme. Alves mueve apenas los labios, como si bisbiseara un suspiro. Jimena, aun de espaldas, la oye y la entiende. Me asegura que es una mujer culta, que perteneció un tiempo a la mejor sociedad de Lisboa. Yo no he entrado aún en el mundo de este ser introvertido y discreto, refugiado en permanente mutismo. No le conozco la voz a Mme. Alves. Pasa delante de mí como ante una columna de humo, lo que atribuyo a respeto y timidez, no a despreciativa indiferencia. Conjeturo que puede ser descendiente o pariente, acaso la hija de Rutilio Alves, compañero de generación y amigo de Fernando Pessoa, el gran poeta de *Antinous*. No me he atrevido a preguntárselo. Rutilio Alves murió pobre y olvidado en París. Su hija nos prepara la comida.

La vieja casa restaurada resurgió ante mis ojos poco a poco, y sólo entonces fue cuando reparé en su aire de antigüedad reciente. El zumbido del viento en la rota chimenea me resulta una música sedante. La ruinosa *ferme* de algún *maitre de maison* local, vasta, oscura, se ha convertido en esta casa-museo, el lugar ideal para el encuentro de dos seres como Jimena y yo, dos Géminis a escasos días de diferencia entre sí, con parecidos gustos y distintos disgustos pero unidos en un mismo sentimiento de mutuo afecto y comprensión.

—¡Ah, nuestra flamante ruina! —contó Jimena que fue lo primero que dije cuando recobré el conocimiento. No sé, no lo recuerdo. Ciertas sombras de amnesia rondan todavía mi mente, y me hacen estar entre el día y la noche de un tiempo que transcurrió sin mí. Salí del hospital oliendo a intemperie. Sólo he traído conmigo mi maltrecha salud y el indeleble olor del quirófano.

Del Rothschild lo único que se me quedó grabado es esa tumba del general La Fayette, al pie de mi ventana. El sol del atardecer la reflejaba invertida en los vidrios como si la lápida estuviese incrustada en el cielo, entre nubes, con su verja enana de hierro forjado y su pequeño seto de lirios. Es la tumba más pequeña e insignificante que conozco de un general. La contemplaba a través de la mascarilla y de los tubos que penetraban en mi cuerpo por todos los orificios. Después dejé de verla. Lo único que oía todo el tiempo era el chirriante estruendo de los trenes del *métro* al remontar la rampa exterior de la estación Courteline hasta Nation. Pero también ese rumor se me fue haciendo cada vez más difuso y acabó reabsorbiéndose en mi ensueño comatoso. Los médicos no daban ya la mitad de un *sou* por mis míseros despojos.

Mi muerte clínica estaba decretada. El jefe de sala ordenó desconectar los aparejos. Jimena, todo el tiempo a mi lado, camino ya a la morgue, me raptó con la complicidad de los enfermeros que transportaban la camilla. Alquiló una ambulancia, me cargó en ella, con ayuda de los mismos enfermeros sensibilizados por la buena propina. Condujo ella misma y en pocas horas me devolvió a nuestra incomparable Nevers. El doctor Maurel, nuestro viejo amigo y protector, completó el salvamento de emergencia. "¡Esto es un milagro! —dijo—. Bueno, es lo que siempre sucede. Cada hombre vive en su milagro hasta que Dios decide retirarle su confianza."

Sólo me enteré de todo varios días después. Jimena me había preparado un lecho junto al alféizar de nuestra Ventana del Poniente, la pequeña mezquita de nuestro culto particular. ¡Ah, esa ventana! Pasaba la mano cadavérica por el maderamen que recubre el vano de la arcada, tan ancho como el espesor del muro. No lo quería creer. El sitio de nuestras lecturas al sol de la tarde. Lecho de amor cuando la noche se pegaba a los cristales a espiarnos. Teníamos que correr las cortinas para escondernos del guiño cómplice de las estrellas. Siento ahora mismo latir en esas maderas y piedras rugosas el pulso de tantas cosas inolvidables. No somos más que el recuerdo de necesidades perdidas; de momentos irrecuperables, de lo que fuimos y ya no somos. De tarde en tarde viene el doctor con su larga barba y su pesado bastón de roble con empuñadura de plata y cadenilla a la muñeca. Entra y me mira como a un hombre que le parece imposible que siga estando allí.

—*Encore vous ici? Ce revenant!* —mascullaba y se iba como fastidiado por un fenómeno antinatural que contradecía sus viejos principios. Maurel me tenía afecto personal pero me detestaba como enfermo que alteraba los plazos mortales tan bien distribuidos en la economía de la naturaleza, en los cuadros de la ciencia médica y en las tablas de expectativas de vida de las compañías de seguros. En este aspecto yo no era para él sino *el aparecido*.

Una vez que se iba el médico me oía farfullar a un

ritmo endiablado sin entender lo que decía, como queriéndome recuperar de la enorme cantidad de silencio en la que había naufragado durante un tiempo incalculable. A Jimena no se le perdía un solo sonido de ese galimatías egoísta y feroz de los resucitados cuya velocidad de pensamiento y de voz sólo es posible en el estado de absoluto reposo. Jimena me traducía mis palabras, despojadas de su incoherencia y de ese moho viscoso que uno trae de los lugares de muerte. Oírla a ella era todo lo que me importaba por el momento para sentir que la vida seguía.

Después de algunos meses, como no tenía otra que hacer, empecé a escribir esta especie de diario íntimo al que le pondré un título cualquiera; acaso el título de uno de los libros del danés de *Temor y Temblor*: *Papeles póstumos de alguien que todavía vive*. Es exactamente el que le conviene. Registran impresiones y sucesos del momento que pasa (eso que podría llamarse la engañosa memoria del presente), algunos recuerdos y presentimientos no del todo nítidos: el desvaído olor de la memoria. No son en absoluto un texto literario; la literatura que pretende ser más honesta e imaginativa que la vida me parece abominable. Estos papeles póstumos no son sino el material en bruto de mi no siempre dichosa experiencia humana. Están trabajados con el carácter abrupto, deshilvanado, de vaga espontaneidad, que tienen las cartas escritas al apuro en un momento de gran tensión emotiva, o el hablar de alguien que intenta narrar un mal sueño del que ha olvidado lo principal salvo la angustia inexpresable.

La realidad del mundo, de un ser humano, es esencialmente fragmentaria, como si estuviera reflejada en un espejo roto. Los escritos póstumos se parecen a esos fragmentos que brillan en la oscuridad. Tratan de contar una historia en ruinas. Son fragmentos de ruinas ellos mismos. Ofrecen un lugar de residencia adecuado a lo que ya no volveremos a ser. Y esto sucede con mayor razón en el gran espejo roto de la historia de un país, de la humanidad, sembrada de ruinas, entre las cuales caminan desorientados los muertos de este mundo como si estuvieran vivos. Quisiera demoler esas ruinas. "La demolición de una ruina es siempre un espectáculo hermoso y aterrador", escribía Djuna Barnes: En cierto sentido, todas las obras son póstumas. Algunas están destinadas a sobrevivir a sus autores, lo que algunas veces sucede. Las otras no son más que ruinas. Uno acaba aprendiendo de ellas la inmovilidad resignada.

Estos papeles, Morena, te están destinados, cuando yo ya no esté. Te contarán desde el pasado algunos hechos que ignoras y otros que no se han producido todavía. No son un diario íntimo ni la exaltada crónica de una resurrección. Menos aún, ese género espurio de una autobiografía. Detesto las autobiografías en las que el *yo* se regodea en su vacua autosuficiencia profiriendo sentenciosos aforismos inventados para la posteridad, o haciendo gorgoritos de una moral o de un cinismo igualmente inventados. La imagen cosmética de quien se toma ante el espejo de la escritura como modelo de una "vida ejemplar" es la forma más burda de engaño narcisista que pueden urdir los literatos; aun aquellos que simulan la modestia y discreción más opacas o el rigor autocrítico más despiadado. Algunos simulan ser mediocres y monótonos; no les cuesta ningún esfuerzo puesto que lo son. Me incluyo a fe mía. "... *e di questi cotai son io medesmo*..." (Inf, IV, 46). Todo lo que cuentan está desmentido por lo que no cuentan; y la doble engañifa resulta a su vez desmentida por los hechos reales, y éstos, por la infinita y esencial irrealidad del mundo.

Quien pretende "retratar" su vida tendría que inventarse un lenguaje propio, distinto de lo que se entiende por literatura, esa actividad ilusoria de monederos falsos. Nadie conoce su verdad íntima. Sólo esto les impide a algunos morir de vergüenza. Únicamente en la incertidumbre de lo que uno es puede encontrarse el comienzo de alguna revelación. No puede uno escribir de sí sin esconderse. Siempre se tiene algo de misteriosamente falseado que uno mismo ignora, que enfurece a quienes no nos quieren y molesta a quienes no nos conocen. Si tuviera uno que relatar su vida tendría que hacerlo como si se tratara de la vida de otra persona; pedir a los demás datos, recuerdos, opiniones; recoger de aquellos que nos quieren o nos aborrecen las imágenes flotantes que guardan de nosotros. El arte del biógrafo, ha dicho lúcidamente el no siempre lúcido André Maurois, es sobre todo saber olvidarse. La sola selección ya es un arte pero este arte no lo domina el memorioso. Como en el suicidio en que uno siempre se mata contra alguien, la autobiografía también se escribe, por lo general, contra alguien. Y hay odios obsesivos, originados por la envidia y el resentimiento, que son capaces de simular talentos y hasta vocaciones que de otro modo no existirían. La fauna de los literatos que anhelan con afán enfermizo ser siempre los primeros del curso es la más detestable que infesta la zoología fantástica. Lo único admirable que tienen es la descomunal desmesura de su egoísmo y narcisismo de atletas afeminados.

El espejo más nítido y honrado es sin duda el odio del otro: uno se ve reflejado en ese metal frío e implacable tal como uno es. Pero no todos tenemos la suerte de contar con el espejo de un odio desinteresado y honesto. Debemos ganarlo y fomentarlo con mil pequeñas astucias aguijoneando la envidia, los celos, la malignidad innata de los mediocres. Tal es el fermento que acaba por destruirlos. Trabajo descorazonador y fatigoso a la larga.

Únicamente los amigos más queridos están realmente en condiciones de aborrecernos. Cuento con dos o tres de esta especie a quienes debo la gratitud de saber que todavía existo. No necesito nombrarlos. Cada uno sabe que es a ellos a quienes me estoy refiriendo. Me sufren de lejos como una enfermedad incurable. En fin, ¡qué haríamos sin estos amigos, defendidos por su tenaz y acolchada imbecilidad, que atenúan a nuestro favor los porrazos de la fatalidad! Y de estos tales soy también yo mismo.

A mi muerte leerán poemas y elogios fúnebres, y escribirán en los periódicos exégesis laudatorias con la satisfacción del deber cumplido, sacudiéndose las manos al final como de un polvo molesto. O no dirán nada, se alegrarán por dentro, y a otra cosa. A idos no hay amigos ni conocidos. Muerto el perro, acabada la rabia. La muerte de un hombre, que es su única y última verdad, provoca indefectiblemente una humareda de los más extravagantes y mentirosos elogios. La muerte es la misma para todos, pero cada uno muere a su manera, decía Novalis. Rilke tomó este pensamiento del autor de *Los himnos de la noche* como fundamento de su concepto poético de la muerte propia.

La historia de una vida no existe sino en amalgama con otras vidas. Entonces la historia que relata de la suya el que se desnuda en público con el impudor de una vieja meretriz es la que menos interesa y hace desear las que no cuenta. Cuánto más noble sería dejar a la verdad en paz por deforme que sea. La verdad sólo es verdad cuando permanece oculta, aun entre los afeites de los poetas seniles y proféticos que abundan en las tierras nuevas todavía sin una gran tradición literaria; que únicamente poseen una literatura sin pasado y acaso sin futuro.

En estos apuntes hay párrafos que desde luego suprimiré por esa irremediable tendencia de nuestra condición de querer ocultar siempre algo de la verdad. No lo haría por Jimena, desde luego; ella adivinaría los párrafos faltantes, sabría leer las entrelíneas y hasta por debajo de las tachaduras. Eliminaría únicamente estos párrafos por un motivo de elemental discreción, de delicadeza. Una de las cualidades de Jimena es la finura de su manera de sentir, pese a sus modales en apariencia algo toscos y autoritarios con los que disfraza su timidez, su desconfianza de un medio del que no se siente parte. ¡Qué le vamos a hacer! —me dijo una vez—. Es un viejo trauma de antes de nacer... Nacer en exilio es como no haber nacido. Mi defensa vital es atacar cuando me siento atacada.

A través de mis relaciones con ella es como me he confirmado en la idea de que a nadie le importa mucho uno por lo que es o deja de ser, salvo en la mente de alguien. Yo me siento *alguien* en la mente de Jimena, y acaso de manera un poco más fantasmal en su corazón. Y ese *alguien* que soy lleva la marca de esta mujer excepcional, pues el hombre, cualquier hombre, sólo vale por la mujer que le acompaña.

Al comenzar los apuntes de esta historia, he dudado entre escribirlos desde el ángulo del narrador impersonal o desde el punto de vista del que utiliza el yo, siempre engañoso y convencional; el primero permite la visión precisa y neutra, aparentemente desinteresada; el segundo otorga al texto el beneficio de la divagación sinuosa, según los estados de ánimo y la inspiración o desgana del momento. Prevaleció en mí, finalmente, la intención primera de "narrar" mis confidencias en un largo relato oral; o mejor, en una ininterrumpida carta "póstuma" a una sola destinataria: Jimena. Los que lleguen a leer estos papeles lo tendrán que hacer al sesgo como quien viola furtivamente, con el rabillo del ojo, el secreto de la correspondencia privada que alguien va leyendo a su lado.

Trato de escribirlos con el máximo de franqueza y lealtad que Jimena se merece. No es que padezca el temor de engañarme y engañarla aun involuntariamente, sino el de simular la sinceridad con aparentes reticencias u olvidos; esos cortes y veladuras que el narrador profesional practica por artificio todas las veces que le es necesario para acomodar el relato a sus intereses particulares; para decir la verdad como si mintiera, ocultándose él mismo en la comodidad e impunidad del testigo excluido. El procedimiento del narrador "omnisciente" me parece más engañoso aún. Una convención fraudulenta que nos viene de la epopeya antigua, o desde más lejos aún: desde la Biblia y aun de los Evangelios. La parábola del Hijo Pródigo, la más melosa y falaz de las que contienen el Nuevo Testamento, es un ejemplo de ello.

Ningún hijo pródigo o impródigo ha regresado jamás al solar paterno. Si vuelve, lo hace como un extraño o como un intruso molesto e inoportuno. Y esto, el propio Cristo lo supo mejor que nadie. Lo pagó con su sangre y tuvo que morir en la cruz para volver a su Reino celestial donde seguramente sigue siendo un extraño. Como lo es en la miserable sociedad que Él pretendió redimir. No redimió a los seres humanos. No evitó ni purificó los horrores de la vida, la estulticia del mundo, los rigores del destino. No en vano el místico Tomás de Kempis, como copiando el Eclesiastés y el Libro de Job, escribió en su *Imitación de Cristo* con espíritu transido: "Vivir en esta tierra es la peor de las desgracias".

Además de los *Papeles póstumos* me inventé también un juego, el viejo juego infantil de la linterna mágica, con un calidoscopio que compré en una tienda de antigüedades. Mediante linternas y diapositivas proyecto pequeños "cortos" coloreados sobre la cal del muro. Inocente esparcimiento de cineasta fracasado. La oscuridad alternativamente iluminada por los colores del espectro me relajan con su movilidad en una especie de ensoñación que anula el paso del tiempo.

El destierro mató en mí al hombre de cine. Ocurrió esto cuando se proyectó y hubo de realizarse, a medias, el filme sobre Solano López y Madama Elisa Lynch, que llegó a ser la virtual emperatriz del Paraguay. Uno de los grandes temas épicos del Paraguay y de América del Sur, donde la mujer es siempre el personaje principal detrás de algún gran hombre; a veces, al lado y en muchos casos hasta llevándole la delantera.

El guión inicial fue escrito por mí. Traté de relatar en él, con el mayor rigor y fidelidad posibles, la historia de estos personajes, ponerlos a la altura del papel histórico que desempeñaron en el martirologio de un pueblo. Al escribir ese libreto, no más importante como libreto que el de una ópera cualquiera, sentí en todo mi ser, sin poder evitarlo, el tremendo poder de los mitos de una raza, amasados con la sangre y el sacrificio de un pueblo mártir. Experimenté el estremecimiento de una revelación que anula de golpe todas nuestras dudas e incredulidades. Comprendí el inconcebible misterio —el de Solano López— de un alma sin freno, sin fe, sin ley, sin miedo, y que sin embargo luchaba ciegamente consigo misma más allá de los límites humanos. Luchó hasta el último aliento para evitar su caída en la degradación extrema de la cobardía o del miedo.

Ese miedo y esa cobardía le llegaron al final. El superhombre, el semidiós, huyó como el más común y timorato de los mortales. Huyó como un ciervo, herido en el vientre por la lanza de un corneta de órdenes. El gran hombre lanzó su cabalgadura a todo galope en dirección al río. Los intestinos desplegándose en el aire formaban una estela sanguinolenta en la crizada carrera. El caballo desbocado se detuvo de golpe ante las barrancas, volteó al huyente mariscal que rodó hasta caer de bruces en el fangoso arroyo. Logró girar aún hasta ponerse de costado enfrentando a sus perseguidores. Éstos se detuvieron atónitos al borde del barranco. El sol de la mañana arrancó destellos cegadores al corvo espadín que se alzó desde el barro en el temblor del puño moribundo, y de la boca brotó, entre espumarajos de sangre, el clamor que estremeció las selvas.

El mariscal estaba muerto. Tres veces muerto, por la colosal derrota, por la irrisoria lanza del corneta de órdenes enemigo, por la asfixia del ahogamiento en las aguas del manso arroyuelo que se encrespó y empezó a rugir como un torrente de lava.

Al llegar a la crucifixión de Solano López por las huestes brasileñas, sentí que esas lanzas despertaban en mí la capacidad del furor continuo y de rabiosa ulceración que llevó a aquel hombre de energía sobrehumana a sobrepasar todos los excesos de una guerra terrible e inútil. Y sin embargo esa derrota final e infamante era la afirmación de un heroísmo singular; era, sin tapujos, una victoria moral (si puede hablarse de moral en la barbarie de las guerras, cualesquiera sean sus causas y objetivos por sagrados que se proclamen).

Solano López obtuvo con su muerte y el exterminio de su pueblo un triunfo incalculablemente mayor que el de los vencedores; un triunfo logrado al precio de innumerables derrotas, de terrores abominables, de un orgullo abominable, de un abominable holocausto. La noche de su asesinato, las mujeres sobrevivientes del campamento fueron violadas por la soldadesca enemiga. Noche de alaridos, de espantosas escenas, de crueldades y sevicias inenarrables al resplandor vacilante de las fogatas. La ebriedad de la victoria celebró el obsceno aquelarre en el anfiteatro de Cerro-Corá, ante el cadáver del mariscal clavado en una cruz de ramas.

Las mujeres desnudas y espectrales vagaban por el monte masticando raíces y gordos gusanos silvestres, bebían en los arroyos. Fueron reconstituyendo poco a poco el éxodo en una peregrinación al revés, bordeando los acantilados, vadeando los ríos y los torrentes, sin más brújula que los brotes migratorios que volaban hacia el sur. Peregrinaban atadas a la ruta del sol. Por las noches, se tumbaban bajo los árboles, turnándose por grupos en la guardia del errante campamento. Cazaban en las selvas alimañas silvestres y se refugiaban a dormir en las cavernas. La rabia y el furor brillaban en los ojos desde el fondo de las cuencas excavadas en las caras acalaveradas.

A lo largo del camino interminable y sin rumbo iban recogiendo las armas abandonadas, cargaban las cajas de proyectiles y formaron sin ninguna idea preconcebida, sólo por instinto de autodefensa, un batallón que fue creciendo hasta formar un ejército redivivo de mujeres hirsutas, hambrientas y feroces, a las que estaba reservada una nueva guerra más despiadada aún que la anterior. Ésas fueron las últimas y terribles amazonas del Paraguay.

Solano estaba ahí, clavado en la cruz de ramas mal descortezadas, como el Cristo del retablo de Grünewald. Más trágico aún que en aquella espantosa representación. Solano estaba ahí desnudo, emasculado, monstruosamente deforme, la lanza atravesada en el costado. Estaba ahí, negro de moscas y avispas que libaban en las bocas tumefactas de las heridas la vejación del pus. La última iniquidad de los vencedores se cifraba en esa insignificante y miserable enormidad.

En cierto modo, era la realización del vaticinio obsecuente del padre Fidel Maíz, fiscal de los tribunales de sangre y capellán mayor del ejército de López. En una famosa homilía-arenga Maíz había ensalzado al jefe supremo llamándole el Cristo paraguayo. Los enemigos, sin saberlo, no habían hecho más que cumplir la profecía del cura fiscal.

Ahí estaba, sacrificado y muerto, el hombre que no supo redimir ni salvar a su pueblo. Un Redentor asesinado. El símbolo hecho carne. Una basura triunfal de su propia nada. La res exhumana pendiente de la cruz de troncos no era la carroña del Dios hecho hombre pintada por el genio de Grünewald con las tinieblas de su propia alma. Ahí estaba el Cristo de Cerro-Corá, sin aureola, sin nimbo, sin la enmarañada corona de espinas, el cuerpo sembrado de bocas purulentas cuyos grumos oscuros no servían ya mesmo sino pa juntar moscas, dijo el sargento que contaba la historia en el último vivac.

La tosca cruz se hallaba plantada a flor de tierra en

el centro del anfiteatro de Cerro-Corá, rodeada de fogatas cuyos carbones brillaban aún incandescentes despidiendo tenues rizos de humo azulado. El resto del mundo se escapaba en esas volutas con los restos de mi alma. Yo contemplaba hacia lo alto el gólgota montañoso, pero veía el cuerpo crucificado como en lo hondo de un precipicio que ningún sol de justicia iba a iluminar jamás. Estaba ahí ese cuerpo crucificado para el que no había ninguna resurrección posible en toda la eternidad.

Me acerqué a la cruz como en la oscuridad y en el silencio de un templo incendiado. Miré fijamente los ojos inyectados de sangre, vidriosos por la muerte, la enmarañada barba, moteada de grumos rojos, coágulos del último vómito de la agonía, la boca abierta, la mandíbula desquijarada, colgando sobre el pecho. Pequeños trozos del uniforme militar se hallaban pegoteados en las placas de pus por todo atavío sobre la desnudez tumefacta.

Ahí estaba el semidiós de un pueblo convertido en la ignominia de su podredumbre. Lo apostrofé en un estremecimiento de todo mi ser: ¡Has vencido al azar mediante una locura desaforada!... ¿Era necesario este espantoso delirio?... ¿Para qué?... Nadie lo sabe... Nadie podrá responder por ti... Estás aislado de la humanidad..., del tiempo..., de la vida... Has muerto con tu patria... No exhalaste estas palabras con tu último aliento. No las profirieron los profetas ni las escribieron los historiadores. Los hechos hablaron por tu boca llena del barro sangriento del enfurecido arroyuelo. Tu tierra ha desaparecido... Ya no tienes un sitio donde reposar... No lo tienes más ni siquiera en el corazón de tu raza que ha desaparecido contigo...

El bosque se erguía espectralmente a la luz de la luna. La inmensa extensión salvaje, el cuerpo colosal de la vida fecunda y misteriosa parecía contemplar impasible el espectáculo de la muerte de un hombre amarrado a la cruz. Desde sus profundidades surgió de repente, una lamentación trémula y prolongada de lúgubre miedo, de extrema desesperación, acaso como la que va a surgir tras la desaparición de los últimos sobrevivientes sobre la tierra. Cesó el fúnebre réquiem. El silencio volvió a pesar como una losa inmensa sobre la espesura.

La campana del pájaro de la muerte dobló en el monte...

Todos mis prejuicios y viejos anatemas contra López y la Lynch, contra el patrioterismo cimarrón de escarapela y machete, se borraron como bajo un soplo demasiado fuerte. Sólo quedaron en mí el horror y el furor. Arrojé la pluma contra la pared y me lancé con los últimos soldados a defender a ese Titán ya muerto, suprema encarnación de la raza.

Una dama de prodigiosa hermosura, vestida de blanco sin más arma que su blanca sombrilla con empuñadura de oro, salpicada de sangre, estaba al pie de la cruz, como una aparición de trasmundo, rígido el cuerpo, contemplando el cuerpo destrozado sin derramar una lágrima, sin proferir el menor lamento, ni siquiera ese suspiro hondo y último que se exhala cuando ya no hay más lamentación.

Un silencio de muerte sigue pesando sobre el campamento. La soldadesca de negros macacos brasileros se halla totalmente inmovilizada. Los jefes y oficiales del Imperio en traje de gala, rutilantes los pechos de condecoraciones bajo el sol de fuego, pasan ante ella con paso marcial, las espadas en alto, como rindiéndole honores, las barbas trémulas de deseo por esa mujer cuya irrealidad la vuelve ante sus ojos aún más carnal e ilusoria.

Cuando termina el desfile militar de los vencedores, Elisa Alicia, por encima de su duelo, sin derramar una lágrima, hace descender de la afrentosa cruz el cuerpo terriblemente ultrajado y profanado del Cristo paraguayo. Madama Lynch entierra los restos de Solano y del hijo

Panchito, el coronel de quince años, que la ha defendido con su espada antes de ser acribillado a tiros y a lanzazos. Unas pocas mujeres, los ojos calcinados por el llanto, la ayudan a cavar con sus manos esas dos tumbas y plantan sobre ella dos cruces sin nombre.

La mujer de blanco recoge su alba sombrilla tachada de sangre, monta a caballo, se aleja y se pierde al galope, seguida por su escolta de mujeres escuálidas, que van arrastrándose sobre sus pies llagados, los cuerpos esqueléticos apenas cubiertos de harapos. Una de ellas va envuelta en los jirones de una bandera de guerra. La selva se abre y se cierra sobre ellas sin dejar rastros.

La mezcla de tiniebla y de luz, de silencio sepulcral y del fragor del universo, se abatió sobre mí y me sumió en una atonía narcótica. Por un tiempo imprecisable, sólo hubo sombra y silencio. Los bosques formaban una masa impasible, más pesada que la puerta de una cárcel inmensa como la noche. De pronto oí voces que ondeaban acercándose y alejándose en las ráfagas de un viento venido de todas partes y de ninguna, fuera del mundo.

Raza inmemorial...
Tu tiempo ha caído en el vacío...
Desde ahora sólo vivirás en el pasado...

El coro se apagó... Hubo otra pausa pesada y prolongada en la que cayó del cielo un rocío de gotas gruesas con sabor a sal que calcinaba las copas de los árboles. La noche era negrísima. Había desaparecido en su propia oscuridad. No se la veía, como si también estuviera en prisión. Sólo iluminaban el vacío oscuro las gotas de fuego que caían del cielo y el fulgor ceniciento de los carbones. Todo estaba quieto, paralizado. De repente estalló un fragor sordo y continuo, distinto de la lamentación anterior. La selva estaba creciendo sin cesar. Se oía el fragor subte-

rráneo de raíces arrancadas. Los árboles, asfixiados, re-
montaban abandonando la tierra en busca del aire. Los
brotes y las semillas se alejaban en bandadas como aves
migratorias en busca de otras tierras más benignas, de otros
cielos menos enemigos.

Volvió el coro fantasmal. Ahora sólo se oían voces
agudas y chillonas, lamentaciones descompuestas y frenéti-
cas como las que arrastran en sus salmodias las lloronas en
velorios y entierros...

> *Lloremos la muerte de la patria...*
> *Ha muerto... y el simulacro que aún queda de ella*
> *sólo sirve para deshonrarla...*
> *Llegado es el tiempo de los ladrones,*
> *asesinos y sepultureros...*
> *¡Malditos sean por toda la eternidad!...*

La escena se esfumó súbitamente en un estampido
que explotó dentro de mí como si hubiera recibido en pleno
pecho la descarga de un pelotón de fusilamiento.

Vi de pronto mi mano lívida estrujando el libreto.
Lo alisé. Lo leí de nuevo. Me reconcilié con los encontrados sentimientos que combatían mi espíritu. Me dije, está
bien... No es un réquiem funerario. Tampoco un exaltado
canto a la gloria. Es sólo un libreto para una película. Relata los hechos del pasado bañados en el aguafuerte de la
época contemporánea. ¿Se puede pedir más? Sí. Todo. Pero
había que contentarse con poco. El libreto era apenas el
negativo de una historia que no se podía narrar en ningún
lenguaje. Aquel acontecimiento fantasmagórico superaba
todos los límites de la imaginación y las posibilidades de
expresión de la palabra y de la imagen.

Llegó el productor delegado, un norteamericano
del cine *underground*, marcado todavía por el sello de Hollywood. Exigía sensacionalismo y espectacularidad. La

verosimilitud, la fidelidad a la historia documental le tenían sin cuidado. "¡Bah!... —dijo Mr. Bottom—. A más de cien años, nadie podrá decir que esos detalles fueron verdaderos o falsos. Hay que dar a la gente lo que la gente pide como el pan. Terror, sexo, violencia, en sus crispaciones extremas. Éste es el alimento de nuestra civilización. Y no hay otro. Es también una necesidad religiosa. Violencia, sexo, terror son la Santísima Trinidad de nuestro tiempo, base del progreso material, incentivo del poder económico de nuestro mundo de civilización y abundancia..."

Rechazó mi libreto por encima del hombro casi sin haberlo leído. Hizo venir a su propio libretista quien además de no conocer la lengua ignoraba por completo la historia del pequeño e infortunado país. Bob Eyre estaba considerado como uno de los mejores guionistas de su país. En una semana entregó su versión al productor. Aprovechó gran parte del libreto hecho por mí, pero redujo la intriga al juego de dos personajes centrales. Madama Lynch y Pancha Garmendia, en torno a la silueta desvaída del mariscal López, convertido en personaje de opereta que parecía moverse todo el tiempo en ritmo de danza sobre el fondo ininterrumpido de los valses de Strauss.

El nudo argumental propuesto por Bob Eyre consistía en una guerra secreta entre las dos mujeres en contrapunto sobre el fondo de la "guerra grande". Rivales en el amor de un Solano López caricatural, se odiaban como sólo pueden odiarse la gacela y la pantera en la noche del Cazador.

Aparte de las reuniones con los oficiales de su estado mayor y algunas visitas a los frentes en retirada, el Mariscal Presidente imaginado por Bob Eyre se pasaba el tiempo en su tienda de campaña haciéndose cuidar los pies, unos pies femeninos y ridículamente pequeños. Las botas militares, de tacones muy altos, las pierneras inmensas, le llegaban hasta las ingles. El brillo del lustrado charol iba delante de él alumbrándole el camino. Daba la impresión de que el mariscal de los ejércitos paraguayos caminaba en puntillas para compensar su baja estatura, hamacándose como un pistolero del Far West. Solano López y la Lynch "hacían" los protagonistas de la historia y Pancha Garmendia, la agonista muda, la víctima sacrificial.

Era una empresa temeraria y en cierto modo delirante, dado que esos personajes encarnan las más puras glorias nacionales. El tiranosaurio se considera su depositario, continuador y garante perpetuo. Yo estaba seguro de que no iba a llegar a buen fin. Se lo advertí al productor, que se alzó de hombros y me redujo al mínimo e inútil papel de asesor literario. Distribuyó mucho dinero en papeles verdes a los intermediarios del gobierno. El rodaje comenzó en seguida.

Un testigo de la época relató en sus *Memorias* que los hombres, mujeres y niños de la región caminaban a través de las ramas de los árboles, como ardillas, para no perderse el espectáculo jamás visto ni imaginado por ellos, creyendo que se trataba de un nuevo carnaval o de una nueva guerra.

"Todos los monos del Paraguay —escribe— acudieron al anfiteatro de Cerro-Corá, atraídos por los cañonazos, y contribuyeron con sus chillidos a la música de fondo." Detalle que al director le encantó. A las ráfagas de los proyectores las siluetas polvorientas de personas y de simios, arracimados en las ramas de copudos árboles y en las altas palmeras, se confundían en una extraña fraternidad, mientras abajo, en un simulacro más creíble que la propia realidad, los hombres se mataban al resplandor de los proyectores. Estalló el relámpago de un corto circuito que desencadenó el incendio de la selva virgen. La hoguera empujada por el viento se fue expandiendo sobre varias leguas de extensión, ante el desbande enloquecido de personas y de monos que huían en medio de espantosos chillidos y alaridos. Las lenguas de fuego subían hasta las nubes. Los montes y valles del Aquidabán quedaron convertidos en campos de cenizas humeantes.

En el libreto de Bob Eyre, como en el mío, la acción transcurre en las postrimerías de la guerra. Se decidió que el nuevo guión permaneciera secreto. Era la negación de la historia oficial. La había vuelto del revés y había que ocultar el fraude. La película empezó a rodarse en un desorden laberíntico de secuencias, de modo que la farsa desaforada y guiñolesca pasara de contrabando la carga de terror, sexo y violencia, las tres unidades caras a los principios del productor.

La Lynch y Pancha Garmendia, al comienzo, no sólo eran rivales en cuanto al amor del semidiós de la guerra que parecía brotado de una tragedia griega. Lo eran también en cuanto a su hermosura. En lo físico, las diferenciaba el color de sus cabelleras: rojiza en la irlandesa; negra y flotante en la paraguaya. En lo espiritual y humano, las diferencias eran abismales. La belleza de la extranjera pertenecía a una naturaleza altanera y estancada. La aguda, codiciosa e implacable crueldad de sus facciones daba a su cabeza una especie de vibración luminosa. Sobre sus párpados se extendía algo que se asemejaba mucho a una fina capa de hielo. Su rostro era un solo bloque de cálculo bajo el metálico resplandor de sus ojos color turquesa, casi violáceos. Esa belleza imperativa parecía de otro mundo.

La hermosura de la nativa era suave y lunar. El poder de su espíritu estaba concentrado en los ojos del mismo color de su pelo que daban a su rostro un halo de candor y de misterio. De ella decían sus contemporáneos: "Tal vez ninguna mujer en la tierra ha tenido una belleza semejante". Y este proverbio exasperaba la envidia de la cortesana que Solano López trajo de los ambientes elegantes de París e impuso a la sociedad paraguaya como una verdadera emperatriz. Eran supuestamente casados pero realmente concubinarios.

Acaso el mariscal paraguayo, que se declaraba amigo de Napoleón III, quiso emular y superar el ejemplo de Maximiliano de Habsburgo, en México. La historia dio otro rumbo a esas aventuras imperiales casi simultáneas. Maximiliano fue juzgado y mandado fusilar por Juárez, en Querétaro, en 1867. Solano López, como un vulgar bandido de fronteras, fue lanceado en 1870, mientras huía, por un cabo, el corneta de órdenes del jefe brasilero, el desde entonces célebre *Chico Diavo*. Borrachas de alcohol y de victoria, las tropas del conde D'Eu violaron a las mujeres y crucificaron el cadáver del mariscal en medio de una espantosa bacanal.

Los destinos de Carlota Amalia y de Elisa Alicia también fueron semejantes y distintos. Vivieron hasta la vejez, la una en mansa locura, olvidada de todo lo que no fuera su amor por el emperador; la otra, en la obsesión demencial de recuperar el fenecido esplendor de su poder, las tierras que le legara el mariscal, su inmenso tesoro enterrado a lo largo de las rutas del éxodo en los centenares de enormes carretones que los transportaban. Los carreteros tenían que morder el pescuezo de los bueyes ya en pura osamenta para hacerlos avanzar. La custodia militar les hacía depositar los grandes cofres metálicos en los lugares prefijados. La reata de prisioneros cavaba los fosos a enorme profundidad sin que se les sacara las cadenas de los grillos. Carreteros y prisioneros eran arrojados vivos a los fosos que se llenaban de tierra. La selva volvía a crecer pronto sobre los claros hasta ocultar por completo las huellas del "entierro".

Durante mucho tiempo el resplandor de ese nuevo El Dorado enterrado surgió de los acantilados, de los lagos, de las entrañas de la tierra arrasada y produjo nuevos éxodos y peregrinaciones en pos de la divinidad engendrada por la guerra: el *Madama-kuarepotyju-yvyguy*, el "oro enterrado de Madama". Pero esto sucedió mucho después. Y lo relatan mejor que yo otros cronistas.

En el comienzo de la historia, según el libreto de Bob Eyre, cuando la Lynch empezó a reinar, la Pancha (así era conocida en todo el país) se recluyó con su madre en un solitario aislamiento, poco después de la muerte de su padre, de origen argentino y antigua prosapia hispánica, a quien López mandó fusilar por considerarlo implicado en una conjura contra su vida y gobierno. Como en todos los casos similares, también sus bienes le fueron totalmente confiscados. Pancha Garmendia y su madre quedaron reducidas a la extrema pobreza. A muy pocos se les escaparon los verdaderos motivos de este asesinato, manipulados indirectamente por la Lynch. Estas supuestas causas no eran otras sino el hecho de que el respetado estanciero Garmendia fuera el padre de Pancha, con lo que la descarga del pelotón de ejecución también la hirió a ella moral y mortalmente.

Al estallar la guerra, la emperatriz arreció su ofensiva contra la rival plebeya. "Esa mujerzuela descalza caerá en mis manos... Vendrá a pedirme limosna y yo la emplearé como lavandera...", se desahogaba con sus confidentes en la corte de adulonas y soplonas incondicionales que formaban su séquito.

En el rodaje de la película, las actrices, igualmente deslumbrantes, supieron sacar un efecto dramático insuperable de esta rivalidad. Pocas veces se vio en el cine —a juzgar por lo que quedó de la película— la interpretación de un duelo femenino de tales dimensiones, con semejante perfección. Las dos actrices llevaban en cada uno de sus gestos la pasión y el furor de la sangre que arrasaron a las protagonistas. En medio de aquella guerra que acabó con un pueblo, la guerra entre las dos mujeres era aún más inmisericorde y cruel: una historia de lírico y trasnochado romanticismo puesta en abismo dentro de otra escena de indescriptible barbarie.

La derrota había sellado desde el comienzo la lenta y furiosa guerra de exterminio para el orgulloso jefe paraguayo que se consideraba el Napoleón del Plata. Hacia el final de esta bárbara contienda, la guerra invisible y secreta entre las dos mujeres, reveló a los más cercanos de la emperatriz, en un giro inesperado y terrible, la verdadera naturaleza de su enfermiza obsesión. El odio había acabado trans- formándose en su corazón en un amor aún más violento y demencial. La consternación cundió en el campamento. Pero como suele ocurrir, el secreto público se mantuvo mejor guardado que el secreto privado.

Ocurrió otro hecho, no menos significativo, ligado con el anterior. Pancha Garmendia fue también acusada de ser el enlace de una conspiración —una de las tantas— contra el mariscal. Tras interminables interrogatorios y bárbaras sesiones de tortura fue condenada a muerte por los fiscales de sangre, junto con otras cincuenta personas, en su mayor parte mujeres. Era evidente que los testimonios sobre la supuesta conspiración habían sido urdidos por la Lynch, cosa que ésta no trató de ocultar sino que, por el contrario, se empeñó en darle la mayor publicidad posible.

En otra vuelta de prensa, que llevaba su sello, la propia Madama Lynch intercedió para que se suspendiera o se conmutara la pena en favor de Pancha Garmendia, la principal acusada. El plan de la Lynch se hizo evidente para los que se hallaban enterados de esta "conjura", que ya se había hecho cíclica y permanente desde el comienzo mismo de la guerra. Pero también en los tribunales de guerra se guardó celosamente el secreto. Y una manera de ocultarlo con más seguridad y rigor legal fue la de proseguir los interrogatorios y los suplicios cada vez más encarnizados. En los intervalos, el P. Fidel Maíz, director espiritual de los tribunales de sangre, trataba de influir sobre la prisionera bajo sacramento de confesión, sin obtener mejores resultados que la propia Lynch.

En el éxodo de las condenadas, Pancha Garmendia no era ya más que un espectro como las otras millares y millares de mujeres que iban arreadas hacia la muerte. Pero este espectro, apenas cubierto por andrajos, había acabado de enloquecer por completo a la emperatriz. La pasión secreta e inconfesable la había arrasado en la única y ansiosa voluptuosidad que son capaces de experimentar en medio del terror y de la muerte los seres destinados a cohabitaciones ocultas.

La omnipotente y obcecada mujer del Mariscal había ofrecido a Pancha Garmendia una coartada para su salvación: la de convertirla en su "dama de compañía". Ésta se negó hasta el final con un desprecio impasible que la proximidad de la muerte hacía más injurioso. Parecía ignorarla, no verla siquiera cuando la llevaban a su presencia. Al borde del anonadamiento, Pancha Garmendia encontró aún fuerzas para cortarse la lengua con los dientes como hacían los que caían prisioneros del enemigo. Quiso eludir así hasta el último aliento los interrogatorios del tribunal de sangre. Y acaso, con mayor razón, permanecer muda ante la emperatriz extranjera que la acosaba con alucinado empecinamiento.

Hubo un último encuentro con la Lynch. Ésta pidió verla antes de su ejecución. Pancha fue arrastrada a su presencia. Su vida había concluido antes de su muerte. La sostenía sólo esa fuerza sobrenatural de las víctimas inocentes que se resisten a desaparecer antes de ver aniquilados a sus verdugos. La mudez y el desprecio ya irremediables, el fuego de una conciencia insobornable, de su virtud sin tacha, eran las únicas armas que ese cadáver ambulante podía oponer a su rival. La mujer todopoderosa amaba y seguiría amando más allá de la muerte a este ser frágil pero indomable. Amaba todo lo que ella era; amaba en ese espectro todo lo que a ella le faltaba: su femineidad pura e inmarcesible, su espíritu de sacrificio. Le aterraba su espantoso silencio. Su enloquecida pasión no había logrado contaminar a la joven mujer que ella destruyó lentamente sin conseguir apoderarse de su cuerpo y de su alma.

Iba a insistir por última vez. La condenada se desplomó. Creyeron que había querido hincarse de rodillas ante la emperatriz para demandarle una última gracia. La Lynch intentó ayudarla para incorporarse. Lo que quedaba de Pancha le lanzó a la cara un espumarajo de sangre. Trémula de una cólera demente, la emperatriz la castigó rabiosamente con su fusta de campaña hasta que el brazo, muerto de cansancio, se le cayó a un costado. Pancha estaba erguida en una especie de halo rojizo. Cuando la Lynch se le acercó, la agónica silueta volvió a escupir su sangre en el rostro lívido. La Lynch pasó la mano por sus mejillas, se limpió la sangre y la llevó a sus labios cerrando los ojos. Dio orden de que se cumpliera inmediatamente la sentencia. Pancha Garmendia fue lanceada contra el montículo de una trinchera. La emperatriz, en traje de generala, presenció la ejecución montada en su caballo. La rodeaba el batallón de mujeres de su escolta, que aullaban enronquecidas sus gritos de odio y de victoria. La emperatriz bajó la espada y la ejecución comenzó.

Las armas de fuego se habían acabado. Los soldados, niños de diez a quince años (los últimos soldados que le quedaban a Solano López), apenas podían con las lanzas, de modo que la carnicería fue atroz. Petrificados de espanto, los niños-soldados contemplaron aún, tras la ejecución, otra escena inenarrable, ésta ya incomprensible para ellos: vieron desmontar de un salto a la emperatriz y arrojarse de rodillas junto al cuerpo aún caliente de Pancha. La abrazó con desesperación y la besó largamente en la boca como queriendo devolverle la vida que ella había mandado quitarle. Sus edecanes la llevaron en vilo, el uniforme de amazona cubierto de sangre, estremecida por los espasmos de una lamentación interior que estalló en un solo grito de fiera mortalmente herida; "un grito salvaje que no podía salir sino de la vulva de una loba", escribió un cronista de la época.

Pronto el tiranosaurio se enteró del verdadero sesgo que estaba tomando el filme en transgresión del libreto autorizado —el mío—, escena por escena, y censurado en todo lo que iba contra el "honor nacional". El jefe de seguridad del campo de rodaje le relató la escena final entre la Lynch y Pancha Garmendia. Dio orden de que las tropas de asalto acabaran con la "mascarada" del panfleto antihistórico y antiparaguayo. Bajo el fuego de morteros y ametralladoras el centenar de actrices, actores y técnicos y los cinco millares de "extras" que acampábamos en las serranías de Cerro-Corá, tuvimos que huir por la picada del Chirigüelo sembrada de cadáveres y cañones de utilería. Helicópteros de la Fuerza Hemisférica vinieron desde São Paulo a rescatar a las actrices y actores extranjeros. Éstos contemplaron, divertidos, esta otra pequeña guerra, que no figuraba en el libreto, pero que parecía formar parte realmente de la Gran Guerra de hacía más de un siglo.

El libreto de Bob Eyre no ahorró ningún detalle como para que la epopeya sagrada para los paraguayos cayera en el absurdo y el grotesco más infames. Pero ese absurdo y ese grotesco llevados a su máxima exasperación, desde el punto de vista fílmico, eran geniales. No se podía negar que el cine-drama imaginado por Bob Eyre había alcanzado y sobrepasado, al menos en estas secuencias, las cimas del estremecimiento del horror.

Más de cinco mil toneladas de equipos de filmación quedaron abandonados en los acantilados en medio de la selva virgen. El productor regresó a Asunción. Bottom quiso recuperar sus equipos y el millón de dólares que había pagado por la autorización del rodaje. Le hicieron ir de un lugar a otro. No recogía otra cosa que las risotadas y burlas en guaraní de los funcionarios. Cuando la embajada de su país quiso intervenir, fue expulsado sin miramientos.

La historia de aquel segundo Cerro-Corá donde Solano López fue crucificado por los enemigos cien años antes como el Cristo paraguayo, según la historia del P. Fidel Maíz, capellán general del ejército y fiscal mayor de los tribunales de sangre, no pasó de ser un melodrama. En la película trunca se llegó hasta la escena de la crucifixión. Guardo un fragmento de esta secuencia. Suelo contemplar de vez en cuando en mi linterna mágica los fotogramas del Cristo de Cerro-Corá, que horrorizó a Jimena cuando los vio por primera vez reflejados en la cal del muro.

Hay algunos rollos de la filmación que circulan clandestinamente por las cinematecas internacionales: una mescolanza indescifrable de escenas de barbarie y de terror alumbradas por el fuego de las batallas. Pudo esta epopeya fílmica constituir el mayor testimonio sobre aquella alucinante hecatombe de un pueblo, de un país. Las cosas sucedieron de otra manera. Aquella aventura que quiso registrar en imágenes el "duro siglo de la Patria", es ahora menos que un sueño para mí. No se repetirá.

Con los demás componentes del equipo paraguayo fui capturado y llevado a las siniestras mazmorras de la Secreta. La operación de "limpieza antisubversiva" terminó como de costumbre en el más espeso silencio nacional e internacional. Ya habían más de un millón de proscritos. Unos cuantos más no importaban demasiado ni alteraban la estadística de los grandes números con la que se maneja el tirano, incluso en sus finanzas personales muy superiores a las del país.

Recuerdo que tras una de las últimas sesiones de picana eléctrica y repetidos baños de inmersión en la pileta pestilencial de la cámara de torturas, creí morir. Trataba de recordar el procedimiento que usaban los prisioneros en la Guerra Grande para tragarse la lengua y morir por asfixia. Mis esfuerzos terminaban siempre en arcadas y vómitos. En la pared de la celda con la punta de un dedo tinto en mi sangre escribí un epitafio que era a la vez una despedida. Decía simplemente: "Estoy bien". Un año después lograba fugarme de la enfermería policial donde me habían internado casi moribundo y donde pasé varios meses encadenado a la camilla de hierro empotrada en el cemento del sótano.

Aquel epitafio era también el de mi vida. Siempre estoy bien. He vivido como quien viaja. Incluso en los largos periodos de inmovilidad. Nunca tuve la sensación de pertenecer por completo a algún lugar, a un grupo, a una raza. Extranjero en todas partes, me sentía especialmente extraño, aislado aun en medio en la multitud, siempre solo, únicamente en mí, hasta que encontré a Jimena.

Con mi calidoscopio y el pequeño triángulo de espejos estroboscópicos mato ahora el tiempo contra la pared. Practico mi entretenimiento de sombrografías. De tanto en tanto, cuando me acomete el melancólico reflujo de recuerdos que parecen ya de otra vida, suelo proyectar la secuencia de la crucifixión (la única que logré rescatar de la frustrada película de Bottom y Bob Eyre). La imagen llena la oscuridad de un siniestro resplandor de infierno. La música del réquiem de Mozart da a las imágenes mortuorias una tensión por momentos intolerable. A veces se me escapan sollozos. Me río a carcajadas para disimularlos. En realidad, la imagen del Cristo paraguayo no es más que la imagen de una ruina. ¿Y qué es una ruina sino una imagen estancada en el Tiempo? El tiempo liberado de su duración.

En realidad, esa imagen atroz no es más que la ruina de un alma, tal vez de la mía, puesto que no existe en el individuo un tiempo mensurable sino innumerables tiempos que entretejen la maraña del cosmos, incomprensible a los ojos humanos. Los sueños no podrán descifrar jamás esa vorágine infinita del caos matemático. No vemos sino un pueril juego de sombras que se acercan y se separan. La locura y el delirio no perciben el paso del tiempo. Tampoco lo percibe la pequeña muerte de la cópula. En esas fracciones de segundos franqueamos el umbral de lo invisible... Nos sentimos caer en el vacío. Por un instante el ritmo del cuerpo se acompasa con los espasmos de la tierra. Queremos hundirnos para siempre en ese blando misterio, infinito y efímero del cuerpo del otro. Despertamos de la muerte fugaz con la sensación de haber realizado un esfuerzo terrible al haber cohabitado a la vez con las hermanas gemelas de la felicidad y la desdicha, con los dioses mellizos del goce y del sufrimiento.

Jimena trabaja en la preparación de sus clases. Busca en los códices esa cuarta dimensión del pasado precolombino, el sentido del sacrificio y de la muerte en los pueblos vencidos. Ha creído encontrar, entre los mayas, que sus mitos de origen consideraban el tiempo como elemento indisociable del espacio material. Tiempo era para ellos el rito del sacrificio pero también la piedra sacrificial; los movimientos ceremoniales de matemática exactitud coreográfica, los ritmos, las voces, los cánticos guturales, pero también el espacio de las ceremonias; la sangre corriendo sobre la piedra, pero también la duración del fuego, las figuras de las volutas de humo a la luz de luna.

—Sé que nuestra mente racional no descifrará ja más este misterio —decía—. Pero es reconfortante pensar que la cultura sólo es el cultivo de las diferencias entre los grupos humanos en su relación con la naturaleza.

Yo disentía en silencio, pero no podía seguirla en estas divagaciones a un mismo tiempo lentas y vertiginosas. Jimena explora como una arqueóloga apasionada esta increí- ble facultad de percepción del cosmos en las culturas llamadas "primitivas". En su animismo cosmogónico conocían el origen y la edad del universo cuyo rostro se reveló para ellos en la abstracción del cero, en la materia del tiempo formando parte del espacio inmaterial. Esto exalta a Jimena. Me dice que encontró algo parecido entre los guaraníes. Para ellos "las hermosas palabras del principio" inauguraron el tiempo juntamente con la creación del mundo por el Primer Padre-Último-Último-Primero. Jimena estuvo en Paraguay y recorrió las rutas de peregrinación, los confiscados territorios y lugares sagrados de las antiguas etnias, que hasta ahora vagan por ellos, perseguidas y diezmadas en un éxodo interminable.

—¡Félix!... —me gritaba desde la cocina, removiendo los leños en la hornalla. Nunca quiso tener una cocina eléctrica, ni televisor ni ninguno de esos *gadgets* electrónicos, símbolos del consumismo en la sociedad de la opulencia. Usa la llama viva. Y cuando faltó el carbón, empezó a usar leños que ella misma trozaba en el bosque y arrastraba en un trineo de patín y ruedas que le sirve en invierno y verano sobre nieve y cemento para traer las provisiones del supermercado.

—Ven a comer. Pareces un encapuchado envuelto por la niebla.

Volvía el rostro hacia esa voz que parecía llegarme desde muy lejos a través de un acueducto. Y era ella la que se hallaba envuelta por el humo. Morena Tarsis convertida en una silueta transparente y brumosa. Ese humo con olor a especias aromáticas, a resinas de árboles añosos, el aroma del pan dorándose en el horno, se volvían perfume impalpable en su ropa, en su cabellera, en su piel.

En Nevers todo es distinto. Por la mañana y hacia el atardecer veo subir entre los árboles, a lo lejos, los vapores del Loira. Oigo pasar por el cielo bandadas de pájaros migratorios. Mientras escribo llegan hasta mí los olores tempranos de la primavera. La primavera en Nevers es incomparable. Se diría que se la puede tocar con las manos. Salgo y me tiendo sobre el césped. El aire, los olores, los colores dejan sentir su densidad. Contemplo el cielo y cierro los ojos. Siento pesar entonces suavemente su comba altísima sobre los párpados. Froto la cara en la seda impalpable de esa palpitación luminosa como hacen los gatos en las faldas de sus dueñas. Froto el cuerpo contra la hierba húmeda hasta quedar distendido y elástico como un gato joven.

El aire es azul y tiñe de azul el perfil de las torres, las aristas de los edificios, de las murallas, del palacio ducal. La vieja ciudad se desangra sobre el filo de sus bordes manando una pelusilla de vapor azulado. Lo extraordinario sucede después. El cielo rojo del poniente va borrando rápidamente el diáfano azul que vuelve a teñir el cielo cuando cae la oscuridad, más luminoso aún en las noches sin luna. Palpitan estrellas enormes y gordas, a punto de reventar, al alcance de las manos. La tierra hace un ruido como de flojos suspiros. Luego desaparece en la bruma. No hay más sonido que el rumor del viento, ladridos lejanos, algún mugido, algún balido. Hay la estridulación sorda y soterrada de los grillos, voces rotas a lo lejos, el distante rumor de los motores.

Ayer por la tarde tomamos mate por primera vez en la glorieta que Jimena hizo construir en torno al brocal de un viejo pozo ciego, en los fondos del jardín, mientras yo me hallaba en el hospital. El brocal hexagonal tallado toscamente con motivos irreconocibles y cubierto con un pesado redondel de roca, hace de mesa. Semeja vagamente un dolmen prehistórico sobre el cual está posada la pava de agua hirviendo en la llama azulada del calentador a alcohol. Le he hecho bromas a Jimena sobre su glorieta "gaélica". Las doradas y olorosas argollas de "chipá" en la canastilla adornada de jazmines, ponen una nota exótica sobre la roca cubierta por un albo mantel de *ao-poi*. En realidad, el mate paraguayo, acompañado por trozos del buen chipá casero de Jimena, tiene un gusto muy distinto en estos rincones de antigüedad siempre joven.

—Me gusta Nevers —dije llevado por el aire de serenidad y paz que flotaba a nuestro alrededor—. Suena a *nunca*, en inglés; a *nadie*, en latín; a *siempre*, en guaraní. La muerte parece no existir en Nevers. No se ven cortejos ni coches fúnebres. No se oyen doblar campanas. Es como si la muerte sólo se hubiera transformado en una enfermedad invisible que cada uno la lleva escondida bajo la ropa.

—Sí, todo sucede en silencio —dijo Jimena.

Después, en la casa, trajo un diario viejo (tampoco leemos diarios, ni revistas de actualidades). Lo abrió en la sección del obituario. Había una buena lista de nombres. Pero eran nombres frescos y lozanos de gente que no parecía haber muerto sino que sólo participaba que había ido a tomar sus vacaciones en la playa o en la montaña para hacer esquí o lanzarse en los deltaplanos desde los ventisqueros.

Me repuse insensiblemente como el aparecido que vuelve de un equivocado y prematuro viaje a la Estigia. Hay lugares que curan y hay lugares que matan. Nevers volvió a ser para mí el lugar de vida, de moroso recogimiento. Y los trastos de Jimena no me molestaban en lo más mínimo; al contrario, me acompañaban con su muda presencia en las que el tiempo se había coagulado. Jimena los cuidaba con minuciosa devoción. Esa colección heterogénea era su paisaje interior y yo lo amaba tanto como detestaba el mío, desnudo de todo signo que identificara mis deseos o mis repulsiones.

Comprendo que Jimena haya puesto en ese "museo" un designio de nostalgia anticipada: el de los que se complacen en amontonar recuerdos de una vida en común sin pensar en la vulnerabilidad del futuro que no garantiza las uniones más firmes ni la invulnerabilidad de la memoria. ¿Presentía tal vez que tarde o temprano iba a quedarse sola? Sabía que tarde o temprano yo iba a volver *allá*. Entonces la "personalidad" de la casa se volvería contra ella, convirtiéndola en una figura más, tallada en carne viva. Una virgen alta, blanca y esbelta, de cabellera bruna hasta la cintura, entre las vírgenes enanas de barnices resquebrajados y los toscos angelotes tallados por los neófitos guaraníes de las Misiones jesuíticas en la madera de árboles centenarios. Las vetas agrietadas ponen arrugas de viejo en los rostros mofletudos de esos querubines que volaron desde las ruinas jesuíticas para aposentarse en esta vieja casa de Nevers.

Muy pronto me atacarían de nuevo esas dos obsesiones larvadas en mi segunda naturaleza de "gringo" camuflado: el no saber qué hacer y el querer saber cómo poder hacerlo. Algo útil y no puramente vegetativo en la angustia del exilio. Encontrar un motivo por el cual estuviese dispuesto a morir por los demás y no ser salvado cada vez como un náufrago a la deriva. No regresar después de cada derrota, sano y salvo, al santuario y refugio de posibilidades inéditas para encontrarse uno digno de la indulgente aprobación de los demás. Siempre traté de desarrollar todo mi pensamiento sobre la cosa más mínima hasta sus últimas consecuencias: ir hasta el fondo de mí en ese misterio sin fondo que es uno mismo.

Esta obsesión del regreso es una idea fija. Una idea falsa, perturbadora. Una idea fija que me atraviesa sin descanso y que me sostiene. Una aguja fija que marca un norte errátil dentro de mí. Mi divisa no podía seguir siendo: "Pienso porque ignoro". No ignoraba, no pensaba, no existía. Me asfixiaba.

Pedí con un gesto a Jimena que dejara entrar a *Yaguareté*. Con toda la solemnidad de que fue capaz, el noble dálmata con nombre guaraní entró como si llevara las coronas blancas y negras del río Paraguay sobre su lomo, y empezó a lamerme la mano. Veía mis ojos reflejados en los suyos, brillantes y comprensivos. La esposa del Rector, que nos lo regaló cuando era todavía un cachorrillo, nos previno. Es una raza muy extraña, dijo. Parecen seres humanos. Sólo les falta el habla. Adivinan cosas. La madre de este pequeñín murió de sobreparto y en medio del delirio de la fiebre sus quejidos expresaban claramente su temor a la muerte, sus ansias de que le salvaran la vida. Mientras pudo mantuvo levantadas las patas delanteras como defendiéndose contra algo que la amenazaba de frente. Murió con la cabeza entre las patas apelotonándose en un rollo duro que nadie pudo deshacer. La tuvieron que enterrar en un hoyo redondo y profundo en los fondos del jardín.

La piel sedosa de *Yaguareté* comunica a mis manos el calor de una amistad a cubierto de traiciones y olvidos. Lo mismo que *Laurel*, el pequeño perro criollo de mi infancia en Manorá. Murió mordido por una *ñandurié*, una víbora pequeña, la más pequeña pero una de las más venenosas que reptan en las malezas del Paraguay. Había estado yo a punto de pisarla sin verla. *Laurel* se abalanzó contra ella y los colmillos mortales que me estaban destinados se le clavaron en el hocico. Fue entonces cuando le cambié el nombre al pueblo de Itapé por el de Manorá, que quiere decir en guaraní *Lugar-para-la-muerte*.

Jimena me ayudó pacientemente a recobrar mis movimientos hasta que pude apoyar mi sombra en el suelo. Juré no volver más a París. Esta historia sin embargo, para bien o para mal, ha comenzado en París. Esta historia ha comenzado anoche, con el llamado de Clovis desde París. Ha comenzado con el anuncio de una noticia, pero no tengo aún la menor idea de qué se trata. No sé si esta historia continuará, qué rumbo tomará, si realmente me concierne o me incluye. Jimena ha quedado tan desconcertada como yo. No te preocupes, le dije. Debe de ser una nueva broma de Clovis.

Dos años después de mi frustrada segunda muerte, me sentía de nuevo fuerte y animoso. Acaso porque la vida le preserva a uno para el solo acto, el único e irrepetible que puede justificar una existencia, la más gris y mediocre. He reflexionado muchas veces sobre cuál puede ser para mí este acto extremo y último que me justifique. No he llegado a ninguna conclusión valedera. Nadie tal vez pueda saberlo. Los hechos son los que se encargan de ponernos a prueba llegado el momento. Es un tema sobre el cual no se puede conversar en serio con nadie. Ni siquiera con Jimena siempre dispuesta sin embargo a escuchar mis divagaciones sobre la tierra que a su imagen me hizo para de sí arrojarme, como susurra entre dientes el poema de Luis Cernuda, muerto en destierro.

—Tengo que encontrar *eso*... —murmuré.

No oí mi voz, pero Jimena ya conocía la cantinela. Continuó mi pensamiento como si también reflexionara en su interior. Nunca sabe uno cuándo encuentra *eso* que ha buscado siempre y que aparece cuando ya uno no lo necesita. Como si estuviera condenado a caminar de espaldas, dijo con el aire de una momentánea resignación. Le contesté que aun ciego, sordo y mudo hay momentos en que todo lo que ha sido y es el ser humano puede condensarse en un acto supremo de rescate para sí y para los demás.

Jimena no cree en el azar de ese rescate siempre improbable. Pareces, me dice, un niño poseso, embaucado por la idea de la "redención", vestigio de esas tontainas de la religión católica que absorbiste en tu casa llena de curas, de monjas, de esa gente entre loca y mesiánica que se cree destinada al sacrificio. Esta vez fue un poco más lejos. Pasó la uña por la costura del nervio. ¿Te consideras tú capaz de ese acto supremo? ¿Te consideras el elegido?

Dije que era uno entre cinco millones. Hay una situación límite sin retorno posible en la que todo se juega a cara o cruz, en un relámpago, deslicé sibilinamente tratando de no poner énfasis en esa frase rimbombante y trivial.

—Sí, pero esa situación límite no se presenta a todos, ni todos los días —replicó Jimena—. Tampoco se la puede elegir como en un bazar de fantasías. Esa situación límite, cuando se presenta, lo elige a uno.

No me arredra el peligro. He luchado a brazo partido con la muerte en varias ocasiones y en medio de las circunstancias más increíbles. El riesgo de morir en un atentado contra el ser que se odia profundamente es la confrontación menos excitante que puede arrostrar el hombre menos valiente y temerario. Lo único necesario, lo único que redime es la sola idea de *hacerlo*. Una creencia absoluta en esa idea. Un acto en el que pueda uno ofrendarse en sacrificio. Rematar al tirano puede cambiar por completo la suerte de una sociedad esclavizada. Es éste el objetivo que cuenta. La liquidación de un hombre nefasto y mediocre cuyo poder absoluto sólo ha podido forjarse sobre la absoluta debilidad de los oprimidos es sólo un medio de lograrlo.

La expresión de Jimena era poco aprobatoria. La duda y el difuso temor se mezclaban en ella. Sé que estoy condenado al fracaso, admití. Pero aun así debo persistir como cuando uno está luchando con todas sus fuerzas en medio de una corriente que lo arrastra. La esperanza diferida es mejor que nada. No hay cosa más pérfida y malsana que la esperanza, dijo Jimena con cierta energía. Sobre todo cuando representa lo que no se ha poseído nunca.

Pienso en mi país, sitiado y masacrado. Tiene que producirse ese acto único e irrepetible por el que un individuo o un pueblo se redima del poder inhumano que lo sojuzga. Jimena recuerda el sacrificio del pueblo español en la guerra civil. Un millón de muertos y otro millón de desterrados no evitaron la tiranía de Franco ni tuvieron el peso necesario para hacerlo caer o para hacerlo volar por el aire como a Carrero Blanco.

El tiranosaurio no volará por los aires. He estudiado en detalle los planes del casi centenar de conspiraciones y atentados fallidos que lleva en su haber, y he sacado la conclusión de que el error principal de todos ellos ha sido emplear los métodos rutinarios ya inútiles: las balas, las granadas de mano, los túneles subterráneos bajo el palacio de gobierno o al paso de su itinerario cotidiano; los aviones en picada sobre los palcos oficiales durante los desfiles de las fiestas patrias; los coche-bombas; los francotiradores de élite apostados en los techos al paso de la caravana presidencial.

Todo esto sin contar que en el auto blindado del tirano viaja siempre un sosia convenientemente camuflado, rutilante de estrellas y condecoraciones, mientras él se escapa en un coche común, vestido de paisano, por vericuetos distintos, rastrillados todos los días por las fuerzas de seguridad y vigilados por cuadrillas enteras de supuestos peones de vialidad pero que en realidad son informantes de la policía.

La muerte del tirano no solucionará todo, dijo Jimena. Mejor dicho, no solucionará nada. Lo que venga después será peor. Un baño de sangre y una guerra civil interminable. Como sucedió en España. Aproveché para forzar mi réplica. El ejemplo de España, dije, refuerza la imperiosa necesidad de acabar allá, cuanto antes.

Preguntó cuántos han sido ya los atentados. Le respondí que muchos, pero que no todos se conocían porque los organismos de seguridad se cuidaban muy bien de publicarlos o de que se filtrasen hasta esa multitud oscura que esperaba en el fondo de su miedo esa posibilidad salvadora. Quién te autoriza a pensar que no seguirán fracasando. Es lo que siempre ocurre, dijo sin ánimo de abatirme. Aduje que eso no iba a ocurrir si el complot contaba con el apoyo de una parte muy poderosa de las fuerzas armadas. Se sabe que existe, larvada, una rebelión en ciertos sectores del ejército. El tirano la conoce, pero la tiene controlada. Teme sin embargo desmontarla a cañonazos. Hace años que viene intentando hacerlo gradualmente. Pero este sector militar de la caballería, con tanques y aviones a su disposición, es más fuerte que todo el ejército junto del Supremo. El golpe puede estallar en cualquier momento. Máxime con el tirano muerto.

—A tirano muerto, tirano puesto, suele ser la regla de juego en los golpes palaciegos —murmuró Jimena.

—Una vida libre sin coerciones ni represiones, sin el cáncer de la corrupción, es lo único que puede regenerar a una sociedad enferma hasta los huesos.

—En España ese sueño "político" costó un millón de muertos. Después, los atentados "redentores" sólo sirvieron para fortalecer el poder del tirano. Ya en plena demencia senil murió en la cama con los auxilios de la santa religión cuando no pudieron prolongarle la sobrevida artificial, mientras su cuerpo se iba empequeñeciendo hasta no ser más que una momia del tamaño de un feto.

—Eso es lo que no debe ocurrir con el tiranosaurio. El monstruo debe morir colgado por el pueblo y arrastrado por las calles...

Sentí que estaba recuperando sin querer el tono falsamente rebelde y patriotero de los primeros años de exilio: el "tono" del café Berna, en Buenos Aires, una de nuestras "trincheras" de reuniones clandestinas en las que incubábamos sueños heroicos de revolución y salvación nacional en nuestro enrevesado dialecto hispano-guaraní, que desorientaba y despistaba a los espías de la policía argentina.

—Mira, Félix, los intelectuales "humanistas" nunca hemos servido para esta clase de faenas. No somos más que los "idiotas útiles" de siempre. Los "aliados objetivos" del poder, como decían los antiguos comunistas que se han convertido también ahora en "aliados objetivos" del capitalismo caníbal. No trato de desalentarte. Busco inducirte a que razones sobre la debilidad de nuestra posición.

En esos días, precisamente, habíamos visto de nuevo en un teatro de París *La muerte de Dantón.*

—Büchner la escribió a los veinte años —Jimena se arrebató un poco—. ¡Un niño! Destrozó hace más de un siglo, casi al mismo tiempo que Marx la inventaba, la utopía de la Revolución como un juguete que ya no sirve ni para chicos ni para grandes. La Revolución como obra de mandarines intelectuales. Tenía ese niño más lucidez o por lo menos más honradez que los grandes patriarcas revolucionarios. Cuando surge un verdadero líder revolucionario las cosas toman otro cariz. ¿Ves tú alguno de esta pasta hoy, en el Paraguay?

—Un líder revolucionario auténtico surge de la masa del pueblo.

Apenas pronunciada, la frase se me antojó de una ridiculez insoportable. Sabía yo lo que ella tampoco ignoraba: esa "masa", casi en su totalidad, está comprada por el tirano o con prebendas miserables, o aplastada por el terror de la represión, las torturas y el genocidio sistematizado. Pero era posible que la fuerza de su identidad le hiciera recuperar algún día la conciencia de lo que había sido como pueblo.

—El miedo es la única forma de conciencia pública que existe hoy por hoy en tu país. Como sucedió en el mío mientras duró la dictadura franquista.

—Por eso es necesario liquidar al tiranosaurio.

—Hay cosas más importantes para un pueblo que acuchillar o colgar a un tirano aunque no sea más que en efigie... o en pensamiento. Los tiranos mueren, los pueblos sobreviven. A España no la pudo liquidar Franco. A veces los pueblos resucitan, como el tuyo, después de aquella guerra infernal que lo arrasó a sangre y fuego hasta el último hombre.

—Quedaron las mujeres que lo reconstruyeron.

—Sí. Las mujeres no hacen a veces más que eso: restablecer todo de manera que el hombre venga de nuevo a hacer de ellas, románticamente, las reinas de sus canciones de amor, pero, en la práctica, las resignadas pobladoras de sus serrallos, las irredimibles y complacientes bestias de carga de siempre.

También eso era verdad. El supermacho del Paraguay sólo había comenzado a consolidar su poder cuando convirtió el país en un gran burdel. Sexo, violencia y terror siguen siendo el recurso infalible del poder cuando los vivos miserables se alían con los miserables muertos. El viejo truco, desde la Colonia, que todavía sigue prestando servicio a los dueños del poder. Al método de "dividir para reinar" se ha sumado el más poderoso aún de "corromper y prostituir" para reblandecer la sociedad y convertirla en una ramera complaciente y servil.

—Hay una justicia inmanente y otra práctica, inmediata, que se debe ejecutar en bien de todos —teoricé con cierto automatismo reflejo.

—Ninguna de las dos sirven para gran cosa. El mito de la justicia absoluta es una utopía irrealizable. Una trampa. Un juego de palabras. No existe la más remota posibilidad de enjuiciar ni al individuo, ni a la sociedad, ni al universo, como no existe la posibilidad de juzgarse uno mismo.

—Están los hechos, Jimena. La represión, el genocidio. Existe la ciencia jurídica, el código penal, la experiencia última de los crímenes de lesa humanidad del nazismo y del fascismo juzgados por tribunales especiales.

Conocía el desprecio moral de Jimena por la justicia "justa". Jimena se exaltó. ¿Es eso, dijo, lo que tú llamas justicia justa? ¿Quién puede aplicarla? Si el tiranosaurio cayera prisionero en este mismo instante por un golpe militar o por un levantamiento popular, ¿quién podría juzgarlo? ¿Una justicia absolutista? ¿La misma que practica el Poder absoluto como un privilegio exclusivo y providencial? ¿Un fiscal omnisciente? ¡Vamos, Félix! No sueñes con esa "justicia justa". Ella no existe sino como un sueño que se ha cobrado en la realidad innumerables víctimas.

—El tiranosaurio es un criminal de guerra, Jimena. Todo se hace bajo su estricto control personal y bajo el único estatuto legal de la "Orden superior". Un juicio sumarísimo bastaría para enviarlo al pelotón de ejecución, a la horca o a prisión perpetua, como está ocurriendo con los criminales de guerra nazis cazados por los judíos. ¿O es que Simón Wiesenthal es el último cazador de criminales de guerra que queda en el mundo? En proporción, los holocaustos del Paraguay han superado las mayores atrocidades de todos los tiempos.

—¿Lo vas a cazar y liquidar tú a mano limpia?

—Acostumbro mi mirada a la sangre. Estoy aprendiendo a ver... a buscar la manera de hacerlo...

Me sentí ridículo recitando ante ella el típico versículo "progre" del intelectual "comprometido". Creo que de esta manera terminó aquella tarde de un frío domingo de febrero último nuestro largo diálogo "político".

Desde nuestra Ventana del Poniente, mientras apurábamos pavas y pavas de mate caliente y espumoso, veíamos caer la nieve que borraba los contornos del paisaje y convertía nuestra Ventana en un ábside gótico rodeado de carámbanos de hielo. El dálmata *Yaguareté* dormitaba junto a la chimenea, arrullado por nuestra discusión.

Jimena parecía angustiada, como a la espera de un acontecimiento inminente. Acaso le preocupaba el llamado de Clovis. Veía en sus ojos rodar en rápida sucesión la sombra de sus visiones interiores. Me miró un instante a los ojos. Bajó un instante los párpados. Se inclinó sobre mí. Le tomé el rostro con las manos y la besé largamente en los labios. Se levantó y se dirigió a la cocina.

—Voy a preparar un chocolate bien caliente.

Las dos veces que intentamos con Jimena entrar clandestinamente en Asunción nos expulsaron. El famoso comisario Cantero, el más temible de los sabuesos de la

Secreta, dirigió el operativo de expulsión. Nos auscultaron todo el tiempo con su olfato sanguinario de perro de presa. Consultaba el rollo del prontuario policial que pedía de tanto en tanto a uno de sus esbirros. Las impresiones dactilares no dieron ningún resultado. No me reconoció. "¡Éste es un gringo pata sucia!... Y soltó una expresión soez, que para nosotros resultó liberadora."

Fue una prueba difícil pero útil. Nos hicieron desnudar en la comisaría y nos revisaron de arriba abajo sin ahorrarle a Jimena el ultraje de hurgarle el ano y los genitales en busca de algún mensaje secreto. Yo llevaba en el ombligo la cápsula de cianuro para casos extremos. Fue el único lugar que no se les ocurrió revisar. Nos dejaron partir. Otros no tuvieron esa suerte. Simplemente fueron "empaquetados" y enterrados vivos en cualquier lugar. El Paraguay está cribado, trufado, de tumbas sin nombre, de desaparecidos, de fantasmas errantes. Durante la Guerra Grande el éxodo de los vencidos enterraba sus tesoros. Ahora se entierran los huesos de los torturados. Los fuegos fatuos continúan zigzagueando por encima de las sepulturas. Esos destellos fosfóricos balizan los lugares que nadie se animaría a remover.

El Paraguay fue llamado por los cronistas Tierra de Promisión, Tierra de Profecía, la *Tierra-sin-mal* de los antiguos guaraníes. Abundaron en ella profetas carismáticos, revoluciones, sacrificios rituales, holocaustos interminables, las formas más primitivas de canibalismo. Un pueblo siempre en peregrinación, en romerías, en éxodos, como en busca de una evasión salvadora.

Siempre tuve la sensación de que el tiempo en el Paraguay es inmóvil, el tiempo de la fijeza, el tiempo petrificado, seco, vacío, fósil. Y que lo que se mueve en esa isla rodeada de tierra es la gente en incesantes peregrinaciones, en éxodos de nunca acabar. El tiempo quieto, inexistente. Sólo la multitud silenciosa de espectros camina noche y día en busca del alimento de horror. Una gran palpitación popular, herida de muerte, pero que continúa avanzando arrastrándose de rodillas hacia alguna crucifixión ya preparada, ya ejecutada, o que está por ejecutarse en los grandes anfiteatros selváticos.

Las dos veces que llegamos con Jimena al Paraguay esas peregrinaciones se nos antojaron detenidas, ancladas en un pavor malsano. Estaban prohibidas las procesiones y romerías religiosas, las manifestaciones políticas, salvo naturalmente las del partido del poder. Se reprimían con toda violencia las migraciones internas del campo a la ciudad en busca de trabajo, de comida. Las aglomeraciones eran dispersadas con el asalto de los carros antimotín. El alud humano era rechazado a través de bretes de alambradas de púas. Bretes interminables como los que se usan para cargar el ganado en los vagones rumbo a los mataderos.

A Jimena le hacen daño estos temas. Alta y maciza, con su rostro de niña, muestra en los instantes de tensión la fuerza de su naturaleza a un tiempo salvaje y refinada. Por temperamento, es una criatura primitiva que se niega a aceptar la despiadada crueldad del mundo. Un ser excepcionalmente dotado y al mismo tiempo extremadamente sensible y vulnerable. Su destino es el de las personas que han nacido desprovistas de todo, salvo de generosidad. Se da entera en cada cosa que hace, incapaz de contenerse, pero como nada reclama para sí puede ser dura y exigente con los demás. No tolera el engaño. Y como no es inocente, su instinto más que sus ojos *ve* con todo su cuerpo lo que quiere saber como si una facultad que no fuese la de la vista estuviera aposentada bajo esos delgados párpados orlados de largas pestañas. Se resarce tal vez así de todos los deseos que ha tenido que reprimir pero que moran latentes en su intimidad más profunda.

Acaso también vive, sin saberlo, en una situación límite. Pero para ella, al menos, hay una salida de retorno: la de los hijos que quiere tener, ese verdadero acto de rescate que la superioridad biológica de la mujer le tiene reservada como privilegio de origen. Jimena anhela esos hijos que yo no le puedo dar. Suele entrarme a veces la congoja de que, más que el amante de Jimena, su compañero, su amigo en la amistad profunda del amor, no soy sino el hijo adoptado por ella. Lo sé, lo siento en mí; no se lo diría jamás a ella. Le sonaría a chantaje moral. Sería como querer coaccionarla con una sinceridad que siempre le sonaría a falso.

—¿Sabes una cosa? —le dije un día—. Siempre he pensado que una mujer, la mujer, por el hecho de que *puede* parir hijos, tiene un cierto don de profecía del que los hombres carecemos.

—El tener hijos es una función biológica natural. ¿Por qué habría de producir un don sobrenatural como el de la profecía? En todo caso, vosotros los hombres sois partícipes, cómplices genéticos de este "don" de profecía.

Me sentí tocado en lo más vulnerable de mi condición de hombre por las palabras de Jimena. Las dijo sin recordar o darse cuenta de esta "muerte" mía en lo más vital del hombre. Las picanas eléctricas y los golpes "clínicos" de los especialistas de la Secreta se habían encargado de extirpar este "don" de dones. La miré humillado en la actitud lisiada de los condenados.

—Perdón... —dijo doblemente contristada.

—No te preocupes —repuse—. Guardémonos de lamentar el hecho ya hecho. Nadie es su padre ni su madre. Tengo mala semilla. Y aunque la hubiera tenido buena, no hubiera querido tener un hijo. Y si fuese su padre no hubiera querido tener ese hijo y él no habría querido que yo fuese su padre.

Jimena me atrajo hacia sí y me besó en la frente como queriendo disipar mis malos recuerdos.

—Algo tan disparatado como tener hijos —insistí para restituirme al tema—; ser poseedora de la semilla genética, le permite a la mujer saberlo todo. Solamente una locura así puede engendrar una verdadera sabiduría.

—En todo caso —se burló ella—, los hombres han sido siempre los únicos profetas. No sé de ninguna mujer que haya merecido este título en los libros sagrados. Es algo que me tiene sin cuidado. Cada uno sabe lo que tiene que saber y con eso basta —altercó ella poniendo punto al asunto.

Su ardiente sensualidad, en la que su inteligencia se ha encarnado, ha concentrado todos sus deseos en el más poderoso de todos: la descendencia de su carne y de su sangre, la prolongación, a través de esos retoños, de las antiguas raíces familiares (jamás habla de estirpe, linaje o genealogías) que le vienen de Castilla por su madre y de Aragón por su padre. Suele viajar a Veguillas, en los altos de Teruel, el pequeño y rústico poblado natal de su padre, en la Cruz de los Tres Reinos, y a Valladolid, cuna de su madre.

Estos lugares son para Jimena lo que para mí, a otra escala y del otro lado del mar, representan Asunción y Manorá, estaciones para otra clase de peregrinación: la procesión personal de una fe laica, no el imposible retorno a las fuentes. Los mismos acentos, los mismos sonidos, los mismos paralelismos míticos de origen, de término y de pérdida. Nuestra unión reposa sobre esas afinidades. Jimena ha rechazado siempre la idea del matrimonio.

—Me parece inmoral delegar en el cura y el juez la voluntad y la responsabilidad de una pareja de vivir juntos su amor y su destino, y para el amor no hay prohibiciones ni tabús que no puedan ser transgredidos por dos seres que se aman de verdad.

Vio en la adolescencia llegar en París el frustrado mayo del 68. Viajó a México y vio los muertos que ese mismo "mayo" mexicano tumbó a balazos en la plaza de Tlatelolco. Las huellas fantasmagóricas de Artaud, entre los tarahumaras, treinta años atrás, se le aparecieron equivocadas y terribles. Todavía ardían vivas en el vía crucis del mezcal. Optó por seguir su propia peregrinación. Se internó en el pasado legendario de los nahuas. Aprendió la lengua con los naturales, siguiendo el vía crucis de los códices del P. Sahagún, saqueados, fragmentados, destazados, dispersos, como si hubieran sido sometidos al potro de los descuartizamientos de Hernán Cortés. Se sabía casi de memoria a los principales cronistas del imperio. Mejor conocía los relatos de los cronistas naturales que hablaban de otras historias; de esas historias que sólo pueden ser contadas en voz alta —solía decir Jimena—. Y mejor aún si lo son por la voz colectiva.

Pasó al Paraguay y aprendió el guaraní. Le deslumbró la cara oscura de la gente campesina que no habla español ni es ya indígena. Le impresionó ese misterio racial, no personal, de esas mujeres descalzas más fuertes que la fatalidad, silenciosas, como envueltas en una emanación protectora de algo mudo y oscuro que no les impedía la risa y el humor mientras fumaban su gran cigarro de hoja del tabaco más fuerte, el *pety-pará*, ése que está cubierto de abultados lunares blancos parecidos a ojos de perdiz.

Entre el sol calcinante y la tiniebla del infortunio colectivo los pies de esas mujeres pisaban la tierra como teñida de sangre y se llevaban las huellas de sus pasos sin dejar rastros. Andaban de un lado a otro con ojos en peregrinación pero siempre volvían a esos lugares del desconsuelo donde estaban sus *tapyi*. Había que levantar otra vez los horcones caídos, un poco de paja, barro, atados con lianas silvestres. O llevarlos a otra parte. La ventaja de los ranchos es que sus ruinas son transportables. Los hombres arribeños llegaban y se iban después de saciar su hambre, sus instintos bestiales, su rabia de ser hombres.

Jimena vivió dos años con una anciana del lugar, dejándose penetrar por el magnetismo de la tierra, de la gente, del tiempo inmóvil, aprendió a hablar y amar la lengua vernácula y a odiar con toda su alma la ciega perversidad y abyección de los hombres.

—A veces llegan los arribeños, ahora más que antes —cuenta Jimena que la anciana decía sin cambiar de tono y sin que una sola de sus innumerables arrugas se moviera—. Pero antes los arribeños no tenían armas. Ahora los arribeños llegan con uniforme, con fusiles y armas de todo calibre. Ahora los arribeños son violadores. Llegan borrachos y gritando. Vienen de ametrallar a los campesinos sin tierra que se han metido de contrabando en los terrenos grandes de los *poguasús*. Llegan, buscan y arrastran a las mujeres jóvenes. Entonces no hay más remedio que dejar que ellos hagan lo que quieran. A veces pasa un batallón entero sobre los cuerpos de las mujeres más jóvenes. No se salvan ni las criaturas. Después van a lavarse la sangre en el arroyo, mientras las más viejas tenemos que prepararles la comida con los frutos del país robados de las chacras ajenas. Esos violadores se llevan entre sus piernas la hermosura de las muchachas y ellas se quedan a amamantar los hijos de esos padres desconocidos y a cuidar los hijos de las que se van muriendo.

Para esos inocentes, se "plagueaba" la anciana, la única esperanza que les queda es morir lo más pronto posible. Eso, aquí, es más seguro que vivir. Si no mueren en seguida pronto se hace tarde y ya no hay remedio. Muchos de ellos también se vuelven después violadores, y de los peores. Violan a sus madres, a sus hermanas y hasta a veces a las abuelas, a ésas que no se les ve la edad y se ponen más lindas con el tiempo. Los soldados se van como vinieron, sin recordar nada, sin reconocer a nadie, sin que les importe nada de nada.

La anciana campesina inició a Jimena en la historia oral del país. Le contaba los casos y las cosas de antes y de siempre, cuentos, leyendas, como si se trataran de pequeños milagros cotidianos que se estaban produciendo en ese mismo momento. La anciana desdentada, casi centenaria, no tenía más que la piel y los huesos bajo sus guiñapos, no sabía leer, no sabía escribir, no demostraba sufrir y acaso hasta se había olvidado de morir. Pero sabía de esas cosas del otro lado de la vida. Sentía miedo, pero su miedo callado y lento era como un elemento de la naturaleza que le venía del exterior, como el viento, el calor o el frío, y que se iba como el viento, el calor, el frío o como el humo espeso de su cigarro.

Esas mujeres habían perdido sus lazos familiares, sus chozas, sus nombres, la conciencia de sus necesidades. Habían olvidado sus vínculos con las cosas y con las fases sensibles de la naturaleza. El monte no tenía límites. Los hombres y sus campamentos de exterminio aparecían y desaparecían. Bajo el sol de fuego que incineraba sus sombras habían regresado al primitivo misterio de la oscuridad, del anonimato, del olvido. No parecían necesitar otra cosa que un alma. Pero aun *eso* habría resultado ahora un estorbo para sus cuerpos en los que milagrosamente se mantenía el ardor de la vida. Sólo precisaban de ese coraje callado cuyo áspero uso las había igualado desde tiempo inmemorial. Se llamaban unas a otras con gritos de pájaros cuyos ecos rodaban y morían en los acantilados, en las "picadas", en los desfiladeros.

Con un saber lento y memorioso la anciana del Alto Paraná, entre una fumada y otra de su "pucho" despachurrado, enseñó a Jimena la manera de dormir para estar más despierta en el sueño y ver en la oscuridad de la noche el fondo de la realidad que la luz del día oculta.

—Aunque esté dormida profundamente —le había dicho la anciana—, usted va a ver lo que pasa antes de que esté pasando. Puede ser un tiempo largo. Es como un recuerdo que está esperando afuera, tumbado como un perro que no se ve ni ladra, pero que es muy efectivo. Le avisa despacio, sin ruido, del peligro, del amenazo. Pero entonces, tiene usted el tiempo justo de esconderse, de escapar, de salvar su mortalidad mortal. Un cristiano puede morir en cualquier momento, cuantimás si es mujer sola y sin defensa. Y usted es todavía demasiado joven, *che ama*, y debe salvarse de la perdición, porque de las mujeres depende la vida de este país y todo.

Jimena aprendió ese duermevela poblado de imágenes difusas desde el fondo de las "salamancas" donde doña Encarnación la ocultaba por las noches en el temor de los ataques.

—La memoria, *che ama*, tiene su peso. *Amome* es más pesada que la piedra —contaba Jimena que la anciana le había dicho con la voz temblona—. Entonces hay que pegar el oído a esa piedra que cada uno lleva adentro y saber su secreto. Lo que la gente ha olvidado es la memoria del daño. Y de qué le sirve al cristiano pensar en la vida eterna, como quieren los *Paí*, si no sabe ni siquiera recordar lo que acaba de pasar...

Jimena volvió a Francia con una nostalgia indecible de aquellas tierras salvajes y castigadas. Cuando se quedó sola, supo que tenía que comenzar todo desde el principio. Nos conocimos en una Universidad del Sur. Hacíamos largos paseos por ese paisaje lleno de árboles y de agua. Esta vez el deslumbramiento fue mutuo.

Yo acababa de separarme de mi ex mujer. Más correcto sería decir que ella me abandonó. Me negué a hipotecar la vida de Jimena. Hice todo lo posible para que me despreciara y olvidara. Me puse otra máscara: la del libertino y desalmado corruptor de muchachas jóvenes. Me hice amante de una putilla de barrio y la hacía asistir a mis clases pagándole en buena moneda su aburrimiento "intelectual". El escándalo había comenzado a circular. Se preparaba un sumario administrativo que acabaría seguramente en expulsión y cárcel.

No logré engañar a Jimena. Me esperó una tarde, a

la salida de la Facultad. Me tomó de la mano delante de mi amante. En voz alta, sin importarle que le oyeran, me dijo:

—No voy a permitir que te hundas.

—No puedo darte un hogar.

—Podemos construirlo entre los dos.

—Mi destino es no tenerlo —le dije sin amargura, sin reproche.

Se acercó a la muchacha que contemplaba la escena con aire ausente. Vi que le hablaba con aire bondadoso. Le puso la mano en un hombro. La otra se alejó llorando como si la hubieran arrojado de un empellón por una escalera.

Huí al otro extremo del Hexágono. Caí en el alcohol y en la indiferencia absoluta del *clochard* sin serlo del todo todavía. Tiempo después, por verdadero azar, me llegó una carta en la que me decía:

"Eso que llaman destino es lo que nosotros hacemos de él. No necesitamos pedir permiso a Dios o a quien sea para vivir y para amarnos como se nos antoje dentro de las pasiones permitidas. No conozco una sola que esté prohibida siempre que sepamos usarla, y seamos dueños de elegirla y vivirla a nuestro modo...".

La carta se me perdió en mis andares. La escribo de memoria. Ésa fue la primera vez que salvó mi vida en pleno tirabuzón hacia la nada.

Cuando recobré cierto aspecto humano volví y le propuse refugiarnos en Nevers para vivir juntos, a nuestro modo. Pero ese "modo nuestro" sólo es peculiarmente "nuestro" en la medida en que hemos sido nosotros quienes lo hemos elegido y lo hemos reinventado todas las veces que hizo falta en un juego constante de afinamientos y ajustes, en ocasiones demasiado lentos; esos que exigen la paciencia de un orfebre ensimismado en la imagen de su pasión y de su obra, la que no siempre corresponde a su iluminación interior.

Diez años han transcurrido desde entonces. Los ciclos decenales que dividen mi vida en tajadas como las de un melón pasado de estación no me han tratado nunca demasiado bien. Los diez años con Jimena han transcurrido como un pensamiento. Leves, serenos, intemporales.

Reanudé mis clases en la Facultad. Me entregaba a ellas con la felicidad de las tareas que se hacen no bajo la compulsión y la monotonía de la rutina sino en la exaltación de una actividad verdaderamente creativa. Daba cursos sobre civilización y cultura latinoamericanas. Hablaba apenas de su literatura actual. Durante estos años de destierro sólo me ha interesado frecuentar la lectura de los autores antiguos: griegos y latinos, los clásicos europeos, los cronistas del Nuevo Mundo, que son en rigor de verdad sus auténticos clásicos. Y naturalmente, la relectura de gigantes como Dante, Cervantes, Shakespeare, Goethe, Rabelais, las grandes escritoras mujeres del siglo XVII y XVIII, Tolstoi, Proust, Stendhal, Flaubert, Conrad, Joyce, Beckett. Y entre los norteamericanos, Melville, Hawthorne, Poe, Faulkner (traído de la mano por Conrad), Emily Dickinson, Eudora Welty, Djuna Barnes, el misterioso y mágico Ambrose Bierce de los *Cuentos de soldados*, cuya vida idéntica a su obra marcó el derrotero de la mía. Nadie elige su época. Pero él eligió la peor. Huyó y desapareció en la vorágine de la Revolución Mexicana, como quien se arroja al cráter de un volcán.

Nada sabía de lo que se estaba escribiendo actualmente en los países latinoamericanos, la mayor parte de ellos sometidos a dictaduras, a persecuciones y represiones de toda índole. Sus culturas de la resistencia, pugnando por sobrevivir, poco podían hacer por un arte y por una literatura que no sirvieran más que de esparcimiento para niñas de las clases acomodadas. No tenían ninguna utilidad práctica inmediata. No existía. Inventaba yo esos libros de autores contemporáneos que estaba obligado a leer, pero que probablemente nunca iba a leer ni nunca serían escritos. Me llegaban algunos nombres, algunos libros. No sabía quiénes eran. No tocaba esos libros que apestaban a exilio interior, a asfixia represiva.

A los más nuevos y desconocidos por mí, los situaba en el capítulo de las "obras maestras desconocidas". Hablaba sobre ellas, como si las hubiera leído de verdad, con la secreta certidumbre de que esas obras maestras existían o serían escritas alguna vez y que mis versiones imaginarias coincidirían con los textos reales. En algún momento esas coincidencias debían producirse puesto que la combinatoria de las variantes posibles en literatura es más bien limitada. Recordaba el chistoso aforismo citado por Borges que afirmaba: "Si diez mil monos se ponen a escribir en diez mil máquinas de escribir durante diez mil años es inevitable que surja de pronto la Divina Comedia". Creo que esta variante improbable es el mayor incentivo de la portentosa y desenfrenada producción de libros que pocos leen pero que abruman nuestra época. De hacer muchos libros no hay fin, dice el Eclesiastés. Prefería leer en la imaginación esos libros abstractos y puros que no existían pero que se podían inventar cada vez de manera diferente. Si existe una literatura de ficción no puede haber otra que ésta, me decía hojeando estos libros ficticios cuyos precursores se hallaban todos en el futuro.

Sentía a mis alumnos bastante reacios al comienzo ante esa materia irreal de conocimiento que no les iba a aportar ninguna ventaja inmediata. Las chicas y los muchachos de hoy sienten hacia la literatura una indiferencia más bien despectiva. Los dejaba familiarizarse con la idea de lo inútil como un lujo inofensivo. Trataba de crear para ellos la reverberación de un centro de interés, despertando su apatía con el espejuelo de mi propio entusiasmo. Excitaba su curiosidad y su amor propio con pequeños desafíos en los que uno debe saber dejarse vencer en ocasiones. También el orgullo tiene su agradecimiento, como la oscura estimación que posee un hermoso cuerpo de sí mismo, o los sentimientos que no dudan de su firmeza y quieren ser reconocidos.

Detrás de los ojos entornados observaba yo rotaciones curiosas, cambios tan variados, tan libres y, sin embargo, aún tímidos y limitados. No tenían todavía la audacia suficiente de llegar a ese punto a la vez luminoso y oscuro del delirio entre la realidad y el deseo, entre el vértigo y el miedo. Entraban finalmente en la atmósfera de encantamiento que sólo puede brotar de la aceptación y de la entrega, de la suspensión de la incredulidad. Se producía un fenómeno de contagio entre los más sensibles del grupo, no precisamente entre los más inteligentes. Lo observaba en sus ojos brillantes, en la actitud tensa de sus cuerpos olvidados de sí, cautivos de lo que oían y experimentaban con una emoción nueva. Veía esa especie de halo sonrosado que hace subir la sangre en un rostro joven cuando algo lo seduce verdaderamente.

La partida entre un enseñante y los alumnos sólo está ganada si éstos lo encuentran digno de su aprobación. No la reclamaba yo. Nunca está uno seguro de merecerla. Más bien la rehuía dejando que me la dieran espontáneamente y que hasta me exigieran recibirla. Sin esta aprobación ningún enseñante podría explicar ni enseñar nada. Yo sentía que la iba ganando poco a poco, a través de pequeños núcleos, a veces de una o dos víctimas propiciatorias, a contracorriente de los más díscolos y altaneros. La comunicación se establecía de manera insensible. Los campos de resistencia, incluso la hostilidad, son útiles para esa especie de transferencia hipnótica que está en la base de la experiencia pedagógica.

No había horarios para nosotros. Cuando la sala debía ser ocupada por otros cursos, salíamos al jardín y nos sentábamos sobre el césped. O los que podíamos permitirnos el lujo de vagabundear un rato más, nos fugábamos por las callejuelas antiguas en el atardecer. El movimiento de la marcha se acompasa con el ritmo del corazón y del pensamiento. Los estimula y exalta, como éstos a su vez se mueven con el movimiento de la tierra y de los astros. Nos volvíamos invisibles para los demás, pero nosotros nos veíamos cada vez más claramente en la penumbra a la luz de una amistad naciente; de esa amistad en libertad que tanto se parece al amor, pero que no sufre la ansiedad de la carne, la angustia de la pérdida, el temor a la desconfianza ni a la infidelidad.

—Recuerden —les decía—. Lo que no se sabe se pierde una vez. Pero lo que se sabe y se olvida se pierde dos veces... Contemplen esto y estotro. Ven algo, ¿no es verdad? Hay que aprender a saber lo que se ve y sobre todo a verlo dentro de uno mismo.

Seguían los ejemplos sacados de la realidad circundante. Y todos competían en ver más y saber mejor sobre las cosas más insignificantes. La juventud no ama el orden artificial de las cosas sino la incoherencia natural del mundo. Me instalaba en ese espacio bien conocido por mí y ellos entraban sin darse cuenta en el círculo imantado. Mientras hablábamos, viajábamos. Les hablaba de pájaros míticos, de dioses, de desiertos, de selvas vírgenes, de ceremonias salvajes que tienen la sabiduría de lo inescrutable, de sacrificios que juntan la carne, la sangre y el fuego en un misterio elemental; de la evolución del amor y la religión a lo largo de las edades; del sentido de lo genuinamente erótico en las culturas antiguas, tan opuesto a las aberraciones a que ha sido llevado en nuestros tiempos "consumistas". Un mero artículo de excitación enfermiza, en lo más bajo de la escala moral y social. Las muchachas y los muchachos citaban ejemplos de estos desvíos y aberraciones sacados del cine y la televisión. El amor convertido en mercancía y sus secretos más íntimos manipulados como materia prima de la publicidad. El éxtasis erótico como fórmula del éxito comercial; el hastío de lo erótico como fórmula del fracaso de la pareja.

Contemplábamos de pronto desde lejos una casa con las ventanas iluminadas en la noche. Oíamos el ruido de una fiesta lejana. Risas, voces, música de ritmo vivo, canciones alegres. Tratábamos de captar lo esencial de ese sonido. En ocasiones era el espectáculo de un saltimbanqui callejero en cuyas contorsiones la tensión de los músculos y la perfección de los movimientos podían alcanzar a veces, en fracciones de segundos, la belleza imperecedera de las estatuas más perfectas.

Nos arracimábamos en torno al joven y sonriente acróbata comunicándonos nuestras risas y el calor de nuestros cuerpos. Lo aplaudíamos a rabiar para descargar la tensión. Un rato después teníamos que separarnos. Me tendían sus manos húmedas y un poco trémulas. Nos despedíamos en silencio. Yo miraba alejarse el grupo hasta que se perdía en la sombra y sus voces y sus risas se apagaban en un recodo. El desquite era burlarse un poco del profesor, tomarlo a broma; neutralizar la embriaguez momentánea, que habían experimentado al descubrir con él caminos nuevos y desconocidos. Esta distensión era lo más adecuada y saludable.

Sentí la punta de un cuchillo en la nuca. Una voz dura en el argot del Magreb me intimó:

—Quédate quieto. Suelta todo lo que tengas en tus sucios bolsillos. La billetera... Arrójala en la calzada.

La furiosa y enérgica orden, la aguda punta del cuchillo clavada en el occipucio, eliminaba toda tentación de réplica o resistencia. Extraje mi billetera casi indigente. La tiré hacia atrás con deliberada parsimonia como de alguien que otorga generosamente un don sin el menor asomo de temor.

—¡Rápido! Tus zapatos... tus calcetines...

Me los saqué y los tiré también por encima del hombro, tratando de que dieran en el blanco invisible, no para agredirlo en un desquite burlón, sino para que me enfrentara y pudiera verle el rostro. Oí que uno de los zapatos le daba en plena cara.

—¡Vamos, cabrón! ¡No hagas bromas! —hizo correr la punta del cuchillo sobre las vértebras abriéndome un tajo—. Tu chaqueta... tus pantalones... tu camisa... ¡Rápido!

Mientras me desnudaba pensé que el asaltante debía ser muy alto, flaco y muy joven. La hoja del cuchillo estaba asestada en la nuca de arriba hacia abajo. Su voz de dientes apretados sonaba sobre mi cabeza sordamente. Tendría enfundada la cabeza en una media de mujer, o llevaría puesta una capucha. Por la rudeza de sus manos al palpar mi cuerpo al comienzo, deduje que su fuerza muscular y sus reflejos nerviosos eran los de un verdadero atleta. Pensé en el acróbata. Sus movimientos eran los de un danzarín. Se me ocurrió que esa sombra invisible correspondía al cuerpo del contorsionista callejero. En ningún momento pude ver su cara ni distinguir su silueta.

—Le vimos hace un rato trabajar en la calle... Nos gustó mucho... —dije sin ninguna intención indiscreta, sólo como buscando abrir un resquicio de comunicación.

—¡Cállate, mierda!

Sentí el dolor ardiente de un nuevo tajo en la espalda y de otro más marcándome una cruz sobre la paletilla.

—Esto para que aprendas a no ser soplón... —volvió a farfullar la voz camuflada.

Mi vestimenta quedó reducida al calzoncillo.

—Sácate ese mugriento taparrabos.

Lo arrojé con premura antes de que el contorsionista me despellejara vivo.

El asaltante recogió el botín con celeridad pasmosa y desapareció como si lo hubiese tragado la tierra. Tuve la sensación de que había sido asaltado por un fantasma, salvo por las evidencias materiales del atraco y por la sangre que me corría desde el omóplato hacia las nalgas. No sentí ningún rencor hacia el asaltante. Consideré que había hecho algo natural. Sólo me pareció un poco raro que me hubiese elegido a mí y que me diese cuchilladas como a un enemigo cuando yo le había aplaudido con mis alumnas hacía un momento. Me hubiera gustado verle la cara y darle la mano. No al asaltante, al artista.

Hacía frío y comenzó a llover. Crucé las manos sobre las partes pudendas y avancé a la deriva, en busca de un improbable taxi, o al menos de una ayuda de emergencia. Un par de polizontes surgió de una bocacalle avanzó hacia mí, tomándome cada uno de un brazo. Me pidieron documentos. No los tengo encima, dije, como ustedes lo pueden ver. Les mostré la espalda que sangraba como por dos espitas. Creí que eso evitaba toda ociosa explicación. Lo interpretaron al revés. Uno de los agentes recogió de la calzada el calzoncillo con la punta de su cachiporra y me lo tendió. Me lo puse ahora con el pudor que no sentí cuando me lo hicieron sacar. El polizonte oscuro y corpulento cerró un par de esposas sobre mis muñecas. El otro fue a buscar un vehículo.

—¡*Merde!*... ¡Estos pederastas crecen como hongos! Debieran quemarlos a todos... —oí que farfullaba al irse uno de los "canas". A los pocos minutos apareció una camioneta policial barriendo la tortuosa callejuela con sus potentes faros que hendían la cortina oblicua de la lluvia. Me embutieron en el asiento trasero a empellones y puntapiés.

El mito del ombligo como cicatriz del nacimiento y como centro erótico del cuerpo es la fuente de la vida prenatal y el cráter sin fondo del deseo donde convergen y se funden los dos sexos restableciendo la unidad originaria, dicen los especialistas. Lo cual sólo es verdad en parte. El misterio onfálico es más complejo de lo que en realidad parece, raíz de muchos ritos de fertilidad y de divinidades femeninas o andróginas.

En el hombre, sin embargo, cortado el cordón umbilical, el ombligo siempre protuberante no es más que el muñón del primer falo que pierde al nacer; del mismo modo, las tetillas ornadas de falsas aureolas no cumplen ninguna función. En la mujer el ombligo se repliega en un hoyo profundo, el cóncavo vaso de luna del Cantar, en el vientre de la Sulamita, lleno siempre del licor exquisito en el que el rey Salomón se placía abrevar, sin saciar jamás sus ansias, y en el que yo, plebeyo y agnóstico, agoto las mías, no menos intensas e inagotables que las de un rey. Mi vaso de luna está excavado en el vientre de Jimena, mi *Sul Ama*, que sabe entregarse al sueño del amor misterioso como si muriera cada vez en el transporte del goce.

La cicatriz del nacimiento. Me viene obsesionando este mito desde hace ya muchos años. En Manorá, mi pueblo natal, cuando yo era niño, ocurrió un hecho, a medias real y fantástico. Un hombre de tamaño liliputiense nació o creyó haber nacido ya adulto. Se hacía llamar Nonato. Pero todos le decían don Chiquito. No era un nonato; era un hijo nacido de mujer como todos; un proyecto inacabado de hombre. Cuando nació, el feto parecía muerto. Revivió y ya tenía la cara de viejo que no cambiaría después. La comadrona y la gente del lugar creyeron que a medida que fuera creciendo iría recobrando la juventud con lo que se corregiría así, naturalmente, el error de la naturaleza.

—Estas criaturas —sentenció la comadrona sin mucha convicción— nacen viejas y maduran hacia la niñez. Se van enchiqueciendo hacia la edad adulta. En la ancianidad alcanzan la infancia. Se les antoja que son fetos y buscan el regazo de la madre al cual encaramarse. Buscan olvidar que nacieron alguna vez. De allí salió el *ñe´engá*: nadie es más viejo que el que acaba de nacer.

—¡Cierto *ité pa upeva*! —admitió una mujer con una gran verruga en la comisura de los labios.

Don Chiquito nacía cada mañana y desnacía por las noches.

Su inteligencia era excepcional. Llegó a maestro de escuela. Lo conocí allí, en los primeros grados. Era un portentoso narrador de "casos". Su voz de asmático, cavernosa y aguda, nos tenía alucinados y atemorizados. A la cuarentena probable de su edad sin edad llevaba enrollado a su cintura una liana silvestre reseca y curtida en su propio sudor, que él decía que era su cordón umbilical, pero al mismo tiempo creía que seguía viviendo en el claustro materno. Caminaba agachado, casi doblado en dos, mirando siempre el suelo en busca del ombligo que se le había perdido. Se levantaba la astrosa camisa y mostraba el vientre seco, negro y liso sin huella del ombligo. A los que se burlaban o dudaban, don Chiquito solía dar esta prueba de su no nacimiento.

Era un niño viejo que no acababa de crecer. Íbamos por las tardecitas a espiarle cuando "hablaba" con su madre que había muerto hacía muchos años. Para él seguía viva, puesto que estaba convencido de que, al caer la noche, por la que sentía pavor, entraba a refugiarse en el útero materno del que no salía sino al amanecer para concurrir a la escuela en ruinas y dar clase a los pocos escolares rotosos que veníamos por curiosidad, pero que salíamos aprendiendo a leer y a escribir.

Había construido su rancho sobre cuatro pilotes al borde de la laguna muerta que existe junto al puente de las vías del ferrocarril. En las épocas de lluvia, en agosto, la laguna se hinchaba y la cabaña lacustre de don Chiquito parecía flotar sobre el agua estancada que fermentaba espesa de detritos vegetales, de plantas acuáticas y hasta de carroñas de animales muertos.

Desde los durmientes, en el terraplén, podíamos ver a don Chiquito cuando hablaba con su madre y hasta oíamos la voz lejana y borrosa de ésta en la discusión interminable en la que alternaban las dulzuras y reconvenciones maternas, las súplicas incomprensibles del nonato que no quería nacer. Hasta nos parecía oír sollozos y aun los gemidos sofocados de la parturienta. Luego veíamos a don Chiquito subir e introducirse hasta desaparecer por completo en el "útero materno", una especie de bolsón que colgaba del horcón principal. Nos sobrepasaba ese misterio que veíamos representar, silenciosos y alelados, desde el puente.

Una mañana, mientras don Chiquito estaba en la escuela, vadeé la laguna y me colé en el interior del rancho por una abertura de las tablas del piso, entre los pilotes. Me aproximé a la bolsa ovalada y descubrí estupefacto que era en realidad un nido de pájaro, o al menos que estaba construido como el nido de las garzas, el ave que en guaraní se denomina *kuarahy-mimby*, la flauta-del-sol. Estaba hecho con las materias más suaves que se puedan imaginar pero que yo no sabía reconocer. No eran plumones de aves ni pellejos de animales; era más bien como una membrana muy fina pero resistente, semejante a lo que después sabría que es una placenta humana.

Desde el interior pendía una liana gruesa retorcida en nudos y anillos. Acaso fuera un auténtico cordón umbilical disecado y brillante por un continuo frote. Con algo de pavor pasé los dedos sobre esos nudos y circunvoluciones.

No pude seguir. La voz de don Chiquito, primero, luego la de la madre, brotaron nítidamente en alguna parte en un altercado violento. Huí empavorecido. Por la abertura me lancé a la laguna y gané a nado el puente. Desde los durmientes vi a don Chiquito que se venía acercando por el camino, siempre cabizbajo y como ausente del mundo que le rodeaba.

Desde que había memoria don Chiquito vivía apartado de la grey. El cura del pueblo había pedido su excomunión al obispado, pero no pudo lograr que lo echaran de la escuela pues era el único maestro que había en el pueblo. De tanto en tanto, en sus sermones, se refería al viejo loco que vivía en el embuste sacrílego de considerarse un nonato. Y para anatematizarlo repetía las palabras de Nicodemo, el príncipe de los fariseos, a Jesús (Juan 3, 4): "¿Cómo puede el hombre nacer siendo viejo? ¿Cómo puede entrar de nuevo en el vientre de su madre, y nacer?"

Porque a la verdad —tronó el cura desde el púlpito—, un hombre que es un don nadie y casi un don nada, que se hace pasar por una criatura nonata, es lo peor del mundo, un monstruo de la naturaleza... Y si ese falso niño pretende nacer todos los días para venir a la escuela a enseñar a los niños verdaderos es todavía más monstruoso... ¡Un verdadero sacrilegio, sin perdón de Dios, Nuestro Señor!

Ese día don Chiquito había entrado en la iglesia. Su voz se alzó como un chillido. "De cierto, de cierto te digo, dijo Jesús a Nicodemo, que el que no naciere otra vez no puede entrar en el reino de Dios...". Vino el sacristán y lo sacó a empellones mientras iba atontándolo con el sonido de la campanilla. Le vimos perderse entre los remolinos de polvo rojo de la plaza. Nunca más volvió a entrar en la iglesia. Y puede decirse que a pesar de sus bracitos apergaminados don Chiquito le ganó al cura en la pulseada, lo que significaba también, en cierto modo, el triunfo de la escuela laica sobre la Iglesia.

Cuando entré en la Universidad recordé el hecho y comencé a escribir sobre él. Aquel ensayo inconcluso trataba desde el ángulo del psicoanálisis y de la antropología cultural (Freud, Jung, Durkheim, Mircea Eliade, Marcel Mauss y compañía, sin excluir las extensas reflexiones que hace San Agustín, en sus *Confesiones,* sobre sus relaciones intrauterinas con su madre), sobre el misterio del nacimiento. Se titulaba *Contravida.* Quedó abandonado entre tantos otros papeles y libros inútiles de los que felizmente me exoneró el exilio. Otro de los favores que le debo.

Creo que en aquel ensayo, a partir de un hecho a medias real, a medias fantástico, existía el prurito de demostrar que el hombre de todas las épocas, nonato perpetuo, busca succionar con ansias en esa cicatriz del nacimiento la nostalgia del delicado alimento prenatal; acaso el presentimiento de su vida futura. La comezón del mito persistió en mí y creo que se la contagié a Jimena. Mi interés mítico era en ella interés biológico y cultural. Durante unas vacaciones decidimos partir en busca de esa huella primordial de la nacencia. Estuvimos en Londres contemplando durante días y días la Venus del Bronzino, luminosa en su rincón oscuro de la National Gallery. Jimena se enamoró perdidamente de ella hasta no poder contener las lágrimas.

En el Museo Vaticano me enamoré yo de la Afrodita Cnidia de Praxíteles, nacida de sus manos cuatro siglos a.C. Viajamos a Nápoles para admirar el vaso de luna de Onfalia, que según los entendidos es un dechado de suprema perfección. Recordé, sentí en mí, las palabras de Max Aub, que parecían copiadas del *Cantar;* un eco del exaltado cántico de hace más de tres mil años del Amante. "¡Oh muslos suaves, y la blanca dorada superficie lunar del vientre, con la enroscada cueva del ombligo!..."

Claro que, ante la visión del grupo del Museo de Nápoles, no pensaba en Onfalia sino en Jimena, dos mujeres, dos bellezas perfectas, que yo no podría unir nunca en mi imaginación. Las perfecciones también son diferentes y únicas. Son incomparables, salvo desde el cosmos in- abarcable de la belleza absoluta que gira en la mente de los iluminados, de los locos, de los artistas, sólo ellos capaces de percibirla como una revelación a la vez mística y erótica.

Otro ejemplo límite es la figura tallada de Antínoo, el efebo esclavo de Bitinia de quien el emperador Adriano hizo su semidiós doméstico. Es que también en el arte hay un límite infranqueable cuya ruptura provocaría quizás una catástrofe inesperada y terrible. No hay un arte superior a otro; sólo son diferentes como emanación de la belleza y aun como representación de la fealdad diabólica del mundo.

En el mismo Museo de Nápoles nos extasiamos ante la escultura de Hércules y Onfalia, "la del hermoso ombligo". Extasiado, es un decir. Yo estaba muerto de vergüenza ante Jimena, por el humillante espectáculo de Hércules travestido con la vaporosa túnica de Onfalia, los cabellos delicadamente trenzados por las esclavas en un peinado de mujer. Onfalia, en cambio, está vestida con la piel del león de Nemea, la fiera fabulosa caída de la luna, despojo obtenido por el héroe en su primer trabajo, trofeo ahora del último de Onfalia.

Reparé en la falta del dedo que le arrancó el león en la lucha. Señalé con algún disimulo el empequeñecido falo de Hércules, oculto por un pliegue de la clámide; luego la clava de Hércules en manos de Onfalia. Jimena puso el índice sobre los labios y me susurró en voz muy baja en medio de la romería de visitantes que circulaba en religioso silencio:

—¡Tate! A ti no te ocurrirá esto...

En el Museo del Prado fuimos fascinados por las estatuillas de Epimeteo y Pandora, talladas por El Greco. Los hoyuelos umbilicales, pintados de negro, resaltan sobre la blancura de los cuerpos como ojos ebrios de furia mística abiertos en la transparente delgadez de sus vientres.

Jimena había conocido en México la Venus de Xico, encontrada al pie del volcán del mismo nombre. Tiene una copia muy fiel entre sus objetos más queridos. Es pequeñísima pero parece inmensa bajo ciertos efectos de luz. El ombligo redondo, ancho y profundo está excavado en el centro del vientre, entre los senos y el sexo que simula otro ombligo. El hoyo está rodeado por un anillo oval erizado de úvulas umbilicales semejantes a dientes carnosos contrapuestos. Jimena ha contado hasta sesenta de estos dientes defensivos, semejantes en un sentido al mito de la vulva dentada, que Sir James Georges Frazer ponderó sobriamente en *La rama dorada*.

Desde luego hay ombligos con un pezón interno y su correspondiente aureola. Hay ombligos-ojos con párpados entrecerrados, que miran soñadores lo que no pueden ver; hay ombligos ojos-de-gato, oblicuos o verticales, y ombligos horizontales parecidos a una boca muy fina que sonríe dejando entrever la punta de una diminuta lengua bífida. Algo de esto se percibe en el vientre de la reina Nefertiti, que admiramos en el Louvre. Pero el pezón ofídico ha sido roído por el tiempo.

Todos ellos tienen relación con los elementos, los alimentos, los cultos de la procreación y de la fertilidad y, sobre todo, con la música de la tradición más antigua. Jimena, en sus años de México, grabó en Tehuantepec el *Son del ombligo* a cuyo compás bailan todavía los nativos del Istmo. No sería sorprendente que la famosa danza del vientre haya surgido de estos ritmos rituales antiquísimos, marcados por el vaivén cadencioso y sincopado del ombligo en el acto sexual. Los brasileños se jactan de que sus mujeres tienen el ombligo "grano de café", cuya forma, tamaño y color son exactamente los de un grano de la aromática bebida.

Es raro que esta imagen no haya aparecido aún en los afiches y tandas publicitarias gráficas y audiovisuales cuyo oleaje de pornografía barata invade las calles, los hogares, los cuartos de los niños, las mentes que se van cretinizando velozmente en este fenómeno de erotomanía colectiva. Hambre, obsesión, obnubilación, tedio de los amantes sin amor. El fenómeno no tiene límites ni antídotos. Es la depravación del sexo convertido en goce puramente animalesco. No somos más que simios llenos de tedio, movidos por el automatismo reminiscente del deseo. No tiene sentido hablar de la civilización, de decadencia o de fin de época. Asistimos tal vez a la extinción de todo eso.

La peregrinación por la ruta onfálica nos confirmó una verdad simple y peregrina. No se ve lo hermoso que se posee. Se ve siempre "la belleza de los otros", como lo dice mi amigo Ticio Escobar en el libro que ha dedicado a los indios chamacocos del Chaco paraguayo. Es cierto que el antropólogo y crítico de arte respetuoso que es Ticio no se detiene en la grieta umbilical que en las mujeres indígenas se oculta entre los coloridos tatuajes que cubren sus cuerpos. Hay entre ellos y la naturaleza un cordón umbilical vivo y tangible que no se corta jamás, ni siquiera en la muerte.

No paramos hasta visitar en Bihar, en la India, la talla de *Tara*, la virgen madre budista de una perfección casi insoportable para los ojos y la sensibilidad de los "extranjeros" de Occidente. Me pregunté por qué algunas de las prodigiosas representaciones de la Virgen cristiana no producen esta misma impresión. Es obvio que se trata de un problema de visiones y sensibilidades de culturas —dijo Jimena—, no de una perfección artística imposible de percibir en sus límites.

Como etapa final de nuestra peregrinación onfálica, intentamos un viaje a Mauritania donde es fama que existe todavía un culto al ombligo como la deidad o fetiche mayor de una cabila de beréberes o beduinos, ya extinguida. Se supone que este culto deriva de otro aún más primitivo cuya antigüedad se remonta hasta Set, el tercer hijo de Adán. El culto de un monstruoso pez-útero en el que quedó convertido Set por el crimen de haber violado a una de las doncellas de la diosa Ashtar, cuando el desierto del Sahara era aún una inmensa región de selvas vírgenes. Desaparecen las razas y las culturas, las selvas se convierten en desiertos, pero los mitos esenciales sobreviven para crear seguramente nuevas razas y culturas a su imagen y semejanza.

No alcanzamos a llegar. Caímos prisioneros de los guerrilleros del Polisario. Como brotados de la arena nos rodeó de golpe una veintena de hombres con uniformes rotosos, piel y huesos resecos como sarmientos de vid.

—¿Quiénes son ustedes?

—Franceses.

—¿Qué vienen a buscar aquí?

—Queremos llegar hasta la ciudad de Attar.

—¿Y allí?

—Visitar el santuario donde dicen que se venera la diosa del ombligo lunar.

No entendieron. Su dialecto de monosílabos crepitantes era duro e inentendible. Nos repitieron la pregunta. Los tubos nerviosos de sus automáticas oscilaban apuntándonos muy cerca de nuestros pechos.

—Queremos visitar el santuario del pez-útero —contesté dibujando la imagen con gestos lo más gráficos y menos obscenos posibles—. La virgen en forma de un útero humano con senos, doble ombligo y vulva.

Creyeron que nos burlábamos de ellos. Repetí la respuesta en un fraseo y con señas más decentes y conviviales (aquí el galicismo expresa bien lo que quería explicar).

—No existe más. Lo incendiamos —creímos entender que decían.

De todas formas, daba igual. Con incendio o sin incendio, el pez-útero no iba a venir a visitarnos sobre ese mar de arena calcinado por la luz al rojo blanco que parecía congelada en el cielo. El resplandor de pura luz ausente no arrancaba ninguna sombra a las matas peladas, a nuestras figuras, a los guerreros mauritanos, flacos como lanzas, altísimos y hermosos como etíopes con su tez de color leonado y sus rasgos de finura casi femenina.

La atmósfera era abstracta e inmóvil, y a un tiempo, vertiginosa, como en los sueños.

Sospecharon que éramos espías. Ningún turista iba a ir a buscar ídolos eróticos en ese universo de arena, viento y soledad. Nos metieron en una profunda caverna en medio de las dunas donde estuvimos cautivos por un tiempo que nos pareció infinito. Por las noches nos helábamos pese a yacer estrechamente abrazados sobre la arena de un cauce seco y unas matas de hierba rala. Durante el día nos sofocaba el calor.

Siempre estaban apostados en la boca de la cueva dos o tres beduinos armados. De tanto en tanto bajaban a observarnos con sus linternas sordas que nos bañaban por un rato con el polvo de hueso de sus haces de luz blanca. Hacia el amanecer nos traían agua y leche fermentada de cabras. La miraban a Jimena con deslumbramiento y se iban sin dejar de volver el rostro hacia nosotros. Estábamos condenados al hambre, a la abstinencia de la carne y del sueño. Nos poseía una extraña sensación, casi sobrenatural, como de estar enterrados vivos.

Jimena se apretaba a mí. Yo esperaba de un momento a otro lo peor. Lo veía reflejado en los ojos cargados de deseo de los bellos etíopes. Y Jimena temía ver reproducidas en esa caverna africana las escenas que le había relatado la anciana campesina en el Guairá del Paraguay. Veía de nuevo a las muchachas violadas por la soldadesca del tirano, no ya como oyente sino como víctima, ella misma, tras mi previo degüello.

Trataba yo en vano con desesperación de calmar

la suya. Maldecía mil veces mi inconsciencia, mi estupidez, por haber mencionado a los saharauis nuestra búsqueda del fetiche erótico. Como si yo mismo hubiera lanzado el fatal exorcismo del pez infernal contra el cuerpo de Jimena, para hacerlo más visible y deseable a esos hombres del desierto.

Cuando no estaban los centinelas, para ocupar de alguna manera ese tiempo muerto, Jimena se puso a estudiar las piedras de extrañas vetas amarillas que relumbraban en la penumbra. En realidad buscaba un agujero de escape a través de esos embudos como chimeneas que a veces se encuentran en las cuevas rocosas.

Un rayo de luz lívida caía perpendicular a través de algún hueco invisible. Lo buscamos con empeño. Pero lo que descubrimos fue un nido de arañas gigantes. Inmóviles y como al acecho habían girado todas hacia nosotros sus antenas inmensas. Matamos muchas con pedazos de roca. La batalla duró toda la tarde. Jimena lanzó de pronto un grito de horror señalando con el dedo varias arañas muertas patas arriba.

Me acerqué a ver. Sentí que la piel y los cabellos se me erizaban con el horror del grito que había exhalado Jimena. En el vientre de las peludas arañas observé dos botones como los de una protuberancia umbilical unida a una hendidura muy semejante a un orificio vulvar, unido a su vez al ano de los arácnidos situado entre las ocho larguísimas patas. Lo que veíamos se asemejaba bastante a una alucinación de nuestros sentidos calenturientos y agotados.

Era demasiado. El pez-útero de Set, desterrado del Edén, convertido en arañas cainitas, tataranietas oscuras del padre Adán, unidas contra nosotros después de millones de años por el cordón umbilical de la creación, del pecado y de la muerte.

—¡No puede ser!... —murmuraba Jimena, asida a mis brazos.

Retrocedimos hacia un lugar más despejado de la cueva. Corríamos el riesgo de que hubiesen escapado algunas. De pronto la oscuridad inundó el recinto. Estuvimos toda la noche de pie con las espaldas pegadas a la pared de piedra, metidos hasta las rodillas en una laguna pútrida cuyas aguas al ser removidas soltaban un hedor que nos asfixiaba y nos hacía toser sin parar.

Algunas linternas sordas entraron en la cueva hacia el amanecer como en los días anteriores.

Súbitamente dejé de ver a Jimena. Se había escondido en una anfractuosidad. Señalé a los saharauis el centenar de arañas destripadas como para desviar su atención. Ni siquiera se fijaron en los cascarones oscuros. Con señas y voces sordas preguntaron por Jimena. Señalé una dirección falsa. Fueron directamente al lugar donde ella se había ocultado. La extrajeron de la grieta arrastrándola de los brazos. Me lancé contra ellos, impotente. De un fuerte golpe con la culata de su arma en la cabeza alguien me derribó inconsciente.

Cuando recobré el sentido no vi más a Jimena. Me arrastré reptando hacia el exterior. Allí estaba ella, en medio de saharauis, bebiendo de un odre que le habían alcanzado. Me volvió el alma al cuerpo. Jimena se aproximó, me ayudó a incorporarme y me dio a beber de la vasija protegida del calor por un grueso forro de lana. Los saharahuis bromeaban y se reían entre ellos como ante una escena muy divertida.

El sol comenzaba a subir hacia levante sobre la cadena montañosa del Atlas, pintando de un rosado tierno las cumbres nevadas. Desde el cielo del norte bajaba hacia nosotros velozmente una mancha oscura.

Por aviso de los mismos saharauis, un helicóptero español venía a rescatarnos. Nos llevaron, esposados, a Ceuta donde, al principio, nos confundieron con unos traficantes de droga venidos de Marruecos, a los que andaban buscando. Nuestro precario equipaje se había perdido y con él nuestros pasaportes. Hubo que esperar el resultado de consultas y averiguaciones con las autoridades españolas y francesas.

Drogados estábamos nosotros de fatiga, de hambre, de falta de sueño, los ojos inyectados de sangre, los labios y las encías ulceradas por un principio de escorbuto, los cuerpos hinchados y deformes por las picaduras de insectos, en el fondo felices por la imprevista aventura llegada a buen fin. Jimena estaba irreconocible. Pero esa fealdad que le infirió el desierto hacía resplandecer aún más la aureola de su belleza intocada.

La especial sensibilidad en que nos sumieron las vicisitudes de esta peregrinación hizo reflotar en mí la imagen alucinante del políptico de Mathis o Mathaeus Grünewald, que no había contemplado sino en malas reproducciones.

—No podemos dejar de verlo —propuse a Jimena.

Las serviciales tarjetas del *eurailpass* nos llevaron a Colmar. Fuimos directamente al ex convento convertido en museo. Un guía nos condujo por el pasillo que circunda el jardín y entramos en el recinto de una capilla. En el salón, alumbrado fantasmalmente por el claroscuro coloreado de los vitrales, no veíamos el políptico por ninguna parte. Olvidaba yo que el retablo entero, compuesto por numerosas alas plegables, había sido desarmado, al ser traído de Issenheim, su ciudad de origen, en los vaivenes territoriales de las guerras entre Alemania y Francia. No hubiera podido caber de otra manera en la pequeña capilla gótica de Colmar.

—¿Dónde está el Cristo? —preguntamos con gestos al guía esbozando en el aire la señal de la Cruz.

El rudo y parco alsaciano tendió la mano. Giramos la cabeza y vimos avanzar hacia nosotros, como respondiendo a nuestra pregunta, el panel central con la escena de la crucifixión. Una increíble fuerza como de succión magnética nos absorbió hacia el centro mismo del campo óptico del cuadro que irradiaba una fuerza tremenda. La cruz plantada a flor de tierra se combaba hacia nosotros. El cuerpo del Crucificado se hallaba a nuestra misma altura, como saliéndose del marco. Daba la impresión de que en cualquier momento iba a desprenderse de la Cruz. Con un movimiento reflejo tendimos los brazos hacia Él para recogerlo y evitarle la última vejación de la caída.

El Cristo de Mathis Grünewald estaba ahí, vivo, agonizando en la cruz de ramas silvestres hacía más de cuatro siglos o veinte siglos o los eones todos desde que el hombre es hombre, aureolado por la dignidad siniestra de ser el asesino de su hermano. El que engendró la raza cainita, la especie más feroz que habita el planeta. El Hijo de Dios, hecho Hombre, había querido redimirla y salvarla sin lograr otra cosa que hacerla cada vez más feroz y miserable.

Las laceraciones que cubrían el cuerpo de ese cadáver viviente le comunicaban una suerte de doloroso estremecimiento. Temblaban los pectorales con espasmos tetánicos, como si le costara un gran esfuerzo respirar. El pecho, abombado por la putrefacción, soltaba al aire algunas costillas, entre los pedazos de lanzas rotas clavadas en las carnes descompuestas. Las manos grandes y amoratadas se crispaban bajo los clavos enormes. Las rodillas entrechocaban sus rótulas en las piernas retorcidas hasta los pies. ¡Esos pies! Eran horribles esos pies esponjosos y coagulados, puestos uno encima de otro. Se aplanaban y extendían en la putrefacción hasta parecer los de un palmípedo monstruoso. Las negras y cuadradas cabezas de los clavos sobresalían de las carnes amoratadas. El pulgar y el índice, crecidos desmesuradamente, arañaban casi el suelo formando la V de una cruz gamada.

Por encima de este cadáver en ebullición la cabeza enorme y tumultuosa colgaba sobre el pecho, bajo el peso de la enmarañada corona de espinas que se clavaban en la frente. Los ojos entreabiertos y cenicientos manaban una infinita mirada de sufrimiento y de terror. Jimena se cubrió el rostro, sus manos temblaban.

Huysmans, a comienzos de siglo, contempló y describió con inocultable emoción mística, la Crucifixión de Matheus Grünewald, a la que calificó de la mayor obra de naturalismo sobrenatural que produjo el gótico tardío, la más poderosa Crucifixión que se haya pintado jamás. Le dio un título exaltado: "la divina abyección de Grünewald". No podía yo alejar de mi mente ni dejar de sobreimprimir sobre el Cristo del retablo que estábamos contemplando las imágenes evocadas por las palabras del gran escritor de *Allá lejos*, que prefiguraban su conversión.

La sensación que me sobrecogió era de otra naturaleza. Algo extraño perturbaba mi visión. Observé de pronto que a la cabeza gacha le había crecido una espesa barba. Y en ese mismo instante tuve conciencia de que en el Cristo de Colmar había estado contemplando todo el tiempo el Cristo de Cerro-Corá.

Lo extraño es que ese retablo no era conocido en América. Y de seguro lo era menos aún por los sacrificadores. Yo vi una reproducción de ese retablo muchos años después, ya en el exilio europeo. Para los invasores y victimarios del siglo pasado la crucifixión de Solano López no pasó de ser una parodia vengativa y burlesca. Pero la irrisión sacrílega que la soldadesca brasilera ejecutó con el cadáver del enemigo vencido y profanado de la manera más bárbara era, por un misterio inexplicable, la réplica exacta de la crucifixión de Grünewald, pintada cuatro siglos antes. Se trataba indudablemente de una de esas misteriosas simetrías que se encuentran de pronto en la realidad infinita y desconocida del cosmos, entre nuestra realidad miserable y opaca y el transfigurador universo del arte, sin que ninguna ley física ni razón sobrenatural puedan explicar estas coincidencias.

Jimena parecía petrificada. El rostro intensamente pálido, denotaba el choque de contradictorios sentimientos. La tomé de la mano y escapamos de ese calvario. Su hedor sobrenatural se mezclaba con el aroma de las flores que fuimos pisoteando como ebrios y ciegos sin encontrar la salida. Las pesadas manos del alsaciano cayeron sobre nosotros y nos llevaron a empellones hacia las verjas. Discretamente le tendí una cristiana propina. De un manotazo, como quien espanta una mosca, hizo volar el arrugado billete sin que se le moviera un músculo en las pétreas facciones.

Jimena en camisa de dormir se peinaba ante el espejo. La imagen reflejada me la mostró cada vez más parecida a la *Joven peinándose* de Tiziano. Sentí un ansia tremenda de su cuerpo, de su ombligo, de esa sangre caliente que pone rubicundas sus mejillas, de ese óleo de vida que vuelve más negra su larga cabellera. Era una impulsión rabiosa, casi animal. Necesitaba desquitarme y resarcirme de cuevas, de arañas peludas, de ese sabor a muerte que sentíamos escocer como un ácido nuestros cuerpos, luego de haber estado sumidos durante horas en "la divina abyección de Grünewald". Sólo una línea infinitesimal separa la emoción mística del transporte amoroso. La franqueamos en la ingravidez palpitante del deseo.

A la luz de la luna el maravilloso vientre de Jimena resumía y concentraba la entera belleza de su cuerpo, la energía de su ser. Y, en ese vientre, el hoyo del ónfalo brillaba con las partículas de su ámbar, de su néctar. Únicamente la lengua doblada en dos, como un anélido chupador, podía penetrar hasta el fondo y succionar suavemente la ambrosía de ese licor alucinógeno. Yo lo hacía con los ojos cerrados, sin respetar el proverbio árabe: "Por encima del ombligo no hay pecado".

La comba lisa y plena del vientre, en posición horizontal, no tenía ya arriba ni abajo. Ninguna frontera delimitaba zonas de pecado o de impureza. El vaso colmado de luna y de licor se transformaba en el centro erótico del cosmos. Cubría todo el universo de los sueños. Cada partícula, imantada por el deseo, alcanza a reproducir, a *ser* todo el cuerpo. El pliegue húmedo de la comisura del párpado y las sedosas pestañas, las axilas húmedas, los lugares más secretos del cuerpo de una mujer, pueden alcanzar a reproducir en el voluptuoso trance la suave cavidad genital.

Esa foseta mórbida era todo el cuerpo de Jimena. Los cristales de luna con gusto a leche, a miel, a sal de mares profundos, a la miel almizclada de las abejas negras, al óleo de su propio sudor, de sus jugos más recónditos, se disolvían en la boca en un goce indecible. Y cada cristal reproducía como un espejo, a escala cada vez más pequeña, hasta el infinito, el cuerpo de Jimena, su vientre, su ombligo, su sexo, y otra vez su cuerpo, su vientre, su ombligo, su sexo, y yo como un insecto negro peregrinando sobre esas hermosuras, sobre esos óleos, sobre esas sales, sobre esas esencias, libándolos con deleite inagotable.

Ayer tuve un incidente con Jimena, el primero desde que nos conocemos. Un malentendido ajeno a nosotros, absurdo y casi increíble, a propósito de la carta de una estudiante de posgrado a quien dirijo en su tesis sobre literatura hispanoamericana contemporánea.

Leda Kautner es una muchacha alemana que hace sus estudios en París. La carta en verdad nada tiene que ver con la tesis. Bastante ambigua, deja entrever lo obvio: lo que suele ocurrir a veces entre un profesor y sus alumnas jóvenes: esa reversión de lo paternal hacia lo afectivo y aun hacia lo erótico.

La carta, de varias carillas escritas con letra nerviosa e irregular, llegó plegada en finos dobleces en un sobre de gran formato color fucsia y con mi nombre escrito en letras mayúsculas, las de los anónimos y mensajes reservados. También su firma, al final, estaba escrita en letras capitales y bajo la fecha, la palabra subrayada: *Personal*.

Suprimiré o resumiré los párrafos demasiado incoherentes. Como el del sueño obsesivo que la acosa y del que me acusa. Se ve atacada por un hombre que la viola y la apuñala en un descampado. Ese hombre soy yo. Muerta, ve la reconstrucción del crimen que el juez instructor manda hacer.

Leda comenta: "En mi región natal de Transilvania existe una creencia popular ingenua y terrible. Dicen que la sangre de un muerto vuelve a manar de sus heridas si el asesino las toca. ¡Lo terrible es que entre los sospechosos que el juez somete a la prueba *in extremis* está usted, profesor!... Esto es lo que más me martiriza. Pasan uno a uno los presuntos asesinos. Tocan con sus dedos mis heridas, pero éstas siguen secas. Pasa usted, el último, y bajo su dedo tembloroso las heridas empiezan a sangrar. Usted debe decirme algo... Este suplicio del sueño debe terminar... Yo sé que usted me comprenderá y me ayudará a liberarme de él..."

Me hace varias confidencias de carácter íntimo. Cuenta que ha nacido en la ciudad de Tirgu Muresh, en los Cárpatos. Huérfana a los pocos años de padre y madre, muertos en los campos de concentración de Ceaucescu, fue adoptada por una familia alemana, los Kautner, que pudieron huir del horror y la llevaron a Munich. Hasta ahora viven allí entre los recuerdos de Hitler a quien los Kautner a un tiempo odian y veneran. Viven en una casa cercana a la cervecería donde éste inició su utopía milenarista del Superhombre, de la super raza destinada a conquistar el mundo y purificarlo en los hornos crematorios de las razas débiles y enfermas.

La muchacha maldice ese sueño que le ha hecho odiar su sexo, y al que culpa de su soledad y de sus temores. No lo tuve nunca antes, se queja. Habla de una fecha reciente. Me hace responsable de su pesadilla obsesiva. El chantaje es evidente. Relata en detalle algunas de sus fantasías eróticas y al final me formula una extraña pregunta que le han inspirado, según explica, algunos fragmentos del *Zarathustra* de Nietzsche : "¿No cree usted que la mujer es un animal a punto de convertirse en un ser humano y que sólo puede transmutarse a través del amor?... ¿El amor de quién?... ¿Existe el amor?..." Siguen algunas exaltadas reflexiones que claramente me aluden. Finalmente me suplica que la acompañe en la *soutenance* de su tesis por temor al *trac* que le suele sobrevenir en los momentos difíciles.

La inconcebible actitud de Leda trastorna mis ideas sobre la relación hombre/mujer. Siempre sospeché que el hombre usa a la mujer para que la mujer no abuse de él. El gesto desenvuelto, repentino, casi demasiado teatral de Leda, abría la posibilidad inversa: la de que la mujer pueda usar al hombre para afirmar su superioridad frente a él. Yo aceptaba de hecho y de derecho este trueque posible, pues siempre me pareció errado el que la mujer no buscara remontarse a su nivel natural: el de su superioridad biológica frente el hombre. Resignada a su esclavitud inmemorial, la mujer se resiste a ver en el hombre al animal de presa, a su depredador y explotador.

Está además la desproporción inmensa en la relación de fuerzas entre la mujer y el hombre, dueño de las fuentes de trabajo, autor de las leyes, juez y ejecutor de las normas, protagonista exclusivo de la política y del "arte" de gobernar, regulador del universo social hecho a su imagen y semejanza, etc., etc. Toda la retahíla de conceptos y hechos tan transitada por las llamadas "ciencias humanas".

Tiempo atrás yo había escrito para la Revista de la Universidad un artículo sobre este tema. Mejor dicho, sobre la enorme angustia que experimenta el hombre ante el más pequeño avance de la mujer en la recuperación de su libertad y sus derechos, ante la menor manifestación de su independencia. Trataba de describir, apoyado en la documentación de especialistas y en estadísticas actualizadas, los mecanismos de defensa y contra ataque que el "género viril" desencadena contra su "media costilla" al menor conato de rebeldía, al menor amago de subir en derecho de sí al lugar que le corresponde. "Vivimos en un mundo —concluía el artículo— atacado por una enfermedad incurable, llamada hombre."

En aquel ensayo propugnaba yo el estudio y la discusión de una nueva educación sentimental, sexual y moral ante los estragos, en el mundo occidental, de la civilización tecnológica y antihumanista. Preconizaba, dentro del contexto de la civilización de la imagen y de la libido al desnudo, la transformación de la libertad sexual y del epicureísmo burgués en una nueva práctica remodeladora del cuerpo y del espíritu humanos. La esencia de esta transformación debía radicar, en síntesis, en la camaradería ética y estética y en el mutuo respeto de la pareja (la célula más pequeña de la sociedad humana: par de dos solos en la unidad de dos en compañía); en la realización de la fusión sexual y de lo erótico basada en la plena exaltación del deseo como identificación y sinergia de dos voluptuosidades diferentes, a veces antagónicas, en la armonización de dos fuerzas contrarias. En otras palabras: abolir el egoísmo sexual y asumir el cuerpo del otro como centro de gravitación y equilibrio de lo erótico, cualesquiera fuesen los géneros, la naturaleza y la edad de las parejas.

Creo que este artículo fue poco leído en mis cursos. En general, las muchachas no quieren saber nada del "histerismo intelectual" del feminismo, al que consideran una invención paranoica de la secta mujeril "lesbianizada"; acaso una trampa fomentada por los mismos hombres para mejor usar y abusar de las mujeres.

—El feminismo mal entendido es machismo al revés —le oí decir a una de las activistas más recalcitrantes, una especie de virago con la voz abaritonada y espeso bozo oscuro sobre los labios—. El machismo feminista ha producido un choc emocional funesto para las mujeres. Ha creado un nuevo derecho para la mujer: el derecho a ser desgraciada.

—No queremos ser mujeres machistas —adujo otra—. No queremos mandar a los hombres a casa, a la cocina o al diablo. No es nuestra idea convertirlos en capones y hacer que se vuelvan todos eunucos y homosexuales. Esto es asunto suyo. Queremos mandar en nosotras como mujeres. Acabar con el acoso sexual de los hombres, con el chantaje y soborno en los puestos de trabajo, en los que las secretarias deben andar con cinturón de castidad y peto blindado. Queremos competir con los hombres de igual a igual. Elegir al hombre o a la mujer que nos guste, hacer el amor con él o con ella, vivir con él o con ella mientras nos gustemos mutuamente, y que cada uno se vaya por su camino sin hacerse reproches ni pasar falsas facturas...

La discusión entre feminismo y machismo, entre los partidarios de la homo, de la bi y de la heterosexualidad surgió durante el velatorio de dos componentes del seminario y continuó en los cursos los días que siguieron al triste episodio. Dos muchachos homosexuales, que formaban pareja y vivían en la unidad y con la dignidad de un matrimonio en regla, fueron atacados por el sida y murieron casi al mismo tiempo con diferencia de pocas horas. El malafortunado suceso dio pie a que alguien llegara al extremo de sostener que el sida es un invento "gay", una enfermedad venérea engendrada por los homosexuales y que éstos eran los verdaderos "homi-cidas o sex-sidas". El violento y confuso debate no podía llegar a ninguna conclusión razonable.

Por su parte, las mujeres que no querían ser más que mujeres, sostenían que la obsesión de la igualdad a todo trance con el hombre les ha hecho sacrificar sus aspiraciones sentimentales y maternales más legítimas. En todo caso, no les importan demasiado estos vaivenes del péndulo en la lucha de los géneros: lo que los yanquis llaman *"backlash"*, los franceses *"retour de manivelle"* y en español "golpe de culata" o "efecto de retrocarga". Las muchachas y los muchachos sólo coincidieron en que lo único importante era la pulsión sexual del inmediato presente. La fugacidad del "vértigo horizontal" de la encamada era lo único que podía exigírsele al amor homo, bi o heterosexual. Fuera de esto, afirmaron en su mayoría, no hay nada. No nos importa nada. Salvo repetir el juego hasta que el *croupier* de la ruleta cante: "¡No va más!".

Ignoro las ideas que tiene Leda Kautner al respecto. Por su carta creo entender que se está produciendo en ella un despertar algo tardío de su condición de mujer, de la larva del sexo en el sueño letárgico en que estaba sumida. Un despertar en verdad un poco alarmante y flamígero. Se pueden adivinar las raíces del mal en su lejana y pesadillesca infancia transilvana bajo la tradición gótica del vampirismo, el régimen de terror de Ceaucescu, gemelo en cierto modo del de Stroessner, los cuales se podían resumir en el aforismo: "Si estás invitado a cenar por un vampiro debes contribuir con tu sangre".

Revisé el *Zarathustra*. En el capítulo titulado *Del conocimiento inmaculado*, se lee: "Cuando vi salir la luna anoche, tan abultada y preñada sobre el horizonte, creí que iba a parir un sol. Pero esa pretendida preñez era falsa. Antes creeré hombre a la luna, que mujer..." La parábola del filósofo nihilista y misógino destila su pequeño veneno: "En la luna hay un monje lascivo y envidioso, que se pasea por los tejados rondando y espiando las ventanas entornadas. Lascivo de todo lo que hay de más obsceno en la noche... envidioso de todos los placeres y alegrías de los amantes..."

Leda Kautner pregunta en la carta con una ingenuidad o un cinismo bien poco nietzscheanos: "Lo de la luna-hombre no me extraña puesto que en alemán luna, *mond*, es voz masculina. Lo que me intriga es el concepto negativo del placer (está tachado 'el goce') que propone Nietzsche. ¿Es que el placer es sólo gozar con el placer de los otros 'mirando', espiando, a través de las ventanas entornadas como ese monje oscuro y encapuchado?" (Hay otra tachadura muy compacta bajo la cual se adivina más que se lee: "¿O hay que entrar directamente en las alcobas por las ventanas entornadas...?" (El resto, ilegible.)

La gata sobre el tejado de zinc caliente... pensé con cierto humor recordando la pieza de Tennessee Williams. Imaginaba a Leda en los tejados espiando furtivamente las ventanas entornadas. Y es verdad que en algunos momentos surge en Leda algo como un aura animalesca: esa voluptuosidad de una gata de angora en periodo de celo con la pelambre tornasolada y erizada al doble de su tamaño, cuyas miradas son capaces de hipnotizar un árbol. He rastreado en las enciclopedias el origen y la historia de la raza gatuna en todas sus especies y variedades. Las gatas de Transilvania son las más terribles, las caprichosas e imprevisibles.

Pero este aspecto de la personalidad de Leda Kautner no dura sino como una efímera y turbia reverberación de su intimidad. Podría pensarse en la latencia de un vicio remoto e inalcanzable, no revelado todavía en ella como vicio, y que curiosamente constituye por ahora la fuerza de su carácter solitario, la base de su virtud de reserva, de apartamiento; para decirlo todo, de su castidad intransigente, si es que efectivamente la guardaba por temor a lo desconocido o por el prurito de una soberanía mal entendida de mujer aún inmadura.

"¿Puede usted, querido Profesor, aclararme esta duda? —seguía la carta—. Los libros siempre son más engañosos que los hechos de la vida real ¿no es cierto? ... Voy caminando por la orilla de mi cuerpo pero no lo encuentro. Tal vez esté en poder de otro o no lo he tenido nunca. No encuentro mi cara. No sé quién soy... ¿Puede usted ayudarme? Prometo no crearle problemas de ninguna índole y me someto desde ahora por completo a su voluntad, experiencia y sabiduría..., a lo que usted quiera hacer conmigo..."

Me sorprendió enormemente esta carta a la vez tan risiblemente infantil e "intelectual". Leda Kautner me impresionó siempre por su inteligencia, por una gran timidez que suele llenar de rubor sus mejillas y cortar por completo su capacidad de comunicación. Hay momentos en que su silueta grácil, su rostro sonrosado y pequeño de finas facciones en proporción a su estatura y largo cuello, tendieran a apagarse, como si se replegara hacia su interioridad, absorta en una idea fija o en un recuerdo. Al principio pensé que era miope, pero nunca le vi usar lentes.

En otros momentos relampaguea en sus ojos dorados esas ráfagas de ansiedad brotadas de una profunda sensualidad que no se aviene en absoluto, al menos en apariencia, con la modalidad de su carácter, como si hubiese en ella algo misteriosamente falseado. Su rostro sensible y asustadizo deja adivinar una niña ultrajada por un oscuro drama del que seguramente no guarda memoria, o por la sospecha del deseo carnal del que tampoco debe de tener conciencia y que aumenta en ella el temor al sexo y la rebelión contra sí misma por no aceptarlo.

Puedo recordar por separado cada uno de sus rasgos, la nariz recta de aletas palpitantes, la barbilla firme, los dientes perfectos, la cabellera larga hasta la cintura, de un rubio oro con destellos rojizos, las pupilas del mismo color en los ojos rasgados y oblicuos, casi caucásicos, el torso breve, las piernas largas y bien torneadas de montañesa, el pequeño lunar junto a la comisura de los labios, el gesto de las manos cruzadas cuando duda o se resiste a hablar entrecerrando los ojos hasta convertirlos en dos hendiduras que dejan filtrar su brillo dorado. Lo que en ella causa más impresión es su voz completamente ronca de un registro grave que cae a menudo en un ronroneo gutural, como si estuviera siempre a punto de interrumpirse. Recuerdo todo eso. Pero me resulta imposible reconstituir el conjunto de su figura o de su rostro, cosa que raramente me suele ocurrir con mis alumnos a quienes recuerdo por años en los menores detalles de su presencia física, de su personalidad, de su carácter. A Leda Kautner la solía llamar en clase con el apodo latino de Fulva, por su color dorado, leonado.

Desde que la conocí, al comienzo de los cursos, se estableció entre nosotros una comunicación ambigua, dividida entre la simpatía y la hostilidad. Sus labios finos pero bien formados dejan entrever una necesidad de bondad y aun de dulzura en la lenta y apenas esbozada sonrisa que desaparece en seguida en su permanente seriedad. Atrae y repele a la vez por esa manera de tornarse incolora hasta parecer espectral. Un ser evanescente. Una vez tuve que llamarla por su nombre para descubrirla en clase. Se levantó en su pupitre, entre sorprendida y altiva.

—Ah, estaba usted ahí... —le dije con cierto tono de ironía y reproche—. Parece que a usted le agrada meterse bajo su sombra. Deje un aviso cuando esté ausente.

No dijo nada, pero se quedó mirándome fijamente como si ella también me hubiera descubierto de pronto y no acabara de reconocerme. Permaneció callada con su aspecto de adolescente herida, su semblante asustadizo y hosco, su actitud a la vez desdeñosa, exasperada, de ostensible agresividad. De haber estado cerca de ella pienso que me hubiese dado una bofetada. Hondas rayas le cruzaron la frente como si hubiera envejecido de golpe. Esa actitud duró sólo un instante. Tras el oscuro relámpago, volvió a adoptar en seguida su expresión de ausencia y de reserva, de áspero e intratable retraimiento. Recordé en ese momento que ella era la única que no participaba de nuestros paseos. Acabadas las clases se retiraba furtivamente, nadie la veía desaparecer. Leda Kautner era sin embargo una de las mejores alumnas, cosa que tampoco le perdonaban sus compañeras.

Pese a este desentendimiento inicial, me pidió poco después que la dirigiera en su tesis. En todo el tiempo que llevamos trabajando juntos jamás se insinuó el menor atisbo de lo que ahora sucede. O quizás uno, vagamente premonitorio. Una tarde, en la salita de estudios de la Facultad, nos hallábamos solos mientras trabajábamos con las fichas. En un momento dado me rozó la mano sin querer. Me pidió disculpas con un monosílabo gutural y enfurruñado. Se le cayó el lápiz; nos agachamos los dos a recogerlo. Nuestras cabezas chocaron con cierta violencia. Pasé mi mano por su frente, en el sitio donde se veía el rosetón del golpe, pidiéndole a mi vez que me disculpara. Se levantó impulsivamente, con la cara al rojo vivo. Recogió sus libros y carpetas y se marchó sin despedirse.

Al día siguiente nos volvimos a ver. Parecía completamente olvidada del incidente. Me dio a leer el capítulo final sobre el silencio como expresión de un discurso subyacente en la narrativa latinoamericana, el correspondiente al sustrato cultural indígena y africano. Ha estado trabajando durante dos años principalmente en México y Brasil. Sus análisis temáticos se basan en las obras de los principales autores latinoamericanos, con referencia y en oposición dialéctica a los cronistas de Indias más representativos, a los que considera como los verdaderos clásicos de las letras americanas. Su tesis es de lo mejor concebido y escrito por estudiantes europeos dedicados a la cultura y literatura latinoamericanas, que he leído en estos últimos años.

Leda habla correctamente siete idiomas y conoce varios dialectos transilvanos y eslavos. Posee el don de lenguas. El texto de la carta revela una inteligencia poco común, pero a la vez un espíritu atormentado, lleno de meandros incomprensibles. La obsesión habita su mundo cerrado y sombrío. La tesis y la carta, sin embargo, parecen provenir de dos personas no sólo diferentes sino antagónicas.

Por la ausencia total de sobrentendidos, la carta podía ser tomada como la expresión de un auténtico candor. Pero también, a la inversa, de ser premeditada, como la obra maestra de la astucia para simular este candor y valerse de él con algún fin preconcebido. La manipulación descarada, casi desafiante, de una intimidad que no existe entre nosotros, anula toda presunción de candidez o de inadvertencia. En cualquier caso, no pude leer la carta sin experimentar la sensación de un golpe bajo bastante artero y vil. No supe distinguir al comienzo entre lo que podía ser el producto de un trastorno moral o psíquico o un vengativo ajuste de cuentas, acaso por el distanciamiento en el que se habría sentido relegada por mí pero que ella misma establece con los demás.

Después de todo yo he hecho lo posible por ayudarla, y no recordaba ninguna desatención que la excluyera. Por el contrario, en ocasiones, incluso, la he puesto ante los demás como ejemplo de inteligencia y modestia. Lo cierto es que al principio, al menos, consideré su carta como una agresión inmotivada y gratuita, que me irritó sobremanera con una mezcla de cólera y resentimiento que me costó mucho superar. La actitud de Leda habría que leerla del revés y en función de su peculiar modo de ser. Yo no supe hacerlo.

Mostré la carta a Jimena, a quien no suelo ocultarle estas peripecias un poco histéricas del oficio, que ella por su parte también conoce con respecto a sus alumnos varones y aun con respecto a alguna de sus alumnas, esas que suelen caer en lo que comúnmente se suele llamar, con algún eufemismo, "confusión de sentimientos". Mientras leía la carta, el rostro de Jimena se fue poniendo serio y sus facciones se endurecieron.

—¿Algo anda mal? —me preguntó con una voz distinta de la habitual.

—En la mente o en el cuerpo de esa muchacha se me antoja que sí —dije por decir algo porque yo mismo no sabía tomar la cosa sino con una mezcla de humor y desazón—. Esquizofrénica, paranoica tal vez. Quiere probarse a sí misma de que es capaz de ser normal como las otras. Pero le falta valor para afrontar la realidad y se siente perseguida por todos y por todo.

Esa muchacha, Leda Kautner, es muy rara, conté como quien se refiere a un hecho común. Sus compañeros se burlan de ella diciendo que es hermosa como el Paraíso pero tonta como un conejo. No le gusta hacer vida de grupos. No va a juergas ni a discotecas ni a las orgías de grupos. No fuma marihuana ni hachís ni se acuesta con nadie, se mofan los varones. Las compañeras no son más complacientes y aprovechan la menor ocasión para ridiculizar sus modos de ser, de vestir, de comportarse. Se burlan de la ronquera extraña de su voz que algunas atribuyen a vicios inconfesables. Le ponen a escondidas jeringas y cajas de preservativos en el bolso, fotos, las más obscenas, recortadas de revistas pornográficas, agresiones que ella ignora o que, por lo menos, no tienen ninguna reacción de su parte.

—Tal vez se droga en secreto —dijo una—, con ese aspecto de mosquita muerta que tiene.

La niña montañesa de los Cárpatos no ha sabido adaptarse a la vida moderna, y menos aún al ritmo alocado, cada vez más disoluto, lleno de cinismo y de libertinaje en la vida estudiantil de las grandes ciudades. La libertad de las costumbres es el supremo don que hay que conquistar hasta la exasperación, ya que no existen otros a la vista.

—Leda Kautner no entra en el juego por ñoñez, por cobardía o por alguna disfunción glandular —comenté a Jimena sin convicción—. Es una bala perdida, que no tiene remedio —dije creyendo que ponía con ello punto final al desagradable *affaire* de la alumna que había cogido una repentina calentura hacia el profesor.

Al decir esto sentí que mentía un poco ignominiosamente, de modo directo e indirecto, con un cinismo más hipócrita que el de las muchachas y los muchachos que yo acababa de criticar. Jimena me escuchaba como ausente. Leda Kautner no es así en absoluto; peca más bien de parquedad y de reserva. Pero bajo esa apariencia un poco fantasmal late una firmeza y una seguridad inconmovibles, un valor que puede llegar hasta el delirio. Poco después iba a dar pruebas de ello. Hablaba yo en ese momento tal vez bajo la impresión de la carta; quizás también para tranquilizar a Jimena con un comentario irónico y desvalorizador, inútil para su perspicacia, a veces excesiva.

—¿Te acuerdas de Brunilde, la de Ginebra?...

Me interrumpí sin terminar la frase porque comprendí de inmediato que había cometido una *gaffe* completamente torpe, agravada por el recuerdo de Brunilde, la adolescente suiza que pasó un mes en nuestra casa con su tesis bajo la dirección de Jimena. Un paralelo de tal índole (Brunilde nos había propuesto una noche con toda naturalidad y desparpajo acostarse con nosotros "para saber cómo era *eso*"), no resultaba en verdad lo más apropiado para aclarar y apaciguar la situación.

Aquella noche (lo recuerdo aún con estupor) Jimena llamó a Brunilde. La muchacha apareció en bata de dormir.

—Desnúdate —le ordenó imperativamente—. Ven y métete en la cama con nosotros para "ver cómo es eso".

Brunilde se encogió en su bata, dejó caer la cabeza sobre el pecho y se echó a llorar.

—Vete a dormir —le dijo Jimena en el mismo tono—. Y no tengas malos sueños. Mañana con el primer tren te vuelves a Ginebra. Y no te metas más en lo que no entiendes y debes descubrirlo por ti misma. Cuéntales a tus *papis* el motivo de tu regreso. Quedarán muy satisfechos y orgullosos.

Jimena me devolvió la carta después de plegarla doblez por doblez con una lentitud que disimulaba su indignación. No agregó una sola palabra y se encerró en un mutismo también poco habitual en ella. La apariencia de celos que a veces puede aparecer en sus sentimientos no son los celos vulgares provocados por el afán enfermizo de posesión o por la humillación del engaño y de la infidelidad. Jimena no siente nada de eso.

—Un amor adulto como el nuestro no puede ser adúltero —dijo una vez ella misma sorteando con un juego de palabras una situación análoga a la que se acaba de producir—. No adulteraré nuestra unión.

—Sí, Jimena —le respondí en el mismo tono—. Creo que ambos nos hallamos por encima de esa triste posibilidad. Estamos unidos por el amor *fati*, el amor de la pareja en la existencia real tal cual es. Y aún más: en el amor hecho destino. Un destino hecho por nosotros, como tú misma sueles decir.

—No podemos estar seguros de acertar siempre. La vida no es un banco de préstamos a largo plazo y a bajo interés. Vienen de pronto los descubiertos y los ajustes de cuenta. Siempre hay despilfarros imprevistos, pequeños devaneos que a veces suelen resultar caros —agregó con el retintín de cierta intención.

—Ni tú eres tan simple como para que te dejes engañar por las apariencias ni yo soy lo bastante idiota como para que mi amor por ti excluya la posibilidad de que puedas amar a otro. Quiero decir el derecho de que pongas en juego tu libertad. La libertad no admite imposiciones ni esclavitudes, se debilita y desaparece en la costumbre. Es su peor enemiga.

—Nadie desea verdaderamente su libertad. Cuando la tiene en plenitud busca el modo de perderla de otra manera.

—Siempre habrá alguien mejor que yo, simplemente por ser otro, que te está esperando en alguna esquina del universo.

—¡No seas tonto!

—Te debo la vida. Mientras ella dure seré tuyo...

—¡Basta! ¡Por favor! —me interrumpió de nuevo con la voz metálica—. No vuelvas a repetir ese sonsonete idiota que me hace sentir tu verdugo. Eres tan libre como yo y mi amor no exige el tuyo en exclusividad como retribución por haberte "salvado la vida". Y menos el tenerte aquí como un rehén en reclusión perpetua a la que tú mismo te has condenado.

—Yo la he elegido mientras no pueda hacer otra cosa.

Jimena me miró a los ojos profundamente y moviendo con reprobación la cabeza me dijo en un susurro de dientes apretados:

—¡Estás lleno de remordimiento! Tras la infidelidad viene el arrepentimiento. Pero yo sé que eres el hombre más fiel del mundo. Probablemente más que yo misma con respecto a ti. El día que no te ame más, te lo diré con la misma sinceridad.

—Lo sé. En ella descansa la seguridad de nuestra unión.

Jimena se levantó y dio unos pasos con los brazos cruzados, como hablando para sí.

—Y en cuanto a la fidelidad, la única fidelidad que cuenta es la que está segura de sí misma. Una verdadera fidelidad exige una lealtad que ninguna astucia por refinada que sea puede traicionar. No hay auténtica fidelidad más que la que acepta el amor del otro sin exigirle reciprocidad y sin juzgarlo cuando falta a la suya y pone con ello punto final a una relación acabada.

Se apoyó de espaldas en la pared y se volvió hacía mí; su entonación era crispada y apenas podía disimular su malestar íntimo.

—¿Lo harías tú, me exigirías tú esa reciprocidad?

—En este momento te diría que no —repuse ante su gesto inquisitivo—. Pero lo que para mí cuenta verdaderamente es tu generosidad.

—¿Por qué has de reprocharme a cada momento el que te haya puesto los calcetines cuando tú no podías hacerlo?

—¡Ah, si hubieran sido solamente los calcetines!

—Las mujeres paraguayas se someten enteramente a sus hombres, además de las otras esclavitudes atávicas que ellas mismas se imponen con humildad y amor verdaderamente aberrantes. ¡Las constructoras de templos, las mujeres de los éxodos y peregrinaciones, no son más que bestias de carga para todo servicio! No te salvé la vida. Hice simplemente lo que debí hacer, como tú lo hubieras hecho por mí en una situación semejante.

La cabeza alta y erguida, más hermosa aún por la ira sorda que hacía palpitar sus senos bajo la liviana camisa, se volvió hacia mí con aire compasivo. La miré en sus ojos enormes donde las pupilas contraídas eran apenas un punto oscuro, y la mordí en los labios, suavemente. Jimena cerró los ojos y me besó apasionada y largamente hasta perder el aliento mientras se dejaba caer sobre el diván.

—Tus escenas de celos me producen ternura —le dije—. Son tu manera de recordarme tu amor pero también lo que le falta. O tal vez lo que ya sobra de él. Herrumbre de la costumbre; es la enfermedad del metal pero también de nuestra frágil condición humana. Te lo previne un día. Hay para todo una edad límite. ¿No estará el de nuestro amor tocando esa raya final?

Volvió a sellar mis labios con un largo beso.

En realidad, estos desajustes en el equilibrio emotivo de Jimena responden a otras causas más profundas y sutiles. Son la parte de inseguridad, de temor, que ella no ha logrado dominar totalmente en su naturaleza sin embargo tan compacta y armoniosa. Conozco yo sus momentos de desesperación tranquila y temeraria. Odia la mentira y la hipocresía.

Hija del exilio, sin haber salido de ninguna parte, como ella misma suele decir, se siente exiliada por dentro. Nací en destierro y no salí de él, suele quejarse como en burla. Después de la batalla del Ebro, su padre y otros muchos llegaron a duras penas a la frontera con las armas en la mano. Los fugitivos fueron desarmados e internados en campos de concentración. Su madre con más de cuatrocientos niños de una escuela, de la que era directora, pudo fugarse en un barco de pesca un poco antes del sitio de Bilbao por las tropas rebeldes. Llegaron a Burdeos. De allí fueron conducidos a Prades donde el gran violoncelista Pau Casals tenía su colonia de niños refugiados.

Jimena conoce y aborrece sus limitaciones. La debilidad en los otros o en sí misma no le inspira ninguna compasión. Desprecia la piedad pero sobre todo la autocompasión. Cuando duda sobre algo o sobre alguien, es de ella misma de quien duda, y sólo en esos raros momentos de exasperación surge en ella el ser ciego y humillado que la violencia de la realidad ha injertado en la parte más oscura de su carácter. Jimena, tan carnal, tan terrena, no tiene un suelo firme que pueda considerar suyo y sobre el cual logre al fin hallar seguridad y paz del corazón. Se siente de pie sobre una estrecha cornisa al borde de un abismo. Se ve caer teniéndome a mí como testigo mudo que nada puede hacer para evitarlo. No teme la caída, aborrece perder su intimidad, incluso ante mí. Mi compañía la fortalece en su ansiedad de vivir pero también debilita la razón misma de esa ansiedad.

Necesita a veces exasperarse, "salirse" de sí, criticar y autocriticarse cuando descubre que amar ciegamente a alguien implica la entrega de lo más suyo sin posibilidad de construirse en compensación una fe, reprimiendo la autopiedad tanto como la estima de sí misma. ¿No es eso lo que le ocurre conmigo? Pienso que "inventa" sus celos para infligirse un castigo o cobrarse algunas cuentas del pasado. Se macera constantemente en purgar supuestos errores y faltas, suyas y de los otros, como si únicamente el castigo existiera como una aberración de la naturaleza humana. Estas rupturas pasajeras de su equilibrio la inmunizan por un tiempo contra sus dudas a costa del daño que le producen. Su hermosura serena, su perfil de medalla griega se alteran entonces como bajo los vapores de un ácido que manan de su interior. Su voz cambia de diapasón. Su cara de querer a todo el mundo puede llegar a tener en esos momentos una expresión implacable. Odia, detesta, con un sentimiento irreductible, las mentiras. Hay algo de infección de muerte en las mentiras, dijo una vez; algo de hedor a putrefacción de la dignidad humana. No las puedo soportar. Prefiero el silencio a las palabras falsas, porque comprendo que no todo puede decirse por infinitas, poderosas o pueriles razones.

Encontrarás muchos de esos silencios en este largo relato que ahora empieza, mi querida Morena. Leerás en lo escrito lo que no puede decirse de viva voz cuando falta el soplo del espíritu.

—¿Qué vas a hacer con esa muchacha? —me preguntó

—Nada —dije—. Ya se le pasará. Los cólicos eróticos de la adolescencia no duran. Se calman con los primeros sudores nocturnos y un leve frote del pubis con las sábanas. Luego se dedican a ejercicios más serios. Las mujeres jóvenes no saben todavía qué hacer con la libertad sexual que les trajeron dos guerras mundiales. Se hunden en el sexo, en toda su gama de matices, acabando por aburrirse o por buscar las variantes más absurdas de la homosexualidad y de la bisexualidad. Y el punto omega *gay* está aún lejos de ser alcanzado.

Jimena esperó a que se me bajara la espuma. Sin ánimo inquisitivo repitió su pregunta:

—¿Qué vas a hacer con tu alumna? Tendrás que ayudarla, supongo.

—No creo que esta muchacha esté en esto; al contrario, la creo en el extremo opuesto. Se arreglará sola.

—Hazla venir aquí.

—¿Con qué objeto?

—Ella necesita hablar contigo. Eres su director de tesis.

—Mi trabajo de dirección ha terminado.

—Es ahora cuando comienza, en lo más importante. Considero inmoral que esa chiquilla deslenguada se mofe de tu trabajo, de tu autoridad de profesor, de tu condición de hombre. Deberías enseñarle a distinguir y separar las cosas. La literatura nada tiene que ver con esto, o apenas de un modo indirecto. No todas las mujeres saben lo que quieren. Pero casi todas quieren lo que saben, aunque lo sepan torcidamente. Hazla venir y muéstrale que las cosas son normales cuando hay mutuo respeto y consideración.

Acepté de inmediato su propuesta porque yo mismo estaba interesado en aclarar una situación tan equívoca en la que yo no tenía arte ni parte pero en la que todas las apariencias parecían acusarme. Juzgaba descabellado dejar a Jimena en la sospecha de que yo era el seductor y mi alumna la víctima.

Jimena me atribuye la facultad de seducir con una suerte de "calculado desinterés", de "indiferencia hechizada", creando un espacio de lejanía y resistencia. Ve en mi comportamiento con las mujeres una actitud a la vez de respeto y de rechazo que excita la curiosidad de la gente joven del otro sexo y también de los efebos a los que no puedo ver y tratar sino como a hijos míos.

Creo que Jimena se equivoca en esto. Es cierto que adoro la belleza y la juventud de los cuerpos, pero no hay mayor placer que el comienzo de la curva del goce en el que el erotismo de la carne se sublima y nos transforma y podemos disfrutar de él sin ceder a las tentaciones de la fugacidad del sexo. Voluptuosidad de la sensualidad, sí, pero no de la sexualidad, cuya exacerbación se vuelve triste y tediosa a la larga, insaciable, devoradora y salvaje.

—Eres más callado que Aquiles. Pero tus pies son más ligeros. Tienes una manera de seducir que seduce por la manera. Abstención. Miradas llenas de una lejanía innominada. Quieres que te quieran, que te mimen, no que te compadezcan. Un lobo estepario que busca a la oveja joven y la ubica por el olor de la lana y del pis, que suelta el aroma de la carne tierna.

—¡Diagnóstico irrefutable! —dije por decir algo tomándolo a risa.

Tal vez ésta fue la experiencia inicial que Jimena tuvo conmigo —pensé—. Teme quizás que la virtud cautivadora de mi "indiferencia hechizada" produzca nuevas "víctimas".

Llamé a Leda por teléfono invitándola a venir. Llegó al día siguiente. Jimena no estaba. Cuando volví de la Facultad encontré un mensaje en el que me decía que se iba a Sevilla por unos días a terminar un trabajo de investigación que estaba haciendo en el Archivo de Indias.

Por la ventana divisé a Leda sentada en un banco del jardín palmeando el lomo del dálmata mientras esperaba con el aire contrito y humillado de quien se siente convocado a un tribunal. Los rayos del sol producían reflejos rojizos en su pelo dorado y liso que le cubría la espalda como una cascada y que la brisa del atardecer removía en ondas muy suaves. El dálmata le lamía una mano y ella le acariciaba con la otra el largo hocico. Luego te tocará hacer el cisne, me dije con ironía entre el temor y el fastidio.

Tuve un sobresalto momentáneo, pero no le di importancia. Después de todo, nunca he sabido reconocer los síntomas de la fatalidad cuando inicia uno de sus ciclos malafortunados. Lo tengo suficientemente probado. Las premoniciones no funcionan para mí. Y aquí, con esta muchacha, pese a lo extraño de su carta, de su actitud, de su gesto inexplicable, no había ningún riesgo que temer, salvo el no poder ofrecerle ninguna ayuda de las que ella me pide y necesita.

Los seres humanos no son malvados ni perversos; sólo son torpes o desdichados, me dije para tranquilizarme y neutralizar el malestar que esa visita me causaba. El rechazo que me produjo la carta, la repugnancia moral de sentirme "usado" por la súbita pasión de la joven, que amenazaba transformarse en insistente acoso, se apaciguaron un poco. Pensé que hay seres que envejecen prematuramente. Quizás sólo el alma de Leda era vieja. Medí la audacia, el valor y la desesperación de esa adolescente que venía arrastrada por un capricho enfermizo. O, peor aún, por el "terrible amor" con el que la casualidad la había herido como con un lanzazo. Esos amores equivocados y desgraciados desde su origen no toman a un hombre, a cualquier hombre, sino como pretexto para su revelación. Leda me había elegido mal y en mal momento, y este error fatal hacía doblemente desdichada su elección.

Tuve un vago presentimiento de lo que me esperaba al menor descuido, ante cualquier actitud que pudiera teñir de ambigüedad mi comportamiento con ella. En una situación semejante, hasta la rectitud y probidad más rigurosas podían resultar ambiguas. ¿O es que todo esto ya había estado sucediendo en mis relaciones con esta muchacha, sin darme cuenta de ello? En tal caso, sólo yo era el culpable de este equívoco; pero él prueba a su vez la poca importancia que yo concedía a esta supuesta intimidad. No sentía que esta intimidad, al menos como intentaba sugerir Leda en su carta, existiese en realidad, y menos aún, que la hubiera yo fomentado de manera inadvertida por mí. Me sentía al margen de todo remordimiento por el supuesto delito de haber infringido o estimulado lo prohibido. El trato con mis alumnos, sin ninguna excepción, se rige por una moral, no puritana sino simplemente humana, de respeto, de consideración, de libertad y tolerancia. No entendía que algo inexistente me exigiera lo que un hombre, en mi situación —una situación que Leda conoce bien—, no puede conceder.

Empecé a sentir cierta conmiseración por esa muchacha de remoto origen, por su infancia destruida en el reino de terror de Ceaucescu. ¿No estaba tratando de justificarla para ocultar la erupción de mi vanidad y poncrla a salvo de toda sospecha, incluso de la mía? O acaso la intimidad, la familiaridad que la carta reclamaba sorpresivamente y fuera de toda lógica, incluso de la caprichosa lógica sentimental, ¿no era más que el S.O.S. de un ser acorralado por la soledad, por la falta de confianza en sí misma, por el orgullo, por el terror? ¿Quién era Leda Kautner?

La observé un largo instante. Después fui a abrir la puerta.

Leda Kautner hizo honor a la confianza de Jimena. Quiero decir que ésta había vuelto a acertar con su intuición infalible. No había en Leda el menor vestigio de la perturbación que le había hecho escribir esa carta. Ni siquiera insinuó la menor alusión a ella. Traía otra clase de desasosiego más calmo pero contenido a duras penas.

Miraba en torno de sí, temerosa, y como al acecho de una sorpresa desagradable.

—Tranquilícese y póngase cómoda. Vamos a trabajar —le dije con voz firme y neutra—. Estoy solo en la casa. Pero aunque estuviera Jimena, mi mujer, no nos molestaría en absoluto. Ella recibe también aquí a sus alumnos de tesis.

No hizo el menor gesto. Sólo noté que las finas aletas nasales le palpitaban con ritmo más rápido que de costumbre. El rubor, en cambio, no subía a sus mejillas como otras veces, o por lo menos no conseguía teñir la palidez de su tez, atenuar las profundas ojeras que le excavaban el rostro sin maquillar. En la desazón que la dominaba ni siquiera pareció oírme.

Abrí los brazos disponiéndome a escucharla.

—¿Por dónde comenzamos?

Me tendió en silencio los libros y un fichero que le había prestado. Me entregó también la Revista de la Universidad en la que había aparecido mi artículo sobre feminismo y machismo muy favorable desde luego a la causa de la mujer frente a la "enfermedad incurable" del hombre. Leda venía simplemente a devolvérmelos. Con la voz más ronca que nunca y con un tartamudeo casi inaudible me agradeció mi ayuda y dijo que había desistido de presentar su tesis. No traía las dos gruesas carpetas de cuero negro.

—¿Dónde las tiene?

—Las quemé anoche.

—¿Por qué hizo eso?

Tardó mucho en responderme, como si no pudiera salir del estado de humillación y abatimiento que se advertía en su voz, en sus gestos, en su cuerpo vibrátil, despojado por entero del aura de sensualidad que suele manar de ella a veces fugazmente. Estaba agitada y no podía mirarme de frente. Se mordía los labios. Mantenía los ojos bajos, las manos enlazadas sobre las rodillas cubiertas por la ridícula y larga falda escocesa que deformaba por completo la armonía de su cuerpo.

—¿Por qué hizo eso? —insistí sin reproche.

—Todo esto es muy... *unheimlich*... —murmuró retorciéndose las manos y cerrando los ojos.

—¿Desagradable, quiere usted decir?

—Mucho peor que eso... ¡Abominable!

Salí para traerle un refresco. Cuando volví se había marchado. La vi alejarse velozmente entre los setos del jardín. Por el movimiento de su cabeza observé que iba corriendo seguida por el perro con un trotecito cómplice. Sólo veía la parte alta de su cabeza avanzando entre el follaje. A la luz oblicua del sol, las crenchas de su pelo lucían ahora un rubio airado y su movimiento de vaivén era rápido y crispado como el de un niño con rabieta que escapa de una reprimenda injusta e intolerable. Abrió el cancel y se lanzó a campo traviesa. La seguí con el auto porque me di cuenta de que había equivocado el camino de la estación.

—Suba. La llevo.

Denegó con la cabeza y siguió caminando con paso firme y acelerado, casi marcial, por el camino de tierra. Tropezó con un tronco y cayó. Hundió y refregó la cara contra la arena. Bajé para ayudarla a levantarse. Me ordenó en alemán que me fuera y soltó una interjección salvaje como el quejido de un animal herido mientras golpeaba la tierra con los puños. Me acerqué y le di dos enérgicas bofetadas en las mejillas embadurnadas con el barro de sus lágrimas. Un golpe de viento desnudó sus corvas. Levanté el ruedo de su falda, me incliné y volví a propinarle dos fuertes nalgadas que resonaron en la carne dura y reluciente. Se irguió lentamente como si despertara de un mal sueño. Caminó como borracha y se perdió en la bruma que comenzaba a espesarse. Me limpié lentamente el barro de las manos frotándolas contra el césped. Vi que la palma y el dorso estaban rojos y sentí que me ardían. También ella, pensé, viajará sentada en el tren sobre el culo rojo y ardido.

Unos jubilados que jugaban a la petanca en la plaza observaban inmóviles la escena. Algo me gritaron. No los oí. Arranqué con furia. Los neumáticos iban dando alaridos sobre la grava. Una procesión de encapuchados muy semejante a las de Semana Santa en Sevilla avanzaba por la calle. La densa fila me obligó a frenar. Detuve el coche junto al bordillo para dar paso a los penitentes. Canturreaban sordamente una letanía ininteligible. Las voces huecas se reabsorbían en sí mismas sin ninguna resonancia. Subí los cristales. La confusa salmodia se apagó. Los penitentes pasaban apretujándose blandamente contra el coche sin hacer la menor presión sobre él, como si en lugar de cuerpos humanos fuesen una masa de algodonosas siluetas revestidas de hábitos religiosos. Un golpe de viento levantó algunas capuchas. No eran rostros humanos vivientes. Vislumbré caras angulosas como esculpidas en madera barnizada con colores muy oscuros, petrificadas en una mueca idéntica en todas ellas. Únicamente en las cuencas profundas fosforescían destellos parpadeantes. Sin querer cerré los párpados, estupefacto. Un chasquido breve, repentino, golpeó el espejo retrovisor. Abrí los ojos. Como si se hubiera invertido el orden del tiempo, primero oí el chasquido. Segundos después alcancé a ver la trayectoria de un grumo rojizo como el de un escupitazo que se aplastó contra el cristal rectangular. La procesión de penitentes había desaparecido. Con redoblada furia los perseguí dando varias vueltas por las calles adyacentes sin sentir los alaridos de los neumáticos ni el olor a goma quemada. Tuve todo el tiempo la mancha delante de mí en el retrovisor. Me seguía como un agujero rojizo en mi propia visión. Nunca había visto en Nevers procesiones de esta naturaleza. Las calles estaban casi desiertas. Unas pocas mujeres volvían del supermercado con sus carritos repletos de provisiones.

Aparqué el coche en el garaje y comprobé que el plasto adherido al espejo era una mancha de sangre. La raspé con un palito concienzudamente. Los hematíes penitenciales se resistieron poseídos por la genuina obstinación de la fe. Los limpié como pude con los dedos untados de saliva. Entré y eché agua en la bañera. Mientras se llenaba esculqué los libros, ficheros y papeles que me había devuelto Leda, por si hubiera entre ellos alguna otra carta tan delirante como la primera. Nada encontré por suerte. Vi mi artículo muy subrayado y cribado de signos de interrogación, de anotaciones al margen en alemán, lengua que no domino, y de otras marcas que no alcancé a descifrar. Me sumergí en el agua fría. Se me representó de nuevo en un flash subliminal el trasero rojo y ardido de Leda hasta el nacimiento de las bragas. Es todavía más hermoso que su rostro, pensé. Experimente cierta excitación, que desapareció pronto. Creo que me dormí en seguida con un sueño sin imágenes.

Cuando desperté era noche cerrada. Tiritaba de frío en el agua. Salí, me vestí el albornoz y me cubrí la cabeza con el capuchón. Encendí la luz y vi que en la bañera flotaban dos medusas lechosas. Pensé en la espuma del jabón, pero yo no había usado jabón. Dejé correr el agua y repasé con la esponja la bañera hasta dejar la losa reluciente. Bebí media botella de ron y me dejé caer pesadamente en el lecho de la ventana occidental, mi pequeña ermita, mi refugio contra las tentaciones prohibidas.

La música de la boda está en su apogeo. La pareja de los recién casados, muy jóvenes, bailan al ritmo del *Danubio azul*. En el escenario de los invitados especiales, sentados en altas butacas, los padres los contemplan embelesados de dicha familiar. Sobre los vientres rechonchos de los papás oscilan gruesas leontinas de oro. Las mamás lucen enormes sombreros de rafia y se abanican con pantallas de plumones que se mueven como pájaros vivos. Los esponsales son el acontecimiento mayor de la comarca. La multitud pueblerina se apiña absorta y deslumbrada tras las rejas de los grandes ventanales abiertos de par en par al calor y a la oscuridad de la noche. El muchacho, desorientado, angustiado, baila con su flamante esposa como si llevara entre sus brazos una sombra. Busca con los ojos a alguien en medio de la batahola frenética. Una pareja se acerca a la de los recién casados y se entrelaza con ella. La extraña y bella muchacha rubia sin dejar de bailar con su compañero forcejea por alcanzar con el suyo el rostro del recién casado. Sus cabezas se juntan por fin. Sus labios se unen y no se separan más. Las dos parejas entrelazadas continúan bailando en medio de una explosión de aplausos, de risas y de gritos. Los padres se han puesto de pie, gesticulan y se desgañitan indignados, humillados, rojos de ira. No se escuchan sus voces. Las grandes bocas se abren y cierran con la asfixia de cuatro gordos peces coleando de agonía en la playa de arena del Danubio azul. La orquesta ataca con nuevos bríos. La recién casada va arrastrada en los giros del vals, llorando a lágrima viva. Baila aferrada al esposo tempranamente infiel. La diadema nupcial se desliza sobre el velo y le cubre los ojos. La larga cola de tules se arrastra pisoteada por centenares de tacos. La recién casada huye. La cola trabada por los tacos le hace perder el equilibrio. Cae de rodillas. Se levanta y sigue huyendo, la cabeza entre las alas, con el pavor de un ave herida. El bailarín de la pareja intrusa también ha desaparecido. Sólo quedan la muchacha rubia y el recién casado bailando solos, muy apretados, sin dejar de besarse. Se ha formado en torno un ruedo de centenares de personas que aplauden y chillan erizadas de oscura sensualidad. Los amantes se besan como para hacerse llagas. Se besan con frenesí, con desesperación, en los giros de un beso interminable. Se besan infinitamente buscando entrar el uno en el otro, transfundirse, desaparecer juntos en medio de la algarabía que va en aumento al ritmo de la música. El inmenso salón va quedando vacío, silencioso, distante. En la oscuridad sólo palpita el fulgor de una gargantilla de diamantes caída en el piso.

Plácidamente el sueño me retomó entre sus brazos.

Jimena volvió tres días después. Su rostro resplandecía de serenidad. Nada preguntó. No se habló más del asunto, ni siquiera cuando encontró sobre el diván el arrugado pañuelo de Leda de un fucsia rabioso con el que se había enjugado las lágrimas. Acaso estaría húmedo todavía. Discretamente Jimena pasó el aspirador que se tragó pedazos de papeles arrugados y también el pañuelo.

Esa noche, en un estado de euforia especial, repetimos todo el ritual de Onfalia. Enajenados, arrebatados por la pasión sin nombre, recorrimos una vez más el camino de las caravanas que avanzan hacia el pequeño cráter lunar. Sorbí hasta la última gota del redondo hoyuelo lleno hasta los bordes. No hubo lugar, ni comisura ni pliegue del cuerpo de Morena por el cual no reptara y saltara mi lengua como el pez vivíparo del *Cantar*, el delfín de Delfos, en procura de ese néctar que enloquece por igual a reyes y labriegos. Sus cristales infinitesimales sabían a sales secretas de cuevas marinas. Veía surgir de ellas el cuerpo blanco de luna de Jimena. Lo acaricié arrobado. La contemplaba recorrida por pequeños temblores en la embriaguez final del sueño hasta que se inmovilizó en un largo suspiro que surgió desde el vientre y le arañó al salir las fosas nasales con una especie de ronquido muy suave.

Algo en mí, sin embargo, anulaba o enturbiaba mi felicidad. Sentía como si yo mismo pudiera generar el fracaso de un instante perfecto que había transcurrido como fuera del tiempo. No tanto su fugacidad. Siempre se puede disfrutar en un relámpago de lo transitorio. Y nosotros, Jimena y yo, lo habíamos gozado como nunca antes había sucedido en un transporte fuera del tiempo.

Otra era la causa de mi anegante desasosiego. Un angustioso impulso de negar algo que estaba sucediendo allí mismo pero en el plano de una dimensión desconocida. Me sofocaba un sentimiento independiente de cualquier rebeldía de mi carne o de mi espíritu, que suspendía y paralizaba todo impulso de mi voluntad y de mis fuerzas. Traté en vano de superar este misterioso fenómeno de insensibilidad, que dejaba la duda en suspenso. Pero, por otra parte, la incredulidad agudizaba la expectativa anhelante de percibir *eso* que estaba ocurriendo como separado por un abismo de lo que podía considerarse como natural, como lo que era *posible* que ocurriese en el mundo: algo como un deslizamiento insano hacia lo inexplicable, lo nunca oído, lo nunca visto.

Me pareció oír una respiración contenida que no era el suave y pausado respirar de Jimena en el sueño. Sentí cada vez con más nitidez que *alguien* estaba adentro desde antes. Me dejé rodar lentamente desde el borde del lecho hasta la alfombra que asordinó mi caída. Escuché un ruido sordo y rítmico que se desvaneció en seguida. Me orienté en puntillas hacia el crujido. Podía ser el de un ratón buscando su comida. Me levanté de un salto y fui a cerrar la puerta y echarle llave. Me quedé pegado a ella, de espaldas. Pensé de pronto en la puerta que daba a la cocina. Estaba entreabierta. Por allí entraba el aroma del pan horneado en la tarde, que flotaba en la habitación. Corrí a atrancarla con la barra de hierro.

La noche estaba adentro. Me encontré aislado, sitiado, acosado, indefenso, porque me habían desarmado los contrastes. También por los presentimientos y por el sentido de culpa que la proximidad de Jimena hacía más dolorosa y punzante. Pero, sobre todo, me sentía desarmado por un deseo inexpresable que latía dentro de mí sin que pudiese reprimirlo ni olvidarlo. El horror, no revelado todavía como horror, ya se había apoderado de mí y me tenía paralizado. El horror, sí, pero el horror de la fascinación me iba invadiendo gradualmente como en las pesadillas.

A través de los cristales, como el sarcasmo de un recuerdo, veía la luna con las formas de una mujer gorda y desnuda, sentada en la cornisa de un tejado. Habituado a la penumbra, muy pronto distinguí las formas de los árboles corpulentos del jardín. La rebelión de la incredulidad se había desvanecido casi tan rápidamente como el estupor inicial del descubrimiento. Lo primero que percibí, hacia un rincón de la habitación, fue un vaho de mujer. Un vaho de mujer joven, extraño, distinto; no el inconfundible aroma del cuerpo de Jimena. Pero lo más extraño era que ese vaho también yo lo conocía.

El perfume del cuerpo de una mujer es su más genuina seña de identidad; el signo inconfundible de su edad, de su carácter, de sus gustos más íntimos, de su personalidad, de su nacionalidad, de su raza, de sus estados de ánimo. Con los ojos cerrados, con sólo husmearla, uno puede describir la mujer desconocida que se tiene delante. Aunque me lo negaba todavía, con un resto de renuencia pasiva, podía admitir que, antes de ver a la que estaba allí, ya la había reconocido por ese vaho que manaba de ella. Me aproximé un poco más. A la tenue luminosidad de un reflejo lunar vi tendida una silueta desnuda retorciéndose con el rostro pegado a la alfombra. Ahí, a dos pasos, delante de mí, estaba la imagen de la joven de encanto temible que yo creía lejos de allí, envuelta en su propia desesperación, recluida en su misérrimo cuarto de hotel. Veía los destellos rojizos de su cabellera cubriéndole los senos. La hermosura de su cuerpo desnudo resplandecía en la penumbra. Se volvió de costado y me miró con una angustia infinita.

Muy pronto fue demasiado tarde para tratar de impedir lo que había comenzado a suceder. *Supe* que el poder femenino iba a llevar sus designios hasta el fin sin la menor vacilación. No había fuerza humana capaz de impedirlo; al menos, esa fuerza no existía en mí o se había bloqueado en una especie de total impotencia. Me negaba a ver pero lo que estaba sucediendo se me imponía con fuerza arrolladora cuanto más cerraba los ojos.

En el primer instante no supe qué hacer. Era un descubrimiento demasiado turbador que impedía toda reacción de mi parte. Me abrumaba una sorda y creciente enajenación de los sentidos. El sólo encarar la posibilidad de lo que ocurría se volvía aterrador. Jimena tenía el sueño muy liviano. Sabía dormir despierta. Podía despertarse en cualquier momento... y entonces ¿qué haría yo?... ¿qué sería de mí?... ¿qué sería de ella?...

El paroxismo de la duda no impidió no obstante que *eso* que estaba sucediendo, a medias adivinado, presentido a medias, repugnara a mi imaginación hasta la náusea, chocara con mis sentimientos de honradez y fidelidad hacia Jimena, hacia mí mismo, y me llenara de amarga autocondenación. En un último conato de incredulidad pensé con esfuerzo que cuando parecían ocurrir cosas fuera de lo común, en ciertas disposiciones de ánimo, todo en realidad suele suceder naturalmente fuera de nuestra percepción anormal. Pero ahí y en ese momento era al revés: las cosas eran todavía mucho más extrañas de lo que se podía imaginar con la mente alterada y el espíritu completamente confuso.

Quería convencerme aún de que sólo estaba preso de una pesadilla. ¡Basta!... pensé con rabia. Todo era demasiado ambiguo, fantasmal. Tal vez la fantasmagoría estaba en mí. Tal vez esa figura femenina, desnuda, estremeciéndose en espasmos por las ansias del deseo, no era más que la proyección de una fantasía corporizada por el alucinador poder de la fiebre. Me toqué la frente. Ardía. Pero todo mi ser ardía en una calentura insensata y malsana. Esto no sucede así en la realidad, me dije. Pero los colgajos de sentido común, a los que trataba de asirme como último recurso, no bastaban para destruir esta escena fantásticamente irreal, desgraciadamente real. El run run de la duda me decía aún que *era* otra especie de realidad, que el mundo de lo posible estaba lleno de misterios indescifrables y que el poder embaucador del sueño o de la fiebre puede tramar las escenas más extravagantes.

En medio del vértigo de la desesperación pasé revista mentalmente a las posibilidades *reales* de su presencia. La imprevisible y extraña muchacha, desde aquella tarde, pudo permanecer en un hotelucho de Nevers, espiar mis movimientos y entrar esta noche en la casa con la complicidad del dálmata, se habían hecho amigos, sin saber que Jimena había regresado. Pudo volver incluso aquella misma tarde de su frustrada visita; merodear la casa, entrar mientras yo dormía en la bañera, y quedarse escondida en el granero donde Jimena acostumbra colgar ristras de dátiles para secarlos.

Durante el sueño en el agua creí, en efecto, tener la sensación de que alguien se inclinaba a mirarme. Debí suponer que Jimena había regresado y que entraba en el baño para asegurarse de que yo estaba allí. Me habría visto dormido y salió sin despertarme. Luego olvidé por completo esta engañosa visión del duermevela en el agua casi helada.

La muchacha de los Cárpatos estaba allí. La frase de su carta, "¿...o es que para espiar el placer de los otros hay que entrar directamente por la chimenea...?", revelaba ahora toda su fuerza de intención. No tuvo necesidad de espiar por la ventana como el monje lascivo. La puerta trasera de la casa nunca está cerrada con llave. Mientras yo le traía el refresco, antes de marcharse furtivamente, pudo haber explorado esta posibilidad.

Después, los bofetones y las nalgadas en público no habrían hecho sino exasperar su humillación y su deseo de vengar ese castigo, que no tuvo, por mi parte, más intención que la de volverla a la realidad, sacarla de ese embrujo violento que la poseía. ¿Venía también ahora a cobrarse la muerte que yo le había dado en su sueño apuñaleándola en la garganta, según me acusaba en la carta?

Nunca había elegido mejor momento para cumplir su venganza. No hubiera debido olvidar yo las extrañas palabras de su carta: "¿No cree usted que la mujer es un animal a punto de convertirse en un ser humano y que sólo el amor puede transmutarlo?..." Como animal joven, como mujer virgen pero no inocente, desde el fondo de su perversidad natural o de algún trauma que la había marcado a fuego, la temeraria muchacha había calculado su venganza a puro instinto con la perfección propia de los animales débiles. Mi indignación iba en aumento. Mi repugnancia, mi rebelión contra ella, crecieron en mí, arrolladoramente, pero no podían quebrar mi impotencia.

¿Cómo había podido entrar? Fracciones de segundo. Posibilidades que chocan y se fragmentan en infinidad de astillas mentales. Ideas incoherentes. Fogonazos de alternativas probables como ráfagas de luz lívida me confundían aún más. No me llevaron a ninguna aclaración aceptable ni reveladora. Entrar era relativamente fácil. Lo difícil, lo imposible, era todo lo que pasó después. Las dos puertas de la habitación estaban entornadas. La tenebrosa muchacha se introdujo sin obstáculos, mientras Jimena y yo viajábamos por la ruta onfálica en el sueño más pesado de los durmientes que no duermen: el ensueño en llamas del transporte amoroso.

La visitante de la noche pudo contemplarnos a su sabor durante horas desde la oscuridad de la alcoba. La naturaleza de aquel engaño —seguía insistiendo tercamente para autoconvencerme—, tenía algo de maleficio diabóli-

co que me dejó sin respiración. El anhélito de una angustia
de muerte empezó a rasparme la garganta. Un temblor in-
coercible se apoderó de mis miembros y un sudor frío me
bañaba todo el cuerpo. Empecé a oscilar en medio de un
mareo que me subía desde los pies como si la tierra se hubiese puesto a girar repentinamente en sentido contrario o
como si se resquebrajara en el temblor de un silencioso ca-
taclismo.

Me incliné y le toqué la cabeza. Era *ella*. Tembló
bajo mi mano todo su cuerpo hasta los pies como en una
convulsión eléctrica. Salté y la aferré por las muñecas. Iba
a decir algo pero le mordí los labios con bestial ferocidad.
Invadió mi boca el sabor de su sangre. La arrastré por los
cabellos al otro extremo de la habitación hasta ocultarla
detrás de una mampara.

Ya no pude incorporarme ni separarme de ese
cuerpo flexible como el de una bailarina. Me había aferra-
do el cuello con sus brazos largos y finos pero de una fuerza descomunal. Pegó mi rostro al suyo y comenzó a be-
sarme. Me besaba con una furia creciente. Me besaba infinitamente. Me besaba como para sacarme llagas en los labios, como para trozarme la lengua, como para cortarme
la respiración. Tomaba con esos besos el resto de mis fuerzas. Sometía mi voluntad. Sellaba mi silencio. Su sensualidad devoradora me excavaba como en una absorción que
me iba dejando vacío. Me sentía violado por un fantasma
del que no podía o no quería desprenderme, que se aferra-
ba a mí con una fuerza sobrehumana. Me sentí totalmente
inmovilizado, prisionero de sus brazos, de su cuerpo que
ondulaba sobre el mío tratando de penetrarme.

Acercó sus labios a mis oídos. Me mordió levemente el lóbulo de una oreja. Comenzó un ronco bisbiseo con
su respiración ardiéndome hasta el fondo del tímpano. Su
aliento olía a dátiles secos. Me arañaba todo el cuerpo con
sus largas uñas como si hubiera querido despellejarme, des-

vestirme de la piel, abrir un canal para entrar dentro de mí. Pareció que me concedía un momento de tregua. Me embaucó de nuevo con una actitud de súplica humilde, de momentánea resignación, que simularon devolverme el derecho a la iniciativa viril que en mí estaba tan muerta como el deseo.

—Ah... si un hombre quiere... si tú quieres... Una mujer puede ser la una... y ser la otra —musitó desde muy adentro de ella misma—. Tú has dicho que el hombre puede ver a una mujer como es y como la desea... Y que cada una es única y verdadera... en el momento en que la ama... Tú has dicho... abolir el egoísmo sexual y tomar el cuerpo del otro como centro de su propio deseo... Tú sabes cómo soy y yo sé que me deseas...

—¡Cállate maldita!

—Ámame ahora a mí..., que soy la *única* por un instante... por este momento que no se volverá a repetir... Si sólo piensas en la que *ya no es*, amas una fantasía... Piensa en la que yo soy ahora... aquí... a tu lado... ¡Ponme tu dedo sobre mi herida para que sangre! Y si quieres, puedes beber hasta la última gota de mi sangre que tú hiciste correr para ti!... Me apretó la cabeza y la boca sobre la herida de su cuello. Pero yo me resistía a tragar esa sangre que sabía al ácido de un cuchillo herrumbrado.

Abrió su cuerpo para que la poseyera por mi voluntad y mi propio deseo. Se entregó como en una ofrenda sacrificial.

En un descuido me incorporé de un salto con el resto de mis fuerzas. Mi peso era mayor ahora porque ella había trepado a horcajadas a mis espaldas entrelazando sus piernas sobre las mías y apresándolas como una tenazas. Mantenía siempre sus brazos aferrados a mi cuello. Sentía que sus duros pezones me raspaban las vértebras y que sus descargas ardientes llegaban hasta la misma médula, mientras yo iba perdiendo el aliento. Con la punta de sus pies frotaba y trataba de excitar mis genitales que se replegaban y reducían, vacíos por completo hasta del último vestigio de deseo, fláccidos de miedo, de horror. El aroma del pan que en la puerta del horno se nos quema hacía más monstruoso el horror.

En una pirueta de danza giró sobre el eje de mis caderas y me enfrentó. Perdí el pie y caí. Ella trepó sobre mí, me cubrió con su cuerpo y acomodó su sexo sobre el mío. Empezó a ondular y hamacarse con la habilidad y plasticidad de la ramera más experimentada en las magias y manipulaciones de la cópula. Se agachó sobre mi sexo y se empeñó en animarlo ayudándose con la lengua, los labios y los dientes. La tironeé de la larga y lacia cabellera que despedía pequeñas chispas fosforescentes. En el tirón acerqué su rostro al mío, barboté otra maldición en el hueco de su boca y la volví a morder en los labios que se hallaban al borde del grito. Un mechón de su cabellera se me quedó en las manos.

El horror de la fascinación se había transformado en el horror de la abominación. Experimenté de pronto una idea ciega. Sentí estallar en mí un odio apasionado, un rencor sin nombre, un furor homicida. Llevé mis dos manos al cuello de la muchacha. Iba a estrangularla. Sólo con su muerte iba a poder sacar su cuerpo que se había adherido al mío como con ventosas. No podía decir que yo la penetraba. Ella me hacía entrar en su cuerpo con la fuerza de succión que brotaba del suyo, cada vez más poderosa. Sólo con su muerte iba a poder liberarme de esa representación diabólica del pez-útero que habíamos buscado con Jimena en la inmensidad del Sahara, y que ahora estaba allí devorándome a través de su ombligo-vagina, jadeando en un orgasmo interminable que se alimentaba de mi abstención y de mi odio. Oprimí mis dedos crispados sobre su cuello con salvaje violencia. Perdió el aliento, los ojos comenzaron a girar casi ya fuera de las órbitas. Su cuerpo se fue ablandando y cesaron sus roncos gemidos. Me miré las manos. A la turbia luz de la luna vi que las tenía manchadas de sangre.

La levanté en brazos para sacarla de la habitación y arrojarla afuera, a la noche, de donde había salido. Tendió ella los suyos alrededor de mi cuello en un suspiro agónico. Pero en ese mismo momento tuve la sensación de que su peso disminuía rápidamente y que su cuerpo pegajoso y frío se ablandaba como desgonzado en todas sus articulaciones. Se me cayó de los brazos como algo inerte e ingrávido. Me agaché a buscarla. Había desaparecido. Corrí hasta la puerta, pero tenía echada la llave. No habría podido huir por allí.

Sólo quedó en mis brazos, en mi pecho, en todo mi cuerpo el sudor apelmazado con la sangre de esa lucha nocturna. El olor inconfundible de su piel, de su cabellera, la humedad de su sexo virgen, impregnaban mi cuerpo. La inconsciencia de ese instante parecía ya un recuerdo. Quedé inmóvil, convertido en un solo temblor de pies a cabeza, extenuado, al borde del anonadamiento. Empecé a temer de mí. Temía la repetición de otro ataque. Lo temía más que antes. ¿O lo deseaba? Podía ella estar ahí al acecho con demoniaca obstinación. Y yo ya no podría luchar contra ella en la extinción total de mis fuerzas, como si yo mismo me extinguiera en una nebulosa oscura. El horror había crecido porque ahora sólo tenía el vacío a mi alrededor. Nada que hiciera resistencia a mi ciego afán de destrucción. Me sentí de pronto desamparado, abandonado. Podía morirme en ese momento ahí mismo y nadie encontraría los restos de mi cuerpo del mismo modo que había desaparecido el suyo.

Me atacó un pavor súbito. ¿Y si estuviera desplomada, muerta, en el jardín? Entre la náusea de cólera que me llenaba de espumarajos la boca y el miedo a esa muerte cuyas consecuencias no había previsto, una idea se me clavó en el pecho como un cuchillo. Debía encontrar *a todo trance* el cuerpo de la fugitiva estrangulada y hacerlo desaparecer... Recordé de improviso el antiguo pozo cegado en los fondos del jardín... ¡La glorieta de Jimena!... Por esa noche arrojaría el cuerpo de la muchacha en el pozo. Después buscaría la forma de hacerlo desaparecer definitivamente.

En ese momento oí aullar al dálmata. Abrí la puerta y me lancé al exterior en busca de la infernal muchacha, que a mi juicio ya debía de estar muerta. El perro seguía aullando entre los cipreses. La luna volaba sobre esos aullidos en los que había algo de alarido humano, como recogiéndolos entre las nubes que comenzaban a ocultarla. No divisé ninguna sombra humana, nada que se pareciese a la silueta de la fugitiva. El perro vino saltando hacia mí. Me puso las patas en el pecho. Al muriente resplandor lunar, vi que también las tenía rojas y húmedas. De la lengua le goteaban largos hilos de baba manchada de sangre como si hubiese lamido las heridas de alguien. Le intimé con gestos a que me indicara por dónde había escapado la desaparecida. El dálmata seguía ladrando a la luna con aullidos cortos y estrangulados.

Corrí como un demente por todos los vericuetos del jardín, seguido por el perro que ya no ladraba. No se me ocurrió revisar el granero. Con el frío de la noche el sudor se me helaba sobre el cuerpo desnudo. Me desmoroné sobre la hierba húmeda. Empecé a restregarme contra ella para sacarme la suciedad viscosa que se endurecía en la piel, en los miembros, en el cabello, escarchada bajo el sudor frío. Desprendí con un tirón un mechón de pelo rubio que se me había pegado en el ombligo con la plasta de esperma y sangre. Lo arrojé entre unas matas como si se tratara de un reptil ponzoñoso. Caí exánime. Cuando recobré el sentido, estaba despuntando el amanecer. El dálmata velaba a mi lado. Traté de incorporarme y me quedé sentado sobre el césped.

En la niebla reptante del amanecer vi de pronto una silueta femenina enfundada en una larga túnica oscura y tocada con el sombrero cónico y puntiagudo de las brujas de los relatos góticos. La silueta venía avanzando cautelosamente desde la puerta del fondo con una escoba bajo el brazo. Me abalancé hacia ella, la cargué en brazos y me dirigí hacia el pozo. La figura fantasmal casi no tenía peso. Oí una voz entrecortada y empavorecida:

—¡Señor, don Félix!... ¿Adónde me lleva usted?...

El estupor me paralizó un instante. Abrí los brazos y dejé caer el cuerpo de la pobre mujer sobre los agudos cantos del sendero. No tuve fuerzas ni valor para pedir disculpas a Mme. Alves, ni para ayudarla a levantarse. Cuando cegado por el furor la alcé en mis brazos no sabía que era ella. Creí que era la *otra*. Temí una nueva estratagema de la fugitiva. Me volví. Reconocí a Mme. Alves. Logró ponerse de rodillas. Me miraba aterrada como desde una alucinación. Recogió su escoba y se alejó corriendo. Pude al fin zafarme de la parálisis. Tenía la lengua dura, hinchada, incapaz de barbotar un grito o una palabra. Con el cuerpo fuera de mí, bamboleándome como un ebrio, me encaminé hacia la casa.

Entré y caí de rodillas. Oí muy lejana la voz de Jimena como entre las resonancias de un sótano. Lentamente salí de la inconsciencia en la que me parecía estar embutido como dentro de una funda de goma. Necesité imperiosamente asirme de algo. Tendí los brazos. Jimena acudió en mi ayuda y me llevó a rastras hacia el arco de la ventana, musitándome palabras de cariño y haciéndome preguntas totalmente ininteligibles para mí.

—¿Qué ha sido, Félix? ¿Te has hecho daño?

—No sé... no sé...

Jimena dio luz. Se asustó. Me hizo recostar lentamente en el lecho.

—¡Tienes manchas de sangre!... ¿Qué ha sido, por Dios?

—No sé.... He matado a alguien... Creo que he matado a alguien... ¿Qué era? ¿Qué fue? No sé... no sé...

Era nada.... nada....

—Nada... —sollocé—. Era nada... nada...

Nos miramos como dos desconocidos, tan dividi-
dos en la fugacidad de esa mirada, por primera vez en largo tiempo, que ninguno de los dos era capaz de comprender
los sentimientos del otro, y menos aún de saber y entender
lo inexplicable que había sucedido.

Durante más de diez días volé en una fiebre altísima
que no quería remitir. Jimena hizo llamar al doctor Maurel.
Me auscultó con desconfiada parsimonia y diagnosticó una
pulmonía con complicaciones broncopulmonares.

—¡Vamos, pero este hombre no tiene remedio!
Siempre está como muerto. *Eppur, si muove!*... —trató de
ironizar—. Su robusta mala salud le sigue dando satisfacciones... *especiales* —subrayo.

Recetó remedios e inyecciones, que me las aplicaba
la propia Jimena. Fui mejorando rápidamente. Cuando recobré la voz, Jimena hizo llamar otra vez al doctor Maurel
para una nueva consulta.

—Claro —agregó Maurel—. Estos enfermos naturales son los que más duran... hasta que les ponen la cu-
chilla al cuello.

Pidió a Jimena que se retirara un instante. Quería tener
algunas palabras conmigo. Maurel se puso íntimo, de "hombre
a hombre", y me habló con la delicadeza y corrección del más
puro francés de la "vieille France". Me preguntó si viajaba mucho.
Le dije que no me movía de la casa. Con discreción quiso enterarse de mi edad. No lo sé, dije. Maurel se encrespó: "¿No sabe
usted su edad?"

—No, exactamente... —balbuceé.

—Ya no es joven —exclamó como si me lo re-
prochara.

—Viejo no soy... —me defendí en retirada.

—¿Piensa usted a menudo en muslos y cosas así? —inquirió sibilino.

Yo no comprendía; no sabía adónde quería ir el médico.

—¿Se refiere usted tal vez a muslos de mujer?

—¡Por supuesto! —bufó—. No voy a preguntarle si piensa usted en muslos de pollo, de pavo, o de otras especies de animales comestibles. Le pregunto si piensa usted con exceso en muslos, culos, sexos de mujer y alrededores. Por supuesto, usted no se come ya una rosca —insinuó imitando el acento de la calle.

—¿Comer una rosca? —repetí totalmente desorientado en la nebulosa de la fiebre.

—El pene, vamos. El órgano genital. ¿Sabe usted qué es el pene, qué son los testículos? —se palmeó la entrepierna como si fuera a coger los suyos para enseñarme con un ejemplo concreto qué era esa *cosa* desconocida por mí.

—Ah eso... —dije parpadeando mucho.

—¡Claro, hombre! ¡Esto! ¿Se hincha aún el suyo? ¿Tiene todavía erecciones? ¿Lo usa usted mucho?

El francés clásico de Maurel había descendido de golpe al argot de provincias. No eran los términos que yo hubiera empleado. No hubiera osado siquiera mencionarlos ante la solemne gravedad del doctor. El ardor de la fiebre ondeaba sobre mí y se mezclaba al hielo de mis extremidades. Sentí un gusto amargo en la boca. El interrogatorio de Maurel me estaba produciendo un sordo resquemor de ira, de vergüenza. *¡Comerse la rosca!*... Era menos y era más que un insulto. Su autoridad de médico, aunque lo hiciese en favor de mi estado de salud, no le autorizaba a este interrogatorio humillante y obsceno, impropio de Maurel.

—Ha cometido usted excesos —dijo, recuperando la dicción de Pascal, de Montaigne, en una frase especialmente bien construida—. Debe ahorrar sus energías vitales si no quiere envejecer pronto o correr riesgos más inmediatos. La juventud es un acto de coraje. ¿De acuerdo?

—De coraje... ¡Oh sí, doctor! Desde luego... Pero yo no me siento cobarde totalmente...

—Un acto de coraje y de abstinencia.

—Tampoco me siento particularmente abstemio, le diría...

—Bueno, bueno. Dejémonos de hacer frases idiotas. Meta ese pene en un estuche de piel de zapa —conminó, volviendo a la rudeza del dialecto callejero—. ¿Leyó usted *Peau de chagrin*, de Balzac?

—Oh sí, doctor. Desde luego...

—Hay ahora preservativos de piel de zapa con pinchos metálicos que evitan el vicio solitario de los tocamientos, de la masturbación y el comercio carnal.

—¿Me habla usted de una especie de cilicios genitales? —pregunté con total ingenuidad.

—Eso... eso... —dijo Maurel—. Recuerde que usted vive en un milagro y que no hay razón para forzar las cosas. Haga penitencia. Ponga la hierba tierna a secar al sol de la mañana y bébasela en tisanas por la noche. Cautela, amigo. La discreción y la prudencia son el mejor cálculo. Y a la larga, el que prodiga los mejores dividendos.

Se abstrajo un momento. Apartó las cobijas. Me recorrió de arriba abajo como escrutándome nudo a nudo y hueso por hueso. Se inclinó sobre mí casi hasta tocar con su pera mi frente. Iba a añadir algo; probablemente algún último consejo sobre el buen uso y ahorro de las energías carnales. Desistió moviendo la cabeza como ante un inútil esfuerzo.

¡Sensacional!, exclamó y se levantó perdiendo el equilibrio. El bastón de roble se deslizó de su mano y cayó sobre la lámpara que estalló con el estruendo de una explosión. Salté en la cama y me cubrí el rostro con la sábana. Jimena acudió en el acto y me tranquilizó. Encendió la vela de un candelabro y miró a Maurel. Éste esbozó en dirección a ella un gesto discreto indicando que se retiraba. En medio de la penumbra salió con el corpachón erguido, su barbita a la Pasteur brillando plateada a la vacilante luz del velón. Jimena le precedía con el candelabro para abrirle la puerta. No los vi más. Sólo oía el murmullo de su conversación en la galería.

Mi temor más grande era el que, inconsciente por la calentura, ese mismo ardor pudiese soltarme la lengua y delatarme ante Jimena con respecto al aquelarre nocturno, si mi propio silencio no fuese ya en sí una confesión reveladora. Si Maurel había notado sus huellas en mi cuerpo, Jimena no podría dejar de encontrarlas en la casa. Habrían quedado demasiados indicios. Acaso los habría descubierto ya y se abstenía de hablar de ello hasta mejor oportunidad.

Pasó el tiempo y la temida amenaza no se cumplió. El rostro y el trato de Jimena seguían siendo indulgentes. No mostraban la menor perturbación. Resplandecían para mí como de costumbre en la transparencia de su afecto, en la fuerza confortadora de su compañía, en la afabilidad de su trato. Era casi evidente que Jimena había interpretado el extraño suceso de la noche, acaecido mientras ella dormía, como la reminiscencia de mis sufrimientos en la prisión, convertida en una terrible pesadilla de la que yo no tenía conciencia ni memoria. Creo que ésa fue, al menos, la explicación que dio a la aterrorizada Mme. Alves, pidiéndole que me excusara por mi inexplicable acción. Con su delicadeza habitual, Jimena omitió referirme las razones que Mme. Alves le dio para renunciar a su puesto. Debieron de ser muy valederas y razonables como para que Jimena no pudiera retenerla pese al afecto que sentía por ella Mme. Alves, y para que prefiriera no mencionármelas. Me veía yo en el pavor de Mme. Alves convertido en un sátiro desnudo atacándola en la penumbra del alba. Un sátiro barbudo con cuernos sulfúricos y cola de diablo tratando de violar a la hija de Rutilio Alves, el poeta muerto en exilio, noble amigo de mi admirado Fernando Pessoa. ¡Ay... per-

dón, Mme. Alves!... ¡Tantos mundos extraños giran y
chocan entre el cielo y la tierra más allá de lo que pueden
soñar nuestras filosofías!...

Cuando me sentí un poco mejor telefoneé a Clovis, pidiéndole disculpas por faltar a la cita comprometida
y anunciándole que en pocos días más iría a visitarle. Re-
tomé mis tareas de jardinero, más que por mero gusto ho-
gareño y profesional, por el deseo culpable de hacer desaparecer cualquier rastro sospechoso que hubiera podido
quedar aún en el campo de batalla. Lo primero que hice
fue verificar el pozo de la glorieta. La pesada tapa circular
había sido removida y vuelta a colocar. El reborde de cemento que la mantenía unida al brocal estaba resquebraja-
do y los fragmentos se hallaban esparcidos a su alrededor.
Evidentemente, Jimena tuvo la misma idea que yo y se me
anticipó a investigar las honduras clausuradas del viejo
pozo. El olor a putrefacción se escapaba por las fisuras; pero
el hedor de los vegetales pudriéndose en la humedad de un
siglo era claramente distinto del de un cadáver joven.
Los vestigios siguieron apareciendo y desaparec-
ciendo en secuencias sobrecogedoras. Ese mismo día —Jimena estaba en la Facultad—, el dálmata se me acercó con
el mechón de pelo rubio entre los dientes, el que yo había
arrojado aquella noche entre unas matas. Cogí el mechón
que con el calor del sol y la humedad se había enrollado en
un bucle dorado y brillante de rocío. Le di vueltas entre
mis dedos con una sensación de repugnancia, de miedo,
no ya de terror, pero sí con ese indefinible sentimiento de
melancolía y de nostalgia que a veces nos dejan hasta las
pesadillas más terribles. Oía la voz de Fulva que musitaba
a mis oídos: "Este momento no se va a repetir... Yo tengo

guardado mi dolor en un lugar seguro... No dejes que se te apague el corazón..."

Se me cayó el bucle al suelo. Se desenroscó y enroscó de nuevo como si tuviera vida propia. Lo recogí. No sabía dónde esconderlo. No era el caso de prenderle fuego; el olor del pelo quemado dura días, se pega al aire para siempre. Lo llevé al baño y lo dejé caer en el retrete. Tiré la cadena y lo vi desaparecer en el remolino del chorro.

Pocos días después Jimena vino a comunicarme riéndose:

—Parece que en el granero hay ratones. Han desaparecido casi todos mis dátiles secos, y los que sobran parecen roídos.

—Habrá que poner raticidas.

—Es que las huellas parecen de colmillos humanos.

Las palabras y el tono de Jimena no dejaban traslucir la menor insinuación de una sospecha o la intención, oculta más allá del estropicio ratonil, de someterme al reactivo de una prueba.

—Los sin techo están comenzando a aparecer en todas partes. Habrá que poner un candado a la puerta del fondo —dije mientras preparaba mi maletín de viaje—. Y darle la llave de la puerta del fondo a Mme. Alves, —agregué, olvidando su huida.

—Ya no hay necesidad de dársela —repuso—. Mme. Alves no vendrá más. ¿Qué pasó con ella esa noche, o mejor, al amanecer de aquella noche? Me contó que tú la habías levantado en vilo y la habías llevado hacia el pozo.

Pensé en el increíble poder del monosílabo para relatar historias inenarrables.

—Lo que me contó Mme. Alves, muy asustada, con respecto al pozo —continuó Jimena— me hizo aún más confusas tus exclamaciones en medio de la fiebre, en las que mencionabas obsesivamente el pozo... ¡El pozo... el pozo!... Y esa fatídica frase: ¡He matado a alguien!... Clamabas desorbitado, como si todavía siguieras bajo los efectos de una pesadilla.

—¡Oh!... —dije solamente, sin querer recordar el incidente.

Llegué temprano a París. En la espera de mi cita con Clovis, me entretuve deambulando por algunos sitios que conozco. La primavera en París suele ser incomparable, cuando las hojas verdes parecen renacer y abrirse en una misteriosa luminosidad interior. Caminé por la calle de Picpus, hasta el Rothschild. Subí a la planta alta y me asomé a la ventana para contemplar una vez más la tumba del marqués de La Fayette. No la pude ver. Habían puesto sobre ella un toldo de colores veraniegos tal vez por alguna reparación no terminada, o quizás para protegerla de los rayos de sol.

—¿Tiene algún enfermo aquí? —preguntó el cabo de guardia.

—Yo soy el enfermo... —tartamudeé.

—¿Viene a visitarse a usted mismo? —repuso con cara de pocos amigos a lo que creía un mal chiste—. No es hora de visita.

El cabo me conminó a abandonar la planta.

Sólo en ese momento me di cuenta de que este viaje a París tenía inconscientemente para mí un trasfondo ritual de peregrinación, digamos de purificación. No descartaba la sorda inquietud de que una de esas inoportunas casualidades me hiciera encontrar con Leda. Como buscando anestesiarme de cansancio deambulé hasta la calle de la Paix y me dirigí hacia las Tullerías. Es uno de los pocos sitios de París que me agradan. Contemplaba los reflejos del sol en el follaje y caminaba a pasos lentos sintiendo el frufrú de la arena en la suela de mis zapatos, el canto de los pájaros, el asordinado rumor de los motores. El sol ponía reflejos dorados en los ojos excavados de los bustos de piedra.

Vagaba sin rumbo y sin un motivo preciso. Sin embargo, una ansiedad que no podía reprimir me empujaba hacia determinado lugar. Al remontar la rue Soufflot, viniendo desde el Panteón, me encontré subiendo las gradas del hotel Senlis donde Leda Kautner solía alojarse en sus temporadas de estudio en París. Pedí hablar con la propietaria, a quien conocía. Me atendió con mucha amabilidad. Hasta el último instante esperé que me dijera que Leda Kautner no se había hospedado allí y que ni siquiera la conocía.

—Vengo a averiguar —le dije— acerca de una alumna mía de posgrado, *mademoiselle* Kautner, ausente de sus cursos desde hace algún tiempo. Quería saber si quizás se halla enferma.

—Ella ha regresado a su país hará unos quince días —me respondió la patrona.

—¿Está usted segura?

—Completamente. Aquí, en el hotel, nos ocupamos de gestionarle el billete de avión para Munich. Partió en el vuelo de medianoche, de Lufthansa. Había otros vuelos durante el día, pero ella insistió en el vuelo nocturno. Parecía enferma y seguramente quería viajar durmiendo.

—¿Podría precisarme el día de su partida?

La patrona revisó el libro de huéspedes. Recorrió con el índice la columna de nombres y se detuvo sobre el de Leda.

—El 6 de marzo.

—¿No dejó ningún mensaje?

—Ninguno, señor. Sólo me dijo, al despedirse, que se iba. Pagó su cuenta y me dejó algún dinero para cancelar su deuda con la Universidad.

Agradecí a la patrona su atención. Dejé reservada una habitación por si el encuentro con Clovis pudiese prolongarse. Pedí la que había dejado vacante la viajera, si aún estaba disponible.

—Sí, lo está —me respondió la patrona con un mohín de lástima—. ¡Pero ésa es muy pequeña para usted! Podemos darle otra mejor, más confortable, sobre el jardín.

—No, gracias —dije—. Es sólo por una noche. Con ésa me arreglaré.

Me retiré. Volví a bajar la escalinata.

Mientras me dirigía hacia los jardines del Luxemburgo coordiné mentalmente las fechas. De pronto surgía un hiato en el tiempo. De ser cierta la información de la patrona del hotel, Leda había partido siete días antes de su embrujada visita a Nevers, el 13 de marzo. No suelo recordar las fechas, pero ésta sí no la iba a olvidar jamás. Algo se desfondó bajo mis pies sumiéndome en una nueva horrible duda. Pero al mismo tiempo fortaleció mi idea de que lo ocurrido aquella noche terrible no había sido más que una fantasmagoría creada por el poder alucinador de una pesadilla. Debía dudar ahora hasta de la misma duda.

Estas fechas de calendario, pensé, marcaban el curso natural del tiempo, y lo que pasó en Nevers había sucedido en el corazón de una hechicería fuera de lo natural. No había otra explicación plausible. Sopesé de nuevo las posibilidades reales de la presencia de Leda en Nevers, como ya lo hiciera aquella noche. Encontraba factible el que la temeraria muchacha retrasara la fecha del billete de avión y se mudase de hotel. En esta imprevista variante radicaba ahora la clave del enigma. Me quedaba, no obstante, un recurso de verificación parcial aunque no absoluta: ir a las oficinas de Lufthansa y comprobar por mí mismo si Leda había partido en la fecha indicada por la patrona del hotel. Lo hice de inmediato. Tomé un taxi y pedí al conductor me llevara hasta las oficinas centrales de la compañía aérea, en les Champs Elysées. Me atendieron amablemente con la angulosa cortesía germana de los funcionarios en el extranjero. Efectivamente, Leda había viajado en el vuelo nocturno del 6 de marzo. La duda quedaba levantada sólo parcialmente. No podía descartar el extremo de que Leda regresara de Munich, dándose el tiempo necesario para cumplir sus obsesivos propósitos.

Me pasaba los dedos por los labios ulcerados aún por las dos fiebres y allí tocaba lo natural de lo sobrenatural. De todos modos, yo tenía que atenerme a la hipótesis de la fantasía pesadillesca. Al fin de cuentas, Leda había vuelto a meterse bajo su sombra. Su ausencia definitiva borraba las huellas de un episodio que nunca debió hacer ocurrido.

Caminé hacia la Rive Gauche. Aspiré hondo el aroma balsámico de las plantas y las flores. Me sentía ingrávido. Experimenté cierto alivio a mi atribulada angustia de la mente y a la tensión anginosa del pecho. Seguía teniendo guardado mi corazón en un lugar seguro. Y todo mi amor era para Jimena. Más profundo aún que el de antes después de la prueba sufrida. Ahora sí podía decir: He soñado. Y al decirlo concentré toda mi voluntad en un punto de la realidad. Allí estaba la imagen de Jimena. Y también en el centro del sueño sano e indestructible se alzaba la imagen más íntima de Morena en la plenitud de su amor y de su belleza.

La llamé bajito, como si pudiera oírme telepáticamente, y le comuniqué mi dicha. ¡Oh Morena... Morena... estamos libres!...

Llegué hasta las puertas del Ministerio de Asunto Exteriores. De pronto alguien me tomó del brazo y me lo agitó enérgicamente. No podía ser otro que Clovis de Larzac: su gesto habitual de aparecer por sorpresa y descoyuntarle a uno el brazo. Antiguo colega en dos o tres universidades, compañero de juergas y del "libertinaje universitario" que sobrevino después del 68, pero sobre todo amigo, el más encantador de los amigos; algo excéntrico y un poco dandy o snob para los que no le conocen bien. En realidad es el hombre de mayor rigor interior que he conocido bajo ese talante de humor voluble y disparatado que usa algunas veces *pour épater le bourgeois* ; o tal vez como una máscara que le permite estar sin estar en cualquier sitio.

Clovis es ahora funcionario del Quay d'Orsay en el Departamento para América Latina. A Clovis debo el haber dejado de ser apátrida. Él se encargó personalmente de los trámites de mi nacionalización. De ese favor él ni siquiera se acuerda. Con el aura de increíble magnetismo que irradia su persona clavó en mí sus ojos de color indefinible que parecen despedir los rayados reflejos del ágata.

—¡Qué tal, salvaje! —me saludó golpeándome la espalda.

—¡Vaya!, me dije, el mismo Clovis de siempre...

Únicamente sobre sus patillas y aladares renegridos ha caído una levísima pátina de nieve otoñal que hace aún más atractivo su fino y tostado rostro.

—¡Mi querido Félix! ¿De quién andas huyendo?

—De quién va a ser. De mí mismo. No tengo otro enemigo declarado ni conocido.

— No se te ve más por París. No se oye nada más de vosotros en ninguna lengua viva o muerta del mundo. ¿Continúa Jimena a tu lado?

—Si las apariencias no engañan creo que sí.

—¡Vaya, por Dios! ¡Pobre muchacha... hasta cuándo te va a soportar! ¡Qué vocación masoquista de la fidelidad! ¿No venís más a París?

—Sabes que ya no aparezco sino por necesidades del servicio. Vine ahora por tu llamado.

—Has hecho bien en venir. Hay una noticia fabulosa para ti proveniente de tu país de origen. *De ton petit pays de merde*... Pero, mira, hoy no te puedo recibir. Tengo una reunión inesperada con el ministro. Ven a verme mañana, a mi oficina, a esta hora. Te mostraré algo que no habrías podido imaginártelo jamás. ¡Es algo genial, sensacional! Besos a Jimena. Te espero.

Me dio un abrazo y se metió como un espolón de proa en medio de una ola de muchachas estudiantes que venían cantando. No dejaron de asediarlo pidiéndole autógrafos y tirándole besos con las puntas de los dedos; alguna más audaz se los dio en plena mejilla. En un esguince de danzarín esquivó el grupo primaveral de las chicas que lo premiaron con aplausos y risas sin que ninguna pudiera identificar al extraño y apuesto personaje al que seguramente confundieron con algún actor de cine o televisión. Clovis tiene algún parecido con Laurence Olivier cuando era joven y buen mozo. La mitad de la sangre inglesa que corre por sus venas ha contribuido tal vez a esta semejanza.

Por ocupar el tiempo de alguna manera me puse a recorrer los bordes "ilustrados" del Sena. Me demoré visitando los puestos de *bouquinistes* a la pesca de ese libro buscado pero inesperado siempre, que a veces suele surgir del hacinamiento de libros viejos engrudados de polvo, de humedad, de olvido, como si la escritura hubiera sido inventada para olvidar la memoria y luego para olvidarse de sí misma bajo la apariencia de perennidad de los libros que los particulares escriben y que los pueblos no leen.

Algunos eran conocidos y clientes míos de hace años. Me reconocieron. Ofrecieron algunas "novedades", siempre las más viejas e impensables. Yo alzaba la mano y pasaba saludándolos con corteses inclinaciones de cabeza.

Hace rato que ando buscando la *Monadología* de Leibniz, en alguna de sus primeras ediciones. Experimenté el deseo de releer, en su versión original, ese principio de la "armonía preestablecida", que es uno de los fundamentos de la comunicación de las sustancias. He hablado a Jimena alguna vez de este principio que puede aplicarse al ejemplo de dos seres perfectamente armonizados en el amor fiel y vitalicio como una joya engarzada a un anillo. Leibniz, ese Leonardo germánico del intelecto, es para mí una mina inagotable de ideas y nociones acerca del ser humano, del mundo, de los animales y del universo. Sobre sus huellas geniales flota aún el polvo matemático que levantaron sus pasos en las bibliotecas del mundo como los de una caravana entera de sabios.

No encontré el tratado de esas misteriosas mónadas de los seres indivisibles pero distintos que componen el universo en la mágica *harmonia praestabilita*, según el descubridor del cálculo infinitesimal. En cambio, emergiendo de una sonrosada valva marina, sobresalía la tapa de un viejísimo volumen con la estilizada viñeta de un ombligo en un vientre de mujer bajo el título impreso en letras góticas. Eran las "monadas" de Bonaventure Des Périers, descritas en su libro *Le blason du beau tétin* (El blasón del hermoso ombligo), compuesto mucho antes que las traducciones y exégesis del *Cantar* de Fray Luis de León, como cántico de las nupcias místicas entre la Iglesia de Cristo y la especie humana redimida por él; anterior a los *Cánticos espirituales* de San Juan de la Cruz; a los inflamados teoremas de amor de la Doctora de Ávila, anterior a los demás místicos enamorados del amor divino que se ocuparon del Vaso de Luna del Cantar.

Margarita de Navarra, la autora de los relatos del *Heptamerón*, era partidaria de la Reforma y acogía en su sede de cultura y libertad a los poetas y escritores perseguidos y hasta a pícaros inteligentes y astutos como aquel Des Périers que dio blasón de nobleza al *beau tétin*, pero también al bello andrógino humano, partido por la mitad: un Entero demasiado feliz, convertido en dos Medios Cuerpos, demasiado lánguidos, paradigma hoy día de nuestros hombres y muchachos epicenos, oficiantes de la nueva religión gay.

Adquirí el *Blasón* a buen precio. Se trataba de una edición facsimilar clandestina, relativamente reciente, pero sin fecha y sin el nombre del autor. Me senté a leer en un recodo solitario, a la sombra de un roble añoso que bañaba sus raíces en el agua oscura. No pude concentrarme en el *beau tétin*. Acaso por asociación de ideas me puse a pensar en la vida un poco fantasmagórica de Clovis. Este Don Juan posmoderno, lleno de civilización interior, toma la fatalidad del mundo y la contrabalancea con un juego orgiástico que en él es un verdadero *ars vitalis*, heredado de las viejas épocas. Este marrullero de fina y templada raza pertenece a una clase de hombres que a mí me agrada, sobre todo por las facetas de su personalidad que más desagradan a los demás.

Clovis es evidentemente un hijo del amor; hijo natural del famoso almirante Webster, que fue guía de Eisenhower durante el desembarco de los aliados en el Canal de la Mancha. Herido en la batalla de Dunkerque, William Webster poco después de la guerra fue nombrado embajador en Francia. Conoció en los ambientes cortesanos a la marquesa de Larsac, linaje antiguo que encubre y rescata con creces la bastardía de Clovis, único hijo de esta unión. La amó breve e intensamente con un amor a la vez carnal y metafísico que únicamente los flemáticos ingleses pueden permitirse sin que se note el fuego de la pasión bajo la parca y helada cortesía exterior. El almirante W.W. fue trasladado como embajador a la flamante República de la India, donde murió asesinado por los independentistas violentos de Paquistán, que habrían sospechado en él la presencia de un nuevo virrey para un nuevo imperio.

La marquesa, rica heredera, poco después hizo un matrimonio de mutuas conveniencias con un marqués borbón de origen español, tronado y ya entrado en años, de los que abundan en París. Los siete hijos varones que nacieron de esta unión "legítima" eran todos desiguales, feos y deformes, como si Clovis les hubiera hurtado por adelantado, a cambio de su bastardía, ese "pequeño milagro" del encanto natural que le ganaba la simpatía de hombres y mujeres.

Clovis no conoció a su padre, el almirante, que jamás se ocupó de él, y el barón, su padrastro, lo gratificó hasta su muerte con una ojeriza seca y furtiva, preñada de odio. Pero odiaba con la misma saña silenciosa a los hermanastros de Clovis.

—El barón, mi padrastro español, era impotente y su francés era detestable. No podía hablar con nadie más de dos frases seguidas que sonaban como ladridos —dijo sin ánimo de burla.

Todas las noches Clovis, elegante y apuesto, cena con amigos en el mejor restaurante de la ciudad. Luego se deja ver en el palco *avant-scène* del teatro de moda de la temporada por diez minutos —ni uno más—. Las mujeres se vuelven hacia esa aparición. Cambian susurros. Clovis cuida al máximo su disfraz de hombre mundano pero siempre solitario y de costumbres irreprochables. Al resto de sus noches nadie sabe qué empleo le da. La intimidad de Clovis es insondable, fuera de lo que él mismo quiera aludir o revelar. Me confesó un día, sin dar mucha importancia a su confidencia, que estaba escribiendo la historia de su familia, en la que hay —me dijo con su inimitable sonrisa— varios envenenadores, mujeres disipadas, un presidente de Consejo y hasta un cardenal.

—En la mía hubo un obispo —dije sin ánimo de competir con esa genealogía de un gentilhombre de los buenos tiempos—. Pero no por eso somos peores, ¿no?

—¡Qué va! Esas púrpuras son las que nos hacen exquisitos sin evitar que seamos austeros —replicó ya con su mente en otra cosa.

Pese a la trágica historia de su madre, estaba orgulloso de ella pero no tomaba en serio su linaje; el linaje que Balzac ya había celebrado en una de sus novelas con el título nobiliario y el nombre levemente modificados de la condesa.

—Cuando la desgracia llega a sus extremos en un

ser humano —dijo— hay que respetarlo por encima de sus vicios y defectos.

Nos contó un día en una francachela de amigos en Amiens que su madre había tenido esos hijos aún en vida del barón franco-español, con distintos amantes, porque no podía soportar que únicamente los hombres disfrutaran de libertad sexual incondicional.

—Luego se volvió lesbiana —reveló Clovis con toda naturalidad un secreto que desde luego era público y notorio en los mentideros de la *haute* de París—. Mi madre puso un instituto de educación corporal que le servía a la vez de gineceo y de fuente de jugosos ingresos.

—Sólo que después —dijo Clovis sin cambiar de acento— se enamoró perdidamente de una adolescente adorable, una verdadera obra maestra de la naturaleza. La niña soportó por un tiempo ese amor que le sacaba el aliento, pero ella a su vez estaba enamorada de un *garçon* que era su prometido. Una tarde huyó del instituto sin más vestimenta que su malla de gimnasia. No volvió más. Desapareció para siempre.

—La condesa —dijo Clovis con voz neutra— no se resignó a esa tragedia. El mundo se le había quebrado en mil pedazos. Acabó suicidándose con un raticida. Tardaron unos días en encontrar su cadáver, presente en todas partes sólo por el insidioso hedor que se filtraba por las rendijas de las puertas. La suicida enamorada se había encerrado en el placard donde guardaba sus abrigos de pieles para beber la pócima en un gesto de final pudor y desesperación. La encontraron desnuda, envuelta en un abrigo de visón, en posición fetal y con la tetina del biberón en el que había bebido el veneno todavía entre sus labios.

La gente no sabía si reír o llorar, si bien algunos verdaderamente lloraban de risa. El narrador no concebía lo trágico sino como una forma de humor, de lo grotesco, de lo absurdo. Pero ese humor tejido de verdades que parecían mentiras, de frases ingeniosas y golpes de efecto era de lo más trágicamente verdadero que podía oírse en boca de un hombre cuyo aspecto ocultaba una suerte de estado de trance permanente y cuya sonriente cortesía no era quizás sino una forma de su desesperación de animal de las grandes profundidades cuando emergía a la superficie.

Clovis es el único hombre capaz de invitar delante de todo el mundo a una mujer que le ha deslumbrado en una fiesta o en una reunión de amigos a desnudarse en el acto y a hacer el amor detrás de una mampara o de un piano. Y más de una vez lo ha conseguido. Clovis manda apagar las arañas. La conmoción de los espectadores los agita nerviosamente ante ese movimiento de danza de dos siluetas entrelazadas confusamente ante un espejo. "No es el desnudo ni el acoplamiento explícito —escribe mi amiga Tununa Mercado en su pautado y melodioso manual erótico *Canon de alcoba*—, sino el color penumbroso, las formas insolentes de la irrealidad, la morbidez de las superficies, la rebeldía de la materia pugnando por salirse y penetrar por el ojo-órgano de la piel hasta el lugar de la cópula."

Como en el ceremonial descrito por Tununa (ella ha escrito también *Corona de castidad*, un austero tratado sobre el delirio erótico de los místicos), en los shows de Clovis la marea del deseo se hincha, crece y se hace progresivamente extensa. Crispa las manos y los rostros. Se insinúa en la penumbra con la luminosidad de una gracia inequívocamente sexual y buscona que hace palpitar el plexo solar de los hombres y los labios entreabiertos de las mujeres. No hay más que eso. Pero se *ve* mucho más que eso. Sólo por un momento. Se enciende la luz y la pareja reaparece. Ambos impecablemente vestidos y sonrientes, cogidos de las manos, como si volvieran de haber realizado una vertiginosa parodia de cine mudo. El simulacro mimético del amor ha brindado una escena de mágica perfección en homenaje a Eros. Una melancólica sátira de costumbres que a Federico Fellini le habría gustado filmar treinta años atrás con música de Nino Rotta. Lo bueno de Clovis es que nunca deja víctimas y siempre está dispuesto a hacer favores. Es un ser al que le gusta ser amado "a distancia y en rotación" —son sus palabras—, sin prometer nada y exigiendo menos aún.

La condesa de Esterhazy, de la nobleza húngara, refugiada en París, dijo a Clovis en una de sus tertulias:

—Tú no amas a nadie.

Clarinka de Esterhazy es una de las mujeres más trivialmente perversas del mundo elegante de París. No podía dejar en paz a su tiempo que ya había cambiado sin que ella se percatara de ello, y sin haber podido tampoco adecuarse al nuevo. Aun así, su belleza casi intacta resplandece sobre la de muchas jóvenes que envidian su *charme* y su astucia casi demoniaca para cazar la presa que más le apetece en el momento apetecido.

—No amas a nadie porque te amas demasiado a ti mismo —le dijo a Clovis oprimiéndole levemente una mano.

—¡Oh sí! —replicó él, riéndose con radiante simpatía—. Me amo con locura... pero me amo siempre en el otro. Estoy permanentemente enamorado, sólo que de una manera muy particular. Lo que se dice estar enamorado, en definitiva, sólo ocurre una vez. Se puede amar a varias mujeres al mismo tiempo a condición de que se las ame de manera diferente pero con la misma intensidad, concentrando todas las fuerzas vitales en una sola como si fuera la única, mientras las otras esperan su turno para ser a su vez cada una en su momento la única. La virtud del caballero enamorado es tratarlas a todas con estricta imparcialidad.

—Esa virtud esconde un abominable egoísmo —sonrió la condesa.

—No lo creas, Clarinka. El orgulloso animal hombre no lo pasa mejor. Por más viril y seductor que sea, está en la misma situación. Debe esperar y rendirse sumisamente a los deseos de la mujer que lo haga selectivamente el único, por un momento. De nada le sirven cien millones de años de arcaica y supuesta superioridad. Y los homo, los bisexuales, los pederastas y anacoretas del sexo están a medio camino entre el todo y la nada.

—Tu evangelio caritativo de *boudoir* es bastante superficial: sólo importa en él la cantidad y una especie de dosaje de oportunidades de buena voluntad entre hombres y mujeres y sus diversas especies y maneras de hacer el amor —dijo la otoñal condesa— Tal es tu justicia distributiva: cantidades por partes iguales a unos y otras para que nadie se queje y la fiesta siga en paz.

—La cantidad no existe, Clarinka —dijo Clovis—. Sólo la unidad es única. Se ama aún más a las que no se conoce todavía pero de las que ya tiene uno la imagen prentida e irrepetible en una absorta premonición.

—Y si al enamorarte de una de estas amantes futuras te confiesa ella, antes de la entrega, que es seropositiva, ¿te alejarías de ella?

—Al contrario, no la soltaría más. Sería la suprema sublimación del amor. El amor único e irrepetible. Amor y muerte siempre han andado juntos. Son dos hermanos siameses que viven bajo una misma piel. Por eso el amor tiene el perfume de la muerte. El amor *es* la muerte. La muerte asumida con el sabor ineluctable de la fatalidad. Después de todo, lo que se vive es lo que se muere. La pequeña muerte del amor, ésa del orgasmo efímero y engañoso, es demasiado poco. Pero la condena definitiva de dos cuerpos encadenados en una larga agonía, ¿qué mayor placer puede haber? ¿Qué mayor prueba de amor podrían darse dos enamorados de por vida a los que sólo la muerte va a separar?

A una amiga nuestra, muy joven, que andaba enloquecida por él, la llevó a su *boudoir*. Estuvieron desnudos en la cama toda la noche, bebiendo y hablando de bueyes perdidos en medio de una nebulosa música de cítaras hindúes. Clovis, afectuoso y tierno pero sin el menor impulso amoroso, no hizo el menor intento de poseerla. Le tuvo oprimida la mano todo el tiempo. Se levantó de pronto hacia el amanecer y la empezó a vestir con su propio atuendo deportivo. Florence era casi tan alta como Clovis. Sus ropas la modelaron como si hubieran sido hechas para ella. Clovis bailó con el "muchacho" unos pasos de danza al ritmo de la *Zarabanda* de Bach. Florence estaba aterrada. "Se me caían lágrimas de amor, de tristeza, de desesperación...", contaba.

Clovis, sin perder la sonrisa, la devolvió a su casa en el Lancia descapotable. Clovis iba feliz en su "amor en rotación y a distancia". Florence no podía contener el llanto. Clovis detuvo el coche frente a su casa, enjugó a besos cada una de sus lágrimas y la acompañó hasta la puerta.

—Estás libre —le dijo—. No te olvidaré jamás. Eres la mujer con quien hubiera querido casarme y vivir para siempre, pero yo no soy el hombre que tú necesitas. No podemos concedernos una noche maravillosa fuera del tiempo y luego encenagarnos en el tedio de la rutina y la costumbre que acabaría por separarnos para siempre.

Esto fue lo que Florence contó. Seguramente no fue exactamente lo que le dijo Clovis. Sus conversaciones no se pueden reproducir. Sólo tal vez sus palabras, no el pulso vital, el silencio cargado de energía, nervio de toda conversación.

Florence quedó sumida por largo tiempo en una especie de desdicha sonámbula. "Fue peor que un mal sueño en el cual por un momento me sentí la mujer más feliz de la tierra y en seguida la más desdichada —nos decía la pobre—. Un sueño se puede contar. Pero yo ni siquiera tengo una realidad de la cual pueda acordarme sino como de algo fantasmagórico. ¡Una escena irreal con el hombre más adorable del mundo!...", gemía y volvía a soltar las lágrimas.

Clovis es así. Ni de Dios ni del diablo. Y su fuerza radica en que ha tomado considerable distancia de sí. Me veo en los otros tanto más nítidamente cuanto más diferentes y lejanos los siento de mí. Cuando la distancia que me separa de ellos es la misma que me separa de mí. El único espejo que no engaña es el espejo del sexo en lo oscuro, como enseña el Eclesiastés, dice a veces como si aludiera a un hecho inalcanzable.

Clovis es un hedonista puro que no se permite sin embargo la menor concesión a sus principios de pureza radical. Tiene firmemente plantados los pies en la realidad, pero en una realidad que él elabora a cada instante mientras saca de ella los estímulos que necesita. Tan pronto como esos estímulos decaen Clovis desaparece, toma forma de oscuridad. El humo de su apagón no se pierde. Deja el hueco magnético de su presencia hacia el cual las mujeres vuelven los ojos brillantes esperando que pueda reaparecer en cualquier momento el cometa fulgurante y oscuro.

Creo que un tiempo Jimena anduvo también inconscientemente enamorada de Clovis. Un día se lo dije en son de broma completamente inocente. "No estoy enamorada de Clovis —me respondió en un murmullo sin acritud alguna—. Estoy enamorada de su finura natural, de su libertad íntima, que son un pequeño milagro en estos tiempos en los que la fealdad, la suciedad y el autodesprecio son los valores supremos en todas partes y en todos los planos de la vida. Por lo demás, ya conoces sus inclinaciones naturales —marcó lo de "naturales" con un gracioso mohín de condescendiente intención—. A Clovis no le interesan particularmente las mujeres." Y en esto Jimena tenía razón. Clarinka, la condesa húngara estaba enamorada en su ocaso de Clovis. Pero Clovis estaba enamorado de su marido, un joven efebo que podía ser el hijo de la condesa. Murió éste de una pulmonía salvando a Clovis de ponerle cuernos a la condesa filicida.

No sé por qué me estoy deteniendo en estos recuerdos sobre la vida de Clovis que su repentina presencia ha despertado en mí. Tal vez porque ignoro cómo voy a reac-

cionar ante este imprevisto encuentro; sobre todo porque
he adivinado desde el comienzo en la sonrisa un poco sar-
cástica de Clovis que en ese mismo instante ha comenzado a
tejerse para mí la trama de un destino, absolutamente inesperado. Él también habría percibido en mí el brusco cambio
de estado de ánimo y aplazó para mañana lo que estaba por
decirme.

Me metí durante toda la tarde en la Biblioteca Nacional. Repasé algunos capítulos de la *Monadología*. A la
salida fui a un cine a ver, creo que por tercera vez, la película de Michael Cimino sobre la guerra del Vietnam con
Robert De Niro en el fabuloso papel del cazador. Cené
opíparamente, al salir, en un restaurante que encontré al
paso en el Quartier Latin. Llegué caminando al Senlis. Tuve
que despertar al sereno. Me dio las llaves y subí hasta la
habitación de la mansarda. Llamé a Jimena por teléfono.

Todavía se hallaba despierta trabajando sobre el
Códice Florentino, de Sahagún.

—Estaba esperando tu llamado —me dijo con su
tono afectuoso de siempre, entre un bostezo y otro—.

—Me quedo en París por esta noche —le dije—.
Clovis sólo puede recibirme mañana.

—Se te oye mejor la voz.

—Sí, parece que el aire de París me curó la afonía.

—Cuídate. Métete en un buen hotel.

—Estoy alojado en el Senlis. Tomaré mañana el tren
nocturno de regreso —el beso de Jimena sonó como el leve
soplo de un eco en el otro extremo del hilo. Ella recibió el
mío. Dos frutos que se desleían a distancia en el sonido de
una suave delicia en la boca de cada uno.

Tuve un sobresalto. La luna, siempre ridícula, estaba del otro lado de los cristales del ventanuco, vigilándome
como el monje lascivo que espía a los amantes, al que men-
cionaba Leda en su carta. Me levanté a cerrar el postigo y
corrí el visillo. Eché llave y cadena de seguro a la puerta.

Contemplé un instante, sin ninguna emoción, la ex alcoba de Leda Kautner. Su aspecto ascético, su irrisoria dimensión, me dieron la impresión de una celda monacal. Pensé que un alma atormentada y nocturna como la de la muchacha de los Cárpatos no habría podido caber en esta buhardilla. Aquí había estado encerrada, prisionera, temiéndose, ignorándose a sí misma en la soledad.

¿Por qué hacía yo este estúpido vodevil, a medias deliberado, a medias inconsciente? ¿Qué me había inducido a este nuevo equívoco suficientemente ambiguo como para que no me hiciera sentir abyecto ni ridículo? ¿Estaba tratando otra vez de engañarme? ¿Qué buscaba afirmar o destruir con esta pantomima de un *voyeur* impotente y frustrado?

Quería verificar tal vez con una última prueba, aparentemente pueril, que todo estaba en orden, que el nudo de un mal recuerdo, ese que la memoria desata sin prisa y con toda naturalidad, había quedado atrás. Pensaba que el hueco de ausencia definitiva dejada por Leda Kautner iba a contribuir a alisar de una vez por todas las turbias aguas del desdichado episodio.

La repugnancia y rebelión que experimenté cuando recibí la carta con la que la imprevisible y extraña muchacha pretendió usarme como cobayo sexual, la furia homicida que me arrasó la noche en que descubrí su presencia en la habitación, el rencor y el resentimiento sordos y persistentes que me abrumaron durante muchos días cuando recuperé mis sentidos, y que se agravaron ante el desfile de indicios acusadores, se habían extinguido por completo. Estos encontrados sentimientos de condenación contra ella y contra mí mismo, esta rabiosa cólera por el extravío insensato de esa muchacha, formaban parte ahora de mi buena conciencia, de mi bienestar actual. Y este bienestar se había acentuado a partir del momento en que entré en su habitación abandonada.

Pasé las manos por el absurdo empapelado en cuyos colores predominaban el fucsia y el azul oscuro, casi negro a la escasa luz del velador. Abrí el placard y el vaho de Leda, acaso imaginario, me envolvió en una sutil y evanescente emanación. Lo aspiré con la naturalidad de lo esperado, sin la menor turbación de los sentidos ni malestar moral alguno. La imagen de Leda se había desvanecido por completo. No podía recordarla en ninguno de sus rasgos: en mi imaginación se habían convertido en el rostro anónimo de la belleza absoluta. No podía *verla* de ninguna manera. Y ni siquiera esa esfumada emanación de su cuerpo me traía su imagen. No volvió a mi memoria el horror de la fascinación. No volví tampoco a sentirme abandonado como cuando ella huyó y desapareció en Nevers dejándome a solas con mi furor homicida como con un cuchillo de dos puntas.

Lo único que me extrañó un poco, en una reacción puramente mental o sensorial, dado que estaba tranquilo y reconciliado conmigo mismo, fue no desear el deseo, no recuperar el deseo totalmente muerto aquella noche. Tal vez habría podido resucitar aquí, en la alcoba abandonada, ahora que todo había pasado. Ese vaho de una ausencia presente que salía del placard resultaba excitante. Era el olor del desgarrado deseo, de la delirante pasión de la joven, de su intransigencia, de su imperiosa necesidad de llegar hasta el fin de sí misma aun cuando fuera a costa de su muerte, sin medir las consecuencias que su acto insensato podía llevar aparejadas para los demás.

En un impulso algo violento me puse a abrir los cajones de la cómoda que se trababan desencuadernados. Estaban vacíos sin más olor que el de la madera laqueada. Abrí el cajón de la mesa de luz. En los intersticios del fondo vi un pequeño fragmento de papel. Lo retiré con las uñas. No había nada en él; nada más que el trazo trunco de algunas letras manuscritas, las características de Leda, grandes y desiguales. Resto de una palabra en alemán, probablemente el fragmento de un borrador que quedó ahí como el vestigio de algo que ahora ya no tenía ninguna importancia.

Traté de adivinar la mutilada palabra. Tal vez dijera ...*wie... der... se... hen...*, o algo así. El roto pedazo de un largo... largo adiós. Entré en el baño llevando entre las uñas el fragmento. Lo arrojé al retrete y tiré la cadena. Me senté en la banqueta a ver precipitarse la turbonada del agua arrastrando la minúscula brizna de papel. El brillo de la losa blanca me hipnotizó ligeramente. Balbuceé una palabra cualquiera y constaté que mi ronquera había desaparecido y que mi voz era límpida y grave como de costumbre. Me levanté y fui a mirarme en el espejo. Deseaba quizás interiormente que me mirara desde la luna una cara distinta de la mía. O que una cara extraña se superpusiese a la mía. Estaba dispuesto a ver con entera calma lo que fuera. Aun lo peor. Y lo peor era eso: mi cara, que no era la mía, con su espesa barba entrecana y sus rasgos falsificados. Pues como dice Lichtenberg: "Cuando un mono mira hacia un espejo, no puede ver a ningún Apóstol mirándole desde el inocente cristal..." Esto era también un progreso definitivo, no una mera casualidad. En Nevers, hasta ayer, sentía temor de mi espejo. Me recortaba la barba sin mirarme en él. La cara de macaco podía aparecer en cualquier momento. Sobre todo aquí.

La sensación de sosiego físico y moral me hacía sentir cada vez más tranquilo y en paz. Conmigo mismo y sobre todo con Jimena. Bajo esa sensación de serenidad me trabajaba el remusguillo de una ligera e innominada tristeza. Pero aun este sentimiento indefinible contribuía a mi distensión. Pensé en Leda. Acaso estaba triste por ella, por el malogrado destino de un ser excepcional destruido por la vida. Lamentaba no haber podido ayudarle a tender un puente entre su fantasmagórico mundo y la realidad natural. Cosas de un alma vieja que había llegado ya a su fin mortal en un cuerpo que apenas había comenzado a vivir.

Ah... si existiera la posibilidad de un injerto de almas... Si a Leda se le hubiese podido injertar un alma correspondiente a su cuerpo... Hubiera sido la más adorable de las mujeres. Algo nuevo e insólito, increíblemente deseable por su misma rareza. Un hombre digno de ella, y libre, la hubiera amado con locura, la hubiera hecho feliz. Hubiesen podido ser felices los dos en una felicidad absoluta y esencial como yo lo soy con Jimena... Pero en su infierno personal, donde vive en intimidad orgullosa con la rebelión y el miedo, la pobre muchacha eligió torcidamente. Me eligió a mí, engañada por el ser falsificado que yo mismo soy.

El sueño y la fatiga me fueron venciendo poco a poco. Miré hacia el placard entreabierto. Ya no percibía la tenue emanación. Me desvestí y me metí desnudo en el angosto lecho. Me tendí boca abajo con el rostro pegado a las fundas. Empecé a frotarme contra las sábanas maquinalmente. Leda me decía en su carta que lo hacía cuando pensaba en mí. Reprimí y contuve el idiota meneo. El olor a colada reciente me asqueó un poco. Retiré las fundas y volví a hundir y refregar la cara en la almohada. Sólo después me di cuenta de que buscaba el olor de la cabeza de Leda, el perfume indefinible de su pelo, de la piel suave de su nuca. Pero allí sólo me atosigó el olor acre del rayón de goma del cojín.

Giré y me volví boca arriba. Traté de encontrar sin conseguirlo las caras imprevistas que suelo buscar antes de dormirme en las manchas de los techos y paredes, en las vetas de la madera, costumbre infantil para escapar de la realidad que ha perdurado en mí más que el recuerdo de aquella edad. Eché una mirada en diagonal a las páginas informativas de *Le Monde*. Leí en algún título el anuncio de la ejecución de Ceaucescu y su mujer condenados a la pena capital por crímenes de lesa humanidad. Dejé caer el periódico.

Apagué la luz. Un pudor de otras épocas inmovilizaba mis manos cruzadas sobre el pecho impidiéndolas reconocer cierta renacida turgencia. En la oscuridad todo seguía en orden y no era posible esperar ni desear más que esa sedante distensión que me predisponía al sueño. Creo que en seguida me dormí con un sueño pesado y sin imágenes. Un ruido me hizo reflotar en un súbito salto a la vigilia. Mi propio pie se había deslizado del estrecho camastro pisando el diario arrugado al pie de la cama.

Me desveló la punzada de un doloroso pensamiento que no se me había ocurrido antes. La voz de Jimena en el teléfono tenía un leve matiz inusual. Acaso la garganta irritada por el sueño y el efecto de los bostezos. Me atravesó la repentina sospecha de que Jimena estaba *enterada* de lo que había pasado. No podía no estarlo. Por lo menos en el fondo de una aprensión crepuscular. Habían quedado demasiadas huellas del horror como para que su extraordinaria capacidad de intuición y percepción no hubiera podido detectarlas: mi entrada del jardín, cubierto de sangre, con la resaca de la terrible lucha sexual pegoteada al cuerpo, y todo lo demás.

Si aquella noche el susto o lo que fuera le ocultó la evidencia, pudo ir descubriéndolo gradualmente, o en una revelación súbita de las que suele tener a menudo. Si lo sabía, lo disimulaba con una discreción que la honraba a ella y aumentaba mi indignidad y mi bajeza. La hipótesis de la presencia real de Leda en Nevers volvió a apoderarse de mí anulando todas las alternativas y atenuantes posibles de carácter onírico, parapsicológico o hechiceril. Y esta posibilidad de que lo sucedido fuese real seguía siendo para mí la más aceptable, la menos culpable, la más deseable. Salvo que, en última instancia, estuviera yo volviéndome loco.

Vino a mi mente aquel comentario de Jimena sobre los dátiles "roídos por dientes humanos". ¿No envolvía un comentario indirecto pero intencional? Recordé las dos largas conversaciones que tuvo con el doctor Maurel en la galería, al retirarse de su última visita. Nunca me refirió lo que habían hablado. Era evidente que una grieta muy fina se había producido entre nosotros. Pero ¿por qué tenía estos miramientos y hasta cuándo podría soportar ella la carga de una simulada ignorancia?

El torcedor apretó su torniquete en torno a mi cabeza y a mi pecho. Ya no pude dormirme, acosado por un nuevo oleaje de horror que me cubría y anegaba como una segunda marea. Más delirante aún que la primera. Ahora no tenía en qué agotar mi desesperación revolviéndome en el angosto lecho de una ramerilla de tres al cuatro, en ese miserable cuartucho en el que todavía se hallaba aposentado el vaho de su encubierta y feroz sensualidad. El horror de aquella noche de abominación volvía a poner de relieve bajo una luz sulfurosa la bruma en que había tratado de vivir desde entonces. Sus halos neblinosos se hacían de nuevo visibles bajo la iluminación espectral de la claridad lunar.

Escuché unos sordos sollozos. Tardé en darme cuenta de que eran míos. Me tumbé estrujando la cara y la boca sobre la almohada empapándola con la espuma de mi angustia, de mi cólera, de una culpa que me resistía a admitir en toda su plenitud. ¿Qué me estaba pasando? Aquel *Nada... Era nada... Nada...* que balbuceé al entrar más muerto que vivo, no era simplemente un eco tenebroso que rebotaba, tardío, hacia mí. Ahora volvía a mí *todo* el horror de aquella noche como girando al revés en cámara lenta. Y en medio de la lentitud mortal de esas escenas, que había creído sobrepasadas para siempre, orlada de una luz lívida, apareció la imagen de Leda, desnuda y cubierta de sangre, mirándome fijamente con sus ojos dorados en su habitual expresión de ausencia y lejanía. Se me escapó un grito. Encendí a ciegas el velador y la imagen desapareció. Descolgué el teléfono para llamar a Jimena, sin saber para qué. Desistí y dejé caer el tubo sobre el mármol de la mesa de noche.

De ahora en adelante viviría yo en la espera sin esperanza de los condenados, aguardando, temiendo sólo el instante en que el rechazo, la indignación, la condenación, henchirían las palabras de Jimena conminándome a la separación, a la ruptura definitiva. Su juicio sería implacable, aun contra su convicción de que la justicia justa es imposible. Volvía a oír sus palabras: "...Estás lleno de remordimiento... Una verdadera fidelidad exige una lealtad que anula cualquier astucia por refinada que sea para traicionarla... La única fidelidad que cuenta es la que está segura de sí misma... No hay auténtica fidelidad más que la que acepta el amor del otro sin exigirle reciprocidad y sin juzgarlo cuando falta a la suya... ¿Me exigirías tú *eso*?... "

Jimena no condena la infidelidad radical del abandono como corte definitivo, como asunto de vida y muerte de cada uno. Aborrece las pequeñas y malvadas infidelidades que se ocultan en los repliegues de las pequeñas y aberrantes mentiras, en los pequeños y miserables silencios de las confesiones que se aplazan indefinidamente en busca de ese momento de sinceridad total que no llegará jamás.

Era inútil que me dijese a mí mismo: no me encuentro culpable sino por omisión, en una mínima parte, de lo que pasó. Estoy lleno de remordimientos, es verdad. Por todos los fracasos de mi vida, pero no por lo que pasó aquella noche. Lo prohibido se me impuso. No supe impedirlo como no se puede impedir la fuerza arrasadora del delirio. Ciertos actos no son elegidos ni aceptados. Los hechos los producen. ¿Consideraba Jimena por ventura esta exención en mi favor? ¿Es esto lo que la ayuda a sobrellevar en silencio el presumible conocimiento de lo que ha sucedido? ¿Me consideraba víctima de una misteriosa confabulación de circunstancias que ella misma no podía descifrar ni explicar? Si es así, debe de ser una carga muy pesada para ella y yo no puedo ayudarla en lo más mínimo.

El sofisma no me producía ningún alivio. Mi sufrimiento no provenía de que me sintiese culpable sólo en mínima medida, sino en el hecho de que no encontrara la manera de revelar a Jimena lo sucedido con toda naturalidad, sin que esta revelación no engendrara en su espíritu una cadena de presunciones y sospechas las que de todos modos acabarían convirtiéndome a sus ojos en responsable absoluto, sin absolución posible, de lo acontecido.

Al callarme aceptaba y me hacía cómplice de la asaltante nocturna hasta sus últimas consecuencias, incluida la de su muerte. ¿Podía a mi vez convertir en cómplice a Jimena? Si la hubiera despertado aquella noche, ¿cuál hubiera sido su reacción más inmediata ante la pavorosa escena? En algún momento, en mi desesperación, estuve a punto de hacerlo. Haberla llamado entonces o haberle revelado después lo que había pasado era lo mismo: anverso y reverso del mismo espanto. El hecho de aplazar la revelación no lo atenuaba ni disminuía mi culpa.

Resistí a la seducción con todas mis fuerzas. Pero resistir a la seducción no significa dejar de estar seducido. Existía la otra hipótesis: la de una fantasmagoría urdida por la trama de los sueños. Y aun en este casi improbable extremo, ¿no revelaría esa fantasmagoría sino otra realidad más profunda y sutil: el hecho de que yo estoy fascinado y enamorado de la bella y extraña muchacha, y que yo escondo esta verdad inconfesable como una enfermedad secreta? Sueño o realidad, igual me quedo vacío como se queda el mar sin la gota de eternidad que le falta.

Yo creo firmemente que todo lo sucedido fue real. Los vestigios que quedaron son ineluctablemente delatores. En el caso de que ella lo ignore todavía, moralmente está implicada de manera indirecta en ese suceso horrible. Y esto es como estar ya *enterada* de todo, aun sin saberlo, en ese limbo de adivinación que posee el amor de las mujeres como Jimena, tanto para el pasado como para el futuro. Incluso para la memoria del presente, que no existe sino como tiempo que pasa y en el cual no se puede fijar ni registrar nada como no se puede escribir con el dedo en el agua que corre. Ese don de adivinación tiene en las mujeres enamoradas dos lóbulos como el cerebro. Los hechos más brutales están cargados de una parte de sueño, de delicados matices espirituales, que únicamente el instinto femenino sabe percibir. La imaginación de estas mujeres está hecha con los deseos y las experiencias íntimas de los seres amados, que ellas asimilan y convierten en su propia intuición.

Las verdades indignas viven en el tiempo como los seres humanos indignos, o sea como casi todo el mundo. La sombra de esa verdad maligna acompaña a Jimena, día y noche, con la sombra de su ominoso secreto. Cuando duerme, se acurruca a sus pies, insobornable, como un perro. No lo ve aún. En algún momento lo descubrirá, si mi silencio no se confiesa entretanto inconscientemente como todo silencio culpable... "Ver de verdad —suele decir— no es más que una verdad verde que no madurará sino en la putrefacción final..."

Te estoy contando la verdad ahora, Jimena. No ha pasado el tiempo puesto que la culpa subsiste. No he aplazado la confesión. La he retenido en mí como castigo. El ver-de-verdad está ahora en tus manos para que madure dentro de ti. Estos papeles te revelarán desde el pasado la maldita verdad en toda la plenitud de su descomposición final. Era yo quien estaba hediendo en el fondo del pozo de tu glorieta. En todo caso, ese pozo está en mí, hiede en mí como un vacío de siglos. Me irás a buscar en el futuro para juzgarme. Pero yo ya no estaré en ninguna parte para aceptar y recibir tu condena. La justicia justa no existe, sueles afirmar con razón. De este modo, el tiempo transcurrido en la ignorancia de la indigna verdad multiplicará para ti el peso y el horror de este ocultamiento. Lo hará mil veces más ruin y cruel. Y entonces ya no sería yo únicamente culpable de omisión sino el culpable convicto y confeso del peor crimen contra la fidelidad: la mentira recelada con premeditación y alevosía en un aplazamiento sin fin. Callar la verdad por temor o por cálculo es la peor de las falsedades porque es deliberada. Detrás de una confesión inconsciente o voluntariamente diferida hay algo verdadero que no se puede traicionar. Y yo lo he traicionado puesto que delego mi confesión a la escritura cuyo sistema de signos es el más engañoso de todos.

Siempre pensé, Jimena —y esto quiero repetírtelo desde lo hondo de mí— que tu amor supera infinitamente al mío porque el don de ti misma es la esencia de tu autenticidad. Y que la miseria sin nombre de mi amor consiste en que es y ha sido siempre la de limitarse como don y extralimitarse como egoísmo. Tu amor no es un "préstamo" a largo plazo y a bajo interés como tú misma has ironizado alguna vez al definirlo. Es, como el mío, un sentimiento de esos que duran toda la vida, y que por lo mismo no puede esperarse que sean perennes puesto que la vida está hecha de momentos fugaces en los que todo, aun lo más intenso y querido, se hunde de improviso sin una razón que lo justifique, y muchos, casi todos, morimos antes de que nos acabe la vida.

Jimena, pronto no seré más que un recuerdo desvaído para ti. Te esperan esos hijos futuros que darán a tu existencia su más noble justificación. Tampoco espero ya ni soy digno de esa gracia, ese esplendor primaveral de los retoños de nuestra sangre que hubiera renovado y salvado mi vida. Me acuerdo en este momento de las personas que he abandonado alguna vez o que me han abandonado, y no comprendo cómo puede dejarse a las personas que uno quiere de verdad y que son insustituibles. Tú eres insustituible para mí y no me apartaría de ti si no fuese por un motivo superior a mi propia vida. Conoces este motivo. Es un pacto sin palabras que hemos sellado entre los dos. Y ese pacto es inapelable.

En mi juventud creía que la vida es más grande y poderosa que el destino. Y que la vida, ella por sí misma, vence en todas las encrucijadas cuando uno pone empeño en ello. No estuve nunca seguro de mí. Quizás mantuve la duda por un tiempo. Pero desde aquella noche mi sangre *sabe* que habita un hombre perdido... y quiere salir... busca desposeerme de ti, de mí... despojarme de todo lo que tenga todavía un sentido de expiación y de rescate en la acción que me propongo, y que de algún modo voy a cumplir.

En el torpor de las arterias, siento que mi sangre no me cree, a pesar de todas las pruebas que le proporciono de mi voluntad de dejarla salir cuanto antes. Es una sangre cavilosa y desconfiada. Mi sangre me conoce. Sabe que no puede esperar de mí el más mínimo gesto de honradez ni de lealtad. Ya no le puedo exigir ahora:

—Calma. Ten un poco de paciencia. Yo quiero liberarte en un chorro caliente como la última supuración de mi odio contra la cara del tirano..., o de mí mismo ante el pelotón de fusilamiento... si vuelvo a fracasar en el único acto que hubiera podido justificarme como hombre, como ciudadano de un pueblo oprimido y vejado hasta el último extremo de la degradación...

A ti, Jimena, sí puedo decirte desde ahora y lo gritaré en el último instante: Guárdame al menos tu amistad. Una amistad como la tuya es para mí idéntica en valor a tu amor. Sé que lo he perdido irremediablemente... lo sé... lo supe siempre... La actriz Cytheris escribe a su amigo y confidente Lucio Mamilio Turrino una carta en la que le cuenta su despedida de Marco Antonio, poco antes de la muerte de Julio César. No encuentro palabras más conmovedoras y ciertas para expresar mis sentimientos. Yo también debo decirte: Desde ahora debo aprender a vivir, por poco tiempo más, sin la amorosa mirada de tus ojos que llenaron mis noches y mis días de una intolerable dulzura... esos ojos a cuyo fulgor soñé morir...

El zumbido del teléfono descolgado taladraba mis oídos, mis pensamientos. Arrojé con rabia el tubo sobre la horquilla. En el ruido que produjo la rotura del micrófono oí el sonido de una voz que me llamaba por mi nombre. Y esa voz era la voz distante de Leda Kautner. Salí, mejor dicho huí de la habitación. Acabé de vestirme en el corredor y bajé.

Toqué el timbre del conserje. Escuché ronquidos que se interrumpían; luego, el rechinar de resortes de alguna litera portátil del otro lado del mostrador. A las cansadas apareció el sereno. Un hombre sin edad, demacrado, pálido; uno de esos seres que continúan viviendo con licencia de la muerte, o que parecen andar buscando, desorientados, la tumba que les han robado. Al hojear el registro, las manos azuladas y huesudas delataban la aceptación de la mortalidad. Pagué la cuenta de esa noche de cuento de hadas, en la que el amor había jugado conmigo como el gato con el ratón. Sonaba otra vez el teléfono en ese momento. El sereno bajó el volumen del pequeño receptor de radio que llevaba cruzado al pecho en banderola y atendió.

—Una llamada de larga distancia para usted. Cabina 3, por favor —me indicó la voz cavernosa.

Me azotó el pecho una oleada de sangre. Le respondí casi gritando:

—Dile que no estoy... que me he ido...

Mis palabras se confundieron con el verso final de *Alfonsina y el mar,* la melancólica canción de Ariel Ramírez y Félix Luna, que en ese momento sonaba en el walkman del sereno. La voz de Mercedes Sosa con olor a valles profundos arrullaba el sueño eterno de Alfonsina. La taciturna Alfonsina Storni entró caminando en el mar buscando la gota de eternidad que a ella le faltaba y que no encontró en su poesía del amor ausente. Yo me estoy ahogando no en el mar del amor ausente sino en el mar de la pasión demente donde navegan sirenas corsarias carnívoras.

Bajé a saltos las gradas hacia la puerta principal. Estaba cerrada con llave. Tuve que esperar a que el sereno viniera a abrirla como desde la eternidad. Avanzó paso a paso dándose puñetazos en las piernas para acallar el monótono chirrido de las articulaciones. Mercedes Sosa arrullaba el sueño de Alfonsina sobre el pecho del conserje en el receptor afónico, desde el acantilado de Mar del Plata.

—¡Aprisa... apúrese! —grité destempladamente.

"Ya voy che... ", gritó con bronca el sereno. "Menos apuro, bacán. No ves que estoy impedido..." Cada palabra olía a vino de taberna, a desgracia, a miseria. Los chirridos de las piernas se detuvieron junto a mí. El hombre las acomodó dando más puñetazos en los trabados resortes de las articulaciones. Consiguió al fin tenerse en pie, se inclinó y abrió la puerta a cámara lenta. Le alargué una luca.

—Viejo, para vos... —dije con remordimiento viéndole tan mal parado.

Dijo "mercí, musiú..." No era del Senlis de París de donde yo iba saliendo. No era el hotel donde yo había dormido en el ex camastro de Leda. Su voz seguiría esperando en el tubo desde Munich. Yo salía de un turbio hotelucho de la Boca en Buenos Aires y me dirigía hacia ninguna parte.

Me senté en un banco de piedra de una plaza. Con las primeras luces del amanecer se me presentaron dos caminos: arrojarme bajo las ruedas de un tren, o acudir a la cita de Clovis. El dilema no se sostenía. Me invadió la amarga satisfacción de una apuesta con el absurdo: dejar que ese destino, en el cual no creía, decidiese por mí sobre cuál de los dos caminos debía tomar. No sé cuánto tiempo pasó. Había olvidado mi reloj pulsera sobre la mesa de noche.

Quedó en pago del teléfono roto. Salí a la calle y me encaminé hacia una estación del metro. El sol brillaba fuerte sobre mí pero yo caminaba a oscuras.

Al descender por la escalera mecánica, una chiquilla argelina o tunecina de corta edad trepaba en sentido
contrario llorando a lágrima viva. Evidentemente se había
perdido entre el gentío y buscaba a los suyos. Se asió a mi
mano y me dijo *¡papá!*..., pero siguió llamando a gritos a
su madre. Le pregunté dónde la había dejado. Indicó una
dirección cualquiera. Acabé de bajar con ella y anduvimos
recorriendo el andén en busca de los padres perdidos. No
tardó en aparecer la madre, una joven magrebí que llo-
raba también muy afligida y asustada. Recuperó a la niña
casi arrancándola de mi mano y echándome una mirada
de repulsión y de odio que delataban sus sospechas. Se
alejaron corriendo hacia la salida.

Estaba llegando un tren. Me abrí paso a empujo-
nes en el sitio donde se apiñaba mucha gente pugnando por
subir y me acerqué al borde mismo del andén. ¿Esperaba
aún el empellón providencial? Vi las ruedas brillantes que
se venían aproximando raudamente. Los frenos rechina-
ron bruscamente antes de lo esperado. El movimiento de
arco iniciado por mi cuerpo para lanzarse a las vías chocó
contra el vagón todavía en movimiento. Sus puertas se
abrían en ese momento. Fui introducido a la fuerza por el
alud humano.

Todo continuaba existiendo con la misma indiferencia de siempre. Comprimido por la masa vociferante me
sentía más solo. La soledad que yo mismo había construido a mi alrededor. Solo en la multitud pero sin la multitud
adentro. Una mano de mujer me tocó la mano. Me volví y
miré un rostro desconocido, ajado y turbio. Se había equivocado. Retiró su mano y pidió disculpas. Pero en ese
mismo instante, en la compensación de un vaivén del péndulo que llevamos en nuestro interior, la calma volvió a

mí. Bajo el estímulo de un presentimiento pensé que algo importante me esperaba en la noticia que iba a darme Clovis.

Barrió con el brazo los legajos que tenía en su mesa, dispuesto a una larga conversación. Me tendió un pliego. Se trataba de una invitación de la presidencia de la República del Paraguay. Por intermedio del Ministerio de Cultura, recientemente creado, invitaba a los países democráticos del mundo a enviar representantes del arte, de las ciencias y de las letras a un Gran Congreso que iba a tener lugar en Asunción durante todo el mes de septiembre, con el título genérico de *Historia, cultura y sociedad en la América Latina del siglo XX*. La invitación impresa en finas hojas de auténtico pergamino ribeteadas de oro y con letras en relieve, esmaltadas de púrpura, estaba refrendada por el propio presidente de la República, general Alfredo Stroessner, y llevaba fecha del 1 de enero de 1987.

—Las cancillerías de Europa y de los Estados Unidos, excepto las de China comunista, de la declinante Unión Soviética y las de sus satélites del Este, se están despepitando de risa —dijo Clovis, serio pero mordaz.

Me fijé en el calendario que estaba sobre la mesa. Marcaba el 27 de marzo de 1987. Mi mente trabajaba velozmente como en la solución de esas charadas que aparecen en los periódicos.

—Sigue leyendo. Vale la pena —dijo Clovis.

En un golpe de vista me enteré de que el maratoniano congreso va a celebrarse en conmemoración del trigésimo aniversario del ascenso al poder del general presidente.

Otros actos de no menor importancia iban a ser la entrega gratuita de tierras, casas, implementos agrícolas y generosos créditos a los inmigrantes de los países europeos, orientales y asiáticos (excepto China comunista y Corea del Norte) que quieran habitar la región occidental del país, exentos de impuestos y gabelas de cualquier naturaleza por treinta años. El gobierno de Stroessner ofrece sufragar todos los gastos de viaje, traslado y alojamiento y otorgar una pensión transitoria de dos mil dólares mensuales hasta su instalación definitiva en las casas que les va a proporcionar en los lugares escogidos por los interesados.

—Inmigrantes europeos, orientales y asiáticos en Paraguay... en el Chaco, entre los fortines militares y bajo la férula de las autoridades castrenses... —no pude menos de reírme—. Cesión gratuita de tierra. Créditos generosos, exención de impuestos por treinta años... ¡Vamos, Clovis! Hay más de cien mil campesinos sin tierra y otros tantos miles de indígenas que son ametrallados cuando invaden los inmensos latifundios vacíos en poder de los militares y capitostes del régimen...

—Eso está bien —me interrumpió Clovis—. Es un estímulo para los futuros propietarios. La defensa de la propiedad es sagrada. Por otra parte, el problema de los cien mil campesinos sin tierra ya ha sido resuelto por el dictador. Los ha puesto a trabajar en masa en la construcción de los trenes de alta velocidad entre Asunción y Brasilia.

—Hacia el norte de la región oriental están las colonias de los brasileños que han establecido un nuevo estado en pleno territorio paraguayo con leyes, autoridades, moneda y lengua brasileños, sus propios juzgados y tribunales de primera instancia. Ya son como un millón. La invasión "pacífica" de los nuevos "bandeirantes" paulistas está avanzando hacia Asunción a banderas desplegadas y van a extender su dominación por todo el país. El Paraguay tiene bastante experiencia con los macacos brasileños, desde hace más de trescientos años.

Clovis iba arrugando la nariz. Detesta los discursos que huelen a panfletos sociales o políticos. Iba a seguir en mi enumeración informativa.

—Todo eso no importa mucho por ahora —me detuvo Clovis—. Deja a los macacos en su sitio. Nadie puede contra el derecho del más fuerte. En cuanto a Stroessner es evidente que quiere cambiar la población del país ya que no puede cambiar el país. Está harto de paraguayos idiotas. A él se le da una higa de la pureza racial. No es un ario *pur sang*. No es indio, ni criollo ni mestizo. Es un hombre de ninguna parte cuya única patria es el poder. Sigamos con el congreso —dijo con voz metálica.

Leo que la invitación encarece expresamente a las cancillerías la formación de comisiones preparatorias para la selección de los representantes que asistirán al congreso. Invita incluso al envío anticipado de observadores que verifiquen sobre el terreno la amplitud, seriedad y proyecciones futuras del congreso. Además de hacerse cargo del alojamiento y traslado en clase de lujo de los invitados, cualquiera sea su número, la invitación compromete el pago de diez mil dólares a cada uno de los participantes por sus respectivas ponencias y comunicaciones.

Continúo leyendo. La invitación recomienda también a las cancillerías la invitación a destacados representantes de la banca, del comercio y de la industria para un congreso paralelo de intercambio, expansión económico-financiera e inversiones de bienes y capitales en Paraguay. Se ha instituido asimismo un premio de un millón de dólares para un concurso de propuestas de inversiones de los más variados tipos, que estará a cargo de un jurado de expertos nacionales e internacionales. En un recuadro impreso decorado por la bandera paraguaya leí: *La energía eléctrica de Itaipú significa la industrialización del país y la ayuda a los países vecinos menos desarrollados.*

—¿Qué dices a esto? —inquirió Clovis.

—Lo obvio —dije—. El tiranosaurio está dando las últimas boqueadas. La guerra fría se acaba y los Estados Unidos han tenido que arrumbar la mentada doctrina de la seguridad nacional en el desván de los trastos viejos.

—Vamos a enviar una avanzadilla de observadores para que vayan a olfatear el cotarro.

—Hijo de padre bávaro y madre paraguaya es un nazi convencido y practicante. Durante un curso de perfeccionamiento militar en Alemania, conoció a Hitler en Munich y aún alardea de que bebió con él una jarra de cerveza en la cervecería donde el futuro *Führer* preparaba el copamiento del poder.

—Todo eso es historia antigua —me interrumpió de nuevo con un ligero gesto de fastidio—. No interesa ya a nadie, ni a los que se salvaron de los hornos.

No tuve necesidad de explayarme en mi panfleto antidictatorial. Clovis disponía de un *dossier* muy completo de la situación del Paraguay, de las actividades de su amo supremo y un informe exhaustivo sobre el sistema represivo, métodos de espionaje, persecución y la práctica sistemática y masiva de la tortura como un elemento de compulsión, de intimidación y de exterminio hasta los últimos confines del país.

Me alcanzó una de las abultadas carpetas. Había una lista de los prisioneros muertos en los más horribles suplicios en las cámaras de la Dirección Nacional de Asuntos Técnicos, popularizada en el run rún del miedo colectivo simplemente con el nombre de "la Técnica", o "la Secreta". Figuraba también en uno de los legajos la nómina de los torturadores principales, de los asesores taiwaneses y, en un principio, hasta de los "técnicos" norteamericanos que estaban adscritos a la Técnica, cuando Stroessner era todavía una baza útil para los Estados Unidos. Vi también una extensa lista de "indeseables" y de "enemigos del gobierno". En ella figuraban mi nombre y mis señas anteriores.

—¿No crees tú que ante este cuadro de horrores la asistencia a ese congreso sería como apoyar y en cierto modo legitimar este aparente viraje "democrático" de la tiranía?

—Ese congreso, si llega a realizarse, será para Stroessner el comienzo del fin.

—¿En qué se funda tu confianza en la repentina conversión de un régimen totalitario, en plena descomposición, en protector de la inteligencia y la cultura? ¿O es que ahora crees en los "valores" humanistas de un régimen implacable como el de tu tiranosaurio?

—Creo en la necesidad de un detonante para hacer estallar una situación explosiva. El carácter particularmente absurdo de este congreso le da aún mayor peso a ese detonante que va a ser infiltrado desde el exterior, a invitación del propio tiranosaurio.

Clovis hacía juegos de prestidigitador con un lápiz entre los dedos. Tras una pausa reflexiva, mirándome fijamente, me preguntó:

—En suma, ¿crees tú que esta invitación es aceptable?

—Sobre tablas.

—Necesitamos verificar todo eso sobre el terreno. Vamos a enviar observadores. Luego estudiaremos si la asistencia al congreso puede ser posible y resultar útil.

Un momento antes había leído yo algo en una nota al pie de la nota del programa que concentró toda mi atención.

—En ese caso —dije, recobrando la voz— te ruego que me incluyas en la lista de invitados.

—No creo que te convenga ir —dijo Clovis torciendo un poco el labio—. Tu nombre continúa figurando en la lista de los peores enemigos del régimen.

—Tengo otro nombre. Soy otro. Las dos veces que estuvimos con Jimena en Paraguay, los sabuesos más renombrados del régimen no me reconocieron.

—Ya veremos. No hagamos planes aún—. Sonó el teléfono. Me despidió con un gesto.

Al bajar la escalinata del palacio, contemplé por

primera vez con simpatía la carroña dorada que dormitaba
a orillas del Sena. Tomé un taxi para regresar al aeropuerto
de Orly. Durante el trayecto volví a pensar en la nota des-
tacada al pie de la invitación, que despertó en mí un súbito
interés, al punto de no oír lo que me estaba diciendo Clovis. La nota decía: *"En el acto de inauguración del Congreso, el Excmo. Señor Presidente de la República del
Paraguay tendrá el placer de saludar personalmente a los
ilustres invitados en el Salón Blanco del Palacio de Gobierno, donde se servirá un vino de honor en su homenaje"*.
    ¡Estrechar la mano al tiranosaurio! ¡Vaya honor!
¿No era esto una de esas figuras increíbles que suele tejer
el azar? No. Era algo bien concreto y definido, una situación marcada a escuadra en tiempo y lugar bien definidos.
Podía ser éste el instante único y excepcional en el que
vengo pensando desde hace bastante tiempo. Todo mi ser
se tendió hacia ese momento definitivo en el que, en un
fogonazo infinitesimal, uno se convierte en lo que debe ser
y hace lo que debe hacer. La aventura suprema, el éxito o
la catástrofe. Sentí que el pulso se me había acelerado con-
siderablemente. Tenía la boca seca. No dejé de beber durante el vuelo, lo que no hizo otra cosa que aumentar el
mareo de una ansiedad casi obnubilada que me dominó
desde que leí la nota sobre el "apretón de manos" en la
invitación presidencial.
    El primer hilo París-Asunción había comenzado a
tensarse. Y la tela de araña podía alcanzar a tener propor-
ciones colosales aun cuando por el momento yo pudiera
tomar a risa el hecho absurdo. Veía a lo lejos agitarse febrilmente las inmensas patas de la araña roja. ¿Se puede escribir
una historia real o imaginaria sobre hechos que aún no han
sucedido o que están empezando a suceder? Acaso es lo
único que puede hacerse. Toda historia real o imaginaria no
es sino una anticipación del presente.

Cuando le referí a Jimena mi encuentro con Clovis, la noticia del grotesco congreso y la posibilidad de viajar a Asunción entre los invitados, su rostro se turbó.

—No debes asistir a ese congreso —me dijo apretándome la mano con la suya en su gesto habitual de prevenirme contra algo, sabiendo de antemano sin embargo que mi decisión estaba tomada. Me abstuve de contarle que el juicio de Clovis coincidía con el suyo. Lo intuyó de todos modos.

—Supongo que Clovis no te alentó a partir —dijo con firmeza.

—No hay ningún riesgo personal —insistí con cierta irritada seguridad, desviando la cuestión.

—No se trata de riesgos personales, Félix —replicó suavemente Jimena—. Razón de más, aunque no haya ninguno, tu sola presencia en ese "congreso de cultura", aunque no sea conocida sino por ti, será un triunfo para el régimen. Y peor aún si te descubren y te aclaman. Y peor aún... —Jimena se mordió los labios y contempló el vacío que parecía extenderse interminablemente a sus pies.

—No iré yo. Irá Félix Moral, "ese extranjero tejido por la trama del destierro", como definió Ricardo Piglia en una de sus novelas, a quienes como tú o como yo o como otros millones de extranjeros convivimos con nuestra naturaleza esquizofrénica. Así andamos a los tumbos con nuestras dos mitades.

—Ese nombre es un seudónimo. Un nombre falso. No te ha cambiado. Te oculta.

—No puedo entrar de otra manera.

—¡Ay Félix, no hagas las dificultades más difíciles! Que la ansiedad de aprovecharte de un retorno aparentemente fácil no turbe tu buen criterio! Al pisar tu tierra natal, la frágil máscara de Félix Moral se desvanecerá y volverás a ser tú mismo a cara descubierta. Aunque no te descubra la policía del tirano, sentirás que un desconocido ha usurpado a traición tu propio lugar, tu propia persona, tu propio ser. ¿Cómo te comportarás ante tus propios compatriotas a quienes estarás engañando como a ti mismo? No los engañarás. Ellos sabrán que *eres* tú.

—Bien, Jimena, tienes razón pero no es necesario que nos pongamos solemnes ante una opción no tomada aún, bastante quimérica por lo demás. Analizaremos los dos, como siempre lo hacemos, este problema en todas sus implicaciones y consecuencias, y luego tomaremos una decisión de común acuerdo.

Jimena acercó su rostro al mío y me dio un beso. Le temblaron ligeramente los labios. En ese beso, y también por anticipado, sentí el sabor de la despedida, no en el espíritu de Jimena sino en el mío. Me dominó de golpe una infinita tristeza como si de pronto todo se hubiera ya consumado.

No ha recuperado Jimena su vivacidad habitual. No hemos vuelto a hablar del congreso, pero es evidente que su sombra se ha interpuesto entre ambos y se ha superpuesto a la historia de Leda, agravando las cosas. Hay manchas que no se pueden borrar ni raspar con las uñas. Mis ocurrencias suenan a hueco y ya no tienen el premio de esa risa fresca que es uno de los mayores encantos de Jimena y que ahora no alcanza a marcar la gracia de sus hoyuelos ni a encender el brillo de sus pupilas. Se ha retirado de mí a una distancia imprecisable. No hemos vuelto a hacer el amor. Hay la excusa de la trombosis, pero es una excusa implícita que ninguno de los dos quiere mencionar. Me siento yacer en un corral de aves, pisoteado por gansos que me atruenan con sus graznidos. Dos gallinas ponen dos inmensos huevos entre mis piernas de gallo muermoso.

Veo a Jimena preparando sus clases en medio de libros y papeles, que son el resguardo visible de su extrañamiento, de su confinamiento en lo hondo de sí. Me gustaría conversar con ella como antes. O simplemente estar juntos en esa comunicación silenciosa que nos unía más que las palabras. No me queda más que entretener el tiempo muerto con mis *sombrografías*. Fabrico siluetas en las que voy copiando con un lápiz las imágenes proyectadas por la sombra de esa luz volátil que gira bajo mis ojos en la mezcla coloreada del rojo, del verde y del amarillo. La idea fija vuelve a rondarme en las noches de insomnio.

¿Qué puede ser ese acto misterioso e inescrutable? Experimentar de pronto una idea, un impulso, por los que uno se sienta lanzado inexorablemente a morir por algo que nos sobrepasa más allá de todo límite, que no podemos comprender pero que nos ilumina al tiempo que nos fulmina como un rayo. Siento que esa idea o ese impulso no va a brotar de golpe como en los héroes de los novelones románticos que rescatan al antihéroe de la víspera. Esa idea tiene que haber nacido con uno, espera y estalla dentro de uno cuando ha llegado el momento. Y casi siempre fracasan. Como en las revoluciones de nuestra América, donde los héroes victoriosos de la víspera terminan asesinados o derrotados. Pienso en el *Che*, como un Cristo yacente en el lavadero de la escuelita en Yacanguazu. Pienso en Bolívar, en su peregrinación final hacia Santa Marta, en José Martí, muerto en combate frente a los españoles, en el propio mariscal López, el héroe máximo de nuestra nacionalidad asesinado en Cerro-Corá por los brasileños.

Recuerdo avergonzado un desatinado gesto mío, que todavía me hace crujir los dientes. En una *Carta abierta al pueblo paraguayo*, que alcanzó a publicarse en un periódico de Asunción, planteaba al tiranosaurio un desafío: "Use usted su soberanía y su poder omnímodo en un acto liberador para el pueblo todo de su país y para usted mismo; el único y último acto de rescate que puede todavía librarlo del anatema infamante de la posteridad. Renuncie usted al absolutismo personal y devuelva el poder a la ciudadanía de la República en elecciones libres, fuera de la represión y coacción de las armas".

En suma, la idiota ingenuidad del reto no sirvió sino como tema de uno de sus discursos "patrióticos". "Uno de los bandidos subversivos —dijo el Gran Tembelo— me exige desde el destierro que yo renuncie y me vaya. Cómo no. Trato hecho. Yo entrego el poder a los comunistas y me voy. ¡Que venga ese bandido a ocupar mi puesto si tiene huevos!... ¡Que venga el mismo Stalin con su Ejército Rojo!..." Cien mil gargantas aullaron en la Plaza de los Héroes durante horas bajo el tórrido sol: "*¡Patria o muerte!.. ¡Estroner presidente!...*

Al tiranosaurio le importa un bledo el juicio de la historia y de la posteridad. En casi medio siglo de poder absoluto, él legitimó el refrán acuñado por un destacado hombre público: "El Paraguay es el único país donde nadie pierde ni gana reputación". Y puede agregarse: "El Paraguay es el único país donde la única reputación válida, hereditaria y perpetua es la de ladrones, asesinos e infames traidores a la patria". Ésta es la gran "tradición nacional" que se perpetúa sobre un pueblo que merece otro destino, lleno de héroes y de mártires anónimos enterrados en cualquier parte sin cruz ni marca que memore sus nombres, como ya lo decretó el Supremo Francia hace más de un siglo.

¿No puedes hacer por tu país algo menos imbécil que una carta abierta al Gran Manitú?, se sublevó mi conciencia. Ante el bofetón de esa pregunta se me ocurrió de pronto una idea estrafalaria: ¿Y si me dedicara a hacer lo más difícil, a cometer el acto más absurdo y descabellado? El acto más inconcebible sería entonces el *acto* fulminante y definitivo. Reflotó en mí, con más fuerza que antes, la idea de matar al tirano. Pero muchos lo han intentado dentro y fuera del país y todos han sido liquidados en medio de terribles suplicios o han desaparecido sin dejar huellas.

Leí todos los procesos de magnicidio de todos los tiempos, que pude encontrar en bibliotecas y archivos especializados. La Roma de la decadencia, la Inglaterra de Cromwell y la Italia del Renacimiento detentan la palma magnicida. Pero el éxito de los Brutos de todos los tiempos era siempre un producto del azar.

Tenía más de mil fórmulas anotadas en una libreta de forro arratonado que guardo escondida en el hueco de una lámpara en mi estudio. La libreta siempre caliente me impulsaba a imaginar variaciones inagotables, pero no prendía en mí la inspiración de ese acto único que dormía en mí con la luz de una estrella extinguida o no nacida todavía. La idea del magnicidio, si se ha de ejecutar con alguna posibilidad de éxito, debe ser concebida como lo más difícil e insensato, anoté en la libreta. Y ello sólo era posible bajo las apariencias de la más extrema facilidad y naturalidad. ¿Era ésta una nueva trampa de la mala conciencia? ¿O era en verdad el acto supremo que yo esperaba de mí, pero que nadie más que yo debía saberlo y esperarlo, hasta que fuera ejecutado?

Clovis ha llamado por teléfono para anunciarme que la asistencia al congreso de "cultura" está decidida y que el viaje a Asunción se realizará el 1° de septiembre. Es la mejor noticia que han podido darme; en cierto modo ella me resarce de los sobresaltos y angustias de estos últimos tiempos y aclara el nebuloso desconcierto, del que no he podido aún recuperarme del todo. Desde ahora en adelante, todo mi pensamiento se concentra en un objetivo central focalizado en un punto deslumbrante, casi enceguecedor: ¡La muerte del tirano!

La inminencia de ese Congreso en Asunción, la

posibilidad de ese viaje, me acercan la oportunidad que ya creía irrealizable: la de cumplir mi proyecto por cualquier método que tuviese a mano. Repetí *a mano*, sin darme cuenta en un primer momento, del sentido que implicaban estas dos palabras, clave de una estrategia acerca de la cual sólo tenía una idea vaga envuelta en presagios e incertidumbres.

Surge ahora con toda nitidez en mi conciencia el papel que puede jugar en tal designio el arma secreta, la más inconcebible y minúscula, de la que hablé a Jimena en días más propicios. Un microcosmos mortal, le dije, que no cabe en la imaginación del más desconfiado pero que calza en un dedo y estalla sin ruido y con acción retardada. Creo que éstas fueron mis palabras. Jimena creyó que bromeaba. No sabía, ni sabe todavía, que al decirle esto —tengo la sensación de que hace ya una enormidad de tiempo— pensaba en el gran anillo del conde de Villamediana que ella guarda, entre sus reliquias familiares, en un estuche de terciopelo rojo sellado con el escudo nobiliario del conde.

Escucho sus risas, el cáustico comentario en los que habría prorrumpido de haberle revelado yo aquella vez cuál es el "arma secreta" en la que pienso. Nada más pueril, en efecto, nada más ridículo ni absurdo que este pensamiento que parecería corresponder al nivel mental de un chico de la primaria, atosigado de novelas policiales y de ciencia-ficción. Para mí mismo lo fue y, en principio, lo sigue siendo. Jimena desconoce o ha olvidado lo que el gran anillo de plata, en forma de áspid que se muerde la cola, puede cobrar como temible arma ofensiva en el designio magnicida. Habría que remontarse un poco a los orígenes de este objeto a la vez histórico y legendario para entender lo que yo espero de él en el futuro, un futuro casi ya "al alcance de la mano".

Las familias de los Tassis y Peralta empiezan a aparecer en los anales del reino a comienzos del siglo XVI. El fundador de una de las ramas, fue el primer conde de Villamediana que acompañó al Rey en Portugal como Correo mayor. Su hijo, don Juan de Tassis y Peralta, nació en Lisboa. Desde muy pequeño dio muestras de cierto talento literario y de un carácter festivo y fogoso pero al mismo tiempo dócil y discreto. Felipe II lo llevó consigo a la corte de Madrid y lo puso a cargo de los preceptores más capaces. Se acordaba especialmente del licenciado don Luis de Tribaldos de Toledo que le descubrió el inagotable y misterioso mundo de la naturaleza y de los animales.

Juan de Tassis y Peralta se formó en el ambiente culterano de la época. Cifraba el emblema de la perfección en la poesía y en el mundo de los animales domesticados por el hombre, en el caballo de pura sangre árabe educado para los torneos. El único con el que el hombre, el caballero, se unifica y consubstancia hasta formar parte de un solo cuerpo, el de un semidiós. El mito del Centauro era para don Luis de Tribaldos, el emblema más hermoso de la Creación. Bajaba la voz para decirle: "Píndaro da al Centauro genealogía divina. Y la gran poesía dice siempre la verdad". Por lo que la poesía y los caballos (sobre todo, los de carrera) formaban una unidad indisoluble en la mente del joven Tassis.

Pronto, el futuro conde frecuentó las tertulias de la Academia a las que concurrían Lope, los hermanos Argensola, Mira de Amescua y otros grandes de la época. Su vena literaria era la sátira, pero su verdadera pasión eran las mujeres, el juego, la colección de joyas, de pinturas y su afición a las carreras de caballos. Arriesgaba apuestas enormes que su sueldo de Correo Mayor, con ser alto, no podía cubrir. A raíz de estos excesos fue desterrado a Valladolid donde fundó otra rama a la que —según las siempre fantasiosas genealogías familiares—, los antepasados de la madre de Jimena pertenecieron. No hay ningún indicio cierto sobre esta descendencia, salvo tal vez el gran anillo del conde, de la que Jimena es la última depositaria.

El anillo desapareció por largo tiempo. Por deudas de juego el conde se vio obligado a empeñarlo a uno de los hijos de la dinastía de los Tasso, fundada por don Francesco Tasso, de Bérgamo, el verdadero zar de los correos de postas en toda Europa. La suma, cogida a cuenta del anillo, era enorme y por lo tanto impagable.

Cuando don Juan de Tassis y Peralta sucedió a su padre en el título de conde, no renunció a su vida agitada. Amigo del conde de Lemos, que apreciaba su ingenio poético, éste le prohijó y le llevó consigo a Nápoles. De esta época es la carta que escribió a su esposa doña Ana Mendoza, con quien casó siendo ambos adolescentes. Le hablaba en esa carta de las dos grandes penas que sufría: la primera, la de haber birlado, sin saberlo, a don Miguel de Cervantes el puesto junto al conde de Lemos al que el gran escritor aspiraba. La segunda cuita se relacionaba con el empeño del anillo. Acababa dándole señas precisas de quién de los Tasso era el poseedor de la joya y le encarecía la necesidad de rescatarlo a cualquier precio. Doña Ana se negó en redondo a ocuparse de la recuperación del anillo, tanto más cuanto que ese anillo de dudoso origen había provocado el primer conflicto matrimonial. Cuando el conde regresó a Madrid, malvendió algunas propiedades y recuperó el anillo pero perdió a la joven y hermosa doña Ana, que ya estaba un poco harta del noble nómada.

Don Juan de Tassis y Peralta se dedicó entonces con más ardor que antes a lanzar los dardos envenenados de sus sátiras contra personajes eminentes pero corrompidos de la corte. Lo que le valió un nuevo destierro a un pueblo de Andalucía. No atemperó esto su ardoroso afán de criticar con epigramas y letrillas muy cáusticas la inmoralidad de la

administración y a sus principales agentes. Cuando Felipe
IV subió al trono hizo llamar a Villamediana y le conminó
a que dejara en paz a la gente de la corte y se dedicara a sus
poemas y comedias, en los que sobresalía como uno de los
primeros poetas culteranos de la corte.

La rehabilitación del segundo conde de Villamediana se produjo en Aranjuez y en presencia del rey, con el es-
treno de su comedia *La gloria de Niquea*, representada por
las damas de la corte. La pieza del conde precedió incluso a
El vellocino de oro, de Lope de Vega, que iba en segundo
término en el programa. La pieza de Lope se interrumpió
apenas comenzó el primer acto, debido al incendio del teatro. En medio del pánico general, el conde de Villamediana
sacó en brazos a la Reina para librarla de las llamas. No era
un secreto la admiración que el conde profesaba a Isabel de
Borbón y que dejó entrever en algunos de sus más intrinca-
dos poemas. Habladurías de época hicieron correr el rumor de que, en testimonio de su gratitud, la Reina se había
sacado del dedo la sortija real y se la había obsequiado.

La maledicencia no es dueña de su retorcida lengua.
Lo cierto —según crónicas dignas de crédito— es que apenas depositó a la Reina a buen recaudo, el conde, rodilla en
tierra, se inclinó exageradamente barriendo la alfombra con
las plumas del sombrero para rendirle pleitesía. Cuando se
levantó, la Reina ya le había vuelto la espalda y se alejaba
con sus tules chamuscados, rodeada por su empavorecido
séquito.

Menudearon los comentarios que sindicaban al
propio conde como instigador del incendio que le había
permitido la increíble hazaña galante. Esa misma noche, al
volver en su coche a su palacio en la calle Mayor, fue apu-
ñaleado por un desconocido. Tanto el origen del incendio
como el asesino del conde no se descubrieron jamás. Lope
de Vega compuso un epigrama que revelaba en cierto modo
lo que se quería ocultar:

—Mentidero de Madrid:
Decidnos: ¿Quién mató al Conde?
—Dicen que le mató el Cid
por ser el Conde lozano.
Disparate chabacano
La verdad del caso ha sido
que el matador fue *Bellido*,
y el impulsor, *soberano*.

Queda en pie el misterio del anillo. De ningún modo podía ser la sortija de la Reina. El gran anillo de plata era digno de un corpulento chambelán de la corte, pero no de Su Alteza Serenísima. Tampoco podía serlo por su naturaleza de arma secreta. En su colección de joyas, don Juan de Tassis tenía varias piezas de tales características, provenientes algunas de ellas, como el anillo en cuestión, del saqueo de Roma. A lo largo de cuatro siglos, el anillo del conde vino resbalando por las ramas del frondoso árbol genealógico de los Tassis y Peralta, hasta que por ley del azar, que también domina en las florestas dinásticas, cayó en el joyero de roble de Clara Tarsis, madre de Jimena.

Esta trayectoria de los objetos errantes es a veces más misteriosa que los itinerarios de los seres humanos. Sugieren pequeños desajustes del cosmos. Órbitas que se muerden la cola. El anillo del conde de Villemediana afecta, precisamente, la forma de una serpiente cuya cola entra en la boca del ofidio de plata bajo el engaste del ópalo que lo corona.

Hay también un vínculo inexplicable en los apellidos de los que componían la extendida corporación de los Correos Mayores. Así los Tassis de Castilla se anudan con los Tasso de Bérgamo. Éstos, a su vez, se convierten en la rama de los Thurn und Thaxis, en la que descuella Alessandrina de Rye, una de las más grandes figuras de los correos de postas cuyo centro estaba en Francfort, Colonia, Hamburgo, Rheinhausen y Venecia, sin excluir la sede pontificia. En el imperio postal de los Tasso, el derecho de sucesión se extendía a la rama femenina. Luego este derecho fue adoptado por todas las empresas de los Correos mayores. Si el imperio hubiera subsistido —le dije una vez a Jimena, a propósito de eso—, te tocaba a ti el derecho de ser la emperatriz de los Correos Mayores. No le hacían mucha gracia estas patochadas genealógicas.

Los Tasso no desdeñaron en ir modificando su apellido según las exigencias de las distintas lenguas y de los países a los que se iba extendiendo su imperio postal. Se pueden advertir las raíces etimológicas y fonéticas principales. Así, los Tasso se convirtieron en Daxen, Taxis, Thaxis, Thassis, Thassus, y por tanto, en el Tassis del primer conde de Villamediana. El célebre poeta Torcuato Tasso no perteneció a la noble secta de los Correos Mayores. Se limitó a escribir *La Jerusalén libertada* en la que celebra la cruzada del magnífico Godofredo de Bouillón. De creer en las crónicas familiares, parece que a don Torcuato le fascinaba viajar en las grandes diligencias de correo ("naves de tierra firme", las llamó en sus poemas), cuyo balanceo le ponía en estado de trance. Algunos de sus biógrafos aseguran —todos tendemos a descubrir el ángulo inédito de la realidad— que el poeta escribió algunos de los cantos de la *Jerusalén* dentro de las diligencias postales en sus frecuentes viajes de Sorrento a Roma. Llevaba en propias manos su gran poema como una carta hacia el futuro en el advenir de los tiempos.

Los Tasso, además, fueron tantos, tan ilustres y ricos en Europa, que un poeta de la talla de don Torcuato no añadía gran cosa a su ejecutoria. Los Tasso de Bérgamo hacían arrancar su origen desde el propio Paulo de Tarso, roca fundadora de la Iglesia Católica Romana. La de los correos de postas es la primera gran epopeya de la comunicación postal universal cumplida por las patas de los caballos, por el ingenio y la tenacidad de los mensajeros, por la visión de los fundadores de un imperio que habría envidiado Mercurio. Es una historia portentosa digna de los poemas homéricos.

En España, en la rama de los Tassis de Valladolid, el apellido cambió una de sus *eses* por una *r*, convirtiéndose en Tarsis, el apellido materno de Jimena. Suele ser ella muy renuente a hablar de esta genealogía que le parece falsa además de presuntuosa. He investigado por mi cuenta en los anales postales, tanto como en la historia familiar de los Peralta Tassis. Y la conclusión parece irrefutable. Leyenda o crónica histórica, estos avatares no niegan la preeminencia que tuvo la descendencia de los Villamediana en los Correos Mayores del Rey, y menos aún la existencia real del anillo.

Después de muchas hesitaciones y con un sentimiento de estar cometiendo una profanación, he sustraído el anillo del costurero de Jimena. Lo he estado observando anoche con el microscopio. La cabeza que muerde la cola tiene un orificio invisible a simple vista. Una cierta presión sobre el ópalo, que finge un ojo de cíclope, dispara por el orificio un aguijón de una centésima de milímetro. No lo hace regularmente; es evidente que el mecanismo debe estar atascado por exceso de polvo y de herrumbre. Acaso por falta de costumbre. Tengo que hacerlo revisar por un experto sin despertar sospechas. El argumento es simple: debo venderlo en las subastas del Sotheby´s. El anillo me va divinamente en el dedo mayor de la diestra, como si yo mismo lo hubiese encargado a un orfebre de Roma, cuatro siglos atrás, para la presente emergencia, que ha de cumplirse en un mes, a más tardar.

Lo raro es que el blasón inscrito en el estuche y que se reproduce microscópicamente en el interior del anillo, no corresponde al escudo de los Villamediana. Hay un tejón

(tejón en italiano es *tasso*), coronado por el cuerno de correos. En el campo azul de la parte inferior hay otro tejón de plata, pero en la parte superior dorada despliega sus alas un águila real, negra como el carbón. El conjunto está dominado por un cuerno de caza tallado en oro. Y esto es lo extraordinario: se trata del blasón de los Tasso, pero no de los Villamediana. Tengo para mí que el hijo de don Francesco devolvió al conde o a su esposa, cuando todavía vivían juntos, gato por liebre. Pero esta liebre, o mejor dicho, el águila negra del escudo, es valiosa porque es única. La llevaré posada en un dedo sin que nadie lo note. El pico más duro que el topacio, hará estallar como un rayo la cabeza del tirano.

Me resultó bastante difícil dar con uno de estos orfebres, entendidos en joyas del Renacimiento. Al fin encontré un joyero italiano afincado en Marsella, verdadero artista y erudito en historia de las joyas. Me contó la historia del anillo con precisión de detalles, y se comprometió en remediar el funcionamiento en pocos días.

—Estos mecanismos microscópicos —diagnosticó— son muy sensibles a la enfermedad del tiempo. A veces por falta de uso. Lo tendrá en tres días. ¿A qué dirección se lo envío?

—Vivo en París. Volveré a buscarlo yo mismo —dije al joyero. Le di una dirección falsa. Me firmó un recibo en buena y debida forma.

Volví un día después del plazo convenido. El orfebre de Marsella me recibió con una cordialidad, que me pareció excesiva.

—El anillo está en perfectas condiciones —dijo—. Es de los que usaban algunos de esos nobles desquiciados del *Quattrocento* para fulminar a sus enemigos o rivales con un apretón de manos en la mayor impunidad. Me hizo ver con rayos X el depósito interior que servía para almacenar el veneno. El ópalo movedizo producía el disparo de la saeta mortal del grosor del cabello de un recién nacido.

Ensayó una prueba con agua destilada. Me apretó la mano y con el pulgar oprimió el ópalo. La delgadísima lengüeta del áspid de plata me penetró en la palma de la mano, sin que sintiera el menor signo de que esto había ocurrido. No quedó ningún rastro del aguijón. Le pedí la cuenta de la reparación. Noté que el joyero hesitaba un poco; luego me propuso directamente:

—Se lo compro por lo que usted pida.

—Imposible, *Signor* —le respondí—. Es una reliquia de familia. Mi madre no se desprendería de él por todo el oro del mundo.

—Entonces usted no me debe nada —dijo el joyero con sinuosa amabilidad—. Objetos como éstos pertenecen al patrimonio artístico del país —insinuó como para intimidarme con la posibilidad de una confiscación y persuadirme a una ventajosa venta clandestina.

—Oh. No se preocupe. Está debidamente registrado —repuse con toda naturalidad—. Mi madre tiene la posesión vitalicia del anillo.

—Si algún día cambia de opinión, vuelva a visitarme con el anillo. Le ofrezco por él cien mil francos contantes y sonantes.

—Vale mucho más —le dije con una sonrisa—. Pero ya veremos. Hay joyas que pasan de moda o que los coleccionistas rechazan, y entonces se vuelven menos... preciosas, y hay que desprenderse de ellas o donarlas a los museo especializados en estas maravillas de amor y muerte.

De Marsella a Turín. Vive en esta ciudad un compatriota amigo, exiliado como yo desde hace muchos años, también enemigo declarado del tiranosaurio. Julio Miñarro, especialista en microbiología y toxicología, trabaja como investigador en el afamado instituto X de Turín. Se alegró mucho de verme. Le expliqué confidencialmente el proyecto. Consideró las dificultades y los riesgos a que me exponía, pero, al notar mi determinación, no intentó disuadirme. Miñarro me habló de un pariente suyo, el doctor Agustín Goiburú, que intentó igualmente liquidar al tirano pero que tuvo la desgracia de caer en manos de los esbirros del régimen mientras pescaba apaciblemente a orillas del Paraná, al otro lado de la frontera. Necesitaba tener constantemente bajo los ojos la tierra natal como incentivo de su obsesión. Yo conocía bien el hecho pues poseía todos los antecedentes de esta conjura, frustrada entre otras tantas. Goiburú sufrió horribles torturas. Tal vez fue "empaquetado", es decir, enterrado vivo, o arrojado desde un avión militar sobre la selva virgen.

Cuando le expliqué a Miñarro el mecanismo y la filosofía del proyecto magnicida celebró la originalidad y el sentido del intento.

—¡Dar la muerte al tirano con un apretón de manos me parece sensacional!... —dijo riéndose con una risa nerviosa y crispada—. Si tu tentativa tiene éxito, pasará a la historia como el acto que puso fin a la infame tiranía con un gesto de cortesía.

—Has acertado —repuse—. Suelo decir que la cortesía no es sino una forma de la desesperación.

—Agustín y los otros héroes que fueron sacrificados como él quedarán vengados —dijo Miñarro—. Dame el chirimbolo ése y veremos cuál es la carga que le conviene. Tiene que ser un tóxico o un virus de acción retardada, por lo menos de tres días, como para que te dé tiempo de ponerte fuera del alcance de las uñas de los matones de la Técnica.

Le dejé el anillo. Lo observó con curiosidad.

—¡Nunca he visto nada semejante! —dijo con un silbido de admiración—. Te espero en una semana.

Me despedí con un abrazo. Julio Miñarro habrá sentido la tensión de ansiedad y de dicha que me embarga.

Llegué a Nevers al atardecer. A la satisfacción de haber recuperado el anillo sano y salvo, se ha sumado la alegría de un notorio cambio en la actitud de Jimena. Me ha recibido con su cariño de siempre. Ha vuelto a ser la misma de antes. Era un día fresco y llovía. Me invitó a tomar mate en la cocina. El aroma del chipá, acabado de hornear, trajo por anticipado el regusto de otros días más felices, que parecían haber regresado. Nada me preguntó sobre mi corta ausencia. Suponía tal vez que había ido a París, a presentar los papeles para el viaje a Asunción. Hablamos de varios asuntos intrascendentes. Luego de un silencio, en el que buscaba la manera de proponerme algo, Jimena me dijo:

—Ya que estás decidido a viajar para asistir a... ese congreso, me gustaría acompañarte. ¿Es esto posible?

La abracé y le di un beso, radiante.

—¡Absolutamente! —respondí sin vacilar—. Voy a llamar ahora mismo a Clovis para pedirle que te incluya en la lista oficial de invitados. Me das una inmensa alegría, Jimena.

Encontré a Clovis en su despacho y no sólo aceptó, risueño y amable, el pedido de Jimena, sino que aplaudió su decisión de acompañarme a Asunción.

La inesperada propuesta de Jimena me ha puesto de nuevo ante un dilema de hierro. Si, por una parte, su gesto de adhesión, de solidaridad, de afecto, me ha dado una inmensa y genuina alegría, por otra, hace recaer sobre mí el peso de un grave problema cuya solución no alcanzo a vislumbrar.

La compañía de Jimena significa que debo abandonar mi proyecto magnicida. Sus decisiones nunca responden a motivos triviales, y esta última tiene todos los visos de que ha determinado jugarse el todo por el todo. Es evidente que sus intenciones van más allá de acompañarme en una gira "turística" o "cultural", sobre todo teniendo en cuenta su radical oposición, desde el comienzo, a esta jugada de tahur del tiranosaurio, y su empeño en hacerme desistir del viaje a Asunción. ¿Es esto lo que ella se propone? El recurso es muy parecido a un chantaje con las mejores intenciones posibles, desde luego, que deberían llenarme de orgullo y de felicidad, pero que a la vez me sumen en una desesperación sin límites.

No puedo revelar a Jimena el motivo real de mi viaje. Si lo hiciera, ella pondría en juego todos los recursos a su alcance para impedírmelo. Por otra parte, es también casi seguro que se ha percatado ya de la sustracción del anillo, lo que le ha permitido reatar cabos y tener una idea clara de mis propósitos. Ella sabe que yo no la complicaría jamás en un acto de esta naturaleza. Su aparentemente ingenua alegría por acompañarme, oculta apenas su decisión de convertirse en "rehén" de mi propia vida poniendo la suya como escudo contra la ejecución de un acto insensato cuyas consecuencias, lo sé, son ineluctables.

La fecha de partida está próxima. Sólo me falta retirar el anillo que Miñarro llenará con la carga letal. Todo está resuelto, pero ¿qué hacer con la decisión de Jimena de acompañarme? He pensado en todas las variantes posibles para resolver la cuadratura del círculo. No encuentro ninguna, excepto cancelar el viaje y usar el anillo contra mí mismo.

El anillo la implica a ella también en la empresa y nos une en un círculo vicioso inescapable. Este círculo, infinito como la misma vuelta del anillo, nos sitúa a los dos antes y más allá del fin de todo. Es cierto que los objetos inanimados no tienen nada en común con los seres humanos, salvo que los seres humanos hagan de ellos el *objeto* de su vida y de su muerte. Yo he robado ese anillo a Jimena, y pienso usarlo para dar muerte con él al tirano. Esto me obliga, por un principio elemental de lealtad hacia ella, a revelarle el hurto. Lo que significa, inevitablemente, revelarle también el proyecto en todos sus detalles. Lo que determina a su vez, en última instancia, su anulación. ¿Logrará ella que el tiranosaurio se me escape de las manos?

No sé... no sé... Sólo sé que acabo de contraer con ella la deuda de otra revelación nuevamente aplazada.

Intento en silenciosa desventura no pensar en el paso del tiempo. Dormir exacerba aún más la angustia. No puedo renunciar a mi proyecto, pero tampoco puedo renunciar a la compañía de Jimena que me brinda con este gesto acaso la última prueba de su verdadero amor. El dilema me ha desgarrado en dos mitades que luchan entre sí con idéntico encarnizamiento. Acaso mi angustia no es más que la desesperación del individuo aislado en su propio egoísmo. ¿Es que el acto único y heroico, con el que pretendo definirme de una vez para siempre en un relámpago, no es más que la expresión de este egoísmo? No puedo detener la marcha del tiempo. No puedo resignarme a vivir medio día, pero ni siquiera un solo minuto, al margen de esa obsesión que domina mis pensamientos, mi voluntad, todo mi ser. ¿Es que no puede uno enardecerse más que por lo absurdo?

En ciertos casos, como en el dilema al cual estoy enfrentado, no se puede elegir: es el resto de la eternidad o nada.

Tres días después se produjo el accidente de Jimena al volver de la Facultad. En el choque de su automóvil con un pesado camión sufrió fracturas de la pierna y del brazo izquierdos y una herida profunda en el rostro. Me telefonearon desde la clínica de traumatología a la que la transportaron de urgencia. Estuve a su lado durante el día desde que le hicieron las primeras curaciones. No podía moverse. Le enyesaron el brazo y la pierna. A ésta la pusieron en alto con la polea y el peso de varios discos de plomo durante algún tiempo. Sentía yo una gran emoción al poder ayudarla y acompañarla ahora que ella necesitaba de mí. Volvía a vivir los días del hospital Rothschild en los que la asistencia de Jimena produjo el milagro de mi "resurrección", celebrado por el doctor Maurel, al haber raptado mi casi cadáver cuando lo llevaban a la morgue.

Permanecía en silencio al lado de su lecho apretándole la mano. El efecto de los calmantes la tuvieron durante tres días en un estado de atonía crepuscular. No era el sueño "despierto" que le enseñó la anciana del Guairá. Tenía una noción difusa de lo que sucedía a su alrededor, pero después no se acordaría de nada de lo que le había pasado, ni siquiera del choque. Supe que había despertado de este trasueño doloroso cuando me sonrió por primera vez y me llamó bajito con la voz de una niña en total desamparo.

—Lástima —le dije, acariciándole la frente perlada de sudor—que no pueda yo a mi vez raptarte y llevarte a nuestra Ventana del Poniente.

Me sonrió tristemente. Cuando pudo hablar, me miró en los ojos con la intensidad de otras veces y me pidió perdón por haber frustrado "nuestro" viaje.

—No te preocupes, Morena —le dije en un murmullo junto a su oído—. Me quedaré a cuidarte. Pronto estarás bien y podremos viajar como lo hemos proyectado.

Sentí en su voz debilitada el acento de una resignada dimisión. Ella y yo *sabíamos* que ese viaje no se iba a hacer. Era mejor no hablar de ello y no tocar más el asunto.

En dos semanas pude llevarla a casa. Pero entretanto sucedió el triste episodio del dálmata. Sucedió así. Hice un rápido viaje a Turín. Julio Miñarro me entregó el anillo y un frasquito hermético conteniendo la toxina viral.

—La carga tóxica, calculada para cien kilogramos de peso, actúa en setenta y dos horas —me dijo con la seguridad del científico pero también con la inocultable inquietud de quien está proporcionando de contrabando un arma para una acción criminal, por justa y justiciera que se pretendiera.

—La especie del Tyrannosaurus Rex pesa más —precisé por las dudas.

—Oh, la acción de la carga cubre el doble del peso previsto.

Miñarro me explicó que el fin es fulminante y que

sobreviene sin ningún síntoma previo igual a un síncope. Hay, dijo, parálisis total de la circulación y del sistema nervioso. El cuerpo del "paciente" quedará rígido y retorcido como si hubiera sido mordido por una cobra. Puede ocurrir incluso que disminuya a la mitad de su tamaño. Me mostró cómo cargar el anillo, la manera de esterilizarlo después del "uso" y me enumeró por escrito las precauciones que debía tomar para evitar los peligros de filtración. Me entregó también un saquito de material infrangible, de los que se usan en toxicología, para guardar el anillo y el frasco sin riesgo de fuga de las moléculas del tóxico.

—Una vez usado —me encareció— debes esconder todo esto en lugar seguro donde no lo encuentre ni el diablo. Borra todo vestigio. Pueden surgir investigaciones. Sé que me meto en un lío padre. Pero lo hago para vengar en cierto modo la memoria de Agustín y de todos los que como él fueron sacrificados en espantosas torturas. El tiranosaurio por lo menos no sufrirá ningún dolor. La montaña de dolor que ha causado a nuestro pobre pueblo caerá sobre él convertida en un chorrito de milésimas de milímetros. Quedará reducido a la altura de sus botas. Tendrán que enterrarlo en un cajón de criatura. Suerte y coraje. Que todo salga bien.

Nos despedimos en silencio como dos cómplices que caminan maniatados hacia el tablón de un cadalso.

Regresé a Nevers. El siguiente paso era ensayar el test de eficacia. Al volver de la clínica, donde estuve varias horas con Jimena, me demoré absorto en preparar el anillo para ensayar la primera prueba. Me lo puse en el dedo. Sentí que el anillo pesaba por lo menos el doble que yo. Llamé a Yaguareté con el silbido de siempre. El noble dálmata entró, parsimonioso y solemne, como si llevara sobre su lomo las coronas blancas y negras del río Paraguay, y empezó a lamerme la mano. Justamente la mano en la que llevaba puesto el anillo. Veía reflejada la sierpe bifronte en los suyos, brillantes y comprensivos. La luz mortecina del atardecer ponía en sus pupilas el resplandor de dos hogueras lejanas y diminutas. Conversamos un rato. Movía su cabeza como si entendiera lo que le iba diciendo.

—Vamos —le dije y salí llevándolo del collar.

Me senté en un banco de la glorieta, y empecé a hablarle de nuevo, como si fuera yo el que necesitara convencerse de que la barbaridad que iba a cometer era un acto inocente y justo.

—No somos nada —le dije al final acariciándole la cabeza—. Y ni siquiera somos dueños de nuestra vida. Tú y yo vamos a morir por una misma causa... Tú vas a morir con la muerte reservada al tirano. Pero no vas a morir como él, que es una bestia feroz. Vas a morir como un hombre. Yo voy a morir como un perro. No podemos evitarlo. Has sido para mí un gran amigo y yo te quiero mucho... Mucho me duele lo que voy a hacer. Mucho te pido perdón... —mis ojos estaban húmedos, mi voz estaba rota.

Ya no veía reflejado el anillo en sus ojos. Se habían cubierto de lagañas fibriculares rojizas como venillas rotas. Me miraba con una mirada tristísima, lejana.

— Dame tu mano... —le pedí, humilde, culpable.

Me tendió la pata derecha con la educación, la paciencia y la confianza sin límites que siente un perro hacia su amo. Se la oprimí fuertemente mientras desplazaba ligeramente con el pulgar el gatillo de ópalo. El dálmata me observaba como adelantándose a mis pensamientos. No se movió un milímetro pero al sentir que el tóxico penetraba en su sangre con voz humana clamó "¡NO!..." De sus fauces entreabiertas colgaban dos finos hilos de baba. Se alejó lentamente y fue a echarse en el lugar de costumbre, ante la puerta cancel donde cumplía su oficio de vigía y guardián. Ya no iba a moverse de allí.

Dije a Jimena que el dálmata estaba enfermo.

—No prueba bocado, no quiere beber. Está arrollado sobre sí mismo, como dormido... Acaso está enfermo de tristeza...

Jimena dobló la cabeza a un costado. Le caían lágrimas. Se deslizaban y reabsorbían sobre el yeso. No dijo nada. Nada preguntó. Se dejó hundir en uno de esos insondables mutismos que a veces le sobrevienen y que parecen alejarla de golpe a una distancia imprecisable.

Cuando la esposa del Rector nos lo regaló, siendo todavía un cachorrillo, nos previno. Es una raza muy extraña, dijo. Parecen seres humanos. Sólo les falta el habla. Adivinan cosas. La madre de este pequeñín murió de sobreparto y en medio del delirio de la fiebre sus quejidos expresaban claramente su temor a la muerte, sus ansias de que le salvaran la vida. Mientras pudo mantuvo levantadas las patas delanteras como defendiéndose contra algo que la amenazaba —dijo la esposa del Rector. Murió con la cabeza entre las patas apelotonándose en un rollo duro que nadie pudo deshacer.

Así murió el dálmata treinta y seis horas justas después de nuestro apretón de manos. Era el tiempo que correspondía a su peso, a su espacio, a su vida, a su muerte.

Murió como su madre, levantando las patas delanteras a un enemigo invisible. Los cincuenta o más kilos quedaron rebajados a mucho menos de la mitad y el cuerpo del dálmata se redujo al de un cachorrillo acabado de nacer. Lo recogí en mis brazos. Lo acuné un poco mientras lo llevaba a enterrar en el hoyo que él me había visto cavar en los fondos del jardín cuando aún vivía y su cuerpo era todavía grande y adulto. El hoyo resultó enorme para ese cuerpecillo disminuido. Tuve que echar mucha tierra encima.

Segunda parte

Hoy, a las dos de la tarde, dentro de veinte minutos, llegaré a mi ciudad natal, si todavía puedo llamarla así. Bajo la luz fuerte y como artificial no consigo percibir el paisaje. Desde el momento en que el avión comenzó a descender, después de sobrevolar la gran represa he pegado la frente a la ventanilla. A nueve mil pies de altitud no me fue dado admirar la poliédrica joya del lago, engarzado como un diamante en la falda de la cordillera. Los siete saltos del Guairá, los más grandes del mundo, amansados, domesticados, confluyen ahora a alimentar esta gema líquida cuya energía mueve el medio centenar de turbinas. A menos de la mitad de esa altura, la visión sigue igual. Los prismáticos no la mejoran. Abajo y arriba todo es opaco y brillante a la vez. No hay nubes, no hay cielo, no hay tierra. En estas capas bajas de la atmósfera flota una inmensidad sin color. La luz del día y la oscuridad de la noche parecen haberse juntado en una niebla de híbrida fosforescencia.

A menos que la memoria me traicione, sumergida ella misma en esta bruma algodonosa que cambia de matices en sus vertiginosos y a la vez quietos remolinos, nada me hace suponer que estemos sobrevolando la tierra natal. La inmensa nave hiende las turbulencias con un levísimo balanceo que es suficiente para aumentar la jaqueca que me oprime las sienes y la sensación de vértigo sobre el diafragma. El brazo izquierdo se me ha entredormido como en un doloroso hormigueo y siento la boca llena con el sabor metálico de una acidez desconocida.

En un primer momento pensé que el raro efecto óptico se debería al material refractario de la ventanilla. Pero el óvalo de fibra de vidrio, de doble fondo, me permite ver con toda nitidez el ala del aparato a babor, los torbellinos de aire en las turbulencias, los chorros de gases en llamas de los turborreactores. En la luz turbia y como artificial no acabo de ver el paisaje a través de las mirillas, pese a que el inmenso Boeing 747 vuela ahora a escasa altura. Tal vez la atmósfera cubierta de cirros y de nimbos no corresponden al cielo subtropical. La salvaje tala de selvas vírgenes sobre una superficie de más de ochocientas mil hectáreas para la construcción de la central hidroeléctrica tal vez sea la responsable de estas perturbaciones de la atmósfera. Puede ocurrir que el vuelo siga otro derrotero para entrar a la capital por una ruta inhabitual y aterrizar en algún nuevo aeropuerto de extrema seguridad.

El avión desciende en espiral. Adentro crece la algarabía de los pasajeros. Desde mi observatorio continúo sin ver nada. Abajo y arriba todo es opaco y brillante a la vez. La máquina hiende el inmenso colgajo de tiniebla blanca. El azul eléctrico de las turbonadas de gas se torna púrpura y el púrpura se apaga de nuevo en la oscuridad luminosa, veteada de manchas violáceas.

El cambio de luz debe de haber comenzado precisamente al entrar en la zona de la central hidroeléctrica. Hasta donde alcanza mi vista, fija en los horizontes ahogados por esa luminosidad que no es diurna ni nocturna, nada me permite vislumbrar el escorzo cercano o lejano de la ciudad. Busco en vano el centelleo del río patrio. Lo que resulta raro en esta época del año, cuando las interminables lluvias de agosto hacen salir de madre al río padre y las inundaciones arrasan las poblaciones ribereñas. No veo el mar de aguas revueltas y barrosas que suelen arrastrar en lentos remolinos ranchos, islas de camalotes, millares de vacunos muertos enormemente hinchados.

En el buen tiempo se suele descubrir, desde el avión que va descendiendo, la curva sensual de la bahía, vientre de agua de la ciudad, coronado por el ombligo inflamado de la casa de gobierno. Diríase un carbunclo a punto de reventar. Con sus torrecillas almenadas y su aire de falso mudéjar, la antigua casa de la dinastía de los López se asemeja al palacio de un sultán miliunanochesco. Antiguamente, el palacio hacía honor a su origen. Ahora está repintado de rojo. Durante el día emite un color ceniza azulado. Por las noches, el rojo sobrenada en lo oscuro y fosforece, frotado de tiza por la luna invisible. A la luz de los reflectores, el palacio centellea como bañado de mica sanguinosa. Se lo ve cortado horizontalmente en dos mitades, desde la base hasta el cimborio y los arbotantes de la cúpula. Las escalinatas de mármol y los minaretes flotan en el aire. La impresión se agrava cuando el movimiento rotatorio de los reflectores hace oscilar la mole entera. Semeja entonces un inmenso galeón anclado en la bahía. Pero no por eso merece el mote peyorativo que le ha dado la inquina maledicente de los opositores. Lo de *casa rosada* o *casa de empeño*, como llaman al antiguo palacio de los López, está relacionado con esa historia del tesoro enterrado de la presidenta del Paraguay, que nos contaron la última vez que estuvimos en Asunción. Acaso el mote satírico se relaciona también con la subasta del país en la que está "empeñado" el tiranosaurio. A éste lo han popularizado con el apodo del Gran Tembelo por su inmenso belfo colgante que se confunde con la papada.

Cuando el avión ha comenzado a descender he pegado la frente a la ventanilla. Trato en vano de otear las altas palmeras, enanas aún por la altura, las viejas quintas, los caseríos de extramuros. En uno de ellos, en medio de la franja boscosa de Villa Morra, se hallaban las casas del clan familiar. En aquella zona de quintas y chacras de principios de siglo se yerguen ahora las fastuosas mansiones de la nueva oligarquía. Hay algunas residencias calcadas sobre el modelo del palacio de gobierno y hasta sobre los castillos del Loira. Los nuevos ricos, jerarcas y funcionarios del poder, remontados por la tromba del contrabando, de los grandes negociados, han reemplazado a los antiguos terratenientes de las doce tribus del patriciado. Y la cosa sólo ha cambiado para empeorar.

Recuerdo nuestro primer viaje, también furtivo como éste, en que veníamos a buscar, tú, una patria; yo, a recuperar la mía. Cuando viste desde lo alto las suaves lomadas de Asunción observaste con ingenuo entusiasmo que esas lomas eran siete y que se parecían a las siete colinas de Roma. Ahora ya no están, o por lo menos no logro divisarlas. Han sido borradas por la aplanadora de sombras que llena el espacio, las que sin embargo ofuscan los ojos con su oscura luminosidad.

Tras la expulsión, el mismo día en que llegamos, ya no tuvimos ocasión ni ganas de mirar ni admirar las colinas de Asunción. Era un día hermoso, de esplendor matinal y mucho cielo; uno de esos días capaces de hechizar a las aves migratorias y de hacerlas retroceder en pleno vuelo. No existía aún esta capa de luz sombría que no cambia de color. Aquella mañana no volví la cara hacia la ciudad esfumada en los vapores luminosos del amanecer. Mucho tiempo ha pasado, pero esa escena continúa viva en mí, llena de felicidad y de desdicha compartidas por los dos. En aquel entonces la luz era natural. Ahora, desde la mirilla, se me antoja que estamos volando en el interior de una gran burbuja opalescente.

Este fragmento inicial debí escribírtelo al final. Quise empezar preguntándote cómo estás, cómo sigue el proceso de recuperación de tu salud tras la malhadada fractura de tu pierna. Siempre me han parecido un poco hipócritas las condolencias y las palabras convencionales de interés por la salud del otro. Tales adhesiones son indecibles. Pero, además, algo semejante a una angustia innominada ante lo que para mí es claro y oscuro a la vez, fue demorando mi deseo de tocar este tema... y otros.

Una razón diferente es la que me impulsa a escribirte estas palabras ininterrumpidas que no cesan de fluir hasta cuando dejo de escribir. Comencé a hacerlo desde mucho antes del despegue, durante las siete horas que me vi obligado a esperar en el aeropuerto de Barajas el avión procedente de Francfort, para no hacerlo desde París, donde se hallaba concentrada la mayor parte de los invitados. Creímos que esto era lo mejor. Clovis aprobó esta medida de cautela.

Apenas el inmenso y supermoderno Boeing, especialmente acondicionado para este viaje, se estabilizó en el cielo de Madrid, proseguí borroneando cuartillas para enviarte este mensaje acaso incoherente y un poco convulso. Es quizás el último que pueda enviarte con alguna seguridad. Te lo alcanzará Clovis, que regresará tras la inauguración del congreso. Es un mensajero adecuado, hasta cierto límite. Nunca se sabe hasta dónde puede uno confiar en estos mercurios un poco mitómanos. Yo confío plenamente en él. Quedó también establecido entre tú y yo que, en caso de no tener un portador de absoluta seguridad, utilizaremos los relativamente inseguros servicios de la valija diplomática. Pero esto solamente en situación de extrema necesidad, pues es seguro que en cualquier caso nuestra correspondencia será revisada, censurada y aprovechada en los informes confidenciales entre los gobiernos.

La necesidad de comunicarme contigo en nuestro lenguaje íntimo me toca ahora, en lo vivo, en lo urgente. Debo revelarte, en lo posible, *todo*. Todo lo que hasta ahora no te he dicho, aunque lo supieras ya en lo hondo de ti. Si callo algo no me reconocerás en lo que te escribo. La erosión del viaje habrá comenzado a actuar sobre mí hasta mi completa desaparición. Después sólo quedará la soñadora memoria del olvido. Hasta que eso suceda, si no soy franco hasta la última gota de mi verdad, subsistirá el riesgo de que todo lo que aquí cuento esté desmentido por lo que no cuento.

Debo agradecerte una vez más (y si tuviera fe debería bendecirte) todo el amor que has sufrido por mí. Tú me has dado la perfecta transparencia de tu comprensión en la que yo pude ver reflejada toda mi oscuridad. Tu sabiduría, tus sentimientos de mujer hicieron que el mismo peligro del amor fuera la razón esencial de nuestro amor y convertiste la pasión carnal en la religión de dos cuerpos que ardían en un mismo fuego sin temor a los goces prohibidos, salvo el de caer en la cenicienta monotonía del tedio. Cómo podré olvidar esa tarde en la que después de haber traspasado los límites de lo permitido caíste en un sueño profundo de varios días. Yo velaba ese sueño que te protegía y transfiguraba en la inocencia profunda de tu cuerpo dormido. Al despertarte te miré abarcándote entera y te pregunté: ¿Te ves reflejada en mis pupilas? Me veo reflejada en la manera en que me miras, respondiste.

La vida no es larga, los seres humanos no son fuertes. Tú me enseñaste a vivir a la manera de la gente sencilla, de la gente de la primera edad del mundo que estaba saliendo de las cavernas y que se ponía de rodillas ante el sol naciente. Me enseñaste a no pensar en el mañana sino como el hoy prolongándose a sí mismo. Me enseñaste a no temer al poder de la última hora y a gozar la felicidad del último minuto.

Es traicionera esta dimensión en la que voy entrando insensiblemente y alejándome de ti. Nada tiene que ver con las horas que pasan, ni con las latitudes que van cegando sus horizontes sucesivos aunque invisibles, a medida que el avión devora distancias. Viajo en lo desconocido hacia lo desconocido sin más certidumbre que la de un acto que debo cumplir a toda costa sin saber cómo ni cuándo ni dónde.

Incómoda sensación ésta de hallarse amarrado por el cinturón de seguridad a una butaca (que se parece a la de un teatro), y saber que uno viaja a fantástica velocidad sin que se note. No se puede abandonar la función en el momento en que a uno le plazca sino en el momento en que ella se cumple y termina con uno.

Hemos convenido un código determinado para el intercambio de nuestros mensajes cifrados. Recuerda: tu *nom de guerre* es Morena. Jimena ya no está. Partió a guerrear contra los moros. Te volveré a llamar Morena, como en nuestra Ventana del Poniente. Este nombre sonaba a conjuro amoroso en la dichosa intimidad. Ahora suena al adiós de Andrómaca en la tristísima despedida, ahora que estás desposada conmigo no por las nupcias sino por la separación. Quedó algo en suspenso entre nosotros. Es lo que voy a intentar decirte en estas cuartillas. Forman parte y son la continuación de los papeles póstumos de un hombre que todavía vive y que te seguirá amando hasta el último suspiro.

Sabes a qué voy al Paraguay. Hemos discutido el proyecto de la *misión* que me he impuesto. Pensé que tú y yo no debíamos discutir mi decisión de venir para cumplirla. No hubiéramos podido hacerlo con la franqueza que siempre hemos puesto en nuestras confidencias. Los dos sentíamos tal vez que lo que más queríamos aclarar y poner al desnudo era precisamente lo que con más astucia y ambigüedad se nos escabullía. Sabíamos intuitivamente que el sentido de esas confidencias se hallaba (y se halla) fuera de nosotros. Toda historia busca su centro, pero nuestras escalas de vida y de experiencia están descentradas. No se trata de un malentendido esencial; se trata más vale, a mi juicio, de razones de vida que se complementan y se sostienen aun a distancia; que se iluminan mutuamente por lo mismo que son diferentes.

Pienso que cada uno entiende las razones o sinrazones de los hechos de la misma manera, sí, pero desde ángulos distintos y, en algunos casos, opuestos. Cada uno dijo sí y no, en los momentos en que debió decir lo contrario. Decidimos entonces dejar librado el problema a las soluciones que los mismos hechos fraguan instruyéndonos sobre lo que debemos hacer. De haber sido idénticos estos ángulos, la visión de los hechos los hubiera superpuesto, confundido y anulado. Géminis vela sobre nuestras naturalezas binarias desde casas diferentes del cosmos. Trece días nos separan y a la vez nos unen sin que seamos mellizos ni gemelos. Esta divergencia de nuestras mentes en la afinidad de nuestros sentimientos es precisamente lo que más nos une en un amor de imposible fin, mientras uno de los dos aliente sobre esta tierra. Este planeta, maravilloso y miserable a la vez, sólo tendrá algún sentido mientras existan en él seres como tú.

Sí, Morena. Ya lo sabías. Voy al Paraguay a matar al tirano. Que sirva esta declaración de puño y letra como testimonio de parte, si no puedo hacerla yo personalmente a los fiscales de la tiranía. He traído el arma secreta de la que te hablaba. Viene conmigo el diminuto cosmos orbicular que calza en un dedo; el anillo en forma de áspid, del conde de Villamediana. Te lo he sustraído. No lo lamentarás demasiado. No formaba parte ya ni siquiera de tus recuerdos y menos aún como reliquia de la estirpe que negabas como tuya. Perdóname este robo material menos grave que los robos afectivos que te he infligido sin querer, y que aun así son imperdonables e irreparables.

Será casi un juicio de Dios —si es que Él existe verdaderamente— el que este anillo de un aristócrata disoluto y poeta cumpla un hecho de bien público, la salvación de un país. Y que lo haga después de cuatro siglos de haber sido tallado por un orfebre profeta, casi al mismo tiempo en que se fundaba este país en el continente recién descubierto.

Por el momento el anillo está descargado de su magia letal. Lo traigo escondido en el doble forro de mi chaqueta en su funda hermética. Está cosido al forro de mi destino. La cápsula metálica con la pócima viene en el maletín, disfrazada de frasco vaporizador para la calvicie. Servirá por ahora para refrescarme de tanto en tanto la barba y la memoria con el suavísimo perfume vengador. Podría decirte ahora que el anillo en forma de áspid y su carga de ponzoña soy yo mismo. La identificación es total y no admite fisuras si quiere ser eficaz. Sólo hay un camino para saber en realidad lo que uno es, lo que uno debe saber, y ese camino es —ya te lo dije— arriesgarlo todo en un acto. El ejecutor de una empresa atroz —sentenciaba Salustio— debe imaginar que ya la ha cumplido. Cuando se descubre un pensamiento de esta naturaleza, se acaban los temores, las fatigas, se disuelve hasta el presentimiento del fracaso. Voy mortalmente enfermo de felicidad.

Hay una verdad irrefutable: no existe en el mundo una cosa inferior a otra. Sólo el poder es inferior a la flaqueza. Voy a destruir con la mía el siniestro poder que oprime a mi patria. Tengo que hacerlo ahora ya que no podré alcanzar la edad de las águilas. Sentimientos como los míos, ciertamente, tienen su locura, pero es esta locura la que engendra felicidad. Siento en lo hondo de mi espíritu esa increíble felicidad de los criminales en potencia, sólo comparable y tal vez superior a la felicidad idiota de los tiranos en acto, que disponen con total impunidad de la vida de un pueblo.

Hay también el placer de la impostura. Hay una embriagadora felicidad en la idea de que se miente y se embauca para su bien a toda una sociedad habituada a ser engañada y subyugada para su mal. En el fondo del alma colectiva existe larvada la necesidad de este engaño. Disfruta y se consuela con las infamias más execrables que se cometen contra ella. Lo que también justifica su miedo que es la única forma de conciencia pública que existe en un país aplastado por la tiranía, degradado por la miseria, por siglos de sufrimiento. Tú lo expresaste muy bien en el único diálogo de carácter "político" que tuvimos aquella tarde en que nos enzarzamos en la discusión sobre la "justicia justa".

La situación inhumana en que vive la colectividad justifica su miedo, su aceptación pasiva del yugo, pues ese tirano es el producto de su consentimiento, de su dimisión, de su aceptación casi gozosa del sufrimiento y la abyección. Yo digo "voy a matar al tirano para liberar a mi pueblo". Pero es una frase vacía, desprovista de historia, de sentido común. Porque ¿quién puede liberar a un pueblo que no quiere ser libre, que ama ser esclavizado? Únicamente se liberan los libres.

De todos modos voy a hacerlo. Soy el juez, el criminal y el verdugo. La trinidad absoluta. No se me mueve un pelo por asumirla entera. Comprenderás que no te estoy hablando de vagas teologías sino del simple sentido común, ese sentido común que es la esencia de los delirios. El sentido común nos da a entender que lo bueno es útil aun cuando parezca malo. ¿Cómo podría contarse una historia si no hubiera un antihéroe virtuoso? Trataré de serlo lo más que pueda.

Admito —te lo he dicho varias veces— que lo que me empuja a este ridículo "miserocidio" (algún nombre debo dar a la ejecución de un miserable) sea una de esas estúpidas obcecaciones que hacen desvariar la mente humana contra la evidencia misma del sentido común y del destino. Pero estas obcecaciones forman parte del sentido común más sólido y pedestre. Son su rostro oculto. La luna lleva el suyo, invisible, a su espalda; pero sin esa cara oculta no podría mover los mares ni enloquecer a los hombres, que por eso se llaman lunáticos.

Nada destruye tanto la lucidez como la obsesión de la desdicha, me has dicho con la mayor razón del mundo, sabiéndome desdichado y lleno de remordimiento. Buscabas liberarme de estas lacras que son las peores que puede sufrir un ser humano. Me has dicho: sé tú mismo, vive y sufre hasta que llegue el don que te dejará desnudo de impurezas. No he podido hacerlo y ahora me llega la hora del anhelo que sólo se calma en la final expiración. Me apoyo en tu madura capacidad de inteligencia, de fidelidad, de sufrimiento, de generosidad. Lo malo de estas cartas en pleno viaje es que predisponen a la efusión sentimentaloide y la verbosidad es la negación más flagrante del sentimiento amoroso que es indecible. Léeme con la sobriedad que soy incapaz de tener en lo que escribo.

No me retires, Morena, tu confianza. Asísteme con tu presencia que me rodeó siempre como una muralla inexpugnable. Ella me ayudará cuando no pueda ya apartar de mí el cáliz lleno de hiel. Sólo me absuelve, en cierta medida, el saber casi con certeza que hiciste el supremo esfuerzo para otorgarme el don de comprender y aceptar finalmente mi decisión. El accidente que sufriste no fue un accidente casual. Fue un recurso acaso premeditado inconscientemente para dejarme partir solo a fin de no entorpecer mis designios. Cómo no agradecerte ese gesto que lleva tu sello en favor de mi pueblo, al que tú amas dos veces más que yo mismo.

En cuanto a las otras confidencias o *revelaciones* que también quedaron en suspenso, ya están dichas y escritas. Las encontrarás —ya las habrás leído— en la carpeta de apuntes. Te la dejé furtivamente sobre la copia facsimilar del *Códice Florentino*, que tienes sobre tu escritorio. Que Fray Bernardino de Sahagún, el héroe más puro de la Conquista Espiritual, me salga de fiador. Las omisiones o supresiones, que anuncio en una de sus páginas, no fueron hechas. Lo que escribí allí para ti, escrito está, y lo dejé en tus manos en su integralidad. Las confesiones últimas no admiten veladuras. Son las confidencias que no me atreví a hacerte de viva voz, por pudor, por cobardía, por la torcida inclinación de mi naturaleza. Nuevamente te pido perdón. No incurriré en más deslealtades. Concentrado en una idea de hierro, me está vedado el más inocente de los placeres permitidos. Debo negar mi propia animalidad de hombre; debo seguir siendo la mitad de un hombre a punto de convertirse en un ser humano pleno y definitivo.

Oiré siempre tus palabras: "He sido muy feliz... muy afortunada... tengo mucho de qué enorgullecerme. Demasiado afortunada. Demasiado feliz durante un breve tiempo. Y ahora soy desdichada por... por toda la vida..." Veo erguida tu apesadumbrada cabeza contra la luz del ocaso como si sintieras orgullo de tu pena, como si me dijeras todavía: "Yo... sólo yo sé cómo voy a llorar tu ausencia... Pero, lejos o cerca, estaré contigo hasta el final..." En tu rostro había un aire tan desolado que tuve la sensación de que ya habías llorado todo lo que podías llorar por una angustia como la tuya, por un hombre como yo que no merece tu llanto. Veía brillar tus ojos llenos de lágrimas, de esas lágrimas que no caerían, de esas lágrimas que se iban a secar detrás de tus ojos...

A medida que se aproxima el momento en que debemos tocar tierra en la ciudad desaparecida o invisible, mi rechazo a llegar aumenta casi hasta las náuseas. Debe de haberme producido una repentina sordera. He dejado de oír la batahola de los demás pasajeros, el zumbar de los motores, la voz del comandante que está dando alguna información por los altavoces.

Un paisaje mineral huye hacia atrás. Un paisaje desierto, desolado, barrido vertiginosamente por la luz pesada, manchada de oscuridad que evoca los resplandores del fósforo disuelto en aceite de negras resinas. Una ciudad asentada sobre un monte no puede desaparecer..., pienso, transhumando inconscientemente algún pasaje de las Escrituras. ¡Asunción no está aquí!..., me oigo murmurar. Tras un violento bandazo en una turbulencia repentina, el avión está haciendo un giro completo de 180 grados.

Siento que he vivido, trabajado y soñado toda mi vida para este minuto de última hora. Y es así como uno trata de querer de golpe todo lo que no ha querido cuando ya todo le está negado. Siento que el arco del viejo trauma tensa su cuerda, que debe de estar tejida con las fibras de todos mis nervios... y que dispara mi ser hacia atrás, hacia atrás...

Tan intenso es su impulso, que experimento la sensación de que esa energía inconcebible se transmite a la nave y la arrastra en su movimiento de retroceso. Comprendo que no se trata más que de alguna perturbación de mis sentidos; o quizás, más simplemente, de un mareo de origen gástrico. Desde el momento mismo de partir la comida ha venido siendo opípara. Ya he ingerido mi puntual pastilla de alkaseltzer. Los viajes en avión nunca me han caído bien. Les debo más de un trance penoso, y este vuelo parece interminable. Los efectos de la indisposición continúan, cada vez con más fuerza.

Desde la mirilla observo que en el mecanismo de los reactores se ha producido un cambio. Los gases en llamas despiden un resplandor de un rojo muy intenso y compacto, semejante al fuego de los semáforos. Se me ocurre que las turbinas se han detenido por algunos segundos, produciendo el efecto de un frenazo, y que han vuelto a ponerse en movimiento, esta vez en sentido inverso, como lo hacen para frenar el aterrizaje. No es el aterrizaje todavía. El vuelo continúa. Sólo que ahora la estela de fuego se proyecta hacia adelante. El paisaje mineral huye hacia adelante. El avión está retrocediendo como los pájaros que vuelan al revés según la leyenda indígena. Creo que he soltado un suspiro de alivio. Prefiero volver a llegar. O lo que es más probable, no llegar jamás.

En el barrio agreste de mi infancia pájaros veía mi aguda vista pasar en sus peregrinaciones migratorias al anuncio del invierno. Me tiraba sobre la hierba y los contemplaba con los ojos volcados hacia atrás. Garzas, golondrinas, aves de la selva y del desierto. Entonces me parecía verlas volar al revés. Me entraban ganas de irme tras ellas. Las seguía con la vista. Casi podía tocarlas con las manos. Veía los ojillos entrecerrados, fijos en su rumbo sin huellas, las plumas frotadas por el viento despedían pequeñísimas chispas eléctricas. Sin la brújula biológica que guía a esas criaturas en su vuelo, yo sólo he conseguido avanzar a contrapelo de los hechos, a contracorriente de la vida fuera de sus órbitas naturales. Ahora sé que la "libertad íntima y última" no existe sino como el sueño del prisionero, del torturado que quiere morir y no puede... Sólo el paralítico de nacimiento puede concebir la perfección de la danza; sólo el deforme congénito, el excluido sin remedio, puede concebir la belleza absoluta.

La nave ha cesado de retroceder. Aterrizamos en el aeropuerto de Río de Janeiro, la penúltima escala del viaje. Allí ha embarcado otra cincuentena de invitados al congreso, procedentes de los países iberoamericanos y del Caribe (excepto Cuba, naturalmente), de Guayanas, Haití, República Dominicana, Puerto Rico, Estados Unidos y Canadá. Somos ahora más de un centenar de invitados: mujeres y hombres de ciencia, escritores, catedráticos de las más importantes universidades, hombres de negocio, industriales, inversores. También, por supuesto, los grandes tiburones de las finanzas internacionales. Los delegados japoneses, otro centenar, arribarán a Asunción en vuelo directo desde su país.

La tripulación ha descendido a tomar relevo. Antes de dejar la nave, el comandante se ha despedido amablemente en cuatro lenguas por los altavoces, deseándonos un feliz término del viaje. Es animada la visión de las dos tripulaciones que se cruzan en las pasarelas. Un cambio de guardia de honor ante la nave que nos conduce. La fatiga y monotonía del viaje se han interrumpido en el espectáculo de una belleza y un esplendor inauditos. ¡Ah, el placer del observador! El Boeing pintado de púrpura debe de tener el aspecto de una nave imperial, anclada en un mar más azul que el de Capri, con la silueta africana del Corcovado en el fondo y las playas rutilantes del Guanabara.

Oficiales en blanco uniforme de gala de la aeronáutica con galones y cordones dorados cambian saludos militares. Los siguen esbeltas walkirias en ceñidos trajes de amazona y birretes color fucsia coronando las blondas y largas cabelleras. Las walkirias paraguayas se hacen notar, entre sus colegas alemanas, en que son rubias de cabellera negra. En lugar de la piel dorada de las alemanas, tienen la tez mate y satinada como las hindúes y las guayabas del verano. Se saludan sonrientes tirándose besos al pasar. Pienso en las mensajeras de Odín, cuya misión era escanciar el hidromel a los guerreros que partían al combate y luego en homenaje a los héroes muertos en él.

La demora se alarga sin embargo más de la cuenta. Clovis comenta irónicamente que se está esperando tal vez a los representantes de los pueblos esquimales y a los indios pieles rojas de Estados Unidos y Canadá. No aparecen los habitantes indígenas de las praderas ni de las regiones polares. Ha entrado en cambio, en nuestra cabina, un extraño personaje, enfundado en una vieja y larga chaqueta de *clergyman*, ceñida por un ancho cinturón de cuero negro. La lustrina muy deslucida está llena de lamparones y zurcidos. Lo he tomado por un pastor protestante, o de cualquier otra congregación similar. Lleva un sombrero de fieltro de alas anchas y rígidas que le hacen sombra al rostro muy pálido, del que sobresalen sus mandíbulas y pómulos puntudos. La larga cabellera que le cae por detrás, quemada por el sol, debe ser completamente blanca. Sobre el cuello de plástico muy ajado aparece la nuez igualmente prominente y huesuda. Pendiente de un collar de metal ordinario, una cruz pectoral de exagerado tamaño le cae sobre el pecho. Porta un maletín oscuro que lleva delante de sí con mucho cuidado como para evitar cualquier choque. Busca el número correspondiente a su plaza y toma asiento en la fila de butacas fronteras a la que yo ocupo.

No se trata evidentemente de un invitado al congreso. Es de esas personas con las que no querría uno encontrarse en ninguna parte. Y menos en esta hermética campana volante. De la presencia de este viajero es imposible desentenderse. Posee un aura y un magnetismo muy especiales. Deposita el maletín sobre el filoso canto de las rodillas. Cruza sus manos sobre él como sobre un objeto de culto, o como sobre algo extremadamente sensible y delicado. Me choca que nuestros maletines sean casi idénticos. Este sentimiento indefinible se agrava cuando me doy cuenta de que somos bastante parecidos, aun cuando su cabellera y su barba de un blanco ceniciento parecen darle más edad. Es muy flaco, casi transparente. Da la impresión de una figura de cera en medio de sus gárrulos vecinos.

Alguien con un movimiento involuntario le ha volcado el sombrero sobre la cara. La coronilla calva ha dejado ver los costurones de viejas cicatrices. El hombre no se ha inmutado en lo más mínimo. Sin prisa, sin fastidio, con la punta del índice ha devuelto el sombrero a su posición natural. Su expresión no es ni altanera, ni desdeñosa, ni despreciativa, sino sencillamente impasible; esa impasibilidad de alguien a quien no le interesa ni le toca nada de lo que ocurre a su alrededor porque se siente ya fuera del mundo. Abre el maletín, saca de su interior lo que debe de ser un sobado Breviario o un Libro de Horas y se enfrasca en una profunda meditación. Su inmovilidad es tan absoluta que da la sensación de una silueta esfumada, como si el hombre mismo hubiese desaparecido en su sombra.

Me ha sorprendido que ese eclesiástico de raída vestimenta pueda viajar en vuelo tan exclusivo. Inexplicablemente, el hombre de iglesia está allí por completo fuera de lugar aunque no como un intruso ni como un polizón. Nadie le ha detenido el paso ni le ha preguntado nada. Simplemente es una pieza que no encaja en el rompecabezas. Fue en ese momento cuando se me ocurrió que el religioso podía pertenecer a la congregación de los mennonitas establecida en los lejanos confines del Chaco boreal desde comienzos de siglo. Han formado en varias zonas falansterios militarizados. Recordé que las colonias mennonitas en el Paraguay son muy ricas y cuentan en cierto modo con la protección oficial. Se me hizo evidente que ese hombre, que esa sombra casi inexistente, es un hijo de la secta de Menno Simon. Un hombre del sol, de la lluvia, del polvo del Poniente, en cuyo pecho arde el fuego pálido y fanático de aquellos cuáqueros del desierto, venidos de Europa en busca de la Tierra Prometida, en nada semejantes a franciscanos y jesuitas.

Durante todo el trayecto no ha probado alimentos ni bebidas que las azafatas sirven a granel. No pronuncia palabra. Cuando le ofrecen algo levanta levemente la mano y agradece con una ligera inclinación de cabeza sin mirar a quien le habla, para recaer en seguida en la actitud de mutismo, aislamiento y meditación en la que viene sumido. Esperé que por lo menos bebiera agua. Tampoco lo hizo. Ese hombre sólo bebe el agua de su estremecimiento y de su anhelo, según dicen las Escrituras. Igual que yo, aunque me permita lo normal y aun algunos excesos para no despertar sospechas.

El pastor mennonita debe de estar muy enfermo, conjeturé. Su agonía impasible sólo se reflejaba en la palidez enfermiza que la canosa barba y el sombrero oscuro volvían aún más lívida. Se me ha antojado que ese hombre lleva sobre el semblante, que exiguamente se dejaba ver, la palidez no de un muerto sino de la misma muerte.

También viaja la ruidosa tribu local. Vuelve de sus dorados viajes de turismo por diversos países del mundo. Ricachones autóctonos, jerarcas y altos funcionarios del régimen leen los periódicos o conversan entre ellos disparando sus voces como tiros. Sus mujeres muy enjoyadas, perfumadas y maquilladas, lucen modelos de revistas de moda, que las vuelven un poco grotescas como criadas en vacaciones que estuvieran disfrazadas de patronas. Hablan como cotorras, todas al mismo tiempo, en el infecto dialecto del *yopará*, esa mezcla obscena de un español que ha dejado de ser español y de un guaraní que insulta al guaraní, acoplados contra natura.

Los espacios que les corresponden están abarrotados por enormes bultos de los que sobresalen brazos de pantallas de cristal de murano, de estatuillas de jade, pies de muebles antiguos, veladores de cerámica, cajones-jaulas con perros y gatos de las razas más finas. Una de las damas, que ocupa militarmente la fila adyacente de asientos cercana a la mía, relata a sus vecinas las nuevas adquisiciones que ha hecho para la mansión que está mandando construir. Coge un álbum de joyas arquitectónicas, encuadernado en vitela. Exhibe diversas reproducciones de los castillos de Francia y de Italia.

—Vean... miren... —se pasa los dedos por la lengua y vuelve las páginas del álbum—. Mi mansión será como ésta. ¡De lo más caté! Ésta... miren ... —señala con la larguísima uña barnizada de cinabrio la fastuosa ilustración—. Julián ha contratado a un arquitecto francés, un famoso especialista en estas cuestiones de castillos y palacetes del Renacimiento. Llegará a Asunción el mes que viene para comenzar los trabajos. Nuestros arquitectos ningó, los pobres, son apenas maestros de obra. Son demasiado chuí todavía. Para qué pa luego vamos a decir otra cosa de ellos.

Extrae de uno de sus grandes bolsos un abultado paquete y empieza a desenvolverlo. Ante los asombrados ojos de las demás van apareciendo varios pares de objetos finamente cincelados que tintinean y relucen con dorado resplandor.

—¿Qué es eso, Felisa? —preguntó una de las más curiosas y movedizas de las contertulias.

—Los pestillos para las salas de baño y aseo de nuestra mansión de Villa Aurelia —contestó la interpelada con la falsa modestia del orgullo—. Son de oro puro.

—Ah picaportes, querrás decir... ¡Qué preciosidad!

—Los mandé labrar por mi joyero de París. Nosotros recibimos muchas visitas importantes luego. Potentados alemanes, franceses, italianos. La otra vez estuvieron un jeque de Arabia Saudita y otro del Kuwait. Ellos están acostumbrados a estas cosas. Para más, vivimos en el barrio presidencial. Traigo otras zonceritas. Ya verán, ya verán. El grueso de la carga viene por barco, ¡para qué les voy a contar!

Las comadres no acababan de acariciar esas cinceladas formas, vagamente fálicas. Pasaban de mano en mano, alumbrando las caras admirativas, envidiosas, falaces, sonrientes. Una verdadera reunión del gran mundo a bordo. Las azafatas participaban y disfrutaban de igual a igual de este aurífico momento. Escuchaban, asentían, sonreían, con la encantadora superioridad de los inferiores que saben ocupar su lugar con inocultable soberanía.

En ese momento han sonado los chirriantes timbres de alarma y se han encendido las rojas luces de alerta sobre la viñeta de una bomba con la mecha encendida. La voz del comandante ordena perentoriamente que todos vuelvan a sus asientos y se ajusten los cinturones de seguridad. Caen ante las caras de los pasajeros las máscaras de oxígeno. Las aeromozas se precipitan a auxiliar a los más torpes que no atinan a imaginar qué está pasando y menos aún qué es lo que deben hacer con esos artilugios que oscilan delante de sus rostros despavoridos propinándoles leves papirotazos en sus narices. En el silencio que hiede a catástrofe sólo zumban sordamente los controles electrónicos como moscardones enfurecidos. Con toda evidencia, buscan detectar y localizar algún misterioso desperfecto o artefacto. Noto que el pastor mennonita no está en su asiento. La máscara oscila ante el asiento vacío.

Cierro los ojos, dispuesto a lo peor. Como en una evocación subliminal me llegan las voces de los actores en la escena de la despedida de Héctor y Andrómaca, en la pieza de Eurípides, que vimos en París, un poco antes de tu accidente. "¡Adiós, amor, un largo adiós!...", entreoigo musitar a Andrómaca sobre el cadáver de Héctor. Y la voz de la comedianta, bastante mediocre, tiene sin embargo la fuerza de un genuino dolor trágico. Acaso más profundo que el que debió sentir la verdadera Andrómaca, hace más dos mil años, de rodillas ante el cuerpo inanimado de su esposo, muerto en el combate al que ella quiso sustraerlo. Como si fuera posible traicionar o esquivar el destino.

La espeluznante expectativa no duró mucho. La señal roja de alerta fue reemplazada por la verde de "pasado el peligro". La voz del comandante, esta vez forzadamente amable y melosa, pidió disculpas y tranquilizó al pasaje explicando que sólo se había tratado de una falsa alarma. Un aplauso multitudinario de varios minutos estalló en las dos cabinas. Varios ¡vivas! exaltados saludaron al comandante y a todos los miembros de la tripulación. El comandante agradeció el homenaje y anunció que seguidamente se servirían los aperitivos y el almuerzo. El ritmo vivo y sincopado de una galopa popular enardeció el entusiasmo de la tribu elegante que continuó con sus gritos y con su palmoteo cada vez más enérgico acompañando el compás de la música. El champán burbujeante, servido por las azafatas como en los movimientos de un volandero pero disciplinado ballet, volvió a espumar en los brindis y en los vivas al Reconstructor. La efigie con el enorme belfo caballuno, bastante retocado en las litografías, se repetía a lo largo de las dos cabinas en marcos y paneles dorados como en una multiplicación de espejos. El rostro mofletudo parecía cobrar relieve estereoscópico celebrado por la aguda algarabía de las mujeres y los ladridos de los perrillos en sus jaulas. Los invitados observaban estupefactos el jaleo indescriptible.

—¡Esto es la civilización de la barbarie! —comentó mi vecino, el profesor belga Jan Kleenewerk, catedrático en Lovaina de culturas y civilizaciones amerindias.

Eugène Ionesco se puso de pie y con muchos visajes y voz tartamudeante pronunció un discurso que nadie entendió pero que todos aplaudieron a rabiar. Su obra *El rey se muere* va a ser puesta en escena en el Teatro Municipal como uno de los números del programa de festejos con motivo del congreso.

Vi avanzar por el pasillo al hombre de negro, siempre con el maletín por delante. Volvió a ocupar su asiento. No le había visto levantarse. Probablemente, en medio de la baraúnda del toque de alarma, habría ido a encerrarse en uno de los gabinetes de aseo. Llevaba ahora unos anteojos oscuros que le volvían más pálido el semblante verdoso y exangüe. Portaba el maletín con movimientos menos meticulosos. El pastor, me dije, ha tenido un cólico de bilis y ha liberado el maletín de alguna carga peligrosa en los gabinetes de aseo.

En ese instante algo desvió y obnubiló mi atención. En alguna parte de la cabina fulguró una chispa azul y percibí en medio del bullicio el siseo como de un suspiro ahogado. Giré los ojos y vi la silueta de una persona que se me antojó conocida. De pie conversaba con un pasajero, inclinada hacia él. No pude reprimir un sobresalto. ¡Allí, a veinte metros, se hallaba Leda Kautner en persona dándome la espalda! ¡Algo increíble y diabólico! ¿No has de dejar en paz mi alma en este mundo?..., murmuré mordiendo mis palabras en un súbito arrebato de indignación y de cólera.

Me negué a seguir mirando. Pero no pude retirar la mirada. Negarse a contemplar una visión que creemos sobrenatural no hace más que aumentar el embrujo de su atracción irresistible. No estaba seguro de que fuese *ella*. En el relevo de Río no la había visto subir al avión. Alguien podía estar disfrazada con sus apariencias. Acaso era una nueva alucinación. La veía de perfil, pero el perfil es la media máscara de una cara y esconde su belleza o su fealdad. No distinguía su rostro pero esa espalda desnuda, combada en la inclinación, la perfección de esa cintura, tenían también una fisonomía. Y esa fisonomía inconfundible era la de Leda. La percibía de nuevo como una silueta de humo a la luz de la luna. Adivinaba en esas grupas finas y mórbidas a la fiera espectral de la temible muchacha. Veía de nuevo en ella al animal mujer en todas las variedades de su especie y de sus razas, en su depravada inocencia, en su perversidad natural, uno de cuyos rasgos era esa inconcebible y casi milagrosa ubicuidad que le hacía estar en todas partes, sobre todo en las menos oportunas.

El temblor que me poseía dejó entrar la noche entre mis costillas... me penetró de nuevo aquella escena de fascinación y de horror. Cuando logré serenarme avancé por el pasillo hacia esa aparición para enfrentarla y negarla. Me detuve muy cerca viendo brillar el pelo como oro hilado de la larga y lacia cabellera. Estaba a un paso. Podía tocarla con las manos. En eso la silueta volvió el rostro hacia mí. Nada tenía de parecido al de Leda. La belleza es múltiple y ninguna se parece a otra. Sólo la fealdad es única y por eso es atroz. La gallarda y airosa figura de una de las azafatas con su uniforme y birrete de color fucsia estaba erguida ante mí en actitud expectante y gentil, con un rostro como dibujado por el genio de Durero. Me preguntó en alemán si necesitaba algo. Su amable sonrisa se me antojó burlona. Denegué con un gesto y volví derrotado a mi asiento. En una risa nerviosa descargué la tensión que me había sobrecogido ante aquel espejismo.

Mi vecino, el profesor Kleenewerk me tocó el brazo.

—¿Qué le sucede? —me preguntó sinceramente interesado.

—Nada... —dije—. Esta luz... esta falta de luz... este ruido...

—¿Está usted preocupado tal vez por el incidente del falso alerta? —me interrogó transfiriéndome su propia preocupación.

—No, particularmente —respondí sin salir aún del todo de la obnubilación que acababa de sufrir.

—¿Qué está pasando con el vuelo? —preguntó el profesor Kleennewerk, inquieto, casi abrumado—. Le oí decir a usted, hace un rato, algo como que no estamos volando en dirección a Asunción.

Tardé un poco en entender. El semblante del profesor belga estaba rubicundo, casi apoplético; los ralos cabellos húmedos de sudor. Se lo veía verdaderamente preocupado, asustado.

—¿Sospecha usted un secuestro? —insistió parpadeando mucho.

Le respondí que no pensaba en un desvío ni en un secuestro por inoportunos piratas del aire.

—¿Cuáles son las razones de su seguridad? —inquirió asiéndose a mi brazo.

Le dije que evidentemente no existe hoy seguridad en ninguna parte. El hombre está expuesto cada vez más a errores terribles. Yo mismo acabo de... Me interrumpí, mordiéndome la lengua. Experimentaba la necesidad de hablar, de decir cualquier cosa con tal de evadirme

de la angustia. El profesor Kleenewerk me daba sin saberlo esa oportunidad.

No hay seguridad en ninguna parte, repetí. En todo
caso, en vuelos muy especiales como éste suelen extremar
las precauciones. Un sistema de control selecciona y limita
rigurosamente su clientela local y extranjera. Habrá notado
usted, le dije, que este avión no trae clase turística. En las
dos cabinas de lujo viajan exclusivamente pasajeros de primera clase. Además del pasaje habitual, venimos los invitados al Congreso, más de un centenar de representantes del
mundo científico, literario y artístico de Occidente.

—¡Por eso mismo el riesgo de represalia es mayor!
—farfulló colérico Kleenewerk.

Hasta donde es posible, han tomado las precauciones necesarias, dije con la fe del incrédulo. El tiranosaurio quiere salir de su caverna, adecentar las apariencias de
su régimen sanguinario, respirar los aires de los nuevos
tiempos. Sería fatal para él que acontezca el menor percan-
ce a este inmenso capital de inteligencia que ha atraído a
su feudo con el pretexto del congreso. Me extendí con cierta
minuciosidad sobre obvios elementos de seguridad, acaso
para descargar mi propia inquietud. Mi voz y mi actitud
eran lo suficientemente impasibles como para simular cierta
neutralidad. Lea usted aquello. Señalé los afiches.

Sobre la imagen de un avión de la Flota Aérea Paraguaya en el óvalo de la bandera nacional, una leyenda inscri-
ta en diagonal con grandes letras rojas y negras asegura: "El
terrorismo internacional no actúa aquí". Y la inscripción se
hallaba multiplicada y distribuida a lo largo de toda la cabina en páneles luminosos.

—No los había visto —dijo mi vecino—. ¡Es increíble!

—Se sabe —dije bajando la voz— que estos aparatos de uso oficial cuentan con dispositivos electrónicos
para la eyección de los asientos, provistos de paracaídas.

Se supone que hay, además, detectores de rayo láser para toda clase de explosivos y armas.

—¡Ah!... —murmuró sin mucha convicción el profesor Kleennewerk—. Uno nunca sabe lo que puede suceder en estos países atrasados y primitivos.

—El secreto de la eficacia y seguridad de estos aviones —continué—, como todo secreto, es público y notorio. Corre el rumor, la empresa misma se encarga de propalarlo, de que el gobierno de este país ha "negociado" la licencia de explotación comercial de estos dispositivos de seguridad con el de los Estados Unidos, o que ya la ha vendido por una suma astronómica a un gran consorcio multinacional de líneas aéreas.

Estaban sirviendo el almuerzo. Kleenewerk y yo volvimos a la realidad y, siguiendo la corriente general, atacamos nuestras respectivas bandejas colmadas de apetitosas viandas y vinos de los sellos más prestigiosos. La música del país seguía poniendo su fondo sincopado y cadencioso a ese almuerzo un poco legendario.

—Fíjese en las azafatas —hice notar a mi vecino—. En su mayoría son muchachas alemanas, de Baviera, la región de origen del dictador. Diga usted, ¿no parecen todas gemelas? Él mismo ha mandado seleccionarlas de acuerdo con una imagen y un modelo únicos. Me enteré en Munich de estos concursos de belleza muy particulares. Son sometidas a un riguroso curso de aprendizaje y luego contratadas con sueldos tan altos como los de las más cotizadas actrices del cine norteamericano. El propio dictador supervisa estos torneos de belleza que no desmerecen a los concursos europeos de las reinas de belleza.

—¡Parece increíble! —dijo Kleenewerk con indignada voz; los ojillos miopes parpadeando mucho tras los espesos cristales.

—No es eso todo —continué con voz neutra—. Murmuraciones dignas de crédito afirman que en el harén del tiranosaurio abundan de hecho las hermanas mellizas. También niñas de corta edad son adoptadas y guardadas bajo la vigilancia de nurses especializadas hasta su pubertad y adolescencia. La satiriasis del tiranosaurio ejercita con singular deleite el derecho feudal de pernada en estas vírgenes vestales.

El profesor Kleenewerk buscó desviar el tema que evidentemente le resultaba desagradable y que ponía a prueba su conciencia de invitado al Congreso de Historia, Cultura y Sociedad en la América Latina del Siglo xx.

—En realidad en el Paraguay puede ocurrir cualquier cosa en cualquier momento —comentó con la expresión de un malestar cercano a la náusea.

Le he respondido que era así, efectivamente. Puede ocurrir cualquier cosa en cualquier momento, pero nunca lo que uno espera que ocurra. Y lo que ocurre es siempre lo más irreal que pueda concebirse y ese momento puede durar siglos. La clave de la realidad paraguaya, a mi entender, es que usted encuentra siempre un hecho imposible, intercalado en el tejido de los hechos supuestamente normales o verosímiles. La existencia del tiranosaurio, por ejemplo. Un hombre infinitamente mediocre, convertido en amo absoluto de un país que ha tenido caudillos de un temple extraordinario.

—¿Por qué llama usted tiranosaurio al presidente de la República?

—No lo llamo yo. Lo llaman así los propios paraguayos oprimidos por el dictador desde hace más de treinta años. Usted sabrá, además, que el más feroz de los dinosaurios que han vivido sobre la tierra ha recibido en las enciclopedias el nombre de *tyrannosaurus rex*. El tiranosaurio paraguayo es también el más antiguo y sanguinario tirano de América Latina. Y el mote grotesco y cruel no está mal elegido. No hago más que repetirlo con los debidos respetos.

Clovis se aproximó y me llamó al pasillo. Su rostro estaba serio y algo crispado, fuera por completo de su aire habitual.

—Tengo malas noticias para ti. Acabo de hablar con el comandante —dijo bajando la voz y hablándome casi al oído—. A propósito del alerta. Me refirió confidencialmente que había recibido un radiograma de Asunción. Los expertos de la Técnica suponen que entre los invitados al congreso viene alguien, un agente terrorista internacional infiltrado, a quien se proponen detener. Suponen que viene armado de explosivos. Temo que sospechen de ti. Ten cuidado. Yo no te sacaré el ojo de encima. Trata de ser cauto en tus conversaciones. Hay micrófonos ocultos en los brazos de las butacas.

Volvió a su sitio. Lo vi alejarse como agobiado por el peso de algo previsible e inevitable.

Comprendí entonces la presencia de esos hombres de anteojos oscuros y vestidos todos con el mismo gris, distribuidos estratégicamente entre el pasaje. Algunos simulaban dormir; otros aparentaban leer los diarios. Se notaba que las propias azafatas no dejaban de escuchar las conversaciones de los pasajeros. Mi buen apetito se había desvanecido por completo. Contemplaba la bandeja del suculento almuerzo como el cuerno de la abundancia repentinamente vacío.

Continuaba sonando la música viva y sincopada. Los pebeteros de mármol manaban tenues guedejas de humo con esencias balsámicas. El almuerzo había concluido y el ballet de las aerobayaderas se afanaba ahora en desembarazar las mesas limpiándolas de las más ínfimas partículas de comida y dejándolas relucientes como espejos.

Entraron en acción tramoyistas y técnicos de luces. En el centro espacioso de la cabina levantaron un transparente pedestal circular, iluminado desde abajo, que empezó a girar entre los pebeteros humeantes y los detalles del horrendo decorado. En la deslumbrante cabina del Boeing, las aerobayaderas se movían ingrávidas sirviendo el café y los licores, en medio de los ritmos gemidores de boleros que derramaban su almíbar por los altavoces. Los olores capitososos de los manjares flotaban aún en el ambiente. La batahola del pasaje se mantenía a pleno. Las caras congestionadas y apopléticas se difuminaban en la niebla aromática.

Rompió a tocar la polca del partido del poder. Estallaron otra vez estruendosos vivas y aplausos al Reconstructor, al Partido Colorado y a las Fuerzas Armadas, el trípode del poder absoluto. Una bella muchacha de estilizada delgadez emergió de una gran caracola groseramente alusiva, subió al podio giratorio y empezó a bailar la danza de la botella. Una de champán, acabada de descorchar, se mantenía en equilibrio sobre la corona de su birrete color fucsia. El podio de cristal coloreado giraba sobre potentes focos de luz que volvían translúcido el cuerpo de la bailarina en sus flexibles y rápidos giros. Los aplausos y los gritos arreciaron en su homenaje. Los hombres más próximos le lanzaban requiebros de embriagada sensualidad; algunos pugnaban por tocar las caderas ondulantes y huidizas. El pasaje se agolpó en torno al ruedo como en un improvisado anfiteatro.

Con provocativos contoneos, la botella como atornillada en la coronilla, la bailarina fue desprendiéndose de su túnica de estameña, semejante a la de una novicia, ceñida por el grueso cordón blanco de la iniciación. Las flexibles contracciones de su cuerpo dejaron caer la túnica hasta que quedó completamente desnuda, sin más atavío que un collar de perlas negras alrededor del largo cuello. Del cilicio atado a la cintura pendía una plaqueta de oro sobre la pelvis amarrada a los muslos. Caireles del mismo metal guarnecían los pezones y el ombligo sonando con el crepitar excitado de crótalos. Por momentos la negra cabellera larga hasta las corvas le envolvía el cuerpo y el rostro como fingiendo ocultarla. Los focos bajos de los reflectores la hacían parecer mucho más alta y como más desnuda. Los vellos del pubis sobresalían del triángulo de oro. La luz plena mostró que la cintura y el vientre empezaban a sangrar bajo las púas del cilicio. Hilos rojos fluían hacia los muslos. Como en estado de trance, los ojos cerrados, la boca entreabierta en una respiración entrecortada y anhelante, la muchacha danzaba sin dejar de apuntar con su barbilla trémula en una determinada dirección delante de sí. Seguí esa dirección. Por juego o por burla, ese punto no era otro que el sitio donde se halla sentado el pastor mennonita, sumido en la lectura de su Breviario, sin darse por enterado de lo que ocurría. La muchacha bailaba para él en ese transporte fingido o real. Sus movimientos fueron disminuyendo. Con temblores en todo el cuerpo, el blanco de los ojos brillando entre las rajas de sus párpados, la muchacha quedó al fin completamente extenuada e inmóvil. Cruzó los brazos sobre el pecho, petrificada como una estatua viva, manchada de sangre.

El delirio machuno estalló en un gemido de gargantas enronquecidas. Las mujeres reían y aplaudían, vengadas por esa airosa Venus del espacio. La botella cayó sobre un hombro de la bailarina proyectando chorros espumosos en todas direcciones. Como despertándose de un doloroso sueño, la muchacha se pasó el dorso de la mano por la frente rociada de sudor, pero todo el cuerpo estaba húmedo y brillante. Se arrancó los caireles de los senos y del ombligo, la placa pelviana, el cinturón de crin erizado de pinchos sangrientos, y los arrojó sobre la alfombra. Se doblegó sobre sí misma hasta ocultar el triángulo oscuro del pubis y se dejó caer en una butaca. Dobló las piernas y se acurrucó en ella en posición fetal. Con las manos húmedas se oprimía los ojos. El movimiento convulsivo de los hombros delató que estaba atacada por sollozos. Una azafata se acercó y la cubrió con una esclavina escarlata. Recogió luego los adminículos ensangrentados. El médico y dos enfermeras acudieron corriendo y se la llevaron en una camilla.

Poco después, a raíz de la infidencia de una de las azafatas, se corrió la voz de que la muchacha había muerto, fulminada por un ataque cardiaco. La dama de los pestillos de oro comentó con pesar:

—¡Pobre María Luz Noguer! Yo la conocía. De buena familia era la inocente. Solía bailar en nuestras fiestas íntimas. Le tocó bailar aquí su canto del cisne. Era una de las ex barraganas del que ya sabemos. La había despedido. No las aguanta por más de un año. Para el Karaí la mujer termina su vida a los dieciocho años como mucho. Cada cual con sus gustos. ¡Y el que puede, puede, che ama kuera! ¡Qué pikó se le va a hacer! Nosotras, a los cuarenta, podemos esperar todavía la tercera juventud.

Dos damas de la tribu se hallaban sentadas en la fila detrás de la nuestra. Le oí contar a una de ellas, en guaraní, otra de las hazañas priápicas del Karaí. Al parecer, la muerte de la bailarina había excitado, sobre todo en las mujeres, la comezón de secretearse entre ellas los chismes sobre las intimidades aberrantes del Gran Hombre, de seguro conocidas y repetidas hasta la saciedad en los sumideros de la *vox populi*, siempre clandestina y maliciosa. La dama malhablaba con toda naturalidad en la creencia de que los gringos que venían delante no entenderían el champurreado dialecto criollo. Agucé de todos modos el oído para no perder una hilacha del relato a la Drácula. Se trataba de una historia espeluznante, una variante increíble de vampirismo sexual.

Una de las pupilas del almácigo de vírgenes púberes, una niña de trece años llamada Purificación Capilla, de una belleza extraordinaria ("...parecía un ángel caído del propio trono del Creador", decía la mujer acollarada en espirales de perlas, diamantes y esmeraldas) era la favorita del Karaí. De tanto en tanto venía al asilo para niñas que no habían cometido todavía ningún pecado. El Karaí tiene allí su habitación privada. Dicen que la mandaba traer, la hacía desnudar y, mientras tomaba sus interminables guampas de tereré, se pasaba acariciándola para constatar que el don primicial permanecía intacto. La dama dijo simplemente "le metía el dedo para saber si seguía siendo virgen".

Cuando Purificación se enteró de cuál era el destino que le esperaba, huyó de la "nursery". Además de hermosa era muy inteligente y decidida. Se escondió durante varios meses en la casa de una conocida de su madre, la que casualmente era amiga de una de mis cocineras, la impagable Candelaria de Jesús, decía la dama bajando la voz. La pobre Candé, temblando de miedo, no aguantó más el temor y me contó la fechoría de la niña. El miedo se me pasó a mí. Era un asunto muy delicado, che ama mi... —musitó la dama—. Yo no podía complicarme y menos todavía complicar a Juan Bautista, a quien el general le acababa de nombrar director general de esa mina de oro que es el Instituto de Previsión Social. Allí el doctor Godoy en poco tiempo se hizo uno de los hombres más ricos del Paraguay. Le conté todo luego a Juan Bautista. Él pasó el dato a la Secretaría de la Presidencia. En un jeep de la Policía fueron a buscar a la chica las guardianas del asilo, entre ellas una monja, o una que se hacía pasar por monja, porque el asilo ese era una especie de Buen Pastor para niñas. Esa misma noche, la muchacha se suicidó tomando el veneno para los ratones. Hasta allí yo sé lo que pasó. Mi cocinera cayó presa y no supe más nada. Después se dijo, no sé yo si es verdad o no, que el Karaí mandó llevar a su refugio privado el cuerpo todavía caliente de Purificación Capilla y que allí mismo violó a la muertecita. Dicen que no se contentó hasta que vio correr la sangre entre las piernas. La dama rió un poco nerviosamente en una especie de fatigada resignación.

—Son calumnias —dijo la otra—. La chica pudo
haber estado con el periodo. A esa edad ya se tiene la regla.
—¡Ea... Benedicta! —protestó la otra—. No tenés
laya luego. No hay que burlarse pues de la desgracia ajena.
—Yo no me burlo, che ama... —se defendió la incrédula—. Digo nomás que eso me parece una exageración
de los opositores chismosos. No pierden el menor detalle
para desacreditar al Karaí en lo más y en lo menos. Lo que
él no permite es que nadie se burle de él. Y ahí estaba esa
chica rebelde tirándole a la cara su cadáver como si los miserables vivos se hubieran aliado en ella con los miserables
muertos para contrariarle.
—Tenés razón. Dicen que después mandó que se
enviara el cadáver de la chica a su madre —dijo la dama de
los collares—. Candé, mi cocinera, la celadora y otras personas complicadas en el asunto desaparecieron para siempre, así que no tuve más quien me contara esas cosas. Se echó
tierra sobre el asunto y sólo siguieron las murmuraciones
de los malhablados.

Vengo concentrado en el hombre de las colonias.
Me resulta cada vez más extraño y al mismo tiempo más
transparente, como si su destino físico estuviera irremediablemente unido al mío en una suerte de oscura identidad y complicidad. Atribuí de nuevo estos desvaríos al
estado de ánimo especial que suelen producirme los viajes
muy largos. La confusión de la azafata con Leda, el alerta
de la bomba y la confidencia de Clovis sobre las sospechas
que la Secreta de Asunción tendría sobre mí como terrorista internacional infiltrado, no han sido desde luego los
mejores estímulos para levantarme el ánimo.
La figura del pastor mennonita me perturba y me

sosiega a la vez. Poco a poco, en el sopor que trataba de reprimir, he sentido que el hilo de una comunicación apenas perceptible se establecía entre nosotros. Esa sensación se ha ido afirmando y haciéndose cada vez más natural. En determinado momento he tenido la impresión nítida y al mismo tiempo borrosa de que yo conocía a ese hombre y de que él me conocía a mí. El hombre de la cruz pectoral me observa como a través de un antifaz casi impenetrable con esa vaga mirada del agonizante que busca un auxilio imposible en los ojos de los que asisten a su doloroso tránsito.

Cuando se volvía hacia mí, yo trataba de mirarle en el centro de la frente, entre los dos ojos oscurecidos por los cristales ahumados. Sólo distinguía vagamente unos puntos como gránulos de pólvora o de sésamo sembrados entre las cejas y en los pómulos quemados al rojo por el sol o por la fiebre. Me pareció que esbozaba un leve ademán queriendo darme a entender algo. No había hecho más que levantar la cruz pectoral y tenerla un instante oprimida en sus manos en mi dirección. Me pareció sentir que dejaba escapar un suspiro muerto y olvidado hacía mucho tiempo en algún rincón de su ánima. El temblor de un párpado, un rictus en la comisura de la boca delataban su fracaso o su desesperanza. Sólo después iba a acordarme de esa señal que teníamos en la prisión: el palito apretado en el puño que significaba peligro.

Tal vez en ese momento se introdujo entre ambos la sensación de una visceral, de una fraternal identidad de destinos cruzados. Yo buscaba no complicar aún más esa situación ambigua. No dejé entrever el menor indicio de sentirme afectado por esas señales, que eran fantasmales porque provenían de un fantasma o de alguien que pronto iba a convertirse en un fantasma. Percibí su decepción. Volvió a mirar fijamente delante de sí con la resignación fatigada de un íntimo desgarramiento, de esos que impiden toda comunicación. Ese hombre, ese religioso, no parecía marcado por el sello de ninguna Iglesia reconocible, aunque sí tal vez por el de una disimulada y, hasta hacía un momento, inquebrantable fe.

Pensé que entre su trasijado maletín y el mío flamante existían secretas simetrías. Entre lo que guardaba adentro, aparte de algunos útiles de aseo, vagos documentos de identidad tal vez falsos, y el grueso anillo con el frasco de ponzoña que yo llevaba ocultos, no habría sino una diferencia de forma, de naturaleza. Recordé en ese momento lo que me habías dicho tú una vez a propósito de Leda: "Se tiene derecho a mentir sobre las apariencias pero no sobre lo esencial".

Las apariencias del pastor eran ésas; lo esencial estaba oculto.

En ese momento fue cuando sonaron los estridentes timbres de alarma. En todos los paneles de la cabina se encendieron señales de una vivísima e intermitente luz roja. Y fue entonces cuando perdí de vista al pastor mennonita hasta que, pasada la señal de alarma, reapareció furtivamente con el maletín evidentemente más liviano al que ya no se cuidaba de proteger de algún probable choque.

Terminado el almuerzo, el comandante está anunciando por los altavoces que la nave va a cruzar la frontera entre Brasil y Paraguay y que en pocos minutos más sobrevolará el área de la central hidroeléctrica. La más grande central hidroeléctrica del mundo, precisa ahuecando mucho la voz. Hay un murmullo de decepción cuando el comandante previene que a trece mil pies de altitud los pasajeros sólo van a poder contemplar el hermoso lago azul de Itaipú resplandeciendo con su propia luz. La luz cenital del sol no es más que la tiniebla blanca del mediodía. Pero está como recubierta y opacada por el resplandor de los millones de kilovatios que genera la central. Nuevamente apelo a mi poderoso Zeiss Ikon cuyos campos de visión parecen naufragar en la niebla algodonosa de la atmósfera.

—Las represas del Niágara, en los Grandes Lagos, la de Asuán sobre el Nilo —clama el comandante con voz estentórea— son pequeños charcos frente a este lago de diez mil kilómetros cuadrados que tienen ustedes ahí abajo... La fuerza generadora de Itaipú triplica la fuerza de las dos juntas...

La voz cavernosa del comandante continúa explicando que la enorme potencia de la central se expande por todo el país proveyendo de luz hasta el más humilde rancho de los confines. Se ha puesto una voz de mando de parada militar, henchida de nacional orgullo, al repetir la cantinela informativa sobre turbinas y megavatios, mechada de vulgarizaciones técnicas. Nadie entiende nada, salvo tal vez el hecho de que la luz de Itaipú no se apaga jamás.

—¡Es una de las grandes obras de la Reconstrucción, inaugurada por el Presidente Stroessner el 5 noviembre de 1982!... ¡Hace apenas cinco años!... —arenga el comandante.

Un aplauso general premia el fervor nacionalista del comandante.

—¿Por qué este despilfarro? —pregunta mi vecino.

De inmediato, como si le hubiera oído, el comandante responde haciendo vibrar la cabina con las resonancias de los altavoces: "¡En el Paraguay no se derrocha nada! ¡La fuerza de la naturaleza es inagotable!... La luz de la central de Itaipú alumbra más que el sol, pero no se apaga como el sol al caer la noche. El cielo nocturno y el cielo diurno han dejado de verse en el Paraguay. No se ven más el sol, la luna ni las estrellas... Siguen existiendo tal vez, pero ni falta que hacen... La luz que nunca se apaga de Itaipú ilumina el Paraguay en un día perpetuo como el poder del Gran Reconstructor..."

Nuevos aplausos, esta vez algo irónicos e incrédulos por parte de los invitados. A mí me inquieta esa voz vieja, acatarrada, del comandante, que tropieza con el escollo de un belfo enorme y colgante de dinosaurio que se prolonga en la papada. Busca mimetizarse en la voz de alguien que lo rebasa infinitamente en la gran oscuridad de la noche del Poder. Pone una cassette con un saludo del dictador dirigido a los invitados al entrar en tierra paraguaya. Es la misma voz del comandante. Éste la imita a la perfección en esa suerte de dialecto teutón, español, guaraní, de confusa dicción, lleno de errores de sintaxis, pero sobre todo empedrado de idiotismos: como en el sonido y la furia de Macbeth, la voz de un idiota que quiere decir algo pero que no significa nada.

Las azafatas se afanan en completar las informaciones sin conseguir otra cosa que confundir aún más a los viajeros autóctonos y extranjeros. Un corpulento y gordo jerarcón, en seductor más o menos ebrio, coge a una de ellas por la cintura y le estampa dos sonoros besos en los cachetes. La muchacha se deshace del abrazo con una agilísima genuflexión y una encantadora sonrisa. Los más curiosos se atropellan y agolpan en las ventanillas para contemplar la oscuridad del sol y el resplandor de la presa. La dama de los pestillos de oro y sus contertulias suben en bandada a la cabina del comandante con chillidos de cotorras barranqueras.

Para sustraerme al efecto monótono pero hipnótico de las aerobayaderas, inconscientemente me he sumergido en un recuerdo penoso: el de los interrogatorios y torturas a que fuimos sometidos un compañero de prisión y yo tras un fallido atentado contra el tirano, hace veinte años. En los "quirófanos" de la Técnica nada había cambiado. El instrumental consagrado a las sevicias, salvo algunos adelantos, seguía siendo el mismo. Estaban allí los mismos viejos aparatos de radio para asordinar los alaridos o amplificarlos a escalas y timbres paroxísticos; la misma bañera (ese extraño baptisterio excremental) desconchada, con el agua hasta los bordes densa de inmundicias, recubierta por fuera de costras de sangre seca entre las manchas de mugre. En aquella época, los métodos "persuasivos" de los torturadores eran aún bastante rudimentarios, pero no por ello menos eficaces y terribles. Esos artilugios, los baños "lustrales" en el agua de esa Estigia nauseabunda, los instrumentos herrumbrados de esa panoplia, se habían cobrado miles de vidas y habían quebrado otras tantas existencias convertidas para siempre en despojos subhumanos. En medio de vómitos incoercibles y de un vértigo lento de mareo, la víctima miraba el agua de la bañera llena de inmundicias y excrementos, en la que apenas cabía el cuerpo de un hombre y ante la cual el próximo "submarino" esperaba, maniatado, su turno.

La tortura, en sí misma, no es sino la continuidad de los tormentos morales y psíquicos que han comenzado mucho antes. Se siente el pavor que toma la forma y el tamaño de la cara de los verdugos y nos confunde con ellos en la fraternidad demoniaca de un mutuo delirio, cuyas fronteras ningún ser vivo podrá descubrir jamás: ese odio del supliciado, transformado en amor contra natura hacia el verdugo en ese instante de impotencia y dolor absolutos. Como entre las resonancias de un acueducto que reverberan en todo el cuerpo machacado, y bajo la tapa del cráneo a punto de estallar, se escuchan lejanos los gritos de los torturadores encapuchados en una rojiza niebla. En la soledad total del sufrimiento, el poder del torturador le convierte en el único y sumo dueño y hace sentir a la víctima violada, triturada, que la humillación infinita del suplicio se transforma en un trance de amor y de muerte. A partir de ese momento no desea otra cosa en el mundo sino llegar hasta el fin de esa entrega.

El avance tecnológico más notorio de las cámaras de tortura era un pequeño aparato no más grande que un receptor de radio. Quizás lo utilizan todavía, pues sus resultados eran infalibles. Acaso lo han perfeccionado aún más. Es un instrumento precursor de la tortura óptica, menos conocido que la "picana", pero mucho más eficaz, aun cuando los riesgos mortíferos de su aplicación son también mayores.

Se trata de un proyector de enceguecedores rayos blancos e infrarrojos que queman las retinas y produce atroces dolores y perturbaciones en el cerebro al mismo tiempo que una parálisis completa del cuerpo y del sistema respiratorio. Los párpados seccionados impiden cerrar los ojos. Una miríada de diminutas partículas semejantes a finas cenizas envuelve el haz negro. Cada partícula se mueve enloquecidamente en torno al núcleo, rodeada, a su vez, por el halo de un diminuto arco iris. Nada hay más terrible que esa luz tenebrosa percibida como a través de una poderosa lupa dentro de uno mismo, corporizada en filamentos infinitesimales, en medio de un dolor que no es de este mundo. El supliciado queda en estado cataléptico, con asfixia y disnea, rígido y duro como hierro pero, a la vez, más sensible a los dolores, al sufrimiento moral, a la humillación. De tanto en tanto, le arrojan chorros de agua salada que arde en las heridas y las llagas descargando un poco la acumulación de los rayos. El electrocutado revive a medias. De regreso, arrastrado a las celdas como un fardo de basura empapada sufre el tormento adicional de una sed de fuego. Se tiene la sensación de haber sido traspasado enteramente desde el cerebro a los talones por el "hueso negro de la luz": la luz invisible que hace visible la oscuridad.

Nunca te he hablado de esto. El recuerdo del suplicio se había escondido para mí mismo en la sombra de un involuntario olvido más fuerte a veces que la memoria voluntaria: "te olvidas de acordarte para huir de tus fantasmas", me reprochabas mis súbitas y prolongadas amnesias. Así era, sin duda. Desde entonces, ese "esqueleto negro", sin yo saberlo, sin que me preocupara en absoluto de él, me acompaña incrustado en el mío. Sólo se hace sentir en ocasiones de extrema tensión. Duerme en los nervios de uno el resto del tiempo, seguro de su presencia y energía latente, como una larva siniestra que anida en la médula.

Mi compañero, Pedro Alvarenga, alias *Pyxäi* (Piquento), un joven de 27 años, el más arrojado de los magnicidas potenciales que surgieron por entonces, le dio este mote al aparato que producía los rayos. Esqueleto negro de la luz. Y la verdad es que la expresión definía con terrible exactitud el fanal de los rayos. En la parafernalia de utensilios de suplicio, es el instrumento sumo de la Técnica, como el violín es el rey de los instrumentos de cuerda. El violín de los rayos es un verdadero *Stradivarius*, particularmente persuasivo en los "solos" de rayos invisibles que tornaban visible la oscuridad de la muerte. Y en la sala de conciertos había varios virtuosos que podían rivalizar con Paganini. ¿De dónde surgió esta maravilla? Se hablaba de un técnico norteamericano que vino a asesorar a la Técnica en tiempos de Dan Mitrione, en el Uruguay. Nadie lo sabe a ciencia cierta. Acaso fuera el mismo Dan Mitrione, que halló su muerte propia en tierra ajena después de haber formado aventajados discípulos.

Pedro Alvarenga (*Pyxäi*), con la cabellera completamente blanca antes de los veinte años y con los pies más que nunca comidos por los piques, salió casi ciego de la prisión. No volví a verlo pues yo también perdí parte de la visión y de la memoria. Una vez, hace años, recibí un mensaje de él, desde el Brasil, en el que me invitaba a planear nuevas "aventuras". No le respondí. Ya estaba en plena cura de aislamiento y desinfección de todo lo que oliera a exilio, a luchas clandestinas, a la carne en descomposición del pueblo natal de cuya carroña se alimenta el tiranosaurio.

Me he preguntado muchas veces qué habrá sido de Pedro Alvarenga, el bravo y animoso muchacho que se formó en la dura escuela del sacrificio y que fue ejemplo de sangre fría y valor en los increíbles episodios de la resis-

tencia, al igual que los Candia, los Soler, los Derliz Villa-
gra, los Agapito Valiente, los Agustín Goiburú, y tantos
otros, hombres y mujeres, millares y millares de heroínas
y héroes anónimos que dieron su vida en la lucha clandestina de la liberación.

Me cuesta un gran esfuerzo, como sabes, recordar
las fisonomías. Prefiero imaginarlas aproximativamente
como un boceto nebuloso y dejar que esos semblantes con-
fusos vayan recuperando sus propios rasgos, sus intensida-
des particulares. Únicamente no podré acordarme jamás de
las caras patibularias de mis torturadores. Cosa curiosa: uno
los llega a olvidar enteramente, sin el menor asomo de rencor y hasta si esos angustiosos e impotentes sentimientos de
venganza.

Conozco casos en que una entrañable amistad y, a
veces, hasta el amor más tierno, han llegado a anudarse entre los torturadores y sus víctimas de otro tiempo. Una
amiga mía y de mi madre, inteligente, combativa y bella a
sus cuarenta años, lo pasó muy mal en las cámaras de tortura de la Secreta. Era enlace de algunos grupos de la resistencia. No la soltaron sino después de arrancarle todo lo
que sabía acerca de la acción clandestina de esos grupos y
hasta los nombres de todos sus responsables.

Después de años de prisión, Marina —tal era su
alias de combate— salió en libertad, destruida, irreconocible, vieja, flotando en la bruma de una apacible locura. Mi
madre la visitaba de tanto en tanto para hacerle compañía.
Mucho tiempo después, hasta su muerte, conservaba un
platónico y melancólico amor por uno de sus torturadores. Un poco antes de morir, entregó a mi madre su diario
íntimo, iniciado a su salida de la cárcel. Esas páginas de un
desolado delirio otoñal estaban enteramente colmadas por
la presencia del fantasma encapuchado cuyo rostro ella
descubrió en el lampo de una revelación, entre un toque y
otro de la picana eléctrica, entre una quemadura y otra del

aparato lumínico, entre la primera y última violación que el encapuchado cometió con ella cuando la arrastraba desnuda a su celda.

La confesión de ese amor surgido del sufrimiento y del odio, perennizado como un sentimiento de rescate y transfiguración, es un testimonio escalofriante y conmovedor. La pobre mujer sublimó su amor en la intensidad de un sentimiento maternal, casi religioso. Vivió en total aislamiento con la fantasía de haber tenido un hijo de su torturador. En esa soledad cuidó a su hijo como un secreto celosamente guardado. En la penumbra de la habitación mi madre sólo alcanzaba a atisbar la cuna del silencioso niño, velado por un dosel de encajes y rotosas sedas. Tan intensa era su obsesión, que a la larga nos convencimos de que ese hijo existía realmente. Mi madre le llevaba alimentos y ropitas para el niño que iría creciendo, que a los dos años debía ya estar caminando por la casa. Cuando la mujer murió, la cuna vacía estaba junto al lecho. En el patio encontraron una pequeña tumba recién excavada. En el interior de un diminuto cajón pintado de blanco, no había más que el fémur ennegrecido de una criatura de unos tres años, que nadie se atrevió a mandar analizar.

Pedro, como los otros iguales a él, habrá desaparecido ya en la vorágine de violencia que eligió para vivir y para morir, como otros eligen la pesadilla que quieren soñar. La última vez que nos vimos en la prisión de Emboscada, en el antiguo castillo de Arekutacuá, me dijo: "Si escapo de ésta volveré a la lucha armada, solo o con el ejército de liberación..." Pedro Alvarenga escapó y sin duda volvió solo al riesgo y a la fascinación de la muerte. El tal ejército de liberación no se formó nunca.

¡Bah... la liberación! ¡Las más bellas palabras se vuelven agrias como la leche cuando nadie la toma! Cómo liberar a un pueblo que no quiere ser liberado. Sólo se liberan los libres... resuena en mí el conjuro maléfico. ¡Libertad... democracia! ¿Qué quieren significar estas dos palabras falsamente míticas que déspotas y oprimidos proclaman como su exclusiva religión? Después de todo, por miserables y corruptos que sean los labios que las pronuncian, esas palabras son la expresión de alguna clase de creencia por la que multitudes y pueblos enteros se han sacrificado y seguirán siendo sacrificados por el insaciable Moloch del poder. Aunque esté llena de infamia y cobardía, esa expresión guarda una apagada nota de rebeldía, envuelta en una extraña mezcla de deseo y de odio, de desesperanza y fascinación.

Estoy tendido en la oscuridad esperando la muerte. Pesa sobre mí la masa de plomo de impenetrables tinieblas que el rayo de luz lívida atraviesa espectralmente. Estoy por decirlo así computado entre los muertos, el primer puesto o el último, poco importa. Pero no me enterraron entonces. He sobrevivido como *otro*, en lugar de otro. Quizás en esto, y solamente en esto, se encuentre toda la diferencia que me separa de Pedro Alvarenga, si es que él existe todavía... Quizás toda la sabiduría, toda la verdad y su final deslumbramiento, están concentrados en ese instante en que damos el paso último y atravesamos el umbral de lo invisible. Yo estoy vivo todavía, cargado de muchas muertes por las que no puedo pagar ningún rescate, ni siquiera con mi sangre, puesto que ella sólo serviría para destruir a un tirano. Lo corrupto sólo con lo corrupto se mata. Pedro no será ya de este mundo. Habrá dado sin duda el último paso. Habrá pasado ya a la otra orilla, mientras que a mí me fue permitido retirar el pie titubeante del borde de ese abismo sin fondo...

No, no fui enterrado entonces. Pero desde ese momento sobrevivo en un tiempo que recuerdo espectralmente como el paso a través de un mundo que no contiene ningún odio, ninguna esperanza, ningún deseo... igual a este viaje que dura ya un día y una eternidad y que debe de ser acaso la grotesca representación o la premonición del último tramo de mi vida. Quiero pensar que la recapitulación que te estoy escribiendo de cosas que ya han sucedido y de otras que están por suceder no es un relato de fingido y despreocupado desprecio. Si he sobrevivido ha sido al precio de innumerables derrotas, de terrores sin nombre, de abominables satisfacciones, de capitulaciones nefandas. No puedo considerar esto como una victoria moral. Pero de todos modos es una victoria: la victoria de la corrupción sobre la corrupción. ¿Puedo llamarla de otra manera?

Observo al pastor que me observa a mí con la misma extrañeza. Entre los dos, el aparato de los rayos, nuestros dos maletines, el vacío brumoso de veinte años. Y no es aquella situación extrema que sufrí en la cámara de tortura la que mejor recuerdo: una visión enceguecedora, repleta de dolor físico y miseria moral. Es la situación extrema de Pedro Alvarenga la que me parece haber vivido en aquellas espantosas sesiones. Es la que siento revivir ahora, a la vista del pastor.

A través del óvalo he divisado el rectángulo violáceo del campo de aterrizaje. El avión va planeando ya casi al ras de la pista de cemento. Todo sucede muy rápidamente, de modo que pocos son los que advierten en el primer momento qué es en realidad lo que está sucediendo. Tras el aterrizaje y el rápido carreteo por la pista central, el inmenso Boeing ha frenado bruscamente, a pocos metros de la torre de control. Un poco más y choca contra ella. Apagan los motores. En el silencio que sigue al rechinar de los tensores, tres golpes sordos resuenan en la puerta delantera de la nave que todavía se columpia por los efectos del frenazo. Golpes rítmicos como los de un bastón de teatro anunciando el comienzo del espectáculo antes de levantarse el telón. La algarabía y el desorden entre los pasajeros aumentan hasta el frenesí. El violento y extraño aterrizaje desata el pavor en el remolino de más de tres centenares de personas.

Los golpes se repiten más violentos y apremiantes. A una orden seca y autoritaria del comandante, el sobrecargo y las azafatas se precipitan sobre el tablero de los mandos electrónicos. La puerta circular semejante a la pesada puerta del tesoro de los bancos comienza a abrirse pero se detiene dejando apenas un resquicio para el paso de una persona. Un hombre armado entra por el orificio, se abre paso entre el amasijo humano y trepa a saltos por la escalera de caracol hacia el puesto de comando del avión.

Las densas filas de pasajeros se agolpan en los pasillos intentando la salida en una marea indescriptible de cuerpos jadeantes y crispados, en medio de empellones, insultos y gritos de terror. Con alaridos histéricos las mujeres se arrojan a lo largo del pasillo donde son pisoteadas por los que vienen detrás. Algunas se enrollan en las espesas alfombras; otras se cubren la cabeza con los bultos y los bolsos. La puerta robotizada rechina y se abre por completo. Hombres armados en uniforme de combate y las caras embadurnadas de negro irrumpen y copan la cabina como en el asalto a una trinchera. La avalancha de "caras pintadas" con una traílla de perros impide que la marea humana se lance al vacío.

La voz colérica del comandante se desgañita en los altavoces tratando de imponer orden. Las azafatas y los oficiales cargan con todas sus fuerzas tratando en vano de contener ese remolino de personas enfurecidas y empavorecidas. Nadie atiende más que a su propio pánico y apuro

por salir. Los hombres armados impiden que ninguno de
los pasajeros desembarque. Las ametralladoras entretejen
una verja amenazadora en la abertura redonda. Yo retro-
cedo y me quedo a la expectativa. Siempre conviene hacerlo en caso de un alboroto imprevisto. Por la escotilla, a
contracorriente de los pasajeros enloquecidos, irrumpen
más "caras pintadas". Reconozco en ellos las facciones
asiáticas de los mercenarios contratados en Taiwán, famosos por su ferocidad y fulmínea rapidez en las acciones an-
tidisturbios. La batahola se ha vuelto infernal.

El pastor mennonita es uno de los primeros en levantarse de un salto con su maletín negro. Con una agili-
dad que no le suponía se abre paso hacia la salida. Un
enorme pastor alemán salta sobre él y lo ataca a dentella-
das. Los taiwaneses acaban de reducir al pastor bajo una
andanada de golpes. Se ensañan con él a puntapiés y bofetones. Le arrancan la barba postiza. En ese momento lo
reconozco. ¡Es él! Pedro Alvarenga está allí. Tiende hacia
mí algunos gestos vagos y tetánicos como de ahogado. Yo
nada puedo hacer por él. Contra la turbia luminosidad
circular de la salida veo que lo llevan arrastrado, sin que
intente el más mínimo gesto de resistencia o de defensa. Al
querer aferrarse a una de las barras de la puerta, lo despren-
den a culatazos y lo arrojan al vacío. Es lo último que veo
de Pedro Alvarenga, vivo.

Una de esas rápidas visiones interiores que a veces
sobrevienen fulgurantes me anticipó lo que iba a ver. Oí
que alguien me llamaba "profesor". Giré como bajo un
choque eléctrico y vi a Leda Kautner en uniforme de azafata y con el birrete fucsia sobre el resplandor de sus cabellos de oro. Me miraba fijamente con los ojos brillantes en
ese rostro infinitamente hermoso y odiado. En mi atónita
estupefacción no supe reaccionar en seguida. De nuevo
todo mi cuerpo temblaba bajo el horror de la fascinación.

Leda llevaba del brazo a una anciana y a una niña de

corta edad. Me ordenó en alemán que me ocupara de ellas y que las ayudara a descender del avión. Me las entregó y al hacerlo su mano rozó la mía. Quise aferrarla pero su mano escapó y me señaló la salida. Dese prisa, me ordenó con su voz inconfundible. Obedecí como un autómata sin poder recobrar el habla. Tomé a la anciana y a la niña del brazo y me volví para hablar a ese ser humano o fantasmal.

—¡Leda! —murmuré con trémula angustia.

Había desaparecido. Tuve la sensación de que esa presencia, que se me había mostrado tan cercana como para hablarme y hablarle, como para tomarle la mano y no abandonarla nunca más, había saltado hacia atrás en las tinieblas, a una distancia inaccesible. La busqué con la vista por todas partes. Se había esfumado otra vez. ¿Volvería a vivir aquella noche embrujada de Nevers en cada uno de sus detalles de deseo, de tentación, de cobarde terror, de renuncia, de dimisión no voluntaria, de desesperación intensa e irremediable?

Recorrí en vano con los ojos, una por una, las siluetas de las azafatas que con rápidos movimientos ayudaban a desembarcar a los últimos grupos de aterrorizados pasajeros. La anciana y la niña lloraban. Traté de calmarlas y avanzamos hacia la puerta. ¿Por qué Leda me había confiado a la anciana y a la niña cuando bien pudo hacerlo ella con menos riesgo que yo? Pero a esta pregunta se unían otras aún más extrañas e incomprensibles. ¿Cómo estaba Leda allí? ¿Cómo había conseguido el puesto de azafata en un avión, precisamente en éste, de las Flotas Aéreas del Estado paraguayo? ¿Cómo sabía ella que yo iba a viajar en este vuelo? El hecho de que la selección y reclutamiento de aeromozas se hacían con preferencia en Baviera, región de origen del dictador, y de que Leda vivía en Munich, no lo explicaba todo. Rehusé el tomar en serio estas respuestas con las que trataba de engañarme a mí mismo. Por otra parte, detesto indagar y menos aún explicar las causas últimas de lo que me acontece. En la ficción, como en la vida, los más ínfimos hechos son inexplicables. Lo misterioso, lo extraño, constituyen su naturaleza y su razón de ser.

Una intuición, sin embargo, iluminó mi mente con respecto a la primera pregunta. Leda no buscó proteger a la anciana y a la niña con mi supuesta inmunidad de invitado al congreso oficial. Ella sabía que esa inmunidad, además de falsa, era irrisoria en situaciones y lugares como éstos. Buscó protegerme *a mí* con el escudo de la anciana y la niña convirtiéndome en la imagen del respetable paterfamilias, igualmente falsa pero al menos inofensiva. ¿Debo agradecerle o maldecirla otra vez?

Fuimos de los últimos en salir. Empezamos a descender la plataforma bajo los rayos entrecruzados de poderosos reflectores. Piquetes de las fuerzas de seguridad se arremolinaban en torno al avión. Había varios jeeps de la guardia de seguridad de la presidencia, y hasta dos tanquetas blindadas del ejército, con los motores en marcha. Cazadores con guanteletes de cuero sujetaban las traíllas de perros que husmeaban con sofocados y furiosos ladridos a los pasajeros que iban bajando. Uno de éstas fieras trepó a saltos los escalones y me saltó a la mano donde llevaba el anillo. Un guardia tiró de la cuerda obligando al perro a retroceder. Sentí que el dedo se hinchaba en el anillo. Me lo saqué y lo repuse en su escondrijo del doble forro. Metí la mano sangrante en el bolsillo de la chaqueta. El dolor de la dentellada, embotada en cierto modo por el grueso anillo, me reveló que estuve a menos del grosor de un cabello de ser descubierto. El escudo imaginado por Leda surtió su efecto. Mientras bajábamos paso a paso busqué con los prismáticos el cadáver de Pedro Alvarenga entre los cuerpos desparramados junto al avión.

De repente lo vi a un costado de la plataforma. Con su vestimenta hecha trizas, Pedro yacía de bruces en su último disfraz. Lo habían estrangulado con la cadena de la cruz pectoral. La cruz estaba enterrada en la espalda hasta la empuñadura. El cuerpo flaco, esquelético, se había extendido en la muerte. Parecía inmensamente largo, casi interminable. Tenía la boca pegada a la tierra como preguntándole si ya podía entrar. Sólo alcancé a ver el maletín destrozado y vacío, el sombrero aplastado bajo la oruga de la tanqueta. Las patrullas que custodiaban el cadáver nos obligaron a seguir avanzando con los tubos de sus automáticas y sus gritos ululantes. La anciana y la niña lloraban desesperadamente. Las ayudé a bajar el último peldaño. Me agaché todo lo que pude tratando de ver de reojo, por última vez, el perfil de ese rostro que había tenido todo el tiempo delante de mis ojos sin poder reconocerlo y que ahora estaba más irreconocible aún puesto que Pedro había pasado al otro lado del umbral de lo invisible.

Ráfagas de viento o del gas de los tubos de escape removían la barba y sus largos cabellos apelmazados por la sangre. Enfoqué los prismáticos sobre el Boeing, sintiendo que el corazón me latía. Pero el avión estaba quedando desierto. En desordenada fila la tripulación, con el comandante a la cabeza, se apresuraba hacia el edificio central portando sus maletines oscuros con un ala fosforescente a los costados. Clavé los prismáticos en la fila de las azafatas. Leda no se hallaba entre ellas. Los maleteros acarreaban en sus furgonetas montañas de equipajes, vigilados por los taiwaneses.

Orienté una vez más los prismáticos hacia el avión. Entonces la vi, acodada en la barandilla de la plataforma, contemplando en actitud pensativa el bárbaro espectáculo que se agitaba a sus pies. El viento hacía revolar la cabellera en torno a su cabeza formándole una especie de yelmo. Su actitud de indiferente placidez me turbó y entristeció sin que supiera por qué. No parecía sufrir. Acaso estaba familiarizada desde que nació con la violencia y el terror. Aquella silueta, en lo alto, parecía saciada y tranquila, incluso satisfecha y divertida, como si para ella la medida de sus emociones estuviera definitivamente colmada. Yo contemplaba sus brazos desnudos sobre el barandal, los ojos entrecerrados y renuentes a la luz tenebrosa.

La niña, llorando, tiraba de mí y yo no podía desprenderme de la silueta leonada e inmóvil que seguramente también me veía. Se irguió suavemente y entró en la cabina. Bajé los prismáticos y con ellos cayó un tiempo que parecía no haber existido. Me pregunté, mejor dicho, una duda que venía de lejos preguntó en mí si realmente había visto y conocido a aquella muchacha alguna vez; si era posible que yo hubiese encontrado a un ser semejante.

Alcé a la niña en un brazo, con el otro cogí a la anciana del suyo, y nos dirigimos hacia el resplandeciente edificio de vidrio. Sentí que un peso intolerable me oprimía el pecho; el olor de la tierra empapada en gasolina y aceite de motores me cortaba la respiración. Jamás había respirado una atmósfera tan vil. La infección de una rapacidad imbécil lo invadía todo como emanaciones de un campo sembrado de invisibles cadáveres en un lugar donde no se había librado ninguna batalla. Era el hedor pestilencial de la corrupción victoriosa.

Me encuentro de nuevo en la ciudad sepulcral, agraviada por la presencia de los mercenarios asiáticos, semejantes a figuras espectrales, camufladas de seres humanos, armados hasta los dientes. Me siento sin embargo más extranjero que ellos.

La penumbra recubierta de perpetua luz artificial encubre innumerables y sutiles horrores. Hay enemigos, criminales de cuello y corbata, personajones de aparatosa presencia. No se ve a la gente común, a los trabajadores, a las mujeres vendedoras de frutas, de chipá, a los niños lustrabotas, a los rebeldes, a los mendigos, que existían antes. ¿Dónde están los fogosos líderes políticos, sociales, sindicales, las combativas mujeres de otro tiempo? ¿Dónde la humanidad joven, de ambos sexos, con menos de quince años, esa edad que marca la frontera entre lo viejo que debe morir y lo nuevo que debe existir, crecer y vivir? ¿Dónde está eso que llamamos pueblo, atado desde hace más de un siglo a voluntaria servidumbre?

¿Qué llegaría a suceder si a este pueblo "empayenado" por el poder se lograra arrancarlo de su abyecto embrujo? ¿No lo sufriría como una doble mutilación, como la nostalgia del gran Padre, que velaba por él y que de pronto ha desaparecido por el agujero de un anillo?

De todos modos, el espectáculo de atroz salvajismo produce cierto alivio puesto que con toda evidencia es lo único que tiene derecho a existir aquí; lo único que puede esperarse que reine en este país como la normal expresión de su monstruosidad. El resto del mundo no está en ninguna parte. No hay más que esta región aislada del mundo, sumergida en sus propios miasmas y horrores, orgullosa de ellos. Y esto no es más que un presagio visible de todo lo que está oculto detrás.

La niña se negó a entrar en el lujoso salón de recepción. Volví a alzarla en brazos, le inventé un nombre, la acaricié un poco, le dije palabras cariñosas. Apretó su pequeño rostro pecoso contra el mío y me embadurnó la cara con sus mocos. Poco a poco se tranquilizó y dejó de llorar. Una fila de nurses aguardaban con coches cunas a un costado del salón. Entregué la niña a una de estas sonrientes oficialas. Noté que el vestido de la niña estaba manchado con la sangre de mi dedo mordido por el perro. Le pedí a la nurse que le cambiaran la ropa. No se preocupe, señor, me dijo. Le presenté a la anciana como abuela de la niña. También se hizo cargo de ella. Me uní a la fila de los invitados. En ese instante recordé la historia de Purificación Capilla, víctima del vampirismo del tiranosaurio, que la mujer del director de Previsión Social había referido a su amiga en el avión. Me precipité para recuperarla pero las serviciales nodrizas del Buen Pastor de Niñas ya se habían retirado por una puerta excusada.

En las escalinatas de mármol las comisiones oficiales de recepción rendían honores a los invitados al congreso. Nos entregaron nuestras respectivas acreditaciones y las lujosas carpetas del congreso, juntamente con los números correspondientes a nuestras habitaciones. Leí en el grueso disco de plata: Habitación Nº 13, Hotel Domingo Faustino Sarmiento, lo que no dejó de sorprenderme. ¿Qué hacía aún don Domingo, en Asunción, a estas alturas, prestando su nombre al congreso patrocinado por el dictador sobre el tema de civilización y barbarie en la América Latina del siglo xx?

Mujeres ataviadas de ceñidas túnicas color escarlata, con vertiginosos peinados y los pechos cruzados por las bandas doradas de la presidencia, nos precedían y flanqueaban hacia los jardines de la rotonda de salida. A la sombra de la avenida de palmeras, que formaban con sus curvas las iniciales del dictador, para ser divisadas desde el espacio —inútil escenografía—, aguardaban varias limusinas blindadas, oscuras y relucientes, rodeadas de guardias en uniforme de húsares a la usanza del Ejército Grande. Se tocaban los altos morriones empenachados de plumas y abrían las portezuelas a los congresales.

Una sorda explosión rompió el aire, estremeció el edificio y produjo un diluvio de fragmentos de metales y cristales rotos. Giré en redondo y orienté los prismáticos hacia el campo. Vi que el Boeing volaba en pedazos. Enormes lenguas de fuego empezaron a proyectarse en todas direcciones desde los depósitos de combustible. Tomados por sorpresa, los carros de asalto y los pelotones de taiwaneses, no tardaron en reaccionar. Empezaron a disparar rabiosamente sus automáticas contra los restos en llamas del aparato. Granadas de mano, obuses de mortero y bazukas redujeron a escombros en pocos minutos lo que quedaba del avión incendiado.

Pensé en Leda Kautner convertida en una brizna de

humo entre esos escombros que iban agigantándose en una esfera ardiente. Pensé en Pedro Alvarenga, en el momento en que sonaba el alerta de la bomba. Le adiviné entrando en los gabinetes de aseo y escondiendo el artefacto en el estante de las servilletas de ñandutí y los frascos de perfumes. La bola de fuego empezó a rodar con creciente rapidez sobre la llanura de cemento propagando una combustión generalizada a los centenares de aparatos estacionados.

En la penumbra de la tarde, turbia de esa luz que no era diurna ni nocturna, la inmensa bola de fuego levantó vuelo dejando una estela de resplandor y de humo. Fue haciéndose cada vez más pequeña hasta desaparecer en el horizonte reducida al fulgor de una estrella errante. El mar de olas de fuego más altas que la torre de control se apagó y convirtió sin transición en una llanura verde y ondeante. Podían divisarse manadas de animales de todas las especies aparecidos desde el principio del mundo paciendo en la neblina primordial. Se movían nebulosos en medio del *tatachiná* del origen, entre el titilar de los pastos cubiertos de rocío, bajo el sol que comenzaba a brillar como en el primer día de la creación.

Por interminables pasillos voy andando a remolque del botones que me precede con la maleta. La habitación es suntuosa; mejor sería decir presuntuosa, inmensa, atiborrada de esa cargazón de mal gusto que es el signo distintivo de la Segunda Reconstrucción en el estilo del Tercer Reich y de la Italia de Mussolini. Arquitectura acromegálica. Hay dos lechos con baldaquinos de raso y encaje. La suite cuenta con una antecámara de recepción, tipo Vip a todo dar. Observo con suspicacia esta gigantesca ergástula de lujo, apropiada para hombres de negocios, nuevos ricos en vacaciones, traficantes de drogas y de armas y participantes de congresos culturales internacionales.

Soy uno de los huéspedes de honor del Reconstructor. Me ha costado entrar en el fastuoso hotel construido sobre la antigua casona de don Domingo Faustino Sarmiento, el patriarca civilizador que vino a morir en Asunción en la casa que le regalaron los paraguayos, en premio a su intervención en la Guerra Grande como exterminador de los últimos soldados de López, que eran niños de diez y doce años de edad. Consideré al botones con mirada retrospectiva:

—Tendrían la edad de éste... —digo para mí.

—Yo tengo catorce años —responde el *groom* sin saber a qué me estoy refiriendo.

Me informa que la casona del prócer ha sido conservada intacta, como una reliquia, en el centro del hotel, que cubre una manzana entera. Le alargo con fingida indiferencia una fuerte propina. El efebo atezado la desliza con astuta indolencia en uno de los bolsillos de su recamado uniforme púrpura y gualda. Su birrete es de color fucsia, que es al parecer el color heráldico de los servidores en este país. El irónico fruncimiento de labios quiere significarme, sin duda: "Ah... usted es de los que pagan al llegar, para no dar más después..."

Experimento una terrible fatiga. Me he sentado a observar con disimulo al muchacho, camuflado en el uniforme del botones. No me había fijado antes en él con detenimiento. Esbelto como un junco, su rostro es de una portentosa hermosura. No se le podía imaginar sino desnudo sobre un zócalo de mármol. Recordé la estatua de Antinoo, el efebo esclavo de Bitinia, que admiramos en el museo de Nápoles. No dudo que el emperador Adriano lo hubiera tomado de inmediato a su servicio como suplente o sustituto de su esclavo favorito. En sus facciones andró-

ginas se han mezclado los rasgos de Antinoo y Nefertiti.
Este lacayuelo es anterior a ellos y también posterior; ha
dado la vuelta completa al fenómeno de la hermosura humana. La piel morena luce satinada por el sol y la luna del
trópico, cuando todavía brillaban en estos parajes incul-
tos, devorados ahora por la luz leprosa de Itaipú. Me observa con cierta malicia por el rabillo del ojo. Es su arma
de seducción.

He aquí, me digo, el resplandor extremo y último
de la belleza de una raza desaparecida: el producto de esos
deslizamientos genéticos que producen los cambios pero
que también preservan la continuidad y contribuyen a la
perfección de la especie, más allá de las hecatombes y los
cataclismos, como si el espejo de la belleza humana no pudiese quebrarse jamás. Este fámulo marrullero es el descendiente de la gente más hermosa que hubo en América.
El rostro, el cuerpo vestigial de un mutante, cortan el
aliento. Es un puñado de ceniza del antiguo fuego, reen-
carnado en este ser asexuado que crece en hermosura en
medio de la corrupción. Lleno de vida, de salud, pero también de una precoz e innata depravación natural.

Está erguido ante mí, los brazos cruzados a la espalda,
como un pequeño príncipe en ropa de esclavo. Ignora su origen,
pero sabe que el universo le pertenece precisamente porque fue
despojado de él sin su consentimiento. He aquí, me digo, el heredero de los Caballero, de los Genes, de los Valdovinos, de los
Talavera, hermosos e imperecederos como semidioses, mezclados a la estirpe del Cid Campeador, de los guerreros indígenas
que llevaban en la frente la estrella de la Tierra sin Mal.

Una voz petulante y cínica como la de un viejo alcahuete interrumpe mi exaltada reflexión.

—¿Va a dormir solo aquí? —me pregunta.

—Sí, ¿por qué? —le pregunto a mi vez.

Con un movimiento de cabeza me señala los dos
amplios lechos.

—La mitad de mi cuerpo en uno, la otra mitad en otro —le digo guiñándole un ojo.

—¿No quiere usted otro cuerpo en medio? —no le entendí al pronto—. Yo le puedo conseguir, si usted quiere, una muchacha muy joven y muy linda para que le haga compañía. No se va a arrepentir.

—No quiero nada. Y menos, muchachas.

—Vea, señor, si usted quiere, yo puedo volver cuando termine mi turno —me propone con ladino gesto de complicidad.

—¿Para qué? —le pregunto adivinando ya lo que va a decirme.

—Para lo que usted quiera... —la voz adopta una entonación de rapaz callejero—. Ya que no le gustan las muchachas, a lo mejor le gusta jugar un rato conmigo. Por veinte dólares le hago todos sus gustitos. Algunos señores me pagan mucho más por unas cosquillitas. Otros, para tomarme fotos desnudo.

Me observa como buscando mi aquiescencia.

—Desnúdate —le ordeno— Voy a tomarte unas fotos.

Lo hizo en un periquete como un gimnasta habituado a contorsiones exhibicionistas. Él mismo eligió las posturas en las que "soy —dijo— más fotogénico". Le hice varias tomas del rostro, del torso de frente y de espaldas. Quiso también que le fotografiara las piernas, las nalgas y los genitales. Los señores de edad se quedan encantados. Dicen que son los más lindos del mundo. Total, la docena de fotos le sale lo mismo. Las que me ha sacado ya van en la propina que me acaba de dar. Después hablamos y le hago precio.

—Vete ya... —le ordené imperativamente.

—Dejo mi turno a las veinte horas. Vengo a traerle un whisky, o lo que sea, y me quedo. Digo..., un suponer, si usted quiere...

Lo miro estupefacto. ¿Es que todo entonces está en descomposición y ya no hay límites entre el bien y el mal, ni siquiera para estos retoños de prodigiosa perfección física de la vieja raza?

—¿Cómo te llamas? —le pregunto con tono paternal, buscando el giro comprensivo.

—Odiseo Aquino —responde sin inmutarse—. Soy hijo de don Ramón Aquino, el jefe de los garroteros.

—Mira, Odiseo —le digo tratando de desactivar sin rupturas el desparpajo de burdel del muchacho—. Yo podría ser tu padre, no puedo ser tu amante.

—Eso va por el gusto de cada uno —dijo la voz de tahúr con una sonrisa pícara, no del todo encanallada aún.

—No creo que tu padre apruebe lo que haces.

—A él le importa un pito lo que yo haga. Él no se ocupa de mí.

—Vamos a ser amigos ¿eh? Y los veinte dólares te los daré por algún otro trabajito que te pediré más adelante. Yo no soy de acá y tú me podrás ayudar a orientarme un poco con respecto a tu ciudad.

—Como guste, señor —la voz de alcahuete vuelve a ser casi infantil—. Yo vivo en la Chacarita. Allí lo van a velar esta noche al terrorista que mataron en el avión en el que venían ustedes.

—¿Dónde? —pregunto disimulando el golpe de ansiedad que me han producido sus palabras.

—En la Chacarita, en casa de su madre, cerca de mi casa. Ha sido un gran triunfo de las fuerzas de seguridad —se fue exaltando—. ¡A estos bandidos hay que quemarlos a todos!

—Te llamaré cuando necesite tus servicios.

—Me voy entonces. Cuando se le ofrezca algo, mándeme llamar nomás en la conserjería.

Le deslizo otro billete de cinco dólares. Odiseo saluda militarmente tocándose con los dedos la visera de charol y se marcha con elásticos movimientos de un puma joven.

Apenas cerró la puerta el desenvuelto botones, me dejé caer en la cama en el estado de la más extrema extenuación. ¡Ah sombra terrible de Facundo!... Voy a evocarte, para que sacudiendo el ensangrentado polvo que cubre tus cenizas, te levantes a explicarme la vida secreta y las convulsiones internas de este noble pueblo... —me encontré farfullando mentalmente el primer exámetro del libro de don Domingo Faustino Sarmiento, que nos obligaban a recitar de memoria en la escuela "República Argentina".

Sonaron tres discretos golpes en la puerta. Me levanté a abrir.

—Hola, Clovis.

—Te perdí de vista —me dijo soplando fuerte con los labios apretados—. ¡De buena nos hemos salvado! Por fracciones de segundo. El terrorista muerto había logrado obtener en el obispado de Sao Paulo una invitación de observador para el congreso. Se hizo pasar como miembro de la secta de Jesús del Gran Poder. Todo parece muy extraño. Los de la Técnica sospechan que el terrorista creía que el presidente iba a estar presente en la recepción de los invitados. La bomba que incendió el avión estaba destinada a tu tiranosaurio.

Yo estaba callado como un muerto.

—¿Cómo te sientes?

—Mortalmente cansado.

—Te vi escribir todo el tiempo durante el viaje.

—Sí, cuando nada se puede hacer se escribe.

—Una carta de amor a tu Jimena, ¿no?

—¿Podrás alcanzársela a tu regreso?

—Hombre, claro. Regreso a París apenas terminen los actos de inauguración.

—¿Cuándo nos recibe el Gran Hombre?

—No se sabe nada aún. Probablemente al cierre del congreso, o en cualquier momento. Sabes que tu dictador es afecto a los sorpresivos golpes de efecto —bajó mucho la voz—. Parece que estás enfermizamente ansioso por dar un apretón de manos a tu tiranosaurio. Querrán dejar que se calme un poco la terrible impresión de la llegada. Los invitados están aterrorizados. Muchos han manifestado su deseo de regresar de inmediato. Las autoridades están tratando de presentar el accidente como un acto de legítima defensa contra el terrorismo internacional.

Clovis no ha perdido su equilibrio ni su buen humor. Siente que está viviendo una aventura de las más extravagantes, en un medio muy extraño. ¡Muy extraño!, ha repetido. A mí, en cambio, me nota muy deprimido y trata de alentarme con sus ocurrencias.

—Supongo que querrás seguir escribiéndole a Jimena —me tiende su estilográfica "que escribe por espejo en oscuro"—. Te la presto. Así no tendrás necesidad de encender la luz.

La cojo sin poder reprimir cierto instintivo impulso de repulsión. Es una gruesa lapicera negra, a pilas, pero increíblemente liviana. No temas, me dice, tomándola de nuevo. Está hecha con la raíz del *amorphophallus*, una especie de planta milenaria, ya extinta, de la antigua Indochina. Es un recuerdo de la guerra de Camboya, el símbolo de la planta sagrada en forma de pez. Ves estas capas superpuestas en forma de escamas de rodaballo, el pez de las profundidades. El mango de la pluma está estriado de venas que parecen dilatarse y contraerse bajo la presión de la mano. Clovis hace girar la pluma entre sus dedos largos y finos. El artefacto es vivo y activo, comenta con entusiasmo. ¿No parece acaso el trabajado miembro de un negro de buena alzada? Sospecho que el taxidermista de Pnom Penh que armó la pluma, no me confesó toda la verdad. Lo bueno es que sea eficaz.

Apaga la luz y me hace una demostración en la os-

curidad. La pluma brilla con el destello azulenco del fósforo. Fíjate, dice Clovis, escribe con tinta simpática. Los trazos duran un instante y se secan sin dejar huellas. Es lo más a propósito para escribir cartas de amor a la esposa lejana... o documentos *top secret*. Enciende la luz y me entrega la pluma. Haz buen uso de ella. Recuerdo que la primera frase que escribí con ella fue la frase de mi maestro Marcel Schwob: "La gente de aquel lejano país dio al día el nombre de tortura y a la noche el nombre de éxtasis..." ¿No parece una descripción de tu propio país? Te dejo. Debo ir a mi embajada.

Salió Clovis. Volví a apagar la luz. Tomé los prismáticos y descorriendo un poco el cortinado me puse a observar el movimiento de la calle. Los vidrios opacos por fuera me permiten ver sin ser visto. Pasan mujeres que parecen tocadas con el velo musulmán. No veo niños en este país de ancianos, sobre el que ha caído el peso de la decrepitud colectiva. Acaso los niños también están atacados de senilidad precoz y se confunden con los adultos provectos. Caminan pegados a la pared como esquivando los riesgos de la calzada donde ruedan autobuses imperiales de tres pisos, abarrotados de pasajeros. Motos y automóviles de lujo pasan como exhalaciones.

Los peatones, de los que no alcanzo a ver los rostros, caminan encorvados, las cabezas gachas, mirando obstinadamente las cerámicas vitrificadas de las aceras. Alguno que otro, al alzar la vista hacia la cúpula del hotel (que es en realidad un gigantesco reloj cuya esfera luminosa refleja la efigie del Reconstructor), deja entrever un rostro impersonal, sin vida, inexpresivo. Un transeúnte aprieta el paso arrastrando una cuerda. El collar va detrás del hombre a la altura de un perro. El aro se detiene y se acerca a la pared. El hombre pega dos o tres tirones a la cuerda, inútilmente. No tiene más remedio que esperar. Un largo chorro amarillo se proyecta contra el zócalo de mármol negro del edificio. Leo en el letrero: "Cambios Guaraní". Sólo cuando el chorro termina, el aro se deja arrastrar de nuevo con evidente mala voluntad. El dueño del perro pierde la paciencia. Arrolla la cuerda con el aro y los mete en su maletín. Se aleja rápidamente con el cuerpo muy inclinado por el peso. Dejo caer los prismáticos. La calle se queda desierta, borrosa. Me acuerdo de aquella frase de las Fábulas de Stevenson: "El viento sopló con tal fuerza que le arrancó la mano de la cara y no había nada ahí..." Detrás de esas manos, de esas siluetas, no hay nadie... no hay nada...

Me confronto con estas sombras del pasado y me descubro repentinamente más envejecido que ellos, despojado de ese tiempo al parecer sin límites que me sobraba en el exilio. Yo que perdí en el extranjero mi lengua, mi aspecto físico y mi modo de ser, no me reconozco en esta gente. No reconozco la ciudad que me fue muy amada en la juventud. Mi vida que gustó aquí del sol y de la luna, se parece a algo que no ha sucedido. Asunción también ha cambiado mucho. Las ciudades donde han ocurrido muchas calamidades son recelosas. Ésta es astuta y desconfiada con los intrusos y advenedizos; sobre todo, con los transgresores de lo prohibido.

Estoy tratando de no ceder a esos pequeños tics de comportamiento, propios de una comunidad gregaria deformada, degradada, en su vieja forma de ser. Ellos forman una especie de atávico mimetismo que ya no domino o que ya no me domina. Igual cosa me ocurre con los giros expresivos de la lengua natal, pero sobre todo con el horrendo dialecto *yopará* derivado de ella, que parece el habla idiota de la senilidad colectiva, el *ñe'ë tavy* del débil mental, de una sociedad enferma, atacada masivamente por el síndrome de Alzheimer. Éste demostró que la demencia senil colectiva (un fenómeno de inmunodeficiencia nerviosa, parienta del Sida) se debe a la degeneración de ciertos sistemas neurotransmisores. La presión de factores represivos del ambiente físico y psico-social bloquean e inhiben los mecanismos de reacción y de defensa del sistema nervioso. Deja de fun-

cionar la sinapsis neuronal, que descubrió el aragonés Ramón y Cajal. El elemento patológico desencadenante del síndrome es la acetilcolina (llamada toxina de la angustia y del miedo), capaz de generar una especie muy extraña de cáncer de los nervios. Su síntoma principal son los delirios colectivos. ¿No es esto lo que está pasando aquí?

Por ahora no cuentan para mí sino el presente y lo desconocido. Dicen que donde lo desconocido existe, también existe la promesa. No creo en ella, salvo en lo que uno es capaz de hacer por sí mismo. No hay día seguro para ninguno. Tal vez con un poco de maña y haciendo de la necesidad virtud, se puedan eludir los azares del día siguiente. Sólo que para mí el "día siguiente" es un solo día fijo y firme, que aún me está negado saber cuándo va a cumplirse. Hasta ese preciso instante debo concentrar todo mi pensamiento y mi voluntad, en la más extrema austeridad. Me está vedado el más inocente de los placeres permitidos. Debo negar mi propia animalidad de hombre, no ser más que la mitad de un hombre a punto de convertirse en un ser humano definitivo y pleno. Siempre me ha costado ser tolerante con los que se desprecian, pierden su autoestima, se niegan o se esconden de sí mismos. Me toca ahora ser todo esto. Te pido que seas tú tolerante con esta forzosa e inevitable humillación mía de despreciarme, de negarme y ocultarme.

Te estoy escribiendo a oscuras con la pluma de Clovis. Hay apenas un rectángulo de luz acuosa, pálida, insidiosa, bajo la cama. No sé de dónde vendrá ese rayo soñoliento. Quizás se filtre por la ventana, aunque yo la he cerrado herméticamente. O tal vez está siempre ahí, echado tenuemente sobre la alfombra, como la sombra de un perro electrónico que me espía desde debajo del lecho. Debe ser el reflejo de algún monitor oculto. No he podido descubrirlo. Te escribo, viendo apenas lo que escribo. Espero que la pluma de Clovis evite los monitores ocultos de detección. En desquite tengo la sensación de estar conversando contigo. En lo oscuro siento o imagino la fuerza de tu mano en la mía.

Dejaré de escribirte por un rato. Me ahogo en esta habitación semejante a una inmensa campana neumática. Saldré a visitar la casona que fue del prócer, embutida en las entrañas del inmenso hotel que lleva su nombre. Sabía que la casona ha sido convertida en escuela. A la sombra de los jazmineros en flor, en medio del denso aroma, percibí los efluvios muy fuertes de dos animales en celo, como el producido por la cópula de dos gatos. Oí sus alaridos de salvaje paroxismo como los vagidos de dos bebés que están siendo degollados. Iba a huir. En un recodo tropecé con los cuerpos de una pareja de camarero y camarera, ocupados en un fornido y desmelenado fornicio. El tufo sexual era casi palpable, repugnante. En confianza, sin querer interrumpir sus jadeantes gemidos, tapándome la nariz, me agaché sobre la bestia de dos espaldas y pregunté dónde quedaba la casa de Sarmiento. Tendió el muchacho un brazo malhumorado y húmedo como sacudiéndose un insecto y salpicándome con gruesas gotas de esperma.

Estaba en el zaguán de la casa patriarcal y no me había dado cuenta. Solamente pude verla por fuera. De noche está cerrada como una tumba. Por las mañanas, hacia el final del curso escolar, asisten a ella como premio, los mejores alumnos, niños y niñas, de las escuelas de la capital. Muchos de estos alumnos, sobre todo las niñas, las más agraciadas, comienzan aquí su carrera de hostelería como camareras, recepcionistas, "nínfulas" de compañía para los señores aburridos y abotagados por el calor. De esta escuela sarmientina han salido ya dos Miss Mundo y varias

misses del Paraguay. Los concursos de belleza constituyen el *chu-chu* del dictador, a quien corresponde de hecho y por derecho la presidencia de honor del jurado desde hace cuarenta años.

Mi abuelo Ezequiel Gaspar conoció al gran sanjuanino aporteñado. Y hasta llegó a ser su amigo. Le llevaba a su estancia de San Ignacio y le hacía visitar las ruinas jesuíticas que el prócer admiraba mucho. Una noche, contaba mi abuelo, el viejo masón se quedó a dormir en las ruinas de Trinidad con la india más bonita de la estancia que yo mismo se la elegí. Amarraron con lazos dos hamacas a los fustes de las columnas y allí se durmieron a la luz de las estrellas. Regresaron al día siguiente a medio día.

—¡Qué tal! ¿Cómo lo pasaron? —pregunté al prócer con respeto, más bien por cortesía, viendo resplandecer de felicidad su ancha cara.

De lo mejor —respondió el brioso anciano, muy jarifo todavía a su edad—. Me hubiera gustado ser Padre Provincial en tiempo de las Misiones y vivir en esa Ciudad de Dios.

"¡Era un putañero bárbaro!...—solía decir mi abuelo—. No podía ver una mujer joven sin que le temblaran las inmensas papadas y se le cortara el aliento. Sufría de asma erótica. Comenzaba entonces a desvariar y a contar sus hazañas amorosas, muy exageradas, para tapar los agujeros del presente considerando que todo tiempo pasado fue mejor."

Es cierto que no se podían tomar en serio todas las anécdotas de Ezequiel Gaspar, que era suelto de lengua y adobaba sus chismes con la sal del diablo sin ningún temor de Dios ni de los Santos Evangelios.

Para la inauguración de la casa don Domingo invitó a su amiga y "ninfa egeria" Mary Mann, la cuñada de Nathaniel Hawthorne, y a varios amigos norteamericanos de alto copete, escritores, financistas, empresarios, con los que trabó relación durante el tiempo en que fue embajador de la Argentina en los Estados Unidos y luego como presidente de la nación. La inauguración se convirtió durante tres días en una verdadera fiesta nacional con bandas de músicos, galopas populares y fuegos de artificio.

La horrible "yanky", según mi abuelo, echaba pestes contra el Paraguay y trató de convencer a Sarmiento de que se fuera a vivir a los Estados Unidos. Mary Mann regresó en seguida, asqueada de la horda de mujeres descalzas "en este país de ilotas salvajes que bien merecía ser raído de la faz de la tierra".

Don Domingo se sentía como un pez en el agua y nadie lo iba a sacar de su glorioso retiro asunceño. Le encantaban los cenáculos y la jocunda fiesta de la charla entre amigos, arte en el que descollaba como un conversador sin parangón. Celebraba en su casa, los sábados, tertulias que eran muy lucidas y concurridas. Presidentes de la República, senadores, diputados, políticos de alto bordo, ricachones y estancieros patricios con sus mujeres o sus barraganas, intelectuales y artistas se reunían en torno al carismático anfitrión que tenía embobados a todos con su humor y su inagotable facundia. "¡Oh el rito eleusino de las tertulias!", solía repetir admirativamente don Domingo Faustino. Oficiaba en ellas como un gurú extrovertido y bonachón.

El fino intelectual, escritor y político, don Manuel Gondra, presidente por un mes y unos días —el único que osó criticar en América la poesía de Rubén Darío en un ensayo admirable—, puso una noche en aprietos a don Domingo Faustino.

—Vea, Excelencia —le dijo—. Quiero hacerle una pregunta, perdóneme el atrevimiento.

—Pregunte no más, Excelencia —le respondió el cuitado con guasa—. Las preguntas son lo único interesante que hay en el mundo de las ideas.

—¿De dónde extrajo Vuecencia esa frase *No se fusilan ni degüellan las ideas*, esculpida en el frontispicio de su casa?

—Si leyó Vuecencia mi libro *Civilización y barbarie*, habrá notado que están indicadas en él las fuentes de esa cita: los grandes republicanos Fortoul y Volney, ellos también sólidos y honestos masones como yo.

—Pues yo leí esa tajante frase en un texto de Diderot, publicado en la *Revue Encyclopédique* —dijo el erudito don Manuel con manso talante—. Luego la leí como suya en un artículo de su diario *El Progreso*. Tenía esta duda...

—Sáquesela de la mente, mi querido Presidente Gondra —le interrumpió don Domingo; su voz de bajo profundo y sus carcajadas estrepitosas resonaron en el salón—. ¿Quién ha dicho algo por primera vez en este mundo? Repetimos lo que ya otros dijeron. Todo ha sido visto, leído, sabido. No hacemos más que ensayar tímidas variantes. Con lo que la literatura está llamada a desaparecer. ¿No lo cree así, Su Excelencia?

Don Manuel Gondra inclinó su cabeza en señal de cortés acatamiento. Su fina y bien recortada barba finisecular tocó la blanca pechera almidonada de su camisa en la que brillaban tres solitarios botones de oro.

—La literatura podrá tal vez desaparecer —agregó don Domingo *ex cathedra* dirigiéndose el concurso—. Mas siempre será verde el árbol verde de la vida, como acaba de decir Rubén Darío, el gran poeta asirio de Nicaragua, que en realidad se llama Félix Rubén García Sarmiento y que hasta es medio pariente mío, si el gran poeta me permite este honor.

Don Domingo Faustino estaba orgulloso de contarse entre los eminentes extranjeros que el Paraguay tuvo el honor de acoger. Desde Bonpland hasta él mismo, pasando por Artigas, los hermanos Robertson, los médicos suizos Rengger y Longchamp, el famoso traductor de *Las mil y una noches*, Sir Francis Richard Burton. Los nombraba a todos con la familiaridad de trato entre viejos conocidos.

—El noble conde y gran pianista polaco Erwin
Brinnicky es para mí el paradigma de los desterrados voluntarios —dijo don Domingo con sincera admiración
mirando como en éxtasis a su hija, la condesa Malwida—.
Dio su vida por el Paraguay.

Le faltó enumerar —don Domingo carecía del don
de profecía— al general Juan Domingo Perón, al sanguinario dictador Somoza, que los terroristas hicieron volar
de un bazucazo cuando regresaba a su residencia. Le faltó enumerar a otros generales y dictadores, dados de baja
transitoriamente, que también se acogerían al asilo de la
tierra purpúrea. Le faltó enumerar a figuras consulares del
nazismo, los Martin Bormann, los Klaus Barbie, el será-
fico Dr. Mengele, llamado el Ángel de la Muerte, médico
personal del tiranosaurio, y a otros nómadas ilustres, de
cuyos nombres en este momento no quiero acordarme.
Enjaulados los llevaron del Paraguay para ser juzgados
por sus crímenes. No solamente los criminales de guerra
del nazismo. También los héroes de la Guerra Grande
fueron llevados prisioneros en jaulas de troncos a Río de
Janeiro. Pensé en Ezra Pound transportado en jaula de
hierro al país que él había repudiado y que lo había repudiado a él. Curioso destino el de estos arcángeles caídos.
Surcan enjaulados los cielos del planeta buscando a sus
fiscales y verdugos.

Mi abuelo Ezequiel Gaspar, a quien debo estas re-
miniscencias (no he tenido más que verificar las fechas, la
ortografía de los nombres propios y agregar algunos), era
desde luego uno de los asiduos parroquianos de las tertulias sarmientinas. El taciturno fiscal del Estado, José Segundo Decoud siempre vestido de luto, pálida y
transparente figura de cristal herido, solía aparecer a veces,
antes de que *Chico Diavo*, el matador de Solano López,
violara y aceptara casarse con su única hija Cordelia. Hablaba apenas el doctor José Segundo Decoud. "Es un

hombre probo que se halla siempre en el fiel de la balanza", solía alabarlo el anfitrión. Don José Segundo se retiraba en seguida sin ser notado dejando un halo de tristeza y elegancia casi espectral en la abigarrada parroquia.

Mi abuelo conocía al dedillo la historia de los Decoud y sentía por ellos gran admiración y amistad. Negaba indignado, por ejemplo, la afirmación que el publicista inglés Cunninghame Graham hace en su libro *Un tirano del Paraguay*. En ese libelo infame y mentiroso —decía mi abuelo— Cunninghame (su pronunciación inglesa era desdichada) atribuye al padre de los Decoud el fraude de un millón de dólares al presidente don Carlos Antonio López, padre de Solano. En aquellos tiempos, el viejo López no disponía de tanto dinero.

—¡Puras calumnias! —exclamaba Ezequiel Gaspar—. ¡Una familia desgraciada la de los Decoud, pero digna y esclarecida! Yo los conocí muy de cerca. Un hijo del primer Decoud, novio de la hermosa Carmelita Recalde, también pretendida por Francisco Solano, fue asesinado en una emboscada nocturna. La cabeza degollada del joven Decoud amaneció en la puerta de la casa de Carmelita. Ésta enloqueció y murió. ¡Aquí no se degüellan las ideas, aquí se degüella a los hombres y a las mujeres, a la vista de todo el mundo... ¡qué carajo! ¡Y todos tan tranquilos!... —bufaba Ezequiel Gaspar. Nadie le hacía caso. Es la ventaja de los simples.

La condesa Malwida Brinnicky-Niëtzsky venía desde su castillo de San Bernardino, construido sobre un acantilado del lago azul de Ypacaraí. Don Domingo la hacía traer y llevar de regreso a su castillo en el landó en el que él mismo salía a pasear por las afueras de la ciudad en los atardeceres primaverales. La castellana de San Bernardino iba y venía en el landó como una reina, custodiada por diez macizos palafraneros vestidos de azul. "Mis esclavos liberales", los llamaba don Domingo. Marchaban en fila detrás del landó en sus caballos enjaezados como para un torneo, responsables de la seguridad de la condesa. La figulina anciana y pequeña, pero bellísima y preciosa aún como un bibelot, subía sonriente al landó sin ayuda y se despedía en lo oscuro, inmaterial y luminosa, como si arrojara con sus manos puñados de luciérnagas.

La condesa era hija del pianista polaco, el conde Erwin Brinnicky, el gran héroe cultural de la Guerra Grande, a quien no se le han rendido aún los honores que ese extranjero ilustre merece. El conde, pianista de fama mundial, huyó de todo ruido y vanagloria y prefirió desterrarse en el Paraguay, a mediados del siglo pasado. Diez años más tarde, tras la guerra y la derrota, acompañó en el éxodo a Madama Lynch hasta Cerro-Corá con el piano de Chopin. Era la figura central de su séquito en aquella peregrinación de la retirada que se dirigía hacia alguna parte fuera de este mundo.

La emperatriz en desgracia cabalgaba en seguimiento de su amado marido concubinario, del indómito jefe de un pueblo, del derrotado más testarudo de la tierra. No podía abandonarle a él, que era la mitad de su vida. No podía separarse del instrumento, que era la mitad de la vida de los sobrevivientes en el éxodo sepulcral. No podía separarse de sus cofres en los que iba encerrado, intacto y entero, el tesoro del país devastado, saqueado a sangre y fuego; ese tesoro que debía ser restituido a las arcas del Estado cuando éste recobrara su soberanía tras el holocausto inmisericorde.

El conde Brinnicky la seguía con el piano. En la fragosa travesía por selvas, cordilleras, ríos y desiertos, el transporte del piano resultaba a veces más difícil y producía más víctimas que el paso de los cañones de grueso calibre, de las vituallas y sobre todo de los centenares de cofres con el tesoro. Éstos, al menos, iban siendo enterrados en lugares inaccesibles a lo largo de la espantosa marcha. Durante las lluvias, el piano era envuelto con las telas en-

gomadas de las tiendas de campaña. Pero, a veces, huía como una embarcación rebelde flotando sobre el desborde de las inundaciones. Tenían que rescatarlo, a costa de muchos ahogados. El ingeniero inglés Thompson era el afinador oficial del piano. Cuando éste desertó y se llevó parte del tesoro, entregándose a los aliados, el conde se dio maña para afinar él mismo el instrumento, a veces en mitad de una ejecución.

Mi padre poseía el oído absoluto, decía la condesa con tímido orgullo acariciando el camafeo de sardónice sobre el cual estaba labrado en relieve el busto del conde cuyo rostro aparecía brumoso entre las vetas oscuras del ágata.

Mientras el conde viviera, el piano debía seguir. Y siguió hasta el fin. En determinadas situaciones ciertos objetos parecen dotados de virtudes inauditas, de una naturaleza casi sobrenatural. El piano, subía montado a los aires por maromas y aparejos de varia invención. Se deslizaba en los acantilados sobre puentes colgantes, entre cañones, cajas de proyectiles, grandes atados de bastimentos y el santo grial de los cofres. El gran pájaro color ámbar planeaba, volaba, se posaba en los nuevos campamentos, sin más alas que las que llevaba en sus cuerdas. En cada una de las estaciones del interminable via crucis, las manos del conde, discípulo y amigo de Chopin, desataba esas alas inmateriales. La música fluía como un misterio de la naturaleza. Las sonatas románticas sonaban ahora en los aduares del mariscal y la emperatriz como himnos de guerra.

El anfitrión eludía astutamente estos temas de la Guerra Grande, pero estimulaba a la anciana y diminuta condesa, a relatar sus remembranzas y a tocar el piano. Lo hacía maravillosamente bien. El genio del virtuoso de su padre había renacido en ella. Sólo que debían ponerle un sillón muy alto de modo que sus brazos quedaran al nivel del teclado. Mientras tocaba, su figura bien modelada y juvenil semejaba a la de una niña de quince años.

Malwida se acordaba de cuando llegó, muy pequeña, a la ciudad de San Bernardino, fundada por pastores lu-
teranos y por gente de la nobleza alemana. Eran los tiempos
de la búsqueda del tesoro de Madama Lynch en el lago de
Ypacaraí. Pronunciaba muy mal el nombre guaranítico del
lago sagrado, pero contaba maravillosamente, como si estuviese relatando un sueño, esas noches de los fuegos flotantes
sobre el lago. Los buscadores del tesoro traían y deposita-
ban sobre el agua montones de paja seca y les prendían fuego
para que les sirvieran de luminarias.

Como en una escena mágica la niña polaca contemplaba a los hombres desnudos en medio de islotes de fuego
sondeando febrilmente las aguas. Lo único que lograban
sacar del lecho profundo y barroso eran grandes moles de
hierro, tornos, calderas, cañones, hundidos por el ejército
paraguayo en la retirada de Caacupé y Piribebuy. A veces
los grupos rivales se enfrentaban en choques sangrientos por
la posesión del inexistente tesoro. Por la mañana Malwida,
ayudándose con los binóculos de teatro de su padre, veía
flotar entre grandes manchas de sangre centenares de cadáveres. Eran los últimos combates de la Guerra Grande veinte
años después de que ella hubiese terminado, comentaba la
condesa con ironía y pesadumbre. ¡Combates enloquecidos
por el oro de Madama, que no aparecía por ninguna parte!

—Ah sí... —comentaba don Domingo Faustino—.
Toda empresa humana, la más altruista como la más cruel,
tiene como clave la búsqueda de un tesoro. Sin esta clave
misteriosa no hubiera existido la tentación de la utopía, no
se hubieran construido los imperios, no hubieran surgido
las religiones ni el gran arte de todos los tiempos. La historia
misma de la humanidad habría sido chata y aburrida a más
no poder. Lo que ocurre es que a veces ciertos grandes hombres, artistas, guerreros, apóstoles de la fe, gobernantes preclaros,
mueren y se llevan a la tumba el resplandor de El Dorado que
moraba dentro de ellos mismos sin que lo supieran...

Un conato de aplauso se insinuó en alguna parte.

—¡Silencio... carajo!... ¡No estamos en una galle-
ra!...—retumbó, incontenible, el rugido de cólera de don
Domingo Faustino, fulminando con miradas de fuego a la
grey zafia e ignorante que inundaba el salón.

En el silencio absoluto que se produjo hasta los cí-
nifes parecían zumbar en humillada sordina. En los altos
sillones, las damas en patas hamacaban los pies, los dedos
cuajados de sortijas, incrustadas de crisólitos.

—Caramba —dijo conciliador don Domingo—. Veo
volar lámpiros sobre los pies de carmelitas descalzas de las
damas...

Todos celebraron con risas descocadas la ocurren-
cia del anfitrión, sin entenderla en lo más mínimo.

—¡Este don Domingo, por Dios, siempre tan gracioso y querendón!... ¡Compararnos con las Carmelitas,
por Dios!..—se congració una de las damas palmípedas
haciendo coruscar en los reflejos de los candelabros los
pedestres anillos.

En un remate de fina ironía, pero cruel para ella
misma, Malwida Brinnicky-Niëtztky relató la historia del
piano de Chopin que la Lynch mandó comprar en un remate de Sotheby's. Mi padre viajó a Londres para inspec-
cionar el instrumento. Él sostenía —dijo Malwida con voz
aniñada— que el tal piano no era de Chopin. Se trataba de
un timo urdido por el rapaz encargado de negocios en París, Cándido Bareiro. De todos modos, dijo mi padre, el
piano tiene buen sonido. Sin decir nada a Madama Lynch,
para no desencantarla, trajo el instrumento a Asunción. No
sospechaba mi buen padre, ni remotamente, el destino que
le esperaba. Así, el falso piano de Chopin era verdadero
para Madame Lynch y resultó ser fantástico para los habitantes de la región, sobrevivientes de la guerra, que jamás
habían visto un piano ni sabían lo que era el extraño instrumento abandonado en el anfiteatro de Cerro-Corá.

Muchos años después me contaron que los indios del Amambay transportaron el piano a la cumbre de su cerro sagrado y lo convirtieron en objeto de culto de sus ceremonias rituales.

—¡Ah Paraguay... mi Polonia sudamericana!... — murmuró la condesa en un gran clamor de su espíritu; se la escuchó claramente en el silencio que reinaba emotivamente en la reunión. Las cintas oscuras del camafeo que ceñían el cuello de alabastro se habían puesto muy tensas. Se veían palpitar bajo ellas las venas azules con rápidos latidos.

Bajó suavemente la tapa del piano y apoyó sobre ella la cabeza como si hubiera caído en un desmayo o en una profunda y dolorosa meditación. Tras algunos instantes la condesa se repuso, se secó los ojos húmedos con un pañuelo de encajes y atacó su Polonesa preferida con increíble energía hasta el final. Las cintas tirantes del camafeo hicieron saltar el broche y la efigie del conde rodó sobre la alfombra con oscuros destellos. Don Domingo se acercó, recogió el glíptico como si se tratara de una reliquia sagrada, y se la alcanzó a la condesa. Ésta dio un tenue beso a la efigie y se ciñó de nuevo el camafeo a la garganta.

Más nítidos y reales eran los recuerdos de Malwida sobre Elisabeth Foster-Nietzsche, la hermana del autor de *Zarathustra*, llegada a San Bernardino en 1886. "Durante cinco años, en mi casa, decía Malwida con su voz trémula y cascada, Elisabeth sufría verdaderos ataques de furia sobre los manuscritos de su hermano en los que éste injuriaba a su madre y a su hermana. Como una poseída, Elisabeth se ponía durante horas a corregir, tachar, falsificar y hasta a arrancar páginas de los manuscritos.

La condesa recordaba que Elisabeth Foster-Nietzsche trajo los borradores de *Ecce Homo*, que se convertiría en una de las obras póstumas de Friedrich Wilhelm. Contó que el padre Fidel Maíz, que la solía visitar en su castillo de San Bernardino, leyó ese manuscrito. El sacerdote, ex fiscal de

los tribunales de sangre, fue el promotor de la idea de exaltar a Solano López como el Cristo Paraguayo. El vaticinio se cumplió con su crucifixión en Cerro-Corá por los brasileros. La condesa contaba que el padre Maíz había exclamado: "El gran filósofo alemán comprendió y retrató muy bien en su autobiografía a Solano López, sin conocerle... Sólo podía hacerlo un hombre que se llamó a sí mismo el Crucificado..."

En otra de las tertulias, retomando los hilos sueltos del tejido que ella devanaba como un relato fantástico sin principio ni fin, la condesa contó que Maíz se había ido arrebatando en una idea que le martirizaba. "¡El Superhombre! —dijo—. ¡El *homo viator*... el hombre del vía crucis que se asume como un destino...! ¡El suicidio de Dios en el Gólgota!... El señor Nietzsche entendió muy bien lo que ocurrió en el Paraguay, que él no conocía. Adivinó el impulso místico y patriótico que me llevó a mí, pobre sacerdote de un país en ruinas, de una Iglesia en ruinas, a proclamar a Solano López, entre lo temporal y lo eterno, el Cristo Paraguayo... Cristo, Dios y Hombre verdaderos, es único. Pero el Cristo humano se reproduce en todos los hombres que se sacrifican por la redención de sus pueblos. Solano fue el Cristo Paraguayo sacrificado en Cerro-Corá...".

La condesa escribió a Lou Andréas von Salomé la última enamorada de Nietzsche. Malwida no conocía a Lou y ésta, en un principio, la confundió con Malwida von Meysenburg. Pero de este inicial enredo iba a surgir una amistad entrañable entre ambas. La condesa, a la sazón en la flor de la edad y de su inteligencia, viajó a Europa. Le preocupaba mucho la suerte de los manuscritos de Nietzsche. Visitó a Lou Andréas Salomé, y le refirió lo que ocurría en San Bernardino, rogándole que interviniera para impedir el afrentoso robo que le estaban haciendo a un genio su propia madre y su hermana. Lou le enseñó el epistolario que había mantenido con Friedrich Wilhem, y le contó confidencialmente los motivos de su ruptura con éste a raíz de la violenta querella que surgió entre Nietzsche y Wagner.

En Triebschen, junto al lago de los Cuatro Cantones, el matrimonio Wagner había acogido con cordialidad y afecto al inestable Friedrich Wilhem. Pero éste quedó perdidamente enamorado de Cósima Listz, hija de Franz Listz y esposa de Richard Wagner. Era otro de sus frecuentes *coups de foudre*. Pronto estalló el conflicto dado el tremendo carácter de los dos protagonistas masculinos. No se debe olvidar, dijo Lou a Malwida, que Nietzsche y Wagner dieron vida entre los dos, en las ideas y en la música, al mito del Superhombre tras la muerte de Dios.

Richard echó en cara su deslealtad a Friedrich Wilhem. Éste se defendía afirmando que sus sentimientos hacia Cósima eran de la más pura admiración y amistad. Pero el amor platónico más sublimado deja de serlo cuando la amada es la mujer de un amigo también admirado y respetado y cuando éste pasa a ser el más abominado enemigo. La filosofía "práctica" de Nietzsche —él mismo lo escribió en uno de sus libros— radicaba en el axioma de que cuando no encontraba lo que necesitaba, debía procurárselo de cualquier modo, aunque fuera artificialmente, por falsificación o invención, aun a costa del dolor de los demás. Así inventó el sofisma de los "espíritus libres". Quiso hacer de Cósima un "espíritu libre"; es decir, quiso separarla de Richard Wagner y esclavizarla bajo su poderosa voluntad como su amante platónica.

Friedrich Wilhem intentó un último artero golpe. Bajo el seudónimo de Dionysos —el viejo dios helénico del que él se había convertido en profeta— envió un delirante mensaje a Cósima. El texto del furtivo billete decía: "¡Ariadna, te amo!..." Cósima y Richard lo mandaron al diablo. Friedrich Wilhelm empezó a atacar furiosamente a Wagner. Éste pasó de héroe a traidor en la mitología de

Nietzsche, fervoroso de Dyonisos, cuando el compositor de los Nibelungos se declara por Apolo, y empieza a concebir su música inspirado en el humanismo y en la moral del cristianismo, basados en la idea de la compasión. "¡Tú también un vencido!..." es la última injuria que Nietzsche arroja a Wagner por encima de su amor a Cósima-Ariadna. Continúa amándola desesperadamente, pero ya no puede llegar hasta ella. El hilo del laberinto se partió en mil pedazos. Friedrich Wilhelm cayó en una atormentada crisis. El colapso mental no tardó en hundir esa mente genial, la más alta del siglo, en la noche definitiva de la locura. La muerte de Dios, preconizada por Nietzsche, no era otra cosa sino la muerte del hombre, víctima de sus propias furias.

—Mi querida Malwida —le dijo Lou apretándola en un fuerte abrazo que la remontó en el aire—. Nada puedo hacer en esta guerra de fantasmas...

Lou Andréas Salomé, la amante platónica pero carnalmente incandescente de tantos hombres célebres, estaba allí hermosa, alta, deslumbrante. La pequeña y generosa Malwida la contempló como la imagen misma de Eros, incorpórea, etérea, intemporal. "En una mujer de temple el sexo alcanza la espiritualidad suma que le está negada al hombre cazador...", escribió Malwida en su *Journal intime*.

Malwida logró convencer a Lou de que visitara el Paraguay. Logró traerla a su castillo de San Bernardino. Visitaron las zonas rurales. Llegaban a los ranchos más pobres donde eran recibidas con la generosidad de la miseria absoluta. Lou quedó embrujada por el magnetismo vital de la tierra, de esas mujeres sin rostros y descalzas, cubiertas por oscuro y rotoso manto, pero cuyos pies eran su verdadera fisonomía arrastrándose a flor de tierra y mostrando lo que eran ellas de pies a cabeza.

—Aquí, en el Paraguay —le había dicho Malwida— las mujeres reconstruyen sin cesar lo que los hombres destruyen...

Malwida y Lou fueron recibidas en palacio por el general Bernardino Caballero, héroe de la guerra, a la sazón presidente de la República. Le expusieron la dramática situación de los manuscritos y le pidieron su mediación. Don Bernardino no había leído jamás un libro, no tenía la menor idea de quién era ese genio alemán de quien las dos mujeres le hablaban con unción casi religiosa. El general Caballero no era un héroe culto. Era algo mucho mejor: era un héroe humano, generoso y carismático. Mandó que la justicia interviniese de inmediato. Foster nada pudo hacer en defensa de los supuestos derechos legales de su mujer sobre la obra inédita. Elisabeth fue obligada a entregar los manuscritos a un juez. Éste los devolvió al Tribunal de Weimar, ciudad en la que se encontraba Nietzsche, paralítico, y donde poco después había de morir. Así se salvaron los manuscritos de *Ecce Homo* en Paraguay, el país de las causas perdidas.

"No puedo olvidar a tus mujeres paraguayas cubiertas con ese manto parecido al *tchador* de las mujeres persas —escribió Lou a Malwida, a su regreso—. No vi de ellas sino los pies descalzos, pero esos pies son su verdadero rostro. En esos pies vive y anda la historia de un país. Esas mujeres son como Janos de pies bifrontes. Dan un paso hacia el futuro, otro hacia el pasado, en un presente inmóvil para ellas."

(Estoy tratando de transcribir de memoria las palabras de Lou Andréas Salomé y de Malwida Brinnicky-Niëtzsky. Sé que te emocionarán. Desde ángulos tan diferentes, las vivencias de estas dos personas de la alta y rancia cultura europea coinciden en cierto modo con las tuyas cuando estuviste en Paraguay, viviste con las mujeres del pueblo y aquella anciana del Guairá te enseñó a dormir despierta...)

"Tu *chateau* sobre el lago sagrado de los indios es hermoso —decía la carta de Lou a Malwida, en otro párrafo—. Tiene cierto parecido con el castillo de Duino donde mi pobre Rainer María escribió sus famosas Elegías." "No podré olvidar tampoco —concluía la carta— la figura del legendario presidente Bernardino Caballero, a quien me presentaste en ese palacio mudéjar que parece surgido de la fantasía de un creyente de Alá. Nadie sabrá jamás que ese guerrero inculto salvó esos manuscritos de los que el mundo se hará lenguas. Herrn Bernardin *(sic)* es de la clase de hombres más hermosos que he visto en mi vida...", gemía Lou a lo lejos con su corazón en perpetua combustión amorosa. "Podría encarnar uno de los personajes míticos de Wagner. No me extraña que cuando lo llevaron prisionero en una jaula y lo tuvieron en exposición en la plaza mayor de Río de Janeiro, las mujeres brasileñas de todas las categorías sociales y hasta la misma esposa del emperador vinieran a contemplar alucinadas ese 'monstruo' de belleza masculina..."

A lo largo de más de un siglo, la historia de la Guerra Grande (llamada de la Triple Alianza), continúa siendo materia de controversias y discusiones, de querellas y duelos interminables. A pesar de haberse escrito sobre ella bibliotecas enteras, sigue siendo totalmente desconocida. La historia oficial de los vencedores no ha hecho sino oscurecerla aún más y tornarla inverosímil como una tragedia que no ocurrió ni pudo haber ocurrido.

Hay, sin embargo, un testigo extranjero, en cierto modo neutral, que levantó con humor y fantasía una de las puntas del velo de la tragedia: se trata de Sir Richard Francis Burton, el más famoso traductor de *Las mil y una noches*, viajero incansable, aventurero de la estirpe de los Marco Polo, héroe de la campaña colonial británica en

Egipto, autor de casi un centenar de libros, la mitad de los cuales destruyó y quemó su mujer lady Effie con saña implacable. *El Libro de la espada* o *Anatomía de la melancolía* son libros que perdurarán como los libros de Plinio, los de Joyce o los de Jorge Luis Borges, pese a sus distintos géneros, naturaleza y extensión, a las diferentes épocas en que fueron concebidos y escritos. Son partes del Libro Único que se sigue escribiendo a lo largo de las edades por el mismo autor con diferentes nombres. Escribe uno para que los particulares lean.

Sir Richard estuvo en el Paraguay a principios y al final de la contienda. Vio sobre el terreno el final de la guerra, se hizo amigo de Francisco Solano López y de Elisa Alicia Lynch. Habló, conoció y entrevistó a los jefes aliados, con los cuales intentó por su cuenta una negociación de paz, la que cayó en el más completo fracaso.

Hacia fines de 1870, poco después de terminada la guerra pero no la destrucción y el saqueo del país bajo las fuerzas de ocupación, Richard Francis Burton publicó su libro *Cartas desde los campos de batalla del Paraguay*, muy inferior a los otros en calidad literaria y magia creativa, pero superior a todos ellos como crónica del holocausto de un pueblo. "Un pueblo que va a desaparecer sin dejar huellas", afirma el autor en el prefacio.

Con lenguaje pintoresco e imaginativo relata en ella episodios de la vida de los campamentos de López y aporta elementos no tratados por los profesionales de la historia sobre el debatido y nunca aclarado final de la contienda. Desde las anfractuosidades de la serranía siguió con su catalejo los últimos combates de un puñado de pigmeos, barbudos y espectrales, armados de lanzas de tacuara, contra los superarmados escuadrones de la caballería brasileña, apoyados por la artillería de grueso calibre.

Cuando llegó Burton, en esa segunda visita, ya no sobrevivían en el Paraguay más que mujeres, ancianos, niños e inválidos. ¿De dónde sacaba aún Solano López esas tropas que Burton veía luchar con tanto denuedo y heroísmo? Esos combates se reproducían en todas partes, en medio de los espejismos y torbellinos de polvo del desierto, en los laberintos selváticos, en las cavernas infranqueables de la cordillera, bajo el sol de hierro del verano, bajo los chaparrones diluviales del invierno.

"Yo tenía la impresión —dice Burton en una de sus *Cartas*— de que un solo y único puñado de hombres era el que aparecía y desaparecía en todos los lugares a la vez. Esos pigmeos no eran hombres adultos. No eran más que muchachos púberes, que se habían pegado a las caras unas hirsutas barbas "fabricadas" con crines y colas de caballos mediante el indestructible látex del *mangaisy* (en guaraní en el original). Mucho de esos niños iban acompañados por sus madres, disfrazadas de la misma guisa. Esos dos mil niños, que 'sobraban', iban a ser aplastados por los cascos de los caballos aliados. Así lo ordenó, hacia el final de la guerra, el coronel Domingo Faustino Sarmiento —sucesor del general Bartolomé Mitre en la presidencia, y director de la guerra—, en una proclama famosa." Burton la transcribió en el apéndice. Dejó en castellano la palabra "sobraban" referida a los niños-soldados que debían ser aplastados por los cascos de la caballería aliada.

Por momentos no se sabe si Sir Richard está relatando lo que vio realmente, o si está traduciendo con palabras, necesariamente más pobres que las imágenes y como deformadas groseramente, las visiones de delirio de Cándido López, el pintor de la tragedia. Burton vio y admiró esos cuadros que iban saliendo "del natural" pero también de una visión de ultratumba; incluso vio pintar a Cándido López, sentado entre los muertos, al final de una batalla. "Parecía un sordomudo o un sonámbulo completamente fuera del mundo real —escribe en una de sus cartas (la décimo tercera), totalmente dedicada al pintor."

Burton, por entonces, era cónsul de su país en la corte del Brasil. Tenía carta blanca para recorrer el país en guerra. Traía instrucciones reservadas del emperador para convencer a Solano López de que aceptara renunciar a su investidura de jefe de Estado y al mando de sus fuerzas armadas a fin de que el alto mando aliado pudiese negociar, con el sucesor que él mismo designase, el cese de la guerra. El emperador comprometió su autoridad en asegurarle todas las garantías de protección a su persona, a su familia y a sus bienes, con la sola condición de abandonar el país eligiendo el que más le conviniera para solicitar asilo fuera de América del Sur.

El cónsul, viajero y capitán inglés, buscador impenitente de mundos y de seres extraños, visitó al mariscal presidente y a su consorte Madama Lynch en el errante cuartel general en plena retirada cuando ya su fin estaba próximo. Conversó mucho con ambos en las largas sobremesas de campamento a la luz de las cercanas estrellas y en la trepidación de los lejanos combates. En su gabinete de trabajo, Solano explicó al cónsul, documentos a la mano, que la inicua guerra que estaba devastando el país, había sido instigada y financiada por el imperio británico, empeñado en la expansión del librecambio.

En la buena tradición filibustera de la Reina de los Mares —escribe en su *Carta primera* que Solano le dijo—: "El Imperio trocó la enseña corsaria de Sir Francis Drake y sus congéneres por la patente de corso de la 'independencia protegida', invento del nuevo pacto neocolonial cocinado entre gallos y medianoche por el Foreing Office y las cancillerías de Buenos Aires y del Imperio del Brasil". El cónsul traduce los insultos que bramó el mariscal en una verdadera explosión de furia. En ella se mezclaron, según el cónsul, expresiones en el castellano más castizo que había oído en América y también en el dialecto paraguayo de la lengua vernácula. Burton no entendió muy bien el discurso bilingüe del mariscal, pese a que había estado ya durante dos largos periodos en el país. El cónsul se jactaba de hablar en treinta y cinco idiomas, incluidos sus dialectos, y de soñar en diecisiete. "Ese hombre me apostrofaba —escribe— en una germanía inextricable."

Burton cuenta que sonrió ante la desenfrenada invectiva. Sabía todo lo que Solano sabía. Sabía cosas que Solano no sabía. Se las iba transmitiendo oblicuamente, sin comprometerse demasiado. Su pasión era estar enterado de las cosas. Sabía que no se podía torcer el curso de los hechos ya consumados, pero que se debían conocer sus causas primeras y, sobre todo, los elementos imperceptibles y aparentemente anodinos que los habían desencadenado. Encontró natural que el mariscal paraguayo se batiera como un tigre acorralado por la jauría. Comprendió que palabras como "renuncia", "abdicación", "rendición", no tuvieran ningún sentido para esa fiera acosada. Su lema era vencer o morir. Pero la victoria no fue más que un espejismo apagado, hacía cinco años, con los fuegos del primer combate. La muerte aleteaba ya, agoreramente, sobre el aura de ese hombre que sentía día y noche la corrosión del tiempo y del universo.

"Le abrí desde el comienzo —escribe el capitán inglés— amplio crédito y justificación a todos sus excesos y me guardé la irrisoria propuesta del emperador en el forro de mis guantes. Sabía yo que los principales jefes de las fuerzas federales de la mesopotamia y del noroeste argentinos, en guerra contra Buenos Aires, habían propuesto a Solano, reiteradamente, incorporarse con sus tropas al ejército paraguayo y hacer la guerra juntos contra la alianza. ¿Por qué no aceptó usted esa ayuda?, le pregunté. Solano me respondió un poco brutalmente. Primero, dijo, porque el ejército paraguayo se basta solo para luchar contra esos piratas. Segundo, porque el ejército regular de un país civilizado no puede admitir el concurso de fuerzas irregulares. La anarquía y la mezcla no son buenas en ningún caso, y menos aquí. Estado y nación, pueblo y ejército son, en este país, un cuerpo orgánico y disciplinado. Un solo cuerpo y una sola cabeza: ¡ésta! Se golpeó el kepis y mostró los dientes amarillos por el tabaco. En lo hondo de la espesa barba, casi azulada de tan negra, esa mueca de soberbia duró sólo un instante. La mano de Solano se tendió hacia los mapas y los croquis de batallas que tachonaban la lona de la tienda, fijados con alfileres.

"Los nuevos filibusteros —barbotó Solano— quieren aniquilarme para convertir al Paraguay, la única nación libre y soberana de América del Sur, en un país de esclavos. La alianza me hace la guerra sobre la base de un pacto secreto tan inicuo, que no se atrevieron a publicarlo. Yo les he declarado la guerra como se debe, ante la faz de las naciones, cuando armé la expedición en defensa del Uruguay contra la invasión del Brasil. Cumplí con todas las normas del derecho internacional. Hice el honor al presidente Mitre de pedir permiso a su gobierno para que esta expedición cruzara el territorio argentino. Pero ya estaba él coaligado con el Brasil y, en lo interior, con el general Urquiza, que simulaba mantener estricta neutralidad. Pronto me enteré de que Urquiza ya había apresado a los principales jefes federales para impedir su adhesión militar al Paraguay. La traición de Urquiza y la venta de su 'neutralidad' en el conflicto le valieron los trescientos mil caballos para la remonta de su ejército y el millón de dólares que le envió por adelantado la banca Mauá.

"Mi error táctico y estratégico —reconoció Solano López— fue no atacar y aplastar a Urquiza mientras mis fuerzas, muy superiores a las de la alianza, cerraban una tenaza de hierro y de fuego sobre el Brasil por el norte hacia Mato Grosso y por el sur hacia el Plata sobre Buenos Aires. Tanto el general humanista Mitre como el general hacendado Urquiza debían grandes favores a mi padre (éste era inclusive compadre del vencedor de Caseros) y a mí mismo. Yo fui el mediador de la unificación argentina. Fui llevado en andas por las calles de Buenos Aires. Me entregaron un Libro de Oro con el homenaje de las mujeres y hombres más eminentes de aquel país. Mitre y Urquiza eran considerados leales amigos del Paraguay. La varita mágica del oro inglés los convirtió en enemigos jurados pero ocultos. Pude atropellarlos a mansalva como hicieron ellos y hacerles morder el polvo de la derrota desde el primer minuto. No quise cometer esta felonía que me habría igualado a mis enemigos."

Mostró al cónsul una copia del tratado secreto de la Triple Alianza. "¡De la triple infamia! —masculló Solano, abofeteando el arrugado papel. Pretenden anexar mi patria, por partes iguales, al imperio esclavócrata del Brasil y al vice-imperio de Inglaterra en el Plata, que esclaviza a las provincias argentinas. Eso únicamente podrán imponerlo sobre mi cadáver, en el último combate, sobre la última frontera."

No era una bravuconada —comenta Sir Richard. Ese hombre no se volvió loco en ese momento. Ya lo estaba. No era un malvado. Era un hombre de honor. El cónsul preguntó al mariscal sobre el por qué de esa obcecación inútil, contra la evidencia de un destino sellado inexorablemente, mientras se consumaba la destrucción de su país. Cuenta que, echando lumbre por los ojos, Solano le respondió: "Lo que llaman destino es una coartada de los débiles y pusilánimes. No conozco otro destino que el forjado por mi voluntad. Mientras yo pise un palmo de esta tierra, mi patria existirá y sus enemigos no prevalecerán contra ella".

Solano se había erguido en su silla. A Burton le pareció que había crecido de golpe, sin levantarse, hasta tocar con su cabeza el techo de la tienda. Se oía hacia el sur el lejano tronar de los cañones de la artillería brasileña. Se escuchó un sordo tumulto en el tráfago del cuartel general. Empezaron a granear los disparos. Solano se levantó y salió llevando del brazo a Burton.

—Venga a ver el globo de los aliados.

"Globo" es un modismo porteño que significa

embuste, inflada mentira. Llevado por la brisa, un aeróstato con los colores del Brasil sobrevolaba el campamento, tripulado por dos hombres que observaban con catalejos las posiciones de retaguardia. "¡Vea usted a los mirones corsarios!..", comentó, divertido. Los fusiles de chispa y los cohetes Congreve nada podían contra ese espejismo que reverberaba al sol con los colores del espectro. Suavemente, como una pompa de jabón, la esfera desapareció tras la cresta de los montes. "¡No tardará en caer en mis manos y entonces yo le daré otro uso!...", dijo Solano.

"Ese hombre —comenta Burton— odiaba la derrota con un odio absoluto e implacable. Odiaba esa guerra furiosa y lenta que ya duraba un siglo; una guerra que no tenía parangón con ninguna otra en la historia del Nuevo Mundo. En ésta no había que evitar la derrota, sino que había que prolongarla en la duración de los tiempos. Pero quizás este odio era la única voluptuosidad que podía atravesar aún el temple de acero del que su alma se hallaba revestida. Necesitaba seguir derramando ríos de sangre, la de todo su pueblo, para calmar la apoplejía de su furor sobrehumano. Tomarse a sí mismo como destino era su peor desatino." La prosa de Richard Francis Burton olvidaba, a veces, el tono descriptivo y jovial de los viajeros ingleses y se inflamaba de un arrebato trágico de segunda mano.

Sir Francis relata su viaje a Asunción para entrevistar a los jefes aliados y persuadirles a la concesión de una salida decorosa en favor del vencido mariscal. El cónsul anota que el generalísimo brasileño le respondió secamente: "El armisticio se hará sobre la muerte de ese monstruo". Encontró, en cambio, que el generalísimo argentino sentía hacia Solano gran respeto y hasta cierta admiración. "Ese hombre es un tirano —traduce *ad literam* las palabras de Mitre—. Un tirano aplastado por la montaña del poder absoluto, pero también es un hombre que ama a su patria y la defiende a su modo." Burton añade por su cuenta que "en definitiva nada hay más terrible que el espectáculo de un pueblo sacrificado por la estulticia de la historia. Quizás era esto, añade, lo que fascinaba a Mitre, militar, político, intelectual y poeta, en la indomable ferocidad del jefe paraguayo. Alucinado por la utopía napoleónica, éste se creía forjado para la guerra, pero para una guerra a la medida de sus fantasías. Podía decirse que sus propias fantasías eran las que lo habían derrotado y que esas mismas fantasías le obligaban a mantener en la derrota el penacho de su gloria mientras él viviera y combatiera, ya que él sabía mejor que nadie que la victoria era imposible."

El cónsul describe las bombardeadas casas de Asunción, cuyo incendio sirvió para iluminar las noches de saqueo. Burton no menciona el palacio blanco, digno de un alcázar moruno. No se fijó en él, salvo para contar el hecho de que los caballos enjaezados de los jefes aliados mordisqueaban su ración de alfalfa en la gran sala de recepciones. "Asegurados por el cabestro a las columnas de mármol y alabastro, rumiaban su ración de forraje. También el caballo dice 'pienso luego existo' —escribe socarronamente—. Sobre los fardos de forraje, que olían a llanuras verdes, a inagotable abundancia, a bucólica paz, los palafreneros dormitaban hirviendo de moscas."

En una nota añade: "Aunque se excave hasta el centro de la Tierra no se encontrarán aquí, ni en los siglos ni en los milenios que vengan, las ruinas de una ciudad. El arqueólogo Heinrich Schliemann acaba de descubrir hace tres años, luego de más de tres mil años, las ocho ciudades de Ilión superpuestas como los recuerdos de un hombre o como un palimpsesto de piedra anteriores a Príamo y a Hércules. Aquí, en Paraguay, en Ilión-Asunción, lo sagrado no va a confundirse con la antigüedad sino con la ausencia del tiempo, con la perennidad del sacrificio humano."

La guerra estaba en todas partes. Sir Francis la olía con delectación en la naturaleza quemada, en las casas incendiadas, en las roñas, en las carroñas esparcidas por todas partes, en el terror de las poblaciones diezmadas. Al leer las *Cartas* de Richard Francis Burton se tiene la sensación de que el guerrero de Egipto se anticipó en un siglo a la filosofía bélica de Erich von Ludendorff. Para éste y para Burton la guerra es la expresión más alta de la voluntad vital de los pueblos.

"La guerra, escribe, no puede hacerse sin una férrea dictadura militar. Exige la tiranía absoluta. El mundo no puede moverse sin el estado de guerra permanente. Todos los países son beligerantes y no pueden dejar de luchar un solo instante unos contra otros. El territorio entero del planeta es un inmenso e interminable campo de batalla. Cuando todo ajetreo bélico haya cesado, la humanidad misma es la que habrá desaparecido."

En notas extraviadas en el ritmo endiablado de sus "impresiones de viaje", el Burton mujeriego vuelve una y otra vez, como furtivamente, a la imagen de la mariscala. No oculta la fuerte impresión que le han producido su belleza y su fuerte personalidad. "Conocí a muchas mujeres —anota— de una hermosura semejante. Pero la de *Ela* era única. La belleza es múltiple, pero la multiplicidad de los paradigmas de belleza no permite distinguir cuál es su límite de perfección. La hermosura de *Ela* rozaba ese límite o acaso lo trascendía. Sus cabellos, del color del cobre recalentado al rojo, estaban peinados en forma de una diadema en torno a su cabeza; el rostro, velado por tenue luminosidad, daba la sensación de lejanía, de ausencia. Parecía un ser de otro mundo. Y lo era. Las formas puras de esa mujer eran su única pureza. Su cuerpo era su única alma."

Burton dedica un largo párrafo al tocado, a las joyas, a las finas maneras de anfitriona de Madama Lynch en las tertulias de campamento, que hacían olvidar la guerra y trasladaban en la imaginación la escena, que se jugaba en la jungla salvaje, al ambiente cortesano de París. Destaca irónicamente el contraste entre la gran dama de corte por las noches y su apostura de amazona, durante el día, sus órdenes en la aterciopelada voz de contralto idéntica a la maravilla de su cuerpo, sus briosos galopes en la fajina bélica, ceñida en su uniforme de mariscala, color hoja seca, bicornio de raso negro, altas botas charoladas de granadero y su sombrilla de mango de oro, engastado de fina pedrería, que empuñaba a sol y a sombra. Cuando cabalgaba la llevaba colgada de su cinturón como un espadín de oro enfundado en albo raso.

"En el nacimiento del primer hijo, Panchito —escribe el cónsul—, Solano le había obsequiado el bastón de oro incrustado de diamantes (fastuoso homenaje, a su vez, de las damas de Asunción, al comienzo de la guerra). Elisa despreciaba a esas damas patricias de horrible indumentaria, que andaban descalzas con los dedos de los pies relumbrantes de sortijas. Las despreciaba con agresiva ostentación como esas damas caricaturales del patriciado la habían despreciado, en su zafia ignorancia y bajas maneras, desde su llegada al Paraguay. Ordenó a su orfebre que convirtiera el bastón de oro en empuñadura de su sombrilla. El disgusto y la cólera del mariscal, al enterarse del despropósito, fueron homéricos; pero la mariscala, según su arte de armonizar las tensiones contrarias que hacen sonar la lira y disparar el arco, ganó la primera y única batalla que hubo entre ambos. El mariscal no dominaba el arte de la guerra (Solano López, ¡hélas! era un pésimo estratego), y el arte de la mariscala no podía sustituir en los campos de batalla la inepcia del jefe absoluto sin riesgo de empeorar las cosas."

"La sombrilla con el astil del bastón de mando era empuñada como un cetro por la mariscala, con lo cual la voluntad del mariscal presidente quedó cumplida por encima y más allá de las apariencias" —anota Burton con benévolo sarcasmo. La edición príncipe de las *Cartas* apareció ornada con varios dibujos del propio Burton. Uno de ellos muestra la imagen ecuestre de Elisa con su famosa sombrilla posando para él, al borde de un acantilado boscoso. La carta concluye con una trivialidad: "El abismo llama al abismo..."

A Solano lo retrata de un solo trazo. Lo ve de baja estatura, abultado abdomen, nariz chata de leopardo, los ojos de cuarzo ribeteados de una orla de sangre, la cara enormemente hinchada por el dolor de muelas. "La lleva vendada —escribe el cónsul— con un pañuelo rojo, del que fluye un hilo de baba manchado de tabaco." Con humor típicamente inglés, Burton refiere los accesos de dolor que le arrancan del sueño y le hacen rugir como un tigre. "Bebía entonces —añade— desaforadamente, y el aguardiente le sumía en borracheras embrutecedoras. Salía de ellas para entrar en otra embriaguez aún más brutal: la atmósfera siniestra de las conspiraciones. El mariscal presidente mandaba reprimir esos conatos con castigos atroces y con fusilamientos en masa de los supuestos complotados. Sus propios hermanos, el obispo, sus funcionarios más leales y sus oficiales más aguerridos, pagaron con la vida estos accesos de rabiosa locura que desencadenaban inauditas matanzas. Los tribunales de sangre —dice Burton— redoblaban entonces su actividad bajo la dirección y el celo del cura Maíz, convertido en Torquemada criollo. El propio Maíz fue quien glorificó a Solano como el Cristo paraguayo. Cuando se describen los rasgos de un malvado no caben el sarcasmo ni la indignación, menos aún cuando se desarrolla el tema de la desintegración de un carácter. Y Solano, ya lo dije, no era un malvado sino un iluminado que se creía traicionado por sus manes."

Burton encuentra justificada esta actitud y otras del mismo jaez del capellán mayor del ejército y fiscal director de los tribunales de sangre. "Ante la tragedia que estaba padeciendo el pueblo —razona el cónsul— éste tenía necesidad de que su jefe militar se convirtiera en un Mesías carismático, envuelto en la aureola de inmortalidad de la fe religiosa."

En contraste con los rasgos monstruosos que atribuye a Solano, el cónsul admite que poseía unos pies pequeños, blancos, casi femeninos, "los más pequeños y mejor cuidados que yo hubiese visto en un hombre". Esos pies le obligaban a un andar de pasos muy cortos, balanceándose sobre los altos tacones de sus botas, caricaturiza Burton. "En los momentos de reposo, uno de sus asistentes se arrodillaba ante esos pies, los lavaba, los masajeaba con ungüentos vegetales aromatizados y pulía las uñas. Finalmente los depositaba con sumo cuidado sobre un almohadón escarlata en un acto de verdadera adoración hacia el amo, profundamente dormido, que se quejaba en sueños de esa caries monumental."

El autor de las *Noches* no siempre es sarcástico con la "concubinaria" pareja. En sus *Cartas* hace la apología de Solano López y de Elisa Alicia Lynch con exaltado entusiasmo. "Un hombre tan hombre y una mujer tan mujer, que en ellos estaba restablecido el equilibrio de la especie por lo más alto. Hombre de inmensa energía, Francisco Solano López se había entregado a todos los excesos de esa guerra terrible y los había sobrepasado sabiendo que lo hacía para nada. Más que amo de su pueblo era su vicediós. Sabía que estaba arando en el mar, como dijo Bolívar de su acción en las guerras de la independencia, pero esto no disminuía ni su fe ni su ferocidad. La 'mariscala' ejercía sobre él ese tipo de dominio que se asemeja al hechizo. Los ojos glaucos, la mirada insondable de la irlandesa tenían más poder que los ojos inyectados de sangre de la fiera humana."

Burton no refiere que Elisa Alicia, divorciada del médico francés Quatrefages, al que había repudiado, no podía casarse con Solano, según las normas de la ley y los ritos de la Iglesia Católica Romana. Ella lo amaba a su modo. Elisa Alicia seguramente no podía amar a ningún hombre en los términos triviales del amor conyugal. No lo podía amar sino como al mediador y realizador de su desmesurada ambición. Esta desmesura era la naturaleza y la medida de su amor por Solano López. La magnífica razón de su amor era la aventura misma de ese amor, la loca empresa de construir juntos el imperio que el amor había inspirado a esta mujer de recio temple nacida para emperatriz. En ciertos estados de concentración y complejidad, la materia más fría siempre tiene un alma. La ambición de *Ela* tenía el alma que faltaba a su cuerpo.

A Sir Richard le fascinaba el cuerpo de *Ela;* sabía que su alma tenía dueño, y ésta le interesaba mucho menos.

Se oyó un campanilleo entre el sordo rumor del campamento.

—Vamos a cenar —dijo el mariscal.

Regresaron al amplio pabellón donde Madama Lynch los aguardaba como en un palacio. "La tertulia de sobremesa estuvo más animada que nunca —escribe Burton en la Carta XVII—. Mesa suntuosa, vinos finos de Francia, vajilla y cubiertos de plata con las iniciales entrelazadas de Elisa y Francisco, montadas en oro sobre el escudo nacional: un león parado en campo de gules, con una zarpa apoyada en una palmera real, y la estrella roja de Marte brillando en uno de los cuarteles."

"Me pareció vivir la noche de las noches: la Noche del Poder, pero también la Noche de la desventura y de la dicha, de la tragedia y de la felicidad. Relaté algunos episodios de la campaña de Egipto amañándolos un poco para levantar el ánimo decaído del Mariscal. No probó bocado. Sólo mandó que le desanudaran el pañuelo que vendaba la cara cada vez más hinchada para beber aguardiente puro con el que hacía largos buches antes de tragarlos. La fatiga y el dolor eclipsaban el temple sanguíneo y poderoso de ese hombre cuyo destino no era sino la fuerza de su voluntad.

"Madama Elisa me pidió que relatara algunas historias de las *Mil y una noches*. Empecé con algunas de las más anodinas. Poco afecto a las ficciones, el mariscal, vencido por el sueño, empezó a roncar, sacudido de tanto en tanto por temblores palúdicos. La mariscala, completamente inmóvil, escuchaba contemplando el cielo encendido con todos sus fuegos.

"En respetuoso silencio, la servidumbre también escuchaba desde la penumbra, hincada de rodillas sobre la hierba. Esas sombras mutiladas por la mitad me hicieron pensar que a mis historias les faltaban las piernas. Inventé otros relatos más intencionados y picantes en una delicada gradación. Sentía que me iba internando en un terreno minado, pero no podía ni quería volverme atrás. No podía olvidar aquella mañana en que, paseando por el campamento, sorprendí a Madama Elisa saliendo desnuda del baño, asistida por sus doncellas, en el improvisado tenderete de aseo levantado entre copudos árboles. Yo estaba viviendo interiormente la aventura de otra historia que no pertenecía al Libro de las Noches; una aventura en la que el riesgo de la seducción era su mayor incentivo.

"Inventé el relato del derviche enamorado de una de las siete doncellas de Shcherazad. El derviche embauca al jardinero del palacio para entrar en él secretamente. El derviche busca la manera de introducirse en el palacio de Arún Al-Rachid, blanco como la helada y la neblina, en busca de la doncella de sus sueños. El jardinero barre las hojas muertas del jardín. El derviche lo llama y le muestra a través de las rejas un espejo que refleja de un lado escenas licenciosas y del otro la manera de entrar en el espejo y de participar en ellas. Le dice que se lo va a regalar si le deja entrar. El jardinero le franquea la entrada y se va con el espejo apretado al pecho, enajenado por la anticipada dicha de esos placeres prohibidos. Es noche de luna llena. El derviche sabe que su enamorada toma baños de luna en la terraza de un ala interior del palacio, protegida contra las miradas indiscretas por cendales de humo aromático. El derviche vaga por los jardines toda la noche sin poder entrar en el palacio cerrado a cal y canto por el fulgor plateado por la luna. Con las primeras luces del amanecer desemboca en una especie de acuario y ve la espalda desnuda de la doncella, perlada de gotitas de agua, al salir de una inmensa jofaina de mármol negro. El derviche adivina por la hermosura escultural de esa espalda el rostro de la hurí que ama. Va a precipitarse hacia ella con los brazos abiertos. Pero al girar ésta para vestirse el albornoz, el derviche descubre que la mujer desnuda es la propia Sheherazad...

"Me detuve un instante embargado por la originalidad del imprevisto hallazgo narrativo (la narradora convertida en personaje de un cuento desconocido para ella, de una historia que no está en el Libro). Iba a continuar... Un golpe seco como el chasquido de la cuerda de una guzla que se rompe, interrumpió lo que iba a decir. Miré parpadeando en derredor. El mariscal seguía roncando en su sueño agitado de sobresaltos. La anfitriona estaba de pie. Con un gesto imperioso mandó levantar la mesa dando por terminada la tertulia. Es resbaloso el mundo, me dije. Uno tropieza sin querer. Mi corazón se puso en blanco. La miré como buscando una explicación a su intempestiva actitud. Estaba muy seria. Los seres dichosos son serios, pensé. Pero esa seriedad no ocultaba la dicha sino algo más profundo. Los seres como *Ela*, me dije, desprecian cualquier emoción por creerla indigna. Esos sentimientos se congelan en su interior. Su helado silencio me hizo estornudar. Con los brazos cruzados sobre el pecho la expresión de su rostro se había vuelto impenetrable. Una máscara mineral había surgido por debajo de ese rostro. La vi más altanera y despreciativa que la reina de Saba del Tintoretto. No parecía esperar sino que yo tuviese la dignidad de marcharme. No podía despegarme de ese hechizo. La represión de algún oscuro impulso tornaba aún más hermoso el crispado semblante. Cerré los ojos. En fracciones de segundos vi desfilar en esa mujer al animal mujer en todas las variedades de su especie y de sus razas: desde la sirena mítica hasta las no menos míticas amantes siamesas unidas por el vientre. Traté de imaginar desnudo ese cuerpo hecho para el amor, pero el rostro de una sombría ferocidad era capaz de paralizar el deseo más ardiente. Dije *Good night, Madame...* y me retiré afelpado y sonriente con el aire de la más candorosa inocencia."

Sir Francis, como se advierte en las frases nada elípticas que acabo de transcribir, estaba fascinado por Madama Lynch. Continúa recordándola en constantes alusiones. En otras dos cartas (la XIX y la XX) habla de ciertos amoríos que tuvo en Harrar "con una princesa etíope muy parecida a la divina *Ela* —escribe con el fingido temblor de un embuste—, sólo que en una versión de mujer de piel sedosa y oscura como la tinta del café de cardamomo..." Burton era un hábil manipulador del subterfugio narrativo. Poseía el arte de la insinuación capciosa en la manera de decir que dice por la manera. Sería razonable, empero, no fiarse excesivamente de las garrulerías del cónsul. La guerra y los placeres prohibidos eran sus temas favoritos. Es natural que lady Effie, la pacata mujer de Sir Richard, se sintiera con todo el derecho de destruir los centones de "obscenidades eruditas" que escribió su aventurero marido. Las *Cartas* se salvaron porque las hizo imprimir en secreto con su editor Tinsley de Londres. La primera edición apareció bajo la protección vicaria de un seudónimo.

Las fantasías eróticas de Sir Richard Francis Burton no se detenían, como se ve, ante ningún obstáculo, así fuesen la frágil muralla del sueño del mariscal y la dignidad inexpugnable de la mariscala en su condición de mujer. Pero, al margen de ellas, la mediación del cónsul, en un aspecto puramente cultural, no debería ser descartada. El Paraguay, isla rodeada de tierra, de infortunios, de tiempo detenido, es un país completamente cerrado a las nocivas y permisivas influencias foráneas. No hay indicios ni memoria de que los cuentos de las *Mil y una noches* se conocieran en el Paraguay antes de la Guerra Grande.

La mediación del cónsul pudo ser ésta: servir de puente por el cual las historias de las Noches de Oriente pasaron al imaginario colectivo paraguayo a través de las mujeres de servicio de la mariscala. El propio Sir Richard cuenta en sus *Cartas* que oyó repetir a una de esas mujeres, en una versión muy extraña y desfigurada (él ya había aprendido el guaraní), la historia de la Undécima Noche. Burton no se sorprende. Para él hay un solo mito de origen que se bifurca y que atraviesa en constante mutación y proliferación de narraciones las culturas de todos los pueblos y todas las edades. "La memoria de un individuo o de un pueblo, en trance de muerte —anota en una digresión—, recobra de golpe los recuerdos del pasado y del porvenir, aun de los más remotos y desconocidos acontecimientos, por ínfimos que sean: un personaje, una palabra, un sueño, la cara de la maldad, que es lo único que queda cuando todo lo demás se ha perdido."

Habrá que convenir, con Sir Richard, que los cuentos de las *Mil y una noches* entraron en el Paraguay por la puerta de servicio de Madama Lynch, no ya de su incendiado palacio de Asunción sino de las tiendas de campaña del cuartel general. Con lo que las guerras más terribles, aun las del holocausto de todo un pueblo, siempre dejan un remanente cultural que con el tiempo se acendran y se incorporan a la esencia de su identidad.

En el apéndice documental de las *Cartas* Burton refiere, retrospectivamente, la captura de un globo de reconocimiento aliado, acaso el mismo que el mariscal le mostrara navegando plácidamente sobre la floresta paraguaya. Este inane triunfo, inflado apenas con aire caliente, produjo gran alegría en el cuartel general. Los tripulantes, dos oficiales argentinos, confesaron que habían huido de las fuerzas brasileñas de las que estaban hartos por su trato desconsiderado y humillante. Con evidente placer comunicaron a los ayudantes de Solano López todos los datos de utilidad militar que poseían; datos que, desdichadamente ya de nada servían al mariscal. Sus informes, espontáneos y plenos, no alteraron la temperatura del día siguiente.

Sir Richard conversó con los desertores y encontró que eran dos hombres cultos que se habían formado en Europa. La captura del globo restableció también la fluidez de las relaciones entre Sir Richard y la mariscala, las que a raíz del relato del derviche enamorado, húmedo por el relente nocturno, quedaron algo resfriadas. No ahorra el cónsul sus dardos sutiles contra "la mujer de limitado y arbitrario universo pero singularmente tenso". Cuenta, como si se tratara de un triunfo personal, que Madama Lynch le invitó a una nueva cena seguida de tertulia. "También nosotros, a nuestro modo —escribe—, hacíamos historia al estilo de París o de Londres en un medio escuálido y salvaje".

Esta vez, cuenta Sir Richard, la anfitriona se pasó la velada absorta y silenciosa, toda de negro vestida, la gorguera alechugada y los puños de encaje blanco. La imagen misma de la melancolía. "En esa imagen se inspiró mi libro *Anatomía de la melancolía*. Me pasé la noche relatando las sucesivas encarnaciones de Buda como grados espirituales sucesivos en el estado de castidad y purificación total a que el Gautama aspiraba. La máscara mineral volvió a aparecer bajo el rostro hermosísimo. Supongo que la misteriosa e imprevisible Elisa tomó mis fábulas búdicas como un desquite punitivo de mi parte, lo que no fue sino un acto de urbanidad y cortesía. El universo de las mujeres es vasto e impenetrable como una noche sin estrellas. Pero Alá sabe más."

Lo notable del retrato que de Madama Lynch hace Sir Richard en esta Última Cena corresponde, con un siglo de anticipación y mágica exactitud, al retrato de Virginia Woolf que hará el gran dibujante Rothestein. Por su parte, Virginia Woolf retrató en *Orlando* un siglo después a Sir Richard Francis Burton, a quien evidentemente no podía conocer. ¿Qué vínculos inextricables unen los espíritus afines a través del tiempo y del espacio? No creo mucho en las simetrías o asincronías panteístas. Pienso que las más flagrantes no pasan de ser simples coincidencias. Así como los historiadores escriben sus obras no para explicar el pasado sino para justificar el presente, los escritores y artistas andan buscando siempre a sus precursores en el futuro, fiados en la sustancia del porvenir. Es una fe con muchos apóstoles pero sin ningún mártir. Sospecho que se trata de una mera astucia por parte de estos creadores de mundos imaginarios para salvaguardar cronológicamente ese bien tan preciado pero inexistente de la originalidad absoluta, de lo inédito, de lo intocado. Y aquí tocamos de nuevo el mito de la virginidad impoluta que no permite ir más lejos y que no existe en la literatura porque no tiene himen aunque produzca himeneos.

Con respecto al globo cautivado, Sir Richard relata: "Pocos días le bastaron al coronel inglés Thompson (mimado de López y futuro desertor) para formar un grupo de aeronautas y adiestrarlos en el uso del artefacto. Los desertores argentinos colaboraron con su mejor entusiasmo y voluntad. El globo quedó listo para ser usado. Solano López ordenó una incursión nocturna sobre el puesto de comando brasileño. Los dos tripulantes, excelentes baqueanos y ojeadores, que conocían al dedillo la posición enemiga, hicieron descender el globo en una isleta próxima. Franquearon audazmente el cordón de seguridad del campamento y se arrastraron en la maleza hacia el pabellón del marqués de Caxías, generalísimo del imperio, llevando los sables entre los dientes. Los cuerpos desnudos de los incursores, teñidos de achiote negro, eran invisibles, excepto los ojos y el brillo de los sables que delataron su presencia y alertaron a los centinelas. Los dos cayeron heridos. Todavía vivos, los despellejaron por gusto, para ver si eran negros de verdad y para arrancarles algunos datos militares. Los prisioneros, mudos bajo el suplicio, murieron de repente por asfixia. Estaban ejercitados para tragarse la lengua y morir en una emergencia semejante. Bajo banderas de parlamento el alto mando brasileño hizo llegar los desollados cadáveres al cuartel general de Solano. Recibieron cristiana sepultura. El mariscal prendió a las toscas cruces las medallas del valor militar. Ante el mástil del pabellón izado a media asta, los restos de sus tropas harapientas, formadas en cuadro, apenas podían tenerse en pie y sostener sus armas al hacer los disparos de reglamento."

Uno de los incursores sin embargo había logrado penetrar en la antecámara del generalísimo brasileño, donde decapitó al secretario. El marqués de Caxías se salvó por mero azar, pues se hallaba negociando necesidades íntimas en el retrete. Hay un testimonio irrefutable de esta hazaña, que no es una invención del obnubilado Sir Francis. Entre las escenas de guerra, pintadas por Cándido López, existen dos cuadros de colores sombríos; en el primero se recorta en escorzo la forma esférica del globo contra la vaga luminosidad de la noche. En la barquilla sólo viaja el lívido fulgor de dos machetes ("dos criminales alfanjes con vida propia", dice el conde de Orleans).

De los tripulantes no se ve más que el brillo de los

sables entrando sigilosamente en el pabellón del generalísimo brasileño, que escribe a la luz de una bujía. Un imperceptible efecto óptico produce la impresión de que la cabeza del jefe, demudada de horror, se halla separada del tronco por una delgada estría. Se ha vuelto, implorante, hacia sus invisibles asaltantes, es decir, hacia el relumbrar de los sables, ingrávidos en el aire, uno de ellos con tachas de sangre. La escena parece tomada del natural. El espacio se halla focalizado en torno a la estría que secciona el cuello, alrededor del cual gira el dinamismo interno del cuadro. Un golpe de viento ha entrado en la tienda y remueve la voluta de humo del cigarro caído en el suelo. A través de ella, como dos ectoplasmas, se perfilan las siluetas opacas, bordeadas por un halo, de los dos hombres que van a morir.

Cándido López pintó el cuadro del globo hacia el final de la contienda, cuando su cuerpo mutilado por la metralla estaba reducido a menos de la mitad. El pintor no era ya solamente una metáfora corporal del pueblo diezmado, exterminado por la guerra. Pero Sir Richard Francis Burton nada escribió, no hizo la menor alusión al final de ese pintor que se despedazaba lentamente mientras iba pintando.

En estos despojos vivientes, quemados por la destilación del mal, suele habitar la presciencia de lo justo. Cándido López pintó en cuadros memorables la tragedia de la guerra, pero su propio cuerpo era el comentario más terrible de ella. El pintor se hizo cargo en su arte del martirologio colectivo y lo "pasó" a los cuadros de la segunda época. Éstos niegan el marcial esplendor de las primeras, algo retóricos todavía. Acaso estos cuadros, según un enigma no aclarado aún, fueron la obra de otro pintor, un paraguayo llamado también Cándido López. El argentino pintó el avance triunfal de las tropas empenachadas de púrpura y gualda, la marea incontenible de barcos y armas pesadas, el galope de escuadrones con sus lanzas resplandecientes y sus banderines flameando a todos los vientos, las figuras ecuestres de los jefes aliados, erguidas en las cumbres y señalando con el sable corvo la dirección de la victoria. El Cándido López paraguayo se ocupó de la vasta y oscura pululación de los vencidos.

Un trozo de metralla le arranca el brazo derecho. Pronto aprende a pintar con el izquierdo, ayudado por su amigo y protector, el indio guayakí Jerónimo, el mismo que le ha enseñado a tejer sus lienzos con fibras silvestres y a moler los colores de las plantas tintóreas, mezclados con polvos minerales y el fuego machacado de los lámpiros. El indígena le trae miel de lechiguanas, huevos de perdiz, agua con plantas medicinales y hasta pichones asados. Le unta el cuerpo, ya mediado, con grasa de cerdo salvaje y de tapires del río, que cura sus heridas. Con aparejos de lianas del monte, Jerónimo iza todas las noches hasta el lecho de ramas que le prepara en la copa de los árboles. Ahorquetado en las ramas vecinas, el indio con su arco y sus flechas vela el sueño de su amigo, que reposa al resguardo de alimañas e insectos, del ojeo de las patrullas enemigas y hasta del husmeo del tigre. A las primeras luces del amanecer, lo transporta a hombro, en la misma red de lianas, hasta los lugares donde Cándido debe pintar, esos lugares donde el sufrimiento y la muerte hacen su trabajo: el paso de las caravanas de fugitivos, los combates, las emboscadas, las torturas en los tribunales de sangre, las ejecuciones sumarias, los lanceamientos infamantes de conspiradores, desertores y traidores.

Cándido López es la única figura real, pero invisible, en medio de esa trituración espectral que mezcla el alba con la noche, los seres vivientes con los minerales y el horror, las penurias y la muerte con la potencia invencible de la vida. La presencia constante y silenciosa del pintor menguante se ha convertido en un elemento anodino del paisaje. No, desde luego, para el ojo implacable del Cazador que lo vigila. Un casco de obús le vuela el brazo izquierdo, que ya empezaba a ser diestro. Jerónimo lo lleva a las cavernas donde los curanderos indígenas lo atienden. Aprende a pintar con el pincel encastrado entre los dedos de los pies. Sucesivamente pierde ambas piernas a la altura de las rodillas. Aprende a pintar con el pincel apretado entre los dientes.

Todo sucede como si la pasmosa puntería del cazador invisible fuese esculpiendo poco a poco ese cuerpo inagotable, esa piltrafa humana animada por un espíritu indómito. Su cabeza no se levanta ya a más de un palmo sobre el suelo. Lo que es una ventaja para él, pues ahora puede pintar escondido en la maleza, al abrigo de ese cazador que lo persigue desde la muerte. El pintor decrece en la misma medida en que los sobrevivientes van siendo cazados y diezmados. Pero de esa mutilación incesante crece una obra inmensa, bajo el signo de la irredimible locura humana. La imagen final es la de un pueblo reducido al hombre último parecido a todos los hombres muriendo.

La captura del globo y de sus tripulantes fue la única y última acción de guerra exitosa que el azar brindó a Solano López en sus últimos días. Pero los caprichos del azar fueron igualmente los que convirtieron este misérrimo triunfo en un sarcástico réquiem de sus armas. Poco después, el coronel Silvestre Carmona, ayudante de campo del mariscal, ex fiscal de sangre, y uno de sus oficiales más valerosos, engrosó la fila de desertores que iban a entregarse a las fuerzas enemigas. Con el pretexto de enterrarlos en lugar seguro, llevó una buena parte de los cofres del tesoro en pago del asilo que le brindaron los brasileños. El mismo Silvestre Carmona, después de haber sido quien sugirió al mariscal el emplazamiento del cuartel general junto a la caverna del eco, iba a ser el guía de las tropas brasileñas en su ataque al bastión de Cerro-Corá, que terminó con el asesinato de Solano López.

El día antes el mariscal reunió por última vez a los decaídos oficiales de su Estado Mayor. Solano les refiere que ha recibido al gran cacique de las tribus Caynguá. Seguido por numeroso séquito de guerreros y servidores, éste ha traído alimentos y ofrece ocultar al Tendotá, a sus oficiales y al resto de sus efectivos y armamentos, en las profundas e impenetrables cavernas de la cordillera del Amambay. Desde esos refugios inexpugnables podrían seguir la guerra de guerrillas indefinidamente. Requiere la opinión de todos. Alguien le pregunta si a las mujeres del éxodo también se les permitirá refugiarse en las cavernas. Solano López no responde. Pero su silencio da la respuesta.

Tras una larga pausa cargada de malos presagios, Solano López volvió a demandar la opinión de todos y de cada uno. El general Aveiro dijo lenta y agoreramente: "Nuestro deber de soldados nos impone obedecer las órdenes de nuestro Jefe Supremo. Lo que S.E. diga se hará. Pero, a mi juicio, amontarnos, escondernos en las cavernas de la serranía no sería sino prolongar, días más, días menos, nuestra determinación de morir por la patria..." Todos aplaudieron las palabras del nuevo ayudante de campo. Solano López aceptó complacido la decisión de sus subordinados. Recordó y ratificó su juramento de no abandonar el suelo de la patria mientras quedase un combatiente para defenderla con las armas en la mano sin dar ni pedir cuartel. Profirió duros juicios de condenación contra los traidores y desertores.

—¡A ese miserable Carmona, mil veces traidor, yo mismo lo hubiera destrozado a latigazos! —gritó furioso golpeando varias veces con el taco el asperón rojo del anfiteatro. Un grito de repulsión y condenación unánime enardeció las gargantas de los oficiales y se multiplicó en mil ecos de trueno en la caverna.

—¡Esperaremos aquí y moriremos todos hasta el último hombre sobre el último combate!... —exclamó con voz enérgica e inexorable...

Era el atardecer del 28 de febrero de 1870.

Solano López se rehizo y se mostró cordial y festivo. Contó chistes sobre los cobardes fanfarrones que cargan todas las cicatrices de sus heridas en la espalda. "¡A ver! —ordenó— ¡Quién tiene la espalda más llagada! Voy a condecorarlas con la roja insignia del valor!" Los oficiales se sacan las guerreras en harapos y enseñan sus espaldas al mariscal con respetuoso pudor. Éste va descargando sobre ellas con su látigo de cola de lagarto fuertes zurriagazos que marcan sobre los lomos combados sangrientos cardenales.

—¡Esto para que no muestren la espalda al enemigo! —grita entre sonoras carcajadas y los ecos se propagan en las anfractuosidades del anfiteatro.

En actitud obsecuente, el capellán y fiscal Fidel Maíz recuerda la decisión de Julio César, aconsejada por el astrónomo Sosígenes de Alejandría, de añadir un día más al mes de 28 días. Su gesto de adulonería y erudición es celebrado por el mariscal y coreado por todos.

—Así —sentencia doctamente el padre Maíz—, el mes más corto del año se convirtió en bisexto kalendas Martii —y dirigiéndose al mariscal—: ¡Con más poder que Julio César, S.E. puede remodelar el calendario!

Solano, entre solemne y chispeante, acepta con humor el consejo y, palmeando a Maíz en el hombro, dice parodiándole:

—Tomemos pues al tiempo un poco de su preciosa sustancia. Así tendremos un día más en este nuestro Huerto de los Olvidos, como le gusta repetir al padre Maíz, especialista en Gólgotas y Crucifixiones.

Todos se pusieron de pie y aclamaron largamente al mariscal. Los laberintos de la Caverna del Eco que desemboca en el anfiteatro, empezaron a devolver, como si retrocedieran al principio, las voces, las risas, los gritos, los murmullos apenas audibles y hasta el soplo acezante de las respiraciones. El mariscal estornudó en ese momento y la caverna lo amplificó en el ruido de un trueno que fue propagándose por los acantilados.

Por la noche, en la vela de armas, el mariscal procedió a la entrega de condecoraciones. Las medallas de latón, apresuradamente batidas por los herreros, llevaban la inscripción: "A los que vencieron penurias y fatigas en la campaña del Amambay". Pendían de cintas tricolores con moños y escudos cosidos por manos de Madama Lynch. El mariscal firmó el decreto respectivo con fecha del 29 de febrero de 1870, transfiriendo a las condecoraciones el día ganado al tiempo calendárico por sugerencia del padre Maíz. Revestido con los santos ornamentos, éste bendijo las medallas y pronunció una breve pero inflamada oración patriótica. El mariscal las fue prendiendo al pecho de la treintena de oficiales según un riguroso orden de antigüedad, de servicios y de méritos. Casi todos ellos habían comenzado su carrera militar como jefes de policía de Asunción y habían integrado como fiscales los tribunales de sangre. El mariscal los nombró uno por uno y ellos iban respondiendo: "¡Presente!" La multiplicación de los ecos sugirió la presencia de un Estado Mayor de un millar de oficiales que no alcanzaban a una treintena.

—Estas medallas de vil latón valen más que el oro y que la plata porque están hechas del metal de vuestro honor y de vuestra bravura militar —dijo Solano echando lumbre por los ojos y escupiendo baba amarilla por los hinchados labios.

En la privacidad de la tienda del comando en jefe el mariscal mandó redactar por el anciano vice-presidente Sánchez su testamento. En él legaba a Madama Elisa Lynch, "para siempre jamás", cinco mil leguas de tierra. "En este espacio —hacía constar el documento— están incluidos los centenares de miles de hectáreas de yerbales, chacras y estancias de la patria, que no deben caer en manos extranjeras. Elisa Lynch le recordó que era extranjera. Solano le respondió vivaz y enamorado que con su lealtad y su sacrificio había ganado el derecho y el honor de ser paraguaya. Firmó el testamento con fecha 29 de febrero y se lo entregó con un beso. Madama Lynch le devolvió el documento y le pidió que corrigiera la fecha. "No conviene hacer cosas en un día que no existe...", le dijo con suave disentimiento pero inflexible convicción. Solano corrigió la fecha, volvió a firmar ratificando la enmienda, y se lo entregó con marcial orgullo.

El redoble del tambor enemigo con aire de jolgorio macumbero no cesó de sonar del otro lado del monte. La derrota es huérfana, parecía decir. Vosotros, hijos del diablo coludo y dientudo, nacisteis sin padre ni madre en tiempos en que los animales ya no eran hombres y quedasteis en puros chanchos de monte...

Cayó polvo de neblina blanqueando la tibia noche de febrero que ardía de luciérnagas y de astros. Lo que pasó después ya no sirve contar porque no hubo nada más sino una mala palabra que iba a durar cien años.

La derrota duraba un tiempo que no se podía contar por años. El mariscal derrotado, pero no vencido, trataba de convertir esa retirada en una guerra de resistencia, sin más generales que un puñado de fieles y un ejército de ancianos, inválidos y niños. En los sucesivos altos del éxodo, en torno a la gran tienda roja del cuartel general, surgía una nueva capital del país trashumante. La vida del campamento trataba de recobrar en ella el ritmo normal de un pueblo de fantasmas que se movían como en una agitada pesadilla.

El conde pianista ejecutaba durante el día polonesas y mazurcas. Sus himnos y marchas triunfales sonaban como peón de combate. El mariscal aparecía en la abertura de la tienda exigiéndole con gestos imperiosos acentos más briosos y marciales. Su enorme cara hinchada por el dolor de muelas se ponía violácea en los gritos. El conde machacaba entonces como enloquecido las teclas luchando a brazo partido con la misma muerte. Sus tocatas furiosas horadaban el aire muerto del campamento con crepitar de huesos que entrechocaban entre sí. La danza macabra tenía así la virtud de poner en pie hasta a los agonizantes que aferraban sus lanzas y atacaban a enemigos imaginarios.

Por las noches, surgían suaves, evanescentes, los valses de Chopin, que hacían suspirar soñadoramente a la emperatriz errante evocando los amores del gran músico taciturno y tuberculoso con la enérgica y deslumbrante George Sand en Palma de Mallorca. Luego, cuando todo se aquietaba en el selvático anfiteatro, empezaba a oírse un enlutado tambor cuyo monótono son duraba hasta el amanecer. El mariscal y la mariscala no podían dormir, enloquecidos por ese fúnebre redoble que hacía retemblar sordamente la tierra. Todas las patrullas que se enviaron para secuestrarlo, volvían derrotadas o no volvían más. No lo podían ubicar. Siempre sonaba delante de ellos o detrás, en cualquier parte, en el sitio más imprevisible, atrayendo a los patrulleros a las emboscadas. Los componentes de la última patrulla regresaron heridos y fueron fusilados. Pero el tocador ubicuo del tambor continuó batiendo el cuero a más y mejor. Y esto ocurrió hasta el mismo día de la muerte del mariscal.

En el campamento brasilero bulle ruidosa la macumba en invocación al *Padre Echú*. Oficia de "sacerdote" el cabo de órdenes, capoeira y jinete de circo, el mulato *Chico Diavo* a quien el *Gran Changó*, el *Padre Echú* y otras divinidades afro-brasileiras le untan con los óleos salvajes del Gran Poder. *Chico Diavo* sera el que logre asestar a Solano López el lanzazo mortal, ganándose con ello las cien libras esterlinas de la prima, ofrecida por el jefe de la vanguardia, general Núñez Tavares da Silva, pero que nunca le será pagada.

El gran tambor entró en el anfiteatro con las fuerzas invasoras.

Sobre el historiado piano el conde fue lanceado por los brasileros unos minutos antes de que lancearan a Solano

López. Cuando éste oyó el terrible estrépito de teclas y cuerdas que estallaron como somatén de sálvese quien pueda, dicen que exclamó: "¡Ay... me lo han matado al músico!... ¡Ya todo está perdido!..." Montó en su corcel de guerra y huyó hacia el río. Pasó frente al carretón donde estaban prisioneras su madre y sus hermanas por el delito de conspiración y tentativa de asesinato del mariscal con un chipá envenenado.

—¡Por Dios, Solano! ¡Sálvanos, hijo mío!... ¡Somos mujeres!... —le grita doña Juana coreada por los alaridos de las hijas envenenadoras.

Sin detener su carrera, el interpelado le respondió: "¡Fíese de su sexo, señora!... ¡Es lo único que las puede salvar!..." Continuó en su despavorido galope, seguido muy cerca por el caballo del corneta de órdenes. *Chico Diavo* logra al fin aparejársele, se le adelanta y le asesta su lanza en el vientre. El caballo desbocado del mariscal se detiene de golpe ante la barranca del arroyo despidiendo por el aire al jinete que rueda hasta el lecho del profundo cauce. De esas aguas fangosas emerge el espadín de oro y la cabeza sanguinolenta del mariscal. La boca llena de barro lanza el ronco proferimiento de "¡Muero con mi Patria!..." Lo ultiman a tiros de fusil. El agua espesa y roja de tierra del arroyuelo se vuelve púrpura.

El tambor de la macumba retumba enloquecidamente entre los gritos de júbilo de quince mil gargantas y las salvas de victoria.

Desde las jaulas armadas con ramas en que han sido encerrados, los jefes sobrevivientes del Estado Mayor de Solano contemplan impotentes, con lágrimas en los ojos, ese entierro fantasmal del hombre que ha muerto con el clamor de "¡Muero con mi patria!". En humillante contradicción con ellos, el padre Maíz, de rodillas en su jaula, pide clemencia al conde D'Eu, jefe supremo de las fuerzas brasileñas. Clama a gritos y entre sollozos, en su honor, las mismas loas que hasta hace poco tiempo rendía al mariscal asesinado. Sólo que ahora, en lugar de consagrar al conde D'Eu como al Cristo brasileño lo proclama Redentor del Paraguay y del género humano.

Elisa Alicia Lynch, vestida de riguroso blanco nupcial, sube a la carreta que ha de llevarla al destierro. Su condición de extranjera la salva de ser ejecutada. Sobre el piano destrozado ve el cadáver del conde Brinnicky, atravesado por una lanza. Sus quijadas descoyuntadas muestran la dentadura, la que por un efecto óptico de la resolana se prolonga desmesuradamente en el desdentado teclado del piano. Elisa Alicia Lynch se asombra del rostro con la sombrilla manchada de sangre. La carreta se pone en marcha. Los picadores tienen que morder el testuz a los bueyes y aguijarlos en los traseros para hacerlos avanzar. La cerrazón de polvo rojo de esa tierra cargada de hierro va oscureciendo la blanca silueta entre la indiferencia de un sol de fuego y la curiosidad lasciva de la soldadesca.

La Dama del Paraguay, erguida entre el polvo y las reverberaciones, se va esfumando en la bruma escarlata.

Las *Cartas desde los campos de batalla del Paraguay*, de Sir Richard Francis Burton, se publicaron un mes después de terminada la guerra. Es un libro de historia, pero al mismo tiempo de ficción, de delirante fantasía creativa, muy superior a la simple traducción del Libro de las Noches. La estilizada viñeta que exorna (o exorciza) el *ex libris* muestra en filigrana el escorzo de una mujer que repite la imagen de Elisa Alicia Lynch, dibujada por el propio Burton. El cuerpo nebuloso, envuelto por la larga cabellera, termina en una cola de sirena y lleva al pie la siguiente leyenda:

Ex nihilo nihil...

Hay que volver al libro del traductor de las *Mil y una noches* para saber algo más sobre algunos de los extraños personajes de la Guerra Grande. Los cronistas locales y extranjeros, por alguna razón de pudor histórico tal vez, han preferido no ocuparse de ellos. O lo han hecho con tal ambigüedad, que estos personajes semejan *aparecidos* de una historia fantástica. En las extensas notas del apéndice el autor de las *Cartas* justifica los actos en apariencia más aberrantes del poderoso capellán y fiscal.

Sir Francis Richard Burton menciona, por ejemplo, la circular del padre Maíz que al final de la guerra envió a los capellanes del ejército exhortándoles a fomentar la "prostitución patriótica" de las mujeres en los campos de batalla. "No vacilen los curas —transcribe el cónsul— en el ejercicio de su ministerio desde el púlpito o en sus recorridas diarias por la retaguardia a incitar a las mujeres jóvenes a convivir con los combatientes y a darles todo el placer que necesiten. Esto no será desorden moral ni acto de concupiscencia cuando sea a favor de los defensores de la patria cuya felicidad en este mundo es el primer deber de las conciudadanas".

No se trata de una mistificación de Burton. El cónsul francés Laurent Cochelet, en un extenso informe que envía a su gobierno sobre los últimos hechos de la guerra, confirma la existencia de dicha circular y la califica de un extravío verdaderamente demoniaco del fiscal y capellán mayor.

"Desde los lugares aún libres del invasor —informa Sir Francis y Cochelet confirma, en casi textual coincidencia—, llegaron nutridas caravanas de mujeres mozas, un batallón entero de jóvenes concepcioneras y de otras localidades del norte. Estos batallones de 'prostitutas pa-

trióticas' fueron enviadas, en los intervalos de los combates, a convivir con los combatientes para darles un poco de
'felicidad' al filo de la muerte. No eran rameras profesionales. Eran madres lactantes voluntarias. El cura Maíz in-
terpretó correctamente la inversión del mito nutricio. A
estos hombres-niños que iban a morir, esas mujeres-ma-
dres debían ir a brindar voluntariamente el postrer alimento
que existía para ellos: la felicidad del placer, el extremo
éxtasis del sexo como el único antídoto contra la angustia
del fin último."

"El cura Maíz no hizo otra cosa —arguye Burton,
pero Cochelet condena con encendida indignación este acto
censurable— que implantar, como una necesidad de guerra en los frentes de combate, el tráfico sexual que de hecho existía en las zonas 'liberadas': las violaciones masivas,
las brutales orgías a las que de hecho se vieron forzadas las
mujeres paraguayas por los invasores en los territorios
conquistados. Durante los cinco años de guerra y los siete
de ocupación por las fuerzas vencedores, la mujer paraguaya tuvo que asumir la prostitución —la forma extrema
de servidumbre, la del sexo—, como la única manera de
escapar a las violaciones en masa y de sobrevivir en la retaguardia.

"El precio en especies por cópula era ridículo pero
mágico: dos bolachas, un poco de sal y de azúcar, una tira
de tasajo. Las más bonitas y menos esqueléticas, elegidas
por los oficiales, eran más afortunadas. A veces recibían
raciones de carne vacuna recién faenada. Tal era la tarifa
variable en que su sexo estaba tasado. Este comercio les
permitió alimentarse y alimentar a sus hijos, a inválidos y
ancianos. Surgió una especie de matriarcado: el de las
madres prostitutas. El más viejo oficio de la tierra se impuso
para ellas como un dilema de vida o muerte del que no
podían escapar. Ya no existía la patria. Sobrevivían las
matrias rameras.

"La prostitución forzada y forzosa impuesta por los enemigos —al revés de la 'prostitución patriótica voluntaria' en favor de los defensores que iban a morir— no impidió el florecimiento de idilios y noviazgos de verdadero amor entre las matriarcas rameras y los enemigos de la víspera. Este amor —verdadero desquite de la vida contra la muerte—, iba a engendrar parejas indisolubles, familias dinásticas de apellidos carioca-paraguayos, hogares e hijos, sellados por el pacto de sangre en el nuevo mestizaje forjado en el terrible crisol.

"¿Por qué no prosperó este matriarcado de genuina raigambre social?"

Con esta quemante pregunta lanzada a la posteridad —pero que la posteridad no pudo, no supo o no quiere contestar hasta hoy—, el cónsul extranjero cerró el capítulo de sus *Cartas*, referente a la prostitución patriótica y a su otra cara: la prostitución voluntaria de las matriarcas meretrices, en medio de la corrupción y la depravación general, otro de los estigmas que marcan a un pueblo vencido.

Habría que preguntarse además si tal destino no arrastra a esta colectividad a un exceso de vida futura o a la ausencia paulatina de una futura extinción, como ha ocurrido tantas veces en el caos de las sociedades humanas aplastadas por la violencia y el horror, por la estulticia de la historia, comadrona, alcahueta, mancebía de los chulos del poder.

Algunos políticos proscritos habían vuelto con la Legión Paraguaya a "liberar" al país del tirano, coludidos con los aliados, con los miserables vivos y con los miserables muertos. El resto de esta piara de demolición arribó, apenas terminada la guerra. Los oficiales que sobrevivieron a Solano López se aliaron con estos "redentores" ungidos por el exilio en tierras del Plata o en el Viejo Mundo. Entre todos retomaron el gobierno bajo la égida de las fuerzas de ocupación y continuaron la destrucción final del país.

La Prostitución Patriótica, preconizada por el padre Maíz, se transformó en la mascarada de la Reconstrucción Patriótica, que en realidad no fue otra cosa que una demolición de ruinas. Empezaron a venderse por bolachas las tierras públicas, las mujeres continuaron vendiéndose por bolachas. Era la ley de los condenados a perpetuidad a la corrupción de la servidumbre voluntaria. A caballo de los forzados montaron los tiranuelos, los sátrapas, los vendepatrias, primos hermanos en todas partes.

Una figura histórica compacta y compleja como la del padre Fidel Maíz, un hombre como él, forjado a imagen de esta tierra y nutrido con sus esencias y sus escorias, no ha sido aún comprendido. En su degradación, en sus crímenes, en sus pecados, es el antihéroe más puro y virtuoso del Paraguay. Fue un genuino soldado de Cristo, el Judas de la Última Cena, un apóstol que juró en falso infinidad de veces, un antisanto sin corona de martirio surgido del cristianismo de las catacumbas que tuvo en el Paraguay su último refugio. Nadie entendió a este hombre, a este sacerdote, que eligió cometer los pecados y los sacrilegios más execrables ofreciéndose como víctima propiciatoria, un negro y rijoso cordero pascual, el más infame y miserable, para que la sangre de Cristo, vertida en el Gólgota, tuviera algún sentido fuera de la imposible redención humana. De otra manera habría que tomar en serio el chiste ateo de Stendhal de que la única disculpa de Dios es que no existe.

El antihéroe virtuoso, el antisanto sin corona, quiso recoger en sus manos ensangrentadas el soplo de vida que aún le quedaba a su pueblo moribundo. Quiso salvar a su Iglesia prisionera de las maquinaciones de una secta de esbirros de la Fe, a la que no quiso reconocer como una congregación digna de Cristo. Los capuchinos, primero, luego el solio oscuro y oscurantista del Vaticano, por mediación de su internuncio en Río de Janeiro (un verdadero sátrapa de la religión romana), interpusieron todo su poder y declararon una guerra implacable al cura rebelde y revolucionario. Trataron de aplastarlo pero no lograron prevalecer sobre el cordero rebelde e indómito. Tuvieron que devolver al Paraguay su Iglesia tomada en rehenes como diócesis sufragánea de la Iglesia de los enemigos. La victoria del curita Maíz está ahí, brillando en la oscuridad como un cabo de vela sobre la lápida de una inmensa sepultura. Sólo donde hay sepulcros las resurrecciones son posibles. Pecó el blasfemo, se arrastró el apóstata hasta la más extrema degradación, para que la justicia de Dios, si existe de verdad, pudiera resplandecer en los justos. Que sus pecados le sean perdonados...

Perdóname, Morena, el socrático interludio sarmientino y este último, extenso *intermezzo* bélico de Sir Richard Francis Burton. No tendrán ningún interés para ti. No los quise omitir sin embargo. Estoy escribiéndote al hilo de los momentos que voy viviendo. Hay cosas de la historia y de la gente de este país que sólo ahora, cuando ya es demasiado tarde para mí, se me van revelando en su profundidad y complejidad. Lo curioso es que las veo y las comprendo mejor en el prisma un poco especular de los relatos de extranjeros. Acaso porque yo mismo soy un extranjero y no puedo ya ver lo que fue mío sino desde fuera de mí. En el doble forro de mi casaca escocesa, sobre los latidos del corazón, abulta apenas el pequeño bolso con el anillo y el frasquito de veneno. No me separo de ellos un solo instante. Y cuando llevo la mano al corazón, son el anillo y el frasquito los que toco. Llevo también adonde vaya las páginas que te escribo en el portafolios, que así me sirve de memento y de escudo.

Me hace bien escribirte en lo oscuro. No veo sino el punto fosfórico de la pluma en el momento en que imprime el trazo que se seca y desvanece. Mi amor por ti es como esta escritura espectral: se inscribe y muere para resucitar en tu lectura. Te siento a mi lado, aunque estés muy lejos. Te escribo como en una dulcísima coagulación del tiempo. Esta larga e ininterrumpida carta te llegará desde el pasado cuando el futuro no tenga ya ningún sentido para mí y estas líneas no sean más que la corta memoria de un presente que desaparece como el trazo de la pluma. ¿Qué más puedo esperar sino que todo esté consumado? Mientras te comentaba hace un rato las palabras de Malwida Brinnicky-Niëztky y de Lou Andréas Salomé, a propósito del drama de Nietzsche, el *Crucificado*, recordé lo que el malogrado genio escribió en *Ecce homo* sobre el poema que Lou compuso para que él mismo le pusiera música. La perfidia de su hermana Elisabeth no pudo falsificar ni borrar este epitafio.

Dice Nietzsche: "Alguna vez, en el futuro, se cantará este himno en memoria mía. Es la asombrosa inspiración de una joven rusa, apátrida universal, con quien entonces mantenía una amistad sin parangón posible. Cuando me separé de Lou porque sentí que no podía ofrecerle felicidad, ella me dijo: *Aún tienes tu sufrimiento*... La magnífica muchacha no consideraba el sufrimiento como una objeción contra la vida. Pero, al filo de la muerte, yo no podía darle ya ni vida, ni felicidad, ni sufrimiento..."

Noto mientras te escribo, no sé si con alegría o con tristeza, que se me está borrando la lengua del exilio injertada a lo largo de tantos años en la lengua natal. Pero ésta no reaparece. La lengua es el último refugio de los fugitivos pero es también lo primero que se pierde. Mi estilo se me va pareciendo cada vez menos. Me enfrenta y me contradice negándome pero todavía me incluye. Tú recuperarás en la lectura lo que falta de mí.

Desde el exterior oigo que sube en oleadas una música de arpas extrañamente agigantada. Salgo al balcón con los prismáticos. El comité de recepción está tirando la casa por la ventana. Un conjunto de más de un centenar de tocadoras de arpa, ataviadas del blanco *typoi* popular, ubicadas en las escalinatas de la explanada, nos trae el saludo de la clásica serenata. Este número no figura en el programa de agasajos, de modo que debe ser tomado como una primicia y una sorpresa.

Las hermosas y gallardas arpistas forman con sus cuerpos y sus instrumentos las letras en espiral de la palabra *¡Bienvenidos!* Pertenecen a la Escuela Nacional del Arpa Criolla, el conservatorio musical más importante del país. Proyectores de luces especiales dan un aire ingrávido a las arpistas. Parecen flotar en la nube de humo de grandes pebeteros que mezclan a la música el aroma del jazmín y la reseda. El binóculo me permite tener a las musicantes al alcance de la mano, como sentadas en los arriates de la balconada. Los aires nacionales se suceden sin solución de continuidad. Los invitados se apiñan en la *loggia*. Están como en suspenso, deslumbrados y seducidos por ese espectáculo feérico que supera, si no en magnificencia, por lo menos en exotismo, a los mejores festivales mundiales de luz y sonido, habituales en los escenarios de las ruinas milenarias de Grecia, Italia o España. Algo semejante vimos en Avignon, el año pasado. Pero éste es, de lejos, el más sorprendente y original.

De pronto descubro a mi antigua amiga, la bellísima Fulvia Marcia con su arpa de brazo enchapado en escamas de plata y el cabezal labrado en forma de cabeza de serpiente. Fulvia es la directora de la Escuela y, en este momento, la directora del conjunto que ofrece el recital en nuestro homenaje. En los cambios de ritmos, todas siguen el movimiento de los brazos, el balanceo suave pero imperativo de su cabeza ceñida por una guirnalda de jazmines

sobre la larga cabellera color de miel silvestre. El sonido
metálico de su instrumento está dotado de una resonancia
especial. Supongo que ella no me ve. A través del cordaje
de su instrumento siento sin embargo sus miradas fijas en
mí. En un gesto instintivo me aliso el pelo y retoco el nudo
de la corbata. Veo sus ojos rasgados, las pestañas larguísimas y negras por el rimel de henequén, los párpados pla-
teados como cubiertos de escarcha, moda que impuso hacía
cien años Madama Lynch en Paraguay y, dos mil años
antes, Cleopatra, en Egipto y Roma.
    Fulvia Marcia está allí como la imagen misma de la
juventud. La primera del curso, siempre, la abanderada de
los desfiles, el fetiche de nuestra Facultad, la belleza y la gracia juntas, la inteligencia hecha mujer. No ha cambiado. Es
la misma de siempre. El tiempo trabaja a su favor. La contemplo como olvidada de sí, arrastrada en su inmovilidad
por los giros de la música rítmica y sensual. Afrodita tocando el arpa que los jesuitas enseñaron a labrar y a tocar a los
neófitos guaraníes. La veo marchar gallarda en las mañanas
de los grandes desfiles, envuelta en los pliegues de la enseña
nacional. Vuelvo a contemplar estático su silueta afinada por
el ceñidor de dormir cuando aparecía en el balcón de su alcoba para agradecer las serenatas que sus compañeros de
curso le llevábamos en noches de verano plateadas por la
luna llena. Con la punta de los dedos echaba a volar besos
que nos disputábamos en el aire como si se tratara realmente de besos corpóreos, de pedazos latientes de su propio
aliento. Todos estábamos locos por ella y esa rivalidad nos
unía en la hermandad de los excluidos, pues Fulvia tenía
otras miras más allá de nuestro destino de jovenzuelos pobres que iban para farmacéuticos, contables o abogadillos.
    Odiseo Aquino surgió a mi lado de repente.
    —Parece que le gusta la señora Fulvia —dijo po-
niéndose íntimo—. Es la esposa del señor Ministro del Interior.

Me hice el desentendido. No experimenté la menor emoción. Esa presencia del ídolo de mi juventud no contaba para mí sino como un detalle del decorado irreal. Debo darte razón, Jimena, una vez más: el pasado no existe. No existe más que la memoria del presente, tan efímera como el presente mismo. La música de arpas y el coro de voces femeninas llenaban de resonancias suaves la noche turbia y sin estrellas. Se apagaron las fuentes de luz y sonido. En la penumbra aún llena de vibraciones, las siluetas blancas fueron descendiendo en fila por la rampa y desaparecieron en la explanada como siluetas ascéticas de penitentes. La última en desaparecer, abrazada a su arpa semejante a un gran pez de plata, fue Fulvia Marcia. El silencio reinó de nuevo en torno al fastuoso hotel. Sólo entonces me volví hacia el botones.

—Quiero que me guíes a la Chacarita.

—A su orden, señor. No es lejos. Podemos ir a pie.

Tomé mi cámara fotográfica, la colgué en banderola y nos fuimos.

—¿Quiere ir al velorio del terrorista? No entiendo para qué.

—Voy a sacarle unas fotos —le dije.

—Ah..., ya entiendo...

Pasada la catedral, anduvimos un buen rato por callejuelas de tierra bordeando el parque Bernardino Caballero. Bajamos las barrancas de la bahía y entramos en esa hoya de inundaciones y desgracias. En medio de una jungla de plantas acuáticas se escalonaban los ranchos sostenidos por enclenques pilotes. Perros esqueléticos ladraban cavernosamente a nuestro paso. También aquí el lugar había cambiado de aspecto, aunque permanecía esquivo, impenetrable. Pasamos frente a un edificio moderno de dos plantas, impensable en ese lugar.

—Es la casa de mi padre —dijo Odiseo con inocultable respeto.

Lo contorneaba un cercado de alambradas de púas sostenidas por pilotes simbólicos semejantes a las pesadas porras de los batallones paramilitares liderados por el chacaritense don Ramón.

—No se pueden tocar los alambres —dijo Odiseo—. Están electrizados con corrientes de alta tensión. Al principio, por las mañanas, mi padre tenía que desconectar los alambres y venía con sus garroteros a despegar de las alambradas a los borrachos y los perros que se habían quedado fritos pegados allí.

Pensé en el héroe de esos zanjones que había empezado a destacarse al disolver con sus legiones, a garrotazo limpio, las manifestaciones políticas y estudiantiles, en el ataque al convento de Cristo Rey, en el desmantelamiento de casas de opositores y en el asesinato a garrote de líderes de la resistencia. La única acción en la que había sido derrotado fue la huelga del Hospital de Clínicas. Los estudiantes, médicos y enfermeros le tomaron en rehenes. Durante cuarenta días lo mantuvieron narcotizado en un quirófano haciendo creer a su gente que había sido operado del corazón y que estaba grave. No se le debía molestar. Al final su plana mayor tuvo que pactar y ceder. Don Ramón resucitó y salió del hospital como un enfermo dado de baja. Le dieta postoperatoria le rebajó cuarenta kilos de peso y de coraje. Salió que se apoyaba en su sombra. Los estudiantes de medicina y los enfermeros le iban sosteniendo para que no se cayera. Por un tiempo don Ramón se recluyó en cuarteles de invierno por orden del dictador.

Odiseo se cansó de tratar de reanudar la charla. Absorto en mis pensamientos, no le hacía ningún caso. Finalmente tuvo que adaptarse a mi silencio. El crujir de las suelas de mis zapatos en la costra dura de las pendientes y en los playones de arena se reabsorbían de inmediato en la atmósfera esponjosa del lugar que hedía a restos de pescado y plantas en putrefacción. Un perro sarnoso saltó sobre Odiseo y le lamió la cara.

—Es Floro, mi perro —dijo Odiseo sin excesivo orgullo pero con evidente afecto—. Antes se llamaba Manfloro porque tiene malas costumbres. Floro es más corto y más lindo y nadie se burla cuando se le llama.

A través de la abertura de una choza descubrí los destellos temblorosos de las velas.

—Aquí es —dijo el botones—.Yo no entro en el velorio de un asesino...

—Quédate aquí, a esperarme —le ordené y entré—. O mejor, vete a tu casa.

—No, señor. Le voy a esperar.

En torno al cuerpo yacente algunas mujeres lloraban o rezaban sus monótonas y sordas letanías de difunto. A la cabecera del muerto, una mujer que debía de ser su madre, hincada de rodillas, inmóvil, casi espectral, murmuraba la fúnebre melopea con los dientes apretados. El destello de las velas alumbraba parte de su rostro seco y anguloso que el manto dejaba ver y hacía brillar el mechón de vello corto y ríspido que le había crecido exageradamente en la barbilla. Me aproximé y le pedí permiso para sacar una foto al cadáver de su hijo. Asintió con un gesto de tristísima resignación. Le prometí entregarle una copia de la toma cuando estuviese revelada. La mujer no me oyó o no entendió; en todo caso, eso no tenía importancia para ella. Volvió a su sorda melopea.

Me acerqué al catre donde estaba depositado el cadáver. Me costaba unir los tres rostros del muerto: el casi adolescente de Pedro Alvarenga en la cámara de tortura, el rostro barbudo del pastor mennonita, en el Boeing, oculto por la barba postiza y los anteojos oscuros, y el de ahora, deformado por los golpes, violáceo por la muerte. Esos rostros separados en el tiempo y en experiencias diferentes resistían a juntarse. Rechazaban esa alianza monstruosa de la noche, la soledad, el silencio del propio muerto, inmóvil, desasido de todo lo que no fuera esa impasibilidad que lo tenía ocupado.

El rostro de Pedro Alvarenga, muerto, era distinto ahora, sobre todo porque su férvida sangre valerosa había sido desarmada para siempre de todo su acero. La desigualdad era demasiado grande. El coraje de un hombre como Pedro no fue hecho para tan áspero uso. Pero ese rostro allí, el último, conservaba una serenidad casi sonriente, pese a las deformidades y a los hematomas. Estaba ahí con los ojos cerrados, como dormido en una paz infinita. Ese hombre yacente se permitía ignorar el universo, y si algún pensamiento había en su silencio, ese pensamiento que atribuimos a los estados de la vida después de la muerte, no podía ser sino la expresión de una felicidad absoluta y esencial.

Me aproximé un poco más. Una sombra muy densa cruzó la cara del muerto, la puso luminosa, volvió a pasar sobre ella y la oscureció como cuando las nubes ocultan la luna llena de cráteres. Oprimí el botón del obturador y el relámpago del flash alumbró vívidamente la pobre habitación. El triple rostro se había juntado en uno y esa fusión produjo el efecto de que el muerto se había movido bruscamente en el momento mismo de la toma. De modo que volví a sacar otras dos como resguardo. Las caras de las mujeres se habían inmovilizado semejantes a tallas de piedra en los fogonazos del flash.

La vista de los muertos con sus caras de arcilla verdosa, los cuerpos rígidos como si de pronto se hubieran mineralizado, la raja del blanco de los ojos entre los párpados, su inmovilidad ultraterrena, me han resultado siempre intolerables. Siento por ellos una antipatía irracional, algo más que la vulgar repugnancia que comúnmente se experimenta ante ellos. Siempre he sido incapaz de mirar un cadáver sin repugnancia y sin un profundo disgusto. A la muerte sólo se la puede odiar. Pero ahora, ante el cadáver de Pedro Alvarenga, estos sentimientos luchan contra mis recuerdos, contra mis sentimientos de camaradería, de fraternal afecto.

Un golpe de viento apagó algunas velas. Una densa penumbra cayó sobre la cara del muerto. De repente me pareció ver en ella la cara angulosa de la madre, que ahora tenía un parecido extraordinario con la de su hijo, como si el muerto hubiese envejecido de golpe en la cara de su madre y como si de pronto le hubiera crecido a él también una híspida mecha de pelo canoso en el mentón. Desde la cara de la madre, Pedro me miraba con los ojos cerrados. Seguía observándome con más fuerza que veinticuatro horas atrás desde su asiento en el Boeing. Me miraba con el mismo sufrimiento que veinte años atrás en la cámara de tortura de la Técnica.

La tenebrosa conspiración de la noche parecía tomar a cada instante nuevas formas de acecho y acorralamiento. El universo entero era un misterio de oscuridad; sobre todo en esta oscuridad enchapada de esa luminosidad artificial que ocultaba el cielo de la noche. El silencio estaba lleno de susurros semejantes a ecos de sonidos muertos hacía mucho tiempo. Había sonidos vivos también, imprecisables, indefinibles. El leve azotar del aire por las alas de los murciélagos. ¿Por qué esos chillidos de extraños pájaros nocturnos que buscan su presa, gritos de pequeños animales en súbitos encontronazos con enemigos furtivos más poderosos? ¿Por qué el aleteo bajo y aterrado de ese matorral lleno de pájaros invisibles?...

Hubo de repente algo como un apagón de la luz turbia y rojiza. La noche emergió de golpe, esplendorosa, en lo alto, tachonada de astros, el arco de la luna clavado en el azul del cielo. Invadió el rancho, oscureció las caras orantes bajo los mantos rotosos. Un grito indescriptible se levantó del coro de mujeres y se rompió en agudas voces de incrédula ferocidad y profundo reproche. Los rostros velados se volvieron unánimes hacia mí con los ojos frenéticos y centelleantes, como haciéndome responsable por el eclipse que acaba de ocurrir.

—¡Cállense! —gritó la madre en guaraní y su voz resonó por todo el erial, entre los ranchos lacustres, sobre los zanjones repletos de putrefacción y de basura.

La silueta de Odiseo se asomó desde el exterior a la abertura que hacía de puerta. La madre del muerto prorrumpió otra vez en alaridos angustiosos. Las demás mujeres se abalanzaron contra él, le arañaron la cara con la furia de oscuras euménides y lo arrojaron fuera, llenándole de insultos. Se replegaron en un silencio sobresaltado como en espera de algo mucho peor. Sólo el muerto permanecía impasible. Afuera los árboles se pandeaban golpeados por el viento, un viento que estaba allí en un remolino inmóvil, que parecía no venir de ninguna parte ni soplar en ninguna dirección.

Terminado el apagón, la luz turbia y rojiza volvió a reflotar y a reinar. La comba azul y estrellada, la luna en cuarto menguante, desaparecieron taponadas, comidas por esa luminosidad que no era diurna ni nocturna. Entre el bisbiseo de las plegarias surgió a mis espaldas un suspiro de alivio exhalado por muchas gargantas, como si todo hubiera vuelto a la normalidad.

Salí. Traté de orientarme entre las malezas. En el camino de tierra Odiseo me alcanzó. Trató de explicar el ataque de las mujeres del velorio.

—Esas mujeres me odian porque soy hijo de Ramón Aquino —dijo despreciativamente—. Son todas terroristas de lo peor. Más de una vez, mi padre tuvo que arrearlas a garrotazos y meterlas en la cárcel.

Yo no salía de mi silencio. Me preguntó si me había

dado cuenta del cortocircuito que se había producido hacía un rato. Denegué con un movimiento de cabeza. Es la primera vez que se produce un corte de luz en Itaipú.

–¡No le va a gustar nada esta falla al Karaí, con lo cara que ha salido la represa!... —dijo con aire agorero, como pensando en responsables concretos que iban a recibir su castigo por algo tan grave como un fenómeno sísmico.

Durante todo el trayecto de la excursión nocturna había percibido la caída de unas partículas blandas y olorosas como gotas de una lluvia intermitente. Tenía la cabeza, la barba y los hombros cubiertos de esa capsulillas que el viento arrastraba en sus remolinos. Recogí un puñado de esas simientes y las mostré a Odiseo.

—¿Qué es esto? —le pregunté.

—Son brotes de helechos. Hay también de otros árboles. Siguen volando todavía de noche y de día. Caen en cualquier parte y vuelven a prender donde encuentran buena tierra.

Creí que el jovenzuelo inventaba otra de sus historias. Le pregunté de dónde venían esos brotes.

—De las selvas del Alto Paraná. Para construir la represa tuvieron que voltear las selvas. Voltearon millones de hectáreas. Ya no hay más monte virgen. Esos brotes de helechos y de otras especies de árboles escaparon de la mortandad de la madera. Escapan y vuelan con los vientos del este y del norte en busca de las tierras que perdieron. Pero no tienen memoria. Vuelan a ciegas. El viento los lleva adonde quiere. Menos mal que vuelan los brotes no más. Si hubieran volado los árboles ya nos hubieran aplastado a todos.

Un piquete de hombres armados nos dio el alto. El sargento que los comandaba me pidió documentos. Le alargué mi pasaporte.

—El señor está invitado al congreso oficial —abogó Odiseo, como si hubiera zumbado un mosquito. Nadie reparó en él.

—¿Qué vino a hacer aquí? —me preguntó el sargento.

—Vine a tomar unas fotos al terrorista que mataron en el aeropuerto. Tengo que hacer un informe para el congreso.

—Muéstreme su autorización del jefe de Policía.

Le dije que no la tenía, que no se me hubiera ocurrido tampoco solicitarla en un país libre como éste. El sargento me exigió que le entregara la cámara fotográfica. Se la di. Extrajo el rollo de películas y me devolvió el aparato. Los vi desvanecerse del mismo modo en que aparecieron.

—Están muy rigurosos en estas cosas —comentó Odiseo—. Hablaré con mi papá. A lo mejor él consigue que le devuelvan los negativos. Es muy amigo del Señor Presidente.

Dije al muchacho que se podía quedar, que ya conocía el camino y que iba a volver solo al hotel.

—Como usted quiera, señor —aceptó el muchacho.

Le di los veinte dólares prometidos.

—Si me consigues los negativos, te daré otro tanto.

Agradeció llevándose la mano a la visera y se alejó con zancadas de triunfador.

Entre el puntear de los ladridos lejanos y los remezones del viento, una melodía muy suave venía de alguna parte. Me penetró una sensación vaga. No era miedo. Era más bien el sentimiento de lo sobrenatural que he experimentado más de una vez pero que siempre consideré con desconfianza como una reacción irracional o imaginaria ante lo desconocido.

La visión del cadáver de Pedro Alvarenga hizo reflotar en mí el recuerdo de Leda Kautner. Mis dudas persistían desde el momento mismo de la tragedia, no hacía aún doce horas. Me rebelaba contra la idea de que la muchacha de los Cárpatos hubiese quedado incinerada en la explosión del Boeing. Era extraño el hecho de que viniera en ese avión. Más inexplicable aún me parecía el que se hubiera quedado en él a esperar la muerte. Contra todas las evidencias, perseveraba en mí la sensación, el presentimiento oscuro pero imperioso de que Leda estaba *viva*.

Desde que vi estallar y arder el avión, me rondó el pensamiento de que ella debió haber descendido un momento antes. No pudo no hacerlo aunque yo no la viera desembarcar. En ningún momento había perdido de vista la escalera y plataforma de desembarco. No la vi bajar, es cierto, pero pudo haberlo hecho en un momento de descuido mío. Milímetro a milímetro, segundo tras segundo, reviví ese intervalo angustioso. Sólo quedaba un lapso de unos treinta segundos en el que pude haber despegado los ojos o los prismáticos de ese lugar: el momento en que entregué la niña a la nurse y le presenté a la anciana, esos dos seres desamparados que la propia Leda había puesto a mi cargo para ayudarlas a bajar. En esos treinta segundos la ágil muchacha montañesa pudo abandonar la cabina que estaba a punto de convertirse en una masa ardiendo.

Tal es mi certidumbre, que he decidido hacer las indagaciones del caso. Dispongo de una mediadora eficaz: una de las monitoras responsables de nuestro piso, Dalila Mieres. La joven se ha mostrado desde el principio muy amable conmigo. Las monitoras residen en el mismo hotel haciendo guardia permanente. Me ha dado su nombre y el número de teléfono de su habitación, rogándome que la llamara ante cualquier emergencia en la que pudiera necesitarla, a cualquier hora del día o la noche.

La melodía seguía sonando en alguna parte como el sonido de esas flautas que los chicos pobres se fabrican con canutos de caña de castilla. Reproducía ahora las tres notas de la melopea fúnebre del velorio. Me tapé los oídos y apreté el paso. Remonté la barranca y salí a través de un desagüe excavado por los raudales a los pies de la catedral. Esos raudales habían desmoronado ya dos veces la vieja catedral que ahora era nueva, aunque no se notara, y habían arrastrado hacía un siglo al mismísimo Cabildo. Las furias naturales imponen también su dictadura. Tomé por Independencia hacia Sarmiento.

Apenas subí a mi habitación, llamé a Dalila Mieres. Me atendió ella misma. Le pedí disculpas por lo avanzado de la hora. Me dijo que no dormía y que estaba con mucho gusto a mis órdenes, preguntándome en que idioma prefería yo que siguiéramos hablando. En español, le dije, eludiendo apenas el lapsus de responderle "en el nuestro". Le expliqué, resumiéndole como pude, el caso de Leda Kautner, alumna mía de posgrado en Francia y ahora azafata en la Flota Aérea del Estado. Le di sus datos biográficos, su dirección y número de teléfono en Munich.

Introduje un pretexto capcioso, como elemento de presión psicológica: el de haberle entregado un frasco con unas vacunas contra la fiebre amarilla, que no podía dejar de aplicármelas por tratarse de la segunda dosis. Insinué que el frasco no me había sido devuelto por la mencionada azafata, debido tal vez —la excusé— a los incidentes del arribo.

Le confié, además, la inquietud que tenía por haberla visto entrar de nuevo en el avión, cuando toda la tripulación ya había desembarcado, un momento antes de la explosión. Con voz atenta y preocupada, la monitora me dijo haber tomado nota de todo lo que le había expresado. Se comprometió a que desde las primeras horas de la mañana haría las averiguaciones pertinentes y me aseguró que el frasco de vacuna me sería devuelto de inmediato. La seguridad profesional pero sobre todo el acento humano de Dalila Mieres en su voz de timbre cálido y agradable me resultó de buen augurio.

Hay sonidos vivos, me dije antes de dormirme.

Hoy, jueves 28, han comenzado los actos del congreso. A las 9 de la mañana fuimos conducidos al Panteón de los Héroes para depositar nuestra ofrenda floral. La comitiva oficial, encabezada por el Ministro de Cultura, nos esperaba al pie del monumento, bastante reducido para permitir el paso de los tres centenares de invitados locales y extranjeros. Ante la atónita curiosidad del gentío, aglomerado en las inmediaciones, los que quedamos fuera nos entretuvimos en vagar por las calles Palma y Estrella, tomando fotos. Yo reconocía esos lugares como si estuvieran dentro de mí.

La banda de músicos de la Policía, famosa en los anales históricos del país, ejecutó marcialmente el himno nacional. De esta banda salieron los más grandes músicos del país. Una escuadra de fusileros, del cuerpo de tropas que rendía honores, avanzó un paso y disparó al aire la descarga reglamentaria. Tras la nota bélica, 279 coronas de flores, una por cada invitado, eran depositadas en el peristilo. El Ministro de Cultura, en representación del presidente, pronunció una alocución, que resultó interminable y soporífica en torno a los tópicos de rigor. Hizo resaltar la importancia cultural, social y política del Congreso de Historia, Cultura y Sociedad de América Latina en el Siglo xx, el primero en su género que se celebra, afirmó, en nuestro continente. Destacó que el acontecimiento estaba destinado a proyectarse como un llamado a la convivencia pacífica de los pueblos, a la alianza e integración entre los países de la región, y como un mensaje de paz y amistad a los países de Europa, los Estados Unidos y el Canadá. De jaulas artísticamente forjadas, el ministro fue sacando, una por una, 279 palomas mensajeras, y las fue soltando al aire turbio de la mañana. En las patas rosadas llevaban anillos metálicos con el saludo de las autoridades nacionales, de la Iglesia, de las Fuerzas Armadas, del Partido de la Reconstrucción, de los invitados al congreso y del pueblo todo de la República. Levantaron el vuelo en dirección a los departamentos y regiones del país. Algunas palomas se extraviaron y penetraron en el hueco de ventilación de un vasto restaurante al paso, llamado El Lido. El extractor de aire comenzó a asperjar la ceremonia con una fina llovizna de sangre, de salsas y refrescos de todos colores.

La complicidad entre anfitriones y huéspedes, entre los antihéroes vivos allí presentes y los héroes del pasado histórico, allí inhumados, entre la inteligencia democrática de Occidente y los halcones de la barbarie totalitaria del Cono Sur, quedaba de este modo sellada con sangre de palomas y sustancias de cocina al pie del más solemne y austero monumento nacional.

Este hecho fue comentado en todos los tonos de la ironía, del humor, de la obsecuencia y de la condenación más airada, en la rueda de prensa que se realizó poco después. Entre los congresales se destacaba ahora un extravagante personaje, totalmente tullido, que parecía atornillado a una resplandeciente silla de ruedas de metal cromado. Fue el instrumento tronitonante de la indignación surgida en el acto de la ofrenda floral. La voz metálica y chirriante del tullido llenó de resonancias el inmenso salón. De su boca emerge un aparato, mezcla de micrófono y altavoz. El tullido, de vaga apariencia humana, crispado en un nudo de venas, de nervios y de músculos, sostiene sobre las rodillas una computadora pequeña. Con una uña larga y corva compone sobre el teclado las frases que quiere pronunciar. El altavoz pequeño pero poderoso resuena con ensordecedora potencia. Es probablemente el discapacitado de voz más estentórea del mundo.

Pregunté a una de las monitoras quién era el baldado. Me dijeron que se le conocía como El Bastardo. Supe después que era bisnieto de Francisco Lacerda, apodado *Chico Diavo*, el corneta de órdenes que lanceó a Solano

López en Cerro-Corá. El general Correa da Cámara, jefe de la vanguardia del ejército brasileño que perseguía a López, había instituido una prima de cien libras esterlinas para quien capturara vivo o muerto al mariscal fugitivo. El corneta de órdenes de Correa da Cámara, elegido por el azar para cazar a López, nunca pudo cobrar la prima. Correa da Cámara se la quedó como blasón honorífico por el asesinato del jefe paraguayo.

Terminada la guerra, *Chico Diavo* permaneció en Paraguay en las fuerzas de ocupación que el imperio de los Braganza mantuvo durante siete años sobre el devastado país. No habían quedado más que inválidos, mujeres y niños, pero aún tenía algunas riquezas naturales que los vencedores querían aprovechar haciendo funcionar al máximo la trituradora de la ocupación. Por otra parte, Argentina y Brasil, los dos mayores aliados, estaban también al borde de la guerra y la repartija del botín y del territorio no estaba aún resuelta. Mitre se había retirado dejando el campo libre al imperio. El generalísimo brasileño recibió órdenes estrictas de mantener el dominio militar y político sobre los vencidos.

Otra de las hazañas del corneta de órdenes fue violar a la hija de una familia patricia de Asunción. El padre de la niña, que era a la sazón fiscal general del Estado, no pudiendo soportar la afrenta del macaco brasileiro, se suicidó. Francisco Lacerda tuvo la nobleza de unirse en matrimonio con la doncella violada y huérfana, que heredó el castillo de Arekutakuá, actual presidio de Emboscada. *Chico Diavo* se hizo además ciudadano paraguayo de adopción.

De esa unión, que tuvo larga descendencia, el único sobreviviente era El Bastardo, lisiado y mudo, pero poseedor de la fortuna que heredó de sus padres. Ahora lo teníamos delante, sentado en su silla de ruedas llevando por delante a todo el mundo con su descomunal inteligencia y su laringe de trueno. El bisnieto del asesino de López era el único ser vivo inmune e invulnerable a los rigores del poder absoluto. Dueño de una poderosa inteligencia y de una formación teórica realmente alucinante en física de partículas y astrofísica, es miembro correspondiente de varios centros e institutos tecnológicos mundiales, incluso de la NASA. Un niño prodigio, un genio innato capaz de presidir una asamblea de sabios, pero capaz también de convertirse en un diabólico genio del mal.

En las limusinas blindadas nos llevaron a conocer la ciudad, "madre de pueblos y nodriza de ciudades". A los invitados les pareció exótica y llena de misterio. Como broche de oro, o de bronce, de la excursión matutina, subimos hasta la cumbre del Tacumbú, cerro sagrado de los antiguos carios, centinela del *Río-de-las-Coronas* que dio su nombre al país. El cerro redondo y turgente como un seno sirve ahora como pedestal de la gran estatua del Reconstructor, levantada allí por el arquitecto español, el mismo que por encargo del generalísimo Franco, diseñó y construyó el nuevo escorial del Valle de los Caídos. Las simetrías no podían ser más felices. El hombre todavía vivo estaba allí, en la estatua, más magníficamente muerto que todos los que había mandado matar y seguiría haciendo matar. Recta la diestra señalaba el norte como tendiendo la mano a un interlocutor colosal. Eugène Ionesco, sin poder contener su genio burlón, se prosternó ante la estatua y besó la roca del zócalo como lo suele hacer el papa en sus visitas apostólicas a los pueblos más pobres de la tierra.

—¿Por qué se agachó usted a besar los pies del tirano? —le preguntó alguien celebrando la chulería del rumano.

—No me agaché yo. Los pies del tirano subieron hasta mi boca y me hizo tragar todos los dientes —contestó el dramaturgo con su guasa habitual.

Jan Kleenewerk me comunicó su sorpresa de ver esta estatua pedestre y no la ecuestre como suelen ser las de todos los generales. Señalé el gran cañón de bronce, también en tamaño natural, que se hallaba a la derecha del Reconstructor.

—El tiranosaurio es artillero —expliqué—. Prefirió el cañón, símbolo de su arma, en lugar del gran caballo heráldico de los caudillos. Hay un *ñe'engá* que afirma maliciosamente como toda *vox populi* que aquí los caballos del ejército tienen más raza que el trasero de sus jinetes.

Los ojos miopes de Kleenewerk divisaron el cañón.

—Debieron pues montarlo encima —dijo.

Desde lo alto del cerro se divisa a lo lejos una fila interminable de hormigas que se mueven hasta donde alcanza la vista en el horizonte cegado por el ardor de las reverberaciones. Son parte de la legión de cien mil hombres que está construyendo las vías para los trenes de alta velocidad que van a cubrir los tres mil kilómetros entre Asunción y Brasilia. Sobre los durmientes brillan con el filo de cuchillos las dos rectas paralelas de los rieles que se juntan en el horizonte a lo largo de puentes, terraplenes, túneles, cordilleras, promontorios y ríos. El tiranosaurio está orgulloso de esta obra inmensa, par de la central hidroeléctrica. Él mismo ha elegido el nombre para los bólidos que van a circular por esas vías: *Tatá-vevé* o Fuego Volador. El nombre forma las siglas de TAV (trenes de alta velocidad). Sobre un puente colgante de más de diez kilómetros de largo y cien metros de altura esos fuegos voladores van a cruzar sobre la represa a 300 kilómetros por hora, alimentados con la energía eléctrica de sus turbinas. Pensé en la ruina traqueteante del Paraguay Central Railway Company, construido un siglo atrás por el ingeniero de puentes y caminos Sir Charles

Percival Farquhar I. Sus trenes circulan aún con la pertina-
cia de fósiles de la Revolución Industrial. En esos trenes del
Ferrocarril del Sur, venía yo a Asunción desde mi aldea de
Iturbe del Manorá para continuar la escuela y el colegio. De
aquellos viajes sólo recuerdo el aroma apetitoso de los chi-
pás de Pirayú.

El TAV es obra de Sir Charles Percival Farquhar II,
bisnieto del primero.

Tres conquistas adicionales aumentan la satisfacción y el orgullo del dictador: los créditos astronómicos
que ha obtenido de los bancos mundiales para la realización de esta empresa faraónica. Lo que representa el regreso del feudo paraguayo al redil de los países más favorecidos
por la ayuda del BID, del Fondo Monetario Internacional y
del Banco Mundial, bajo el signo de la democracia imperial, en conexión con otros centros financieros europeos y
asiáticos. El lema del dictador "Abrir los brazos al capital
extranjero" se cumple de esta manera generosamente. Es
el único elemento foráneo al que se permite la entrada.

Un segundo logro de carácter social alimenta me-
recidamente su autosuficiencia de estadista probo y moderno: el haber resuelto de golpe el problema de los cien mil
campesinos sin tierra, causa permanente de un gasto super-
fluo de energía represiva. Los ha puesto en su totalidad a
trabajar en la construcción del TAV bajo la vigilancia de las
tropas de un cuerpo del ejército. Diez mil hombres con tanques y helicópteros para "custodiar" a cien mil hombres
armados de pala, pico, miseria e impotencia, alimentados
con cien toneladas diarias de poroto y bastimentos, no es
un mal negocio.

A lo largo de las vías las familias de los nuevos esclavos
ferroviarios han formado un pueblo ambulante. En casetas de
cartón o de paja las mujeres preparan la comida para sus hombres.
Columnas de humo, cuerdas con las ropas lavadas, puestas a
secar, perros flacos, criaturas con los vientres enormes por la

anquilostomiasis, siguen el avance de los rieles. Enormes camiones de la intendencia del ejército van y vienen rugiendo en pos de la errante caravana, que más se parece a una peregrinación multitudinaria como la de Caacupé, el 8 de diciembre, y la de Cerro-Corá, los 1º de marzo, hasta el santuario de Francisco Solano López erigido sobre el lugar de su muerte. El tiranosaurio restableció la fecha del 1º de marzo para la peregrinación anual al santuario de Héroe máximo. Antes ésta se realizaba cada cuatro años según el falso bisiesto del 29 de febrero de 1870, sugerido a Solano López por el padre Maíz, pausa nociva y debilitante para el espíritu patriótico.

Las dos grandes empresas binacionales, la central hidroeléctrica y el TAV, sellaban así la alianza económico-militar de Paraguay y Brasil. El sueño secreto del dictador es incorporarse a los Estados Unidos del Brasil como un nuevo y floreciente estado. Más de un millón de colonos brasileños han levantado ya por su cuenta el borrador de este nuevo estado sobre las mejores tierras de la región oriental con bandera, lengua, escuelas y leyes propias, bajo el signo monetario del cruzeiro. Por fin el fiel de la balanza había encontrado, bajo el genio del Reconstructor, el adecuado contrapeso al equilibrio del Plata, neutralizando la permanente amenaza argentina. La posteridad le tenía reservado el sitial de los próceres egregios.

El dictador agradecía y bendecía la llegada al Paraguay del ingeniero inglés, Sir Percival Farquhar II, que le había presentado el proyecto delineado en todos sus detalles. Ahora Sir Percival dirige los trabajos, recio, compacto, ingrávido, desde su helicóptero privado. Acaba de pasar raudo hacia su puesto de comando. No despega sus labios del micrófono que le comunica todo el tiempo con una red de emisoras de radio y televisión de circuito cerrado.

Años antes, Sir Percival había logrado recuperar con un método de cateo de su invención a rayos láser, el tesoro nacional y lo que quedó del tesoro privado de Madama Lynch, enterrados durante la Guerra Grande en lugares inaccesibles. La exhumación de esos tesoros, a cargo de un cuerpo de ingenieros de puentes y caminos contratados en Inglaterra, bajo la protección de la propia escolta presidencial, duró cinco años. Algunas versiones filtradas del Estado Mayor de Sir Percival aseguraban que el conjunto de estos tesoros recuperados equivalían o superaban el volumen y el valor del tesoro enterrado por el general Yamashita en enormes pirámides subterráneas de cemento y acero durante la Segunda Guerra Mundial, en una de las islas del Japón.

El genio imaginativo y pragmático de Sir Percival entregó al dictador, deducido el tercio pactado a su favor en concepto de honorarios, el fabuloso tesoro que las manos de una mujer habían sepultado cien años antes en los arcanos de la tierra paraguaya. Madama Lynch, pese a su amistad con Eugenia de Montijo y el patrocinio diplomático de Napoleón III, no logró recuperar ese nuevo y secreto El Dorado, que concitaba la codicia nacional e internacional. Tampoco rescató las cinco mil leguas de tierra que le obsequió el mariscal en un legado casi póstumo, como antes le había hecho el presente principesco de su bastón de mando, que ella convirtió en el mango de su sombrilla.

Cuando volvió, para reconquistar los derechos y los bienes de los que había sido despojada, la expulsaron como a una vulgar mujer de mala vida. Estuvo a punto de ser linchada por una concentración de millares de mujeres que la llenaron de injurias y ultrajes, al grito de *"¡A Madama Lynch la ley del lynch!... ¡Ya yucama la Madama!..."*(*) Protegida por las fuerzas de ocupación, logró huir y se refugió en el barco que la había traído.

Regresó a París. Vivió y murió pobremente. La funeraria municipal la enterró como a una mendiga en el

*¡Matemos a la Madama!

Père-Lachaise. Todo eso era historia antigua. Las cenizas de Madama Lynch reposan ahora en el Panteón de los Héroes junto a las de su amado mariscal. Desde ese solio glorioso, como desde ultratumba, la legendaria mujer asiste al renacer de la patria solana. La que ella había visto sucumbir con el mariscal en el barroso arroyo del Aquidabánnigüí. Los lampadarios perpetuos del Panteón alumbran su féretro recamado de oro y piedras preciosas.

El pensar en las circunvoluciones idiotas de la historia me ha infligido un fortísimo dolor en las mías. Me acerqué a la estatua. El Reconstructor me tendía la mano de bronce. Saqué del pequeño bolso el anillo, me lo puse en el dedo mayor y ensayé el apretón de manos magnicida. El metal del anillo sonó contra el metal de la mano enguantada. Esa figura estaba puesta ahí con el solo y exclusivo fin de que yo pudiese ejercitar el gesto liberador del aguijón y la ponzoña. Un grito lejano me hizo volver la cabeza. Retiré la mano con la confusa presteza de un criminal sorprendido *in fraganti* puñal en mano. Miré en derredor. No había nadie. Desde abajo, minúsculo, desmirriado, inoportuno, el chófer de la limusina gritó que me estaba esperando si quería regresar al hotel. Lentamente, tropezando con las piedras, empecé a bajar la ladera del cerro dos veces sagrado.

Por la tarde, luego de un almuerzo campestre a orillas del lago Ypacaraí, el Ministro de Cultura invitó a una visita a las galerías de arte del Museo Nacional, de la que él mismo se constituyó en guía. Muy pocos fuimos los voluntarios que nos atrevimos a aliviar la pesada digestión de los más famosos platos típicos del país ante los previsibles horrores que íbamos a contemplar.

La sala de entrada lleva una inscripción en la que se lee: Cándido López pinta la Guerra de la Triple Alianza contra el Paraguay (1865-1870). Esta leyenda, como toda leyenda, sólo dice la verdad a medias. La gran sala alberga el centenar de cuadros de esta crónica pictórica de la primera guerra internacional de América Latina. El Ministro, verboso, pesado, ignorante de toda solemnidad en materia de arte pictórico, explicó que en la exposición realizada en Asunción hacía muchos años, en ocasión de la inauguración de la Casa Sarmiento, un gran pintor paraguayo (cuyo nombre se mantiene en secreto) se afanó por las noches, mientras se mantuvo abierta la exposición, en copiar el centenar de cuadros y en sustituir los auténticos por las copias logradas mediante su ingeniosa industria. Los intérpretes del Ministro, dislálicos y ceceosos a más no poder, sumían a los invitados extranjeros en inextricable confusión. Ionesco iba de un cuadro a otro, observándolos detenidamente con una inmensa lupa que llevaba colgada al pecho, y tomando fotos de los que atraían su interés.

Cándido López había venido a la guerra del Paraguay como valido y en cierto modo como ordenanza del generalísimo Mitre, sostuvo el ministro. Sin embargo, contra lo que sostiene la historia oficial argentina, el pintor no regresó a Buenos Aires con su jefe cuando éste abandonó el teatro de operaciones en 1868. Fíjense ustedes: ¡Dos años antes de la terminación de la guerra que produjo la ruina total del Paraguay!, el Ministro se iba exaltando de fervor nacionalista.

El museo de Buenos Aires demandó al Estado paraguayo ante las cortes internacionales por falsificación y apropiación indebida de patrimonio artístico, sin el menor resultado, informó el Ministro con despectiva suficiencia. Nada probaba tal extremo. Tampoco prosperó la acusación de plagio masivo. Los mejores expertos de la época se confesaron incapaces de descifrar el enigma. Se habló de un portentoso fenómeno de coincidencia creativa y de otras variantes más o menos teóricas y técnicas, pero el asunto no pasó de estas divagaciones completamente estériles, sentenció el guía, sabihondo y enfervorizado.

Lo más extraño del caso, dijo el Ministro, es que el museo de Buenos Aires sólo había enviado una treintena de cuadros. Se le devolvió un centenar con la misma temática que éstos: la naturaleza, el ambiente de guerra, el paisaje después de las batallas, la insondable melancolía de la muerte. Esto es: el museo de Buenos Aires recibió en obsequio unos setenta cuadros más sobre otros combates y batallas que Cándido López no pintó. Había entre ellos cuadros que ya no podían ser originales del pintor argentino, entre ellos el de la crucifixión del mariscal López en Cerro-Corá. Hemos dicho que Cándido López no estuvo en aquel lejano y último escenario de la tragedia. Tal crucifixión de Solano López simplemente no existió. Fue un *bluff* de los eternos enemigos del héroe máximo de la nación paraguaya.

Por otra parte, aunque la técnica, el estilo y el empaste del pintor paraguayo fuesen muy parecidos a los de Cándido López, incluso en la evolución de la pintura durante los cinco años de guerra, los soportes y las materias tintóreas, los óleos de origen vegetal y mineral que el paraguayo utilizó en la mayor parte de sus cuadros, son diferentes de los del pintor argentino. Se notaba que el Ministro recitaba de memoria con total ignorancia de la jerga pictórica un libreto turístico que le habían preparado.

—Existen cuadros —dijo el Ministro señalando un templete oval—, que no son reproducciones de batallas. Son pinturas, tomadas del natural, en los tribunales de sangre. Algunos registran escenas del suplicio en el "cepo Uruguayana", uno de los más terribles de la Guerra Grande. En ellas aparecen el padre Fidel Maíz y los demás fiscales de guerra Centurión, Aveiro, Resquín, Goiburú, Carmona, ordenando y presenciando los suplicios. El fiscal Juan

Crisóstomo Centurión, que había estudiado en las academias de Londres, era novelista y pintor.

Habló el ministro de los atentados y conspiraciones contra el mariscal López y de los procesos sumarísimos que se instruían a los culpables de estos atentados y conspiraciones. Pasó por alto uno de los más sonados que terminó con el fusilamiento del anciano obispo Palacios y de los otros veinte reos por el delito de traición a la patria. Vean ustedes, allí están los padres Maíz y Román, que condujeron el juicio del obispo. Desde un ángulo del cuadro contemplan la ejecución. Estos cuadros tampoco pudieron ser pintados por el argentino Cándido López que no tenía acceso a tales recintos de extrema seguridad. El ministro también omitió pudorosamente mencionar suplicios tales como el descortezamiento de las plantas de los pies de los desertores recapturados, el de los párpados seccionados para dejar los ojos inermes ante la calcinante luz solar en el estaqueo, y la lenta trituración de los reos, a cada vuelta de las barras, en las prensas de tabaco. Surgieron gritos y alaridos de horror.

—¡El estremecimiento del terror es la más alta felicidad de la humanidad!... Lo afirmó el genio apolíneo de Goethe en la segunda parte del Fausto... —clamó Ionesco en francés; nadie le prestó la menor atención; los intérpretes optaron por no intentar la traducción de esas frases ininteligibles por el tartamudeo del autor a quien el ministro le atribuía una y otra vez la obra *Esperando a Godot*.

Parte de las copias apócrifas del museo de Buenos Aires, dijo el ministro reanudando la marcha, fue reproducida no hace mucho por un editor italiano de libros de arte. Es una preciosa edición para bibliófilos. Lleva el nombre del pintor argentino como título y pertenece a una colección producida bajo el signo genérico de *La imagen del hombre*. El libro, de un gran valor artístico y polémico, está prologado por un escritor compatriota nuestro. Cándido López volvió con Mitre a Buenos Aires antes del fin de la guerra, afirmó el guía. Existe la leyenda de que hubo otro pintor, llamado también Cándido López, éste oriundo del Paraguay. Debió de permanecer en los campos de batalla hasta terminar la crónica pictórica de esa guerra, la más sanguinaria y cruel en toda la historia de nuestra América. A este pintor se le atribuye la Crucifixión de Cerro-Corá. Pero, como digo, se trata de una leyenda inventada por los enemigos del mariscal.

—*Elle est où cette fameuse Crucifixion?* —demandó Eugène Ionesco.

—No está aquí ni en Buenos Aires —tartamudeó el Ministro.

—*Et alors?* —protestó el dramaturgo del absurdo.

El ministro se las vio negras para explicar la ausencia de esa pieza única. Con una serie de circunloquios evasivos dijo que cuando el presidente Perón, un poco antes de su caída, vino al Paraguay para devolver los trofeos de aquella infausta guerra de hacía un siglo, quedó fascinado por el cuadro. El general Perón, ante una muchedumbre de un millón de personas, entregó solemnemente su espada al ejército paraguayo como símbolo de imperecedera alianza. El gesto era contra el Brasil, pero fortalecía la posición del Paraguay.

El presidente Stroessner, brasilerista adicto y confeso, se vio moralmente obligado a obsequiar a su colega argentino el cuadro de la Crucifixión del mariscal López. Algún tiempo después, el general Perón fue derrocado por la llamada Revolución Libertadora, que liberó a los conservadores del populismo peronista. El presidente Stroessner envió una cañonera al puerto de Buenos Aires en su busca. El almirante libertador quiso impedir su salida. Ordenó al acorazado Belgrano que cañoneara y hundiera la nave de guerra paraguaya. Los generales lograron disuadirle de ese acto desaforado y fuera de lugar. El acorazado Belgrano fue hundido en la guerra de las Malvinas, con los ingleses, en el

82, en una suerte de castigo póstumo y como un bofetón a la junta de militares y almirantes, dijo el ministro con acento vindicativo.

La cañonera pudo zarpar al fin, dijo impertérrito el Ministro. El general Perón hizo un corte de manga a los libertadores y vino a refugiarse en Asunción por muchos años. Entre los herrumbrosos trofeos históricos del Museo Militar, le esperaba su espada que no servía ya ni para cortar el asado. El pobre general Perón, con lo grande que era, llegó con lo puesto, y yo casi les diría en calzoncillos. No trajo la Crucifixión. La casa privada del general Perón, no la Quinta de Olivos, fue incendiada. El cuadro se quemó con todo lo que había adentro.

—*Eh bien, quelle belle connerie!* —bufó Ionesco.

El discurso del Ministro no era descabellado. La Crucifixión es en realidad un cuadro de Cándido López, pero no del pintor argentino sino de su homónimo paraguayo. Leyenda o mito, el cuadro de la Crucifixión es verdadero. Yo lo había visto en el Museo Nacional de Asunción pero no en el Museo Mitre de Buenos Aires durante los años de exilio que pasé en esa ciudad que yo amo mucho. Hay pues dos Cándidos López. O en todo caso, hay dos historias diferentes de Cándido López y de sus cuadros: una, la del pintor argentino que estuvo en la Guerra Grande, hasta 1868 como asistente del general Bartolomé Mitre, y que regresó con él; otra, la del pintor paraguayo con este mismo nombre que imitó a la perfección los cuadros del primero, o que los adivinó sin conocerlos, hasta transfundirse con su estilo y con el misterioso mundo de sus imágenes. Existe una pequeña diferencia artística: el argentino prefirió lo pintoresco; el paraguayo, lo pictoresco. Y un leve escollo lógico en cuanto a su identidad: los dos pintores semejantes, casi gemelos, en sus nombres y en sus obras, no podían haberse conocido ni tener el uno la menor idea de la existencia del otro. Los cuadros del Cándido López argentino no estuvieron nunca en Paraguay. Es falsa la referencia del Ministro a una exposición que se habría realizado en Asunción, durante los años del plácido retiro de Sarmiento en esta ciudad.

El Cándido López paraguayo estuvo en Cerro-Corá, el 1º de marzo de 1870, o el 29 de febrero del falso bisiesto inventado por Maíz y decretado por Solano López. Presenció el asesinato del mariscal y el posterior simulacro de crucifixión de su cadáver. Pintó esa terrible escena en un día inexistente. La pintó sin saber tampoco que estaba copiando no la inexistente Crucifixión del argentino, sino otra más remota y antigua: la de Matías Grünewald, que él jamás podía haber visto ni en el original ni en reproducciones del panel central del retablo. Esos lujos culturales no existían en el Paraguay de aquella época. Tampoco en la presente, salvo en las catacumbas culturales de la resistencia. Lo cierto fue que el oscuro hiato de ese día revolvió la historia real y originó incluso la duda de que esa guerra atroz hubiese tenido lugar. Por la grieta de un día pueden desaparecer siglos.

En los tiempos de mi trabajo como periodista en Asunción y en Buenos Aires realicé una exploración a fondo de este enigma sin llegar a ninguna conclusión válida. No existe ninguna mención periodística, ningún estudio de los más acreditados críticos de arte sobre este segundo Cándido López; sobre esta especie de misteriosa "transmigración" pictórica. Pero sus cuadros están ahí, mágicamente idénticos a los del primero. Es asombrosa, por inexplicable pero también por su perfección (más allá de sus relativos valores pictóricos), esta semejanza que une indisolublemente a los dos pintores coetáneos, casi anónimos aún a comienzos del siglo.

El Ministro nos arrastró a las volandas hacia la galería llamada "El jardín de los magnicidas". Ésta es, en cierto modo, la continuación de la primera en época actual. Hospeda murales y cuadros que reproducen los atentados (una cincuentena) perpetrados contra el tiranosaurio y los castigos impuestos a los frustrados magnicidas. Es una especie de círculo infernal donde los condenados siguen sufriendo los suplicios a los que fueron sometidos en vida. Estas escenas han sido pintadas, grabadas o esculpidas por artistas mercenarios del país y del extranjero, ineptos y obsecuentes practicones. El Ministro no hizo ningún comentario sobre esa serie negra y roja.

Se nota que estos cuadros y murales están imitados groseramente de las pinturas del Bosco o de Peter Huys; algunos de ellos copiados directamente del natural. La atmósfera de horror es realmente insoportable. Hubo muchos desmayos y hasta crisis de histeria en las mujeres, que llenaron de alaridos la altísima y resonante bóveda del museo. Los más decididos exigieron perentoriamente al ministro volver al hotel. Algunas delegadas de cierta edad, las de Puerto Rico y México, entre otras, fueron retiradas en camillas. La bella y joven representante del Brasil, que aventajaba a todos en estatura, enganchó sus tacones altísimos en los peldaños de un rellano y rodó desnuda sobre la alfombra dejando una estela de mosaicos de colores muy vivos en los que se abrió su vaporoso vestido. La cubrieron con una cortina y la retiraron también en una camilla.

—¡Esta visita ha sido bárbara y agraviante! —dijo a mi lado, en la ambulancia, un sociólogo español, a quien en un primer momento confundí con Fernando Savater.

—Creo que fue una buena demostracion de las bondades del régimen —insinué tímidamente—. Ionesco ha citado a Goethe: "El estremecimiento del terror es la más alta felicidad de la humanidad..." Podría ser el epígrafe de esta colección de magnicidios.

—Si la sentencia de Goethe fuese verdadera —siguió divagando el sociólogo parecido a Savater—, debería haber un gran arte de los campos de concentración, de los hornos crematorios, de las masacres colectivas de todos los tiempos.

—No la hay —dije tornando naturalmente femenino el sustantivo arte.

—No la puede haber —sentenció el sosias de Savater—. No puede haber un arte de la muerte. La imaginación no puede penetrar en esa realidad de ultratumba y producir un arte genuino. El Bosco, Peter Huys, Goya, Picasso, han revelado en sus cuadros no el horror físico de los supliciados sino el horror moral de los supliciadores: la antropofagia del monoteísmo del poder político o religioso, la atroz indiferencia del universo ante la especie condenada que mora en él.

En medio de la picante ensoñación producida por las oleadas de éter llegamos al hotel. Nos transportaron en camillas a nuestras respectivas habitaciones.

Cuando desperté, después de no sé cuantas horas de pesado sueño sin imágenes, Odiseo Aquino estaba ante mi cama con el rollo de las fotos tomadas en el velorio.

—Mi padre consiguió en la Técnica que le devolvieran las fotos de usted —me tendió triunfalmente el rollo.

Los negativos habían sido revelados; algunos de ellos, los más nítidos, estaban marcados a lápiz con una cruz roja. También lo estaban los que mostraban las caras de las mujeres del velorio. Sin querer me había convertido en informante oficioso de la policía. Mientras iba mirando las fotos, el botones me informó como al desgaire que el Ministro de Cultura había sido destituido y que estaba preso.

—Parece que hubo quejas de la comisión organizadora del congreso... —dijo alzando mucho las cejas y arrugando el morro.

Las supuestas fotos del cadáver de Pedro Alvarenga no eran tales. Sólo se veía en ellas el amasijo de un cuerpo destrozado en la tortura y fotografiado desde diversos ángulos: no eran más que reproducciones de alguno de los cuadros que acabábamos de ver en "El jardín de los magnicidas". Tomé la intencionada atención como una advertencia de la Secreta. Tuve que pagarle de todos modos al botones la suma convenida. Me puso el brazo al cuello y me hizo agachar la cabeza. Creí que iba a soplarme algún aviso confidencial. Me introdujo la lengua en el orificio de la oreja con el beso golondrino de las putillas de burdel, y salió disparando. Creí que había atravesado la puerta como un ectoplasma. No vi que la abriera ni que la volviera a cerrar. Mientras restañaba con repugnancia la saliva, recordé que la suite tenía varias salidas de emergencia ocultas por el cortinado. Arrojé el clinex húmedo en el water closet, oprimí el botón del agua y le eché una maldición al lúbrico botones.

Me derrumbé en el inmenso lecho, humillado, vencido, lleno de repugnancia.

Sonó el teléfono. Era Dalila Mieres. Me preguntó si podía recibirla por unos instantes para hablarme sobre las cuestiones que le había formulado. Le dije que con todo gusto, creo que con acento de excesiva amabilidad tal vez para disimular mi ansiedad.

Llegó en seguida.

—Buen día, señor —dijo inclinándose encantadoramente—. Le traigo buenas noticias. Aquí está su frasco de vacuna. Debería aplicársela de inmediato. En el hotel tenemos un buen gabinete médico con los mejores especialistas del país.

Cuando recuperé la voz, la invité a tomar asiento. Eligió el rincón más apartado de la lujosa suite. Revisó su cuadernillo de notas.

—En cuanto a la azafata mencionada por usted como Leda Kautner, efectivamente los datos que usted me dio coinciden con los de una nueva camarera del servicio especial que integró la tripulación del vuelo de ayer, FAE 747-27 de septiembre de 1987. Fue su primer vuelo al Paraguay. Pero esta camarera está registrada con el nombre de Paula Becker. También es verdad lo observado por usted. La camarera Paula Becker fue la última en desembarcar. Se demoró en el avión, por inexperiencia. Recogió su equipaje de mano y descendió de la máquina momentos antes de producirse la explosión.

—Le agradezco su atención... —dije tartamudeando.

—Espero que la buena nueva sobre su ex alumna Paula Becker le haya tranquilizado a usted. Esta mañana ha emprendido el vuelo regular del servicio hasta Francfort. Estará de regreso en dos días. Si usted quiere hablar con ella, yo misma le transmitiré el recado para que se comunique con usted.

—Oh... gracias... muchas gracias... —murmuré, dislálico.

La monitora Dalila Mieres se levantó suavemente. Dijo "siempre a sus gratas órdenes", se despidió con una inclinación de cabeza y se retiró con la satisfacción del deber cumplido. La vi alejarse por el pasillo, erguida y con pasos casi marciales. Dalila Mieres ha venido no a cortarme los cabellos sino a producirme con la "buena nueva" una total calvicie. Continúo estando pues a merced de Leda Kautner. Ahora se llama Paula Becker. Me persiguen las apariencias y los nombres seudónimos. En dos días estará de regreso. Contemplo el frasquito que contiene la vacuna contra la fiebre amarilla. ¿Debo tomarlo como una guiñada irónica de Paula Becker? La monitora no tiene por qué saber que mi pretexto era falso. Su trabajo es el de velar por la buena imagen de los servicios. En los hoteles hay siempre existencia de estas vacunas. ¿No habrá una vacuna contra la peste de las muchachas de amarillo oro que están en todas partes y en ninguna?

Me invade una preocupación mortal. Comprendo ahora por qué, cuando ocupo la suite, cierro las puertas a doble llave y con las cadenas de seguridad. Decidí confiar a Clovis el endemoniado entuerto. Siempre dueño de sí y amable sustentador del ánimo en las angustias ajenas, confiaba en que él me ayudaría a encontrar una salida. Le llamé a su habitación. Acababa de entrar. Me dijo que subiera.

—Déjame ver —me dijo cuando le hube resumido la historia de Leda Kautner, eludiendo algunos episodios como el de la noche de Nevers.

Trajeron dos vasos de whisky. En la superficie del líquido flotaban dos carbones encendidos de llama azul. Aquí, en los aperitivos, en lugar de cubos de hielo, utilizan prismas congelados de hidrófana, la variedad del ópalo que arde en el agua y cuyo fuego helado hormiguea placenteramente en los labios. Brillaban irisados como espejuelos en llamas. Entreví en ellos mi rostro demudado y nebuloso, la barba roja, los cabellos de escarcha, la expresión pálida y sombría.

—Me hablas de una historia que se parece más bien a una alucinación. Hay caprichos femeninos más obsesivos y testarudos que éste. Conozco algunos. Sin ir más lejos, el de mi excelente madre, que Dios tenga en su gloria. Cuando una mujer cree amar de verdad es más dura que la obsidiana y arde en el agua como esos diminutos témpanos de fuego. Sobre todo cuando es una mujer joven sin los anticuerpos que da la experiencia. La locura de amar la invade con toda su ponzoña transformándose en un odio terrible. Cree que el hombre a quien ama le ha robado su cuerpo, su lugar en el mundo, su pasión de vivir y hasta su derecho a morir. No le dejará en paz hasta verle muerto o hasta que ella misma muera.

Mientras Clovis iba hablando, sentí que él sospechaba la existencia de una causa más profunda de la que no había alcanzado a darme cuenta. Él estaba haciendo tiempo para saber por medio de lo que yo mismo le contase.

—Me dijiste que tu ex alumna y pertinaz enamorada Leda Kautner se llama ahora Paula Becker.

—Es lo que ha sacado en limpio la monitora —repuse.

Precisamente por el hecho de haberla yo omitido, me pareció que él intuía la experiencia de Nevers. El instinto de Clovis es infalible.

—¿Te has acostado ya con tu ex alumna?

—No —le respondí sin vacilar.

Me escrutó con una sonrisa sibilina. Luego de reflexionar un instante, entre dos sorbos de whisky, me preguntó si yo había tratado en los cursos o conversado personalmente con Leda Kautner sobre el poeta alemán Rainer María Rilke. Me sorprendió la pregunta. Pero en seguida recordé que, efectivamente, Leda Kautner en dos o tres ocasiones me había hablado con interés de Rilke y de su libro los *Cuadernos de Malte Laurids Brigge*. Con motivo de la finalización de su tesis le obsequié la biografía de Rilke, escrita por Lou Andréas Salomé, una de sus ex amantes.

—He aquí probablemente la punta del ovillo —dijo Clovis, categórico.

Mencionó el hecho de que en la colonia de artistas de Worpswede, Rilke conoció a Paula Becker y se enamoró perdidamente de la rubia y hermosa pintora. Rilke no estaba "hecho" para el amor carnal, dijo Clovis con una sonrisa. Se inventó en desquite el arquetipo de las doncellas virginales. La belleza de Paula le indujo a identificarla con estas amantes platónicas y etéreas a fin de poseerlas en exclusividad, "lejos de los groseros arrebatos de la sexualidad", en el reino de la pura poesía. Una vez que Rilke comprobó que Paula era virgen —lo cual era extraño e inaudito en una comunidad de artistas que se había congregado precisamente bajo la enseña del amor libre—, la condenó a morir con su virginidad intacta y se constituyó en cancerbero de esa "joya que sólo se pierde una vez". Ocurrió sin embargo —continuó Clovis tras apurar el vaso— que Paula Becker se cansó de ser virgen y pasiva vestal de este poeta al que la espina de una rosa iba a asesinar. Lo abandonó. Se olvidó de Rilke, que se casó con Clara Westhoff, y se unió en matrimonio a Otto Modersohn. Paula murió al ser madre. Lo que por doble motivo produjo en Rilke una profunda depresión. Por perder a una de sus vestales y también porque el fin de Paula contradecía y desacreditaba su doctrina de la "muerte propia". A Paula la había matado la cohabitación carnal, ergo el embarazo, ergo el nacimiento de su hija.

Rilke ya había querido hacer lo mismo con Camille Claudel, continuó Clovis, cuando estuvo en París como secretario de Rodin. Pretendió convertirla en una de sus vestales. Pero Camille era vestal exclusiva del escultor. El poderoso fauno velaba por ella y la tenía muy "ocupada" en la esclavitud de su amor. Camille ni siquiera se dio cuenta de la existencia del poeta-secretario, no concebía otra existencia humana que la de su Júpiter tonante.

—Mi madre —dijo Clovis como cerrando un episodio sin importancia— conocía bien la historia del famoso trío.

Se rió un poco y me observó con la fijeza irónica que le era característica.

—Leda Kautner se ha identificado con Paula Becker, pero no con Camille Claudel —dijo Clovis—. Ha tomado el nombre de Paula y te ha consagrado su virginidad. Si esta historia es real y no una alucinación, sólo te queda una alternativa, mi querido Félix Moral —dijo Clovis palmeándome el hombro comprensivamente—. O la olvidas o te acuestas con ella, que eso es lo que anda deseando desde que te conoció.

—No podría hacerlo jamás. Está Jimena. No podría injuriarla con este acto de infidelidad completamente gratuito y absurdo, ahora que estoy lejos de ella, quizás para siempre.

—Te has puesto sentimental. Tomas muy en serio el sentido, el "sonido" ético de tu apellido. En el transporte carnal no hay infidelidad. Sólo si tú también amas a Leda Kautner o a Paula Becker, traicionarías a Jimena. Si te dejas someter a los caprichos de esa muchacha enloquecida, desdoblada ahora en dos, es que tú también *amas* una fantasía falsa y peligrosa. Esa ninfa erotizada *no es* ni puede llegar a ser una relación normal en tu vida. Conoces mi filosofía amatoria: una mujer *única* cada vez. Si Jimena es la mujer única de tu vida de una vez para siempre, no la juegues por un espejismo. Leda Kautner y Paula Becker no son más que fantasmas de una libido exasperada y extenuada como la tuya. Ponte fuerte en lo tuyo y olvídalas.

La conminación razonable y a la vez un poco irracional pero profundamente sagaz de Clovis no ha hecho sino confundirme aún más, precisamente porque su opinión coincide punto por punto con la mía. Llegaron hasta mí en ese momento como un eco lejano las palabras de Leda aquella noche en Nevers: "Ah... si un hombre quiere... Si tú quisieras... Estoy aquí como soy y como me deseas..."

¿Volverán a repetirse la escena y el horror y la fascinación?

Poco después de nuestra breve conversación, me llamó Clovis para darme, según él, una "buena noticia".

—La comisión organizadora me acaba de anunciar que mañana, después de la reunión inaugural del congreso, tu tiranosaurio nos recibirá a las 12 horas en el Palacio de Gobierno para el besamanos previsto. Por fin tus ansias cortesanas quedarán satisfechas. Con respecto a tu obstinada Caperucita fucsia convertida en lobo feroz, no te preocupes. Tendrá que hacerse a un lado y guardar la necesaria compostura. Ahora comienza el ajetreo. Que lo pases bien. Regresaré a París al día siguiente. Prepárame lo que he de llevar a Jimena.

Refrené el golpe de amarga emoción que me produjo el anuncio, llamé a la operadora para que bloqueara todo llamado, eché cerrojo y cadena a las puertas y me dispuse a preparar el anillo. Vi el rectángulo de luz acuosa bajo la cama. Le eché encima dos gruesas colchas, pero el rectángulo semejante a la pantalla oculta de un circuito cerrado de televisión, continuó flotando sobre ellas. Me encogí de hombros y me encerré en el baño trabando el pestillo.

Una hora me ha llevado instalar en el anillo la carga mortal. Guardé en el frasquito una dosis de reserva en previsión de cualquier emergencia. Puedo necesitarla yo mismo. Durante esta operación simple y a la vez complicada no he podido despegar de mi vista los ojos comprensivos del dálmata, su noble cabeza, el signo de interrogación de su largo y fino cuello, el momento en que a mi pedido me tendió la pata peluda y obediente. Le dediqué aún algunas palabras de afecto y gratitud. Su sombra se desvaneció. Me puse el anillo en el dedo, me recosté en el lecho y me puse a mirarlo fijamente hasta que me invadió una especie de modorra un poco hipnótica.

Alguien golpeó levemente la puerta. Me incorporé bruscamente y una oleada de sangre me golpeó el rostro. Cuídate de no hacerle un hijo, me había dicho Clovis, porque es evidente que esa muchacha de los Cárpatos no ha nacido para ser madre. Enséñale a ser al menos una buena amante.

Se repitió el discreto llamado por dos veces más. Dispuesto a todo, me encaminé hacia la puerta, decidido a usar el anillo, una primera vez, si era *ella*. Dalila Mieres me había dicho que hoy era su día de regreso. Tras un estrépito de cerrojos y cadenas, abrí la puerta. No había nadie. Recorrí velozmente el largo pasillo de punta a punta. Sólo me topé con un camarero del *room service*. El choque estuvo a punto de derribar el carrito repleto de botellas y fuentes cubiertas con tapas relucientes. Cayeron algunas de ellas. El olor de apetitosas viandas se esparció por el pasillo. El camarero recogió las tapas, las repasó y pulió con su servilleta.

—¿No se cruzó usted con una muchacha rubia? —le pregunté, sintiéndome un poco ridículo.

—No vi a nadie, señor —me respondió obsequioso el camarero.

Nos pedimos disculpas mutuamente y volví a mi suite. Guardé el anillo en el bolso protector y me eché de nuevo en la cama sabiendo que no iba a poder conciliar el sueño. Resolví levantarme y seguir escribiéndote.

Ignoro lo que irá a suceder. Una suerte de *fatum*, demasiado repetido e infalible para ser considerado como una suerte de milagro (Dios, si existe, no debe sentir especiales simpatías hacia los tiranos) ha salvado siempre a éste de las emboscadas de la casualidad. Es probable que la inauguración del congreso sea para mí el día del fin último. En tal eventualidad Clovis te referirá lo que en este momento no puedo prever aún. De todos modos, yo permaneceré aquí, "al pie del cañón", en espera de los acontecimientos. Los seguiré con la empecinada fe del incrédulo que está hecha con la sustancia del porvenir según la definición de San Pablo. Dispongo de 72 horas de plazo mientras la acción retardada del anillo produzca los cambios del futuro y forme a la vez su leyenda.

Además de estas páginas de "puño y letra, de latidos de corazón", te envío un video en que he registrado las escenas resaltantes de la semana transcurrida desde nuestra llegada. Incluyo un ejemplar del lujoso álbum-programa para que te diviertas un rato con los datos sobre el congreso y la nómina de los invitados. Reconocerás entre ellos a viejos conocidos nuestros, los componentes de esa fauna perpetua de autoinvitados a los coloquios, ansiosos de buena comida, de "ligues" siempre posibles, de exhibicionismo intelectual.

En un recipiente especial en el que he puesto un poco de la tierra de estas comarcas te llegarán unos brotes de la "selva migrante", de los que te hablo en otra parte. Son semillas y brotes escapados de las selvas originarias sacrificadas en el altar de la civilización y del progreso de este país que "progresa hacia atrás". Los retoños que te envío son ya un bosque en miniatura. Si les tomas cariño, siémbralos en uno de los tiestos que guardan el humus de la tierra natal en nuestra Ventana del Poniente. Podrás regalar a Nevers una selva de helechos gigantes. Espero que ella sabrá albergarlos en alguno de sus hermosos parques, pese a las normas contra la inmigración clandestina. Continuaré mañana con las últimas noticias de la inauguración y del apretón de manos presidencial.

Viernes 1° de septiembre. La reunión inaugural se desarrolló como la escena de una pieza de Ionesco. Decididamente, este congreso de rinocerontes y dinosaurios está hecho a la medida del creador del absurdo teatral. Te la resumo. Luego de un discurso muy prudente y excesivamente elogioso del nuevo Ministro de Cultura en honor de los participantes y en pro de los objetivos del congreso que durará un mes, se realizó la votación para elegir presidente del primero de los tres turnos. La elección recayó en un pastor mennonita paraguayo, residente en Sao Paulo, Brasil, Filomeno Simón, en mérito a su obra de evangelización y de cultura en las regiones del Chaco Boreal. No se hallaba presente entre los asistentes a la reunión. Era totalmente desconocido. Cundió la sospecha general de que tal nombre y tal persona eran fraguados. Tras aceleradas averiguaciones la comisión organizadora que trabaja en conexión con el servicio de inteligencia de la cúpula, llegó a la fulgurante conclusión de que Filomeno Simón, el supuesto y fraudulento pastor mennonita, no era otro que el terrorista internacional Pedro Alvarenga que viajó desde Río entre los invitados, provisto de documentos falsos y de una invitación para asistir al congreso con carácter de observador, también falsa. Ya conoces la historia de Pedro Alvarenga y su trágico fin.

Pasado el momento de estupor y restablecida la calma, fue nombrado presidente de la asamblea por aclamación Eugène Ionesco. Como saliendo de una pesadilla, éste agradeció el honor que se le confería. Confesó su satisfacción de conocer un país que él creía inexistente y que, según todas las apariencias, seguía siendo para él inexistente. Formuló augurios en el sentido de que tan bello y misterioso país existiera en el futuro a partir del Congreso de Historia, Cultura y Sociedad de América Latina en el Siglo I de la Nueva Era. En la alucinación en marcha de la historia, dijo citando a su compatriota Ciorán y cerrando su alocución, las naciones, los países y los pueblos sólo existen en la imaginación de un demiurgo violento y lleno de odio contra la humanidad. Es necesario, dijo, destruir ese demiurgo demencial para que los humanoides se vayan humanando (empleó el verbo neológico "humanar" en español). Fue ovacionado.

El aria de bravura estuvo a cargo de El Bastardo. El tullido expuso su teoría de destrucción del mundo por la cultura y el arte, ilustrándola con numerosos diagramas y fórmulas físico-matemáticas que resultaron incomprensibles para los asistentes. Dio varios ejemplos de un probabilismo práctico espeluznante con otros vectores del arte aliados con la cibernética, lindantes con los hallazgos más delirantes de la ciencia ficción. Hizo volar por el cielo del salón en graciosas evoluciones una bandada de servopalomas y de satélites en miniatura. Por telecomando extendió en el cielo del salón algo semejante a una capa sutilísima de cirro y metal inervada de poros y esporas de latente luminosidad.

La teoría del científico Lacerda sostiene que, utilizando una de las capas (dio el nombre) de la biosfera como refractor de sonido, se puede proyectar una emisión permanente de música sobre el haz del planeta, inmune a todo contraataque de defensa y represalia. Los sonidos de esta emisión serían de tal magnitud de volumen que en diez días habrían borrado todo vestigio de vida humana sin dañar en lo más mínimo la masa de la civilización material, ciudades, edificios, templos, usinas nucleares, etc. Habló de "una operación de cirugía de precisión matemática, dedicada exclusivamente a extirpar el tumor de la miserable raza humana". Eligió los dos primeros compases de la *Heroica* de Beethoven y realizó una prueba de pocos segundos, a todo volumen, con el aparato de su prótesis vocal, aprovechando como refractor la bóveda del salón recubierta por la tela porosa. Los asistentes estuvieron a punto de enloquecer. Hubo muchos que se arrojaron al piso, tapándose los oídos y dando terribles alaridos que la tremenda masa sonora impidió escuchar. El Bastardo sonreía con una expresión de indecible felicidad. Abrió los ojos completamente estrábicos e interrumpió su ordalía burlesca. El silencio que siguió fue casi tan terriblemente ensordecedor como la potencia de los decibeles que hicieron retemblar el salón lleno de bote en bote. El Bastardo condescendió a explicar que la experiencia acabada de realizar había utilizado sólo unas cien millonésimasavas partes del volumen que la *Heroica* de Beethoven podría alcanzar en los altavoces del cosmos.

En la pausa para el café me acerqué a Fulvia Marcia. Me observó atentamente pero no me reconoció. Lo que me dio buena espina con respecto a la eficacia de mi seudónimo aspecto. Fulvia, el ídolo de nuestra juventud, la novia romántica de los excluidos, no me reconoció pese al pequeño frote que le hice con la uña del índice en la palma de la mano. Era nuestro santo y seña en los encuentros furtivos o en medio de numerosa concurrencia. Olvidadiza como la palma de la mano, es un refrán bastante acertado. Además de excelente música, Fulvia es fundadora y presidenta del Centro de Estudios de Geopolítica para el Cono Sur. En la sesión de mañana debe presentar su ponencia sobre "La función geopolítica del eje Paraguay-Uruguay-Bolivia en el equilibrio del Plata".

Correspondió luego el uso de la palabra al antropólogo norteamericano, el profesor Edward Jensen. Con prolijos análisis, datos estadísticos computarizados y estudios sobre el terreno, el profesor Jensen demostró la posibilidad e inminencia de extinción de la sociedad paraguaya al mismo tiempo que los pueblos indígenas. Estableció parámetros muy precisos de esta simetría. El profesor Jensen y su colega y compatriota el profesor E.R. Wolf escribieron en colaboración y publicaron hace poco el libro *The human condition in Latin America*. Búscalo entre mis libros de antropología. Es una obra fundamental. Te resultará muy útil para la redacción de tu ensayo sobre Hegel y América.

La exposición del antropólogo norteamericano produjo un evidente malestar entre los miembros de la comisión organizadora. La plana mayor de las autoridades universitarias se removió en sus asientos con ostensible disgusto y hostilidad. Al término de su conferencia y entre los aplausos de los invitados, se oyeron silbidos e insultos en guaraní contra el profesor norteamericano, autoridad mundial en la materia.

No hubo tiempo para más. Faltaban apenas treinta minutos para la audiencia presidencial, que estaba prevista estrictamente para sesenta minutos. Las limusinas blindadas nos condujeron hasta el palacio mudéjar. Subimos las escalinatas y pasamos bajo un arco de honor. Bien se veía que no era otra cosa que un detector de rayos X y láser, análogo al de los aeropuertos aunque muy ampliado y camuflado en su ornamentación barroca... Cumplía además la función de tomar fotos de los que iban entrando. Las esbeltas monitoras nos introdujeron en el vasto y rojo salón de audiencias. Con suaves y amables gestos nos distribuyeron y colocaron en tres filas, por orden alfabético de apellidos, ante un estrado al que se subía por tres afelpados escalones. A un costado se hallaba el palco de los ministros y secretarios de Estado; al otro, el de los embajadores, del nuncio apostólico y de los representantes de la jerarquía eclesiástica local.

Al sonar en la catedral las primeras campanadas del mediodía, se abrieron las puertas del gabinete privado. Precedido y seguido por su disciplinada cohorte de ayudantes y edecanes, lenta y majestuosamente apareció el tiranosaurio, vestido de gran gala. El abombado pecho se hallaba pavimentado de cruces y condecoraciones hasta el abdomen no menos abultado. El uniforme militar le caía muy holgado, lo que aumentaba la desproporción de su cuerpo contrahecho, grande y fofo. La guerrera floja permitía adivinar bajo las condecoraciones y la banda presidencial el chaleco antibalas. Al principio se tenía la sensación de ver reflejada la imagen del tiranosaurio en la convexidad de un espejo deformante. La cabeza coronada de pelo ralo y casi cano mostraba su media sangre teutona. La senectud no lo trataba bien. Las típicas facciones bávaras se amontonaban ahora sobre el belfo colgante y éste se confundía con la voluminosa papada y la sotabarba de rubios mechones teñidos, de modo que parecía tener el bigote por debajo de la boca. El rostro mofletudo estaba fijo en un punto indeterminado delante de sí. En ningún momento dijo una sola palabra y no iba a decirlas porque no podía. De pie y en una actitud marcial bastante forzada, su figura copiaba la actitud de su estatua que coronaba la cima del cerro Tacumbú.

El Ministro de Cultura pronunció breves palabras y el ceremonial se desarrolló con matemática exactitud.

Comenzó para mí la angustiosa cuenta regresiva de minutos y segundos. Cada apretón de manos duraba un promedio de 13 segundos. Los 279 invitados cubrían un total de 1 hora 13 segundos. A éstos habría que agregar el lento desplazamiento de las tres filas, la subida y bajada de los escalones hasta el estrado, el retraso de algunos a causa de un tropezón y hasta la caída de la representante de Puerto Rico. Lo que suponía un suplemento de 14 minutos 6 segundos y fracciones. Mis cálculos me dieron la evidencia de que el anillo no iba a llegar a tiempo a esa mano inmóvil y rígida en su gesto, idéntico al de la estatua. Sospeché con horror que esa mano, que ese brazo fueran realmente ortopédicos. Me encontraba en mitad de la segunda fila y necesitaba ganar el tiempo de por lo menos cinco lugares más adelante para tener una remota probabilidad de emplear el anillo. Con la voluntad de hacerme invisible, que a veces me da resultado, me deslicé en la fila y gané siete lugares, ubicándome detrás de la hermosa representante del Brasil, lo que me aportaba ciertas garantías de camuflaje táctico.

Mientras me iba acercando al estrado la figura del tiranosaurio se me fue haciendo cada vez más definida. Advertí entonces que la cara amontonada y nebulosa estaba protegida por un velo casi impalpable de protección antibacteriana. En ese momento me di cuenta con espanto de que llevaba calzados unos guantes blancos muy gruesos. Miré el anillo y me dije que la microscópica saeta no iba a traspasar la tela anticontagio del guante. El aguijón del anillo tenía una posibilidad de penetración de una décima de milímetro. De nada servía hacer más enérgico el apretón de manos ni oprimir con más fuerza el gatillo de ópalo. Con ese atavío de protección el tiranosaurio se me aparecía como un extraterrestre, o en todo caso, más o menos semejante al primer hombre llegado a la luna, revestido de una escafandra de metal selenita y tubos de oxígeno a la espalda.

Recordé en ese mismo instante que no había traído conmigo el cartapacio de seguridad donde guardo mis papeles. Lo dejé olvidado en la suite del hotel. Me brotó un repentino sudor frío en la espalda. De todos modos lo habría tenido que dejar a la entrada, en la oficina de control de la entrada, donde el riesgo de un eventual escrutinio y secuestro eran aún mayores. Espero que mi cartapacio con cierre inviolable no haya sido robado ni violado ni... escrutado, pero mi confianza no es muy firme.

Reuní el resto de fuerzas y esperé; o mejor dicho avancé paso a paso, muy breves y cada vez más cortos y lejanos, hacia lo que decidiera el destino, la necesidad o el azar. Estábamos llegando. Deseé que la mujer cuya estatura me aventajaba en una cabeza tropezara y cayera en los escalones enganchada de sus tacones altísimos, como ya le había ocurrido en el museo cuando recorríamos "El jardín de los magnicidas". Sucedió algo mejor. La representante del Brasil subió airosamente al estrado erguida en esos tacones que parecían tornarla ingrávida. Al verla, el Gran Tembelo, el grande amigo del Brasil, la reconoció y sonrió por primera vez con la afabilidad que le permitían sus aprestos de protección facial. Se sacó el guante y apretó la mano de la bella brasileña. La mujer se irguió y aproximó su rostro al del presidente. Creí que iba a darle un beso y que ese beso rasgaría el velo. Se limitó a decirle dos palabras al oído con la más encantadora de sus sonrisas. La mujer bajó o saltó ágilmente los escalones. Yo ya estaba en su lugar y pude estrechar la mano desnuda, todavía tendida, del tiranosaurio, con el más férvido apretón de manos que en mi vida había dado. Sentí la mano blanda y fofa. Iba a retirarla. Pero él me la retuvo y me observó fijamente bajo sus párpados espesos, caídos. Yo clavé la mirada en el centro de la frente, entre ceja y ceja, donde el cáncer de piel mostraba sus gránulos rojizos. Levantó mi mano a la altura de sus ojos y observó con curiosidad el anillo. Su gesto era casi amistoso. Sentí al fin que me soltaba la mano. Descendí los escalones como si no los pisara.

Seguí a los que iban saliendo. En el palco de los diplomáticos vi a Clovis que me guiñó un ojo de festiva

aprobación. Almorzaré con él y le alcanzaré mi envío.
Dentro de 72 horas Clovis ya te lo habrá entregado en
Nevers y yo sabré aquí si el anillo del noble conde de Villamediana ha cumplido honradamente la misión magnicida que le he encomendado.

Ahora sólo me queda esperar los resultados... Seguiré, si puedo, escribiéndote hasta la partida de Clovis.
Es lo único que me consuela y me hace sentir que estamos
juntos... Si esto es imposible, Morena, un largo, largo adiós...

DE JIMENA TARSIS A LA MADRE DE FÉLIX MORAL

Querida señora:

Le extrañará sin duda mi largo silencio. Acabo de
regresar del Paraguay después de dos años de ausencia.
Como le contara en una carta anterior a mi partida, no pude
acompañar a Félix en el viaje que emprendió a fines de
agosto de 1987 a causa del accidente que sufrí. Ya sabrá
usted lo peor, de modo que me limitaré a esbozarle la crónica de aquel desventurado viaje. Le envío los manuscritos de Félix y, en una remesa bancaria sobre Madrid, el
saldo de los haberes que existía en nuestra cuenta conjun-
ta. Sólo he dejado para mí la última carta que él me escribió, de la cual le envío copia.

Félix asistió a las dos primeras reuniones del congreso, inaugurado el 1º de septiembre de 1987. Desapareció dos días después (el 3 de septiembre) sin dejar huellas.
Clovis de Larzac, a su regreso de Asunción, me entregó
un paquete de cartas y de efectos personales que Félix me
envió por su intermedio; incluso un pequeño recipiente con

semillas y brotes de las "selvas migrantes" (como él las llamaba), que el cálido viento del norte arrastra y esparce a lo largo y a lo ancho del territorio paraguayo.

Clovis de Larzac postergó su estancia en Asunción por dos días más para ocuparse de la suerte de Félix, amigo suyo dilecto y ciudadano nacionalizado francés, fiel a su afecto y a la tradición de este país, de no privar de asistencia a persona en peligro, incorporada al derecho de gente y a su código penal.

Clovis de Larzac me refirió y me mostró las pruebas de todos los recursos a que había apelado para encontrar a toda costa a Félix. Conversó largamente con el Ministro del Interior quien, con recomendaciones especiales, lo derivó a las instancias gubernamentales y policiales correspondientes. Como era de prever, no obtuvo ningún resultado y nada pudo sacar en limpio. Clovis fue acosado por llamados telefónicos y billetes anónimos con noticias y datos evidentemente falsos sobre el paradero del desaparecido, a fin de despistar su acción. Las fuentes de estas interferencias, me dijo, eran previsibles, y no se podía sacar de ellas ninguna referencia útil.

Lo evidente era que Félix había sido reconocido por los organismos de seguridad. Se hallaba detenido en un lugar indeterminado. Ningún contacto con él, aun indirecto, era posible. Se hallaba totalmente incomunicado en alguna de las dependencias de la policía secreta, llamada allá Dirección Nacional de Asuntos Técnicos, o más brevemente la Técnica, el antro más siniestro de investigaciones y torturas.

Clovis presentó una enérgica protesta en la cancillería paraguaya y encomendó el seguimiento del asunto a dos abogados de probada honestidad y gran prestigio internacional, uno paraguayo y otro suizo, miembros ambos de una entidad de Derechos Humanos para el área de América del Sur, con sede en Ginebra. Los participantes del congreso suscribieron un apremiante reclamo, dirigido al presidente de la nación y patrocinador del congreso, reclamando la inmediata libertad de Félix, como invitado oficial, y responsabilizando al gobierno del Paraguay por cualquier daño que pudiera sufrir. Esta declaración pública no mereció ninguna respuesta. En un comunicado también público los organizadores oficiales se desligaron de toda responsabilidad ante las pruebas concluyentes de que Félix, en presunta complicidad con terroristas internacionales, se hallaba preparando un atentado contra el primer magistrado. Los jueces instructores del juicio se basaron efectivamente en la carta que Félix me había escrito y de la cual habían obtenido copia.

Apenas me sacaron el yeso de la pierna y pude moverme con ayuda de una muleta viajé al Paraguay, luego de anunciar mi partida a la entidad de Derechos Humanos de Ginebra y de consultar con el abogado suizo que había tomado a su cargo el asunto de Félix. Llegué a Asunción el 27 de septiembre. Me puse de inmediato en contacto con el abogado paraguayo. Muy desanimado y atemorizado éste no había podido avanzar un solo paso en el esclarecimiento de la desaparición. Me comunicó que había recibido por teléfono varias amenazas de muerte si no dejaba caer el caso y que, por esa razón, se veía obligado a abandonarlo haciéndome entrega de todos los recursos, testimonios y pruebas que había conseguido reunir en favor de la causa de Félix.

Clovis de Larzac me había proporcionado las señas de un coronel del servicio de inteligencia, un tal Pedro Abad Oro. Lo visité en su despacho y me atendió con excesiva y falsa cordialidad. Desde el primer momento su actitud escondía apenas sus torpes propósitos de galanteo, e incluso de chantaje. Seguí el juego y pude aprovecharme, a mi vez, de las debilidades del coronel Abad Oro. Empezó por entregarme copia de un legajo con todos los papeles que secuestraron a Félix. Le expresé mi deseo de verlo de inmediato. Me dijo evasivamente que había que esperar; que él gestionaría las autorizaciones de los jueces y que me avisaría el momento en que podría hacerlo.

En días posteriores el coronel Pedro Abad Oro me acompañó al castillo de Arekutakuá, actual presidio de Emboscada. Luego de una larga recorrida por patios y celdas de un verdadero laberinto de fosas subterráneas, en los que se hallan hacinados millares de prisioneros en estado de consunción extrema, el coronel me señaló a un hombre que se venía arrastrando a gatas. Era una piltrafa humana, semidesnuda y mutilada, con rastros de salvajes castigos y torturas. Al no poder ocupar sus manos, llevaba apretado entre los labios por los bordes el abollado plato de hojalata del "rancho" de los presos.

—Éste es... —dijo Abad Oro con voz inexpresiva—. ¿Lo reconoce usted?

Asentí. Era él sin ninguna duda. Me aproximé y le llamé por su nombre. No recibí ninguna respuesta. Sus ojos turbios y sin vida me miraron y no me reconocieron. Emitió un confuso sonido, algo como un quejido estrangulado. Se le cayó el plato. Me arrodillé y levanté su mugrienta y leonina cabeza. Descubrí que le habían arrancado todos los dientes. Los rastros de ultrajes y torturas eran visibles en todo su cuerpo. Descubrí con horror que tenía descortezadas las plantas de los pies, el castigo que infligen en la Técnica a los prisioneros de mayor peligrosidad para que no puedan evadirse. Le saqué varias fotos sin que Abad Oro se mostrara excesivamente renuente. Por momentos tenía la impresión de que actuaba incluso con instrucciones de que el caso se hiciera público, por mi intermedio, para brindar a la opinión internacional una prueba flagrante de la acción subversiva, a la vez que como un ejemplo escarmentativo y disuasivo.

Exigí al coronel Pedro Abad Oro que Félix fuera trasladado de urgencia a un hospital a fin de que recibiera la atención necesaria. Con las fotos tomadas presenté un rela-

torio bastante completo sobre su situación al congreso de
intelectuales y escritores que estaba llegando a su fin. De los
279 congresales no quedaban sino 13, en su mayor parte
viejos intelectuales y escritores locales de marcada tendencia fascista que se ratificaron como partidarios acérrimos del
gobierno. De modo que no pude obtener de ellos el menor
apoyo. Por el contrario, estos "intelectuales" del régimen
publicaron el mismo día a toda página en los diarios una
declaración de agradecimiento al gobierno por la celebración del congreso y un enfervorizado manifiesto de adhesión a "su preclara acción de gobierno y a su resuelta lucha
antisubversiva y antiterrorista".

Querida señora, compréndame. Me cuesta mucho
escribirle esta carta llena de reprobación y de horror sintiendo al mismo tiempo que agravio sus más íntimos sentimientos. Trataré de abreviar en lo posible esta dolorosa
crónica, dejando para un encuentro posterior en Madrid
los detalles de la pesadilla que continúa siendo real para mí
como ha de serlo para usted.

Félix fue transferido al hospital de policía con gran
despliegue de fuerzas de seguridad, pero también de medios de publicidad. Ante un gran gentío, agolpado ante el
hospital, bajaron de la ambulancia la camilla en que Félix
era transportado mientras iba siendo acribillado por los
flashes de multitud de fotógrafos locales y extranjeros. No
me separé un solo momento de su lado y me aseguré de
que se le prestaran todos los auxilios. En los días que siguieron, ante mi apremiante insistencia, le injertaron en las
plantas de los pies tejidos que fueron tomados de mi propia carne. Desde ese día encadenaron sus piernas al lecho
de hierro empotrado en el piso de cemento. Durante el día,
pese a la hostilidad y a las humillantes restricciones que me
oponían los enfermeros y enfermeras de guardia, incluidos los médicos de turno, me daba maña para no abandonarle. Durante la noche iba al hotel donde tenía que

soportar el permanente asedio de Abad Oro quien me invitaba a cenar y se obstinaba en llevarme a las discotecas de moda. No acepté jamás estas invitaciones que trataban de exhibirme como elemento adicto a los servicios de inteligencia y como testigo de cargo en la causa de Félix, después de presentarme en la causa como su delatora y principal acusadora sin permitírseme asistir a la mascarada de juicio.

Poco a poco logré al menos hacer que Abad Oro me respetara. Sentí que iba ganando sobre él cierto influjo que mucho se parecía a un hechizo. No era un mérito personal. Las circunstancias fantasmagóricas que rodeaban el caso, pensaba yo, habían contribuido a que se produjera en él ese "estado de alma", si esto es posible en un desalmado, astuto y moralmente depravado.

Pasaron cinco meses. Estaban a punto de darle el alta a Félix en el hospital y devolverlo a la prisión. Había recuperado apenas los vestigios de sus facultades más elementales sin poder empero mantenerse aún en pie sobre esas plantas atrozmente rebanadas que iban cicatrizando muy lentamente. A partir de ese momento, sólo tuve yo un objetivo preciso y al mismo tiempo obsesivo: la huida. Saqué a escondidas un molde de yeso de sus pies. Le hice fabricar por un artesano un par de zapatos con suelas elásticas pero firmes y forros interiores de crepé muy blandos que le sirvieran de amortiguadores. Tuve la fraternal ayuda de jóvenes médicos de la resistencia.

La huida por avión era absolutamente impensable. Existía una sola y única posibilidad: la peregrinación del 1º de marzo al santuario de Solano López, en Cerro-Corá, y de allí al Brasil. Mi idea era mezclarnos a esa muchedumbre y cruzar la frontera por la ciudad de Pedro Juan Caballero en el extremo norte. La proximidad de la fecha (estábamos a fines de febrero) me hizo pensar en esa remota probabilidad de escapatoria, una en un millón. Recogí toda la información que pude y armé un plan cuya realización sólo era relativamente posible por ser totalmente inverosímil. Logré con Abad Oro que el traslado de Félix a la prisión se hiciera el 27 de febrero pues yo debía viajar de regreso a Francia en los primeros días de marzo.

Voy a ahorrarle los últimos siete días de tremenda tensión, de sobresaltos, de angustias: la terrible lucha contra las imprevisibles maquinaciones del azar. No podía compartirla con Félix sumido todavía en un estado mental y anímico casi crepuscular, cercano a la ausencia y a la falta casi total de reflejos y de motilidad. Era una masa casi inerte que apenas podía sostenerse y moverse como un autómata apoyado en mí, en la pared, en el cabezal de la camilla.

Con fuertes primas logré la complicidad de dos enfermeros del turno de la noche. En los días anteriores, provista de una pequeña lima, había venido aserrando, a hurtadillas, poco a poco un eslabón tras otro de la cadena que sujetaban los tobillos de Félix al lecho de hierro empotrado en el piso. La noche del 26, con delantal y cofia de las médicas de guardia, entré en la sala. Me acerqué al lecho de Félix, hice saltar los eslabones semiaserrados, logré hacerle incorporar y lo llevé paso a paso hacia los retretes. Con la ayuda de los enfermeros cómplices lo cargamos en la ambulancia, subí al volante y conduje a toda velocidad abriéndome paso gracias al estridente sonido de la sirena y a los faros giratorios que iban barrenando la luz tenebrosa, el tráfico, los grupos de viandantes y sobrepasando en una exhalación, una tras otra, las garitas policiales.

Entré en la zona del puerto. Estacioné frente a los depósitos de la aduana, donde a esa hora comenzaba el tráfico de los camiones y vehículos que sacan los lotes de mercadería del contrabando menor. Llevé lentamente a Félix hasta el muelle donde estaba atracado el pequeño buque de pasajeros y cargas que hacía viajes hacia el norte. El comisario nos esperaba a bordo. Nos condujo a la camareta que nos había destinado. Deposité a Félix en la cucheta y volví a salir. Vuelvo en seguida, dije al comisario y le alargué la mitad de la suma prometida. Llevé la ambulancia y la dejé estacionada frente al palacio de gobierno con las luces encendidas. Volví a pie y encontré a Félix dormido y tranquilo en el camastro. Tendí en el piso una colchoneta y me acosté a su lado. El sol alto aunque invisible por la invariable y espesa luz de Itaipú me despertó. Fui a traer el desayuno. Estábamos llegando al puerto de San Pedro. En un día más arribaríamos a Concepción. Por teléfono había alquilado allí, en una agencia de coches de alquiler, el vehículo que nos llevaría a Horqueta. Y desde esa localidad nos incorporaríamos a la peregrinación de los concepcioneros rumbo a Cerro-Corá en la confluencia de las caravanas que acuden de todas partes del país. Elegí un Toyota de todo terreno y nos pusimos en camino hacia las estribaciones de las serranías.

Todo fue transcurriendo con una lentitud desesperante pero sin inconvenientes mayores, salvo pequeños desajustes en el plan de marcha. Recuerdo ese viaje como un sueño y se lo estoy relatando como un sueño del cual se me escapa casi todo excepto la angustia y la desesperación. Félix, absorto en su obsesión, se dejaba llevar como en otro sueño aún más irreal que el mío.

Por su bien y por el mío debo terminar pronto el relato de este vía crucis. En medio de la muchedumbre de peregrinantes que iban entonando roncamente cantos marciales y religiosos estábamos llegando al desfiladero de Cerro-Corá, a la caída de la noche. Desde una altura del monte vimos la meseta iluminada por centenares de fogatas. Poderosos reflectores y aparatos parecidos a cámaras de televisión enfocaban el anfiteatro donde se desarrollaba una confusa escena. Algo como la semi inconsciencia de un recuerdo se iba despertando en Félix. Agitaba sus brazos y se esforzaba por seguir avanzando. En un tiempo imprecisable llegamos al borde del anfiteatro. No se podía adelantar más. Una masa humana rodeaba el espacio sagrado. Un rito extraño se estaba celebrando en él. Poseído por una ansiedad trémula e innominada, Félix me tironeaba de los brazos para seguir avanzando. Desde un promontorio cercano contemplamos la escena inenarrable: la crucifixión de Solano López ejecutada por hombres disfrazados de "macacos brasileiros".

A los pies de la cruz se hallaba Madama Lynch, vestida de blanco, erguida como el personaje de una tragedia antigua, que recibe en sus brazos el cuerpo del esposo crucificado. La actriz principal era extraordinariamente parecida a Madama Lynch, según la iconografía que de ella conocemos. Pero esa actriz no era otra que Leda Kautner, la extraña muchacha ex alumna de Félix. Lo observé con estupor. Intuí que él también la había reconocido. Levantó los brazos hacia ella y la llamó vagamente. Avanzó unos pasos pero tropezó en lo que parecía una gruesa liana y cayó de bruces sobre el suelo rocoso. Era un grueso cable de los muchos que alimentaban los aparatos de filmación.

Un militar en traje de campaña se aproximó seguido por un pelotón de "caras pintadas". Era el coronel Pedro Abad Oro. Con un rictus de burla despreciativa me saludó militarmente. Dijo: "He seguido todos sus pasos, desde la huida del hospital. Viajé con ustedes en el barco hasta Concepción... Sólo he querido prolongar un poco más la ilusión de la fuga..." Volvió el rostro hacia el cuerpo yacente de Félix y escupió sobre él. "¡Ese pobre infeliz ya está muerto antes de morir..." Levantó la mano y la patrulla acribilló con sus armas automáticas el cuerpo de Félix, que se estremeció como en una convulsión tetánica y quedó quieto, la cara hundida en la maleza. Quise precipitarme sobre él. Me derribaron de un culatazo.

A partir de aquel momento no importaba ya en absoluto lo que a mí pudiera sucederme. Me transportaron, esposada, en helicóptero a Asunción. Fui juzgada sumariamente y condenada a prisión perpetua por asociación con terroristas y por el delito de atentar contra la vida del jefe de Estado. Félix murió sin saber que la escena de la crucifixión de Solano López no era un fragmento real de la historia que creyó revivir, sino la escena ficticia del rodaje de una película, tal como él mismo la había imaginado y plasmado en el *script* que fue rodado a medias hace bastante tiempo y que originó su primer apresamiento.

Durante dos años estuve presa en la cárcel de mujeres del Buen Pastor. Me destinaron a la limpieza de cloacas y retretes. La directora me preguntó un día qué otras tareas sabía hacer. Pensé que se habría apiadado de mí, o quizás algo peor. "Sé bordar", le dije. Me pasaron al obrador del penal. Allí empecé a bordar de memoria la larga franja de tapicería de la reina Mathilde, que existe en el Museo de Bayeux. En mis tiempos de enseñante de liceo en esa ciudad, me había encariñado con aquella obra mítica que recordaba la conquista de Inglaterra por los normados. En un año la franja, que se iba arrollando sobre sí misma, había alcanzado más de cien yardas de extensión. La directora me confesó con un temblor de obsecuencia en la voz que tenía la idea de obsequiarla, cuando estuviese terminada, al Excelentísimo Señor Presidente de la Nación. "A lo mejor, dijo, ese gesto te valdrá una disminución del tiempo de tu condena aunque vos no sos ya sino una efectiva N. N." Me entró el deseo angustioso de que el trabajo no tuviera nunca fin y de que quedara para siempre arrollado, invisible, arrumbado en los sótanos de la cárcel.

En la madrugada del 3 de febrero de 1989, una insurrección militar derrocó al dictador. Dos días después fui liberada por orden del nuevo Presidente de la República. El golpe palaciego venía, si no a legitimar, por lo menos a justificar la obsesión tiranicida de Félix que lo había arrastrado a su horrible muerte. Me contaron que el propio ex dictador estuvo a punto de ser volado por una granada de mano del oficial que comandó el operativo al intimarle rendición. El jefe de la insurrección, en la proclama lanzada ese mismo día, comprometía a las fuerzas armadas a inaugurar y custodiar un proceso de transición democrática, a defender las libertades públicas y los derechos humanos. Al término de ese proceso, según la proclama, va a convocarse a elecciones y el gobierno provisorio de las fuerzas armadas entregará el poder a los candidatos civiles que resulten electos. Esperemos que los plazos y las palabras se cumplan en favor de esta colectividad que ya ha sufrido demasiado.

El derrocado dictador, hasta ayer todopoderoso a lo largo de más de cuarenta años de poder discrecional y absoluto, fue obligado a abandonar el país. En compañía del hijo mayor, de unos pocos fieles y bajo fuerte custodia, fue conducido a la estación de trenes de alta velocidad, inaugurada con gran pompa el último día del congreso. El ex dictador fue el primer usuario de este servicio en un viaje directo hasta Brasilia, donde le fue otorgado asilo. Le dieron la bienvenida rindiéndole honores de jefe de Estado en funciones.

Al golpe militar siguió una insurrección civil de carácter pacífico que lanzó una autoconvocatoria a elecciones municipales. Los movimientos independientes de la resistencia tomaron la comuna de la capital juntamente con los principales ayuntamientos del país. Un viento de justicia fuenteovejuna ha empezado a soplar fuerte en todo el país. Las nuevas autoridades comunales de Asunción, seguidas por una inmensa multitud, subieron hasta la cumbre del cerro Tacumbú. Desmontaron la estatua de bronce del dictador y la echaron a rodar cerro abajo en una gran explosión de júbilo colectivo que duró tres días.

Fue una gigantesca celebración de carácter casi ritual. Centenares de miles de manifestantes de todos los sectores sociales en fraternal unión con los pueblos indígenas, arrastraron la estatua por las calles de la ciudad al ritmo de varias bandas de músicos, de conjuntos folclóricos y de tambores indígenas, venidos desde los más lejanos confines. En la Plaza de los Héroes, junto al Panteón Nacional, la estatua fue colgada en una inmensa horca, reliquia de los viejos tiempos. La iluminaban 43 velones encendidos, uno por cada año del poder absoluto que ejerció el dictador. Acaba de celebrarse una Convención Nacional Constituyente de la cual ha surgido una nueva Carta Magna.

La nueva Suprema Corte de Justicia ha solicitado la extradición del ex dictador para que sea juzgado en Asunción. No vendrá. Es difícil que culmine este paso legal necesario como punto final a la dictadura y a la insurgencia de nuevos regímenes de fuerza. Si el ex dictador llegara a venir para afrontar a los jueces de la democracia recientemente instaurada pero aún demasiado frágil, la voz popular vaticina que la estatua de bronce tendrá compañera. No comparto este anhelo. Los sentimientos de odio o de venganza no han mejorado nunca "la alucinación en marcha de la historia". Félix fue una víctima de esta alucinación. Duéleme la desgracia que sufrimos y me conduelo con toda mi alma de su aflicción.

Téngame en su recuerdo y cariño como yo la tengo a usted en la memoria de Félix.

En la composición de *El fiscal* se emplearon
fuentes tipográficas Stempel Garamond y
Garamond de 11/14 y 14/16 puntos.
Terminó de imprimirse el 17 de septiembre de 1993
en Compañía Editorial La Prensa, Basilio Vadillo 29,
9o piso, Col. Tabacalera, México, D.F.
La edición estuvo al cuidado de Marisol Schulz Manaut.
Se tiraron 7,000 ejemplares más sobrantes
para reposición.